Fixed Income

CFA® PROGRAM CURRICULUM • VOLUME 5

**LEVEL II
2007**

PEARSON

Custom
Publishing

Cover photograph courtesy of Robert Essel NYC/Corbis Images.

Printed in the United States of America

10 9 8 7 6 5 4 3 2

ISBN 0-536-17196-3

2005160780

BK/JS

Please visit our web site at *www.pearsoncustom.com*

PEARSON CUSTOM PUBLISHING
75 Arlington Street, Suite 300, Boston, MA 02116
A Pearson Education Company

CONTENTS

READING 63

HOW TO USE THE CFA PROGRAM CURRICULUM

Congratulations on passing LI of the Chartered Financial Analyst (CFA®) Program. This exciting and rewarding program of study reflects your desire to become a serious investment professional. You are participating in a program noted for its requirement of ethics and breadth of knowledge, skills, and abilities.

The credential you seek is respected around the world as a mark of accomplishment and dedication, and each level of the program represents a distinct achievement in professional development. Successful completion of the program is rewarded with membership in a prestigious global community of investment professionals. CFA charterholders are dedicated to life-long learning and maintaining currency with the ever-changing dynamics of a challenging profession.

Curriculum Development

The CFA Program curriculum is grounded in the practice of the investment profession. CFA Institute regularly conducts a practice analysis survey of investment professionals around the world to determine the knowledge, skills, and abilities that are relevant to the profession. The survey results define the Candidate Body of Knowledge (CBOK™), an inventory of knowledge and responsibilities expected of the investment management professional at the level of a new CFA charterholder. The survey also determines how much emphasis each of the major topic areas receives on the CFA examinations.

A committee made up of practicing charterholders, in conjunction with CFA Institute staff, designs the CFA Program curriculum to deliver the CBOK to candidates. The examinations, also written by practicing charterholders, are designed for you to demonstrate mastery of the CBOK as set forth in the CFA Program curriculum. As you structure your personal study program, you should emphasize mastery of the CBOK and the practical application of that knowledge. For more information on the practice analysis, CBOK, and development of the CFA Program curriculum, please visit www.cfainstitute.org/course.

Organization

The 2007 Level II CFA Program curriculum is organized into 10 topic areas. Each topic area begins with a topic level learning outcome that summarizes the broad objective of the material to follow and indicates the depth of knowledge expected. Each topic area is then divided into one or more study sessions, each devoted to a sub-topic (or group of sub-topics) within that topic area. The 2007 Level II curriculum is organized into 18 study sessions. Each study session begins with a purpose statement defining the content structure and objective of that session. Finally, each study session is further divided into reading assignments. *The outline on the inside front cover of each volume should further illustrate this important hierarchy.*

The reading assignments are the basis for all examination questions. The readings are selected or developed specifically to teach candidates the CBOK. Readings are drawn from textbook chapters, professional journal articles, research analyst reports, CFA Program-commissioned content, and cases. Many readings include problems and solutions as well as appendices to help you learn.

Reading-specific Learning Outcome Statements (LOS) are listed in the study session opener page as well as prior to each reading. Reading-specific LOS indicate what you should be able to accomplish after studying the reading. It is important, however, not to interpret LOS narrowly by focusing on a few key sentences in a reading. Readings, particularly CFA Program-commissioned readings, provide context for the learning outcome and enable you to apply a principle or concept in a variety of scenarios. Thus, you should use the LOS to guide and focus your study, as each examination question is based explicitly on one or more LOS. We encourage you to thoroughly review how to properly use LOS and the list and descriptions of commonly used LOS command words at www.cfainstitute.org/toolkit. The command words signal the depth of learning you are expected to achieve from the reading.

Features for 2007

- ▶ **Required vs. Optional segments** - Several reading assignments use only a portion of the original source textbook chapter or journal article. In order to allow you to read the assignment within its full context, however, we have reprinted the entire chapter or article in the curriculum. When an optional segment begins, you will see an icon. A vertical solid bar in the outside margin will continue until the optional segment ends, symbolized by another icon. Unless the material is specifically noted as optional, you should assume it is required. Keep in mind that the optional material is provided strictly for your convenience and will not be tested. *You should rely on the required segments and the reading-specific LOS in preparing for the examination.*

- ▶ **Problems/Solutions** - When appropriate, we have developed and assigned problems after readings to demonstrate practical application and reinforce understanding of the concepts presented. The solutions to the problems are provided in an appendix at the back of each volume. Candidates should consider all problems and solutions required material as your ability to solve these problems will prepare you for exam questions.

- ▶ **Margins** - We have inserted wide margins throughout each volume to allow for easier note taking.

- ▶ **Two-color format** - To enrich the visual appeal and clarity of the exhibits, tables, and required vs. optional treatments, we have printed the curriculum in two-color format.

- ▶ **Six- volume structure** - To improve the portability of the curriculum, we have spread the material over six volumes.

- ▶ **Glossary and Index** - For your convenience, we have printed a comprehensive glossary and index in each volume. Throughout the curriculum, a **bolded blue** word in a reading denotes a glossary term.

Designing your personal study program:

Create a schedule - An orderly, systematic approach to preparation is critical to successful completion of the examination. You should dedicate a consistent block of time every week to reading and studying. Complete all reading assignments and the associated problems and solutions in each study session. Review the LOS both before and after you study each reading to ensure that you have mastered the applicable content and can complete the action(s) specified. Upon completion of each study session, review the session's purpose statement and confirm that you thoroughly understand the subject matter. When you complete a topic area, review the topic level learning outcome and verify that you have mastered the objectives.

CFA Institute estimates that you will need to devote a minimum of 10-15 hours per week for 18 weeks to study the assigned readings. Allow a minimum of one week for each study session spread over several days, with completion scheduled for at least 30-45 days prior to the examination. This schedule will allow you to spend the final four to six weeks before the examination reviewing the assigned material and taking multiple on-line sample examinations. At CFA Institute, we believe that candidates need to commit to a *minimum* of 250 hours reading and reviewing the curriculum and taking online sample exams to master the material. This recommendation, however, may substantially underestimate the hours needed for appropriate exam preparation depending on individual circumstances and academic background.

You will undoubtedly adjust your study time to conform to your own strengths and weaknesses and academic background, and you will probably spend more time on some study sessions than on others. You should allow ample time for both in-depth study of all topic areas and additional concentration on those topic areas for which you feel least prepared.

Candidate Preparation Toolkit - We have created the online toolkit to provide a single comprehensive location for resources and guidance for candidate preparation. In addition to in-depth information on study program planning, the CFA Program curriculum, and the online sample exams, the toolkit also contains curriculum errata, printable study session outlines, sample exam questions, and more. We encourage you to use the toolkit as your central preparation resource during your tenure as a candidate. Visit the toolkit at www.cfainstitute.org/toolkit.

Online Sample Exams - After completing your study of the assigned curriculum, use the CFA Institute online sample exams to measure your knowledge of the topics and improve your exam-taking skills. After each question, you will receive immediate feedback noting the correct response and indicating the assigned curriculum for further study. The sample exams are designed by the same people who create the actual CFA exams, and reflect the question formats, topics, and level of difficulty of the actual CFA examinations, in a timed environment. Aggregate data indicate that the CFA examination pass rate was higher among candidates who took one or more online sample examinations than for candidates who did not take the online sample exams. For more information on the online sample exams, please visit www.cfainstitute.org/toolkit.

Review Programs - After you enroll in the CFA Program, you may receive numerous solicitations for preparatory courses and review materials. Although preparatory courses and notes may be helpful to some candidates, you should view these resources as *supplements to the assigned CFA Program curriculum.* The CFA exams reference *only* the 2007 CFA Institute assigned curriculum; no preparatory course or review course materials are consulted or referenced.

Furthermore, CFA Institute does not endorse, promote, review, or warrant the accuracy of the products or services offered by preparatory organizations. CFA Institute does not verify or endorse the pass rates or other claims made by these organizations.

Feedback

At CFA Institute, we are committed to delivering a comprehensive and rigorous curriculum for the development of competent, ethically grounded investment professionals. We rely on candidate and member feedback as we work to incorporate content, design, and packaging improvements. You can be assured that we will continue to listen to your suggestions. Please send any comments or feedback to curriculum@cfainstitute.org. Ongoing improvements in the curriculum will help you prepare for success on the upcoming examinations, and for a lifetime of learning as a serious investment professional.

ANALYSIS OF FIXED INCOME INVESTMENTS

STUDY SESSIONS

Study Session 14   Valuation Concepts
Study Session 15   Fixed Income Investments: Structured Securities

TOPIC LEVEL LEARNING OUTCOME

The candidate should be able to estimate risk and returns for fixed income instruments, analyze fixed income instruments with unique features, and value fixed income instruments with embedded options.

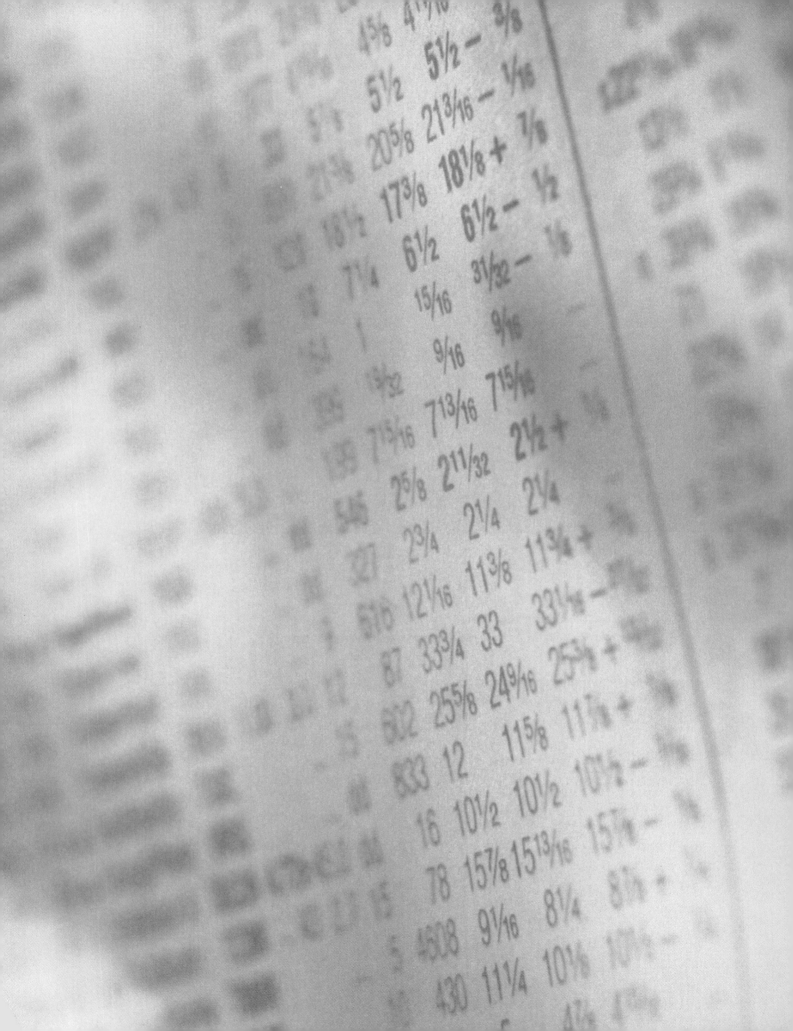

STUDY SESSION 14
FIXED INCOME INVESTMENTS:
Valuation Concepts

READING ASSIGNMENTS

Reading 58   General Principles of Credit Analysis
Reading 59   Term Structure and Volatility of Interest Rates
Reading 60   Valuing Bonds with Embedded Options

This study session describes the primary skills needed for the valuation of fixed income investments. It begins with a study of the key valuation tools used in credit analysis, is followed by a thorough study of interest rate analysis, and concludes with an introduction to embedded options in fixed income securities.

LEARNING OUTCOMES

Reading 58: General Principles of Credit Analysis
The candidate should be able to:

a. distinguish among default risk, credit spread risk, and downgrade risk;

b. illustrate how credit analysis encompasses assessing the borrower's character (including the quality of management) and capacity to repay (including sources of liquidity), and the issue's underlying collateral and covenants;

c. calculate the key ratios used by credit analysts to assess the ability of a company to satisfy its debt obligations, and explain the limitations of these ratios;

d. evaluate the credit quality of an issuer of a corporate bond, given such data as key financial ratios for the issuer and the industry;

e. analyze why and how cash flow from operations is used to assess the ability of an issuer to service its debt obligations and to assess the financial flexibility of a company;

f. explain the typical elements of the debt structure of a high-yield issuer, the interrelationships among these elements, and the impact of these elements on the risk position of the lender;

g. explain the importance of the corporate structure of a high-yield issuer that has a holding company;

h. discuss the factors considered by rating agencies in rating asset-backed securities (i.e., collateral credit quality, seller/servicer quality, cash flow stress and payment structure, and legal structure);

i. explain how the creditworthiness of municipal bonds is assessed, and contrast the analysis of tax-backed debt with the analysis of revenue obligations;

j. discuss the key economic and political risks considered by Standard & Poor's in assigning sovereign ratings;

k. explain why two ratings are assigned to each national government, and discuss the key factors emphasized by Standard & Poor's for each rating;

l. contrast the credit analysis required for corporate bonds to that required for 1) asset-backed securities, 2) municipal securities, and 3) sovereign debt.

Reading 59: Term Structure and Volatility of Interest Rates

The candidate should be able to:

a. illustrate and explain parallel and nonparallel shifts in the yield curve, a yield curve twist, and a change in the curvature of the yield curve (i.e., a butterfly shift);

b. describe the factors that have been observed to drive U.S. Treasury security returns, and evaluate the importance of each factor;

c. explain the various universes of Treasury securities that are used to construct the theoretical spot rate curve, and evaluate their advantages and disadvantages;

d. explain the swap rate curve (LIBOR curve) and discuss the reasons that market participants have increasingly used the swap rate curve as a benchmark rather than a government bond yield curve;

e. illustrate the various theories of the term structure of interest rates (i.e., pure expectations, liquidity, and preferred habitat) and the implications of each theory for the shape of the yield curve;

f. compute and interpret the yield curve risk of a security or a portfolio, using key rate duration;

g. compute and interpret yield volatility, given historical yields;

h. distinguish between historical yield volatility and implied yield volatility;

i. explain how yield volatility is forecasted.

Reading 60: Valuing Bonds with Embedded Options

The candidate should be able to:

a. evaluate whether a security is undervalued or overvalued, given an appropriate benchmark, using relative value analysis;

b. evaluate the importance of the benchmark interest rates in interpreting spread measures;

c. illustrate the backward induction valuation methodology within the binomial interest rate tree framework;

d. compute the value of a callable bond from an interest rate tree, given the call schedule and the rule for calling a bond;

e. illustrate the relationship among the values of a callable (putable) bond, the corresponding option-free bond, and the embedded option;

f. explain the effect of volatility on the arbitrage-free value of an option;

g. interpret an option-adjusted spread with respect to a nominal spread and to benchmark interest rates;

h. illustrate how effective duration and effective convexity are calculated using the binomial model;

i. calculate the value of a putable bond, using an interest rate tree;

j. describe the basic features of a convertible bond and compute the value of the following for a convertible bond: conversion value, straight value, market conversion price (conversion parity), market conversion premium per share, market conversion premium ratio, premium payback period, and premium over straight value;

k. discuss the components of a convertible bond's value that must be included in an option-based valuation approach;

l. compare and contrast the risk-return characteristics of a convertible bond to the risk-return characteristics of ownership of the underlying common stock.

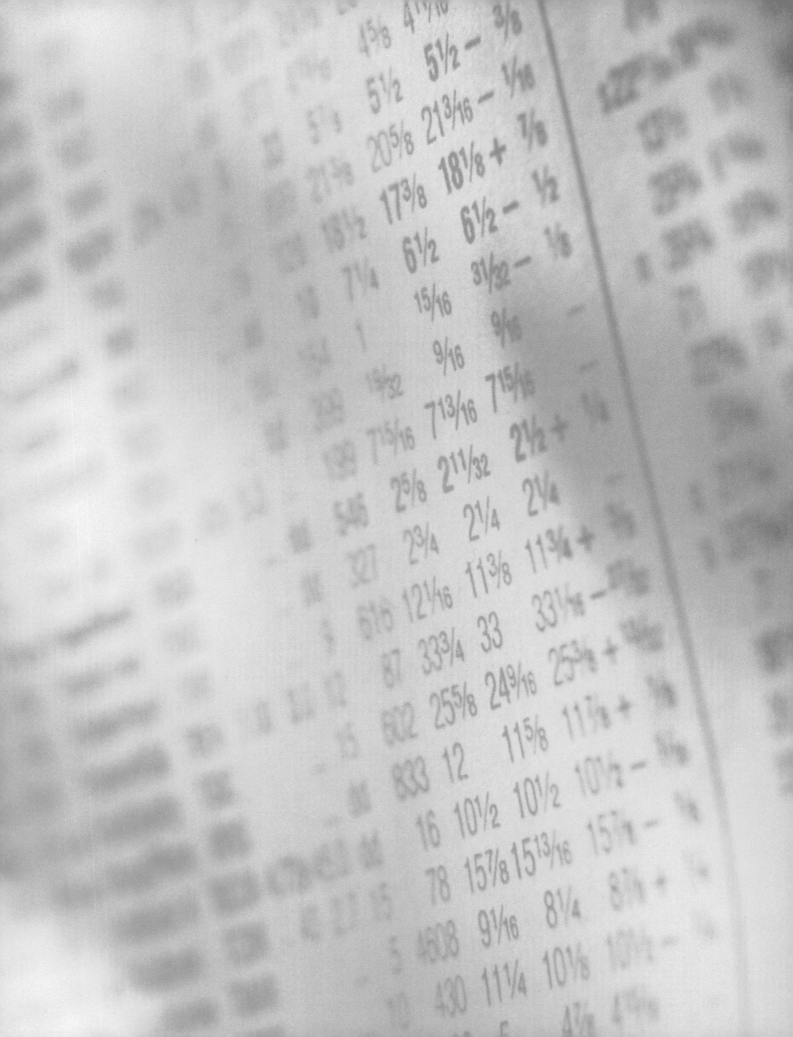

GENERAL PRINCIPLES OF CREDIT ANALYSIS

by Frank J. Fabozzi

LEARNING OUTCOMES

The candidate should be able to:

a. distinguish among default risk, credit spread risk, and downgrade risk;

b. illustrate how credit analysis encompasses assessing the borrower's character (including the quality of management) and capacity to repay (including sources of liquidity), and the issue's underlying collateral and covenants;

c. calculate the key ratios used by credit analysts to assess the ability of a company to satisfy its debt obligations, and explain the limitations of these ratios;

d. evaluate the credit quality of an issuer of a corporate bond, given such data as key financial ratios for the issuer and the industry;

e. analyze why and how cash flow from operations is used to assess the ability of an issuer to service its debt obligations and to assess the financial flexibility of a company;

f. explain the typical elements of the debt structure of a high-yield issuer, the interrelationships among these elements, and the impact of these elements on the risk position of the lender;

g. explain the importance of the corporate structure of a high-yield issuer that has a holding company;

h. discuss the factors considered by rating agencies in rating asset-backed securities (i.e., collateral credit quality, seller/servicer quality, cash flow stress and payment structure, and legal structure);

i. explain how the creditworthiness of municipal bonds is assessed, and contrast the analysis of tax-backed debt with the analysis of revenue obligations;

j. discuss the key economic and political risks considered by Standard & Poor's in assigning sovereign ratings;

k. explain why two ratings are assigned to each national government, and discuss the key factors emphasized by Standard & Poor's for each rating;

l. contrast the credit analysis required for corporate bonds to that required for 1) asset-backed securities, 2) municipal securities, and 3) sovereign debt.

Fixed Income Analysis for the Chartered Financial Analyst® Program, Second Edition, edited by Frank J. Fabozzi, Copyright © 2005 by CFA Institute. Reprinted with permission.

1   INTRODUCTION

The credit risk of a bond includes:

(1) the risk that the issuer will default on its obligation and

(2) the risk that the bond's value will decline and/or the bond's price performance will be worse than that of other bonds against which the investor is compared because either (a) the market requires a higher spread due to a perceived increase in the risk that the issuer will default or (b) companies that assign ratings to bonds will lower a bond's rating.

The first risk is referred to as **default risk**. The second risk is labeled based on the reason for the adverse or inferior performance. The risk attributable to an increase in the spread, or more specifically the credit spread, is referred to as **credit spread risk**; the risk attributable to a lowering of the credit rating (i.e., a downgrading) is referred to as **downgrade risk**.[1]

Credit analysis of any entity—a corporation, a municipality, or a sovereign government—involves the analysis of a multitude of quantitative and qualitative factors over the past, present, and future. There are four general approaches to gauging credit risk:

► credit ratings

► traditional credit analysis

► credit scoring models

► credit risk models

In this reading, we discuss each approach. Our primary focus is on the credit analysis of corporate bonds.

2   CREDIT RATINGS

A **credit rating** is a formal opinion given by a specialized company of the default risk faced by investing in a particular issue of debt securities. The specialized companies that provide credit ratings are referred to as "rating agencies." The three nationally recognized rating agencies in the United States are Moody's Investors Service, Standard & Poor's Corporation, and Fitch Ratings. The symbols used by these rating agencies and a summary description of each rating can be found elsewhere.

---

[1] These types of credit risk are discussed in detail at Level 1.

A. Rating Process, Surveillance, and Review

The rating process begins when a rating agency receives a formal request from an entity planning to issue a bond in which it seeks a rating for the bond issue (i.e., an "issue specific credit rating"). The cost associated with obtaining a credit rating is paid by the entity making the request for a rating. The request for a rating is made because without one, it would be difficult for the entity to issue a bond. The rating assigned applies to the specific bond to be issued, *not* to the entity requesting the rating. A rating agency may also be requested to provide a rating for a company that has no public debt outstanding (i.e., an "issuer credit rating"). This is done for companies that are parties in derivative transactions, such as swaps, so that market participants can assess counterparty risk.[2]

Once a credit rating is assigned to a corporate debt obligation, a rating agency monitors the credit quality of the issuer and can reassign a different credit rating to its bonds. An "upgrade" occurs when there is an improvement in the credit quality of an issue; a "downgrade" occurs when there is a deterioration in the credit quality of an issue. As noted earlier, downgrade risk is the risk that an issue will be downgraded.

Typically, before an issue's rating is changed, the rating agency will announce in advance that it is reviewing the issue with the potential for upgrade or downgrade. The issue in such cases is said to be on "rating watch" or "credit watch." In the announcement, the rating agency will state the direction of the potential change in rating—upgrade or downgrade. Typically, a decision will be made within three months.

In addition, rating agencies will issue rating outlooks. A **rating outlook** is a projection of whether an issue in the long term (from six months to two years) is likely to be upgraded, downgraded, or maintain its current rating. Rating agencies designate a rating outlook as either positive (i.e., likely to be upgraded), negative (i.e., likely to be downgraded), or stable (i.e., likely to be no change in the rating).

B. Gauging Default Risk and Downgrade Risk

The information available to investors from rating agencies about credit risk are: (1) ratings, (2) rating watches or credit watches, and (3) rating outlooks. Moreover, periodic studies by the rating agencies provide information to investors about credit risk. Below we describe how the information provided by rating agencies can be used to gauge two forms of credit risk: default risk and downgrade risk.

For long-term debt obligations, a **credit rating** is a forward-looking assessment of (1) the probability of default and (2) the relative magnitude of the loss should a default occur. For short-term debt obligations (i.e., obligations with initial maturities of one year or less), a credit rating is a forward-looking assessment of the probability of default. Consequently, credit ratings are the rating agencies assessment of the default risk associated with a bond issue.

Periodic studies by rating agencies provide information about two aspects of default risk—default rates and default loss rates. First, rating agencies study and make available to investors the percentage of bonds of a given rating at the beginning of a period that have defaulted at the end of the period. This percentage is referred to as the **default rate**.[3] For example, a rating agency might

---

[2] Counterparty risk is the risk that a party to a financial transaction will default on its obligation.

[3] There are several ways that default rates can be measured. These are described at Level I.

report that the one-year default rate for triple B rated bonds is 1.8%. These studies have shown that the lower the credit rating, the higher the default rate. Rating agency studies also show default loss rates by rating and other characteristics of the issue (e.g., level of seniority and industry). A **default loss rate** is a measure of the magnitude of the potential of the loss should a default occur.[4]

A study by Moody's found that for a corporate bond, its ratings combined with its rating watches and rating outlook status provide a better gauge for default risk than using the ratings alone.[5] The authors of the study looked at one-year and three-year default rates from 1996 through 2003 for senior unsecured rated bonds and within each rating by rating watch (watch upgrade and watch downgrade) and rating outlook status (positive, stable, and negative). The one-year default rate results for three selected ratings are shown below:

Rating	Watch up	Positive	Stable	Negative	Watch Down
Baa3	NA	0.20%	0.60%	1.25%	2.26%
B1	NA	0.98%	2.53%	5.07%	12.03%
Caa1	3.7%	3.82%	8.43%	14.93%	42.21%

Notice that as one moves from left to right for a given credit rating in the above table that the default rate increases. Look at the Caa1 rating. For issues that were on rating watch for a potential upgrade at the beginning of the period, 3.7% defaulted in one year. However, for those on rating watch for a potential downgrade at the beginning of the period, 42.21% defaulted in one year. This suggests that rating watches contain useful information in gauging default risk. Look at the rating outlook status for Caa1. Issues that had a negative rating outlook at the beginning of the year had a one-year default rate that was almost four times greater than issues that had a positive rating outlook.

Moody's makes the following suggestion as to how an analyst can combine the information contained in rating watches and outlook rating status to adjust the senior unsecured rating of a corporate bond:

For issues on:	*Suggestion:*
downgrade watch	reduce current rating by two rating notches[6]
upgrade watch	increase current rating by two rating notches
negative outlook	reduce current rating by one rating notch
stable outlook	keep current rating
positive outlook	increase current rating by one rating notch

Of course, portfolio managers may elect to develop their own system for adjusting the current rating of a bond based on their assessment of the findings of the study by Moody's. What is essential, however, is that in assessing the default risk when using credit ratings, portfolio managers should take into consideration rating watches and rating outlook status.

---

[4] The default loss rate is described at Level I.

[5] David T. Hamilton and Richard Cantor, *Rating Transitions and Defaults Conditional on Watchlist, Outlook and Rating History,* Moody's Investors Service, February 2004.

[6] A rating "notch" is a rating based on the modified rating (i.e., in the case of Moody's with the "1", "2", and "3" modifiers). For example, if an issue is rated Baa2, then a reduction of one rating notch would be a rating of Baa3. A reduction of two rating notches would be a rating of Ba1.

While the discussion above has focused on default risk, other studies by rating agencies also provide information. At Level I, the rating transition matrix published periodically by the rating agencies was explained. A rating transition table shows the percentage of issues of each rating at the beginning of a period that was downgraded or upgraded by the end of the time period. Consequently, by looking at the percentage of downgrades for a given rating, an estimate can be obtained of the probability of a downgrade and this can serve as a measure of downgrade risk.[7]

TRADITIONAL CREDIT ANALYSIS ⬛ 3

In traditional credit analysis, the analyst considers the four C's of credit:

- ▶ capacity
- ▶ collateral
- ▶ covenants
- ▶ character

Capacity is the ability of an issuer to repay its obligations. **Collateral** is looked at not only in the traditional sense of assets pledged to secure the debt, but also to the quality and value of those unpledged assets controlled by the issuer. In both senses the collateral is capable of supplying additional aid, comfort, and support to the debt and the debtholder. Assets form the basis for the generation of cash flow which services the debt in good times as well as bad. **Covenants** are the terms and conditions of the lending agreement. They lay down restrictions on how management operates the company and conducts its financial affairs. Covenants can restrict management's discretion. A default or violation of any covenant may provide a meaningful early warning alarm enabling investors to take positive and corrective action before the situation deteriorates further. Covenants have value as they play an important part in minimizing risk to creditors. They help prevent the transfer of wealth from debt holders to equity holders. **Character** of management is the foundation of sound credit. This includes the ethical reputation as well as the business qualifications and operating record of the board of directors, management, and executives responsible for the use of the borrowed funds and repayment of those funds.

A. Analysis of the Capacity to Pay

A corporation will generate the funds to service its debt from its cash flow. The cash flow is generated from revenues and reduced by the costs of operations. Therefore, in assessing the ability of an issuer to pay, an analysis of the financial statements as discussed later in this reading is undertaken. In addition to management quality, the factors examined by analysts at Moody's are:[8]

1. industry trends
2. the regulatory environment

---

[7] An illustration of a rating transition matrix and the calculation of the probability of downgrade were provided at Level I.

[8] "Industrial Company Rating Methodology," Moody's Investors Services: Global Credit Research (July 1998), p. 3.

3. basic operating and competitive position

4. financial position and sources of liquidity

5. company structure (including structural subordination and priority of claim)

6. parent company support agreements

7. special **event risk**

In considering industry trends, analysts look at the vulnerability of the company to economic cycles, the barriers to entry, and the exposure of the company to technological changes. For firms in regulated industries, proposed changes in regulations must be analyzed to assess their impact on future cash flows. At the company level, diversification of the product line and the cost structure are examined in assessing the basic operating position of the firm.

In addition to the measures described later in this reading for assessing a company's financial position over the past three to five years, an analyst must look at the capacity of a firm to obtain additional financing and back-up credit facilities. There are various forms of back-up credit facilities. The strongest forms of back-up credit facilities are those that are contractually binding and do not include provisions that permit the lender to refuse to provide funds. An example of such a provision is one that allows the bank to refuse funding if the bank feels that the borrower's financial condition or operating position has deteriorated significantly. (Such a provision is called a **material adverse change clause**.) Non-contractual facilities such as lines of credit that make it easy for a bank to refuse funding should be of concern to the analyst. The analyst must also examine the quality of the bank providing the back-up facility.

Analysts should also assess whether the company can use securitization as a funding source for generating liquidity. Asset securitization involves using a pool of loans or receivables as collateral for a security. The decision of whether to securitize assets to borrow or use traditional borrowing sources is done on the basis of cost. However, if traditional sources dry up when a company faces a liquidity crisis, securitization may provide the needed liquidity. An analyst should investigate the extent to which management has considered securitization as a funding source.

Other sources of liquidity for a company may be third-party guarantees, the most common being a contractual agreement with its parent company. When such a financial guarantee exists, the analyst must undertake a credit analysis of the parent company.

In the analysis of an issuer's ability to pay, the analyst will analyze the issuer's financial statements (income statement, balance sheet, and statement of cash flows), project future financial statements based on certain assumptions, and compute various measures. These measures include traditional ratio measures and cash flow measures. Below we review these measures and explain how an additional analysis of cash flows provides a better early warning alarm of potential financial difficulties than traditional ratios.

1. Traditional Ratios

Traditional ratios to evaluate the ability of an issuer to meet its obligations include:

► profitability ratios

► debt and coverage ratios

a. Profitability Ratios

Equity analysts focus on the earnings of a firm, particularly the earnings per share. While a holder of the debt obligation of a firm does not have the opportunity to share in the economic growth of the firm, this does not mean that a credit analyst should ignore a firm's profitability. It is from revenues that a firm will continue to grow in order to generate cash flow to meet obligations.

Profitability ratios are utilized to explore the underlying causes of a change in the company's earnings. They show the combined effects of liquidity and asset and debt management on the profitability of the firm. These ratios break earnings per share into its basic determinants for purposes of assessing the factors underlying the profitability of the firm. They help to assess the adequacy of historical profits, and to project future profitability through better understanding of its underlying causes.

Standards for a given ratio will vary according to operating characteristics of the company being analyzed and general business conditions; such standards cannot be stated as fixed and immutable. It is assumed that the analyst has made all adjustments deemed necessary to reflect comparable and true earning power of the corporation before calculating the ratios discussed below. It is important to stress that ratios are utilized to raise significant questions requiring further analysis, not to provide answers.

Equity analysts use the DuPont formula (explained in textbooks on equity analysis) to assess the determinants of a company's earnings per share. The profitability ratios analyzed to assess earnings per share are:

► return on stockholders' equity

► return on total assets

► profit margin

► asset turnover

Each of these measures and their limitations are explained in textbooks on financial statement analysis and equity analysis so they will not be repeated here.

b. Debt and Coverage Analysis

There are three sets of ratios that are used by credit analysts as indicators to assess the ability of a firm to satisfy its debt obligations:

► short-term solvency ratios

► capitalization (or financial leverage) ratios

► coverage ratios

i. Short-Term Solvency Ratios   Short-term solvency ratios are used to judge the adequacy of liquid assets for meeting short-term obligations as they come due. A complete analysis of the adequacy of working capital for meeting current liabilities as they come due and assessing management's efficiency in using working capital would require a thorough analysis of cash flows and forecasts of fund flows in future periods that will be discussed in the next section. However, ratios provide a crude but useful assessment of working capital. The following two ratios are calculated to assess the adequacy of working capital for a firm:

► the current ratio

► the acid-test ratio

The current ratio is calculated by dividing current assets by current liabilities:

$$\text{current ratio} = \frac{\text{current assets}}{\text{current liabilities}}$$

The current ratio indicates the company's coverage of current liabilities by current assets. For example, if the ratio were 2:1, the firm could realize only half of the values stated in the balance sheet in liquidating current assets and still have adequate funds to pay all current liabilities.

A general standard for this ratio (such as 2:1) is *not* useful. Such a standard fails to recognize that an appropriate current ratio is a function of the nature of a company's business and would vary with differing operating cycles of different businesses. The **operating cycle** of a company is the duration from the time cash is invested in goods and services to the time that investment produces cash.[9]

A **current asset** is one that is expected to be converted into cash in the ordinary operating cycle of a business. Inventory, therefore, is a current asset. In a tobacco or liquor manufacturing company, inventory may be as much as 80% to 90% of current assets. However, for a liquor company that inventory may have to age four years or more before it can be converted into a salable asset. Such a company typically would require a much higher current ratio than average to have adequate liquidity to meet current liabilities maturing in one year. For a public utility company where there is no inventory or receivables collection problem, a current ratio of 1.1 or 1.2 to 1 has proved satisfactory. Industry averages are published by organizations such as Dun & Bradstreet and Robert Morris Associates. While industry averages have their faults, they are preferable to general standards that do not recognize operating differences among classes of companies.

The current ratio has a major weakness as an analytical tool. It ignores the composition of current assets, which may be as important as their relationship with current liabilities. Therefore, current ratio analysis must be supplemented by other working capital ratios.

Since the problem in meeting current liabilities may rest on slowness or even inability to convert inventories into cash to meet current obligations, the **acid-test ratio** (also called the **quick ratio**) is recommended. This is the ratio of current assets minus inventories to current liabilities; that is:

$$\text{acid-test ratio} = \frac{\text{current assets} - \text{inventories}}{\text{current liabilities}}$$

This ratio does assume that receivables are of good quality and will be converted into cash over the next year.

ii. Capitalization Ratios   Credit analysts also calculate **capitalization ratios** to determine the extent to which the corporation is using financial leverage. These ratios, also called **financial leverage ratios**, can be interpreted only in the context of the stability of industry and company earnings and cash flow. The assumption is that the greater the stability of industry and company earnings and cash flow,

---

[9] For example, a firm that produces and sells goods has an operating cycle comprising of four phases: (1) purchase of raw material and produce goods, investing in inventory; (2) sell goods, generating sales, which may or may not be for cash; (3) extend credit, creating accounts receivable; and, (4) collect accounts receivable, generating cash. The four phases make up the cycle of cash use and generation. The operating cycle would be somewhat different for companies that produce services rather than goods, but the idea is the same—the operating cycle is the length of time it takes to generate cash through the investment of cash.

the more the company is able to accept the risk associated with financial leverage, and the higher the allowable ratio of debt to total capitalization (the total dollar amount of all long-term sources of funds in the balance sheet).

There are many variations to be found within the industry to calculate capitalization ratios. Two such ratios are shown below:

$$\text{long-term debt to capitalization} = \frac{\text{long-term debt}}{\text{long-term debt} + \text{shareholders' equity including minority interest}}$$

total debt to capitalization

$$= \frac{\text{current liabilities} + \text{long-term debt}}{\text{long-term debt} + \text{current liabilities} + \text{shareholders' equity including minority interest}}$$

where shareholders' equity includes preferred stock.

For both ratios, the higher the ratio, the greater the financial leverage. The value used to measure debt in both ratios is book value. It is useful to calculate stockholders' equity at market as well as at book value for the purpose of determining these ratios. A market calculation for common equity may indicate considerably more or less financial leverage than a book calculation.

Commercial rating companies and most Wall Street analysts rely heavily upon the long-term debt to capitalization ratio, and this is often provided in research reports sent out to clients. While this ratio can be useful, it should be noted that in recent years, given the uncertain interest rate environment, many corporations have taken to financing a good deal of their business with short-term debt. Indeed, an imaginative treasurer with a keen insight into money market activities can earn as much for a company as a plant manager, simply by switching debt from long term to short term and vice versa, at the right time.

Other considerations in using the long-term debt to capitalization ratio involves leased assets. Many corporations rent buildings and equipment under long-term lease contracts. Required rental payments are contractual obligations similar to bond coupon and repayment obligations. However, assets acquired through leasing (i.e., those leases classified as operating leases) may not be capitalized and shown in the balance sheet. Two companies, therefore, might work with the same amount of fixed assets and produce the same profits before interest or rental payments, but the one leasing a high proportion of its productive equipment could show significantly lower financial leverage.

iii. Coverage Tests   **Coverage ratios** are used to test the adequacy of cash flows generated through earnings for purposes of meeting debt and lease obligations. The four most commonly used coverage ratios are:

▶ EBIT interest coverage ratio
▶ EBITDA interest coverage ratio
▶ funds from operations/total debt ratio
▶ free operating cash flow/total debt ratio

EBIT stands for "earnings before interest and taxes." The **EBIT interest coverage ratio** is simply EBIT divided by the annual interest expense. (Interest expense includes "capitalized interest." This is effectively interest expense imputed for capitalized assets, the most important of which is leased assets.) Interest expense is tax deductible and, therefore, all earnings before taxes are available for paying such charges. Also, the interest should be added back to determine the amount available to meet annual interest expenses.

EBITDA stands for "earnings before interest, taxes, depreciation, and amortization." The **EBITDA interest coverage ratio** is simply the ratio of EBITDA divided by the annual interest expense.

The last two ratios listed above indicate the amount of funds from operations relative to the amount of total debt. The funds from operations includes net income plus the following: depreciation, amortization, deferred income taxes, and other noncash items. The definition of free operating cash flows varies by rating agency. In the next section we describe one variant of free operating cash flow.

Suggested standards for coverage ratios are based on experience and empirical studies relating the incidence of defaults over a number of years to such ratios. Different standards are needed for a highly cyclical company than for a stable company. In the case study presented in the appendix to this reading, benchmark ratios (as measured in terms of median ratios) by credit rating are presented for the coverage ratios described above, as well as for the capitalization ratios.

2. Cash Flow Analysis

Will the ratios just described be sufficient to help an analyst identify companies that may encounter financial difficulties? Consider the study by Largay and Stickney who analyzed the financial statements of W.T. Grant during the 1966–1974 period preceding its bankruptcy in 1975 and ultimate liquidation.[10] They noted that financial indicators such as profitability ratios, turnover ratios, and liquidity ratios showed some down trends, but provided no definite clues to the company's impending bankruptcy. A study of cash flows from operations, however, revealed that company operations were causing an increasing drain on cash, rather than providing cash.[11] This necessitated an increased use of external financing, the required interest payments on which exacerbated the cash flow drain. Cash flow analysis clearly was a valuable tool in this case since W.T. Grant had been running a negative cash flow from operations for years. Yet none of the traditional ratios discussed above take into account the cash flow from operations.

The need to look at cash flow is emphasized by Standard & Poor's:

> Cash flow analysis is the single most critical aspect of all credit rating decisions. It takes on added importance for speculative-grade issuers. While companies with investment-grade ratings generally have ready access to external cash to cover temporary shortfalls, junk-bond issuers lack this degree of flexibility and have fewer alternatives to internally generated cash for servicing debt.[12]

S&P also notes that: "Discussions about cash flow often suffer from lack of uniform definition of terms."[13] Below we describe how S&P's terminology with respect to four cash flow concepts: operating cash flow, free operating cash flow, discretionary cash flow, and prefinancing cash flow. In addition, we discuss the various ratios employing these cash flow measures.

---

[10] J.A. Largay III and C.P. Stickney, "Cash Flows, Ratio Analysis and the W.T. Grant Company Bankruptcy," *Financial Analysts Journal* (July–August 1980), pp. 51–54.

[11] For the period investigated, a statement of changes of financial position (on a working capital basis) was required prior to 1988.

[12] Standard & Poor's, *Corporate Ratings Criteria*, undated, p. 26.

[13] *Corporate Ratings Criteria*, p. 27.

a. Cash Flow Measures

Prior to the adoption of the statement of cash flows in 1987, the information regarding a firm's cash flows was quite limited. The **statement of cash flows** is a summary over a period of time of a firm's cash flows from operating, investing, and financing activities. The firm's statement of cash flows lists separately its

- ► cash flows from operating activities
- ► cash flows from investing
- ► cash flow financing activities

Typically the corresponding cash flows are referred to as:[14]

- ► Cash provided by operating activities
- ► Cash provided by/(used for) investing activities
- ► Cash used for financing activities

"Cash provided by operating activities" is also referred to as "cash flow from operations."

By analyzing these individual statement of cash flows, creditors can examine such aspects of the business as:

- ► The source of financing for business operations, whether through internally generated funds or external sources of funds.
- ► The ability of the company to meet debt obligations (interest and principal payments).
- ► The ability of the company to finance expansion through cash flow from its operating activities.
- ► The ability of the company to pay dividends to shareholders.
- ► The flexibility the business has in financing its operations.

A firm that generates cash flows only by selling off its assets (obtaining cash flows from investing) or by issuing more securities (obtaining cash flows from financing) cannot keep that up for very long. For future prosperity and the ability to meet its obligations, the firm must be able to generate cash flows from its operations.

Analysts have reformatted the information from the firm's income statement and statement of cash flows to obtain what they view as a better description of the company's activities. S&P begins with what it refers to as funds from operations. The **funds from operations** is defined as net income adjusted for depreciation

---

[14] Some firms use different labels. For example, Microsoft refers to these cash flows as: Net cash from operations, Net cash used for financing, and Net cash used for investing.

and other noncash debits and credits. Then from the funds from operation, the following cash flow measures are computed:[15]

> **Funds from operations**
>> Decrease (increase) in noncash current assets
>> Increase (decrease) in nondebt current liabilities
> ─────────────────────────────────────
> **Operating cash flow**
>> Decrease by capital expenditures
> ─────────────────────────────────────
> **Free opearting cash flow**
>> Decrease by cash dividends
> ─────────────────────────────────────
> **Discretionary cash flow**
>> Decrease by acquisitions
>> Increase by asset disposals
>> Net other sources (uses) of cash
> ─────────────────────────────────────
> **Prefinancing cash flow**

Operating cash flow is therefore funds from operations reduced by changes in the investment in working capital (current assets less current liabilities). Subtracting capital expenditures gives what S&P defines as **free operating cash flow**. It is this cash flow measure that can be used to pay dividends and make acquisitions.[16] Reducing free operating cash flow by cash dividends gives **discretionary cash flow**. Adjusting discretionary cash flow for managerial discretionary decisions for acquisition of other companies, the disposal of assets (e.g., lines of business or subsidiaries), and other sources or uses of cash gives **prefinancing cash flow**. As stated by S&P, prefinancing cash flow "represents the extent to which company cash flow from all internal sources have been sufficient to cover all internal needs."[17]

b. Cash Flow Ratios

S&P uses the following cash flow ratios (based on its cash flow definitions described above) in analyzing a company in addition to the measures described earlier for coverage ratios:

$$\frac{\text{Funds from operations}}{\text{Total debt (adjusted for off-balance sheet liabilities)}}$$

$$\frac{\text{Free operating cash flow} + \text{Interest}}{\text{Interest}}$$

$$\frac{\text{Free operating cash flow} + \text{Interest}}{\text{Interest} + \text{Annual principal repayment obligation}}$$

(the above ratio is referred to as the "debt service coverage ratio")

---

[15] *Corporate Ratings Criteria*, p. 27.

[16] One of the most popular measures of cash flow in equity analysis is the "free cash flow." This cash flow measure is defined as "the cash flow available to the company's suppliers of capital after all operating expenses (including taxes) have been paid and necessary investments in working capital (e.g., inventory) and fixed capital (e.g., equipment) have been made." (See, John D. Stowe, Thomas R. Robinson, Jerald E. Pinto, and Dennis W. McLeavey, *Analysis of Equity Investments: Valuation* (Charlottesville, VA: Association for Investment Management and Research, 2002), p. 115.) Analysts will make different adjustments to the statement of cash flows to obtain the free cash flow depending on the accounting information that is available. The procedure for calculating free cash flow starting with net income or statement of cash flows is explained in Stowe, Robinson, Pinto, and McLeavey, *Analysis of Equity Investments: Valuation*, pp. 119–124.

[17] *Corporate Ratings Criteria*, p. 27.

$$\frac{\text{Total debt}}{\text{Discretionary cash flow}}$$

(the above ratio is called the "debt payback period")

$$\frac{\text{Funds from operations}}{\text{Capital spending requirements}}$$

The particular cash flow ratios that S&P focuses on depends on the type of company being analyzed. According to S&P:

> Where long-term viability is more assured (i.e., higher in the rating spectrum) there can be greater emphasis on the level of funds from operations and its relation to total debt burden. These measures clearly differentiate between levels of protection over time. Focusing on debt service coverage and free cash flow becomes more critical in the analysis of a weaker company. Speculative-grade issuers typically face near-term vulnerabilities, which are better measured by free cash flow ratios.[18]

B. Analysis of Collateral

A corporate debt obligation can be secured or unsecured. In our discussion of creditor rights in a bankruptcy at Level I, we explained that in the case of a liquidation, proceeds from a bankruptcy are distributed to creditors based on the absolute priority rule. However, in the case of a reorganization, the **absolute priority rule** rarely holds. That is, an unsecured creditor may receive distributions for the entire amount of his or her claim and common stockholders may receive something, while a secured creditor may receive only a portion of its claim. The reason is that a reorganization requires approval of all the parties. Consequently, secured creditors are willing to negotiate with both unsecured creditors and stockholders in order to obtain approval of the plan of reorganization.

The question is then, what does a secured position mean in the case of a reorganization if the absolute priority rule is not followed in a reorganization? The claim position of a secured creditor is important in terms of the negotiation process. However, because absolute priority is not followed and the final distribution in a reorganization depends on the bargaining ability of the parties, some analysts place less emphasis on collateral compared to the other factors discussed earlier and covenants discussed next.

At Level I we discussed the various types of collateral used for a corporate debt issue and features that analysts should be cognizant of in looking at an investor's secured position. Other important features are covered in our discussion of covenants below.

C. Analysis of Covenants

Covenants deal with limitations and restrictions on the borrower's activities. Some covenants are common to all indentures, such as

▶ to pay interest, principal, and premium, if any, on a timely basis

▶ to pay all taxes and other claims when due unless contested in good faith

---

[18] *Corporate Ratings Criteria*, p. 27.

> ▶ to maintain all properties used and useful in the borrower's business in good condition and working order

> ▶ to submit periodic certificates to the trustee stating whether the debtor is in compliance with the loan agreement

These covenants are called **affirmative covenants** since they call upon the debtor to make promises to do certain things.

Negative covenants are those which require the borrower not to take certain actions. There are an infinite variety of restrictions that can be placed on borrowers, depending on the type of debt issue, the economics of the industry and the nature of the business, and the lenders' desires. Some of the more common restrictive covenants include various limitations on the company's ability to incur debt, since unrestricted borrowing can lead a company and its debtholders to ruin. Thus, debt restrictions may include limits on the absolute dollar amount of debt that may be outstanding or may require a ratio test—for example, debt may be limited to no more than 60% of total capitalization or that it cannot exceed a certain percentage of net **tangible assets**.

There may be an interest or fixed charge coverage test. The two common tests are:

> ▶ **maintenance test**: This test requires the borrower's ratio of earnings available for interest or fixed charges to be at least a certain minimum figure on each required reporting date (such as quarterly or annually) for a certain preceding period.

> ▶ **debt incurrence test**: only comes into play when the company wishes to do additional borrowing. In order to take on additional debt, the required interest or fixed charge coverage figure adjusted for the new debt must be at a certain minimum level for the required period prior to the financing. Debt incurrence tests are generally considered less stringent than maintenance provisions.

There could also be **cash flow tests** (or **cash flow requirements**) and **working capital maintenance provisions**.

Some indentures may prohibit subsidiaries from borrowing from all other companies except the parent. Indentures often classify subsidiaries as restricted or unrestricted. **Restricted subsidiaries** are those considered to be consolidated for financial test purposes; **unrestricted subsidiaries** (often foreign and certain special-purpose companies) are those excluded from the covenants governing the parent. Often, subsidiaries are classified as unrestricted in order to allow them to finance themselves through outside sources of funds.

Limitations on dividend payments and stock repurchases may be included in indentures. Often, cash dividend payments will be limited to a certain percentage of net income earned after a specific date (often the issuance date of the debt, called the "peg date") plus a fixed amount. Sometimes the dividend formula might allow the inclusion of the net proceeds from the sale of common stock sold after the peg date. In other cases, the dividend restriction might be so worded as to prohibit the declaration and payment of cash dividends if tangible net worth (or other measures, such as consolidated quick assets) declines below a certain amount.

D. Character of a Corporation

Character analysis involves the analysis of the quality of management. In discussing the factors it considers in assigning a credit rating, Moody's Investors Service notes the following regarding the quality of management:[19]

> Although difficult to quantify, management quality is one of the most important factors supporting an issuer's credit strength. When the unexpected occurs, it is a management's ability to react appropriately that will sustain the company's performance.

In assessing management quality, the analysts at Moody's, for example, try to understand the business strategies and policies formulated by management. Following are factors that are considered: (1) strategic direction, (2) financial philosophy, (3) conservatism, (4) track record, (5) succession planning, and (6) control systems.

In recent years, focus has been on the corporate governance of the firm and the role of the board of directors.

1. Corporate Governance

The bylaws are the rules of governance for the corporation. The bylaws define the rights and obligations of officers, members of the board of directors, and shareholders. In most large corporations, it is not possible for each owner to participate in monitoring of the management of the business. Therefore, the owners of a corporation elect a board of directors to represent them in the major business decisions and to monitor the activities of the corporation's management. The board of directors, in turn, appoints and oversees the officers of the corporation. Directors who are also employees of the corporation are called **inside directors**; those who have no other position within the corporation are **outside directors** or **independent directors**.

It is the board of directors that decides whether to hire, retain, or dismiss the chief executive officer, to establish the compensation system for senior management, and to ensure that the proper internal corporate control systems are in place to monitor management. Generally it is believed that the greater the proportion of outside directors, the greater the board independence from the management of the company. The proportion of outside directors on corporate boards varies significantly.

Recently, there have been a number of scandals and allegations regarding the financial information that is being reported to shareholders and the market. Financial results reported in the income statements and balance sheets of some companies indicated much better performance than the true performance or much better financial condition than actual.[20] Along with these financial reporting issues, the independence of the auditors and the role of financial analysts have been brought to the forefront.

The eagerness of managers to present favorable results to shareholders and the market appears to be a major factor in several of the scandals. Personal enrichment at the expense of shareholders seems to explain some of the scandals. Whatever the motivation, chief executive officers (CEOs), chief financial

---

[19] "Industrial Company Rating Methodology," p. 6.

[20] Examples include Xerox, which was forced to restate earnings for several years because it had inflated pre-tax profits by $1.4 billion, Enron, which is accused of inflating earnings and hiding substantial debt, and Worldcom, which failed to properly account for $3.8 billion of expenses.

officers (CFOs), and board members are being held directly accountable for financial disclosures. For example, in 2002, the U.S. Securities and Exchange Commission ordered sworn statements attesting to the accuracy of financial statements. The first deadline for such statements resulted in several companies restating financial results.

The accounting scandals are creating an awareness of the importance of corporate governance, the importance of the independence of the public-accounting auditing function, the role of financial analysts, and the responsibilities of CEOs and CFOs.

2. Agency Problem

Corporate financial theory helps us understand how the abuses that diminish shareholder value arise and the potential for mitigating the abuse. In a publicly traded company, typically the managers of a corporation are not the major owners. The managers make decisions for owners. Thus, the managers act as agents. An **agent** is a person who acts for—and exerts powers on behalf of—another person or group of persons. The person (or group of persons) the agent represents is referred to as the **principal**. The relationship between the agent and his or her principal is an **agency relationship**. There is an agency relationship between the managers and the shareholders of corporations.[21]

In an agency relationship, the agent is charged with the responsibility of acting for the principal. As a result, it is possible that the agent may not act in the best interest of the principal, but instead act in his or her own self-interest. This is because the agent has his or her own objective of maximizing personal wealth. In a large corporation, for example, the managers may enjoy many fringe benefits, such as golf club memberships, access to private jets, and company cars. These benefits (also called perquisites, or "perks") may be useful in conducting business and may help attract or retain management personnel, but there is room for abuse. The abuse of perquisites imposes costs on the firm—and ultimately on the owners of the firm. There is also a possibility that managers who feel secure in their positions may not bother to expend their best efforts toward the business. Finally, there is the possibility that managers will act in their own self-interest, rather than in the interest of the shareholders when those interests clash. For example, management may fight the acquisition of their firm by some other firm even if the acquisition would benefit shareholders. This is because in most takeovers, the management of the acquired firm generally lose their jobs. Consequently, a manager's self-interest may be placed ahead of those of shareholders who may be offered an attractive price for their stock in the acquisition.

There are costs involved with any effort to minimize the potential for conflict between the principal's interest and the agent's interest. Such costs are called **agency costs**, and they are of three types: monitoring costs, bonding costs, and residual loss.

Monitoring costs are costs incurred by the principal to monitor or limit the actions of the agent. In a corporation, shareholders may require managers to periodically report on their activities via audited accounting statements, which are sent to shareholders. The accountants' fees and the management time lost in preparing such statements are monitoring costs. Another example is the implicit cost incurred when shareholders limit the decision-making power of managers.

---

[21] The seminal paper on the agency-principal relationship in corporate finance is Michael Jensen and William Meckling, "Theory and the Firm: Managerial Behavior, Agency Costs and Ownership Structure," *Journal of Financial Economics* (October 1976), pp. 305–360.

By doing so, the owners may miss profitable investment opportunities; the foregone profit is a monitoring cost.

The board of directors of corporation has a fiduciary duty to shareholders; that is, the legal responsibility to make decisions (or to see that decisions are made) that are in the best interests of shareholders. Part of that responsibility is to ensure that managerial decisions are also in the best interests of the shareholders. Therefore, at least part of the cost of having directors is a monitoring cost.

Bonding costs are incurred by agents to assure principals that they will act in the principal's best interest. The name comes from the agent's promise or bond to take certain actions. A manager may enter into a contract that requires him or her to stay on with the firm even though another company acquires it; an implicit cost is then incurred by the manager, who foregoes other employment opportunities. Even when monitoring and bonding devices are used, there may be some divergence between the interests of principals and those of agents. The resulting cost, called the **residual loss**, is the implicit cost that results because the principal's and the agent's interests cannot be perfectly aligned even when monitoring and bonding costs are incurred.

3. Stakeholders and Corporate Governance

When managers of a corporation assess a potential investment in a new product, they examine the risks and the potential benefits and costs. Similarly, managers assess current investments for the same purpose; if benefits do not continue to outweigh costs, they will not continue to invest in the product but will shift their investment elsewhere. This is consistent with the goal of shareholder wealth maximization and with the **allocative efficiency** of the market economy.

Discontinuing investment in an unprofitable business may mean closing down plants, laying off workers, and, perhaps destroying an entire town that depends on the business for income. So decisions to invest or disinvest may affect great numbers of people. All but the smallest business firms are linked in some way to groups of persons who are dependent to a degree on the business. These groups may include suppliers, customers, the community itself, and nearby businesses, as well as employees and shareholders. The various groups of persons that depend on a firm are referred to as its **stakeholders**; they all have some *stake* in the outcomes of the firm. For example, if the Boeing Company lays off workers or increases production, the effects are felt by Seattle and the surrounding communities.

Can a firm maximize the wealth of shareholders and stakeholders at the same time? Probably. If a firm invests in the production of goods and services that meet the demand of consumers in such a way that benefits exceed costs, then the firm will be allocating the resources of the community efficiently, employing assets in their most productive use. If later the firm must disinvest— perhaps close a plant—it has a responsibility to assist employees and other stakeholders who are affected. Failure to do so could tarnish its reputation, erode its ability to attract new stakeholder groups to new investments, and ultimately act to the detriment of shareholders.

The effects of a firm's actions on others are referred to as **externalities**. Pollution is an important example. Suppose the manufacture of a product creates air pollution. If the polluting firm acts to reduce this pollution, it incurs a cost that either increases the price of its product or decreases profit and the market value of its stock. If competitors do not likewise incur costs to reduce their pollution, the firm is at a disadvantage and may be driven out of business through competitive pressure.

The firm may try to use its efforts at pollution control to enhance its reputation in the hope that this will lead to a sales increase large enough to make up for the cost of reducing pollution. This is a market solution: the market places a value on the pollution control and rewards the firm (or an industry) for it. If society really believes that pollution is bad and that pollution control is good, the interests of owners and society can be aligned.

It is more likely, however, that pollution control costs will be viewed as reducing owners' wealth. Then firms must be forced to reduce pollution through laws or government regulations. But such laws and regulations also come with a cost—the cost of enforcement. Again, if the benefits of mandatory pollution control outweigh the cost of government action, society is better off. In such a case, if the government requires all firms to reduce pollution, then pollution control costs simply become one of the conditions under which owner wealth-maximizing decisions are to be made.

4. Mitigating the Agency Problem: Standard and Codes of Best Practices for Corporate Governance

Let's focus on just shareholders and the agency problem as it relates to shareholders. There are three ways that shareholders can reduce the likelihood that management will act in its self interest. First, the compensation of the manager can be tied to the price performance of the firm. Second, managers can be granted a significant equity interest in the company. While an interesting solution, in practice most CEOs and boards have an extremely small equity interest in their firms. For example, a study of 1,000 of the largest U.S. corporations found that the median holdings of CEOs was less than 0.2% of the outstanding equity.[22]

Finally, the firm's internal corporate control systems can provide a means for effectively monitoring the performance and decision-making behavior of management. The timely removal of the CEO by the board of directors who believe that a CEO's performance is not in the best interest of the shareholders is one example of how an internal corporate control system can work. In general, there are several key elements of an internal corporate control system that are necessary for the effective monitoring of management. It is the breakdown of the internal corporate control systems that lead to corporate difficulties and the destruction of shareholder wealth.

Because of the important role placed by the board of directors, the structure and composition of the board is critical for effective corporate governance. The key is to remove the influence of the CEO on board members. This can be done in several ways. First, while there is no optimal board size, the more members the less likely the influence of the CEO. With more board members, a larger number of committees can be formed to deal with important matters of the firm. At a minimum, there should be an auditing committee, a nominating committee (for board members), and a compensation committee. Second, the composition of the committee should have a majority of independent directors and the committees should include only independent directors. Third, the nominating committee should develop sound criteria for the selection of potential directors and the retention of current board members. The nominating committee should use the services of recruiting agencies to identify potential independent board members rather than rely on the CEO or management to put forth a slate of candidates. Fourth, the sole chairman of the board of directors should not be the CEO. This

---

[22] Michael Jensen, "The Modern Industrial Revolution, Exist, and the Failure of Internal Control Systems," in Donald H. Chew, Jr. (ed.), *The New Corporate Finance: Second Edition* (New York, NY: McGraw-Hill, 1999).

practice allows the CEO to exert too much influence over board members and set agenda items at board meetings. A compromise position is having the chair of the board being jointly held by the CEO and an independent board member.

The standards and codes of best practice for effective corporate governance are evolving. Unlike securities laws or regulatory requirements (such as exchange listing requirements) which set forth rules that affect corporate governance, standards and codes of best practice go beyond the applicable securities law of the country and are adopted voluntarily by a corporation. The expectation is that the adoption of best practice for corporate governance is a signal to investors about the character of management. The standards of best practice that have become widely accepted as a benchmark are those set forth by the Organisation of Economic Cooperation and Development (OECD) in 1999. The OECD Principles of Corporate Governance cover:

▶ the basic rights of shareholders

▶ equitable treatment of shareholders

▶ the role of stakeholders

▶ disclosure and transparency

▶ the role of the board of directors.

Other entities that have established standards and codes for corporate governance are the Commonwealth Association for Corporate Governance, the International Corporate Governance Network, and the Business Roundtable. Countries have established their own code and standards using the OECD principles.[23]

A survey of more than 200 institutional investors throughout the world conducted between April and May 2002 by McKinsey & Company found that investors "put corporate governance on a par with financial indicators when evaluating investment decisions."[24] The investors surveyed indicated that they were prepared to pay a premium for the stock of companies that they felt exhibited high governance standards.

5. *Corporate Governance and Bond Ratings*

Empirically, there have been several studies that have investigated the impact of corporate governance on stockholder returns.[25] Our interest in this reading is the relationship between corporate governance and bond ratings (and hence bond yields). A study by Bhojraj and Sengupta investigates this relationship using a large sample of 1,001 industrial bonds for the period 1991–1996.[26]

They note that a firm's likelihood of default can be decomposed into two risks, information risk and agency risk. **Information risk** is the risk that the available information for evaluating default risk is not credible. There are two studies that support the position that corporate governance mechanisms reduce information risk. Beasley found that the greater the proportion of a board composed of

---

[23] The World Bank updates country progress on corporate governance on its web site: www.worldbank.org/html/fpd/privatesector/cg/codes.htm.

[24] *McKinsey & Company's Global Investor Opinion Survey,* May 2002.

[25] For a review of the impact of various corporate governance mechanism on shareholder returns, as well as the experiences and perspective of the California Public Employee Pension Fund (CalPERS), see Chapter 22 in Mark J.P. Anson, *Handbook of Alternative Assets* (Hoboken, NJ: John Wiley & Sons, 2002).

[26] Sanjeev Bhojraj and Partha Sengupta, "Effect of Corporate Governance on Bond Ratings and Yields: The Role of Institutional Investors and Outside Directors," *Journal of Business,* Vol. 76, No. 3 (2003), pp. 455–476.

outsiders, the lower the probability of financial statement fraud.[27] Sengupta found that the higher the quality of corporate disclosure, the higher the bond rating.[28] **Agency risk** is the risk that management will make decisions in its own self interest, thereby reducing firm value. There is mixed evidence on how the different types of corporate governance mechanism affect equity returns.

Bhojraj and Sengupta argue that if corporate governance mechanisms reduce agency risk and information risk, the result is that strong corporate governance should be associated with superior bond ratings and therefore lower yields. They find that companies that have greater institutional ownership and stronger outside control of the board benefitted from lower bond yields and higher ratings on their new bond issues. Bhojraj and Sengupta conclude that their findings "are consistent with the view that institutional owners and outside directors play an active role in reducing management opportunism and promoting firm value."

They also investigate the effect of governance mechanisms on lower rated corporate bonds. Bhojraj and Sengupta argue that the monitoring role of governance mechanisms would be more important when dealing with such bonds because traditional measures for assessing default risk described earlier in this reading (profitability ratios, debt and coverage ratios, and cash flow measures) may not be informative about future prospects for satisfying debt obligations. Their results are consistent with a greater role for corporate governance mechanisms in reducing default risk for corporations that issue lower rated bonds.

6. *Corporate Governance Ratings*

Several firms have developed services that assess corporate governance. One type of service provides confidential assessment of the relative strength of a firm's corporate governance practices. The customer for this service is a corporation seeking external evaluations of its current practice. The second is a service that rates (or scores) the corporate governance mechanisms of companies. Generally, these ratings are made public at the option of the company requesting an evaluation. The motivation for developing a corporate governance rating is described by one of the firms that provides this service, Governance Metrics International (GMI), as follows:

> Why are we undertaking this challenge? Our premise is simple: companies that focus on corporate governance and transparency will, over time, generate superior returns and economic performance and lower their cost of capital. The opposite is also true: companies weak in corporate governance and transparency represent increased investment risks and result in a higher cost of capital. Our hope is that GMI research and ratings will help diligent investors and corporations focus on governance on an ongoing basis, identify companies and particular items that need improvement and, just as important, recognize companies that are clearly trying to set the best example with a positive rating.[29]

Firms that provide corporate governance ratings for companies fall into two categories. The first are those that provide ratings for companies within a country. Examples of countries where firms have produced or plan to produce corporate

---

[27] M. Beasley, "An Empirical Analysis of the Relation Between the Board of Director Composition and Financial Statement Fraud," *Accounting Review* (October 1996), pp. 443–465.

[28] Partha Sengupta, "Corporate Disclosure Quality and the Cost of Debt," *Accounting Review* (October 1998), pp. 459–474.

[29] Howard Sherman, "Corporate Governance Ratings," *Corporate Governance* (January 2004), p. 6.

governance ratings are Australia, Brazil, Greece, India, Malaysia, Philippines, Russia, South Korea, and Thailand.[30] The second category includes firms that rate across country borders. Examples of firms that fall into this category are Standard & Poor's, Governance Metrics International, The Corporate Library, and Deminor. We discuss each below.

Standard & Poor's produces a Corporate Governance Score which, at the option of the company, may be disclosed to the public. The score or rating is based on a review of both publicly available information, interviews with senior management and directors, and confidential information that S&P may have available from its credit rating of the corporation's debt.

S&P believes that its Corporate Governance Score helps companies in the following ways:

▶ Benchmark their current governance practices against global best practices

▶ Communicate both the substance and form of their governance practices to investors, insurers, creditors, customers, regulators, employees, and other stakeholders

▶ Enhance the investor relations process when used as part of a program designed to highlight governance effectiveness to both potential and current investors, thus differentiating the company from its competitors[31]

The score is based on four key elements evaluated by S&P:[32]

1. *Ownership structure and external influences*
   ▶ Transparency of ownership structure
   ▶ Concentration and influence of ownership and external stakeholders

2. *Shareholder rights and stakeholder relations*
   ▶ Shareholder meeting and voting procedures
   ▶ Ownership rights and takeover defenses
   ▶ Stakeholder relations

3. *Transparency, disclosure and audit*
   ▶ Content of public disclosure
   ▶ Timing of and access to public disclosure
   ▶ Audit process

4. *Board structure and effectiveness*
   ▶ Board structure and independence
   ▶ Role and effectiveness of the board
   ▶ Director and senior executive compensation

Based on the S&P's analysis of the four key elements listed above, its assessment of the company's corporate governance practices and policies and how its policies serve shareholders and other stakeholders is reflected in the Corporate Governance Score. The score ranges from 10 (the highest score) to 1 (the lowest score).

---

[30] Sherman, "Corporate Governance Ratings," p. 5.

[31] Standard & Poor's, *Corporate Governance Evaluations & Scores*, undated, p. 2.

[32] *Corporate Governance Evaluations & Scores*, p. 2.

Governance Metrics International (GMI) provides two types of ratings. The first is what GMI refers to as a its "basic" rating; the information for this rating is based on publicly available information (regulatory filings, company websites, and news services); no fee is charged to a company receiving a basic rating. The second is a fee-based "comprehensive" rating obtained from interviews with outside directors and senior management. The seven categories analyzed by GMI are shareholder rights, compensation policies, accountability of the board, financial disclosure, market for control, shareholder base, and corporate reputation. There are more than 600 metrics that are used in generating the rating. GMI's scoring model calculates a value between 1 (1 lowest score) and 10 (highest score). The scores are relative to the other companies that are included in the universe researched by GMI. The ratings provided include a global rating (which allows a comparison to all the companies in the universe), a home market rating (which allows a comparison to all of the companies in the home country or region), and corresponding ratings for each of the seven categories analyzed by GMI.

The Corporate Library (TCL) has a rating service it calls "Board Effectiveness Rating." Rather than using best practice standards or codes in developing its corporate governance indicators, ratings are based on what this firm believes are "proven dynamics indicators of interest to shareholders and investors."[33] The indicators include compensation, outside director shareholdings, board structure and make-up, accounting and audit oversight, and board decision-making. The focus is on "which boards are most likely to enhance and preserve shareholder value, and which boards might actually increase investor risk."[34] The ratings are expressed on a scale ranging from A (highest effectiveness) to F (lowest effectiveness). TCL does not intend for its ratings to be used on a stand alone basis. Rather, the ratings are intended to improve current investment research methods employed by investors.

Finally, Deminor focuses on corporate governance ratings for Western European firms. The rating is based on 300 corporate governance indicators obtained from public and non-public information provided by the company being rated, as well as on interviews with members of the board of directors and executive committee. The ratings are based on standards that are internationally recognized such as the OECD Principles of Corporate Governance. The four categories analyzed are (1) rights and duties of shareholders, (2) commitment to shareholder value, (3) disclosure on corporate governance, and (4) board structure and functioning. The ratings range from 1 (lowest) to 10 (highest). There is an overall rating and a rating for each of the four categories.

E. Special Considerations for High-Yield Corporate Bonds

The discussion thus far has focused on credit analysis for any issuer regardless of credit rating. There are some unique factors that should be considered in the analysis of high-yield bonds. We will discuss the following:

► analysis of debt structure

► analysis of corporate structure

► analysis of covenants

---

[33] www.thecorporatelibrary.net/products/ratings2003.html.

[34] Indicators that best practice might suggest such as a split chairman of the board/CEO role or a lead independent director are not considered by TCL because the firm does not believe they are significant in improving board effectiveness.

In addition, we will discuss the reasons why an equity analysis approach to high-yield bond issuers is being used.

1. Analysis of Debt Structure

In January 1990, the Association for Investment Management and Research held a conference on high-yield bonds. One of the presenters at the conference was William Cornish, then President of Duff & Phelps Credit Rating Company.[35] In his presentation he identified a unique factor in the credit analysis of high-yield issuers—the characteristics of the types of debt obligations comprising a high-yield issuer's debt structure.[36]

Cornish explained why it was necessary for an analyst to examine a high-yield issuer's debt structure. At the time of his presentation, new types of bonds were being introduced into the high-yield market such as deferred coupon bonds. He noted that the typical debt structure of a high-yield issuer includes:

▶ bank debt

▶ brokers loans or "bridge loans"

▶ reset notes

▶ senior debt

▶ senior subordinated debt

▶ subordinated debt (payment in kind bonds)

Cornish then went on to explain the importance of understanding the characteristics of the diverse debt obligations that are included in a typical high-yield debt structure.

Consider first bank loans. While investment-grade issuers also have bank debt in their capital structure, high-yield issuers rely to a greater extent on this form of debt because of a lack of alternative financing sources. Banks loans have three key characteristics. First, holders of bank debt have a priority over other debt holders on the firm's assets. Second, bank debt is typically short-term (usually it is not greater than two years). Finally, the rate on bank debt floats with the level of interest rates.

There are three implications of these characteristics of bank debt for the analysis of the credit worthiness of high-yield issuers. First, because the cost of this source of debt financing is affected by changes in short-term interest rates, the analyst must incorporate changing interest rate scenarios into cash flow projections. A rise in short-term interest rates can impose severe cash flow problems for an issuer heavily financed by bank debt.

Second, because the debt is short term, bank debt must be repaid in the near future. The challenge that the analyst faces is determining where the funds will be obtained to pay off maturing bank debt. There are three sources available:

1. repayment from operating cash flow

2. refinancing

3. sale of assets

---

[35] Duff & Phelps was acquired by Fitch.

[36] William A. Cornish, "Unique Factors in the Credit Analysis of High-Yield Bonds," in Frank K. Reilly (ed.), *High-Yield Bonds: Analysis and Risk Assessment* (Charlottesville, VA: Association for Investment Management and Research, 1990).

Typically, it is a combination of the above three sources that a high-yield issuer will use. The implication is that the analyst must carefully examine the timing and amount of maturing bank debt and consider the sources for repayment.

If the repayment is to come from operations, the projections of cash flow from operations become even more critical than for a high-grade issuer which can rely on a wider range of funding sources such as commercial paper. When refinancing is the source of funds for loan repayment, there is the issue discussed earlier that future conditions in the financial market must be incorporated into the analyst's projections in order to assess future funding costs.

If the source of the loan repayment is the sale of assets, the analyst must consider which assets will be sold and how the sale of such assets will impact future cash flow from operations. If key assets must be sold to pay off maturing bank debt, management is adversely impacting the ability to repay other debt in the future from cash flow from operations. In leveraged buyouts, the new management will have a specific plan for the disposal of certain assets in order to pay off bank debt and other debt or related payments. One credit analyst, Jane Tripp Howe, suggests that the analyst ask the following questions regarding asset sales:[37]

> Can the company meet its cash obligations if the sale of assets is delayed?
> How liquid are the assets that are scheduled for sale?
> Are the appraised values for these assets accurate?

Banks will not provide short-term funds where there are insufficient assets to cover a loan in the case of liquidation. If short-term to intermediate-term funds are needed, a high-yield issuer will turn to broker loans (or bridge loans) and/or reset notes. At Level I we covered reset notes. A reset note is a security where the **coupon** rate is reset periodically such that the security price will trade at some specified premium above par value. The presence of reset notes in the debt structure is of particular concern to the analyst for two reasons. First, there is the need to analyze the impact of future interest rates and spreads to assess the impact of higher borrowing costs. Second, to avoid a higher reset rate when interest rates rise due to rising interest rates in general and/or because of a higher spread demanded by the market for the particular issuer, the issuer may seek to dispose of assets. Again the assets sold may have an adverse impact on future cash flow from operations.

While there are typically longer **term bonds** referred to as "senior bonds" in a high-yield issuer's debt structure, the term "senior bonds" is misleading in the presence of bank loans. Moreover, there are deferred coupon bonds. One such bond structure is a zero-coupon bond. Deferred coupon bonds permit the issuer to postpone interest payment to some future year. As a result, the interest burden is placed on future cash flow to meet the interest obligations. Because of this burden, the presence of deferred coupon bonds may impair the ability of the issuer to improve its credit quality in future periods. Moreover, if senior bonds have deferred coupon payments, the subordinated bonds will be adversely affected over time as the amount of senior bonds increases over time relative to the amount of subordinated bonds. For example, one type of deferred coupon bond that was commonly issued at one time was the payment-in-kind (**PIK**) bond. With this bond structure, a high-yield issuer has the option to either pay interest in cash or pay the equivalent of interest with another bond with the same coupon rate. If the issuer does not have the ability to pay the interest in cash,

---

[37] Jane Tripp Howe, "Credit Considerations in Evaluating High-Yield Bonds," Chapter 21 in Frank J. Fabozzi (ed.), *Handbook of Fixed Income Securities* (Burr Ridge, IL: Irwin Professional Publishing, 1997), p. 408.

payment with another bond will increase future interest expense and thereby adversely impact the issuer's future cash flow. If the PIK bonds are senior bonds, subordinated bonds are adversely affected over time as more senior bonds are added to the capital structure and future interest expense is increased further.

2. *Analysis of Corporate Structure*

High-yield issuers usually have a holding company structure. The assets to pay creditors of the holding company will come from the operating subsidiaries. Cornish explains why it is critical to analyze the corporate structure for a high-yield issuer. Specifically, the analyst must understand the corporate structure in order to assess how cash will be passed between subsidiaries and the parent company and among the subsidiaries. The corporate structure may be so complex that the payment structure can be confusing.

Cornish provides an illustration of this. At the time of his presentation (January 1990), Farley Inc. had the following debt structure: senior subordinated debt, subordinated notes, and junior subordinated debt. The question raised by Cornish was where Farley Inc. was going to obtain cash flow to make payments to its creditors. One possibility was to obtain funds from its operating subsidiaries. At the time, Farley Inc. had three operating subsidiaries: Fruit of the Loom, Acme Boot, and West Point Pepperell. An examination of the debt structure of Fruit of the Loom (20% owned by Farley Inc.) indicated that there was bank debt and no intercompany loans were permitted. While there were restrictions on dividend payments, none were being paid at the time. An examination of the Acme Boot (100% owned by Farley Inc.) showed that there was bank debt and while there were restrictions but no prohibitions on intercompany loans, Farley Inc. had in fact put cash into this operating subsidiary. Finally, West Point Pepperell (95% owned by Farley Inc.) had bridge loans that restricted asset sales and dividend payments. Moreover, any payments that could be made to Farley Inc. from West Point Pepperell had to be such that they would not violate West Point Pepperell's financial ratio requirements imposed by its bridge loan. The key point of the illustration is that an analyst evaluating the ability of Farley Inc. to meet its obligations to creditors would have to look very closely at the three operating subsidiaries. Just looking at financial ratios for the entire holding company structure would not be adequate. At the time, it was not likely that the three operating subsidiaries would be able to make any contribution to assist the parent company in paying off its creditors.

3. *Analysis of Covenants*

While an analyst should of course consider covenants when evaluating any bond issue (investment grade or high yield), it is particularly important for the analysis of high-yield issuers. The importance of understanding covenants was summarized by one high-yield portfolio manager, Robert Levine, as follows:[38]

> Covenants provide insight into a company's strategy. As part of the credit process, one must read covenants within the context of the corporate strategy. It is not sufficient to hire a lawyer to review the covenants because a lawyer might miss the critical factors necessary to make the appropriate decision. Also, loopholes in covenants often provide clues about the intentions of management teams.

[38] Robert Levine, "Unique Factors in Managing High-Yield Bond Portfolios," in *High-Yield Bonds*, p. 35.

4. Equity Analysis Approach

Historically, the return on high-yield bonds has been greater than that of high-grade corporate bonds but less than that of common stocks. The risk (as measured in terms of the standard deviation of returns) has been greater than the risk of high-grade bonds but less than that of common stock. Moreover, high-yield bond returns have been found to be more highly correlated to equity returns than to investment grade bond returns. This is why, for example, managers hedging high-yield bond portfolios have found that a combination of stock index futures contracts and Treasury futures contracts has offered a better hedging alternative than just hedging with Treasury bond futures.[39]

Consequently, some portfolio managers strongly believe that high-yield bond analysis should be viewed from an equity analyst's perspective. As Stephen Esser notes:[40]

> Using an equity approach, or at least considering the hybrid nature of high-yield debt, can either validate or contradict the results of traditional credit analysis, causing the analyst to dig further.

He further states:[41]

> For those who work with investing in high-yield bonds, whether issued by public or private companies, dynamic, equity-oriented analysis is invaluable. If analysts think about whether they would want to buy a particular high-yield company's stock and what will happen to the future equity value of that company, they have a useful approach because, as equity values go up, so does the equity cushion beneath the company's debt. All else being equal, the bonds then become better credits and should go up in value relative to competing bond investments.

We will not review the equity analysis framework here. But, there has been strong sentiment growing in the investment community that an equity analysis approach will provide a better framework for high-yield bond analysis than a traditional credit approach.

F. Credit Analysis of Non-Corporate Bonds

In this section we will look at the key factors analyzed in assessing the credit of the following non-corporate bonds:

▶ asset-backed securities and non-agency mortgage-backed securities
▶ municipal bonds
▶ sovereign bonds

---

[39] Kenneth S. Choie, "How to Hedge a High-Yield Bond Portfolio," Chapter 13 in Frank J. Fabozzi (ed.), *The New High-Yield Debt Market* (New York, NY: HarperBusiness, 1990).

[40] Stephen F. Esser, "High-Yield Bond Analysis: The Equity Perspective," in Ashwinpaul C. Sondhi (ed.), *Credit Analysis of Nontraditional Debt Securities* (Charlottesville, VA: Association for Investment Management and Research, 1995), p. 47.

[41] Esser, "High-Yield Bond Analysis: The Equity Perspective," p. 54.

1. Asset-Backed Securities and Non-Agency Mortgage-Backed Securities

Asset-backed securities and non-agency mortgage-backed securities expose investors to credit risk. The three nationally recognized statistical rating organizations rate asset-backed securities. We begin with the factors considered by rating agencies in assigning ratings to asset-backed securities. Then we will discuss how the agencies differ with respect to rating asset-backed securities versus corporate bonds.

a. Factors Considered by Rating Agencies

In analyzing credit risk, the rating companies focus on: (1) credit quality of the collateral, (2) quality of the seller/servicer, (3) cash flow stress and payment structure, and (4) legal structure.[42] We discuss each below.

i. Credit Quality of the Collateral Analysis of the credit quality of the collateral depends on the asset type. The rating companies will look at the underlying borrower's ability to pay and the borrower's equity in the asset. The latter will be a key determinant as to whether the underlying borrower will default or sell the asset and pay off a loan. The rating companies will look at the experience of the originators of the underlying loans and will assess whether the loans underlying a specific transaction have the same characteristics as the experience reported by the issuer.

The concentration of loans is examined. The underlying principle of asset securitization is that the large number of borrowers in a pool will reduce the credit risk via diversification. If there are a few borrowers in the pool that are significant in size relative to the entire pool balance, this diversification benefit can be lost, resulting in a higher level of default risk. This risk is called **concentration risk**. In such instances, rating companies will set concentration limits on the amount or percentage of receivables from any one borrower. If the concentration limit at issuance is exceeded, the issue will receive a lower credit rating than if the concentration limit was not exceeded. If after issuance the concentration limit is exceeded, the issue may be downgraded.

Based on its analysis of the collateral and other factors described below, a rating company will determine the amount of credit enhancement necessary for an issue to receive a particular rating. Credit enhancement levels are determined relative to a specific rating desired for a security and can be either internal or external. External credit enhancement can be either insurance, corporate guarantees, letters of credit, or cash collateral **reserves**. Internal **credit enhancements** include reserve funds, overcollateralization, and senior/subordinated structures.

ii. Quality of the Seller/Servicer All loans must be serviced. Servicing involves collecting payments from borrowers, notifying borrowers who may be delinquent, and, when necessary, recovering and disposing of the collateral if the borrower does not make loan repayments by a specified time. These responsibilities are fulfilled by a third-party to an asset-backed securities transaction called a **servicer**. The servicer may be the originator of the loans used as the collateral.

In addition to the administration of the loan portfolio as just described, the servicer is responsible for distributing the proceeds collected from the borrowers to the different bondholders according to the payment priorities. Where there are floating-rate securities in the transaction, the servicer will determine the

---

[42] Suzanne Michaud, "A Rating Agency Perspective on Asset-Backed Securities," Chapter 16 in Anand K. Bhattacharya and Frank J. Fabozzi (eds.), *Asset-Backed Securities* (New Hope, PA: Frank J. Fabozzi Associates, 1997).

interest rate for the period. The servicer may also be responsible for advancing payments when there are delinquencies in payments (that are likely to be collected in the future) resulting in a temporary shortfall in the payments that must be made to the bondholders.

The role of the servicer is critical in a securitization transaction. Therefore, rating agencies look at the ability of a servicer to perform its duties before assigning a rating to the bonds in a transaction. For example, the following factors are reviewed when evaluating servicers: servicing history, experience, underwriting standard for loan originations, servicing capabilities, human resources, financial condition, and growth/competition/business environment.

As explained in the reading on asset-backed securities, the issuer is the special purpose vehicle or trust. There are no employees. The trust simply has loans and receivables. The servicer therefore plays an important role in assuring that the payments are made to the bondholders. Shortly we will see how the characteristics of the servicer affect the way in which an issue is evaluated in terms of credit quality in comparison to the rating of a corporate bond issue.

iii. Cash Flow Stress and Payment Structure   As explained in the reading on asset-backed securities, the waterfall describes how the cash flow (i.e., interest and principal payments) from the collateral will be distributed to pay trustee fees, servicing fees, other administrative fees, and interest and principal to the bondholders in the structure. In determining a rating for bond class, the process begins with an analysis of the cash flow from the collateral under different assumptions about losses and delinquencies and economic scenarios established by the rating agency. (That is, the rating agencies perform a scenario analysis.) Then in each scenario, the cash flow is distributed to all bond classes in accordance with the structure's waterfall. Once a determination of what loss to the different bond's in the structure can occur, a rating can be assigned.

iv. Legal Structure   A corporation using structured financing seeks a rating on the securities it issues that is higher than its own corporate bond rating. If that is not possible, the corporation seeking funds would be better off simply issuing a corporate bond.

The corporation seeking funds will sell collateral to a special purpose vehicle (SPV). The corporation selling the collateral to the SPV is called the "seller." It is the SPV that issues the securities and is therefore referred to as the "issuer." The SPV is used so that the collateral is no longer an asset of the corporation that sold it and therefore available to the seller's creditors. The key in a securitization is to protect the buyers of the asset-backed securities issued by the SPV from having a bankruptcy judge redirect the collateral to the creditors of the selling corporation. Consequently, the rating agencies examine the legal structure and the underlying legal documents to assure that this will not happen in a bankruptcy.

b. Corporate Bond versus Asset-Backed Securities Credit Analysis

Let's look at how the rating of an asset-backed security differs from that of a corporate bond issue. To understand the difference, it is important to appreciate how the cash flow that must be generated differs for a corporate bond issue and a securitization transaction from which the asset-backed securities are created.

In a corporate bond issue, management through its operations must undertake the necessary activities that will produce revenues and collect revenues. Management will incur costs in creating products and services. These costs include management compensation, employee salaries, the costs of raw materials, and financial costs. Consequently, in evaluating the credit risk of a corporate bond issue, an analyst will examine the factors discussed earlier in this reading regarding the corporation's capacity to pay and the corporation's character.

In contrast, in a securitization transaction, there are assets (loans or receivables) that are to be collected and distributed to bondholders (i.e., investors in the asset-backed securities). There are no operating or business risks such as the competitive environment or existence of control systems that are needed to assess the cash flow. What is important is the quality of the collateral in generating the cash flow needed to make interest and principal payments. The assurance of cash flow based on different scenarios regarding defaults and delinquencies that the rating agencies will review. The rating agencies will review the likelihood of the cash flow based on different scenarios regarding defaults and delinquencies. The greater predictability of the cash flow in a securitization transaction that will be distributed to each bond class issue due to the absence of operational risks that distinguishes it from a corporate bond issue. It is the greater predictability of the cash flow in an asset-backed security transaction due to the absence of operational risks that distinguishes it from a corporate bond issue.

In a "true" securitization transaction, the role of the servicer is to simply collect the cash flow. There is no active management with respect to the collateral as is the case of the management necessary to operate a corporation to generate cash flow to pay bondholders. Standard & Poor's defines a "true securitization" as follows:

> In a true securitization, repayment is not dependent on the ability of the servicer to replenish the pool with new collateral or to perform more than routine administrative functions.[43]

There are securitization transactions where the role of the servicer is more than administrative. Where the role of the servicer is more than administrative, Standard & Poor's, for example, refers to such transactions as **hybrid transactions**. This is because such transactions have elements of an asset-backed security transaction and a corporation performing a service. According to Standard & Poor's:

> In a hybrid transaction, the role of the servicer is akin to that of a business manager. The hybrid servicer performs not only administrative duties, as in a true securitization, but also . . . [other] services that are needed to generate cash flow for debt service.[44]

Moreover, Standard & Poor's notes that:

> Unlike a true securitization, where the servicer is a fungible entity replaceable with few, if any, consequences to the transaction, bondholders depend on the expertise of the hybrid servicer for repayment. . . . Not coincidentally, these are the same attributes that form the basis of a corporate rating of the hybrid servicer. They also explain the rating linkage between the securitization and its hybrid servicer.[45]

Standard & Poor's provides an illustration of the distinction between a true asset-backed securitization transaction and one requiring a more active role for the servicer.[46] Consider a railcar company that has several hundred leases and

---

[43] Standard & Poor's, "Rating Hybrid Securitizations," *Structured Finance* (October 1999), p. 2.

[44] "Rating Hybrid Securitizations," p. 3.

[45] "Rating Hybrid Securitizations," p. 3.

[46] "Rating Hybrid Securitizations," p. 3.

the leases are with a pool of diversified highly rated companies. Suppose that each lease is for 10 years and it is the responsibility of the customers—not the railcar company—to perform the necessary maintenance on the leased railcars. If there is an asset-backed security transaction backed by these leases and the term of the transaction is 10 years, then the role of the servicer is minimal. Since the leases are for 10 years and the securities issued are for 10 years, the servicer is just collecting the lease payments and distributing them to the holders of the securities. In such a transaction, it *is* possible for this issue to obtain a high investment-grade rating as a true asset-backed security transaction.

Suppose we change the assumptions as follows. The securities issued are for 25 years, not 10 years. Also assume that the railcar company, not the customers, is responsible for the servicing. Now the role of the servicer changes. The servicer will be responsible for finding new companies to release the railcars to when the original leases terminate in 10 years. This is necessary because the securities issued have a maturity of 25 years but the original leases only cover payments to securityholders for the first 10 years. It is the releasing of the railcars that is required for the last 15 years. The servicer under this new set of assumptions is also responsible for the maintenance of the railcars leased. Thus, the servicer must be capable of maintaining the railcars or have on-going arrangements with one or more companies that have the ability to perform such maintenance.

How do rating agencies evaluate hybrid transactions? These transactions will be rated both in terms of a standard methodology for rating an asset-backed security transaction and using a "quasi-corporate approach" (in the words of Standard & Poor's) which involves an analysis of the servicer. The relative weight of the evaluations in assigning a rating to an asset-backed security transaction will depend on the involvement of the servicer. The more important the role of the servicer, the more weight will be assigned to the quasi-corporate approach analysis.

2. Municipal Bonds

At Level I we discussed **municipal bonds** available in the United States—tax-backed debt and **revenue bonds**. However, municipal governments in other countries are making greater use of bonds with similar structures to raise funds. Below we discuss the factors that should be considered in assessing the credit risk of an issue.

a. Tax-Backed Debt

In assessing the credit risk of tax-backed debt, there are four basic categories that should be considered. The first category includes information on the issuer's debt structure to determine the overall debt burden.[47] The second category relates to the issuer's ability and political discipline to maintain sound budgetary policy. The focus of attention here usually is on the issuer's general operating funds and whether it has maintained at least **balanced budgets** over three to five years. The third category involves determining the specific local taxes and intergovernmental revenues available to the issuer, as well as obtaining historical information both on tax collection rates, which are important when looking at property tax levies, and on the dependence of local budgets on specific revenue sources. The final category of information necessary to the credit analysis is an assessment of the issuer's overall socioeconomic environment. The determinations that have to be made here include trends of local employment distribution

---

[47] For municipalities, the debt burden usually is composed of the debt per capita as well as the debt as percentages of real estate valuations and personal incomes.

and composition, population growth, real estate property valuation, and personal income, among other economic factors.

b. Revenue Bonds

Revenue bonds are issued for either project or enterprise financings where the bond issuers pledge to the bondholders the revenues generated by the operating projects financed, or for general public-purpose financings in which the issuers pledge to the bondholders the tax and revenue resources that were previously part of the general fund.

While there are numerous security structures for revenue bonds, the underlying principle in assessing an issuer's credit worthiness is whether the project being financed will generate sufficient cash flows to satisfy the obligations due bondholders. Consequently, the analysis of revenue bonds is similar to the analysis of corporate bonds.

In assessing the credit risk of revenue bonds, the **trust indenture** and legal opinion should provide legal comfort in the following bond-security areas: (1) the limits of the basic security, (2) the flow-of-funds structure, (3) the rate, or user-charge, covenant, (4) the priority-of-revenue claims, (5) the additional-bonds tests, and (6) other relevant covenants.

i. Limits of the Basic Security   The trust indenture and legal opinion should explain the nature of the revenues for the bonds and how they realistically may be limited by federal, state, and local laws and procedures. The importance of this is that while most revenue bonds are structured and appear to be supported by identifiable revenue streams, those revenues sometimes can be negatively affected directly by other levels of government.

ii. Flow of Funds Structure for Revenue Bonds   For a revenue bond, the revenue of the enterprise is pledged to service the debt of the issue. The details of how revenue received by the enterprise will be disbursed are set forth in the trust indenture. Typically, the flow of funds for a revenue bond is as follows. First, all revenues from the enterprise are put into a **revenue fund**. It is from the revenue fund that disbursements for expenses are made to the following funds: **operation and maintenance fund**, **sinking fund**, **debt service reserve fund**, **renewal and replacement fund**, **reserve maintenance fund**, and **surplus fund**.

There are structures in which it is legally permissible for others to tap the revenues of the enterprise prior to the disbursement set forth in the flow of funds structure just described. For example, it is possible that the revenue bond could be structured such that the revenue is first applied to the general obligation of the municipality that has issued the bond.

Operations of the enterprise have priority over the servicing of the issue's debt, and cash needed to operate and maintain the enterprise is deposited from the revenue fund into the operation and maintenance fund. The pledge of revenue to the bondholders is a net revenue pledge, "net" meaning after operation expenses, so cash required to service the debt is deposited next into the sinking fund. Disbursements are then made to bondholders as specified in the trust indenture. Any remaining cash is then distributed to the reserve funds.

The purpose of the debt service reserve fund is to accumulate cash to cover any shortfall of future revenue to service the issue's debt. The specific amount that must be deposited is stated in the trust indenture. The function of the renewal and replacement fund is to accumulate cash for regularly scheduled major repairs and equipment replacement. The function of the reserve maintenance fund is to accumulate cash for extraordinary maintenance or replacement costs that might arise. Finally, if any cash remains after disbursement for operations, debt servicing, and reserves, it is deposited in the surplus fund. The entity issuing the bond can use the cash in this fund in any way it deems appropriate.

iii. Rate, or User-Charge, Covenants   There are various restrictive covenants included in the trust indenture for a revenue bond to protect the bondholders. A **rate covenant** (or **user charge covenant**) dictates how charges will be set on the product or service sold by the enterprise. The covenant could specify that the minimum charges be set so as to satisfy both expenses and debt servicing, or to yield a higher rate to provide for a certain amount of reserves.

iv. Priority-of-Revenue Claims   The legal opinion as summarized in the official statement should clearly indicate whether or not others can legally tap the revenue of the issuer even before they start passing through the issuer's flow-of-funds structure.

v. Additional-Bonds Test   An **additional-bonds test covenant** indicates whether additional bonds with the same lien (i.e., claim against property) may be issued. If additional bonds with the same lien may be issued, the conditions that must first be satisfied are specified. Other covenants specify that the facility may not be sold, the amount of insurance to be maintained, requirements for recordkeeping and for the auditing of the enterprise's financial statements by an independent accounting firm, and requirements for maintaining the facilities in good order.

vi. Other Relevant Covenants   There are other relevant covenants for the bond-holder's protection that the trust indenture and legal opinion should cover. These usually include pledges by the issuer of the bonds to have insurance on the project, to have accounting records of the issuer annually audited by an outside certified public accountant, to have outside engineers annually review the condition of the facility, and to keep the facility operating for the life of the bonds.

c. Corporate Versus Municipal Bond Credit Analysis

The credit analysis of municipal bonds involves the same factors and quantitative measures as in corporate credit analysis. For tax-backed debt, the analysis of the character of the public officials is the same as that of the analysis of the character of management for a corporate bond. The analysis of the ability to pay in the case of tax-backed debt involves looking at the ability of the issuing entity to generate taxes and fees. As a corporate analyst would look at the composition of the revenues and profits by product line for a corporation, the municipal analyst will look at employment, industry, and real estate valuation trends needed to generate taxes and fees.

The credit analysis of municipal revenue bonds is identical to that of a corporate bond analysis. Effectively, the enterprise issuing a municipal revenue bond must generate cash flow from operations to satisfy the bond payments. For example, here are the types of questions that a municipal analyst evaluating a toll road, bridge, or tunnel revenue bond would ask. As you read these questions you will see that they are the same types of questions that a corporate analyst would ask in evaluating a corporate issuer if it could issue a bond for a toll road, bridge, or tunnel.[48]

1. What is the traffic history and how sensitive is the demand to the toll charged? Equivalently, does the toll road, bridge, or tunnel provide a vital

---

[48] Sylvan G. Feldstein and Frank J. Fabozzi, *The Dow Jones-Irwin Guide to Municipal Bonds* (Homewood, IL: Dow Jones-Irwin, 1987), p. 72.

transportation link or does it face competition from interstate highways, toll-free bridges, or mass transportation?

2. How well is the facility maintained? Has the issuer established a maintenance reserve fund at a reasonable level to use for such repair work as road resurfacing and bridge painting?

3. What is the history of labor-management relations, and can public employee strikes substantially reduce toll collections?

The covenants that are unique to a municipal revenue bond and impact the credit analysis are the rate covenants and the priority-of-revenue covenants. The former dictates how the user charges will be set to meet the bond obligations. Also, just as in the case of a bond issue of a regulated corporate entity, restrictions on pricing must be recognized. In a municipal revenue bond the analyst must determine whether changes in the user charge require approval of other governmental entities such as the governor or state legislature. Priority-of-revenue covenants specify if other parties can legally tap the revenue of the enterprise before the revenue can be passed through to bondholders.

3. Sovereign Bonds

While U.S. government debt is not rated by any nationally recognized statistical rating organization, the debt of other national governments is rated. These ratings are referred to as **sovereign ratings**. Standard & Poor's and Moody's rate sovereign debt. We will first look at the factors considered by rating agencies in assigning sovereign ratings and then look at a structured approach that an analyst familiar with corporate credit analysis can use in assessing sovereign credits.

The categories used by S&P in deriving their ratings are listed in Exhibit 58-1. The two general categories are economic risk and political risk. The former category represents S&P's assessment of the ability of a government to satisfy its obligations. Both quantitative and qualitative analyses are used in assessing economic risk. Political risk is an assessment of the willingness of a government to satisfy its obligations. A government may have the ability to pay, but may be unwilling to pay. Political risk is assessed based on qualitative analysis of the economic and political factors that influence a government's economic policies.

There are two ratings assigned to each national government. One is a **local currency debt rating** and the other is a **foreign currency debt rating**. The reason for distinguishing between the two types of debt is that historically, the default frequency differs by the currency denomination of the debt. Specifically, defaults have been greater on foreign currency denominated debt.[49]

The reason for the difference in default rates for local currency debt and foreign currency debt is that if a government is willing to raise taxes and control its domestic financial system, it can generate sufficient local currency to meet its local currency debt obligation. This is not the case with foreign currency denominated debt. A national government must purchase foreign currency to meet a debt obligation in that foreign currency and therefore has less control with respect to its exchange rate. Thus, a significant depreciation of the local currency relative to a foreign currency in which a debt obligation is denominated will impair a national government's ability to satisfy a foreign currency obligation.

The implication of this is that the factors S&P analyzes in assessing the credit worthiness of a national government's local currency debt and foreign currency

---

[49] David T. Beers and Marie Cavanaugh, "Sovereign Ratings: A Primer," Chapter 6 in Frank J. Fabozzi and Alberto Franco (eds.), *Handbook of Emerging Fixed Income & Currency Markets* (New Hope, PA: Frank J. Fabozzi Associates, 1997).

EXHIBIT 58-1	S&P Sovereign Ratings Methodology Profile

Political Risk

► Form of government and adaptability of political institutions
► Extent of popular participation
► Orderliness of leadership succession
► Degree of consensus on economic policy objectives
► Integration in global trade and financial system
► Internal and external security risks

Income and Economic Structure

► Living standards, income, and wealth distribution
► Market, non-market economy
► Resource endowments, degree of diversification

Economic Growth Prospects

► Size, composition of savings, and investment
► Rate, pattern of economic growth

Fiscal Flexibility

► General government operating and total budget balances
► Tax competitiveness and tax-raising flexibility
► Spending pressures

Public Debt Burden

► General government financial assets
► Public debt and interest burden
► Currency composition, structure of public debt
► Pension liabilities
► Contingent liabilities

Price Stability

► Trends in price inflation
► Rates of money and credit growth
► Exchange rate policy
► Degree of central bank autonomy

Balance of Payments Flexibility

► Impact on external accounts of fiscal and monetary policies
► Structure of the current account
► Composition of capital flows

External Debt and Liquidity

► Size and currency composition of public external debt
► Importance of banks and other public and private entities as contingent liabilities of the sovereign
► Maturity structure and debt service burden
► Debt service track record
► Level, composition of reserves and other public external assets

Source: David T. Beers and Marie Cavanaugh, "Sovereign Ratings: A Primer," Chapter 6 in Frank J. Fabozzi and Alberto Franco (eds.), *Handbook of Emerging Fixed Income & Currency Markets* (New Hope, PA: Frank J. Fabozzi Associates, 1997), p. 67.

---

debt will differ to some extent. In assessing the credit quality of local currency debt, for example, S&P emphasizes domestic government policies that foster or impede timely debt service. The key factors looked at by S&P are:

► the stability of political institutions and degree of popular participation in the political process,
► income and economic structure,
► fiscal policy and budgetary flexibility,
► monetary policy and inflation pressures, and
► public debt burden and debt service track record.[50]

For foreign currency debt, credit analysis by S&P focuses on the interaction of domestic and foreign government policies. S&P analyzes a country's balance of payments and the structure of its external balance sheet. The area of analysis with respect to its external balance sheet are the **net public debt**, total net external debt, and net external liabilities.

---

[50] Beers and Cavanaugh, "Sovereign Credit Ratings: A Primer," p. 68.

CREDIT SCORING MODELS

The previous section described the traditional ratios and other measures that credit analysts use in assessing default risk. Several researchers have used these measures as input to assess the default risk of issuers using the statistical technique of multiple discriminant analysis (MDA). This statistical technique is primarily a classification technique that is helpful in distinguishing between or among groups of objects and in identifying the characteristics of objects responsible for their inclusion in one or another group. One of the chief advantages of MDA is that it permits a simultaneous consideration of a large number of characteristics and does not restrict the investigator to a sequential evaluation of each individual attribute. For example, MDA permits a credit analyst studying ratings of corporate bonds to examine, at one time, the total and joint impact on ratings of multiple financial ratios, financial measures, and qualitative factors. Thus, the analyst is freed from the cumbersome and possibly misleading task of looking at each characteristic in isolation from the others. MDA seeks to form groups that are internally as similar as possibly but that are as different from one another as possible.

From the above description of MDA it can be seen why it has been applied to problems of why bonds get the ratings they do and what variables seem best able to account for a bond's rating. Moreover, MDA has been used as a predictor of bankruptcy. While the steps involved in MDA for predicting bond ratings and corporate bankruptcies are a specialist topic, we will discuss the results of the work by Edward Altman, the primary innovator of MDA for predicting corporate bankruptcy.[51] The models of Altman and others involved in this area are updated periodically. Our purpose here is only to show what an MDA model looks like.

In one of Altman's earlier models, referred to as the "Z-score model," he found that the following MDA could be used to predict corporate bankruptcy:[52]

$$Z = 1.2 \, X_1 + 1.4 \, X_2 + 3.3 \, X_3 + 0.6 \, X_4 + 1.0 \, X_5$$

where

X_1 = Working capital/Total assets (in decimal)
X_2 = Retained earnings/Total assets (in decimal)
X_3 = Earnings before interest and taxes/Total assets (in decimal)
X_4 = Market value of equity/Total liabilities (in decimal)
X_5 = Sales/Total assets (number of times)
Z = Z-score

Given the value of the five variables for a given firm, a Z-score is computed. It is the Z-score that is used to classify firms with respect to whether or not there is potentially a serious credit problem that would lead to bankruptcy. Specifically, Altman found that Z-scores less than 1.81 indicated a firm with serious credit problems while a Z-score in excess of 3.0 indicated a healthy firm.

---

[51] See Chapters 8 and 9 in Edward I. Altman, *Corporate Financial Distress and Bankruptcy: A Complete Guide to Predicting and Avoiding Distress and Profiting from Bankruptcy* (Hoboken, NJ: John Wiley & Sons, 1993). For discussion of MDA applied to predicting municipal bond ratings, see Michael G. Ferri and Frank J. Fabozzi, "Statistical Techniques for Predicting the Credit Worthiness of Municipal Bonds," Chapter 44 in Frank J. Fabozzi, Sylvan G. Feldstein, Irving M. Pollack, and Frank G. Zarb (eds.), *The Municipal Bond Handbook: Volume I* (Homewood, IL: Dow-Jones Irwin 1983).

[52] Edward I. Altman, "Financial Bankruptcies, Discriminant Analysis and the Prediction of Corporate Bankruptcy," *Journal of Finance* (September 1968), pp. 589–699.

Subsequently, Altman and his colleagues revised the Z-score model based on more recent data. The resulting model, referred to as the "Zeta model," found that the following seven variables were important in predicting corporate bankruptcies and were highly correlated with bond ratings:[53]

▶ Earnings before interest and taxes (EBIT)/Total assets

▶ Standard error of estimate of EBIT/Total assets (normalized) for 10 years

▶ EBIT/Interest charges

▶ Retained earnings/Total assets

▶ Current assets/Current liabilities

▶ Five-year average market value of equity/Total capitalization

▶ Total tangible assets, normalized

While **credit scoring** models have been found to be helpful to analysts and bond portfolio managers, they do have limitations as a replacement for human judgment in credit analysis. Marty Fridson, for example, provides the following sage advice about using MDA models:

> ... quantitative models tend to classify as troubled credits not only most of the companies that eventually default, but also many that do not default. Often, firms that fall into financial peril bring in new management and are revitalized without ever failing in their debt service. If faced with a huge capital loss on the bonds of a financially distressed company, an institutional investor might wish to assess the probability of a turnaround—an inherently difficult-to-quantify prospect—instead of selling purely on the basis of a default model.[54]

Fridson then goes on to explain that credit analyst must bear in mind that "companies can default for reasons that a model based on reported financial data cannot pick up" and provides several actual examples of companies that filed for bankruptcy for such reasons.

5   CREDIT RISK MODELS

Historically, credit risk modeling has focused on credit ratings, default rates, and traditional credit analysis. In recent years, models for assessing credit risk to value corporate bonds have been introduced. The models can be divided into two groups: structural models and reduced form models. In this section we briefly describe these models.

A. Structural Models

Structural models are credit risk models developed on the basis of option pricing theory presented by Fisher Black and Mryon Scholes[55] and Robert

---

[53] Edward J. Altman, Robert G. Haldeman, and Paul Narayann, "Zeta Analysis: A New Model to Identify Bankruptcy Risk of Corporations," *Journal of Banking and Finance* (June 1977), pp. 29–54.

[54] Martin S. Fridson, *Financial Statement Analysis: A Practitioner's Guide, Second Edition* (Hoboken, NJ: John Wiley & Sons, 1995), p. 195.

[55] Fischer Black and Myron Scholes, "The Pricing of Options and Corporate Liabilities," *Journal of Political Economy* (May-June 1973), pp. 637–654.

Merton.[56] The basic idea, common to all structural-type models, is that a company defaults on its debt if the value of the assets of the company falls below a certain default point. For this reason, these models are also known as "firm-value models."[57] In these models it has been demonstrated that default can be modeled as an option to the stockholders granted by the bondholders and, as a result, an analyst can apply the same principles used for option pricing to the valuation of risky corporate securities.[58]

The use of the option pricing theory set forth by Black-Scholes-Merton (BSM) provides a significant improvement over traditional methods for valuing default risky bonds. Subsequent to the work of BSM, there have been many extensions on both a theoretical and practical level. The BSM framework has been used by a number of credit software/consulting companies, including Moody's KMV Corporation and JP Morgan's Credit Metrics (co-developed with Reuters). Both systems use the BSM approach to model defaults and obtain the probability of default. (Moody's KMV refers to this probability as the "expected default frequency.") To make the BSM model operational, model developers define default occurring when the equity price falls below a certain barrier. This simplification is due to the fact that equity prices are much more available than asset values of the company.

B. Reduced Form Models

In structural models, the default process of a corporation is driven by the value of its assets. Since the value of any option depends on the volatility of the underlying (the volatility of the asset value in structural models), the probability of default is explicitly linked to the expected volatility of a corporation's asset value. Thus, in structural models both the default process and recovery rates should a bankruptcy occur depend on the corporation's structural characteristics.

In contrast, **reduced form models** do not look "inside the firm," but instead model directly the probability of default or downgrade.[59] That is, the default process and the recovery process are (1) modeled independently of the corporation's structural features and (2) are independent of each other.

The two most popular reduced form models are the Jarrow and Turnbull model[60] and the Duffie and Singleton model.[61] The statistical tools for modeling the default process and the recovery process are a specialized topic.[62]

---

[56] Robert Merton, "Theory of Rational Option Pricing," *Bell Journal of Economics and Management* (Spring 1973), pp. 141–183, and "On the Pricing of Corporate Debt: The Risk Structure of Interest Rates," *Journal of Finance*, Vol. 29, No. 2 (1974), pp. 449–470.

[57] For a more detailed discussion of these models, see Chapter 8 in Mark J.P. Anson, Frank J. Fabozzi, Moorad Choudhry, and Ren Raw Chen, *Credit Derivatives: Instruments, Applications, and Pricing* (Hoboken, NJ: John Wiley & Sons, 2004).

[58] For the underlying theory and an illustration, see Don M. Chance, *Analysis of Derivatives for the CFA Program* (Charlottesville, VA: Association for Investment Management and Research, 2003), pp. 588–591.

[59] The name "reduced form" was first given by Darrell Duffie to differentiate these models from the structural form models of the Black-Scholes-Merton type.

[60] Robert Jarrow and Stuart Turnbull, "Pricing Derivatives on Financial Securities Subject to Default Risk," *Journal of Finance*, Vol. 50, No. 1 (1995), pp. 53–86.

[61] Darrell Duffie and Kenneth Singleton, "Modeling Term Structures of Defaultable Bonds," *Review of Financial Studies*, Vol. 12 (1999), pp. 687–720.

[62] For a further discussion of reduced form models, see Chapter 9 in Anson, Fabozzi, Choudhry, and Chen, *Credit Derivatives: Instruments, Applications, and Pricing;* Darrell Duffie and Kenneth J. Singleton, *Credit Risk: Pricing Measurement, and Management* (Princeton, NJ: Princeton University Press, 2003), or Srichander Ramaswamy, *Managing Credit Risk in Corporate Bond Portfolios* (Hoboken, NJ: John Wiley & Sons, 2003).

SUMMARY

► There are three types of credit risk: default risk, credit spread risk, and downgrade risk.

► Default risk is the risk that the issuer will fail to meet its obligation to make timely payment of interest and principal.

► Credit spread risk is the risk that the spread that the market demands for an issue will increase or widen, resulting in inferior performance of an issue relative to other issues.

► Downgrade risk is the risk that the issue will be downgraded, resulting in an increase in the credit spread demanded by the market.

► For long-term debt obligations, a credit rating is a forward-looking assessment of (1) the probability of default and (2) the relative magnitude of the loss should a default occur. For short-term debt obligations (i.e., obligations with initial maturities of one year or less), a credit rating is a forward-looking assessment of the probability of default.

► A rating agency monitors the credit quality of the issuer and can reassign a different credit rating to its bonds (an upgrade or a downgrade).

► Before an issue's rating is changed, typically a rating agency will place on rating watch or credit watch that it is reviewing the issue with the potential for upgrade or downgrade.

► Rating agencies issue rating outlooks, a projection as to whether an issue in the long term is likely to be upgraded, downgraded, or maintain its current rating.

► A credit analyst must consider the four C's of credit—character, capacity, collateral, and covenants.

► Character relates to the ethical reputation as well as the business qualifications and operating record of the board of directors, management, and executives responsible for the use of the borrowed funds and its repayment.

► Capacity deals with the ability of an issuer to repay its obligations.

► Collateral involves not only the traditional pledging of assets to secure the debt, but also the quality and value of those unpledged assets controlled by the issuer.

► Covenants are important because they impose restrictions on how management operates the company and conducts its financial affairs.

► The statement of cash flows is used in the analysis of an entity's ability to repay its financial obligations and to gain insight into an entity's financing methods, capital investment strategies, and dividend policy.

► To assess the ability of a company to meet its financial obligations, an analyst looks at profitability ratios that help explain the underlying causes of a change in the company's earnings.

► One of the best ways an analyst can predict future downward earnings is through a careful analysis of accounts receivable and inventories; two signs that can indicate problems are a larger than average accounts receivable balance situation and/or a bloated inventory.

► There are three sets of ratios that are used by credit analysts as indicators to assess the ability of a firm to satisfy its debt obligations: (1) short-term solvency ratios which assess the ability of the firm to meet debts maturing over the coming year, (2) capitalization (or financial leverage) ratios which assess the extent to which the firm relies on debt financing, and (3) coverage ratios which assess the ability of the firm to meet the fixed obligations brought about by debt financing.

▶ Analysts have reformatted the information from the firm's income statement and statement of cash flows to obtain what they view as a better description of the company's activities; these measures include funds from operations, operating cash flow, free operating cash flow, discretionary cash flow, and prefinancing cash flow.

▶ Negative covenants are covenants which require the borrower not to take certain actions; some of the more common restrictive covenants include various limitations on the company's ability to incur debt.

▶ There are two types of interest or fixed charge coverage tests: (1) a maintenance test which requires the borrower's ratio of earnings available for interests or fixed charges to be at least a certain minimum figure and (2) a debt incurrence test when the company wishes to do additional borrowing; in addition, there could be cash flow tests or requirements and working capital maintenance provisions.

▶ In assessing management quality, analysts consider the corporation's (1) strategic direction, (2) financial philosophy, (3) conservatism, (4) track record, (5) succession planning, and (6) control systems.

▶ Corporate financial theory helps us understand how the abuses that diminish shareholder value arise (agency problem) and the potential for mitigating the abuse.

▶ The corporate bylaws are the rules of governance; independent organizations have developed corporate governance ratings.

▶ In analyzing the credit worthiness of high-yield corporate bond issuers, the analyst will want to pay close attention to the characteristics of the debt obligations in the capital structure.

▶ The corporate structure is particularly important to investigate when assessing the credit worthiness of high-yield corporate bond issuers where there is a holding company structure because of potential limitations or restrictions on cash flow from operating subsidiaries to the parent company and among operating subsidiaries.

▶ Covenants in high-yield corporate bond issues should be reviewed in conjunction with the issuer's overall strategy.

▶ Some analysts believe that in assessing the credit quality of a high-yield corporate bond issuer an equity analysis approach is more informative than simply a traditional credit analysis approach.

▶ In analyzing the credit risk of an asset-backed security, rating companies basically look at four factors: (1) the credit quality of the collateral; (2) the quality of the seller/servicer, (3) cash flow stress test and payment (financial) structures, and (4) legal structure.

▶ A key factor in assessing the quality of the collateral is the amount of equity the borrower has in the asset.

▶ To reduce concentration risk in an asset-backed security, rating companies impose concentration limits.

▶ Based on their analysis of the four factors in assigning ratings, rating companies will determine the amount of credit enhancement needed for an issue to receive a particular rating.

▶ Fundamentally, because of the absence of operational risk, an asset-backed security transaction generally has greater certainty about the cash flow than a corporate bond issue.

▶ A true asset-backed security transaction involves minimal involvement by the servicer beyond administrative functions.

▶ In a hybrid asset-backed security transaction, the servicer has more than an administrative function; the greater the importance of the servicer, the more the transaction should be evaluated as a quasi-corporate entity.

▶ In assessing the credit risk of tax-backed debt, four basic informational categories should be considered: (1) information on the issuer's debt structure to determine the overall debt burden; (2) information on the issuer's ability and political discipline to maintain sound budgetary policy; (3) information on the specific local taxes and intergovernmental revenues available to the issuer; and, (4) information on the issuer's overall socioeconomic environment.

▶ While there are numerous security structures for revenue bonds, the underlying principle in rating is whether the project being financed will generate sufficient cash flows to satisfy the obligations due bondholders.

▶ The principles involved in analyzing the credit risk of a revenue bond are the same as for a corporate bond.

▶ In assessing the credit risk for revenue bonds, the trust indenture and legal opinion should provide legal comfort in the following bond-security areas: (1) the limits of the basic security, (2) the flow-of-funds structure, (3) the rate, or user-charge, covenant, (4) the priority-of-revenue claims, (5) the additional-bonds tests, and (6) other relevant covenants.

▶ Sovereign credits are rated by Standard & Poor's and Moody's.

▶ In deriving ratings, the two general categories analyzed are economic risk (the ability to pay) and political risk (the willingness to pay).

▶ There are two ratings assigned to each central government: a local currency debt rating and a foreign currency debt rating.

▶ Historically, defaults have been greater on foreign currency denominated debt.

▶ In assessing the credit quality of local currency debt, rating agencies emphasize domestic government policies that foster or impede timely debt service.

▶ For foreign currency debt, rating agencies analyze a country's balance of payments and the structure of its external balance sheet.

▶ Analysts familiar with corporate credit analysis can build a structure for the analysis of quantitative and qualitative information of a sovereign issuer.

▶ Analysts must assess qualitative factors in assessing the credit risk of both a sovereign and corporate entity.

▶ A structure developed for corporate credit analysis can be developed for assessing the credit risk of a sovereign.

▶ Multiple discriminant analysis, a statistical classification technique, has been used by some analysts to predict corporate bankruptcies.

▶ Credit risk models for assessing credit risk to value corporate bonds include structural models and reduced form models.

Case Study: Bergen Brunswig Corporation

The purpose of this case is to illustrate how the analysis of financial statements based on traditional ratios discussed in this reading can be used to identify a corporate issuer that might be downgraded. The corporation used in the illustration is Bergen Brunswig Corporation.

BACKGROUND INFORMATION

Bergen Brunswig Corporation is a supply channel management company that provides pharmaceuticals, medical-surgical supplies, and specialty products. The company also provides information management solutions and outsourcing services, as well as develops disease-specific treatment protocols and pharmaco-economic initiatives to assist in the reduction of healthcare costs.

The original corporate bond rating was BBB+. On December 17, 1999, S&P lowered the company's rating to BBB− citing "disappointing results at the company's two recently acquired businesses, PharMerica and Statlander." PharMerica, an institutional pharmacy, suffered from changes in Medicare reimbursement policies which reduced hospital patient occupancy and the use of high-margin drugs.

On February 2, 2000, S&P decided to downgrade the company's corporate rating again to BB. S&P's rationale was "deteriorating conditions in the company's core drug distribution business as well as continued losses at Statlander, a specialty drug distributor acquired in 1999."

ANALYSIS

Exhibit 58-A1 shows the financial data for the 1996–1999 fiscal years and various financial ratios. (The financial ratios are shaded in the exhibit.) The company's fiscal year ends on September 30th. Since each rating agency uses slightly different inputs for the ratios it computes, we have included the ratio definitions used by S&P in Exhibit 58-A2.

Exhibit 58-A3 provides a summary of all the ratios that show a deteriorating trend of Bergen Brunswig's financial condition. The eight ratios shown in the exhibit strongly suggest that Bergen Brunswig was losing its financial strength and could possibly be a candidate for downgrade. To show the degree of deterioration, Exhibit 58-A3 also displays for the eight ratios the median ratios for BBB and BB ratings.

Exhibit 58-A4 highlights the trending of two key ratios—EBIT interest coverage and funds from operations/total debt—relative to the BBB benchmark. For 1999, the EBIT fell below 4 times, the median for BBB rated firms. For 1999, the ratio of funds from operations to total debt fell below the median for BB rated firms.

EXHIBIT 58-A1	Financial Data and Selected Ratios for Bergen Brunswig: Fiscal Years 1996–1999 Based on 10K Data			

		1999	1998	1997	1996
1	Revenue	1	$17,244,905	$13,720,017	$11,659,127	
	COGS	1	$(16,145,378)	$(12,969,752)	$(11,004,696)	
	SG & A		$(837,700)	$(534,119)	$(479,399)	
	EBIT		$261,827	$216,146	$175,032	
	Interest Expense	2	$74,143	$39,996	$30,793	
	EBIT interest coverage		3.53	5.40	5.68	
2	EBIT		$261,827	$216,146	$175,032	
	Depreciation & Amortization		$66,031	$37,465	$40,756	
	EBITDA		$327,858	$253,611	$215,788	
	Interest Expense		$74,143	$39,996	$30,793	
	EBITDA interest coverage		4.42	6.34	7.01	
3	Net Income		$70,573	$3,102	$81,679	
	Depreciation & Amortization		$66,031	$37,465	$40,756	
	Current Deferred Income Taxes		$10,840	$41,955	$10,577	
	Other Noncash Items					
	Deferred Compensation		$2,552	$2,809	$2,266	
	Doubtful Receivables		$85,881	$11,934	$11,899	
	Writedown of goodwill			$87,271		
	Abandonment of capitalized			$5,307		
	Funds from operations		$235,877	$189,843	$147,177	
	Long Term Debt		$1,041,983	$464,778	$437,956	$419,275
	Lease Debt Equivalent		$82	$53	$59	$43
	Long Term Debt*		$1,042,065	$464,831	$438,015	$419,318
	Current Maturity of LTD		$545,923	$6,029	$1,021	1,125
	Total Debt		$1,587,988	$470,860	$439,036	$420,443
	Funds from operations/Total debt		14.85%	40.32%	33.52%	
4	Funds from operations		$235,877	$189,843	$147,177	
	Capital Expenditure		($305,535)	($52,361)	($23,806)	
	Working Capital		$1,199,527	$518,443	$474,910	$643,607
	Change in WC		$(681,084)	$(43,533)	$168,697	
	Free operating cash flow	3	$(750,742)	$93,949	$292,068	
	Total Debt		$1,587,988	$470,860	$439,036	
	Free operating cash flow/Total debt		−47.28%	19.95%	66.52%	
5	EBIT		$261,827	$216,146	$175,032	
	Total debt		$1,587,988	$470,860	$439,036	$420,443
	Equity		$1,495,490	$629,064	$644,861	$666,877
	Non-current deferred taxes				$1,791	
	Total Capital		$3,083,478	$1,099,924	$1,085,688	$1,087,320
	Average Capital		2,091,701.10	1,092,806.15	1,086,503.89	
	Pretax return on capital		12.52%	19.78%	16.11%	

(Exhibit continued on next page ...)

EXHIBIT 58-A1	(continued)			
	1999	**1998**	**1997**	**1996**
6 Operating Income	$261,827	$216,146	$175,032	
Sales	$17,244,905	$13,720,017	$11,659,127	
Operating Income/Sales	1.52%	1.58%	1.50%	
7 Long Term Debt*	$1,042,065	$464,831	$438,015	
Long-term debt	$1,041,983	$464,778	$437,956	
Shareholders' equity	$1,495,490	$629,064	$644,861	
Capitalization	$2,537,473	$1,093,842	$1,082,817	
Long-term debt/Capitalization	41.07%	42.50%	40.45%	
8 Total Debt	$1,587,988	$470,860	$439,036	
Shareholders' equity	$1,495,490	$629,064	$644,861	
Capitalization	$3,083,478	$1,099,924	$1,083,897	
Total debt/Capitalization	51.50%	42.81%	40.51%	

* Bergen Brunswig fiscal year ends September 30th.

1. Revenues and Cost of Goods Sold excludes bulk shipment to customers' warehouse sites. The Company only serves as a intermediary and there is no material impact on the Company's operating earnings.

2. (a) Does not include pre-tax distributions on the Company's Preferred Securities.
   (b) Although the S&P formulas call for "Gross Interest Expense" net interest is used because Gross Interest Expense was unavailable in the filings and could not be inferred.

3. Free operating cash flow = Funds from operations + Capital expenditure + Change in WC.

Note for the above formula for free operating cash flow:
(a) Capital expenditure is shown as a negative in the exhibit. That is why it is added to obtain free operating cash flow. (This is consistent with S&P's formula for free operating cash flow as given in formula (4) in Exhibit 58-A2.)
(b) Increase in working capital for 1998 and 1999 is shown as a negative, so is added to free operating cash flow as per the S&P formula (4) in Exhibit 58-A2.

EXHIBIT 58-A2	S&P's Formulas for Key Ratios

1. EBIT interest coverage $= \dfrac{\text{Earnings from continuing operations** before interest and taxes}}{\substack{\text{Gross interest incurred before subtracting (1) capitalized interest and} \\ \text{(2) interest income}}}$

2. EBITDA interest coverage $= \dfrac{\substack{\text{Earnings from continuing operations** before interest and taxes,} \\ \text{depreciation, and amortization}}}{\substack{\text{Gross interest incurred before subtracting (1) capitalized interest and} \\ \text{(2) interest income}}}$

3. Funds from operations/total debt $= \dfrac{\substack{\text{Net income from continuing operations plus depreciation,} \\ \text{amortization, deferred taxes, and other noncash items}}}{\substack{\text{Long-term debt* plus current maturities, commercial paper, and} \\ \text{other short-term borrowings}}}$

4. Free operating cash flow/total debt $= \dfrac{\substack{\text{Funds from operations minus capital expenditures, minus (plus) the} \\ \text{increase (decrease) in working capital (excluding changes in cash)}}}{\substack{\text{Long-term debt* plus current maturities, commercial paper, and} \\ \text{other short-term borrowings}}}$

5. Pretax return on capital $= \dfrac{\text{EBIT}}{\substack{\text{Average of beginning of year and end of year capital, including short-term debt,} \\ \text{current maturities, long-term debt*, non-current deferred taxes, and equity}}}$

6. Operating income/sales $= \dfrac{\substack{\text{Sales minus cost of goods manufactured (before depreciation and} \\ \text{amortization), selling, general and administrative, and} \\ \text{research and development costs}}}{\text{Sales}}$

7. Long-term debt/capitalization $= \dfrac{\text{Long-term debt*}}{\substack{\text{Long-term debt + shareholders' equity (including preferred stock)} \\ \text{plus minority interest}}}$

8. Total debt/capitalization $= \dfrac{\substack{\text{Long-term debt* plus current maturities, commercial paper, and other} \\ \text{short-term borrowings}}}{\substack{\text{Long-term debt* plus current maturities, commercial paper, and other} \\ \text{short-term borrowings + shareholder's equity (including preferred} \\ \text{stock) plus minority interest}}}$

---

* Including amount for operating lease debt equivalent

** Including interest income and equity earnings; excluding nonrecurring items.

 Summary of Ratios Showing Deteriorating Trend and Median Ratio for S&P BBB and BB Ratings					
	1999	**1998**	**1997**	**BBB Median**	**BB Median**
EBIT interest coverage	3.53	5.40	5.68	4.10	2.5
EBITDA interest coverage	4.42	6.34	7.01	6.30	3.9
Funds from operations/total debt	14.85%	40.32%	33.52%	32.30%	20.10%
Free operating cash flow/total debt	−47.28%	19.95%	66.52%	6.30%	1.00%
Pretax return on capital	12.52%	19.78%	16.11%	15.40%	12.60%
Operating income/Sales	1.52%	1.58%	1.50%	15.80%	14.40%
Long-term debt/Capitalization	41.07%	42.50%	40.45%	40.80%	55.30%
Total debt/Capitalization	51.50%	42.81%	40.51%	46.40%	58.50%

EXHIBIT 58-A4 Trending of EBIT Interest Leverage and Funds from Operating/Total Debt Ratios Relative to BBB and BB Benchmark

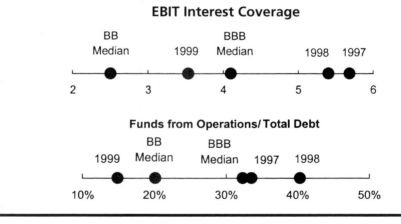

CONCLUSION

An analysis of the key ratios would have clearly signaled by December 1999 that Bergen Brunswig was a candidate for downgrading. As noted earlier, S&P lowered the company's corporate credit rating from BBB+ to BBB− on December 17, 1999 and then lowered it again on February 2, 2000 to BB. Among the reasons for the downgrade, S&P indicated that it expected EBITDA/interest to drop below 4 times in fiscal year 2000.

While we have demonstrated that traditional analysis could have identified a potential downgrade, what we did not address was the timing of information for preparing the analysis and reaching our conclusion. Specifically, S&P downgraded Bergen Brunswig the first time on December 17, 1999, but the company did not file its 10K (annual filing with the SEC) until December 29, 1999. Although we use the 10K numbers (since they are more accurate) for this project, an analyst would most probably estimate the ratios by looking at the 10Qs (the quarterly filings with the SEC).

Exhibit 58-A5 shows how this would be done for the first two ratios (EBIT interest coverage and EBITDA interest coverage). An analyst would add the results from the first 9 months of 1999 (fiscal year) to the last quarter of 1998 in order to estimate the annual ratio and show the trend.

As we can see from Exhibit 58-A5, the annualized EBITDA interest coverage ratio (5.65) is much lower than the 1998 ratio. If we take a closer look, the ratio for the first nine months of 1999 is even lower. This strongly suggests a deteriorating trend. Bergen Brunswig filed its 1999 third quarter 10Q on August 17, 1999, so the information was available to the analyst before December 1999.

We believe S&P further lowered Bergen Brunswig's rating because of the first quarter result. Again, S&P's action date (February 2) is slightly earlier than the date that the company filed with the SEC (February 17). However, the weakening of Bergen Brunswig's financial position is apparent by the fact that the full-year 1999 ratios are even weaker than those for the first nine months of 1999.

EXHIBIT 58-A5	Using Quarterly Financial Data from Bergen Brunswig to Compute EBIT and EBITDA Interest Coverage Ratios		
	1999 9 months	1998 4Q	Annualized Estimate
Revenue	$12,716,939	$3,666,166	$16,383,105
COGS	$(11,938,185)	$(3,466,355)	$(15,404,540)
SG & A	$(559,142)	$(144,725)	$(703,867)
EBIT	$219,612	$55,086	$274,698
Interest Expense	$47,906	$9,657	$57,563
EBIT interest coverage	4.58	5.70	4.77
EBIT	$219,612	$55,086	$274,698
Depreciation & Amortization	$40,497	$9,847	$50,344
EBITDA	$260,109	$64,933	$325,042
Interest Expense	$47,906	$9,657	$57,563
EBITDA interest coverage	5.43	6.72	5.65

PROBLEMS FOR READING 58

1. Explain whether you agree or disagree with the following statement: "The credit risk of a bond is the risk that the issuer will fail to meet its obligation to make timely payment of interest and principal."

2. **A.** In addition to credit ratings, what other information is provided by rating agencies that investors can use to gauge the credit risk of an issuer?

   B. How do long-term credit ratings differ from short-term credit ratings?

3. What are some of the major factors considered by rating agencies in assessing the quality of management?

4. **A.** There are various forms of back-up credit facilities available to a corporation. What factors should an analyst consider in assessing the back-up credit facilities available to an issuer?

   B. What is a "material adverse change clause provision" in a back-up credit facility and what is its significance in terms of the strength of a back-up credit facility?

5. In 1998 there were several developments in Europe leading to the liberalization of the European telecommunication industry. In October 1998, Moody's Investors Service published a report ("Rating Methodology: European Telecoms") addressing the issues in the rating of European telecommunication companies. Below are quotes from the report followed by questions that should be answered.

   A. "We look carefully at a company's general funding strategy—the debt and equity markets the company accesses, and the sources of bank financing it arranges.... This becomes more important the lower down the rating scale, particularly in the case of high yield issuers . . ." Why is the funding strategy of high-yield issuers of particular concern to Moody's analysts?

   B. "As a very general rule of thumb, the larger the company's cushion of cash and assets above fixed payments due, the more able it will be to meet maturing debt obligations in potentially adverse conditions, and the higher the rating. In many cases, the size of this cushion may be less important than its predictability or sustainability. Moody's views the telecom industry as having generally very predictable revenue streams, which accounts for the relatively high level of ratings of the telecom industry compared to other industries." Explain why "predictability and sustainability" may be more important than size of a coverage ratio.

   C. In discussing the financial measures it uses, the report explains the importance of "cash flow to debt figures." The report stated, "We also look at adjusted retained cash flow which includes any items which we view as non-discretionary to gauge the financial flexibility of a company, . . ." What is meant by "financial flexibility of a company"?

   D. The quote in the previous part ends with "as well as adjusted debt figures which include unfunded pension liabilities and guarantees." Why would Moody's adjust debt figures for these items?

   E. In the report, Moody's looks at various measures considered in ratings such as coverage ratios and capitalization ratios, and shows these ratios for a sample of European telecom companies. In each case when discussing ratios, Moody's notes the "loose correlation" between ratings and ratios;

that is, it is not necessarily the case that companies with the best ratios will always receive a better rating. Moody's noted that "inconsistencies underscore the limitations of ratio analysis." Explain why one might expect a loose correlation between ratios and ratings.

6. What type of information can a credit analyst obtain from an analysis of the statement of cash flows?

7. **A.** Using S&P's definitions, what is the relationship between free cash flow, discretionary cash, and prefinancing cash flow?

   B. What is the meaning of free cash flow, discretionary cash flow, and prefinancing cash flow?

8. **A.** Why is the analysis of covenants important in credit analysis?

   B. What is a negative covenant?

   C. Why is covenant analysis particularly important for assessing the credit worthiness of high-yield corporate issuers?

9. What is meant by agency risk?

10. **A.** What is the motivation for corporate governance ratings?

    B. What are some of the characteristics of a firm considered in assigning a corporate governance rating?

11. Explain the following two statements made by Robert Levine in "Unique Factors in Managing High-Yield Bond Portfolios," in Frank K. Reilly (ed.), *High-Yield Bonds: Analysis and Risk Assessment* (Charlottesville, VA: Association for Investment Management and Research, 1990), p. 36.

    A. "One must understand the structure because not all debt that is listed as senior is actually senior debt."

    B. "Intellectually zero-coupon bonds are troublesome when they are not at the bottom of the capital structure . . . From a credit standpoint, it is not desirable to have more senior debt growing faster than the subordinated cash-pay securities, thus offering less protection to the subordinated holders in bankruptcy. We prefer to see less debt that is less senior growing faster than the debt that is more senior—e.g., less above us in the event of bankruptcy."

12. Explain why an understanding of the corporate structure of a high-yield issuer that has a holding company structure is important.

13. The following statement was made by Stephen Esser in "High-Yield Bond Analysis: The Equity Perspective," in Ashwinpaul C. Sondhi (ed.), *Credit Analysis of Nontraditional Debt Securities* (Charlottesville, VA: Association for Investment Management and Research, 1995), p. 54: "An equity perspective on high-yield bond analysis can be an important edge for an active manager." Explain why.

14. In the analysis of an asset-backed security, the analysis of the collateral allows the analyst to project the cash flow from the underlying collateral under different scenarios. However, this is not sufficient to assess the credit worthiness of an asset-backed security transaction. Explain why?

15. Why is it necessary for an analyst to assess the financial condition of a servicer in an asset-backed security transaction?

16. **A.** Some asset-backed security transactions may be characterized as "true securitizations," while others may be more properly classified as "hybrid transactions." What is the distinguishing feature of a "true securitization" and a "hybrid transaction"?

    B. How is the credit quality of a "hybrid transaction" evaluated?

17. What are the four basic categories that are considered in assessing the credit quality of tax-backed municipal debt?

18. A. What is the underlying principle in assessing the credit worthiness of municipal revenue bonds?

B. In a municipal revenue bond, what is a "rate covenant" and why is such a covenant included?

19. You are reviewing a publication of Moody's Investors Service entitled "Moody's Approach to Rating Regional and Local Governments in Latin America," published in August 1997. On page 3 of the publication, the following was written:

"A Moody's credit rating is an independent opinion of the relative ability and willingness of an issuer of fixed-income securities to make full and timely payments of amounts due on the security over its life."

Why in the case of a sovereign entity is the "willingness" of an issuer to pay important?

20. A. Why do rating agencies assign both a local currency debt rating and a foreign currency debt rating to the bonds of a sovereign government?

B. How do the factors considered in deriving a local currency debt rating differ from those for a foreign currency debt rating?

21. Comment on the following statement: "The difficulty with analyzing bonds issued by foreign governments is the intangible and non-quantitative elements involved in the credit analysis. I would not encounter such complexities when analyzing the credit worthiness of domestic corporate bonds or domestic municipal bonds."

22. Krane Products Inc. is a manufacturer of ski equipment. The company has been in operation since 1997. Ms. Andrews is a credit analyst for an investment management company. She has been asked to analyze Krane Products as a possible purchase for the bond portfolio of one of her firm's accounts. At the time of the analysis, Krane Products Inc. was rated BB by S&P. The bonds of the company trade in the market with the same spread as other comparable BB bonds.

Ms. Andrews collected financial data for Krane Products Inc. for the years 2000 and 1999 and computed several financial ratios. Information for selected ratios is given below:

Ratios	2000	1999
EBIT interest coverage	3.8	2.7
EBITDA interest coverage	5.9	4.1
Funds from operations/total debt	28.3%	24.5%
Free operating cash flow/total debt	19.2%	1.2%
Pretax return on capital	24.4%	17.1%
Operating income/sales	25.5%	19.5%
Long-term debt/capitalization	55.0%	57.4%
Total debt/capitalization	57.1%	59.5%

Based on the first three quarters of fiscal year 2001, Ms. Andrews projected the following ratios for 2001:

Ratios	2001
EBIT interest coverage	4.5
EBITDA interest coverage	6.9
Funds from operations/total debt	41.5%
Free operating cash flow/total debt	22.5%
Pretax return on capital	24.2%
Operating income/sales	25.12%
Long-term debt/capitalization	40.5%
Total debt/capitalization	45.2%

Ms. Andrews obtained from S&P information about median ratios by credit rating. These ratios are reproduced below:

	AAA	AA	A	BBB	BB	B
EBIT interest coverage	12.9	9.2	7.2	4.1	2.5	1.2
EBITDA interest coverage	18.7	14.0	10.0	6.3	3.9	2.3
Funds from operations/total debt	89.7	67.0	49.5	32.3	20.1	10.5
Free operating cash flow/total debt	40.5	21.6	17.4	6.3	1.0	(4.0)
Pretax return on capital	30.6	25.1	19.6	15.4	12.6	9.2
Operating income/sales	30.9	25.2	17.9	15.8	14.4	11.2
Long-term debt/capitalization	21.4	29.3	33.3	40.8	55.3	68.8
Total debt/capitalization	31.8	37.0	39.2	46.4	58.5	71.4

What do you think Ms. Andrews' recommendation will be with respect to the purchase of the bonds of Krane Products Inc.? Explain why.

23. Credit scoring models have been found to be helpful to analysts and bond portfolio managers. What are their limitations as a replacement for human judgment in credit analysis?

24. What are the two types of credit risk models used to value corporate bonds?

TERM STRUCTURE AND VOLATILITY OF INTEREST RATES

by Frank J. Fabozzi

LEARNING OUTCOMES

The candidate should be able to:

a. illustrate and explain parallel and nonparallel shifts in the yield curve, a yield curve twist, and a change in the curvature of the yield curve (i.e., a butterfly shift);

b. describe the factors that have been observed to drive U.S. Treasury security returns, and evaluate the importance of each factor;

c. explain the various universes of Treasury securities that are used to construct the theoretical spot rate curve, and evaluate their advantages and disadvantages;

d. explain the swap rate curve (LIBOR curve) and discuss the reasons that market participants have increasingly used the swap rate curve as a benchmark rather than a government bond yield curve;

e. illustrate the various theories of the term structure of interest rates (i.e., pure expectations, liquidity, and preferred habitat) and the implications of each theory for the shape of the yield curve;

f. compute and interpret the yield curve risk of a security or a portfolio, using key rate duration;

g. compute and interpret yield volatility, given historical yields;

h. distinguish between historical yield volatility and implied yield volatility;

i. explain how yield volatility is forecasted.

INTRODUCTION　　　1

Market participants pay close attention to yields on Treasury securities. An analysis of these yields is critical because they are used to derive interest rates which are used to value securities. Also, they are benchmarks used to establish the minimum yields that investors want when investing in a non-Treasury

Fixed Income Analysis for the Chartered Financial Analyst® Program, Second Edition, edited by Frank J. Fabozzi, Copyright © 2005 by CFA Institute. Reprinted with permission.

security. We distinguish between the on-the-run (i.e., the most recently auctioned Treasury securities) Treasury yield curve and the term structure of interest rates. The on-the-run Treasury yield curve shows the relationship between the yield for on-the-run Treasury issues and maturity. The term structure of interest rates is the relationship between the theoretical yield on zero-coupon Treasury securities and maturity. The yield on a zero-coupon Treasury security is called the Treasury spot rate. The term structure of interest rates is thus the relationship between Treasury spot rates and maturity. The importance of this distinction between the Treasury yield curve and the Treasury spot rate curve is that it is the latter that is used to value fixed-income securities.

At Level I we demonstrated how to derive the Treasury spot rate curve from the on-the-run Treasury issues using the method of bootstrapping and then how to obtain an arbitrage-free value for an option-free bond. In this reading we will describe other methods to derive the Treasury spot rates. In addition, we explained that another benchmark that is being used by practitioners to value securities is the swap curve. We discuss the swap curve in this reading.

At Level I, the theories of the term structure of interest rates were explained. Each of these theories seeks to explain the shape of the yield curve. Also at Level I the concept of forward rates was explained. In this reading, we explain the role that forward rates play in the theories of the term structure of interest rates. In addition, we critically evaluate one of these theories, the pure **expectations theory**, because of the economic interpretation of forward rates based on this theory.

At Level I we also mentioned the role of interest rate volatility or yield volatility in valuing securities and in measuring interest rate exposure of a bond. In the analytical readings in Level II we will continue to see the importance of this measure. Specifically, we will see the role of interest rate volatility in valuing bonds with embedded options, valuing mortgage-backed and certain asset-backed securities, and valuing derivatives. Consequently, in this reading, we will explain how interest rate volatility is estimated and the issues associated with computing this measure.

In the opening sections of this reading we provide some historical information about the Treasury yield curve. In addition, we set the stage for understanding bond returns by looking at empirical evidence on some of the factors that drive returns.

2   HISTORICAL LOOK AT THE TREASURY YIELD CURVE

The yields offered on Treasury securities represent the base interest rate or minimum interest rate that investors demand if they purchase a non-Treasury security. For this reason market participants continuously monitor the yields on

Treasury securities, particularly the yields of the on-the-run issues. In this reading we will discuss the historical relationship that has been observed between the yields offered on on-the-run Treasury securities and maturity (i.e., the yield curve).

A. Shape of the Yield Curve

Exhibit 59-1 shows some yield curves that have been observed in the U.S. Treasury market and in the government bond market of other countries. Four shapes have been observed. The most common relationship is a yield curve in which the longer the maturity, the higher the yield as shown in panel a. That is, investors are rewarded for holding longer maturity Treasuries in the form of a higher potential yield. This shape is referred to as a **normal** or **positively sloped yield curve**. A **flat yield curve** is one in which the yield for all maturities is approximately equal, as shown in panel b. There have been times when the relationship between maturities and yields was such that the longer the maturity the lower the yield. Such a downward sloping yield curve is referred to as an **inverted** or a **negatively sloped yield curve** and is shown in panel c. In panel d, the yield curve shows yields increasing with maturity for a range of maturities and then the yield curve becoming inverted. This is called a **humped yield curve**.

Market participants talk about the difference between long-term Treasury yields and short-term Treasury yields. The spread between these yields for two maturities is referred to as the steepness or slope of the yield curve. There is no

EXHIBIT 59-1   Yield Curve Shapes

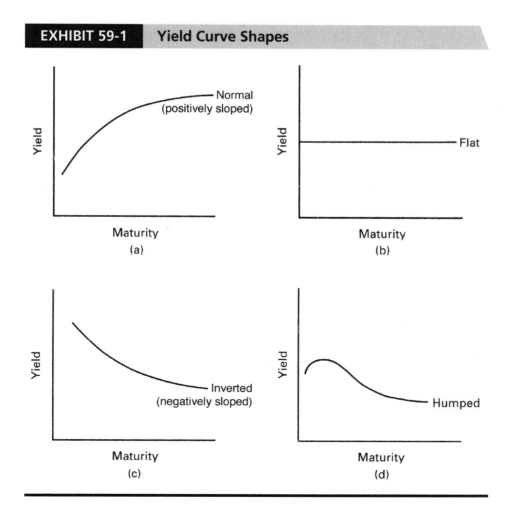

industry-wide accepted definition of the maturity used for the long-end and the maturity used for the short-end of the yield curve. Some market participants define the slope of the yield curve as the difference between the 30-year yield and the 3-month yield. Other market participants define the slope of the yield curve as the difference between the 30-year yield and the 2-year yield. The more common practice is to use the spread between the 30-year and 2-year yield. While as of June 2003 the U.S. Treasury has suspended the issuance of the 30-year Treasury issue, most market participants view the benchmark for the 30-year issue as the last issued 30-year bond which as of June 2003 had a maturity of approximately 27 years. (Most market participants use this issue as a barometer of long-term interest rates; however, it should be noted that in daily conversations and discussions of bond market developments, the 10-year Treasury rate is frequently used as a barometer of long-term interest rates.)

The slope of the yield curve varies over time. For example, in the U.S., over the period 1989 to 1999, the slope of the yield curve as measured by the difference between the 30-year Treasury yield and the 2-year Treasury yield was steepest at 348 basis points in September and October 1992. It was negative—that is, the 2-year Treasury yield was greater than the 30-year Treasury yield—for most of 2000. In May 2000, the 2-year Treasury yield exceeded the 30-year Treasury yield by 65 basis points (i.e., the slope of the yield curve was −65 basis points).

It should be noted that not all sectors of the bond market view the slope of the yield curve in the same way. The mortgage sector of the bond—which we cover in Reading 61—views the yield curve in terms of the spread between the 10-year and 2-year Treasury yields. This is because it is the 10-year rates that affect the pricing and refinancing opportunities in the mortgage market.

Moreover, it is not only within the U.S. bond market that there may be different interpretations of what is meant by the slope of the yield curve, but there are differences across countries. In Europe, the only country with a liquid 30-year government market is the United Kingdom. In European markets, it has become increasingly common to measure the slope in terms of the swap curve (in particular, the euro swap curve) that we will cover later in this reading.

Some market participants break up the yield curve into a "short end" and "long end" and look at the slope of the short end and long end of the yield curve. Once again, there is no universal consensus that defines the maturity break points. In the United States, it is common for market participants to refer to the short end of the yield curve as up to the 10-year maturity and the long end as from the 10-year maturity to the 30-year maturity. Using the 2-year as the shortest maturity, the slope of the short end of the yield curve is then the difference between the 10-year Treasury yield and the 2-year Treasury yield. The slope of the long end of the yield curve is the difference between the 30-year Treasury yield and the 10-year Treasury yield. Historically, the long end of the yield curve has been flatter than the short-end of the yield curve. For example, in October 1992 when the slope of the yield curve was the greatest at 348 basis points, the slope of the long end of the yield curve was only 95 basis points.

Market participants often decompose the yield curve into three maturity sectors: short, intermediate, and long. Again, there is no consensus as to what the maturity break points are and those break points can differ by sector and by country. In the United States, a common breakdown has the 1–5 year sector as the short end (ignoring maturities less than 1 year), the 5–10 year sector as the intermediate end, and greater than 10-year maturities as the long end.[1] In

---

[1] Index constructors such as Lehman Brothers when constructing maturity sector indexes define "short-term sector" as up to three years, the "intermediate sector" as maturities greater than three years but less than 10 years (note the overlap with the short-term sector), and the "long-term sector" as greater than 10 years.

Continental Europe where there is little issuance of bonds with a maturity greater than 10 years, the long end of the yield sector is the 10-year sector.

B. Yield Curve Shifts

A shift in the yield curve refers to the relative change in the yield for each Treasury maturity. A **parallel shift in the yield curve** refers to a shift in which the change in the yield for all maturities is the same. A **nonparallel shift in the yield curve** means that the yield for different maturities does not change by the same number of basis points. Both of these shifts are graphically portrayed in Exhibit 59-2.

Historically, two types of nonparallel yield curve shifts have been observed: (1) a twist in the slope of the yield curve and (2) a change in the humpedness or curvature of the yield curve. A **twist in the slope of the yield curve** refers to a flattening or steepening of the yield curve. A **flattening of the yield curve** means that the slope of the yield curve (i.e., the spread between the yield on a long-term and short-term Treasury) has decreased; a **steepening of the yield curve** means that the slope of the yield curve has increased. This is depicted in panel b of Exhibit 59-2.

The other type of nonparallel shift is a change in the curvature or humpedness of the yield curve. This type of shift involves the movement of yields at the short maturity and long maturity sectors of the yield curve relative to the movement of yields in the intermediate maturity sector of the yield curve. Such nonparallel shifts in the yield curve that change its curvature are referred to as **butterfly shifts**. The name comes from viewing the three maturity sectors (short, intermediate, and long) as three parts of a butterfly. Specifically, the intermediate maturity sector is viewed as the body of the butterfly and the short maturity and long maturity sectors are viewed as the wings of the butterfly.

A **positive butterfly** means that the yield curve becomes less humped (i.e., has less curvature). This means that if yields increase, for example, the yields in the short maturity and long maturity sectors increase more than the yields in the intermediate maturity sector. If yields decrease, the yields in the short and long maturity sectors decrease less than the intermediate maturity sector. A **negative butterfly** means the yield curve becomes more humped (i.e., has more curvature). So, if yields increase, for example, yields in the intermediate maturity sector will increase more than yields in the short maturity and long maturity sectors. If, instead, yields decrease, a negative butterfly occurs when yields in the intermediate maturity sector decrease less than the short maturity and long maturity sectors. Butterfly shifts are depicted in panel c of Exhibit 59-2.

Historically, these three types of shifts in the yield curve have not been found to be independent. The two most common types of shifts have been (1) a downward shift in the yield curve combined with a steepening of the yield curve and (2) an upward shift in the yield curve combined with a flattening of the yield curve. Positive butterfly shifts tend to be associated with an upward shift in yields and negative butterfly shifts with a downward shift in yields. Another way to state this is that yields in the short-term sector tend to be more volatile than yields in the long-term sector.

TREASURY RETURNS RESULTING FROM YIELD CURVE MOVEMENTS

3

As we discussed in Level I, a yield measure is a promised return if certain assumptions are satisfied; but total return (return from coupons and price change) is a more appropriate measure of the potential return from investing in a Treasury security. The total return for a short investment horizon depends critically on how interest rates change, reflected by how the yield curve changes.

EXHIBIT 59-2   Types of Yield Curve Shifts

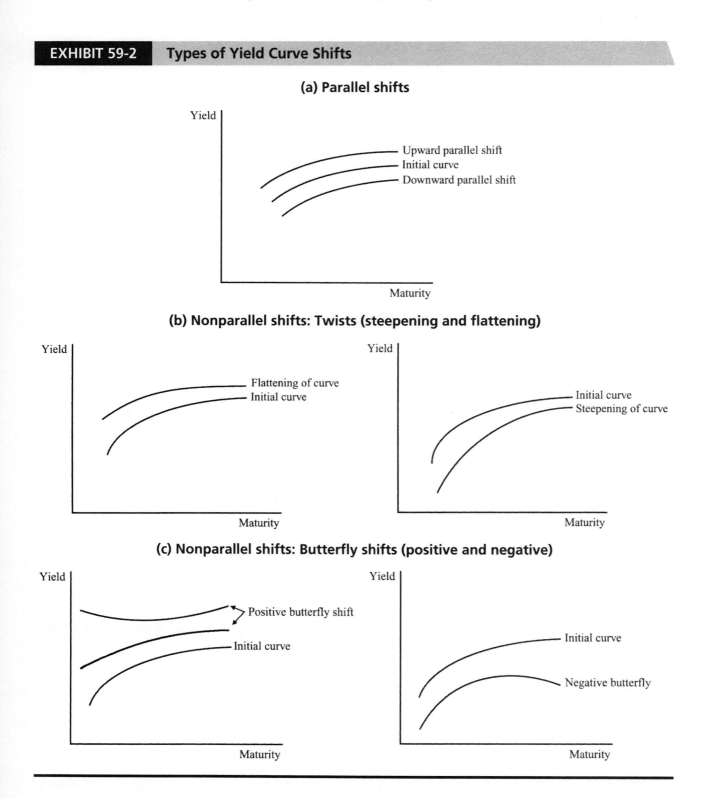

(a) Parallel shifts

Yield

Upward parallel shift
Initial curve
Downward parallel shift

Maturity

(b) Nonparallel shifts: Twists (steepening and flattening)

Yield

Flattening of curve
Initial curve

Maturity

Yield

Initial curve
Steepening of curve

Maturity

(c) Nonparallel shifts: Butterfly shifts (positive and negative)

Yield

Positive butterfly shift
Initial curve

Maturity

Yield

Initial curve

Negative butterfly

Maturity

There have been several published and unpublished studies of how changes in the shape of the yield curve affect the total return on Treasury securities. The first such study by two researchers at Goldman Sachs (Robert Litterman and José Scheinkman) was published in 1991.[2] The results reported in more recent studies

[2] Robert Litterman and José Scheinkman, "Common Factors Affecting Bond Returns," *Journal of Fixed Income* (June 1991), pp. 54–61.

support the findings of the Litterman-Scheinkman study so we will just discuss their findings. Litterman and Scheinkman found that three factors explained historical returns for zero-coupon Treasury securities for all maturities. The first factor was changes in the level of rates, the second factor was changes in the slope of the yield curve, and the third factor was changes in the curvature of the yield curve.

Litterman and Scheinkman employed regression analysis to determine the relative contribution of these three factors in explaining the returns on zero-coupon Treasury securities of different maturities. They determined the importance of each factor by its coefficient of determination, popularly referred to as the "R^2." In general, the R^2 measures the percentage of the variance in the dependent variable (i.e., the total return on the zero-coupon Treasury security in their study) explained by the independent variables (i.e., the three factors).[3] For example, an R^2 of 0.8 means that 80% of the variation of the return on a zero-coupon Treasury security is explained by the three factors. Therefore, 20% of the variation of the return is not explained by these three factors. The R^2 will have a value between 0% and 100%. In the Litterman-Scheinkman study, the R^2 was very high for all maturities, meaning that the three factors had a very strong explanatory power.

The first factor, representing changes in the level of rates, holding all other factors constant (in particular, yield curve slope), had the greatest explanatory power for all the maturities, averaging about 90%. The implication is that the most important factor that a manager of a Treasury portfolio should control for is exposure to changes in the level of interest rates. For this reason it is important to have a way to measure or quantify this risk. Duration is in fact the measure used to quantify exposure to a parallel shift in the yield curve.

The second factor, changes in the yield curve slope, was the second largest contributing factor. The average relative contribution for all maturities was 8.5%. Thus, changes in the yield curve slope was, on average, about one tenth as significant as changes in the level of rates. While the relative contribution was only 8.5%, this can still have a significant impact on the return for a Treasury portfolio and a portfolio manager must control for this risk. We briefly explained in Level I how a manager can do this using key rate duration and will discuss this further in this reading.

The third factor, changes in the curvature of the yield curve, contributed relatively little to explaining historical returns for Treasury zero-coupon securities.

CONSTRUCTING THE THEORETICAL SPOT RATE CURVE FOR TREASURIES

4

Our focus thus far has been on the shape of the Treasury yield curve. In fact, often the financial press in its discussion of interest rates focuses on the Treasury yield curve. However, as explained at Level I, it is the default-free spot rate curve as represented by the Treasury spot rate curve that is used in valuing fixed-income securities. But how does one obtain the default-free spot rate curve? This curve can be constructed from the yields on Treasury securities. The Treasury issues that are candidates for inclusion are:

1. Treasury coupon strips

2. on-the-run Treasury issues

---

[3] For a further explanation of the coefficient of determination, see Richard A. DeFusco, Dennis W. McLeavey, Jerald E. Pinto, and David E. Runkle, *Quantitative Methods for Investment Analysis* (Charlottesville, VA: Association for Investment Management and Research, 2002), pp. 388–390.

3. on-the-run Treasury issues and selected off-the-run Treasury issues

4. all Treasury coupon securities and bills

Once the securities that are to be included in the construction of the theoretical spot rate curve are selected, the methodology for constructing the curve must be determined. The methodology depends on the securities included. If Treasury coupon strips are used, the procedure is simple since the observed yields are the spot rates. If the on-the-run Treasury issues with or without selected off-the-run Treasury issues are used, then the methodology of bootstrapping is used.

Using an estimated Treasury par yield curve, bootstrapping is a repetitive technique whereby the yields prior to some maturity, same m, are used to obtain the spot rate for year m. For example, suppose that the yields on the **par yield curve** are denoted by $y_1, .., y_T$ where the subscripts denote the time periods. Then the yield for the first period, y_1, is the spot rate for the first period. Let the first period spot rate be denoted as s_1. Then y_2 and s_1 can be used to derive s_2 using arbitrage arguments. Next, y_3, s_1, and s_2 are used to derive s_3 using arbitrage arguments. The process continues until all the spot rates are derived, $s_1, ..., s_m$.

In selecting the universe of securities used to construct a default-free spot rate curve, one wants to make sure that the yields are not biased by any of the following: (1) default, (2) embedded options, (3) liquidity, and (4) pricing errors. To deal with default, U.S. Treasury securities are used. Issues with embedded options are avoided because the market yield reflects the value of the embedded options. In the U.S. Treasury market, there are only a few callable bonds so this is not an issue. In other countries, however, there are callable and putable government bonds. Liquidity varies by issue. There are U.S. Treasury issues that have less liquidity than bonds with a similar maturity. In fact, there are some issues that have extremely high liquidity because they are used by dealers in **repurchase agreements**. Finally, in some countries the trading of certain government bonds issues is limited, resulting in estimated prices that may not reflect the true price.

Given the theoretical spot rate for each maturity, there are various statistical techniques that are used to create a continuous spot rate curve. A discussion of these statistical techniques is a specialist topic.

A. Treasury Coupon Strips

It would seem simplest to use the observed yield on Treasury coupon strips to construct an actual spot rate curve because there are three problems with using the observed rates on Treasury strips. First, the liquidity of the strips market is not as great as that of the Treasury coupon market. Thus, the observed rates on strips reflect a premium for liquidity.

Second, the tax treatment of strips is different from that of Treasury coupon securities. Specifically, the accrued interest on strips is taxed even though no cash is received by the investor. Thus they are negative cash flow securities to taxable entities, and, as a result, their yield reflects this tax disadvantage.

Finally, there are maturity sectors where non-U.S. investors find it advantageous to trade off yield for tax advantages associated with a strip. Specifically, certain foreign tax authorities allow their citizens to treat the difference between the maturity value and the purchase price as a capital gain and tax this gain at a favorable tax rate. Some will grant this favorable treatment only when the strip is created from the principal rather than the coupon. For this reason, those who use Treasury strips to represent theoretical spot rates restrict the issues included to coupon strips.

B. On-the-Run Treasury Issues

The on-the-run Treasury issues are the most recently auctioned issues of a given maturity. In the U.S., these issues include the 1-month, 3-month, and 6-month Treasury bills, and the 2-year, 5-year, and 10-year Treasury notes. Treasury bills are zero-coupon instruments; the notes are coupon securities.[4]

There is an observed yield for each of the on-the-run issues. For the coupon issues, these yields are not the yields used in the analysis when the issue is not trading at par. Instead, for each on-the-run coupon issue, the estimated yield necessary to make the issue trade at par is used. The resulting on-the-run yield curve is called the **par coupon curve**. The reason for using securities with a price of par is to eliminate the effect of the tax treatment for securities selling at a **discount** or premium. The differential tax treatment distorts the yield.

C. On-the-Run Treasury Issues and Selected Off-the-Run Treasury Issues

One of the problems with using just the on-the-run issues is the large gap between maturities, particularly after five years. To mitigate this problem, some dealers and vendors use selected off-the-run Treasury issues. Typically, the issues used are the 20-year issue and 25-year issue.[5] Given the par coupon curve including any off-the-run selected issues, a linear interpolation method is used to fill in the gaps for the other maturities. The bootstrapping method is then used to construct the theoretical spot rate curve.

D. All Treasury Coupon Securities and Bills

Using only on-the-run issues and a few off-the-run issues fails to recognize the information embodied in Treasury prices that are not included in the analysis. Thus, some market participants argue that it is more appropriate to use all outstanding Treasury coupon securities and bills to construct the theoretical spot rate curve. Moreover, a common practice is to filter the Treasury securities universe to eliminate securities that are on special (trading at a lower yield than their true yield) in the repo market.[6]

When all coupon securities and bills are used, methodologies more complex than bootstrapping must be employed to construct the theoretical spot rate curve since there may be more than one yield for each maturity. There are various methodologies for fitting a curve to the points when all the Treasury securities are used. The methodologies make an adjustment for the effect of taxes.[7] A discussion of the various methodologies is a specialist topic.

---

[4] At one time, the Department of the Treasury issued 3-year notes, 7-year notes, 15-year bonds, 20-year bonds, and 30-year bonds.

[5] See, for example, Philip H. Galdi and Shenglin Lu, *Analyzing Risk and Relative Value of Corporate and Government Securities*, Merrill Lynch & Co., Global Securities Research & Economics Group, Fixed Income Analytics, 1997, p. 11.

[6] There must also be an adjustment for what is known as the "specials effect." This has to do with a security trading at a lower yield than its true yield because of its value in the repurchase agreement market. As explained at Level III, in a repurchase agreement, a security is used as collateral for a loan. If the security is one that is in demand by dealers, referred to as "hot collateral" or "collateral on special," then the borrowing rate is lower if that security is used as collateral. As a result of this favorable feature, a security will offer a lower yield in the market if it is on special so that the investor can finance that security cheaply. As a result, the use of the yield of a security on special will result in a biased yield estimate. The 10-year on-the-run U.S. Treasury issue is typically on special.

[7] See, Oldrich A. Vasicek and H. Gifford Fong, "Term Structure Modeling Using Exponential Splines," *Journal of Finance* (May 1982), pp. 339–358.

THE SWAP CURVE (LIBOR CURVE)

In the United States it is common to use the Treasury spot rate curve for purposes of valuation. In other countries, either a government spot rate curve is used (if a liquid market for the securities exists) or the swap curve is used (or as explained shortly, the *LIBOR curve*). LIBOR is the London interbank offered rate and is the interest rate which major international banks offer each other on Eurodollar certificates of deposit (CD) with given maturities. The maturities range from **overnight** to five years. So, references to "3-month LIBOR" indicate the interest rate that major international banks are offering to pay to other such banks on a CD that matures in three months. A swap curve can be constructed that is unique to a country where there is a swap market for converting fixed cash flows to floating cash flows in that country's currency.

A. Elements of a Swap and a Swap Curve

To discuss a swap curve, we need the basics of a **generic** (also called a "plain vanilla" interest rate) swap. In a generic interest rate swap two parties are exchanging cash flows based on a **notional amount** where (1) one party is paying fixed cash flows and receiving floating cash flows and (2) the other party is paying floating cash flows and receiving fixed cash flows. It is called a "swap" because the two parties are "swapping" payments: (1) one party is paying a floating rate and receiving a fixed rate and (2) the other party is paying a fixed rate and receiving a floating rate. While the swap is described in terms of a "rate," the amount the parties exchange is expressed in terms of a currency and determined by using the notional amount as explained below.

For example, suppose the swap specifies that (1) one party is to pay a fixed rate of 6%, (2) the notional amount is $100 million, (3) the payments are to be quarterly, and (4) the term of the swap is 7 years. The fixed rate of 6% is called the **swap rate**, or equivalently, the **swap fixed rate**. The swap rate of 6% multiplied by the notional amount of $100 million gives the amount of the annual payment, $6 million. If the payment is to be made quarterly, the amount paid each quarter is $1.5 million ($6 million/4) and this amount is paid every quarter for the next 7 years.[8]

The floating rate in an interest rate swap can be any short-term interest rate. For example, it could be the rate on a 3-month Treasury bill or the rate on 3-month LIBOR. The most common **reference rate** used in swaps is 3-month LIBOR. When LIBOR is the reference rate, the swap is referred to as a "LIBOR-based swap."

Consider the swap we just used in our illustration. We will assume that the reference rate is 3-month LIBOR. In that swap, one party is paying a fixed rate of 6% (i.e., the swap rate) and receiving 3-month LIBOR for the next 7 years. Hence, the 7-year swap rate is 6%. But entering into this swap with a swap rate of 6% is equivalent to locking in 3-month LIBOR for 7 years (rolled over on a quarterly basis). So, casting this in terms of 3-month LIBOR, the 7-year maturity rate for 3-month LIBOR is 6%.

---

[8] Actually the payments are slightly different each quarter because the amount of the quarterly payment depends on the actual number of days in the quarter.

So, suppose that the swap rate for the maturities quoted in the swap market are as shown below:

Maturity	Swap rate
2 years	4.2%
3 years	4.6%
4 years	5.0%
5 years	5.3%
6 years	5.7%
7 years	6.0%
8 years	6.2%
9 years	6.4%
10 years	6.5%
15 years	6.7%
30 years	6.8%

This would be the swap curve. But this swap curve is also telling us how much we can lock in 3-month LIBOR for a specified future period. By locking in 3-month LIBOR it is meant that a party that pays the floating rate (i.e., agrees to pay 3-month LIBOR) is locking in a borrowing rate; the party receiving the floating rate is locking in an amount to be received. Because 3-month LIBOR is being exchanged, the swap curve is also called the **LIBOR curve**.

Note that we have not indicated the currency in which the payments are to be made for our hypothetical swap curve. Suppose that the swap curve above refers to swapping U.S. dollars (i.e., the notional amount is in U.S. dollars) from a fixed to a floating (and vice versa). Then the swap curve above would be the U.S. swap curve. If the notional amount was for euros, and the swaps involved swapping a fixed euro amount for a floating euro amount, then it would be the euro swap curve.

Finally, let's look at how the terms of a swap are quoted. Rather than quote a swap rate for a given maturity, the convention in the swap market is to quote a **swap spread**. The spread can be over any benchmark desired, typically a government bond yield. The swap spread is defined as follows for a given maturity:

swap spread = swap rate − government yield on a bond with the same
                          maturity as the swap

For euro-denominated swaps (i.e., swaps in which the currency in which the payments are made is the euro), the government yield used as the benchmark is the German government bond with the same maturity as the swap.

For example, consider our hypothetical 7-year swap. Suppose that the currency of the swap payments is in U.S. dollars and the estimated 7-year U.S. Treasury yield is 5.4%. Then since the swap rate is 6%, the swap spread is:

swap spread = 6% − 5.4% = 0.6% = 60 basis points.

Suppose, instead, the swap was denominated in euros and the swap rate is 6%. Also suppose that the estimated 7-year German government bond yield is 5%. Then the swap spread would be quoted as 100 basis points (6% − 5%).

Effectively the swap spread reflects the risk of the counterparty to the swap failing to satisfy its obligation. Consequently, it primarily reflects credit risk. Since the counterparties in swaps are typically bank-related entities, the swap spread is a rough indicator of the credit risk of the banking sector. Therefore, the swap rate curve is not a default-free curve. Instead, it is an inter-bank or AA rated curve.

Notice that the swap rate is compared to a government bond yield to determine the swap spread. Why would one want to use a swap curve if a government bond yield curve is available? We answer that question next.

B. Reasons for Increased Use of Swap Curve

Investors and issuers use the swap market for hedging and arbitrage purposes, and the swap curve as a benchmark for evaluating performance of fixed income securities and the pricing of fixed income securities. Since the swap curve is effectively the LIBOR curve and investors borrow based on LIBOR, the swap curve is more useful to funded investors than a government yield curve.

The increased application of the swap curve for these activities is due to its advantages over using the government bond yield curve as a benchmark. Before identifying these advantages, it is important to understand that the drawback of the swap curve relative to the government bond yield curve could be poorer liquidity. In such instances, the swap rates would reflect a **liquidity premium**. Fortunately, liquidity is not an issue in many countries as the swap market has become highly liquid, with narrow bid-ask spreads for a wide range of swap maturities. In some countries swaps may offer better liquidity than that country's government bond market.

The advantages of the swap curve over a government bond yield curve are:[9]

1. There is almost no government regulation of the swap market. The lack of government regulation makes swap rates across different markets more comparable. In some countries, there are some sovereign issues that offer various tax benefits to investors and, as a result, for global investors it makes comparative analysis of government rates across countries difficult because some market yields do not reflect their true yield.

2. The supply of swaps depends only on the number of counterparties that are seeking or are willing to enter into a swap transaction at any given time. Since there is no underlying government bond, there can be no effect of market technical factors[10] that may result in the yield for a government bond issue being less than its true yield.

3. Comparisons across countries of government yield curves is difficult because of the differences in sovereign credit risk. In contrast, the credit risk as reflected in the swaps curve are similar and make comparisons across countries more meaningful than government yield curves. **Sovereign risk** is not present in the swap curve because, as noted earlier, the swap curve is viewed as an inter-bank yield curve or AA yield curve.

4. There are more maturity points available to construct a swap curve than a government bond yield curve. More specifically, what is quoted in the swap market are swap rates for 2, 3, 4, 5, 6, 7, 8, 9, 10, 15, and 30 year maturities.

[9] See Uri Ron, "A Practical Guide to Swap Curve Construction," Chapter 6 in Frank J. Fabozzi (ed.), *Interest Rate, Term Structure, and Valuation Modeling* (NY: John Wiley & Sons, 2002).

[10] For example, a government bond issue being on "special" in the repurchase agreement market.

Thus, in the swap market there are 10 market interest rates with a maturity of 2 years and greater. In contrast, in the U.S. Treasury market, for example, there are only three market interest rates for on-the-run Treasuries with a maturity of 2 years or greater (2, 5, and 10 years) and one of the rates, the 10-year rate, may not be a good benchmark because it is often on special in the repo market. Moreover, because the U.S. Treasury has ceased the issuance of 30-year bonds, there is no 30-year yield available.

C. Constructing the LIBOR Spot Rate Curve

In the valuation of fixed income securities, it is not the Treasury yield curve that is used as the basis for determining the appropriate discount rate for computing the present value of cash flows but the Treasury spot rates. The Treasury spot rates are derived from the Treasury yield curve using the bootstrapping process.

Similarly, it is not the swap curve that is used for discounting cash flows when the swap curve is the benchmark but the spot rates. The spot rates are derived from the swap curve in exactly the same way—using the bootstrapping methodology. The resulting spot rate curve is called the **LIBOR spot rate curve**. Moreover, a forward rate curve can be derived from the spot rate curve. The same thing is done in the swap market. The forward rate curve that is derived is called the **LIBOR forward rate curve**. Consequently, if we understand the mechanics of moving from the yield curve to the spot rate curve to the forward rate curve in the Treasury market, there is no reason to repeat an explanation of that process here for the swap market; that is, it is the same methodology, just different yields are used.[11]

EXPECTATIONS THEORIES OF THE TERM STRUCTURE OF INTEREST RATES

6

So far we have described the different types of curves that analysts and portfolio managers focus on. The key curve is the spot rate curve because it is the spot rates that are used to value the cash flows of a fixed-income security. The spot rate curve is also called the term structure of interest rates, or simply term structure. Now we turn to another potential use of the term structure. Analysts and portfolio managers are interested in knowing if there is information contained in the term structure that can be used in making investment decisions. For this purpose, market participants rely on different theories about the term structure.

We explained four theories of the term structure of interest rates—pure expectations theory, **liquidity preference theory**, **preferred habitat theory**, and market segmentation theory. Unlike the market segmentation theory, the first

---

[11] The question is what yields are used to construct the swap rate curve. Pratitioners use yields from two related markets: the Eurodollar CD futures contract and the swap market. We will not review the Eurodollar CD futures contract here. For now, the only important fact to note about this contract is that it provides a means for locking in 3-month LIBOR in the future. In fact, it provides a means for doing so for an extended time into the future.

Practitioners use the Eurodollar CD futures rate up to four years to get 3-month LIBOR for every quarter. While there are Eurodollar CD futures contracts that settle further out than four years, for technical reasons (having to do with the convexity of the contract) analysts use only the first four years. (In fact, this actually varies from practitioner to practitioner. Some will use the Eurodollar CD futures from two years up to four years.) For maturities after four years, the swap rates are used to get 3-month LIBOR. As notes above, there is a swap rate for maturities for each year 10, and then swap rates for 15 years and 30 years.

three theories share a hypothesis about the behavior of short-term forward rates and also assume that the forward rates in current long-term bonds are closely related to the market's expectations about future short-term rates. For this reason, the pure expectations theory, liquidity preference theory, and preferred habitat theory are referred to as **expectations theories of the term structure of interest rates**.

What distinguishes these three expectations theories is whether there are systematic factors other than expectations of future interest rates that affect forward rates. The pure expectations theory postulates that no systematic factors other than expected future short-term rates affect forward rates; the liquidity preference theory and the preferred habitat theory assert that there are other factors. Accordingly, the last two forms of the expectations theory are sometimes referred to as **biased expectations theories**. The relationship among the various theories is described below and summarized in Exhibit 59-3.

A. The Pure Expectations Theory

According to the pure expectations theory, forward rates exclusively represent expected future spot rates. Thus, the entire term structure at a given time reflects the market's current expectations of the family of future short-term rates. Under this view, a rising term structure must indicate that the market expects short-term rates to rise throughout the relevant future. Similarly, a flat term structure reflects an expectation that future short-term rates will be mostly constant, while a falling term structure must reflect an expectation that future short-term rates will decline.

1. Drawbacks of the Theory

The pure expectations theory suffers from one shortcoming, which, qualitatively, is quite serious. It neglects the risks inherent in investing in bonds. If forward rates were perfect predictors of future interest rates, then the future prices of bonds would be known with certainty. The return over any investment period would be certain and independent of the maturity of the instrument acquired. However, with the uncertainty about future interest rates and, therefore, about

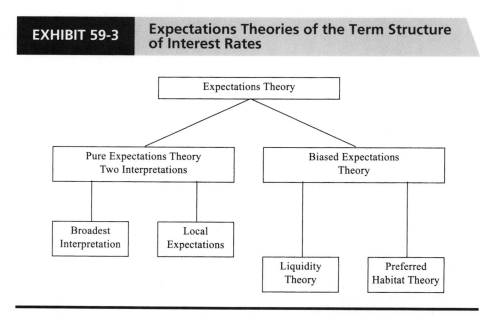

EXHIBIT 59-3   **Expectations Theories of the Term Structure of Interest Rates**

future prices of bonds, these instruments become risky investments in the sense that the return over some investment horizon is unknown.

There are two risks that cause uncertainty about the return over some investment horizon. The first is the uncertainty about the price of the bond at the end of the investment horizon. For example, an investor who plans to invest for five years might consider the following three investment alternatives:

Alternative 1: Invest in a 5-year zero-coupon bond and hold it for five years.
Alternative 2: Invest in a 12-year zero-coupon bond and sell it at the end of five years.
Alternative 3: Invest in a 30-year zero-coupon bond and sell it at the end of five years.

The return that will be realized in Alternatives 2 and 3 is not known because the price of each of these bonds at the end of five years is unknown. In the case of the 12-year bond, the price will depend on the yield on 7-year bonds five years from now; and the price of the 30-year bond will depend on the yield on 25-year bonds five years from now. Since forward rates implied in the current term structure for a 7-year bond five years from now and a 25-year bond five years from now are not perfect predictors of the actual future rates, there is uncertainty about the price for both bonds five years from now. Thus, there is interest rate risk; that is, the price of the bond may be lower than currently expected at the end of the investment horizon due to an increase in interest rates. As explained in Level I, an important feature of interest rate risk is that it increases with the length of the bond's maturity.

The second risk involves the uncertainty about the rate at which the proceeds from a bond that matures prior to the end of the investment horizon can be reinvested until the maturity date, that is, reinvestment risk. For example, an investor who plans to invest for five years might consider the following three alternative investments:

Alternative 1: Invest in a 5-year zero-coupon bond and hold it for five years.
Alternative 2: Invest in a 6-month zero-coupon instrument and, when it matures, reinvest the proceeds in 6-month zero-coupon instruments over the entire 5-year investment horizon.
Alternative 3: Invest in a 2-year zero-coupon bond and, when it matures, reinvest the proceeds in a 3-year zero-coupon bond.

The risk for Alternatives 2 and 3 is that the return over the 5-year investment horizon is unknown because rates at which the proceeds can be reinvested until the end of the investment horizon are unknown.

2. *Interpretations of the Theory*

There are several interpretations of the pure expectations theory that have been put forth by economists. These interpretations are not exact equivalents nor are they consistent with each other, in large part because they offer different treatments of the two risks associated with realizing a return that we have just explained.[12]

---

[12] These formulations are summarized by John Cox, Jonathan Ingersoll, Jr., and Stephen Ross, "A Reexamination of Traditional Hypotheses About the Term Structure of Interest Rates," *Journal of Finance* (September 1981), pp. 769-99.

a. Broadest Interpretation

The broadest interpretation of the pure expectations theory suggests that investors expect the return for any investment horizon to be the same, regardless of the **maturity strategy** selected.[13] For example, consider an investor who has a 5-year investment horizon. According to this theory, it makes no difference if a 5-year, 12-year, or 30-year bond is purchased and held for five years since the investor expects the return from all three bonds to be the same over the 5-year investment horizon. A major criticism of this very broad interpretation of the theory is that, because of price risk associated with investing in bonds with a maturity greater than the investment horizon, the expected returns from these three very different investments should differ in significant ways.[14]

b. Local Expectations Form of the Pure Expectations Theory

A second interpretation, referred to as the **local expectations form of the pure expectations theory,** suggests that the return will be the same over a short-term investment horizon starting today. For example, if an investor has a 6-month investment horizon, buying a 1-year, 5-year or 10-year bond will produce the same 6-month return.

To illustrate this, we will use the hypothetical yield curve shown in Exhibit 59-4. At Level I we used the yield curve in Exhibit 59-4 to show how to compute spot rates and forward rates. Exhibit 59-5 shows all the 6-month forward rates. We will focus on the 1-year, 5-year, and 10-year issues.

Our objective is to look at what happens to the total return over a 6-month investment horizon for the 1-year, 5-year, and 10-year issues if all the 6-month forward rates are realized. Look first at panel a in Exhibit 59-6. This shows the total return for the 1-year issue. At the end of 6 months, this issue is a 6-month issue. The 6-month forward rate is 3.6%. This means that if the forward rate is realized, the 6-month yield 6 months from now will be 3.6%. Given a 6-month issue that must offer a yield of 3.6% (the 6-month forward rate), the price of this issue will decline from 100 (today) to 99.85265 six months from now. The price must decline because if the 6-month forward rate is realized 6 months from now, the yield increases from 3.3% to 3.6%. The total dollars realized over the 6 months are coupon interest adjusted for the decline in the price. The total return for the 6 months is 3%.

What the local expectations theory asserts is that over the 6-month investment horizon even the 5-year and the 10-year issues will generate a total return of 3% if forward rates are realized. Panels b and c show this to be the case. We need only explain the computation for one of the two issues. Let's use the 5-year issue. The 6-month forward rates are shown in the third column of panel b. Now we apply a few principles discussed at Level I. We demonstrated that to value a security each cash flow should be discounted at the spot rate with the same maturity. We also demonstrated that 6-month forward rates can be used to value the cash flows of a security and that the results will be identical using the forward rates to value a security. For example, consider the cash flow in period 3 for the 5-year issue. The cash flow is $2.60. The 6-month forward rates are 3.6%, 3.92%,

---

[13] F. Lutz, "The Structure of Interest Rates," *Quarterly Journal of Economics* (1940-41), pp. 36-63.

[14] Cox, Ingersoll, and Ross, pp. 774-775.

EXHIBIT 59-4	Hypothetical Treasury Par Yield Curve			
Period	**Years**	**Annual Yield to Maturity (BEY)(%)***	**Price**	**Spot Rate (BEY)(%)**
1	0.5	3.00	—	3.0000
2	1.0	3.30	—	3.3000
3	1.5	3.50	100.00	3.5053
4	2.0	3.90	100.00	3.9164
5	2.5	4.40	100.00	4.4376
6	3.0	4.70	100.00	4.7520
7	3.5	4.90	100.00	4.9622
8	4.0	5.00	100.00	5.0650
9	4.5	5.10	100.00	5.1701
10	5.0	5.20	100.00	5.2772
11	5.5	5.30	100.00	5.3864
12	6.0	5.40	100.00	5.4976
13	6.5	5.50	100.00	5.6108
14	7.0	5.55	100.00	5.6643
15	7.5	5.60	100.00	5.7193
16	8.0	5.65	100.00	5.7755
17	8.5	5.70	100.00	5.8331
18	9.0	5.80	100.00	5.9584
19	9.5	5.90	100.00	6.0863
20	10.0	6.00	100.00	6.2169

* The yield to maturity and the spot rate are annual rates. They are reported as bond-equivalent yields. To obtain the semiannual yield or rate, one half the annual yield or annual rate is used.

EXHIBIT 59-5	Six-Month Forward Rates: The Short-Term Forward Rate Curve (Annualized Rates on a Bond-Equivalent Basis)		
Notation	**Forward Rate**	**Notation**	**Forward Rate**
$_1f_0$	3.00	$_1f_{10}$	6.48
$_1f_1$	3.60	$_1f_{11}$	6.72
$_1f_2$	3.92	$_1f_{12}$	6.97
$_1f_3$	5.15	$_1f_{13}$	6.36
$_1f_4$	6.54	$_1f_{14}$	6.49
$_1f_5$	6.33	$_1f_{15}$	6.62
$_1f_6$	6.23	$_1f_{16}$	6.76
$_1f_7$	5.79	$_1f_{17}$	8.10
$_1f_8$	6.01	$_1f_{18}$	8.40
$_1f_9$	6.24	$_1f_{19}$	8.72

and 5.15%. These are annual rates. So, half these rates are 1.8%, 1.96%, and 2.575%. The present value of $2.60 using the 6-month forward is:

$$\frac{\$2.60}{(1.018)\,(1.0196)\,(1.02575)} = \$2.44205$$

This is the present value shown in the third column of panel b. In a similar manner, all of the other present values in the third column are computed. The arbitrage-free value for this 5-year issue 6 months from now (when it is a 4.5-year issue) is 98.89954. The total return (taking into account the coupon interest and the loss due to the decline in price from 100) is 3%. Thus, if the 6-month forward rates are realized, all three issues provide a short-term (6-month) return of 3%.[15]

EXHIBIT 59-6	Total Return over 6-Month Investment Horizon if 6-Month Forward Rates Are Realized

a: Total return on 1-year issue if forward rates are realized

Period	Cash flow ($)	Six-month forward rate (%)	Price at horizon ($)
1	101.650	3.60	99.85265

Price at horizon: 99.85265   Total proceeds: 101.5027
Coupon: 1.65   Total return: 3.00%

b: Total return on 5-year issue if forward rates are realized

Period	Cash flow ($)	Six-month forward rate (%)	Present value ($)
1	2.60	3.60	2.55403
2	2.60	3.92	2.50493
3	2.60	5.15	2.44205
4	2.60	6.54	2.36472
5	2.60	6.33	2.29217
6	2.60	6.23	2.22293
7	2.60	5.79	2.16039
8	2.60	6.01	2.09736
9	102.60	6.24	80.26096
		Total:	98.89954

Price at horizon: 98.89954   Total proceeds: 101.4995
Coupon: 2.60   Total return: 3.00%

(Exhibit continued on next page ...)

---

[15] It has been demonstrated that the local expectations formulation, which is narrow in scope, is the only interpretation of the pure expectations theory that can be sustained in equilibrium. See Cox, Ingersoll, and Ross, "A Re-examination of Traditional Hypotheses About the Term Structure of Interest Rates."

EXHIBIT 59-6	(continued)

c: Total return on 10-year issue if forward rates are realized

Period	Cash flow ($)	Six-month forward rate (%)	Present value ($)
1	3.00	3.60	2.94695
2	3.00	3.92	2.89030
3	3.00	5.15	2.81775
4	3.00	6.54	2.72853
5	3.00	6.33	2.64482
6	3.00	6.23	2.56492
7	3.00	5.79	2.49275
8	3.00	6.01	2.42003
9	3.00	6.24	2.34681
10	3.00	6.48	2.27316
11	3.00	6.72	2.19927
12	3.00	6.97	2.12520
13	3.00	6.36	2.05970
14	3.00	6.49	1.99497
15	3.00	6.62	1.93105
16	3.00	6.76	1.86791
17	3.00	8.10	1.79521
18	3.00	8.40	1.72285
19	103.00	8.72	56.67989
		Total:	98.50208

Price at horizon: 98.50208   Total proceeds: 101.5021

Coupon: 3.00   Total return: 3.00%

c. *Forward Rates and Market Consensus*

We first introduced forward rates at Level I. We saw how various types of forward rates can be computed. That is, we saw how to compute the forward rate for any length of time beginning at any future period of time. So, it is possible to compute the 2-year forward rate beginning 5 years from now or the 3-year forward rate beginning 8 years from now. We showed how, using arbitrage arguments, forward rates can be derived from spot rates.

At Level I, no interpretation was given to the forward rates. The focus was just on how to compute them from spot rates based on arbitrage arguments. Let's provide two interpretations now with a simple illustration. Suppose that an investor has a 1-year investment horizon and has a choice of investing in either a 1-year Treasury bill or a 6-month Treasury bill and rolling over the proceeds from the maturing 6-month issue in another 6-month Treasury bill. Since the Treasury bills are zero-coupon securities, the rates on them are spot rates and can be used to compute the 6-month forward rate six months from now. For example, if the 6-month Treasury bill rate is 5% and the 1-year Treasury bill rate is 5.6%, then the 6-month forward rate six months from now is 6.2%. To verify this, suppose an investor invests $100 in a 1-year investment. The $100 investment in a zero-coupon instrument will grow at a rate of 2.8% (one half 5.6%) for two 6-month periods to:

$$\$100 \ (1.028)^2 = \$105.68$$

If $100 is invested in a six month zero-coupon instrument at 2.5% (one-half 5%) and the proceeds reinvested at the 6-month forward rate of 3.1% (one-half 6.2%), the $100 will grow to:

$$\$100 \ (1.025)(1.031) = \$105.68$$

Thus, the 6-month forward rate generates the same future dollars for the $100 investment at the end of 1 year.

One interpretation of the forward rate is that it is a "break-even rate." That is, a forward rate is the rate that will make an investor indifferent between investing for the full investment horizon and part of the investment horizon and rolling over the proceeds for the balance of the investment horizon. So, in our illustration, the forward rate of 6.2% can be interpreted as the break-even rate that will make an investment in a 6-month zero-coupon instrument with a yield of 5% rolled-over into another 6-month zero-coupon instrument equal to the yield on a 1-year zero-coupon instrument with a yield of 5.6%.

Similarly, a 2-year forward rate beginning four years from now can be interpreted as the break-even rate that will make an investor indifferent between investing in (1) a 4-year zero-coupon instrument at the 4-year spot rate and rolling over the investment for two more years in a zero-coupon instrument and (2) investing in a 6-year zero-coupon instrument at the 6-year spot rate.

A second interpretation of the forward rate is that it is a rate that allows the investor to lock in a rate for some future period. For example, consider once again our 1-year investment. If an investor purchases this instrument rather than the 6-month instrument, the investor has locked in a 6.2% rate six months from now regardless of how interest rates change six months from now. Similarly, in the case of a 6-year investment, by investing in a 6-year zero-coupon instrument rather than a 4-year zero-coupon instrument, the investor has locked in the 2-year zero-coupon rate four years from now. That locked in rate is the 2-year forward rate four years from now. The 1-year forward rate five years from now is the rate that is locked in by buying a 6-year zero-coupon instrument rather than investing in a 5-year zero-coupon instrument and reinvesting the proceeds at the end of five years in a 1-year zero-coupon instrument.

There is another interpretation of forward rates. Proponents of the pure expectations theory argue that forward rates reflect the "market's consensus" of future interest rates. They argue that forward rates can be used to predict future interest rates. A natural question about forward rates is then how well they do at predicting future interest rates. Studies have demonstrated that forward rates do not do a good job at predicting future interest rates.[16] Then, why is it so important to understand forward rates? The reason is that forward rates indicate how an investor's expectations must differ from the "break-even rate" or the "lock-in rate" when making an investment decision.

Thus, even if a forward rate may not be realized, forward rates can be highly relevant in deciding between two alternative investments. Specifically, if an

---

[16] Eugene F. Fama, "Forward Rates as Predictors of Future Spot Rates," *Journal of Financial Economics,* Vol. 3, No. 4, 1976, pp. 361–377.

investor's expectation about a rate in the future is less than the corresponding forward rate, then he would be better off investing now to lock in the forward rate.

B. Liquidity Preference Theory

We have explained that the drawback of the pure expectations theory is that it does not consider the risks associated with investing in bonds. We know from Level I that the interest rate risk associated with holding a bond for one period is greater the longer the maturity of a bond. (Recall that duration increases with maturity.)

Given this uncertainty, and considering that investors typically do not like uncertainty, some economists and financial analysts have suggested a different theory—the liquidity preference theory. This theory states that investors will hold longer-term maturities if they are offered a long-term rate higher than the average of expected future rates by a risk premium that is positively related to the **term to maturity**.[17] Put differently, the forward rates should reflect both interest rate expectations and a "liquidity" premium (really a risk premium), and the premium should be higher for longer maturities.

According to the liquidity preference theory, forward rates will not be an unbiased estimate of the market's expectations of future interest rates because they contain a liquidity premium. Thus, an upward-sloping yield curve may reflect expectations that future interest rates either (1) will rise, or (2) will be unchanged or even fall, but with a liquidity premium increasing fast enough with maturity so as to produce an upward-sloping yield curve. That is, any shape for either the yield curve or the term structure of interest rates can be explained by the biased expectations theory.

C. The Preferred Habitat Theory

Another theory, known as the **preferred habitat theory**, also adopts the view that the term structure reflects the expectation of the future path of interest rates as well as a risk premium. However, the preferred habitat theory rejects the assertion that the risk premium must rise uniformly with maturity.[18] Proponents of the preferred habitat theory say that the latter conclusion could be accepted if all investors intend to liquidate their investment at the shortest possible date while all borrowers are anxious to borrow long. This assumption can be rejected since institutions have holding periods dictated by the nature of their liabilities.

The preferred habitat theory asserts that if there is an imbalance between the supply and demand for funds within a given maturity range, investors and borrowers will not be reluctant to shift their investing and financing activities out of their preferred maturity sector to take advantage of any imbalance. However, to do so, investors must be induced by a yield premium in order to accept the risks associated with shifting funds out of their preferred sector. Similarly, borrowers can only be induced to raise funds in a maturity sector other than their preferred sector by a sufficient cost savings to compensate for the corresponding funding risk.

Thus, this theory proposes that the shape of the yield curve is determined by both expectations of future interest rates and a risk premium, positive or negative,

---

[17] John R. Hicks, *Value and Capital* (London: Oxford University Press, 1946), Second Ed., pp. 141–145.

[18] Franco Modigliani and Richard Sutch, "Innovations in Interest Rate Policy," *American Economic Review* (May 1966), pp. 178-197.

to induce market participants to shift out of their preferred habitat. Clearly, according to this theory, yield curves that slope up, down, or flat are all possible.

7   MEASURING YIELD CURVE RISK

We now know how to construct the term structure of interest rates and the potential information content contained in the term structure that can be used for making investment decisions under different theories of the term structure. Next we look at how to measure exposure of a portfolio or position to a change in the term structure. This risk is referred to as **yield curve risk**.

Yield curve risk can be measured by changing the spot rate for a particular key maturity and determining the sensitivity of a security or portfolio to this change holding the spot rate for the other key maturities constant. The sensitivity of the change in value to a particular change in spot rate is called **rate duration**. There is a rate duration for every point on the spot rate curve. Consequently, there is not one rate duration, but a vector of durations representing each maturity on the spot rate curve. The total change in value if all rates change by the same number of basis points is simply the **effective duration** of a security or portfolio to a parallel shift in rates. Recall that effective duration measures the exposure of a security or portfolio to a parallel shift in the term structure, taking into account any embedded options.

This rate duration approach was first suggested by Donald Chambers and Willard Carleton in 1988[19] who called it "duration vectors." Robert Reitano suggested a similar approach in a series of papers and referred to these durations as "partial durations."[20] The most popular version of this approach is that developed by Thomas Ho in 1992.[21]

Ho's approach focuses on 11 key maturities of the spot rate curve. These rate durations are called **key rate durations**. The specific maturities on the spot rate curve for which a key rate duration is measured are 3 months, 1 year, 2 years, 3 years, 5 years, 7 years, 10 years, 15 years, 20 years, 25 years, and 30 years. Changes in rates between any two key rates are calculated using a linear approximation.

The impact of any type of yield curve shift can be quantified using key rate durations. A level shift can be quantified by changing all key rates by the same number of basis points and determining, based on the corresponding key rate durations, the effect on the value of a portfolio. The impact of a steepening of the yield curve can be found by (1) decreasing the key rates at the short end of the yield curve and determining the positive change in the portfolio's value using the corresponding key rate durations, and (2) increasing the key rates at the long end of the yield curve and determining the negative change in the portfolio's value using the corresponding key rate durations.

To simplify the key rate duration methodology, suppose that instead of a set of 11 key rates, there are only three key rates—2 years, 16 years, and 30 years.[22] The duration of a zero-coupon security is approximately the number of years

---

[19] Donald Chambers and Willard Carleton, "A Generalized Approach to Duration," *Research in Finance* 7(1988).

[20] See, for example, Robert R. Reitano, "Non-Parallel Yield Curve Shifts and Durational Leverage," *Journal of Portfolio Management* (Summer 1990), pp. 62-67, and "A Multivariate Approach to Duration Analysis," *ARCH* 2(1989).

[21] Thomas S.Y. Ho, "Key Rate Durations: Measures of Interest Risk," *The Journal of Fixed Income* (September 1992), pp. 29-44.

[22] This is the numerical example used by Ho, "Key Rate Durations," p. 33.

to maturity. Thus, the three key rate durations are 2, 16, and 30. Consider the following two $100 portfolios composed of 2-year, 16-year, and 30-year issues:

Portfolio	2-year issue	16-year issue	30-year issue
I	$50	$0	$50
II	$0	$100	$0

The key rate durations for these three points will be denoted by $D(1)$, $D(2)$, and $D(3)$ and defined as follows:

$D(1)$ = key rate duration for the 2-year part of the curve
$D(2)$ = key rate duration for the 16-year part of the curve
$D(3)$ = key rate duration for the 30-year part of the curve

The key rate durations for the three issues and the duration are as follows:

Issue	$D(1)$	$D(2)$	$D(3)$	Crash Duration
2-year	2	0	0	2
16-year	0	16	0	16
30-year	0	0	30	30

A portfolio's key rate duration is the weighted average of the key rate durations of the securities in the portfolio. The key rate duration and the effective duration for each portfolio are calculated below:

Portfolio I
$D(1) = (50/100) \times 2 + (0/100) \times 0 + (50/100) \times 0 = 1$
$D(2) = (50/100) \times 0 + (0/100) \times 16 + (50/100) \times 0 = 0$
$D(3) = (50/100) \times 0 + (0/100) \times 0 + (50/100) \times 30 = 15$

Effective duration $= (50/100) \times 2 + (0/100) \times 16 + (50/100) \times 30 = 16$

Portfolio II
$D(1) = (0/100) \times 2 + (100/100) \times 0 + (0/100) \times 0 = 0$
$D(2) = (0/100) \times 0 + (100/100) \times 16 + (0/100) \times 0 = 16$
$D(3) = (0/100) \times 0 + (100/100) \times 0 + (0/100) \times 30 = 0$

Effective duration $= (0/100) \times 2 + (100/100) \times 16 + (0/100) \times 30 = 16$

Thus, the key rate durations differ for the two portfolios. However, the effective duration for each portfolio is the same. Despite the same effective duration, the performance of the two portfolios will not be the same for a nonparallel shift in the spot rates. Consider the following three scenarios:

Scenario 1: All spot rates shift down 10 basis points.
Scenario 2: The 2-year key rate shifts up 10 basis points and the 30-year rate shifts down 10 basis points.

Scenario 3: The 2-year key rate shifts down 10 basis points and the 30-year rate shifts up 10 basis points.

Let's illustrate how to compute the estimated total return based on the key rate durations for Portfolio I for scenario 2. The 2-year key rate duration [D(1)] for Portfolio I is 1. For a 100 basis point increase in the 2-year key rate, the portfolio's value will decrease by approximately 1%. For a 10 basis point increase (as assumed in scenario 2), the portfolio's value will decrease by approximately 0.1%. Now let's look at the change in the 30-year key rate in scenario 2. The 30-year key rate duration [D(3)] is 15. For a 100 basis point decrease in the 30-year key rate, the portfolio's value will increase by approximately 15%. For a 10 basis point decrease (as assumed in scenario 2), the increase in the portfolio's value will be approximately 1.5%. Consequently, for Portfolio I in scenario 2 we have:

change in portfolio's value due to 2-year key rate change	−0.1%
change in portfolio's value due to 30-year key rate change	+1.5%
change in portfolio value	+1.4%

In the same way, the total return for both portfolios can be estimated for the three scenarios. The estimated total returns are shown below:

Portfolio	Scenario 1	Scenario 2	Scenario 3
I	1.6%	1.4%	−1.4%
II	1.6%	0%	0%

Thus, only for the parallel yield curve shift (scenario 1) do the two portfolios have identical performance based on their durations.

Key rate durations are different for ladder, barbell, and bullet portfolios. A **ladder portfolio** is one with approximately equal dollar amounts (market values) in each maturity sector. A **barbell portfolio** has considerably greater weights given to the shorter and longer maturity bonds than to the intermediate maturity bonds. A **bullet portfolio** has greater weights concentrated in the intermediate maturity relative to the shorter and longer maturities.

The key rate duration profiles for a ladder, a barbell, and a bullet portfolio are graphed in Exhibit 59-7.[23] All these portfolios have the same effective duration. As can be seen, the ladder portfolio has roughly the same key rate duration for all the key maturities from year 2 on. For the barbell portfolio, the key rate durations are much greater for the 5-year and 20-year key maturities and much smaller for the other key maturities. For the bullet portfolio, the key rate duration is substantially greater for the 10-year maturity than the duration for other key maturities.

---

[23] The portfolios whose key rate durations are shown in Exhibit 59-7 were hypothetical Treasury portfolios constructed on April 23, 1997.

EXHIBIT 59-7	Key Rate Duration Profile for Three Treasury Portfolios (April 23, 1997): Ladder, Barbell, and Bullet

(a) Ladder Portfolio

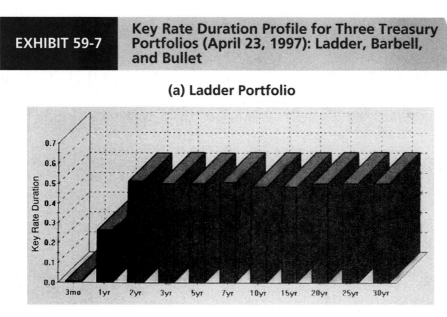

(b) Barbell Portfolio

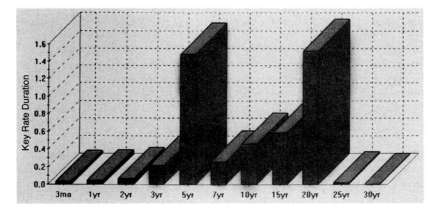

(c) Bullet Portfolio

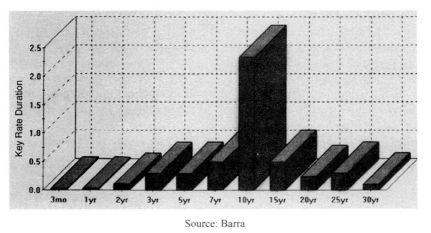

Source: Barra

8   YIELD VOLATILITY AND MEASUREMENT

In assessing the interest rate exposure of a security or portfolio one should combine effective duration with yield volatility because effective duration alone is not sufficient to meaure interest rate risk. The reason is that effective duration says that if interest rates change, a security's or portfolio's market value will change by approximately the percentage projected by its effective duration. However, the risk exposure of a portfolio to rate changes depends on how likely and how much interest rates may change, a parameter measured by yield volatility. For example, consider a U.S. Treasury security with an effective duration of 6 and a government bond of an emerging market country with an effective duration of 4. Based on effective duration alone, it would seem that the U.S. Treasury security has greater interest rate risk than the emerging market government bond. Suppose that yield volatility is substantial in the emerging market country relative to in the United States. Then the effective durations alone are not sufficient to identify the interest rate risk.

There is another reason why it is important to be able to measure yield or interest rate volatility: it is a critical input into a valuation model. An assumption of yield volatility is needed to value bonds with embedded options and structured products. The same measure is also needed in valuing some interest rate derivatives (i.e., options, caps, and floors).

In this section, we look at how to measure yield volatility and discuss some techniques used to estimate it. Volatility is measured in terms of the standard deviation or variance. We will see how yield volatility as measured by the daily percentage change in yields is calculated from historical yields. We will see that there are several issued confronting an investor in measuring historical yield volatility. Then we turn to modeling and forecasting yield volatility.

A. Measuring Historical Yield Volatility

Market participants seek a measure of yield volatility. The measure used is the standard deviation or variance. Here we will see how to compute yield volatility using historical data.

The sample variance of a random variable using historical data is calculated using the following formula:

$$\text{variance} = \frac{\sum_{t=1}^{T}(X_t - \overline{X})^2}{T - 1} \qquad \text{(59-1)}$$

and then

$$\text{standard deviation} = \sqrt{\text{variance}}$$

where

X_t = observation t of variable X
$\overline{X}$ = the sample mean for variable X
T = the number of observations in the sample

Our focus is on yield volatility. More specifically, we are interested in the change in the daily yield relative to the previous day's yield. So, for example, suppose the yield on a zero-coupon Treasury bond was 6.555% on Day 1 and 6.593% on Day 2. The relative change in yield would be:

$$\frac{6.593\% - 6.555\%}{6.555\%} = 0.005797$$

This means if the yield is 6.555% on Day 1 and grows by 0.005797 in one day, the yield on Day 2 will be:

$$6.555\% \ (1.005797) = 6.593\%$$

If instead of assuming simple compounding it is assumed that there is **continuous compounding**, the relative change in yield can be computed as the natural logarithm of the ratio of the yield for two days. That is, the relative yield change can be computed as follows:

$$\text{Ln} \ (6.593\%/6.555\%) = 0.0057804$$

where "Ln" stands for the natural logarithm. There is not much difference between the relative change of daily yields computed assuming simple compounding and continuous compounding.[24] In practice, continuous compounding is used. Multiplying the natural logarithm of the ratio of the two yields by 100 scales the value to a percentage change in daily yields.

Therefore, letting y_t be the yield on day t and y_{t-1} be the yield on day $t-1$, the percentage change in yield, X_t, is found as follows:

$$X_t = 100[\text{Ln}(y_t/y_{t-1})]$$

In our example, y_t is 6.593% and y_{t-1} is 6.555%. Therefore,

$$X_t = 100[\text{Ln}(6.593/6.555)] = 0.57804\%$$

To illustrate how to calculate a daily standard deviation from historical data, consider the data in Exhibit 59-8 which show the yield on a Treasury zero for 26 consecutive days. From the 26 observations, 25 days of percentage yield changes are calculated in Column (3). Column (4) shows the square of the deviations of the observations from the mean. The bottom of Exhibit 59-8 shows the calculation of the daily mean for 25 yield changes, the variance, and the standard deviation. The daily standard deviation is 0.6360%.

The daily standard deviation will vary depending on the 25 days selected. It is important to understand that the daily standard deviation is dependent on the period selected, a point we return to later in this reading.

1. Determining the Number of Observations

In our illustration, we used 25 observations for the daily percentage change in yield. The appropriate number of observations depends on the situation at hand. For example, traders concerned with overnight positions might use the 10 most recent trading days (i.e., two weeks). A bond portfolio manager who is concerned with longer term volatility might use 25 trading days (about one month). The selection of the number of observations can have a significant effect on the calculated daily standard deviation.

---

[24] See DeFusco, McLeavey, Pinto, and Runkle, *Quantitative Methods for Investment Analysis.*

EXHIBIT 59-8		Calculation of Daily Standard Deviation Based on 26 Daily Observations for a Treasury Zero	
(1) t	**(2)** y_t	**(3)** $X_t = 100 [Ln(y_t/y_{t-1})]$	**(4)** $(X_t - \overline{X})^2$
0	6.6945		
1	6.699	0.06720	0.02599
2	6.710	0.16407	0.06660
3	6.675	−0.52297	0.18401
4	6.555	−1.81411	2.95875
5	6.583	0.42625	0.27066
6	6.569	−0.21290	0.01413
7	6.583	0.21290	0.09419
8	6.555	−0.42625	0.11038
9	6.593	0.57804	0.45164
10	6.620	0.40869	0.25270
11	6.568	−0.78860	0.48246
12	6.575	0.10652	0.04021
13	6.646	1.07406	1.36438
14	6.607	−0.58855	0.24457
15	6.612	0.07565	0.02878
16	6.575	−0.56116	0.21823
17	6.552	−0.35042	0.06575
18	6.515	−0.56631	0.22307
19	6.533	0.27590	0.13684
20	6.543	0.15295	0.06099
21	6.559	0.24424	0.11441
22	6.500	−0.90360	0.65543
23	6.546	0.70520	0.63873
24	6.589	0.65474	0.56063
25	6.539	−0.76173	0.44586
	Total	−2.35020	9.7094094

$$\text{sample mean} = \overline{X} = \frac{-2.35020\%}{25} = -0.09401\%$$

$$\text{variance} = \frac{9.7094094\%}{25 - 1} = 0.4045587\%$$

$$\text{std dev} = \sqrt{0.4045587\%} = 0.6360493\%$$

2. Annualizing the Standard Deviation

The daily standard deviation can be annualized by multiplying it by the square root of the number of days in a year.[25] That is,

$$\text{daily standard deviation} \times \sqrt{\text{number of days in a year}}$$

Market practice varies with respect to the number of days in the year that should be used in the annualizing formula above. Some investors and traders use the number of days in the year, 365 days, to annualize the daily standard deviation. Some investors and traders use only either 250 days or 260 days to annualize. The latter is simply the number of trading days in a year based on five trading days per week for 52 weeks. The former reduces the number of trading days of 260 for 10 non-trading holidays.

Thus, in calculating an annual standard deviation, the investor must decide on:

1. the number of daily observations to use.
2. the number of days in the year to use to annualize the daily standard deviation.

The annual standard deviation for the daily standard deviation based on the 25-daily yield changes shown in Exhibit 59-8 (0.6360493%) using 250 days, 260 days, and 365 days to annualize are as follows:

250 days	260 days	365 days
10.06%	10.26%	12.15%

Now keep in mind that all of these decisions regarding the number of days to use in the daily standard deviation calculation, which set of days to use, and the number of days to use to annualize are not merely an academic exercise. Eventually, the standard deviation will be used in either the valuation of a security or in the measurement of risk exposure and can have a significant impact on the resulting value.

3. Using the Standard Deviation with Yield Estimation

What does it mean if the annual standard deviation for the *change in* the Treasury zero yield is 12%? It means that if the prevailing yield is 8%, then the annual standard deviation of the yield change is 96 basis points. This is found by multiplying the annual standard deviation of the yield change of 12% by the prevailing yield of 8%.

Assuming that yield volatility is approximately normally distributed, we can use the normal distribution to construct a confidence interval for the future yield.[26] For example, we know that there is a 68.3% probability that an interval

---

[25] For any probability distribution, it is important to assess whether the value of a random variable in one period is affected by the value that the random variable took on in a prior period. Casting this in terms of yield changes, it is important to know whether the yield today is affected by the yield in a prior period. The term *serial correlation* is used to describe the correlation between the yield in different periods. Annualizing the daily yield by multiplying the daily standard deviation by the square root of the number of days in a year assumes that serial correlation is not significant.

[26] See Chapter 4 in DeFusco, McLeavey, Pinto, and Runkle, *Quantitative Methods for Investment Analysis*.

PRACTICE QUESTION 1

a. The daily yields for 26 days are given below. Compute the daily percentage change in yield for each day assuming continuous compounding.

t	y_t
0	7.17400
1	7.19400
2	7.21800
3	7.15100
4	7.02500
5	7.02400
6	7.03000
7	7.02000
8	6.96400
9	6.90400
10	6.89671
11	6.85300
12	6.87100
13	6.88300
14	6.87500
15	6.87800
16	6.80400
17	6.84300
18	6.79500
19	6.79500
20	6.85400
21	6.81000
22	6.77300
23	6.86700
24	6.88700
25	6.88100

b. Compute the daily standard deviation.

PRACTICE QUESTION 2

Based on the daily standard deviation computed in Practice Question 1, compute the annualized standard deviation based on the following number of days (a) 250, (b) 260, and (c) 365.

between *one* standard deviation below and above the sample expected value will bracket the future yield. The sample expected value is the prevailing yield. If the annual standard deviation is 96 basis points and the prevailing yield is 8%, then there is a 68.3% probability that the range between 7.04% (8% minus 96 basis points) and 8.96% (8% plus 96 basis points) will include the future yield. For *three* standard deviations below and above the prevailing yield, there is a 99.7% probability. Using the numbers above, three standard deviations are 288 basis points (3 times 96 basis points). The interval is then 5.12% (8% minus 288 basis points) and 10.88% (8% plus 288 basis points).

The interval or range constructed is called a "confidence interval."[27] Our first interval of 7.04% to 8.96% is a 68.3% confidence interval. Our second interval of 5.12% to 10.88% is a 99.7% confidence interval. A confidence interval with any probability can be constructed.

B. Historical versus Implied Volatility

Market participants estimate yield volatility in one of two ways. The first way is by estimating historical yield volatility. This is the method that we have thus far described in this reading. The resulting volatility is called **historical volatility**. The second way is to estimate yield volatility based on the observed prices of interest rate options and caps. Yield volatility calculated using this approach is called **implied volatility**.

The implied volatility is based on some option pricing model. One of the inputs to any option pricing model in which the underlying is a Treasury security or Treasury futures contract is expected yield volatility. If the observed price of an option is assumed to be the fair price and the option pricing model is assumed to be the model that would generate that fair price, then the implied yield volatility is the yield volatility that, when used as an input into the option pricing model, would produce the observed option price.

There are several problems with using implied volatility. First, it is assumed the option pricing model is correct. Second, option pricing models typically assume that volatility is constant over the life of the option. Therefore, interpreting an implied volatility becomes difficult.[28]

C. Forecasting Yield Volatility

As has been seen, the yield volatility as measured by the standard deviation can vary based on the time period selected and the number of observations. Now we turn to the issue of forecasting yield volatility. There are several methods. Before describing these methods, let's address the question of what mean value should be used in the calculation of the forecasted standard deviation.

Suppose at the end of Day 12 a trader was interested in a forecast for volatility using the 10 most recent days of trading and updating that forecast at the end of each trading day. What mean value should be used?

The trader can calculate a 10-day moving average of the daily percentage yield change. Exhibit 59-8 shows the daily percentage change in yield for the

---

[27] See Chapter 6 in DeFusco, MacLeavey, Pinto, and Runkle, *Quantitative Methods for Investment Analysis.*

[28] For a further discussion, see Frank J. Fabozzi and Wai Lee, "Measuring and Forecasting Yield Volatility," Chapter 16 in Frank J. Fabozzi (ed.), *Perspectives on Interest Rate Risk Management for Money Managers and Traders* (New Hope, PA: Frank J. Fabozzi Associates, 1998).

EXHIBIT 59-9	10-Day Moving Average of Daily Yield Change for Treasury Zero

10-Trading Days Ending	Daily Average (%)
Day 12	−0.20324
Day 13	−0.04354
Day 14	0.07902
Day 15	0.04396
Day 16	0.00913
Day 17	−0.04720
Day 18	−0.06121
Day 19	−0.09142
Day 20	−0.11700
Day 21	−0.01371
Day 22	−0.11472
Day 23	−0.15161
Day 24	−0.02728
Day 25	−0.11102

Treasury zero from Day 1 to Day 25. To calculate a **moving average** of the daily percentage yield change at the end of Day 12, the trader would use the 10 trading days from Day 3 to Day 12. At the end of Day 13, the trader will calculate the 10-day average by using the percentage yield change on Day 13 and would exclude the percentage yield change on Day 3. The trader will use the 10 trading days from Day 4 to Day 13.

Exhibit 59-9 shows the 10-day moving average calculated from Day 12 to Day 25. Notice the considerable variation over this period. The 10-day moving average ranged from −0.20324% to 0.07902%.

Thus far, it is assumed that the moving average is the appropriate value to use for the expected value of the change in yield. However, there are theoretical arguments that suggest it is more appropriate to assume that the expected value of the change in yield will be zero.[29] In the equation for the variance given by equation (1), instead of using for $\overline{X}$ the moving average, the value of zero is used. If zero is substituted into equation (1), the equation for the variance becomes:

$$\text{variance} = \frac{\sum_{t=1}^{T} X_t^2}{T - 1} \tag{59-2}$$

There are various methods for forecasting daily volatility. The daily standard deviation given by equation (2) assigns an equal weight to all observations. So, if a trader is calculating volatility based on the most recent 10 days of trading, each day is given a weight of 0.10.

[29] Jacques Longerstacey and Peter Zangari, *Five Questions about RiskMetrics™,* JP Morgan Research Publication 1995.

EXHIBIT 59-10	Moving Averages of Daily Standard Deviations Based on 10 Days of Observations

10-Trading Days Ending	Moving Average Daily Standard Deviation (%)
Day 12	0.75667
Day 13	0.81874
Day 14	0.58579
Day 15	0.56886
Day 16	0.59461
Day 17	0.60180
Day 18	0.61450
Day 19	0.59072
Day 20	0.57705
Day 21	0.52011
Day 22	0.59998
Day 23	0.53577
Day 24	0.54424
Day 25	0.60003

For example, suppose that a trader is interested in the daily volatility of our hypothetical Treasury zero yield and decides to use the 10 most recent trading days. Exhibit 59-10 reports the 10-day volatility for various days using the data in Exhibit 59-8 and the standard deviation derived from the formula for the variance given by equation (59-2).

There is reason to suspect that market participants give greater weight to recent movements in yield or price when determining volatility. To give greater importance to more recent information, observations farther in the past should be given less weight. This can be done by revising the variance as given by equation (59-2) as follows:

$$\text{variance} = \frac{\sum_{t=1}^{T} W_t X_t^2}{T - 1}$$

(59-3)

where W_t is the weight assigned to observation t such that the sum of the weights is equal to T (i.e., $\sum W_t = T$) and the farther the observation is from today, the lower the weight. The weights should be assigned so that the forecasted volatility reacts faster to a recent major market movement and declines gradually as we move away from any major market movement.

Finally, a time series characteristic of financial assets suggests that a period of high volatility is followed by a period of high volatility. Furthermore, a period of relative stability in returns appears to be followed by a period that can be characterized in the same way. This suggests that volatility today may depend upon recent prior volatility. This can be modeled and used to forecast volatility. The statistical model used to estimate this time series property of volatility is called an autoregressive conditional heteroskedasticity (ARCH) model.[30] The term "conditional" means that the value of the variance depends on or is conditional on the value of the random variable. The term heteroskedasticity means that the variance is not equal for all values of the random variable. The foundation for ARCH models is a specialist topic.[31]

---

[30] See Robert F. Engle, "Autoregressive Conditional Heteroskedasticity with Estimates of Variance of U.K. Inflation," *Econometrica* 50 (1982), pp. 987-1008.

[31] See Chapter 9 in DeFusco, McLeavey, Pinto, and Runkle, *Quantitative Methods for Investment Analysis.*

SUMMARY

▶ Historically, four shapes have been observed for the yield curve: (1) normal or positively sloped (i.e., the longer the maturity, the higher the yield), (2) flat (i.e., the yield for all maturities is approximately equal), (3) inverted or negatively sloped (i.e., the longer the maturity, the lower the yield), and (4) a humped yield curve.

▶ The spread between long-term Treasury yields and short-term Treasury yields is referred to as the steepness or slope of the yield curve.

▶ Some investors define the slope of the yield curve as the spread between the 30-year yield and the 3-month yield and others as the spread between the 30-year yield and the 2-year yield.

▶ A shift in the yield curve refers to the relative change in the yield for each Treasury maturity.

▶ A parallel shift in the yield curve refers to a shift in which the change in the yield for all maturities is the same; a nonparallel shift in the yield curve means that the yield for all maturities does not change by the same number of basis points.

▶ Historically, the two types of nonparallel yield curve shifts that have been observed are a twist in the slope of the yield curve and a change in the curvature of the yield curve.

▶ A flattening of the yield curve means that the slope of the yield curve has decreased; a steepening of the yield curve means that the slope has increased.

▶ A butterfly shift is the other type of nonparallel shift—a change in the curvature or humpedness of the yield curve.

▶ Historically, the factors that have been observed to drive Treasury returns are a (1) shift in the level of interest rates, (2) a change in the slope of the yield curve, and (3) a change in the curvature of the yield curve.

▶ The most important factor driving Treasury returns is a shift in the level of interest rates. Two other factors, in decreasing importance, include changes in the yield curve slope and changes in the curvature of the yield curve.

▶ The universe of Treasury issues that can be used to construct the theoretical spot rate curve is (1) on-the-run Treasury issues, (2) on-the-run Treasury issues and selected off-the-run Treasury issues, (3) all Treasury coupon securities and bills, and (4) Treasury strips.

▶ There are three methodologies that have been used to derive the theoretical spot rate curve: (1) bootstrapping when the universe is on-the-run Treasury issues (with and without selected off-the-run issues), (2) econometric modeling for all Treasury coupon securities and bills, and (3) simply the observed yields on Treasury coupon strips.

▶ The problem with using Treasury coupon strips is that the observed yields may be biased due to a liquidity premium or an unfavorable tax treatment.

▶ The swap rate is the rate at which fixed cash flows can be exchanged for floating cash flows.

▶ In a LIBOR-based swap, the swap curve provides a yield curve for LIBOR.

▶ A swap curve can be constructed that is unique to a country where there is a swap market.

▶ The swap spread is primarily a gauge of the credit risk associated with a country's banking sector.

▶ The advantages of using a swap curve as the benchmark interest rate rather than a government bond yield curve are (1) there is almost no government regulation of the swap market making swap rates across different markets more comparable, (2) the supply of swaps depends only on the number of counterparties that are seeking or are willing to enter into a swap transaction at any given time, (3) comparisons across countries of government yield curves is difficult because of the differences in sovereign credit risk, and (4) there are more maturity points available to construct a swap curve than a government bond yield curve.

▶ From the swap yield curve a LIBOR spot rate curve can be derived using the bootstrapping methodology and the LIBOR forward rate curve can be derived.

▶ The three forms of the expectations theory (the pure expectations theory, the liquidity preference theory, and the preferred habitat theory) assume that the forward rates in current long-term bonds are closely related to the market's expectations about future short-term rates.

▶ The three forms of the expectations theory differ on whether or not other factors also affect forward rates, and how.

▶ The pure expectations theory postulates that no systematic factors other than expected future short-term rates affect forward rates.

▶ Because forward rates are not perfect predictors of future interest rates, the pure expectations theory neglects the risks (interest rate risk and reinvestment risk) associated with investing in Treasury securities.

▶ The broadest interpretation of the pure expectations theory suggests that investors expect the return for any investment horizon to be the same, regardless of the maturity strategy selected.

▶ The local expectations form of the pure expectations theory suggests that the return will be the same over a short-term investment horizon starting today and it is this narrow interpretation that economists have demonstrated is the only interpretation that can be sustained in equilibrium.

▶ Two interpretations of forward rates based on arbitrage arguments are that they are (1) "break-even rates" and (2) rates that can be locked in.

▶ Advocates of the pure expectations theory argue that forward rates are the market's consensus of future interest rates.

▶ Forward rates have not been found to be good predictors of future interest rates; however, an understanding of forward rates is still extremely important because of their role as break-even rates and rates that can be locked in.

▶ The liquidity preference theory and the preferred habitat theory assert that there are other factors that affect forward rates and these two theories are therefore referred to as biased expectations theories.

▶ The liquidity preference theory states that investors will hold longer-term maturities only if they are offered a risk premium and therefore forward rates should reflect both interest rate expectations and a liquidity risk premium.

▶ The preferred habitat theory, in addition to adopting the view that forward rates reflect the expectation of the future path of interest rates as well as a risk premium, argues that the yield premium need not reflect a liquidity risk but instead reflects the demand and supply of funds in a given maturity range.

▶ A common approach to measure yield curve risk is to change the yield for a particular maturity of the yield curve and determine the sensitivity of a security or portfolio to this change holding all other key rates constant.

- Key rate duration is the sensitivity of a portfolio's value to the change in a particular key rate.
- The most popular version of key rate duration uses 11 key maturities of the spot rate curve (3 months, 1, 2, 3, 5, 7, 10, 15, 20, 25, and 30 years).
- Variance is a measure of the dispersion of a random variable around its expected value.
- The standard deviation is the square root of the variance and is a commonly used measure of volatility.
- Yield volatility can be estimated from daily yield observations.
- The observation used in the calculation of the daily standard deviation is the natural logarithm of the ratio of one day's and the previous day's yield.
- The selection of the time period (the number of observations) can have a significant effect on the calculated daily standard deviation.
- A daily standard deviation is annualized by multiplying it by the square root of the number of days in a year.
- Typically, either 250 days, 260 days, or 365 days are used to annualize the daily standard deviation.
- Implied volatility can also be used to estimate yield volatility based on some option pricing model.
- In forecasting volatility, it is more appropriate to use an expectation of zero for the mean value.
- The simplest method for forecasting volatility is weighting all observations equally.
- A forecasted volatility can be obtained by assigning greater weight to more recent observations.
- Autoregressive conditional heteroskedasticity (ARCH) models can be used to capture the time series characteristic of yield volatility in which a period of high volatility is followed by a period of high volatility and a period of relative stability appears to be followed by a period that can be characterized in the same way.

PROBLEMS FOR READING 59

1. What are the four types of shapes observed for the yield curve?

2. How is the slope of the yield curve defined and measured?

3. Historically, how has the slope of the long end of the yield curve differed from that of the short end of the yield curve at a given point in time?

4. **A.** What are the three factors that have empirically been observed to affect Treasury returns?

   B. What has been observed to be the most important factor in affecting Treasury returns?

   C. Given the most important factor identified in part B, justify the use of duration as a measure of interest rate risk.

   D. What has been observed to be the second most important factor in affecting Treasury returns?

   E. Given the second most important factor identified in part D, justify the use of a measure of interest rate risk in addition to duration.

5. **A.** What are the limitations of using just the on-the-run Treasury issues to construct the theoretical spot rate curve?

   B. Why if all Treasury bills and Treasury coupon securities are used to construct the theoretical spot rate curve is it not possible to use the bootstrapping method?

6. **A.** What are the problems with using the yield on Treasury strips to construct the theoretical spot rate curve?

   B. Why, even if a practitioner decides to use the yield on Treasury strips to construct the theoretical spot rate curve despite the problems identified in part A, will the practitioner restrict the analysis to Treasury coupon strips?

7. What are the advantages of using the swap curve as a benchmark of interest rates relative to a government bond yield curve?

8. How can a spot rate curve be constructed for a country that has a liquid swap market?

9. **A.** What is a swap spread?

   B. What is the swap spread indicative of?

10. **A.** What is the pure expectations theory?

    B. What are the shortcomings of the pure expectations theory?

11. Based on the broadest interpretation of the pure expectations theory, what would be the difference in the 4-year total return if an investor purchased a 7-year zero-coupon bond or a 15-year zero-coupon bond?

12. Based on the local expectations form of the pure expectations theory, what would be the difference in the 6-month total return if an investor purchased a 5-year zero-coupon bond or a 2-year zero-coupon bond?

13. Comment on the following statement made by a portfolio manager to a client:

    > Proponents of the unbiased expectations theory argue that the forward rates built into the term structure of interest rates are the market's consensus of future interest rates. We disagree with the theory because studies suggest that forward rates are poor predictors of future interest rates. Therefore, the position that our investment management firm

takes is that forward rates are irrelevant and provide no information to our managers in managing a bond portfolio.

14. Based on arbitrage arguments, give two interpretations for each of the following three forward rates:

    A. The 1-year forward rate seven years from now is 6.4%.

    B. The 2-year forward rate one year from now is 6.2%.

    C. The 8-year forward rate three years from now is 7.1%.

15. There are two forms of the "biased" expectations theory. Why are these two forms referred to as "biased" expectations?

16. You are the financial consultant to a pension fund. After your presentation to the trustees of the fund, you asked the trustees if they have any questions. You receive the two questions below. Answer each one.

    A. "The yield curve is upward-sloping today. Doesn't this suggest that the market consensus is that interest rates are expected to increase in the future and therefore you should reduce the interest rate risk exposure for the portfolio that you are managing for us?"

    B. "I am looking over one of the pages in your presentation that shows spot rates and I am having difficulty in understanding it. The spot rates at the short end (up to three years) are increasing with maturity. For maturities greater than three years but less than eight years, the spot rates are declining with maturity. Finally, for maturities greater than eight years the spot rates are virtually the same for each maturity. There is simply no expectations theory that would explain that type of shape for the term structure of interest rates. Is this market simply unstable?"

17. Below are the key rate durations for three portfolios of U.S. Treasury securities all with the same duration for a parallel shift in the yield curve.

    A. For each portfolio describe the type of portfolio (barbell, ladder, or bullet).

Key Rate Maturity	Portfolio A	Portfolio B	Portfolio C
3-month	0.04	0.04	0.03
1-year	0.06	0.29	0.07
2-year	0.08	0.67	0.31
3-year	0.28	0.65	0.41
5-year	0.38	0.65	1.90
7-year	0.65	0.64	0.35
10-year	3.38	0.66	0.41
15-year	0.79	0.67	0.70
20-year	0.36	0.64	1.95
25-year	0.12	0.62	0.06
30-year	0.06	0.67	0.01

    B. Which portfolio will benefit the most if the spot rate for the 10-year decreases by 50 basis points while the spot rate for all other key maturities change very little?

    C. What is the duration for a parallel shift in the yield curve for the three portfolios?

18. Compute the 10-day daily standard deviation of the percentage change in yield assuming continuous compounding assuming the following daily yields.

t_t	y_t
0	5.854
1	5.843
2	5.774
3	5.719
4	5.726
5	5.761
6	5.797
7	5.720
8	5.755
9	5.787
10	5.759

19. For the daily yield volatility computed in the previous question, what is the annual yield volatility assuming the following number of days in the year:

A. 250 days?

B. 260 days?

C. 365 days?

20. Comment on the following statement: "Two portfolio managers with the same set of daily yields will compute the same historical annual volatility."

21. Suppose that the annualized standard deviation of the 2-year Treasury yield based on daily yields is 7% and the current level of the 2-year Treasury yield is 5%. Assuming that the probability distribution for the percentage change in 2-year Treasury yields is approximately normally distributed, how would you interpret the 7% annualized standard deviation?

22. A. What is implied volatility?

B. What are the problems associated with using implied volatility as a measure of yield volatility?

23. A. In forecasting yield volatility, why would a manager not want to weight each daily yield change equally?

B. In forecasting yield volatility, what is recommended for the sample mean in the formula for the variance or standard deviation?

VALUING BONDS WITH EMBEDDED OPTIONS

by Frank J. Fabozzi

LEARNING OUTCOMES

The candidate should be able to:

a. evaluate whether a security is undervalued or overvalued, given an appropriate benchmark, using relative value analysis;

b. evaluate the importance of the benchmark interest rates in interpreting spread measures;

c. illustrate the backward induction valuation methodology within the binomial interest rate tree framework;

d. compute the value of a callable bond from an interest rate tree, given the call schedule and the rule for calling a bond;

e. illustrate the relationship among the values of a callable (putable) bond, the corresponding option-free bond, and the embedded option;

f. explain the effect of volatility on the arbitrage-free value of an option;

g. interpret an option-adjusted spread with respect to a nominal spread and to benchmark interest rates;

h. illustrate how effective duration and effective convexity are calculated using the binomial model;

i. calculate the value of a putable bond, using an interest rate tree;

j. describe the basic features of a convertible bond and compute the value of the following for a convertible bond: conversion value, straight value, market conversion price (conversion parity), market conversion premium per share, market conversion premium ratio, premium payback period, and premium over straight value;

k. discuss the components of a convertible bond's value that must be included in an option-based valuation approach;

l. compare and contrast the risk-return characteristics of a convertible bond to the risk-return characteristics of ownership of the underlying common stock.

Fixed Income Analysis for the Chartered Financial Analyst® Program, Second Edition, edited by Frank J. Fabozzi, Copyright © 2005 by CFA Institute. Reprinted with permission.

1   INTRODUCTION

The presence of an embedded option in a bond structure makes the valuation of such bonds complicated. In this reading, we present a model to value bonds that have one or more embedded options and where the value of the embedded options depends on future interest rates. Examples of such embedded options are call and put provisions and caps (i.e., maximum interest rate) in floating-rate securities. While there are several models that have been proposed to value bonds with embedded options, our focus will be on models that provide an "arbitrage-free value" for a security. At the end of this reading, we will discuss the valuation of convertible bonds. The complexity here is that these bonds are typically callable and may be putable. Thus, the valuation of convertible bonds must take into account not only embedded options that depend on future interest rates (i.e., the call and the put options) but also the future price movement of the common stock (i.e., the call option on the common stock).

In order to understand how to value a bond with an embedded option, there are several fundamental concepts that must be reviewed. We will do this in Sections 2, 3, 4, and 5. In Section 2, the key elements involved in developing a bond valuation model are explained. In Section 3, an overview of the bond valuation process is provided. Since the valuation of bonds requires benchmark interest rates, the various benchmarks are described in Section 4. In this section we also explain how to interpret spread measures relative to a particular benchmark. In Section 5, the valuation of an option-free bond is reviewed using a numerical illustration. We first introduced the concepts described in this section at Level I. The bond used in the illustration in this section to show how to value an option-free bond is then used in the remainder of the reading to show how to value that bond if there is one or more embedded options.

2   ELEMENTS OF A BOND VALUATION MODEL

The valuation process begins with determining benchmark interest rates. As will be explained later in this section, there are three potential markets where benchmark interest rates can be obtained:

- the Treasury market
- a sector of the bond market
- the market for the issuer's securities

An arbitrage-free value for an option-free bond is obtained by first generating the spot rates (or forward rates). When used to discount cash flows, the spot rates are the rates that would produce a model value equal to the observed market price for each on-the-run security in the benchmark. For example, if the Treasury market is the benchmark, an arbitrage-free model would produce a value for each on-the-run Treasury issue that is equal to its observed market price. In the Treasury market, the on-the-run issues are the most recently auctioned issues. (Note that all such securities issued by the U.S. Department of the Treasury are option free.) If the market used to establish the benchmark is a sector of the bond market or the market for the issuer's securities, the on-the-run issues are estimates of what the market price would be if newly issued *option-free* securities with different maturities are sold.

In deriving the interest rates that should be used to value a bond with an embedded option, the same principle must be maintained. No matter how complex the valuation model, when each on-the-run issue for a benchmark security is valued using the model, the value produced should be equal to the on-the-run issue's market price. The on-the-run issues for a given benchmark are assumed to be fairly priced.[1]

The first complication in building a model to value bonds with embedded options is that the future cash flows will depend on what happens to interest rates in the future. This means that future interest rates must be considered. This is incorporated into a valuation model by considering how interest rates can change based on some assumed interest rate volatility. In the previous reading, we explained what interest rate volatility is and how it is estimated. Given the assumed interest rate volatility, an interest rate "tree" representing possible future interest rates consistent with the volatility assumption can be constructed. It is from the interest rate tree that two important elements in the valuation process are obtained. First, the interest rates on the tree are used to generate the cash flows taking into account the embedded option. Second, the interest rates on the tree are used to compute the present value of the cash flows.

For a given interest rate volatility, there are several interest rate models that have been used in practice to construct an interest rate tree. An **interest rate model** is a probabilistic description of how interest rates can change over the life of the bond. An interest rate model does this by making an assumption about the relationship between the level of short-term interest rates and the interest rate volatility as measured by the standard deviation. A discussion of the various interest rate models that have been suggested in the finance literature and that are used by practitioners in developing valuation models is beyond the scope of this reading.[2] What is important to understand is that the interest rate models commonly used are based on how short-term interest rates can evolve (i.e., change) over time. Consequently, these interest rate models are referred to as **one-factor models**, where "factor" means only one interest rate is being modeled over time. More complex models would consider how more than one interest rate changes over time. For example, an interest rate model can specify how the short-term interest rate and the long-term interest rate can change over time. Such a model is called a **two-factor model**.

Given an interest rate model and an interest rate volatility assumption, it can be assumed that interest rates can realize one of two possible rates in the next period. A valuation model that makes this assumption in creating an interest rate tree is called a **binomial model**. There are valuation models that assume that interest rates can take on three possible rates in the next period and these models are called **trinomial models**. There are even more complex models that assume in creating an interest rate tree that more than three possible rates in the next period can be realized. These models that assume discrete change in interest

---

[1]Market participants also refer to this characteristics of a model as one that "calibrates to the market."

[2]An excellent source for further explanation of many of these models is Gerald W. Buetow Jr. and James Sochacki, *Term Structure Models Using Binomial Trees: Demystifying the Process* (Charlottesville, VA: Association of Investment Management and Research, 2000).

rates are referred to as "discrete-time option pricing models." It makes sense that option valuation technology is employed to value a bond with an embedded option because the valuation requires an estimate of what the value of the embedded option is worth. However, a discussion of the underlying theory of discrete-time pricing models in general and the binomial model in particular are beyond the scope of this reading.[3]

As we will see later in this reading, when a discrete-time option pricing model is portrayed in graph form, it shows the different paths that interest rates can take. The graphical presentation looks like a lattice.[4] Hence, discrete-time option pricing models are sometimes referred to as "lattice models." Since the pattern of the interest rate paths also look like the branches of a tree, the graphical presentation is referred to as an **interest rate tree**.

Regardless of the assumption about how many possible rates can be realized in the next period, the interest rate tree generated must produce a value for the securities in the benchmark that is equal to their observed market price—that is, it must produce an arbitrage-free value. Consequently, if the Treasury market is used for the benchmark interest rates, the interest rate tree generated must produce a value for each on-the-run Treasury issue that is equal to its observed market price. Moreover, the intuition and the methodology for using the interest rate tree (i.e., the backward induction methodology described later) are the same. Once an interest rate tree is generated that (1) is consistent with both the interest rate volatility assumption and the interest rate model and (2) generates the observed market price for the securities in the benchmark, the next step is to use the interest rate tree to value a bond with an embedded option. The complexity here is that a set of rules must be introduced to determine, for any period, when the embedded option will be exercised. For a callable bond, these rules are called the "call rules." The rules vary from model builder to model builder.

While the building of a model to value bonds with embedded options is more complex than building a model to value option-free bonds, the basic principles are the same. In the case of valuing an option-free bond, the model that is built is simply a set of spot rates that are used to value cash flows. The spot rates will produce an arbitrage-free value. For a model to value a bond with embedded options, the interest rate tree is used to value future cash flows and the interest rate tree is combined with the call rules to generate the future cash flows. Again, the interest rate tree will produce an arbitrage-free value.

Let's move from theory to practice. Only a few practitioners will develop their own model to value bonds with embedded options. Instead, it is typical for a portfolio manager or analyst to use a model developed by either a dealer firm or a vendor of analytical systems. A fair question is then: Why bother covering a valuation model that is readily available from a third-party? The answer is that a valuation model should not be a black box to portfolio managers and analysts. *The models in practice share all of the principles described in this reading, but differ with respect to certain assumptions that can produce quite different values.* The reasons for these differences in valuation must be understood. Moreover, third-party models give the user a choice of changing the assumptions. A user who has not "walked through" a valuation model has no appreciation of the significance of these assumptions and therefore how to assess the impact of these assumptions on the value produced by the model. In Level I, we discussed "modeling risk." This is the risk that the underlying assumptions of a model may be incorrect. Understanding a valuation model permits the user to effectively determine the significance of an assumption.

---

[3]For a discussion of the binomial model and the underlying theory, see Chapter 4 in Don M. Chance, *Analysis of Derivatives for the CFA Program* (Charlottesville, VA: Association for Investment Management and Research, 2003).

[4]A lattice is an arrangement of points in a regular periodic pattern.

As an example of the importance of understanding the assumptions of a model, consider interest rate volatility. Suppose that the market price of a bond is $89. Suppose further that a valuation model produces a value for a bond with an embedded option of $90 based on a 12% interest rate volatility assumption. Then, according to the valuation model, this bond is cheap by one point. However, suppose that the same model produces a value of $87 if a 15% volatility is assumed. This tells the portfolio manager or analyst that the bond is two points rich. Which is correct? The answer clearly depends on what the investor believes interest rate volatility will be in the future.

In this reading, we will use the binomial model to demonstrate all of the issues and assumptions associated with valuing a bond with embedded options. This model is available on Bloomberg, as well as from other commercial vendors and several dealer firms.[5] We show how to create an interest rate tree (more specifically, a binomial interest rate tree) given a volatility assumption and how the interest rate tree can be used to value an option-free bond. Given the interest rate tree, we then show how to value several types of bonds with an embedded option—a callable bond, a putable bond, a step-up note, and a floating-rate note with a cap.

Once again, it must be emphasized that while the binomial model is used in this reading to demonstrate how to value bonds with embedded options, other models that allow for more than one interest rate in the next period all follow the same principles—they begin with on-the-run yields, they produce an interest rate tree that generates an arbitrage-free value, and they depend on assumptions regarding the volatility of interest rates and rules for when an embedded option will be exercised.

OVERVIEW OF THE BOND VALUATION PROCESS

3

In this section we review the bond valuation process and the key concepts that were introduced at Level I. This will help us tie together the concepts that have already been covered and how they relate to the valuation of bonds with embedded options.

Regardless if a bond has an embedded option, at Level I we explained that the following can be done:

1. Given a required yield to maturity, we can compute the value of a bond. For example, if the required yield to maturity of a 9-year, 8% coupon bond that pays interest semiannually is 7%, its price is 106.59.

2. Given the observed market price of a bond we can calculate its yield to maturity. For example, if the price of a 5-year, 6% coupon bond that pays interest semiannually is 93.84, its yield to maturity is 7.5%.

3. Given the yield to maturity, a yield spread can be computed. For example, if the yield to maturity for a 5-year, 6% coupon bond that pays interest semiannually is 7.5% and its yield is compared to a benchmark yield of 6.5%, then the yield spread is 100 basis points (7.5% minus 6.5%). We referred to the yield spread at Level I as the *nominal spread.*

---

[5]The model described in this reading was first presented in Andrew J. Kalotay, George O. Williams, and Frank J. Fabozzi, "A Model for the Valuation of Bonds and Embedded Options," *Financial Analysts Journal* (May–June 1993), pp. 35–46.

The problem with using a single interest rate when computing the value of a bond (as in (1) on the preceding page) or in computing a yield to maturity (as in (2) on the preceding page) is that it fails to recognize that each cash flow is unique and warrants its own discount rate. Failure to discount each cash flow at an appropriate interest unique to when that cash flow is expected to be received results in an arbitrage opportunity.

It is at this point in the valuation process that the notion of theoretical spot rates are introduced to overcome the problem associated with using a single interest rate. The spot rates are the appropriate rates to use to discount cash flows. There is a theoretical spot rate that can be obtained for each maturity. The procedure for computing the spot rate curve (i.e., the spot rate for each maturity) was explained at Level I and discussed further in the previous reading.

Using the spot rate curve, one obtains the bond price. However, how is the spot rate curve used to compute the yield to maturity? Actually, there is no equivalent concept to a yield to maturity in this case. Rather, there is a yield spread measure that is used to overcome the problem of a single interest rate. This measure is the zero-volatility spread that was explained at Level I. The zero-volatility spread, also called the Z-spread and the static spread, is the spread that when added to all of the spot rates will make the present value of the bond's cash flow equal to the bond's market price.

At this point, we have not introduced any notion of how to handle bonds with embedded options. We have simply dealt with the problem of using a single interest rate for discounting cash flows. But there is still a critical issue that must be resolved. When a bond has an embedded option, a portion of the yield, and therefore a portion of the spread, is attributable to the embedded option. When valuing a bond with an embedded option, it is necessary to adjust the spread for the value of the embedded option. The measure that does this is called the option-adjusted spread (OAS). We mentioned this measure at Level I but did not provide any details. In this reading, we show of how this spread measure is computed for bonds with embedded options.

A. The Benchmark Interest Rates and Relative Value Analysis

Yield spread measures are used in assessing the **relative value** of securities. Relative value analysis involves identifying securities that can potentially enhance return relative to a benchmark. Relative value analysis can be used to identify securities as being overpriced ("rich"), underpriced ("cheap"), or fairly priced. A portfolio manager can use relative value analysis in ranking issues within a sector or sub-sector of the bond market or different issues of a specific issuer.

At Level I, two questions that need to be asked in order to understand spread measures were identified:

1. What is the benchmark for computing the spread? That is, what is the spread measured relative to?
2. What is the spread measuring?

As explained at Level I, the different spread measures begin with benchmark interest rates. The benchmark interest rates can be one of the following:

▶ the Treasury market
▶ a specific bond sector with a given credit rating
▶ a specific issuer

A specific bond sector with a given credit rating, for example, would include single-A rated corporate bonds or double-A rated banks. The LIBOR curve discussed in the previous reading is an example, since it is viewed by the market as an inter-bank or AA rated benchmark.

Morever, the benchmark interest rates can be based on either

▶ an estimated yield curve
▶ an estimated spot rate curve

A yield curve shows the relationship between yield and maturity for coupon bonds; a spot rate curve shows the relationship between spot rates and maturity.

Consequently, there are six potential benchmark interest rates as summarized below:

	Treasury market	Specific bond sector with a given credit rating	Specific issuer
Yield curve	Treasury yield curve	Sector yield curve	Issuer yield curve
Spot rate curve	Treasury spot rate curve	Sector spot rate curve	Issuer spot rate curve

We illustrated at Level I how the Treasury spot rate curve can be constructed from the Treasury yield curve. Rather than start with yields in the Treasury market as the benchmark interest rates, an estimated on-the-run yield curve for a bond sector with a given credit rating or a specific issuer can be obtained. To obtain a sector with a given credit rating or a specific issuer's on-the-run yield curve, an appropriate credit spread is added to each on-the-run Treasury issue. The credit spread need not be constant for all maturities. For example, as explained at Level I, the credit spread may increase with maturity. Given the on-the-run yield curve, the theoretical spot rates for the bond sector with a given credit rating or issuer can be constructed using the same methodology to construct the Treasury spot rates given the Treasury yield curve.

B. Interpretation of Spread Measures

Given the alternative benchmark interest rates, in this section we will see how to interpret the three spread measures that were described at Level I: nominal spread, zero-volatility spread, and option-adjusted spread.

1. Treasury Market Benchmark

In the United States, yields in the U.S. Treasury market are typically used as the benchmark interest rates. The benchmark can be either the Treasury yield curve or the Treasury spot rate curve. As explained at Level I, the nominal spread is a spread measured relative to the Treasury yield curve and the zero-volatility spread is a spread relative to the Treasury spot rate curve. As we will see in this reading, the OAS is a spread relative to the Treasury spot rate curve.

If the Treasury market rates are used, then the benchmark for the three spread measures and the risks for which the spread is compensating are summarized below:

Spread measure	Benchmark	Reflects compensation for...
Nominal	Treasury yield curve	Credit risk, option risk, liquidity risk
Zero-volatility	Treasury spot rate curve	Credit risk, option risk, liquidity risk
Option-adjusted	Treasury spot rate curve	Credit risk, liquidity risk

where "credit risk" is relative to the default-free rate since the Treasury market is viewed as a default-free market.

In the case of an OAS, if the computed OAS is greater than what the market requires for credit risk and liquidity risk, then the security is undervalued. If the computed OAS is less than what the market requires for credit risk and liquidity risk, then the security is overvalued. Only using the nominal spread or zero-volatility spread, masks the compensation for the embedded option.

For example, assume the following for a non-Treasury security, Bond W, a triple B rated corporate bond with an embedded call option:

Benchmark: Treasury market
Nominal spread based on Treasury yield curve: 170 basis points
Zero-volatility spread based on Treasury spot rate curve: 160 basis points
OAS based on Treasury spot rate curve: 125 basis points

Suppose that in the market *option-free* bonds with the same credit rating, maturity, and liquidity as Bond W trade at a nominal spread of 145 basis points. It would seem, based solely on the nominal spread, Bond W is undervalued (i.e., cheap) since its nominal spread is greater than the nominal spread for comparable bonds (170 versus 145 basis points). Even comparing Bond W's zero-volatility spread of 160 basis points to the market's 145 basis point nominal spread for option-free bonds (not a precise comparison since the Treasury benchmarks are different), the analysis would suggest that Bond W is cheap. However, after removing the value of the embedded option—which as we will see is precisely what the OAS measure does—the OAS tells us that the bond is trading at a spread that is less than the nominal spread of otherwise comparable option-free bonds. Again, while the benchmarks are different, the OAS tells us that Bond W is overvalued.

C. Specific Bond Sector with a Given Credit Rating Benchmark

Rather than use the Treasury market as the benchmark, the benchmark can be a specific bond sector *with a given credit rating*. The interpretation for the spread measures would then be:

Spread measure	Benchmark	Reflects compensation for ...
Nominal	Sector yield curve	Credit risk, option risk, liquidity risk
Zero-volatility	Sector spot rate curve	Credit risk, option risk, liquidity risk
Option-adjusted	Sector spot rate curve	Credit risk, liquidity risk

where "Sector" means the sector with a specific credit rating. "Credit risk" in this case means the *credit risk of a security under consideration relative to the credit risk of the sector used as the benchmark* and "liquidity risk" is the *liquidity risk of a security under consideration relative to the liquidity risk of the sector used as the benchmark.*

Let's again use Bond W, a triple B rated corporate bond with an embedded call option to illustrate. Assume the following spread measures were computed:

> Benchmark: double A rated corporate bond sector
> Nominal spread based on benchmark: 110 basis points
> Zero-volatility spread based benchmark spot rate curve: 100 basis points
> OAS based on benchmark spot rate curve: 80 basis points

Suppose that in the market *option-free* bonds with the same credit rating, maturity, and liquidity as Bond W trade at a nominal spread *relative to the double A corporate bond sector* of 90 basis points. Based solely on the nominal spread as a relative yield measure using the same benchmark, Bond W is undervalued (i.e., cheap) since its nominal spread is greater than the nominal spread for comparable bonds (110 versus 90 basis points). Even naively comparing Bond W's zero-volatility spread of 100 basis points (relative to the double A corporate spot rate curve) to the market's 90 basis point nominal spread for option-free bonds relative to the double A corporate bond yield curve, the analysis would suggest that Bond W is cheap. However, the proper assessment of Bond W's relative value will depend on what its OAS is in comparison to the OAS (relative to the same double A corporate benchmark) of other triple B rated bonds. For example, if the OAS of other triple B rated corporate bonds is less than 80 basis points, then Bond W is cheap.

D. Issuer-Specific Benchmark

Instead of using as a benchmark the Treasury market or a bond market sector to measure relative value for a specific issue, one can use an estimate of the issuer's yield curve or an estimate of the issuer's spot rate curve as the benchmark. Then we would have the following interpretation for the three spread measures:

Spread measure	Benchmark	Reflects compensation for ...
Nominal	Issuer yield curve	Optional risk, liquidity risk
Zero-volatility	Issuer spot rate curve	Optional risk, liquidity risk
Option-adjusted	Issuer spot rate curve	Liquidity risk

Note that there is no credit risk since it is assumed that the specific issue analyzed has the same credit risk as the embedded in the issuer benchmark. Using the nominal spread, a value that is positive indicates that, ignoring any embedded option, the issue is cheap relative to how the market is pricing other bonds of the issuer. A negative value would indicate that the security is expensive. The same interpretation holds for the zero-volatility spread, ignoring any embedded option. For the OAS, a positive spread means that even after adjusting for the embedded option, the value of the security is cheap. If the OAS is zero, the security is fairly priced and if it is negative, the security is expensive.

Once again, let's use our hypothetical Bond W, a triple B rated corporate bond with an embedded call option. Assume this bond is issued by RJK Corporation. Then suppose for Bond W:

Benchmark: RJK Corporation's bond issues
Nominal spread based on RJK Corporation's yield curve: 30 basis points
Zero-volatility spread based on RJK Corporation's spot rate curve:
  20 basis points
OAS based on RJK Corporation's spot rate curve: −25 basis points

Both the nominal spread and the zero-volatility spread would suggest that Bond W is cheap (i.e., both spread measures have a positive value). However, once the embedded option is taken into account, the appropriate spread measure, the OAS, indicates that there is a negative spread. This means that Bond W is expensive and should be avoided.

E. OAS, The Benchmark, and Relative Value

Our focus in this reading is the valuation of bonds with an embedded option. While we have yet to describe how an OAS is calculated, here we summarize how to interpret OAS as a relative value measure based on the benchmark.

Consider first when the benchmark is the Treasury spot rate curve. A zero OAS means that the security offers no spread over Treasuries. Hence, a security with a zero OAS in this case should be avoided. A negative OAS means that the security is offering a spread that is less than Treasuries. Therefore, it should be avoided. A positive value alone does not mean a security is fairly priced or cheap. It depends on what spread relative to the Treasury market the market is demanding for comparable issues. Whether the security is rich, fairly priced, or cheap depends on the OAS for the security compared to the OAS for comparable securities. We will refer to the OAS offered on comparable securities as the "required OAS" and the OAS computed for the security under consideration as the "security OAS." Then,

if security OAS is greater than required OAS, the security is cheap
if security OAS is less than required OAS, the security is rich
if security OAS is equal to the required OAS, the security is fairly priced

When a sector of the bond market with the same credit rating is the benchmark, the credit rating of the sector relative to the credit rating of the security being analyzed is important. In the discussion, *it is assumed that the credit rating of the bond sector that is used as a benchmark is higher than the credit rating of the security being analyzed.* A zero OAS means that the security offers no spread over the bond sector benchmark and should therefore be avoided. A negative OAS means that the security is offering a spread that is less than the bond sector benchmark and hence should be avoided. As with the Treasury benchmark, when there is a positive OAS, relative value depends on the security OAS compared to the required OAS. Here the required OAS is the OAS of comparable securities relative to the bond sector benchmark. Given the security OAS and the required OAS, then

if security OAS is greater than required OAS, the security is cheap
if security OAS is less than required OAS, the security is rich
if security OAS is equal to the required OAS, the security is fairly priced

EXHIBIT 60-1	Relationship Between the Benchmark, OAS, and Relative Value		
Benchmark	**Negative OAS**	**Zero OAS**	**Positive OAS**
Treasury market	Overpriced (rich) security	Overpriced (rich) security	Comparison must be made between security OAS and OAS of comparable securities (required OAS): if security OAS > required OAS, security is cheap if security OAS < required OAS, security is rich if security OAS = required OAS, security is fairly priced
Bond sector with a given credit rating (*assumes credit rating higher than security being analyzed*)	Overpriced (rich) security (*assumes credit rating higher than security being analyzed*)	Overpriced (rich) security (*assumes credit rating higher than security being analyzed*)	Comparison must be made between security OAS and OAS of comparable securities (required OAS): if security OAS > required OAS, security is cheap if security OAS < required OAS, security is rich if security OAS = required OAS, security is fairly priced
Issuer's own securities	Overpriced (rich) security	Fairly valued	Underpriced (cheap) security

The terms "rich," "cheap," and "fairly priced" are only relative to the benchmark. If an investor is a funded investor who is assessing a security relative to his or her borrowing costs, then a different set of rules exists. For example, suppose that the bond sector used as the benchmark is the LIBOR spot rate curve. Also assume that the funding cost for the investor is a spread of 40 basis points over LIBOR. Then the decision to invest in the security depends on whether the OAS exceeds the 40 basis point spread by a sufficient amount to compensate for the credit risk.

Finally, let's look at relative valuation when the issuer's spot rate curve is the benchmark. If a particular security by the issuer is fairly priced, its OAS should be equal to zero. Thus, unlike when the Treasury benchmark or bond sector benchmark are used, a zero OAS is fairly valued security. A positive OAS means that the security is trading cheap relative to other securities of the issuer and a negative OAS means that the security is trading rich relative to other securities of the same issuer.

The relationship between the benchmark, OAS, and relative value are summarized in Exhibit 60-1.

REVIEW OF HOW TO VALUE AN OPTION-FREE BOND

4

Before we illustrate how to value a bond with an embedded option, we will review how to value an option-free bond. We will then take the same bond and explain how it would be valued if it has an embedded option.

At Level I, we explained how to compute an arbitrage-free value for an option-free bond using spot rates. At Level I, we showed the relationship between spot rates and forward rates, and then how forward rates can be used to derive the same arbitrage-free value as using spot rates. What we will review in this section is how to value an option-free bond using both spot rates and forward rates. We will use as our benchmark in the rest of this reading, the securities of the issuer whose bond we want to value. Hence, *we will start with the issuer's on-the-run yield curve.*

To obtain a particular issuer's on-the-run yield curve, an appropriate credit spread is added to each on-the-run Treasury issue. The credit spread need not be constant for all maturities. In our illustration, we use the following hypothetical *on-the-run issue for the issuer whose bond we want to value:*

Maturity	Yield to maturity	Market Price
1 year	3.5%	100
2 years	4.2%	100
3 years	4.7%	100
4 years	5.2%	100

Each bond is trading at par value (100) so the coupon rate is equal to the yield to maturity. We will simplify the illustration by assuming annual-pay bonds.

Using the bootstrapping methodology explained at Level I, the spot rates are given below:

Year	Spot Rate
1	3.5000%
2	4.2148%
3	4.7352%
4	5.2706%

we will use the above spot rates shortly to value a bond.

At Level I, we explained how to derive forward rates from spot rates. Recall that forward rates can have different interpretations based on the theory of the term structure to which one subscribes. However, in the valuation process, *we are not relying on any theory.* The forward rates below are mathematically derived from the spot rates and, as we will see, when used to value a bond will produce the same value as the spot rates. The 1-year forward rates are:

Current 1-year forward rate	3.500%
1-year forward rate one year from now	4.935%
1-year forward rate two years from now	5.784%
1-year forward rate three years from now	6.893%

Now consider an option-free bond with four years remaining to maturity and a coupon rate of 6.5%. The value of this bond can be calculated in one of two ways, both producing the same value. First, the cash flows can be discounted at the spot rates as shown below:

$$\frac{\$6.5}{(1.035)^1} + \frac{\$6.5}{(1.042148)^2} + \frac{\$6.5}{(1.047352)^3} + \frac{\$100 + \$6.5}{(1.052706)^4} = \$104.643$$

The second way is to discount by the 1-year forward rates as shown below:

$$\frac{\$6.5}{(1.035)} + \frac{\$6.5}{(1.035)\,(1.04935)} + \frac{\$6.5}{(1.035)\,(1.04935)\,(1.05784)}$$
$$+ \frac{\$100 + \$6.5}{(1.035)\,(1.04935)\,(1.05784)\,(1.06893)} = \$104.643$$

As can be seen, discounting by spot rates or forward rates will produce the same value for a bond.

Remember this value for the option-free bond, $104.643. When we value the same bond using the binomial model later in this reading, that model should produce a value of $104.643 or else our model is flawed.

VALUING A BOND WITH AN EMBEDDED OPTION USING THE BINOMIAL MODEL

5

As explained in Section 2, there are various models that have been developed to value a bond with embedded options. The one that we will use to illustrate the issues and assumptions associated with valuing bonds with embedded options is the binomial model. The interest rates that are used in the valuation process are obtained from a **binomial interest rate tree**. We'll explain the general characteristics of this tree first. Then we see how to value a bond using the binomial interest rate tree. We will then see how to construct this tree from an on-the-run yield curve. Basically, the derivation of a binomial interest rate tree is the same in principle as deriving the spot rates using the boot-strapping method described at Level I—that is, there is no arbitrage.

A. Binomial Interest Rate Tree

Once we allow for embedded options, consideration must be given to interest rate volatility. The reason is, the decision of the issuer or the investor (depending upon who has the option) will be affected by what interest rates are in the future. This means that the valuation model must explicitly take into account how interest rates may change in the future. In turn, this recognition is achieved by incorporating interest rate volatility into the valuation model. In the previous reading, we explained what interest rate volatility is and how it can be measured.

Let's see how interest rate volatility is introduced into the valuation model. More specifically, let's see how this can be done in the binomial model using Exhibit 60-2. Look at panel a of the exhibit which shows the beginning or *root* of the interest rate tree. The time period shown is "Today." At the dot, denoted N, in the exhibit is an interest rate denoted by r_0 which represents the interest rate today.

Notice that there are two arrows as we move to the right of N. Here is where we are introducing interest rate volatility. The dot in the exhibit referred to as a *node*. What takes place at a node is either a *random event* or a *decision*. We will see

EXHIBIT 60-2   Binomial Interest Rate Tree

Panel a: One-Year Binomial Interest Rate Tree   *Panel b: Two-Year Binomial Interest Rate Tree*

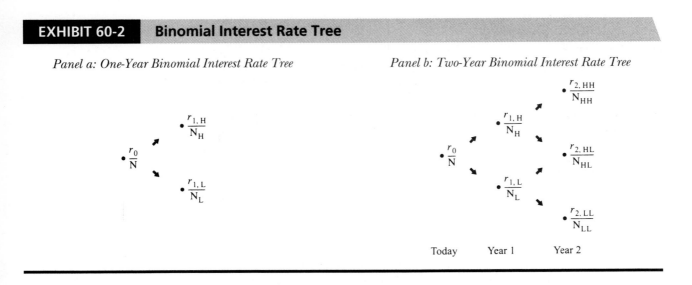

that in building a binomial interest rate tree, at each node there is a random event. The change in interest rates represents a random event. Later when we show how to use the binomial interest rate tree to determine the value of a bond with an embedded option, at each node there will be a decision. Specifically, the decision will be whether or not the issuer or bondholders (depending on the type of embedded option) will exercise the option.

In the binomial model, it is assumed that the random event (i.e., the change in interest rates) will take on only two possible values. Moreover, it is assumed that the probability of realizing either value is equal. The two possible values are the interest rates shown by $r_{1,H}$ and $r_{1,L}$ in panel a.[6] If you look at the time frame at the bottom of panel a, you will notice that it is in years.[7] What this means is that the interest rate at r_0 is the current (i.e., today's) 1-year rate and at year 1, the two possible 1-year interest rates are $r_{1,H}$ and $r_{1,L}$. Notice the notation that is used for the two subscripts. The first subscript, 1, means that it is the interest rate starting in year 1. The second subscript indicates whether it is the higher (*H*) or lower (*L*) of the two interest rates in year 1.

Now we will grow the binomial interest rate tree. Look at panel b of Exhibit 60-2 which shows today, year 1, and year 2. There are two nodes at year 1 depending on whether the higher or the lower interest rate is realized. At both of the nodes a random event occurs. N_H is the node if the higher interest rate ($r_{1,H}$) is realized. In the binomial model, the interest rate that can occur in the next year (i.e., year 2) can be one of two values: $r_{2,HH}$ or $r_{2,HL}$. The subscript 2 indicates year 2. This would get us to either the node N_{HH} or N_{HL}. The subscript "*HH*" means that the path to get to node N_{HH} is the higher interest rate in year 1 and in year 2. The subscript "*HL*" means that the path to get to node N_{HL} is the higher interest rate in year 1 and the lower interest rate in year 2.

Similarly, N_L is the node if the lower interest rate ($r_{1,L}$) is realized in year 1. The interest rate that can occur in year 2 is either $r_{2,LH}$ or $r_{2,LL}$. This would get us to either the node N_{LH} or N_{LL}. The subscript "*LH*" means that the path to get to node N_{LH} is the lower interest rate in year 1 and the higher interest rate in year 2. The subscript "*LL*" means that the path to get to node N_{LL} is the lower interest rate in year 1 and in year 2.

---

[6]If we were using a trinomial model, there would be three possible interest rates shown in the next year.

[7]In practice, much shorter time periods are used to construct an interest rate tree.

Notice that in panel b, at year 2 only N_{HL} is shown but no N_{LH}. The reason is that if the higher interest rate is realized in year 1 and the lower interest rate is realized in year 2, we would get to the same node as if the lower interest rate is realized in year 1 and the higher interest rate is realized in year 2. Rather than clutter up the interest rate tree with notation, only one of the two paths is shown.

In our illustration of valuing a bond with an embedded option, we will use a 4-year bond. Consequently, we will need a 4-year binomial interest rate tree to value this bond. Exhibit 60-3 shows the tree and the notation used.

EXHIBIT 60-3   Four-Year Binomial Interest Rate Tree

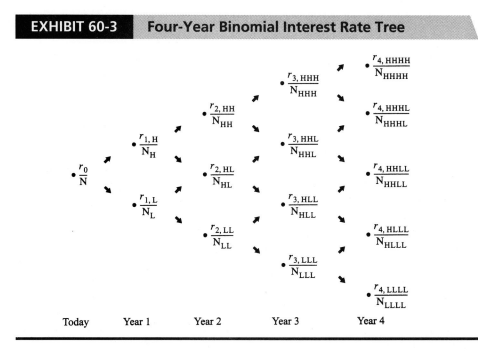

The interest rates shown in the binomial interest rate tree are actually forward rates. Basically, they are the one-period rates starting in period t. (A period in our illustration is one year.) Thus, in valuing an option-free bond we know that it is valued using forward rates and we have illustrated this by using 1-period forward rates. For each period, there is a unique forward rate. When we value bonds with embedded options, we will see that we continue to use forward rates but there is not just one forward rate for a given period but a set of forward rates.

There will be a relationship between the rates in the binomial interest rate tree. The relationship depends on the interest rate model assumed. Based on some interest rate volatility assumption, the interest rate model selected would show the relationship between:

$r_{1,L}$ and $r_{1,H}$ for year 1
$r_{2,LL}$, $r_{2,HL}$, and $r_{2,HH}$ for year 2
etc.

For our purpose of understanding the valuation model, it is not necessary that we show the mathematical relationships here.

B. Determining the Value at a Node

Now we want to see how to use the binomial interest rate tree to value a bond. To do this, we first have to determine the value of the bond at each node. To find the value of the bond at a node, we begin by calculating the bond's value at the high and low nodes to the right of the node for which we are interested in obtaining a value. For example, in Exhibit 60-4, suppose we want to determine the bond's value at node N_H. The bond's value at node N_{HH} and N_{HL} must be determined. Hold aside for now how we get these two values because, as we will see, the process involves starting from the last (right-most) year in the tree and working backwards to get the final solution we want. Because the procedure for solving for the final solution in any interest rate tree involves moving backwards, the methodology is known as **backward induction**.

Effectively what we are saying is that if we are at some node, then the value at that node will depend on the future cash flows. In turn, the future cash flows depend on (1) the coupon payment one year from now and (2) the bond's value one year from now. The former is known. The bond's value depends on whether the rate is the higher or lower rate reported at the two nodes to the right of the node that is the focus of our attention. So, the cash flow at a node will be either (1) the bond's value if the 1-year rate is the higher rate plus the coupon payment, or (2) the bond's value if the 1-year rate is the lower rate plus the coupon payment. Let's return to the bond's value at node N_H. The cash flow will be either the bond's value at N_{HH} plus the coupon payment, or the bond's value at N_{HL} plus the coupon payment.

In general, to get the bond's value at a node we follow the fundamental rule for valuation: the value is the present value of the expected cash flows. The appropriate discount rate to use is the 1-year rate at the node where we are computing the value. Now there are two present values in this case: the present value if the 1-year rate is the higher rate and one if it is the lower rate. Since it is assumed that the probability of both outcomes is equal (i.e., there is a 50% probability for each), an average of the two present values is computed. This is illustrated in Exhibit 60-4 for any node assuming that the 1-year rate is $r*$ at the node where the valuation is sought and letting:

V_H = the bond's value for the higher 1-year rate
V_L = the bond's value for the lower 1-year rate
C   = coupon payment

Using our notation, the cash flow at a node is either:

V_H + C for the higher 1-year rate
V_L + C for the lower 1-year rate

EXHIBIT 60-4   Calculating a Value at a Node

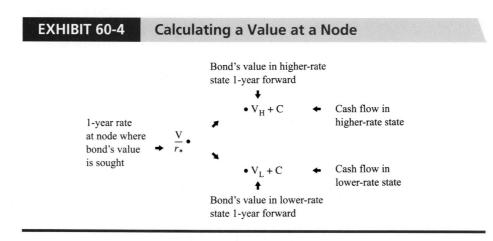

Bond's value in higher-rate
state 1-year forward
↓
• V_H + C   ←   Cash flow in
higher-rate state

1-year rate
at node where $\dfrac{V}{r*}$ •
bond's value →
is sought

• V_L + C   ←   Cash flow in
lower-rate state
↑
Bond's value in lower-rate
state 1-year forward

The present value of these two cash flows using the 1-year rate at the node, r_*, is:

$$\frac{V_H + C}{(1 + r_*)} = \text{present value for the higher 1-year rate}$$

$$\frac{V_L + C}{(1 + r_*)} = \text{present value for the lower 1-year rate}$$

Then, the value of the bond at the node is found as follows:

$$\text{Value at a node} = \frac{1}{2}\left[\frac{V_H + C}{(1 + r_*)} + \frac{V_L + C}{(1 + r_*)} \right]$$

C. Constructing the Binomial Interest Rate Tree

The construction of any interest rate tree is complicated, although the principle is simple to understand. This applies to the binomial interest rate tree or a tree based on more than two future rates in the next period. *The fundamental principle is that when a tree is used to value an on-the-run issue for the benchmark, the resulting value should be arbitrage free.* That is, the tree should generate a value for an on-the-run issue equal to its observed market value. Moreover, the interest rate tree should be consistent with the interest rate volatility assumed.

Here is a brief overview of the process for constructing the interest rate tree. It is not essential to know how to derive the interest rate tree; rather, it should be understood how to value a bond given the rates on the tree. The interest rate at the first node (i.e., the root of the tree) is the one year interest rate for the on-the-run issue. (This is because in our simplified illustration we are assuming that the length of the time between nodes is one year.) The tree is grown just the same way that the spot rates were obtained using the bootstrapping method based on arbitrage arguments.

The interest rates for year 1 (there are two of them and remember they are forward rates) are obtained from the following information:

1. the coupon rate for the 2-year on-the-run issue
2. the interest rate volatility assumed
3. the interest rate at the root of the tree (i.e., the current 1-year on-the-run rate)

Given the above, a *guess* is then made of the lower rate at node N_L, which is $r_{1,L}$. The upper rate, $r_{1,H}$, is not guessed at. Instead, it is determined by the assumed volatility of the 1-year rate ($r_{1,L}$). The formula for determining $r_{1,H}$ given $r_{1,L}$ is specified by the interest rate model used. Using the $r_{1,L}$ that was guessed and the corresponding $r_{1,H}$, the 2-year on-the-run issue can be valued. If the resulting value computed using the backward induction method is not equal to the market value of the 2-year on-the-run issue, then the $r_{1,L}$ that was tried is not the rate that should be used in the tree. If the value is too high, then a higher rate guess should be tried; if the value is too low, then a lower rate guess should be tried. The process continues in an iterative (i.e., trial and error) process until a value for $r_{1,L}$ and the corresponding $r_{1,H}$ produce a value for the 2-year on-the-run issue equal to its market value.

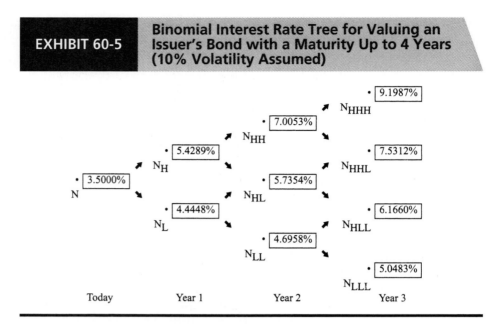

EXHIBIT 60-5 — Binomial Interest Rate Tree for Valuing an Issuer's Bond with a Maturity Up to 4 Years (10% Volatility Assumed)

After this stage, we have the rate at the root of the tree and the two rates for year 1—$r_{1,L}$ and $r_{1,H}$. Now we need the three rates for year 2—$r_{2,LL}$, $r_{2,HL}$, and $r_{2,HH}$. These rates are determined from the following information:

1. the coupon rate for the 3-year on-the-run issue

2. the interest rate model assumed

3. the interest rate volatility assumed

4. the interest rate at the root of the tree (i.e., the current 1-year on-the-run rate)

5. the two 1-year rates (i.e., $r_{1,L}$ and $r_{1,H}$)

A guess is made for $r_{2,LL}$. The interest rate model assumed specifies how to obtain $r_{2,HL}$, and $r_{2,HH}$ given $r_{2,LL}$ and the assumed volatility for the 1-year rate. This gives the rates in the interest rate tree that are needed to value the 3-year on-the-run

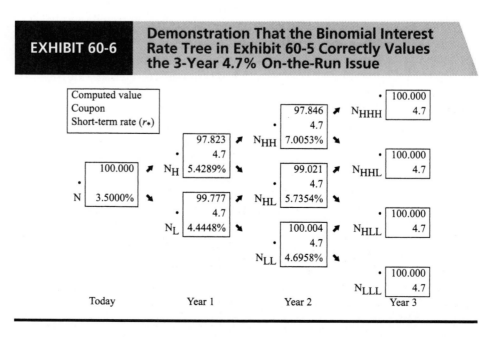

EXHIBIT 60-6 — Demonstration That the Binomial Interest Rate Tree in Exhibit 60-5 Correctly Values the 3-Year 4.7% On-the-Run Issue

PRACTICE QUESTION 1

For the hypothetical issuer whose on-the-run yield was given in Section 4, the binomial interest rate tree below is based on 20% volatility. Using the 4-year on-the-run issue, show that the binomial interest tree below does produce a value equal to the price of the 4-year issue (i.e., par value).

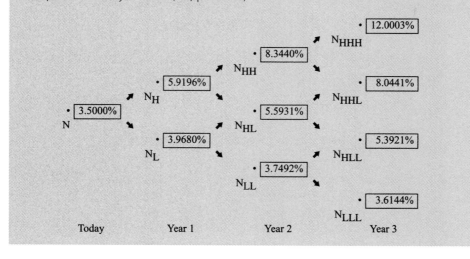

issue. The 3-year on-the-run issue is then valued. If the value generated is not equal to the market value of the 3-year on-the-run issue, then the $r_{2,LL}$ value tried is not the rate that should be used in the tree. At iterative process is again followed until a value for $r_{2,LL}$ produces rates for year 2 that will make the value of the 3-year on-the-run issue equal to its market value.

The tree is grown using the same procedure as described above to get $r_{1,L}$ and $r_{1,H}$ for year 1 and $r_{2,LL}$, $r_{2,HL}$, and $r_{2,HH}$ for year 2. Exhibit 60-5 shows the binomial interest rate tree for this issuer for valuing issues up to four years of maturity assuming volatility for the 1-year rate of 10%. The interest rate model used is not important. How can we be sure that the interest rates shown in Exhibit 60-5 are the correct rates? Verification involves using the interest rate tree to value an on-the-run issue and showing that the value obtained from the binomial model is equal to the observed market value. For example, let's just show that the interest rates in the tree for years 0, 1, and 2 in Exhibit 60-5 are correct. To do this, we use the 3-year on-the-run issue. The market value for the issue is 100. Exhibit 60-6 shows the valuation of this issue using the backward induction method. Notice that the value at the root (i.e., the value derived by the model) is 100. Thus, the value derived from the interest rate tree using the rates for the first two years produce the observed market value of 100 for the 3-year on-the-run issue. This verification is the same as saying that the model has produced an arbitrage-free value.

D. Valuing an Option-Free Bond with the Tree

To illustrate how to use the binomial interest rate tree shown in Exhibit 60-5, consider a 6.5% option-free bond with four years remaining to maturity. Also

PRACTICE QUESTION 2

Show that the value of an option-free bond with four years to maturity and a coupon rate of 6.5% is $104.643 if volatility is assumed to be 20%.

EXHIBIT 60-7	Valuing an Option-Free Bond with Four Years to Maturity and a Coupon Rate of 6.5% (10% Volatility Assumed)

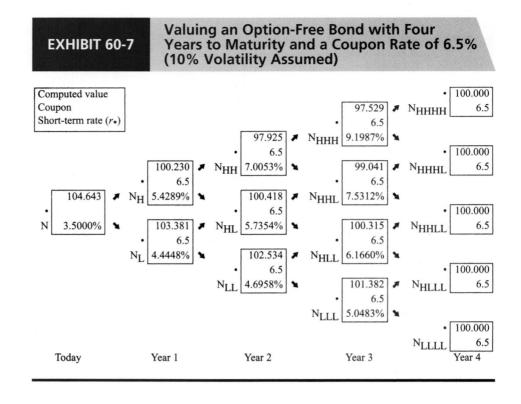

assume that the *issuer's on-the-run yield curve* is the one given earlier and hence the appropriate binomial interest rate tree is the one in Exhibit 60-5. Exhibit 60-7 shows the various values in the discounting process, and produces a bond value of \$104.643.

It is important to note that this value is identical to the bond value found earlier when we discounted at either the spot rates or the 1-year forward rates. We should expect to find this result since our bond is option free. This clearly demonstrates that the valuation model is consistent with the arbitrage-free valuation model for an option-free bond.

6   VALUING AND ANALYZING A CALLABLE BOND

Now we will demonstrate how the binomial interest rate tree can be applied to value a callable bond. The valuation process proceeds in the same fashion as in the case of an option-free bond, but with one exception: when the call option may be exercised by the issuer, the bond value at a node must be changed to reflect the lesser of its values if it is not called (i.e., the value obtained by applying the backward induction method described above) and the call price. As explained earlier, at a node either a random event or a decision must be made. In constructing the binomial interest rate tree, there is a random event at a node. When valuing a bond with an embedded option, at a node there will be a decision made as to whether or not an option will be exercised. In the case of a callable bond, the issuer must decide whether or not to exercise the call option.

For example, consider a 6.5% bond with four years remaining to maturity that is callable in one year at $100. Exhibit 60-8 shows two values at each node of the binomial interest rate tree. The discounting process explained above is used to calculate the first of the two values at each node. The second value is the value based on whether the issue will be called. For simplicity, let's assume that this issuer calls the issue if it exceeds the call price.

In Exhibit 60-9 two portions of Exhibit 60-8 are highlighted. Panel a of the exhibit shows nodes where the issue is not called (based on the simple call rule used in the illustration) in year 2 and year 3. The values reported in this case are the same as in the valuation of an option-free bond. Panel b of the exhibit shows some nodes where the issue is called in year 2 and year 3. Notice how the methodology changes the cash flows. In year 3, for example, at node N_{HLL} the backward induction method produces a value (i.e., cash flow) of 100.315. However, given the simplified call rule, this issue would be called. Therefore, 100 is shown as the second value at the node and it is this value that is then used in the backward induction methodology. From this we can see how the binomial method changes the cash flow based on future interest rates and the embedded option.

The root of the tree, shown in Exhibit 60-8 indicates that the value for this callable bond is $102.899.

EXHIBIT 60-8	Valuing a Callable Bond with Four Years to Maturity, a Coupon Rate of 6.5%, and Callable in One Year at 100 (10% Volatility Assumed)

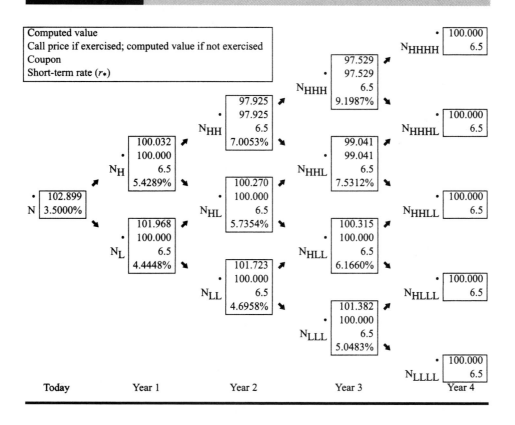

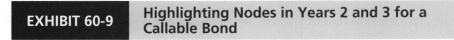

| EXHIBIT 60-9 | Highlighting Nodes in Years 2 and 3 for a Callable Bond |

a. Nodes where call option is not exercised

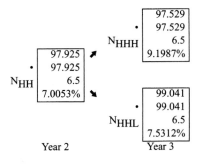

b. Selected nodes where the call option is exercised

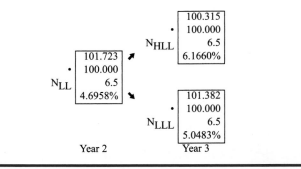

The question that we have not addressed in our illustration, which is nonetheless important, is the circumstances under which the issuer will actually call the bond. A detailed explanation of the call rule is beyond the scope of this reading. Basically, it involves determining when it would be economical for the issuer on an after-tax basis to call the issue.

Suppose instead that the call price schedule is 102 in year 1, 101 in year 2, and 100 in year 3. Also assume that the bond will not be called unless it exceeds the call price for that year. Exhibit 60-10 shows the value at each node and the value of the callable bond. The call price schedule results in a greater value for the callable bond, $103.942 compared to $102.899 when the call price is 100 in each year.

A. Determining the Call Option Value

As explained at Level I, the value of a callable bond is equal to the value of an option-free bond minus the value of the call option. This means that:

value of a call option = value of an option-free bond − value of a callable bond

We have just seen how the value of an option-free bond and the value of a callable bond can be determined. The difference between the two values is therefore the value of the call option.

In our illustration, the value of the option-free bond is $104.643. If the call price is $100 in each year and the value of the callable bond is $102.899 assuming

EXHIBIT 60-10	Valuing a Callable Bond with Four Years to Maturity, a Coupon Rate of 6.5%, and with a Call Price Schedule (10% Volatility Assumed)

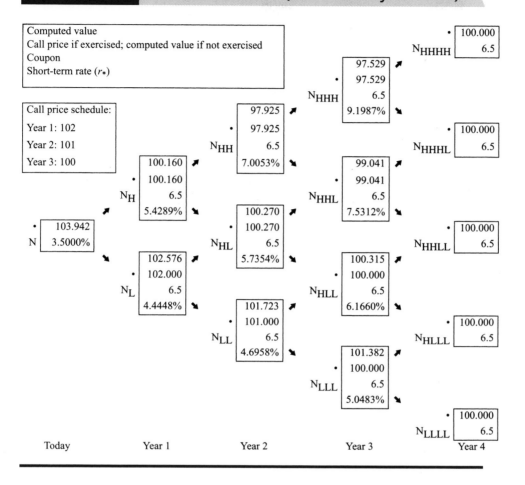

10% volatility for the 1-year rate, the value of the call option is $1.744 (= $104.643 − $102.899).

B. Volatility and the Arbitrage-Free Value

In our illustration, interest rate volatility was assumed to be 10%. The volatility assumption has an important impact on the arbitrage-free value. More specifically, the higher the expected volatility, the higher the value of an option. The same is true for an option embedded in a bond. Correspondingly, this affects the value of a bond with an embedded option.

For example, for a callable bond, a higher interest rate volatility assumption means that the value of the call option increases and, since the value of the option-free bond is not affected, the value of the callable bond must be lower.

We can see this using the on-the-run yield curve in our previous illustrations. In the previous illustrations, we assumed interest rate volatility of 10%. To show the effect of higher volatility, we will assume volatility of 20%. The solution to Practice Question 1 gives the corresponding binomial interest rate tree using the same interest rate model. The solution to Practice Question 2 verifies that the binomial interest rate tree provides the same value for the option-free bond, $104.643.

The solution to Practice Question 3 shows the calculation for the callable bond assuming interest rate volatility of 20%. For the callable bond it is assumed that the issue is callable at par beginning in year 1. The value of the callable bond is $102.108 if volatility is assumed to be 20% compared to $102.899 if volatility is assumed to be 10%. Notice that at the higher assumed volatility (20%), the callable bond has a lower value than at the lower assumed volatility (10%). The reason for this is that the value of an option increases with the higher assumed volatility. So, at 20% volatility the value of the embedded call option is higher than at 10% volatility. But the embedded call option is subtracted from the option-free value to obtain the value of the callable bond. Since a higher value for the embedded call option is subtracted from the option-free value at 20% volatility than at 10% volatility, the value of the callable bond is lower at 20% volatility.

PRACTICE QUESTION 3

Suppose that the volatility assumption is 20% rather than 10% and therefore the binomial interest rate tree is the one shown in Practice Question 1.

a. Compute the arbitrage-free value for the 4-year 6.5% coupon bond callable at par beginning Year 1 based on 20% volatility.

b. Compare the arbitrage-free value for this bond based on 20% volatility and 10% volatility as computed in Exhibit 60-8.

C. Option-Adjusted Spread

Suppose the market price of the 4-year 6.5% callable bond is $102.218 and the theoretical value assuming 10% volatility is $102.899. This means that this bond is cheap by $0.681 according to the valuation model. Bond market participants prefer to think not in terms of a bond's price being cheap or expensive in dollar terms but rather in terms of a yield spread—a cheap bond trades at a higher yield spread and an expensive bond at a lower yield spread.

The **option-adjusted spread** is the constant spread that when added to all the 1-year rates on the binomial interest rate tree that will make the arbitrage-free value (i.e., the value produced by the binomial model) equal to the market price. In our illustration, if the market price is $102.218, the OAS would be the constant spread added to every rate in Exhibit 60-5 that will make the arbitrage-free value equal to $102.218. The solution in this case would be 35 basis points. This can be verified in Exhibit 60-11 which shows the value of this issue by adding 35 basis points to each rate.

As with the value of a bond with an embedded option, the OAS will depend on the volatility assumption. For a given bond price, the higher the interest rate volatility assumed, the lower the OAS for a callable bond. For example, if volatility is 20% rather than 10%, the OAS would be −6 basis points. This illustration clearly demonstrates the importance of the volatility assumption. Assuming volatility of 10%, the OAS is 35 basis points. At 20% volatility, the OAS declines and, in this case is negative and therefore the bond is overvalued relative to the model.

What the OAS seeks to do is remove from the nominal spread the amount that is due to the option risk. The measure is called an OAS because (1) it is a spread and (2) it adjusts the cash flows for the option when computing the spread

EXHIBIT 60-11	**Demonstration That the Option-Adjusted Spread Is 35 Basis Points for a 6.5% Callable Bond Selling at 102.218 (Assuming 10% Volatility)**	

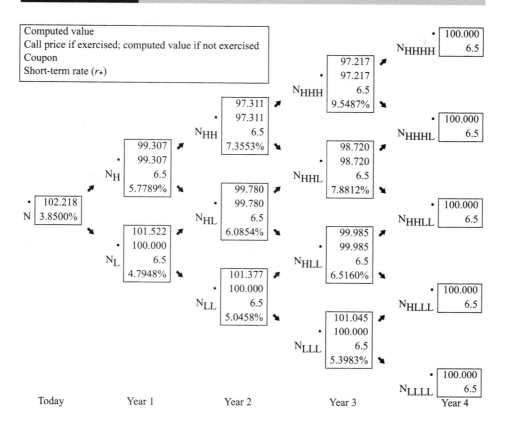

Computed value
Call price if exercised; computed value if not exercised
Coupon
Short-term rate (r_*)

| Today | Year 1 | Year 2 | Year 3 | Year 4 |

*Each 1-year rate is 35 basis points greater than in Exhibit 60-5.

to the benchmark interest rates. The second point can be seen from Exhibits 60-8 and 60-9. Notice that at each node the value obtained from the backward induction method is adjusted based on the call option and the call rule. Thus, the resulting spread is "option adjusted."

What does the OAS tell us about the relative value for our callable bond? As explained in Section 3, the answer depends on the benchmark used. Exhibit 60-1 provides a summary of how to interpret the OAS. In valuing the callable bond in our illustration, the benchmark is the issuer's own securities. As can be seen in Exhibit 60-1, a positive OAS means that the callable bond is cheap (i.e., under-priced). At a 10% volatility, the OAS is 35 basis points. Consequently, assuming a 10% volatility, on a relative value basis the callable bond is attractive. However, and this is critical to remember, the OAS depends on the assumed interest rate volatility. When a 20% interest rate volatility is assumed, the OAS is −6 basis points. Hence, if an investor assumes that this is the appropriate interest rate volatility that should be used in valuing the callable bond, the issue is expensive (overvalued) on a relative value basis.

PRACTICE QUESTION 4

Show that if 20% volatility is assumed the OAS is −6 basis points.

D. Effective Duration and Effective Convexity

At Level I, we explained the meaning of duration and convexity measures and explained how these two measures can be computed. Specifically, duration is the approximate percentage change in the value of a security for a 100 basis point change in interest rates (assuming a parallel shift in the yield curve). The convexity measure allows for an adjustment to the estimated price change obtained by using duration. The formula for duration and convexity are repeated below:

$$\text{duration} = \frac{V_- - V_+}{2V_0(\Delta y)}$$

$$\text{convexity} = \frac{V_+ + V_- - 2V_0}{2V_0(\Delta y)^2}$$

where

Δy = change in rate used to calculate new values
V_+ = estimated value if yield is increased by Δy
V_- = estimated value if yield is decreased by Δy
V_0 = initial price (per $100 of par value)

We also made a distinction at Level I between "modified" duration and convexity and "effective" duration and convexity. **Modified duration** and convexity do not allow for the fact that the cash flows for a bond with an embedded option may change due to the exercise of the option. In contrast, effective duration and convexity do take into consideration how changes in interest rates in the future may alter the cash flows due to the exercise of the option. But, we did not demonstrate how to compute effective duration and convexity because they require a model for valuing bonds with embedded options and we did not introduce such models until this chapter.

So, let's see how effective duration and convexity are computed using the binomial model. With effective duration and convexity, the values V_- and V_+ are obtained from the binomial model. Recall that in using the binomial model, the cash flows at a node are adjusted for the embedded call option as was demonstrated in Exhibit 60-8 and highlighted in the lower panel of Exhibit 60-9.

The procedure for calculating the value of V_+ is as follows:

Step 1: Given the market price of the issue calculate its OAS using the procedure described earlier.
Step 2: Shift the on-the-run yield curve up by a small number of basis points (Δy).
Step 3: Construct a binomial interest rate tree based on the new yield curve in Step 2.
Step 4: To each of the 1-year rates in the binomial interest rate tree, add the OAS to obtain an "adjusted tree." That is, the calculation of the effective duration and convexity assumes that the OAS will not change when interest rates change.
Step 5: Use the adjusted tree found in Step 4 to determine the value of the bond, which is V_+.

To determine the value of V_-, the same five steps are followed except that in Step 2, the on-the-run yield curve is shifted down by a small number of basis points (Δy).

To illustrate how V_+ and V_- are determined in order to calculate effective duration and effective convexity, we will use the same on-the-run yield curve that we have used in our previous illustrations assuming a volatility of 10%. The 4-year callable bond with a coupon rate of 6.5% and callable at par selling at 102.218 will be used in this illustration. The OAS for this issue is 35 basis points.

Exhibit 60-12 shows the adjusted tree by shifting the yield curve up by an arbitrarily small number of basis points, 25 basis points, and then adding 35 basis points (the OAS) to each 1-year rate. The adjusted tree is then used to value the bond. The resulting value, V_+, is 101.621. Exhibit 60-13 shows the adjusted tree by shifting the yield curve down by 25 basis points and then adding 35 basis points to each 1-year rate. The resulting value, V_-, is 102.765.

The results are summarized below:

$$\Delta y = 0.0025$$
$$V_+ = 101.621$$
$$V_- = 102.765$$
$$V_0 = 102.218$$

EXHIBIT 60-12	Determination of V_+ for Calculating Effective Duration and Convexity*

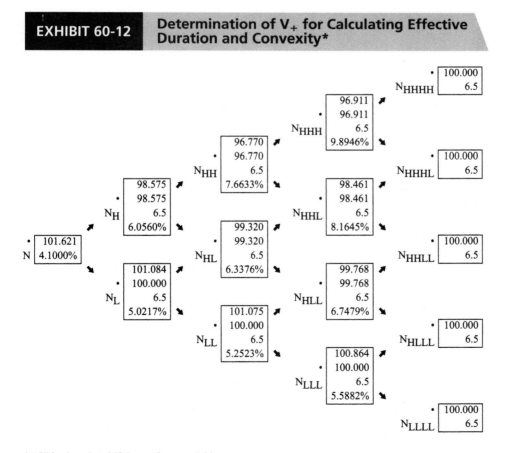

*+25 basis point shift in on-the-run yield curve.

EXHIBIT 60-13	Determination of V_ for Calculating Effective Duration and Convexity*

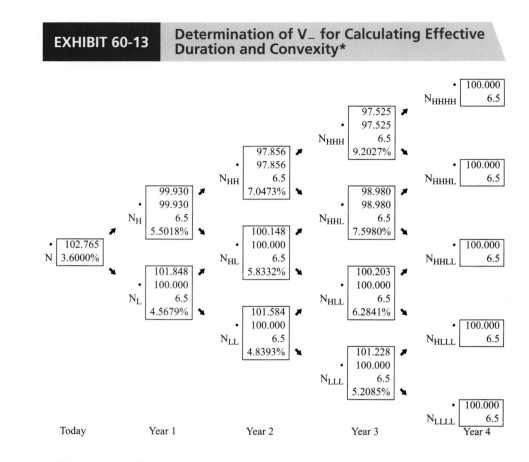

Today	Year 1	Year 2	Year 3	Year 4

*–25 basis point shift in on-the-run yield curve.

Therefore,

$$\text{effective duration} = \frac{102.765 - 101.621}{2(102.218)(0.0025)} = 2.24$$

$$\text{effective convexity} = \frac{101.621 + 102.765 - 2(102.218)}{2(102.218)(0.0025)^2} = -39.1321$$

Notice that this callable bond exhibits negative convexity. The characteristic of negative convexity for a bond with an embedded option was explained at Level I.

7   VALUING A PUTABLE BOND

A putable bond is one in which the bondholder has the right to force the issuer to pay off the bond prior to the maturity date. To illustrate how the binomial model can be used to value a putable bond, suppose that a 6.5% bond with four years remaining to maturity is putable in one year at par ($100). Also assume that the appropriate binomial interest rate tree for this issuer is the one in Exhibit 60-5 and the bondholder exercises the put if the bond's price is less than par.

Exhibit 60-14 shows the binomial interest rate tree with the values based on whether or not the investor exercises the option at a node. Exhibit 60-15 highlights selected nodes for year 2 and year 3 just as we did in Exhibit 60-9. The right

EXHIBIT 60-14 Valuing a Putable Bond with Four Years to Maturity, a Coupon Rate of 6.5%, and Putable in One Year at 100 (10% Volatility Assumed)

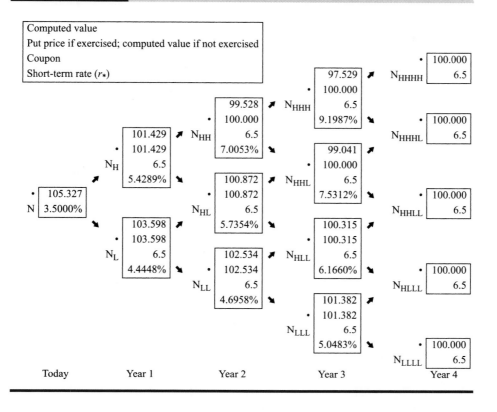

| Computed value |
| Put price if exercised; computed value if not exercised |
| Coupon |
| Short-term rate (r_*) |

Today · Year 1 · Year 2 · Year 3 · Year 4

EXHIBIT 60-15 Highlighting Nodes in Years 2 and 3 for a Putable Bond

(a) Selected nodes where put option is exercised

(b) Nodes where put option is not exercised

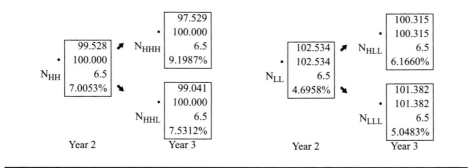

side of the exhibit shows the nodes where the put option is not exercised and therefore the value at each node is the same as when the bond is option free. In contrast, the left side of the exhibit shows where the value obtained from the backward induction method is overridden and 100 is used because the put option is exercised.

The value of the putable bond is $105.327, a value that is greater than the value of the corresponding option-free bond. The reason for this can be seen from the following relationship:

value of a putable bond = value of an option-free bond
+ value of the put option

The reason for adding the value of the put option is that the investor has purchased the put option.

We can rewrite the above relationship to determine the value of the put option:

value of the put option = value of a putable bond
− value of an option-free bond

In our example, since the value of the putable bond is $105.327 and the value of the corresponding option-free bond is $104.643, the value of the put option is −$0.684. The negative sign indicates the issuer has sold the option, or equivalently, the investor has purchased the option.

We have stressed that the value of a bond with an embedded option is affected by the volatility assumption. Unlike a callable bond, the value of a putable bond increases if the assumed volatility increases. It can be demonstrated

EXHIBIT 60-16	Valuing a Putable/Callable Issue (10% Volatility Assumed)

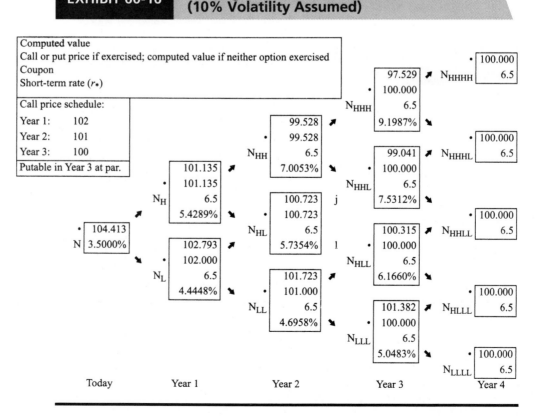

that if a 20% volatility is assumed the value of this putable bond increases from 105.327 at 10% volatility to 106.010.

Suppose that a bond is both putable and callable. The procedure for valuing such a structure is to adjust the value at each node to reflect whether the issue would be put or called. To illustrate this, consider the 4-year callable bond analyzed earlier that had a call schedule. The valuation of this issue is shown in Exhibit 60-10. Suppose the issue is putable in year 3 at par value. Exhibit 60-16 shows how to value this callable/putable issue. At each node there are two decisions about the exercising of an option that must be made. First, given the valuation from the backward induction method at a node, the call rule is invoked to determine whether the issue will be called. If it is called, the value at the node is replaced by the call price. The valuation procedure then continues using the call price at that node. Second, if the call option is not exercised at a node, it must be determined whether or not the put option is exercised. If it is exercised, then the value from the backward induction method is overridden and the put price is substituted at that node and is used in subsequent calculations.

PRACTICE QUESTION 5

Using the binomial interest rate tree based on 20%, show that the value of this putable bond is 106.010. (Assume that the bond is noncallable.)

VALUING A STEP-UP CALLABLE NOTE   8

Step-up callable notes are callable instruments whose coupon rate is increased (i.e., "stepped up") at designated times. When the coupon rate is increased only once over the security's life, it is said to be a **single step-up callable note**. A **multiple step-up callable note** is a step-up callable note whose coupon is increased more than one time over the life of the security. Valuation using the binomial model is similar to that for valuing a callable bond except that the cash flows are altered at each node to reflect the coupon changing characteristics of a step-up note.

To illustrate how the binomial model can be used to value step-up callable notes, let's begin with a single step-up callable note. Suppose that a 4-year step-up callable note pays 4.25% for two years and then 7.5% for two more years. Assume that this note is callable at par at the end of Year 2 and Year 3. We will use the binomial interest rate tree given in Exhibit 60-5 to value this note.

Exhibit 60-17 shows the value of a corresponding single step-up *noncallable* note. The valuation procedure is identical to that performed in Exhibit 60-8 except that the coupon in the box at each node reflects the step-up terms. The value is $102.082. Exhibit 60-18 shows that the value of the single step-up callable note is $100.031. The value of the embedded call option is equal to the difference in the step-up noncallable note value and the step-up callable note value, $2.051.

The procedure is the same for a multiple step-up callable note. Suppose that a multiple step-up callable note has the following coupon rates: 4.2% in Year 1, 5% in Year 2, 6% in Year 3, and 7% in Year 4. Also assume that the note is callable at the end of Year 1 at par. Exhibit 60-19 shows that the value of this note if it *is* noncallable is $101.012. The value of the multiple step-up callable note is $99.996 as shown in Exhibit 60-20. Therefore, the value of the embedded call option is $1.016 (= 101.012 − 99.996).

EXHIBIT 60-17	Valuing a Single Step-Up Noncallable Note with Four Years to Maturity (10% Volatility Assumed)

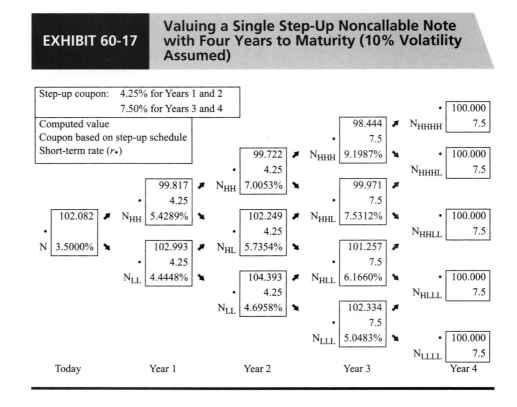

EXHIBIT 60-18	Valuing a Single Step-Up Callable Note with Four Years to Maturity, Callable in Two Years at 100 (10% Volatility Assumed)

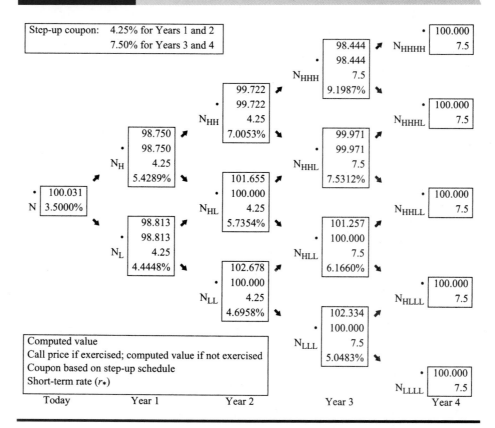

EXHIBIT 60-19 **Valuing a Multiple Step-Up Noncallable Note with Four Years to Maturity (10% Volatility Assumed)**

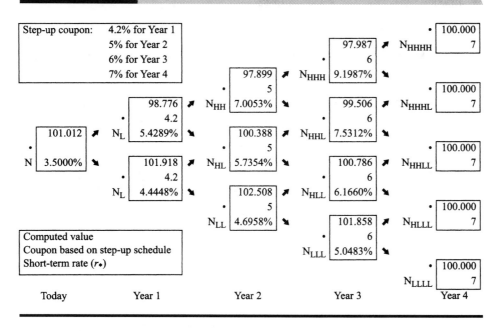

Step-up coupon: 4.2% for Year 1
5% for Year 2
6% for Year 3
7% for Year 4

Computed value
Coupon based on step-up schedule
Short-term rate (r_*)

Today   Year 1   Year 2   Year 3   Year 4

EXHIBIT 60-20 **Valuing a Multiple Step-Up Callable Note with Four Years to Maturity, and Callable in One Year at 100 (10% Volatility Assumed)**

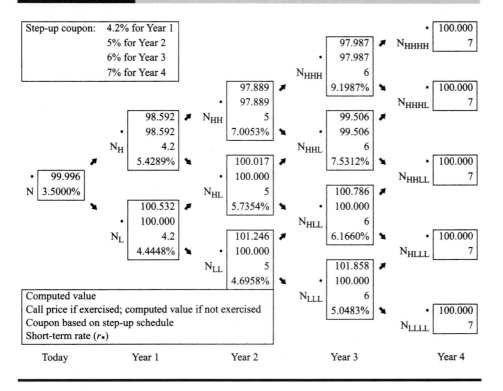

Step-up coupon: 4.2% for Year 1
5% for Year 2
6% for Year 3
7% for Year 4

Computed value
Call price if exercised; computed value if not exercised
Coupon based on step-up schedule
Short-term rate (r_*)

Today   Year 1   Year 2   Year 3   Year 4

9   VALUING A CAPPED FLOATER

The valuation of a floating-rate note with a cap (i.e., a capped floater) using the binomial model requires that the coupon rate be adjusted based on the 1-year rate (which is assumed to be the reference rate). Exhibit 60-21 shows the binomial tree and the relevant values at each node for a floater whose coupon rate is the 1-year rate flat (i.e., no margin over the reference rate) and in which there are no restrictions on the coupon rate.

What is important to recall about floaters is that the coupon rate is set at the beginning of the period but paid at the end of the period (i.e., beginning of the next period). That is, the coupon interest is paid in arrears. We discussed this feature of floaters at Level I.

The valuation procedure is identical to that for the other structures described above except that an adjustment is made for the characteristic of a floater that the coupon rate is set at the beginning of the year and paid in arrears. Here is how the payment in arrears characteristic affects the backward induction method. Look at the top node for year 2 in Exhibit 60-21. The coupon rate shown at that node is 7.0053% as determined by the 1-year rate at that node. Since the coupon payment will not be made until year 3 (i.e., paid in arrears), the value of 100 shown at the node is determined using the backward induction method but discounting the coupon rate shown at the node. For example, let's see how we get the value of 100 in the top box in year 2. The procedure is to calculate the average of the two present values of the bond value

EXHIBIT 60-21   Valuing a Floater with No Cap (10% Volatility Assumed)

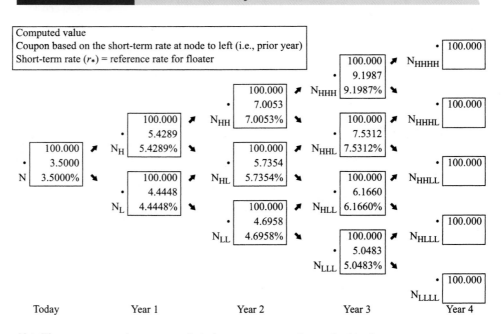

Note: The coupon rate shown at a node is the coupon rate to be received in the next year.

and coupon. Since the bond values and coupons are the same, the present value is simply:

$$\frac{100 + 7.0053}{1.070053} = 100$$

Suppose that the floater has a cap of 7.25%. Exhibit 60-22 shows how this floater would be valued. At each node where the 1-year rate exceeds 7.25%, a coupon of \$7.25 is substituted. The value of this capped floater is 99.724. Thus, the cost of the cap is the difference between par and 99.724. If the cap for this floater was 7.75% rather than 7.25%, it can be shown that the value of this floater would be 99.858. That is, the higher the cap, the closer the capped floater will trade to par.

Thus, it is important to emphasize that the valuation mechanics are being modified slightly only to reflect the characteristics of the floater's cash flow. All of the other principles regarding valuation of bonds with embedded options are the same. For a capped floater there is a rule for determining whether or not to override the cash flow at a node based on the cap. Since as explained at Level I a cap embedded in a floater is effectively an option granted by the investor to the issuer, it should be no surprise that the valuation model described in this chapter can be used to value a capped floater.

EXHIBIT 60-22	Valuing a Floating Rate Note with a 7.25% Cap (10% Volatility Assumed)

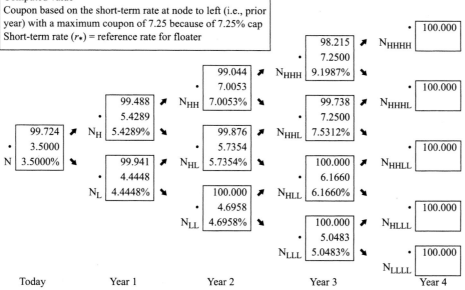

Computed value
Coupon based on the short-term rate at node to left (i.e., prior year) with a maximum coupon of 7.25 because of 7.25% cap
Short-term rate (r_*) = reference rate for floater

Note: The coupon rate shown at a node is the coupon rate to be received in the next year.

10   ANALYSIS OF CONVERTIBLE BONDS

A convertible bond is a security that can be converted into common stock at the option of the investor. Hence, it is a bond with an embedded option where the option is granted to the investor. Moreover, since a convertible bond may be callable and putable, it is a complex bond because the value of the bond will depend on both how interest rates change (which affects the value of the call and any put option) *and* how changes in the market price of the stock affects the value of the option to convert to common stock.

A. Basic Features of Convertible Securities

The conversion provision of a convertible security grants the securityholder the right to convert the security into a predetermined number of shares of common stock of the issuer. A convertible security is therefore a security with an embedded call option to buy the common stock of the issuer. An **exchangeable security** grants the securityholder the right to exchange the security for the common stock of a firm *other* than the issuer of the security. Throughout this reading we use the term convertible security to refer to both convertible and exchangeable securities.

In illustrating the calculation of the various concepts described below, we will use a hypothetical convertible bond issue. The issuer is the All Digital Component Corporation (ADC) 5¾% convertible issue due in 9+ years. Information about this hypothetical bond issue and the stock of this issuer is provided in Exhibit 60-23.

The number of shares of common stock that the securityholder will receive from exercising the call option of a convertible security is called the **conversion ratio**. The conversion privilege may extend for all or only some portion of the security's life, and the stated conversion ratio may change over time. It is always adjusted proportionately for stock splits and stock dividends. For the ADC convertible issue, the conversion ratio is 25.32 shares. This means that for each $1,000 of par value of this issue the securityholder exchanges for ADC common stock, he will receive 25.32 shares.

At the time of issuance of a convertible bond, the effective price at which the buyer of the convertible bond will pay for the stock can be determined as follows. The prospectus will specify the number of shares that the investor will receive by exchanging the bond for the common stock. The number of shares is called the **conversion ratio**. So, for example, assume the conversion ratio is 20. If the investor converts the bond for stock the investor will receive 20 shares of common stock. Now, suppose that the par value for the convertible bond is $1,000 and is sold to investors at issuance at that price. Then effectively by buying the convertible bond for $1,000 at issuance, investors are purchasing the common stock for $50 per share ($1,000/20 shares). This price is referred to in the prospectus as the **conversion price** and some investors refer to it as the **stated conversion price**. For a bond not issued at par (for example, a zero-coupon bond), the market or effective conversion price is determined by dividing the issue price per $1,000 of par value by the conversion ratio.

The ADC convertible was issued for $1,000 per $1,000 of par value and the conversion ratio is 25.32. Therefore, the conversion price at issuance for the ADC convertible issue is $39.49 ($1,000/25.32 shares).

Almost all convertible issues are callable. The ADC convertible issue has a non-call period of three years. The call price schedule for the ADC convertible issue is shown in Exhibit 60-23. There are some issues that have a provisional call feature that allows the issuer to call the issue during the non-call period if the price of the stock reaches a certain price.

Some convertible bonds are putable. Put options can be classified as "hard" puts and "soft" puts. A **hard put** is one in which the convertible security must be redeemed by the issuer for cash. In the case of a **soft put**, while the investor has the option to exercise the put, the *issuer* may select how the payment will be made. The issuer may redeem the convertible security for cash, common stock, subordinated notes, or a combination of the three.

EXHIBIT 60-23	Information about All Digital Component Corporation (ADC) 5¾% Convertible Bond Due in 9+ Years and Common Stock

Convertible bond

Current market price: $106.50   Maturity date: 9+ years

Non-call for 3 years

Call price schedule	
In Year 4	103.59
In Year 5	102.88
In Year 6	102.16
In Year 7	101.44
In Year 8	100.72
In Year 9	100.00
In Year 10	100.00

Coupon rate: 5¾%

Conversion ratio: 25.320 shares of ADC shares per $1,000 par value

Rating: A3/A−

ADC common stock

Expected volatility: 17%   Current dividend yield: 2.727%

Dividend per share: $0.90 per year   Stock price: $33

B. Traditional Analysis of Convertible Securities

Traditional analysis of convertible bonds relies on measures that do not attempt to directly value the embedded call, put, or common stock options. We present and illustrate these measures below and later discuss an option-based approach to valuation of convertible bonds.

1. Minimum Value of a Convertible Security

The **conversion value** or **parity value** of a convertible security is the value of the security if it is converted immediately.[8] That is,

conversion value = market price of common stock × conversion ratio

The minimum price of a convertible security is the greater of[9]

1. Its conversion value, or
2. Its value as a security without the conversion option—that is, based on the convertible security's cash flows if not converted (i.e., a plain vanilla security). This value is called its **straight value** or **investment value**. The straight value is found by using the valuation model described earlier in this chapter because almost all issues are callable.

If the convertible security does not sell for the greater of these two values, arbitrage profits could be realized. For example, suppose the conversion value is greater than the straight value, and the security trades at its straight value. An investor can buy the convertible security at the straight value and immediately convert it. By doing so, the investor realizes a gain equal to the difference between the conversion value and the straight value. Suppose, instead, the straight value is greater than the conversion value, and the security trades at its conversion value. By buying the convertible at the conversion value, the investor will realize a higher yield than a comparable straight security.

Consider the ADC convertible issue. Suppose that the straight value of the bond is $98.19 per $100 of par value. Since the market price per share of common stock is $33, the conversion value per $1,000 of par value is:

conversion value = $33 × 25.32 = $835.56

Consequently, the conversion value is 83.556% of par value. Per $100 of par value the conversion value is $83.556. Since the straight value is $98.19 and the conversion value is $83.556, the minimum value for the ADC convertible has to be $98.19.

2. Market Conversion Price

The price that an investor effectively pays for the common stock if the convertible bond is purchased and then converted into the common stock is called the **market conversion price** or **conversion parity price**. It is found as follows:

$$\text{market conversion price} = \frac{\text{market price of convertible security}}{\text{conversion ratio}}$$

---

[8] Technically, the standard textbook definition of conversion value given here is theoretically incorrect because as bondholders convert, the price of the stock will decline. The theoretically correct definition for the conversion value is that it is the product of the conversion ratio and the stock price *after* conversion.

[9] If the conversion value is the greater of the two values, it is possible for the convertible bond to trade below the conversion value. This can occur for the following reasons: (1) there are restrictions that prevent the investor from converting, (2) the underlying stock is illiquid, and (3) an anticipated forced conversion will result in loss of accrued interest of a high coupon issue. See, Mihir Bhattacharya, "Convertible Securities and Their Valuation," Chapter 51 in Frank J. Fabozzi (ed.), *The Handbook of Fixed Income Securities: Sixth Edition* (New York: McGraw Hill, 2001), p. 1128.

The market conversion price is a useful benchmark because once the actual market price of the stock rises above the market conversion price, any further stock price increase is certain to increase the value of the convertible bond by at least the same percentage. Therefore, the market conversion price can be viewed as a break-even price.

An investor who purchases a convertible bond rather than the underlying stock, effectively pays a premium over the current market price of the stock. This premium per share is equal to the difference between the market conversion price and the current market price of the common stock. That is,

$$\text{market conversion premium per share} = \text{market conversion price} - \text{current market price}$$

The market conversion premium per share is usually expressed as a percentage of the current market price as follows:

$$\text{market conversion premium ratio} = \frac{\text{market conversion premium per share}}{\text{market price of common stock}}$$

Why would someone be willing to pay a premium to buy the stock? Recall that the minimum price of a convertible security is the greater of its conversion value or its straight value. Thus, as the common stock price declines, the price of the convertible bond will not fall below its straight value. The straight value therefore acts as a floor for the convertible security's price. However, it is a moving floor as the straight value will change with changes in interest rates.

Viewed in this context, the market conversion premium per share can be seen as the price of a call option. The buyer of a call option limits the downside risk to the option price. In the case of a convertible bond, for a premium, the securityholder limits the downside risk to the straight value of the bond. The difference between the buyer of a call option and the buyer of a convertible bond is that the former knows precisely the dollar amount of the downside risk, while the latter knows only that the most that can be lost is the difference between the convertible bond's price and the straight value. The straight value at some future date, however, is unknown; the value will change as market interest rates change or if the issuer's credit quality changes.

The calculation of the market conversion price, market conversion premium per share, and market conversion premium ratio for the ADC convertible issue is shown below:

$$\text{market conversion price} = \frac{\$1,065}{25.32} = \$42.06$$

Thus, if the investor purchased the convertible and then converted it to common stock, the effective price that the investor paid per share is $42.06.

$$\text{market conversion premium per share} = \$42.06 - \$33 = \$9.06$$

The investor is effectively paying a premium per share of $9.06 by buying the convertible rather than buying the stock for $33.

$$\text{market conversion premium ratio} = \frac{\$9.06}{\$33} = 0.275 = 27.5\%$$

The premium per share of $9.06 means that the investor is paying 27.5% above the market price of $33 by buying the convertible.

3. Current Income of Convertible Bond versus Common Stock

As an offset to the market conversion premium per share, investing in the convertible bond rather than buying the stock directly, generally means that the investor realizes higher current income from the coupon interest from a convertible bond than would be received from common stock dividends based on the number of shares equal to the conversion ratio. Analysts evaluating a convertible bond typically compute the time it takes to recover the premium per share by computing the **premium payback period** (which is also known as the **break-even time**). This is computed as follows:

$$\text{premium payback period} = \frac{\text{market conversion premium per share}}{\text{favorable income differential per share}}$$

where the favorable income differential per share is equal to the following:

$$\frac{\text{coupon interest} - (\text{conversion ratio} \times \text{common stock dividend per share})}{\text{conversion ratio}}$$

The numerator of the formula is the difference between the coupon interest for the issue and the dividends that would be received if the investor converted the issue into common stock. Since the investor would receive the number of shares specified by the conversion ratio, then multiplying the conversion ratio by the dividend per share of common stock gives the total dividends that would be received if the investor converted. Dividing the difference between the coupon interest and the total dividends that would be received if the issue is converted by the conversion ratio gives the favorable income differential on a per share basis by owning the convertible rather than the common stock or changes in the dividend over the period.

Notice that the premium payback period does *not* take into account the time value of money or changes in the dividend over the period.

For the ADC convertible issue, the market conversion premium per share is $9.06. The favorable income differential per share is found as follows:

coupon interest from bond = 0.0575 × $1,000 = $57.50
conversion ratio × dividend per share = 25.32 × $0.90 = $22.79

Therefore,

$$\text{favorable income differential per share} = \frac{\$57.50 - \$22.79}{25.32} = \$1.37$$

and

$$\text{premium payback period} = \frac{\$9.06}{\$1.37} = 6.6 \text{ years}$$

Without considering the time value of money, the investor would recover the market conversion premium per share assuming unchanged dividends in about 6.6 years.

4. Downside Risk with a Convertible Bond

Unfortunately, investors usually use the straight value as a measure of the downside risk of a convertible security, because it is assumed that the price of the convertible cannot fall below this value. Thus, some investors view the straight value as the floor for the price of the convertible bond. The downside risk is measured as a percentage of the straight value and computed as follows:

$$\text{premium over straight value} = \frac{\text{market price of convertible bond}}{\text{straight value}} - 1$$

The higher the premium over straight value, all other factors constant, the less attractive the convertible bond.

Despite its use in practice, this measure of downside risk is flawed because the straight value (the floor) changes as interest rates change. If interest rates rise (fall), the straight value falls (rises) making the floor fall (rise). Therefore, the downside risk changes as interest rates change.

For the ADC convertible issue, since the market price of the convertible issue is 106.5 and the straight value is 98.19, the premium over straight value is

$$\text{premium over straight value} = \frac{\$106.50}{\$98.19} - 1 = 0.085 = 8.5\%$$

5. *The Upside Potential of a Convertible Security*

The evaluation of the upside potential of a convertible security depends on the prospects for the underlying common stock. Thus, the techniques for analyzing common stocks discussed in books on equity analysis should be employed.

C. Investment Characteristics of a Convertible Security

The investment characteristics of a convertible bond depend on the common stock price. If the price is low, so that the straight value is considerably higher than the conversion value, the security will trade much like a straight security. The convertible security in such instances is referred to as a **fixed income equivalent** or a **busted convertible**.

When the price of the stock is such that the conversion value is considerably higher than the straight value, then the convertible security will trade as if it were an equity instrument; in this case it is said to be a **common stock equivalent**. In such cases, the market conversion premium per share will be small.

Between these two cases, fixed income equivalent and common stock equivalent, the convertible security trades as a **hybrid security**, having the characteristics of both a fixed income security and a common stock instrument.

D. An Option-Based Valuation Approach

In our discussion of convertible bonds, we did not address the following questions:

1. What is a fair value for the conversion premium per share?

2. How do we handle convertible bonds with call and/or put options?

3. How does a change in interest rates affect the stock price?

Consider first a noncallable/nonputable convertible bond. The investor who purchases this security would be effectively entering into two separate transactions: (1) buying a noncallable/nonputable straight security and (2) buying a call option (or warrant) on the stock, where the number of shares that can be purchased with the call option is equal to the conversion ratio.

The question is: What is the fair value for the call option? The fair value depends on the factors that affect the price of a call option. One key factor is the expected price volatility of the stock: the higher the expected price volatility, the greater the value of the call option. The theoretical value of a call option can be valued using the **Black-Scholes option pricing model**. This model will be discussed in Reading 66 and is explained in more detail in investment textbooks. As a first approximation to the value of a convertible bond, the formula would be:

convertible security value = straight value + value of the call option on the stock

The value of the call option is added to the straight value because the investor has purchased a call option on the stock.

Now let's add in a common feature of a convertible bond: the issuer's right to call the issue. Therefore, the value of a convertible bond that is callable is equal to:

convertible bond value = straight value + value of the call option on the stock
− value of the call option on the bond

Consequently, the analysis of convertible bonds must take into account the value of the issuer's right to call. This depends, in turn, on (1) future interest rate volatility and (2) economic factors that determine whether or not it is optimal for the issuer to call the security. The Black-Scholes option pricing model cannot handle this situation.

Let's add one more wrinkle. Suppose that the callable convertible bond is also putable. Then the value of such a convertible would be equal to:

convertible bond value = straight value + value of the call option on the stock
− value of the call option on the bond
+ value of the put option on the bond

To link interest rates and stock prices together (the third question we raise on the previous page), statistical analysis of historical movements of these two variables must be estimated and incorporated into the model.

Valuation models based on an option pricing approach have been suggested by several researchers.[10] These models can generally be classified as one-factor or multi-factor models. By "factor" we mean the stochastic (i.e., random) variables that are assumed to drive the value of a convertible or bond. The obvious candidates for factors are the price movement of the underlying common stock and the movement of interest rates. According to Mihir Bhattacharya and Yu Zhu, the most widely used convertible valuation model has been the one-factor model and the factor is the price movement of the underlying common stock.[11]

---

[10]See, for example: Michael Brennan and Eduardo Schwartz, "Convertible Bonds: Valuation and Optimal Strategies for Call and Conversion," *Journal of Finance* (December 1977), pp. 1699–1715; Jonathan Ingersoll, "A Contingent-Claims Valuation of Convertible Securities," *Journal of Financial Economics* (May 1977), pp. 289–322; Michael Brennan and Eduardo Schwartz, "Analyzing Convertible Bonds," *Journal of Financial and Quantitative Analysis* (November 1980), pp. 907–929; and, George Constantinides, "Warrant Exercise and Bond Conversion in Competitive Markets," *Journal of Financial Economics* (September 1984), pp. 371–398.

[11]Mihir Bhattacharya and Yu Zhu, "Valuation and Analysis of Convertible Securities," Chapter 42 in Frank J. Fabozzi (ed.), *The Handbook of Fixed Income Securities: Fifth Edition* (Chicago: Irwin Professional Publishing, 1997).

E. The Risk/Return Profile of a Convertible Security

Let's use the ADC convertible issue and the valuation model to look at the risk/return profile by investing in a convertible issue or the underlying common stock.

Suppose an investor is considering the purchase of either the common stock of ADC or the convertible issue. The stock can be purchased in the market for $33. By buying the convertible bond, the investor is effectively purchasing the stock for $42.06 (the market conversion price per share). Exhibit 60-24 shows the total return for both alternatives one year later assuming (1) the stock price does not change, (2) it changes by ±10%, and (3) it changes by ±25%. The convertible's theoretical value is based on some valuation model not discussed here.

If the ADC's stock price is unchanged, the stock position will underperform the convertible position despite the fact that a premium was paid to purchase the stock by acquiring the convertible issue. The reason is that even though the convertible's theoretical value decreased, the income from coupon more than compensates for the capital loss. In the two scenarios where the price of ADC stock declines, the convertible position outperforms the stock position because the straight value provides a floor for the convertible.

One of the critical assumptions in this analysis is that the straight value does not change except for the passage of time. If interest rates rise, the straight value will decline. Even if interest rates do not rise, the perceived creditworthiness of the issuer may deteriorate, causing investors to demand a higher yield. The illustration clearly demonstrates that there are benefits and drawbacks of investing in convertible securities. The disadvantage is the upside potential give-up because a premium per share must be paid. An advantage is the reduction in downside risk (as determined by the straight value).

Keep in mind that the major reason for the acquisition of the convertible bond is the potential price appreciation due to the increase in the price of the stock. An analysis of the growth prospects of the issuer's earnings and stock price is beyond the scope of this book but is described in all books on equity analysis.

EXHIBIT 60-24	**Comparison of 1-Year Return for ADC Stock and Convertible Issue for Assumed Changes in Stock Price**

Beginning of horizon: October 7, 1993

End of horizon: October 7, 1994

Price of ADC stock on October 7, 1993: $33.00

Assumed volatility of ADC stock return: 17%

Stock price change (%)	GSX stock return (%)	Convertible's theoretical value	Convertible's return (%)
−25	−22.27	100.47	−0.26
−10	−7.27	102.96	2.08
0	2.73	105.27	4.24
10	12.73	108.12	6.92
25	27.73	113.74	12.20

SUMMARY

▶ The potential benchmark interest rates that can be used in bond valuation are those in the Treasury market, a specific bond sector with a given credit rating, or a specific issuer.

▶ Benchmark interest rates can be based on either an estimated yield curve or an estimated spot rate curve.

▶ Yield spread measures are used in assessing the relative value of securities.

▶ Relative value analysis is used to identify securities as being overpriced ("rich"), underpriced ("cheap"), or fairly priced relative to benchmark interest rates.

▶ The interpretation of a spread measure depends on the benchmark used.

▶ The option-adjusted spread is a spread after adjusting for the option risk.

▶ Depending on the benchmark interest rates used to generate the interest rate tree, the option-adjusted spread may or may not capture credit risk.

▶ The option-adjusted spread is not a spread off of one maturity of the benchmark interest rates; rather, it is a spread over the forward rates in the interest rate tree that were constructed from the benchmark interest rates.

▶ A valuation model must produce arbitrage-free values; that is, a valuation model must produce a value for each on-the-run issue that is equal to its observed market price.

▶ There are several arbitrage-free models that can be used to value bonds with embedded options but they all follow the same principle—they generate a tree of interest rates based on some interest rate volatility assumption, they require rules for determining when any of the embedded options will be exercised, and they employ the backward induction methodology.

▶ A valuation model involves generating an interest rate tree based on (1) benchmark interest rates, (2) an assumed interest rate model, and (3) an assumed interest rate volatility.

▶ The assumed volatility of interest rates incorporates the uncertainty about future interest rates into the analysis.

▶ The interest rate tree is constructed using a process that is similar to bootstrapping but requires an iterative procedure to determine the interest rates that will produce a value for the on-the-run issues equal to their market value.

▶ At each node of the tree there are interest rates and these rates are effectively forward rates; thus, there is a set of forward rates for each year.

▶ Using the interest rate tree the arbitrage-free value of any bond can be determined.

▶ In valuing a callable bond using the interest rate tree, the cash flows at a node are modified to take into account the call option.

▶ The value of the embedded call option is the difference between the value of an option-free bond and the value of the callable bond.

▶ The volatility assumption has an important impact on the arbitrage-free value.

▶ The option-adjusted spread is the constant spread that when added to the short rates in the binomial interest rate tree will produce a valuation for the bond (i.e., arbitrage-free value) equal to the market price of the bond.

► The interpretation of the OAS, or equivalently, what the OAS is compensating an investor for, depends on what benchmark interest rates are used.

► The required values for calculating effective duration and effective convexity are found by shifting the on-the-run yield curve, calculating a new binomial interest rate tree, and then determining the required values after adjusting the tree by adding the OAS to each short rate.

► For a bond with any embedded option or options, application of the binomial model requires that the value at each node of the tree be adjusted based on whether or not the option will be exercised; the binomial model can be used to value bonds with multiple or interrelated embedded options by determining at each node of the tree whether or not one of the options will be exercised.

► With a putable bond, the option will be exercised if the value at a node is less than the price at which the bondholder can put the bond to the issuer.

► The value of a putable bond is greater than the value of an otherwise option-free bond.

► The binomial model can be used to value a single step-up callable note or a multiple step-up callable note.

► To value a floating-rate note that has a cap, the coupon at each node of the tree is adjusted by determining whether or not the cap is reached at a node; if the rate at a node does exceed the cap, the rate at the node is the capped rate rather than the rate determined by the floater's coupon formula.

► For a floating-rate note, the binomial method must be adjusted to account for the fact that a floater pays in arrears; that is, the coupon payment is determined in a period but not paid until the next period.

► Convertible and exchangeable securities can be converted into shares of common stock.

► The conversion ratio is the number of common stock shares for which a convertible security may be converted.

► Almost all convertible securities are callable and some are putable.

► The conversion value is the value of the convertible bond if it is immediately converted into the common stock.

► The market conversion price is the price that an investor effectively pays for the common stock if the convertible security is purchased and then converted into the common stock.

► The premium paid for the common stock is measured by the market conversion premium per share and market conversion premium ratio.

► The straight value or investment value of a convertible security is its value if there was no conversion feature.

► The minimum value of a convertible security is the greater of the conversion value and the straight value.

► A fixed income equivalent (or a busted convertible) refers to the situation where the straight value is considerably higher than the conversion value so that the security will trade much like a straight security.

► A common stock equivalent refers to the situation where the conversion value is considerably higher than the straight value so that the convertible security trades as if it were an equity instrument.

► A hybrid equivalent refers to the situation where the convertible security trades with characteristics of both a fixed income security and a common stock instrument.

► While the downside risk of a convertible security usually is estimated by calculating the premium over straight value, the limitation of this measure is that the straight value (the floor) changes as interest rates change.

► An advantage of buying the convertible rather than the common stock is the reduction in downside risk.

► The disadvantage of a convertible relative to the straight purchase of the common stock is the upside potential give-up because a premium per share must be paid.

► An option-based valuation model is a more appropriate approach to value convertible securities than the traditional approach because it can handle multiple embedded options.

► There are various option-based valuation models: one-factor and multiple-factor models.

► The most common convertible bond valuation model is the one-factor model in which the one factor is the stock price movement.

PROBLEMS FOR READING 60

1. Comment on the following statement:

"There are several arbitrage-free models for valuing callable bonds. These models differ significantly in terms of how interest rates may change in the next period. There are models that allow the rate in the next period to take on only one of two values. Such a model is called a binomial model. There are models that allow the rate in the next period to take on more than two possible values. For example, there is model that allows the rate in the next period to take on three possible values. Such a model is called a trinomial model. All these models represent a significantly different approach to valuation and involve different procedures for obtaining the arbitrage-free value."

2. Why is the procedure for valuing a bond with an embedded option called "backward induction"?

3. Why is the value produced by a binomial model and any similar models referred to as an "arbitrage-free value"?

4. A. When valuing an option-free bond, short-term forward rates can be used. When valuing a bond with an embedded option, there is not one forward rate for a period but a set of forward rates for a given period. Explain why.

   B. Explain why the set of forward rates for a given period depend on the assumed interest rate volatility.

5. The on-the-run issue for the Inc.Net Company is shown below:

Maturity (years)	Yield to maturity (%)	Market price
1	7.5	100
2	7.6	100
3	7.7	100

Using the bootstrapping methodology, the spot rates are:

Maturity (years)	Spot rate (%)
1	7.500
2	7.604
3	7.710

Assuming an interest rate volatility of 10% for the 1-year rate, the binomial interest rate tree for valuing a bond with a maturity of up to three years is shown below:

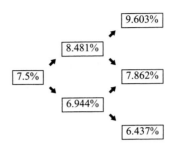

A. Demonstrate using the 2-year on-the-run issue that the binomial interest rate tree above is in fact an arbitrage-free tree.

B. Demonstrate using the 3-year on-the-run issue that the binomial interest rate tree above is in fact an arbitrage-free tree.

C. Using the spot rates given above, what is the arbitrage-free value of a 3-year 8.5% coupon issue of Inc.Net Company?

D. Using the binomial tree, determine the value of an 8.5% 3-year option-free bond.

E. Suppose that the 3-year 8.5% coupon issue is callable starting in Year 1 at par (100) (that is, the call price is 100). Also assume that the following call rule is used: if the price exceeds 100 the issue will be called. What is the value of this 3-year 8.5% coupon callable issue?

F. What is the value of the embedded call option for the 3-year 8.5% coupon callable issue?

6. In discussing the approach taken by its investment management firm in valuing bonds, a representative of the firm made the following statement:

> "Our managers avoid the use of valuation methodologies such as the binomial model or other fancier models because of the many assumptions required to determine the value. Instead, our managers are firm believers in the concept of option-adjusted spread."

Comment on this statement.

7. A portfolio manager must mark a bond position to market. One issue, a callable issue, has not traded in the market recently. So to obtain a price that can be used to mark a position to market, the manager requested a bid from a dealer and a value from a pricing service. The dealer bid's price was 92. The pricing service indicated a bid price of 93 would be a fair value. The manager could not understand the reason for the 1 point difference in the bid prices.

Upon questioning the trader at the dealer firm that gave a bid of 92, the manager found that the trader based the price on the dealer's valuation model. The model used is the binomial model and the benchmark interest rates the model uses are the on-the-run Treasury issues. The manager then contacted a representative from the pricing service and asked what type of valuation model it used. Again, the response was that the binomial model is used and that the on-the-run Treasury issues are used as the benchmark interest rates.

The manager is puzzled why there is a 1 point difference even though the dealer and the pricing service used the same model and the same benchmark interest rates. The manager has asked you to explain why. Provide an explanation to the manager.

8. The manager of an emerging market bond portfolio is approached by a broker about purchasing a new corporate bond issue in Brazil. The issue is callable and the broker's firm estimates that the option-adjusted spread is 220 basis points. What questions would you ask the broker with respect to the 220 basis points OAS?

9. In explaining the option-adjusted spread to a client, a manager stated the following: "The option-adjusted spread measures the yield spread using the Treasury on-the-run yield curve as benchmark interest rates." Comment on this statement.

10. **A.** Explain why the greater the assumed interest rate volatility the lower the value of a callable bond?

    B. Explain why the greater the assumed interest rate volatility the higher the value of a putable bond?

11. An assistant portfolio manager described the process for valuing a bond that is both callable and putable using the binomial model as follows:

    "The process begins by first valuing one of the embedded options, say the call option. Then the model is used to value the put option. The value of the corresponding option-free bond is then computed. Given the value of the call option, the value of the put option, and the value of the option-free bond, the value of the bond that is callable and putable is found by adding to the value of the option-free bond the value of the put option and then subtracting the value of the call option."

    Explain why you agree or disagree with this assistant portfolio manager's description of the process for valuing a bond that is both callable and putable.

12. Explain why, when the binomial model is used to obtain the values to be used in the formula for computing duration and convexity, the measures computed are an effective duration and effective convexity.

13. An assistant portfolio manager is trying to find the duration of a callable bond of FeedCo Corp. One vendor of analytical systems reported the duration for the issue is 5.4. A dealer firm reported that the duration is 4.5. The assistant portfolio manager was confused by the difference in the reported durations for the FeedCo Corp. issue. He discussed the situation with the senior portfolio manager. In the discussion, the assistant portfolio manager commented: "I don't understand how such a difference could occur. After all, there is a standard formula for computing any duration." How should the senior portfolio manager respond?

14. In computing the effective duration and convexity of a bond with an embedded option, what assumption is made about the option-adjusted spread when rates change?

15. Four portfolio managers are discussing the meaning of option-adjusted spread. Here is what each asserted:

    Manager 1: "The option-adjusted spread is a measure of the value of the option embedded in the bond. That is, it is the compensation for accepting option risk."

Manager 2: "The option-adjusted spread is a measure of the spread relative to the Treasury on-the-run yield curve and reflects compensation for credit risk."

Manager 3: "The option-adjusted spread is a measure of the spread relative to the Treasury on-the-run yield curve and reflects compensation for credit risk and liquidity risk."

Manager 4: "The option-adjusted spread is a measure of the spread relative to the issuer's on-the-run yield curve and reflects compensation for credit risk and liquidity risk."

Comment on each manager's interpretation of OAS.

16. Suppose that a callable bond is valued using as the benchmark interest rates the on-the-run yield curve of the issuer and that the yield for the 10-year issue is 6%. Suppose further that the option-adjusted spread computed for a 10-year callable bond of this issuer is 20 basis points. Is it proper to interpret the OAS as meaning that the 10-year callable bond is offering a spread of 20 basis point over the 6% yield on the 10-year on-the run-issue? If not, what is the proper interpretation of the 20 basis point OAS?

17. Suppose that a callable bond has an option-adjusted spread of zero. Does that mean the corporate bond is being overvalued in the market (i.e., trading rich)?

18. In valuing a floating rate note, it is necessary to make a modification to the backward induction method.

A. Why is the adjustment necessary?

B. What adjustment is made?

C. If the floating rate note has a cap, how is that handled by the backward induction method?

19. A. In what sense does convertible bond typically have multiple embedded options?

B. Why is it complicated to value a covertible bond?

20. In the October 26, 1992 prospectus summary of The Staples 5% convertible subordinated debentures due 1999 the offering stated: "Convertible into Common Stock at a conversion price of $45 per share..." Since the par value is $1,000, what is the conversion ratio?

21. Consider the convertible bond by Miser Electronics:

par value = $1,000
coupon rate = 8.5%
market price of convertible bond = $900
conversion ratio = 30
estimated straight value of bond = $700
Assume that the price of Miser Electronics common stock is $25 and that the dividend per share is $1 per annum.

Calculate each of the following:

A. conversion value

B. market conversion price

C. conversion premium per share

D. conversion premium ratio

E. premium over straight value

F. yield advantage of bond

G. premium payback period

22. Suppose that the price of the common stock of Miser Electronics whose convertible bond was described in the previous question increases from $25 to $54.

   A. What will be the approximate return realized from investing in the convertible bond if an investor had purchased the convertible for $900?

   B. What would be the return realized if $25 had been invested in the common stock?

   C. Why would the return be higher by investing in the common stock directly rather than by investng in the convertible bond?

23. Suppose that the price of the common stock declines from $25 to $10.

   A. What will be the approximate return realized from investing in the convertible bond if an investor had purchased the convertible for $900 *and* the straight value does not change?

   B. What would be the return realized if $25 had been invested in the common stock?

   C. Why would the return be higher by investing in the convertible bond rather than by investing in the common stock directly?

24. The following excerpt is taken from an article entitled "Caywood Looks for Convertibles," that appeared in the January 13, 1992 issue of *BondWeek*, p. 7:

   > Caywood Christian Capital Management will invest new money in its $400 million high-yield portfolio in "busted convertibles," double- and triple-B rated convertible bonds of companies whose stock..., said James Caywood, CEO. Caywood likes these convertibles as they trade at discounts and are unlikely to be called, he said.

   A. What is a "busted convertible"?

   B. What is the premium over straight value that these bonds would trade?

   C. Why does Mr. Caywood seek convertibles with higher investment grade ratings?

   D. Why is Mr. Caywood interested in **call protection**?

25. Explain the limitation of using premium over straight value as a measure of the downside risk of a convertible bond?

26. **A.** The valuation of a convertible bond using an options approach requires a two-factor model. What is meant by a two-factor model and what are the factors?

   B. In practice, is a two-factor model used to value a convertible bond?

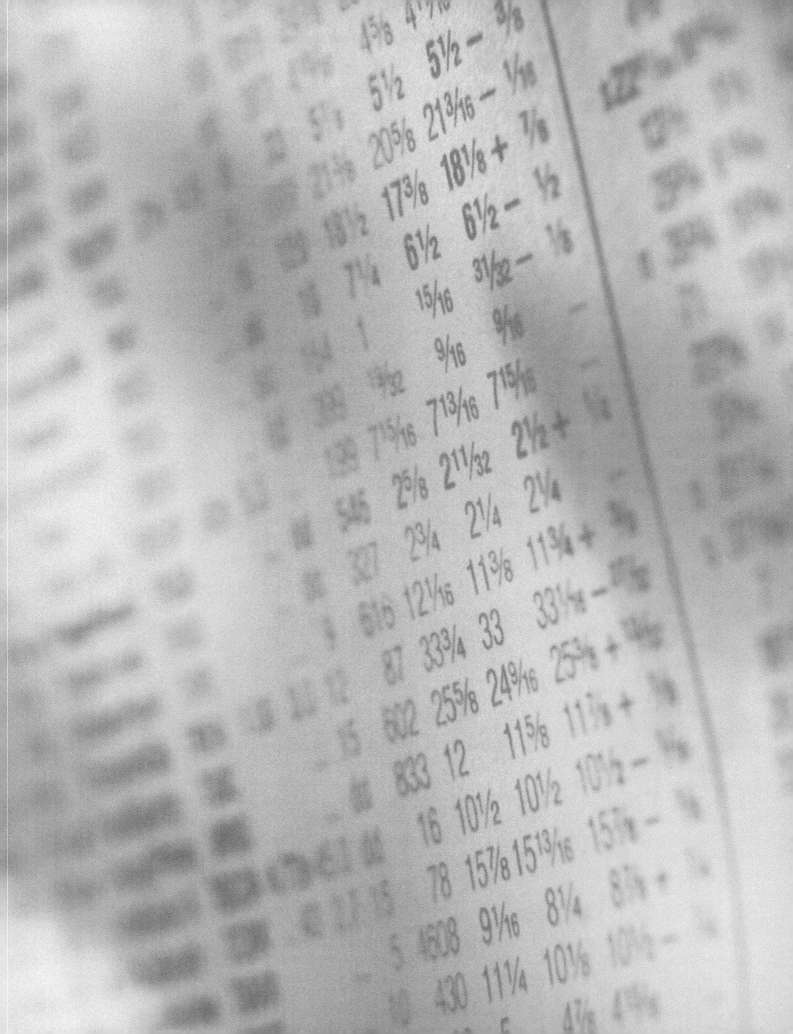

STUDY SESSION 15
FIXED INCOME INVESTMENTS:
Structured Securities

READING ASSIGNMENTS

Reading 61 Mortgage-Backed Sector of the Bond Market
Reading 62 Asset-Backed Sector of the Bond Market
Reading 63 Valuing Mortgage-Backed and Asset-Backed Securities

This study session provides information on the knowledge and skills needed for valuing a unique but growing segment of the fixed income market—structured securities. It begins with an in-depth study of the structure and characteristics of the mortgage-backed and asset-backed markets and securities and concludes with a study of the key valuation tools and techniques for these fixed income instruments.

LEARNING OUTCOMES

Reading 61: Mortgage-Backed Sector of the Bond Market
The candidate should be able to:

a. describe a mortgage loan and illustrate the cash flow characteristics of a fixed-rate, level payment, fully amortized mortgage loan;

b. describe prepayments and how they result in prepayment risk;

c. illustrate the investment characteristics of mortgage passthrough securities;

d. calculate the prepayment amount for a month, given the single monthly mortality rate;

e. compare and contrast the conditional prepayment rate (CPR) to the Public Securities Association (PSA) prepayment benchmark;

f. explain why the average life of a mortgage-backed security is a more relevant measure than the security's maturity;

g. explain the factors that affect prepayments;

h. explain contraction and extension prepayment risks and why they occur;

i. illustrate how a collateralized mortgage obligation (CMO) is created and how it provides a better matching of assets and liabilities for institutional investors;

j. distinguish among the sequential pay tranche, the accrual tranche, the planned amortization class tranche, and the support tranche in a CMO with respect to the risk characteristics and the relative performance of each, given changes in the interest rate environment;

k. explain the investment characteristics of stripped mortgage-backed securities (i.e., principal-only mortgage strips and interest-only mortgage strips);

l. compare and contrast agency and nonagency mortgage-backed securities;

m. distinguish credit risk analysis of commercial mortgage-backed securities from credit risk analysis of residential nonagency mortgage-backed securities;

n. describe the basic structure of a CMBS, and illustrate the ways in which a CMBS investor may realize call protection at the loan level and by means of the CMBS structure.

Reading 62: Asset-Backed Sector of the Bond Market
The candidate should be able to:

a. illustrate the basic structural features of and parties to a securitization transaction;

b. explain prepayment tranching and credit tranching;

c. distinguish between the payment structure and collateral structure of a securitization backed by amortizing assets and non-amortizing assets;

d. distinguish among the various types of external and internal credit enhancements;

e. describe the cash flow and prepayment characteristics for securities backed by home equity loans, manufactured housing loans, automobile loans, student loans, SBA loans and credit card receivables;

f. describe a collateralized debt obligation (CDO) and the different types (cash and synthetic);

g. distinguish among the primary motivations for creating a collateralized debt obligation (arbitrage and balance sheet transactions).

Reading 63: Valuing Mortgage-Backed and Asset-Backed Securities
The candidate should be able to:

a. illustrate the computation, use, and limitations of the cash flow yield, nominal spread, and zero-volatility spread for a mortgage-backed security and an asset-backed security;

b. describe the Monte Carlo simulation model for valuing a mortgage-backed security;

c. describe path dependency in passthrough securities and the implications for valuation models;

d. illustrate how the option-adjusted spread is computed using the Monte Carlo simulation model and how this spread measure is interpreted;

e. evaluate whether mortgage-backed securities are rich or cheap, using option-adjusted spread analysis;

f. illustrate how effective duration is computed using the Monte Carlo simulation model;

g. discuss why the effective durations reported by various dealers and vendors may differ;

h. analyze the interest rate risk of a security given the security's effective duration and effective convexity;

i. explain other measures of duration used by practitioners in the mortgage-backed market (e.g., cash flow duration, coupon curve duration, and empirical duration), and describe the limitations of these duration measures;

j. determine whether the nominal spread, zero-volatility spread, or the option-adjusted spread should be used to evaluate a specific fixed income security.

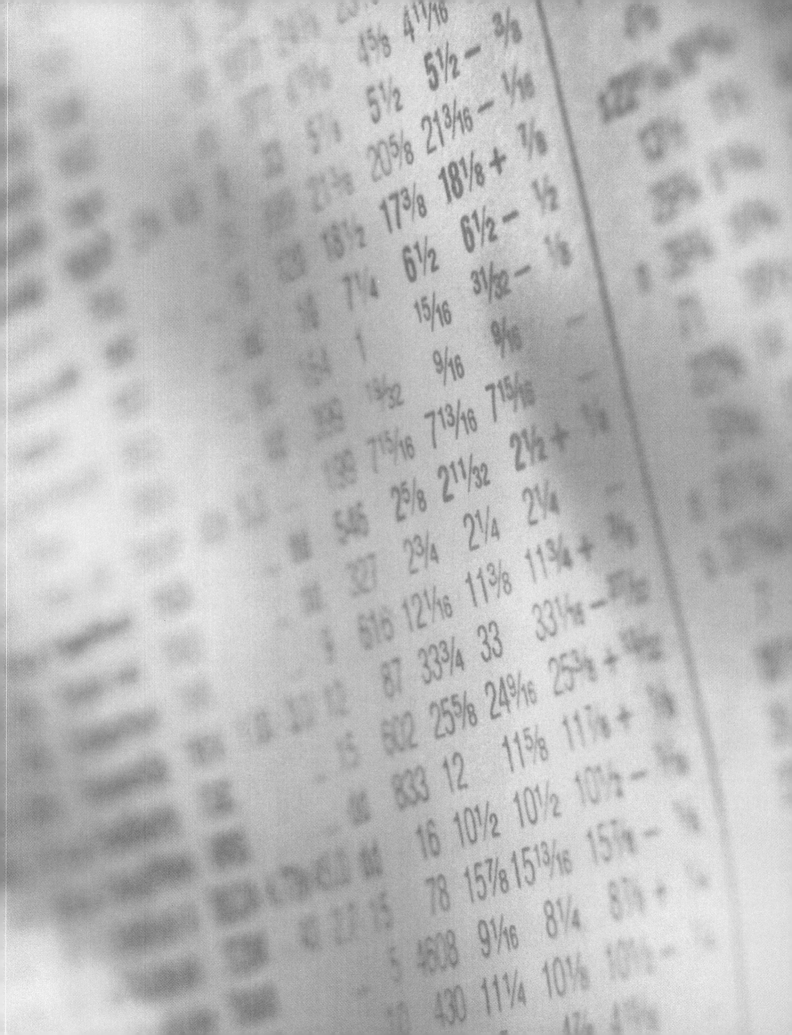

MORTGAGE-BACKED SECTOR OF THE BOND MARKET
by Frank J. Fabozzi

LEARNING OUTCOMES

The candidate should be able to:

a. describe a mortgage loan and illustrate the cash flow characteristics of a fixed-rate, level payment, fully amortized mortgage loan;

b. describe prepayments and how they result in prepayment risk;

c. illustrate the investment characteristics of mortgage passthrough securities;

d. calculate the prepayment amount for a month, given the single monthly mortality rate;

e. compare and contrast the conditional prepayment rate (CPR) to the Public Securities Association (PSA) prepayment benchmark;

f. explain why the average life of a mortgage-backed security is a more relevant measure than the security's maturity;

g. explain the factors that affect prepayments;

h. explain contraction and extension prepayment risks and why they occur;

i. illustrate how a collateralized mortgage obligation (CMO) is created and how it provides a better matching of assets and liabilities for institutional investors;

j. distinguish among the sequential pay tranche, the accrual tranche, the planned amortization class tranche, and the support tranche in a CMO with respect to the risk characteristics and the relative performance of each, given changes in the interest rate environment;

k. explain the investment characteristics of stripped mortgage-backed securities (i.e., principal-only mortgage strips and interest-only mortgage strips);

l. compare and contrast agency and nonagency mortgage-backed securities;

m. distinguish credit risk analysis of commercial mortgage-backed securities from credit risk analysis of residential nonagency mortgage-backed securities;

n. describe the basic structure of a CMBS, and illustrate the ways in which a CMBS investor may realize call protection at the loan level and by means of the CMBS structure.

Fixed Income Analysis for the Chartered Financial Analyst® Program, Second Edition, edited by Frank J. Fabozzi, Copyright © 2005 by CFA Institute. Reprinted with permission.

INTRODUCTION

In this reading and the next we will discuss securities backed by a pool of loans or receivables—mortgage-backed securities and asset-backed securities. We described these securities briefly at Level I. The mortgage-backed securities sector, simply referred to as the **mortgage sector** of the bond market, includes securities backed by a pool of mortgage loans. There are securities backed by residential mortgage loans, referred to as **residential mortgage-backed securities**, and securities backed by commercial loans, referred to as **commercial mortgage-backed securities**.

In the United States, the securities backed by residential mortgage loans are divided into two sectors: (1) those issued by federal agencies (one federally related institution and two government sponsored enterprises) and (2) those issued by private entities. The former securities are called **agency mortgage-backed securities** and the latter **nonagency mortgage-backed securities**.

Securities backed by loans other than traditional residential mortgage loans or commercial mortgage loans and backed by receivables are referred to as **asset-backed securities**. There is a long and growing list of loans and receivables that have been used as collateral for these securities. Together, mortgage-backed securities and asset-backed securities are referred to as **structured financial products**.

It is important to understand the classification of these sectors in terms of bond market indexes. A popular bond market index, the Lehman Aggregate Bond Index, has a sector that it refers to as the "mortgage passthrough sector." Within the "mortgage passthrough sector," Lehman Brothers includes only agency mortgage-backed securities that are mortgage passthrough securities. To understand why it is essential to understand this sector, consider that the "mortgage passthrough sector" represents more than one third of the Lehman Aggregate Bond Index. It is the largest sector in the bond market index. The commercial mortgage-backed securities sector represents about 2% of the bond market index. The mortgage sector of the Lehman Aggregate Bond Index includes the mortgage passthrough sector and the commercial mortgage-backed securities.

In this reading, our focus will be on the mortgage sector. Although many countries have developed a mortgage-backed securities sector, our focus in this reading is the U.S. mortgage sector because of its size and it important role in U.S. bond market indexes. Credit risk does not exist for agency mortgage-backed securities issued by a federally related institution and is viewed as minimal for securities issued by government sponsored enterprises. The significant risk is prepayment risk and there are ways to redistribute prepayment risk among the different bond classes created. Historically, it is important to note that the agency mortgage-backed securities market developed first. The technology developed for creating agency **mortgage-backed security** was then transferred to the securitization of other types of loans and receivables. In transferring the technology to create securities that expose investors to credit risk, mechanisms had to be developed to create securities that could receive investment grade credit ratings sought by the issuer. In the next reading, we will discuss these mechanisms.

Outside the United States, market participants treat asset-backed securities more generically. Specifically, asset-backed securities include mortgage-backed securities as a subsector. While that is actually the proper way to classify these securities, it was not the convention adopted in the United States. In the next chapter, the development of the asset-backed securities (including mortgage-backed securities) outside the United States will be covered.

Residential mortgage-backed securities include: (1) mortgage passthrough securities, (2) collateralized mortgage obligations, and (3) stripped mortgage-backed securities. The latter two mortgage-backed securities are referred to as **derivative mortgage-backed securities** because they are created from mortgage passthrough securities.

RESIDENTIAL MORTGAGE LOANS 2

A **mortgage** is a loan secured by the collateral of some specified real estate property which obliges the borrower to make a predetermined series of payments. The mortgage gives the lender the right to "foreclose" on the loan if the borrower defaults and to seize the property in order to ensure that the debt is paid off. The interest rate on the mortgage loan is called the **mortgage rate** or **contract rate**. Our focus in this section is on residential mortgage loans.

When the lender makes the loan based on the credit of the borrower and on the collateral for the mortgage, the mortgage is said to be a **conventional mortgage**. The lender may require that the borrower obtain mortgage insurance to guarantee the fulfillment of the borrower's obligations. Some borrowers can qualify for mortgage insurance which is guaranteed by one of three U.S. government agencies: the Federal Housing Administration (FHA), the Veteran's Administration (VA), and the Rural Housing Service (RHS). There are also private mortgage insurers. The cost of mortgage insurance is paid by the borrower in the form of a higher mortgage rate.

There are many types of **mortgage designs** used throughout the world. A mortgage design is a specification of the interest rate, term of the mortgage, and the manner in which the borrowed funds are repaid. In the United States, the alternative mortgage designs include (1) fixed rate, level-payment fully amortized mortgages, (2) **adjustable-rate mortgages**, (3) balloon mortgages, (4) growing equity mortgages, (5) reverse mortgages, and (6) tiered payment mortgages. Other countries have developed mortgage designs unique to their housing finance market. Some of these mortgage designs relate the mortgage payment to the country's rate of inflation. Below we will look at the most common mortgage design in the United States—the fixed-rate, level-payment, fully amortized mortgage. All of the principles we need to know regarding the risks associated with investing in mortgage-backed securities and the difficulties associated with their valuation can be understood by just looking at this mortgage design.

A. Fixed-Rate, Level-Payment, Fully Amortized Mortgage

A **fixed-rate, level-payment, fully amortized mortgage** has the following features:

▶ the mortgage rate is fixed for the life of the mortgage loan

▶ the dollar amount of each monthly payment is the same for the life of the mortgage loan (i.e., there is a "level payment")

▶ when the last scheduled monthly mortgage payment is made the remaining mortgage balance is zero (i.e., the loan is fully amortized).

The monthly mortgage payments include principal repayment and interest. The frequency of payment is typically monthly. Each monthly mortgage payment for this mortgage design is due on the first of each month and consists of:

1. interest of $\frac{1}{12}$ of the fixed annual interest rate times the amount of the outstanding mortgage balance at the beginning of the previous month, and

2. a repayment of a portion of the outstanding mortgage balance (principal).

The difference between the monthly mortgage payment and the portion of the payment that represents interest equals the amount that is applied to reduce the outstanding mortgage balance. The monthly mortgage payment is designed so that after the last scheduled monthly mortgage payment is made, the amount of the outstanding mortgage balance is zero (i.e., the mortgage is fully repaid).

To illustrate this mortgage design, consider a 30-year (360-month), $100,000 mortgage with an 8.125% mortgage rate. The monthly mortgage payment would be $742.50. Exhibit 61-1 shows for selected months how each monthly mortgage payment is divided between interest and scheduled principal repayment. At the beginning of month 1, the mortgage balance is $100,000, the amount of the original loan. The mortgage payment for month 1 includes interest on the $100,000 borrowed for the month. Since the interest rate is 8.125%, the monthly interest rate is 0.0067708 (0.08125 divided by 12). Interest for month 1 is therefore $677.08 ($100,000 times 0.0067708). The $65.41 difference between the monthly mortgage payment of $742.50 and the interest of $677.08 is the portion of the monthly mortgage payment that represents the scheduled principal repayment. It is also referred to as the **scheduled amortization** and we shall use the terms scheduled principal repayment and scheduled amortization interchangeably throughout this chapter. This $65.41 in month 1 reduces the mortgage balance.

The mortgage balance at the end of month 1 (beginning of month 2) is then $99,934.59 ($100,000 minus $65.41). The interest for the second monthly mortgage payment is $676.64, the monthly interest rate (0.0067708) times the mortgage balance at the beginning of month 2 ($99,934.59). The difference between the $742.50 monthly mortgage payment and the $676.64 interest is $65.86, representing the amount of the mortgage balance paid off with that monthly mortgage payment. Notice that the mortgage payment in month 360—the final payment—is sufficient to pay off the remaining mortgage balance.

As Exhibit 61-1 clearly shows, *the portion of the monthly mortgage payment applied to interest declines each month and the portion applied to principal repayment increases.* The reason for this is that as the mortgage balance is reduced with each monthly mortgage payment, the interest on the mortgage balance declines. Since the monthly mortgage payment is a fixed dollar amount, an increasingly larger portion of the monthly payment is applied to reduce the mortgage balance outstanding in each subsequent month.

EXHIBIT 61-1	Amortization Schedule for a Level-Payment, Fixed-Rate, Fully Amortized Mortgage

Mortgage loan: $100,000   Monthly payment: $742.50

Mortgage rate: 8.125%   Term of loan: 30 years (360 months)

Month	Beginning of Month Mortgage Balance	Mortgage Payment	Interest	Scheduled Repayment	End of Month Mortgage Balance
1	$100,000.00	$742.50	$677.08	$65.41	$99,934.59
2	99,934.59	742.50	676.64	65.86	99,868.73
3	99,868.73	742.50	676.19	66.30	99,802.43
4	99,802.43	742.50	675.75	66.75	99,735.68
...	...	...	...	...	...
25	98,301.53	742.50	665.58	76.91	98,224.62
26	98,224.62	742.50	665.06	77.43	98,147.19
27	98,147.19	742.50	664.54	77.96	98,069.23
...	...	...	...	...	...
74	93,849.98	742.50	635.44	107.05	93,742.93
75	93,742.93	742.50	634.72	107.78	93,635.15
76	93,635.15	742.50	633.99	108.51	93,526.64
...	...	...	...	...	...
141	84,811.77	742.50	574.25	168.25	84,643.52
142	84,643.52	742.50	573.11	169.39	84,474.13
143	84,474.13	742.50	571.96	170.54	84,303.59
...	...	...	...	...	...
184	76,446.29	742.50	517.61	224.89	76,221.40
185	76,221.40	742.50	516.08	226.41	75,994.99
186	75,994.99	742.50	514.55	227.95	75,767.04
...	...	...	...	...	...
233	63,430.19	742.50	429.48	313.02	63,117.17
234	63,117.17	742.50	427.36	315.14	62,802.03
235	62,802.03	742.50	425.22	317.28	62,484.75
...	...	...	...	...	...
289	42,200.92	742.50	285.74	456.76	41,744.15
290	41,744.15	742.50	282.64	459.85	41,284.30
291	41,284.30	742.50	279.53	462.97	40,821.33
...	...	...	...	...	...
321	25,941.42	742.50	175.65	566.85	25,374.57
322	25,374.57	742.50	171.81	570.69	24,803.88
323	24,803.88	742.50	167.94	574.55	24,229.32
...	...	...	...	...	...
358	2,197.66	742.50	14.88	727.62	1,470.05
359	1,470.05	742.50	9.95	732.54	737.50
360	737.50	742.50	4.99	737.50	0.00

1. Servicing Fee

Every mortgage loan must be serviced. Servicing of a mortgage loan involves collecting monthly payments and forwarding proceeds to owners of the loan; sending payment notices to mortgagors; reminding mortgagors when payments are overdue; maintaining records of principal balances; initiating foreclosure proceedings if necessary; and, furnishing tax information to borrowers (i.e., mortgagors) when applicable.

The servicing fee is a portion of the mortgage rate. If the mortgage rate is 8.125% and the servicing fee is 50 basis points, then the investor receives interest of 7.625%. The interest rate that the investor receives is said to be the **net interest** or **net coupon**. The servicing fee is commonly called the **servicing spread**.

The dollar amount of the servicing fee declines over time as the mortgage amortizes. This is true for not only the mortgage design that we have just described, but for all mortgage designs.

2. Prepayments and Cash Flow Uncertainty

Our illustration of the cash flow from a level-payment, fixed-rate, fully amortized mortgage assumes that the homeowner does not pay off any portion of the mortgage balance prior to the scheduled due date. But homeowners can pay off all or part of their mortgage balance prior to the maturity date. A payment made in excess of the monthly mortgage payment is called a **prepayment**. The prepayment could be to pay off the entire outstanding balance or a partial paydown of the mortgage balance. When a prepayment is not for the entire outstanding balance it is called a **curtailment**.

The effect of prepayments is that the amount and timing of the cash flow from a mortgage loan are not known with certainty. This risk is referred to as **prepayment risk**. For example, all that the lender in a $100,000, 8.125% 30-year mortgage knows is that as long as the loan is outstanding and the borrower does not default, interest will be received and the principal will be repaid at the scheduled date each month; then at the end of the 30 years, the investor would have received $100,000 in principal payments. What the investor does not know—the uncertainty—is for how long the loan will be outstanding, and therefore what the timing of the principal payments will be. This is true for all mortgage loans, not just the level-payment, fixed-rate, fully amortized mortgage. Factors affecting prepayments will be discussed later in this chapter.

Most mortgages have no prepayment penalty. The outstanding loan balance can be repaid at par. However, there are mortgages with prepayment penalties. The purpose of the penalty is to deter prepayment when interest rates decline. A prepayment penalty mortgage has the following structure. There is a period of time over which if the loan is prepaid in full or in excess of a certain amount of the outstanding balance, there is a prepayment penalty. This period is referred to as the **lockout period** or **penalty period**. During the penalty period, the borrower may prepay up to a specified amount of the outstanding balance without a penalty. Over that specified amount, the penalty is set in terms of the number of months of interest that must be paid.

3   MORTGAGE PASSTHROUGH SECURITIES

A **mortgage passthrough security** is a security created when one or more holders of mortgages form a collection (pool) of mortgages and sell shares or participation certificates in the pool. A pool may consist of several thousand or only a few mortgages. When a mortgage is included in a pool of mortgages that is used as collateral for a mortgage passthrough security, the mortgage is said to be **securitized**.

A. Cash Flow Characteristics

The cash flow of a mortgage passthrough security depends on the cash flow of the underlying pool of mortgages. As we explained in the previous section, the cash flow consists of monthly mortgage payments representing interest, the scheduled repayment of principal, and any prepayments.

Payments are made to security holders each month. However, neither the amount nor the timing of the cash flow from the pool of mortgages is identical to that of the cash flow passed through to investors. The monthly cash flow for a passthrough is less than the monthly cash flow of the underlying pool of mortgages by an amount equal to servicing and other fees. The other fees are those charged by the issuer or guarantor of the passthrough for guaranteeing the issue (discussed later). The coupon rate on a passthrough is called the **passthrough rate**. The passthrough rate is less than the mortgage rate on the underlying pool of mortgages by an amount equal to the servicing and guaranteeing fees.

The timing of the cash flow is also different. The monthly mortgage payment is due from each mortgagor on the first day of each month, but there is a delay in passing through the corresponding monthly cash flow to the security holders. The length of the delay varies by the type of passthrough security.

Not all of the mortgages that are included in a pool of mortgages that are securitized have the same mortgage rate and the same maturity. Consequently, when describing a passthrough security, a weighted average coupon rate and a weighted average maturity are determined. A **weighted average coupon rate**, or WAC, is found by weighting the mortgage rate of each mortgage loan in the pool by the percentage of the mortgage outstanding relative to the outstanding amount of all the mortgages in the pool. A **weighted average maturity**, or WAM, is found by weighting the remaining number of months to maturity for each mortgage loan in the pool by the amount of the outstanding mortgage balance.

For example, suppose a mortgage pool has just five loans and the outstanding mortgage balance, mortgage rate, and months remaining to maturity of each loan are as follows:

Loan	Outstanding Mortgage Balance	Weight in Pool	Mortgage Rate	Months Remaining
1	$125,000	22.12%	7.50%	275
2	$85,000	15.04%	7.20%	260
3	$175,000	30.97%	7.00%	290
4	$110,000	19.47%	7.80%	285
5	$70,000	12.39%	6.90%	270
Total	$565,000	100.00%	7.28%	279

The WAC for this mortgage pool is:

$$0.2212\ (7.5\%) + 0.1504\ (7.2\%) + 0.3097\ (7.0\%) + 0.1947\ (7.8\%)$$
$$+ 0.1239\ (6.90\%) = 7.28\%$$

The WAM for this mortgage pool is

$$0.2212\,(275) + 0.1504\,(260) + 0.3097\,(290) + 0.1947\,(285)$$
$$+ 0.1239\,(270) = 279 \text{ months (rounded)}$$

B. Types of Mortgage Passthrough Securities

In the United States, the three major types of passthrough securities are guaranteed by agencies created by Congress to increase the supply of capital to the residential mortgage market. Those agencies are the Government National Mortgage Association (Ginnie Mae), the Federal Home Loan Mortgage Corporation (Freddie Mac), and the Federal National Mortgage Association (Fannie Mae).

While Freddie Mac and Fannie Mae are commonly referred to as "agencies" of the U.S. government, both are corporate instrumentalities of the U.S. government. That is, they are government sponsored enterprises; therefore, their guarantee does not carry the full faith and credit of the U.S. government. In contrast, Ginnie Mae is a federally related institution; it is part of the Department of Housing and Urban Development. As such, its guarantee carries the full faith and credit of the U.S. government. The passthrough securities issued by Fannie Mae and Freddie Mac are called **conventional passthrough securities**. However, in this book we shall refer to those passthrough securities issued by all three entities (Ginnie Mae, Fannie Mae, and Freddie Mac) as **agency passthrough securities**. It should be noted, however, that market participants do reserve the term "agency passthrough securities" for those issued only by Ginnie Mae.[1]

In order for a loan to be included in a pool of loans backing an agency security, it must meet specified underwriting standards. These standards set forth the maximum size of the loan, the loan documentation required, the maximum loan-to-value ratio, and whether or not insurance is required. If a loan satisfies the underwriting standards for inclusion as collateral for an agency mortgage-backed security, it is called a **conforming mortgage**. If a loan fails to satisfy the underwriting standards, it is called a **nonconforming mortgage**.

Nonconforming mortgages used as collateral for mortgage passthrough securities are privately issued. These securities are called **nonagency mortgage passthrough securities** and are issued by thrifts, commercial banks, and private conduits. Private conduits may purchase nonconforming mortgages, pool them, and then sell passthrough securities whose collateral is the underlying pool of nonconforming mortgages. Nonagency passthrough securities are rated by the nationally recognized statistical rating organizations. These securities are supported by credit enhancements so that they can obtain an investment grade rating. We shall describe these securities in the next reading.

C. Trading and Settlement Procedures

Agency passthrough securities are identified by a pool prefix and pool number provided by the agency. The prefix indicates the type of passthrough. There are specific rules established by the Bond Market Association for the trading and

---

[1] The name of the passthrough issued by Ginnie Mae and Fannie Mae is a *Mortgage-Backed Security* or *MBS*. So, when a market participant refers to a Ginnie Mae MBS or Fannie Mae MBS, what is meant is a passthrough issued by these two entities. The name of the passthrough issued by Freddie Mac is a *Participation Certificate* or *PC*. So, when a market participant refers to a Freddie Mac PC, what is meant is a passthrough issued by Freddie Mac. Every agency has different "programs" under which passthroughs are issued with different types of mortgage pools (e.g., 30-year fixed-rate mortgages, 15-year fixed-rate mortgages, adjustable-rate mortgages). We will not review the different programs here.

settlement of mortgage-backed securities. Many trades occur while a pool is still unspecified, and therefore no pool information is known at the time of the trade. This kind of trade is known as a **TBA trade (to-be-announced trade)**. In a TBA trade the two parties agree on the agency type, the agency program, the coupon rate, the face value, the price, and the settlement date. The actual pools of mortgage loans underlying the agency passthrough are not specified in a TBA trade. However, this information is provided by the seller to the buyer before delivery. There are trades where more specific requirements are established for the securities to be delivered. An example is a Freddie Mac with a coupon rate of 8.5% and a WAC between 9.0% and 9.2%. There are also specified pool trades wherein the actual pool numbers to be delivered are specified.

Passthrough prices are quoted in the same manner as U.S. Treasury coupon securities. A quote of 94-05 means 94 and 5 32nds of par value, or 94.15625% of par value. The price that the buyer pays the seller is the agreed upon sale price plus accrued interest. Given the par value, the dollar price (excluding accrued interest) is affected by the amount of the pool mortgage balance outstanding. The **pool factor** indicates the percentage of the initial mortgage balance still outstanding. So, a pool factor of 90 means that 90% of the original mortgage pool balance is outstanding. The pool factor is reported by the agency each month.

The dollar price paid for just the principal is found as follows given the agreed upon price, par value, and the month's pool factor provided by the agency:

$$\text{price} \times \text{par value} \times \text{pool factor}$$

For example, if the parties agree to a price of 92 for $1 million par value for a passthrough with a pool factor of 0.85, then the dollar price paid by the buyer in addition to accrued interest is:

$$0.92 \times \$1,000,000 \times 0.85 = \$782,000$$

The buyer does not know what he will get unless he specifies a pool number. There are many **seasoned issues** of the same agency with the same coupon rate outstanding at a given point in time. For example, in early 2000 there were more than 30,000 pools of 30-year Ginnie Mae MBSs outstanding with a coupon rate of 9%. One passthrough may be backed by a pool of mortgage loans in which all the properties are located in California, while another may be backed by a pool of mortgage loans in which all the properties are in Minnesota. Yet another may be backed by a pool of mortgage loans in which the properties are from several regions of the country. So which pool are dealers referring to when they talk about Ginnie Mae 9s? They are not referring to any specific pool but instead to a generic security, despite the fact that the prepayment characteristics of passthroughs with underlying pools from different parts of the country are different. Thus, the projected prepayment rates for passthroughs reported by dealer firms (discussed later) are for generic passthroughs. A particular pool purchased may have a materially different prepayment rate from the generic. Moreover, when an investor purchases a passthrough without specifying a pool number, the seller has the option to deliver the worst-paying pools as long as the pools delivered satisfy good delivery requirements.

D. Measuring the Prepayment Rate

A prepayment is any payment toward the repayment of principal that is in excess of the scheduled principal payment. In describing prepayments, market participants refer to the **prepayment rate** or **prepayment speed**. In this section we will see how the historical prepayment rate is computed for a month. We then look at how to annualize a monthly prepayment rate and then explain the convention in the residential mortgage market for describing a pattern of prepayment rates over the life of a mortgage pool.

There are three points to keep in mind in the discussion in this section. First, we will look at how the actual or historical prepayment rate of a mortgage pool is calculated. Second, we will see later how in projecting the cash flow of a mortgage pool, an investor uses the same prepayment measures to project prepayments given a prepayment rate. The third point is that we are just describing the mechanics of calculating prepayment measures. The difficult task of projecting the prepayment rate is not discussed here. In fact, this task is beyond the scope of this reading. However, the factors that investors use in prepayment models (i.e., statistical models used to project prepayments) will be described in Section III.F.

1. Single Monthly Mortality Rate

Given the amount of the prepayment for a month and the amount that was available to prepay that month, a monthly prepayment rate can be computed. The amount available to prepay in a month is *not* the outstanding mortgage balance of the pool in the previous month. The reason is that there will be scheduled principal payments for the month and therefore by definition this amount cannot be prepaid. Thus, the amount available to prepay in a given month, say month t, is the beginning mortgage balance in month t reduced by the scheduled principal payment in month t.

The ratio of the prepayment in a month and the amount available to prepay that month is called the **single monthly mortality rate**[2] or simply SMM. That is, the SMM for month t is computed as follows

$$\text{SMM}_t = \frac{\text{prepayment in month } t}{\text{beginning mortgage balance for month } t - \text{scheduled principal payment in month } t}$$

Let's illustrate the calculation of the SMM. Assume the following:

beginning mortgage balance in month 33 = $358,326,766
scheduled principal payment in month 33 = $297,825
prepayment in month 33   = $1,841,347

The SMM for month 33 is therefore:

$$\text{SMM}_{33} = \frac{\$1,841,347}{\$358,326,766 - \$297,825} = 0.005143 = 0.5143\%$$

The SMM_{33} of 0.5143% is interpreted as follows: In month 33, 0.5143% of the outstanding mortgage balance available to prepay in month 33 prepaid.

Let's make sure we understand the two ways in which the SMM can be used. First, given the prepayment for a month for a mortgage pool, an investor can calculate the SMM as we just did in our illustration to determine the SMM for month 33. Second given an *assumed* SMM, an investor will use it to project the prepayment for a month. The prepayment for a month will then be used to

---

[2] It may seem strange that the term "mortality" is used to describe this prepayment measure. This term reflects the influence of actuaries who in the early years of the development of the mortgage market migrated to dealer firms to assist in valuing mortgage-backed securities. Actuaries viewed the prepayment of a mortgage loan as the "death" of a mortgage.

determine the cash flow of a mortgage pool for the month. We'll see this later in this section when we illustrate how to calculate the cash flow for a passthrough security. For now, it is important to understand that given an assumed SMM for month t, the prepayment for month t is found as follows:

prepayment for month t = SMM $\times$ (beginning mortgage balance for month t − scheduled principal payment for month t) **(61-1)**

For example, suppose that an investor owns a passthrough security in which the remaining mortgage balance at the beginning of some month is \$290 million and the scheduled principal payment for that month is \$3 million. The investor believes that the SMM next month will be 0.5143%. Then the projected prepayment for the month is:

$$0.005143 \times (\$290,000,000 - \$3,000,000) = \$1,476,041$$

2. Conditional Prepayment Rate

Market participants prefer to talk about prepayment rates on an annual basis rather than a monthly basis. This is handled by annualizing the SMM. The annualized SMM is called the **conditional prepayment rate** or CPR.[3] Given the SMM for a given month, the CPR can be demonstrated to be:[4]

$$CPR = 1 - (1 - SMM)^{12} \qquad \textbf{(61-2)}$$

For example, suppose that the SMM is 0.005143. Then the CPR is

$$CPR = 1 - (1 - 0.005143)^{12}$$
$$= 1 - (0.994857)^{12} = 0.06 = 6\%$$

A CPR of 6% means that, ignoring scheduled principal payments, approximately 6% of the outstanding mortgage balance at the beginning of the year will be prepaid by the end of the year.

Given a CPR, the corresponding SMM can be computed by solving equation (61-2) for the SMM:

$$SMM = 1 - (1 - CPR)^{1/12} \qquad \textbf{(61-3)}$$

To illustrate equation (3), suppose that the CPR is 6%, then the SMM is

$$SMM = 1 - (1 - 0.06)^{1/12} = 0.005143 = 0.5143\%$$

3. PSA Prepayment Benchmark

An SMM is the prepayment rate for a month. A CPR is a prepayment rate for a year. Market participants describe prepayment rates (historical/actual prepayment rates and those used for projecting future prepayments) in terms of a prepayment pattern or benchmark over the life of a mortgage pool. In the early

---

[3] It is referred to as a "conditional" prepayment rate because the prepayments in one year depend upon (i.e., are conditional upon) the amount available to prepay in the previous year. Sometimes market participants refer to the CPR as the "constant" prepayment rate.

[4] The derivation of the CPR for a given SMM is beyond the scope of this chapter. The proof is provided in Lakhbir S. Hayre and Cyrus Mohebbi, "Mortgage Mathematics," in Frank J. Fabozzi (ed.), *Handbook of Mortgage-Backed Securities: Fifth Edition* (New York, NY: McGraw-Hill, 2001), pp. 844–845.

1980s, the Public Securities Association (PSA), later renamed the Bond Market Association, undertook a study to look at the pattern of prepayments over the life of a typical mortgage pool. Based on the study, the PSA established a prepayment benchmark which is referred to as the **PSA prepayment benchmark**. Although sometimes referred to as a "prepayment model", it is a convention and not a model to predict prepayments.

The PSA prepayment benchmark is expressed as a monthly series of CPRs. The PSA benchmark assumes that prepayment rates are low for newly originated mortgages and then will speed up as the mortgages become seasoned. The PSA benchmark assumes the following prepayment rates for 30-year mortgages: (1) a CPR of 0.2% for the first month, increased by 0.2% per year per month for the next 30 months until it reaches 6% per year, and (2) a 6% CPR for the remaining months.

This benchmark, referred to as "100% PSA" or simply "100 PSA," is graphically depicted in Exhibit 61-2. Mathematically, 100 PSA can be expressed as follows:

if $t < 30$ then CPR = 6% $(t/30)$
if $t \geq 30$ then CPR = 6%

where t is the number of months since the mortgages were originated.

It is important to emphasize that the CPRs and corresponding SMMs apply to a mortgage pool *based on the number of months since origination*. For example, if a mortgage pool has loans that were originally 30-year (360-month) mortgage loans and the WAM is currently 357 months, this means that the mortgage pool is seasoned three months. So, in determining prepayments for the next month, the CPR and SMM that are applicable are those for month 4.

Slower or faster speeds are then referred to as some percentage of PSA. For example, "50 PSA" means one-half the CPR of the PSA prepayment benchmark; "150 PSA" means 1.5 times the CPR of the PSA prepayment benchmark; "300 PSA" means three times the CPR of the prepayment benchmark. A prepayment rate of 0 PSA means that no *prepayments* are assumed. While there are no prepayments at 0 PSA, there are scheduled principal repayments.

In constructing a schedule for monthly prepayments, the CPR (an annual rate) must be converted into a monthly prepayment rate (an SMM) using

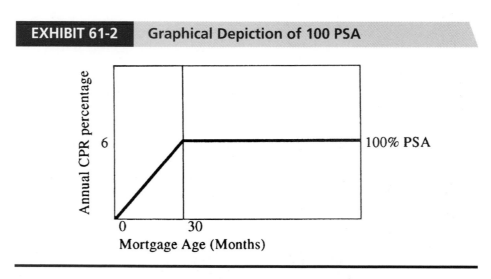

EXHIBIT 61-2   Graphical Depiction of 100 PSA

equation 61-3. For example, the SMMs for month 5, month 20, and months 31 through 360 assuming 100 PSA are calculated as follows:

for month 5:

$$\text{CPR} = 6\% \ (5/30) = 1\% = 0.01$$
$$\text{SMM} = 1 - (1 - 0.01)^{1/12} = 1 - (0.99)^{0.083333} = 0.000837$$

for month 20:

$$\text{CPR} = 6\% \ (20/30) = 4\% = 0.04$$
$$\text{SMM} = 1 - (1 - 0.04)^{1/12} = 1 - (0.96)^{0.083333} = 0.003396$$

for months 31–360:

$$\text{CPR} = 6\%$$
$$\text{SMM} = 1 - (1 - 0.06)^{1/12} = 1 - (0.94)^{0.083333} = 0.005143$$

What if the PSA were 165 instead? The SMMs for month 5, month 20, and months 31 through 360 assuming 165 PSA are computed as follows:

for month 5:

$$\text{CPR} = 6\% \ (5/30) = 1\% = 0.01$$
$$165 \ \text{PSA} = 1.65 \ (0.01) = 0.0165$$

$$\text{SMM} = 1 - (1 - 0.0165)^{1/12} = 1 - (0.9835)^{0.08333} = 0.001386$$

for month 20:

$$\text{CPR} = 6\% \ (20/30) = 4\% = 0.04$$
$$165 \ \text{PSA} = 1.65 \ (0.04) = 0.066$$

$$\text{SMM} = 1 - (1 - 0.066)^{1/12} = 1 - (0.934)^{0.08333} = 0.005674$$

for months 31–360:

$$\text{CPR} = 6\%$$
$$165 \ \text{PSA} = 1.65 \ (0.06) = 0.099$$

$$\text{SMM} = 1 - (1 - 0.099)^{1/12} = 1 - (0.901)^{0.08333} = 0.008650$$

Notice that the SMM assuming 165 PSA is not just 1.65 times the SMM assuming 100 PSA. It is the CPR that is a multiple of the CPR assuming 100 PSA.

3. Illustration of Monthly Cash Flow Construction

As our first step in valuing a hypothetical passthrough given a PSA assumption, we must construct a monthly cash flow. For the purpose of this illustration, the underlying mortgages for this hypothetical passthrough are assumed to be fixed-rate, level-payment, fully amortized mortgages with a weighted average coupon (WAC) rate of 8.125%. It will be assumed that the passthrough rate is 7.5% with a weighted average maturity (WAM) of 357 months.

Exhibit 61-3 shows the cash flow for selected months assuming 100 PSA. The cash flow is broken down into three components: (1) interest (based on the

EXHIBIT 61-3   Monthly Cash Flow for a $400 Million Passthrough with a 7.5% Passthrough Rate, a WAC of 8.125%, and a WAM of 357 Months Assuming 100 PSA

Months from Now (1)	Months Seasoned* (2)	Outstanding Balance (3)	SMM (4)	Mortgage Payment (5)	Net Interest (6)	Scheduled Principal (7)	Prepayment (8)	Total Principal (9)	Cash Flow (10)
1	4	$400,000,000	0.00067	$2,975,868	$2,500,000	$267,535	$267,470	$535,005	$3,035,005
2	5	399,464,995	0.00084	2,973,877	2,496,656	269,166	334,198	603,364	3,100,020
3	6	398,861,631	0.00101	2,971,387	2,492,885	270,762	400,800	671,562	3,164,447
4	7	398,190,069	0.00117	2,968,399	2,488,688	272,321	467,243	739,564	3,228,252
5	8	397,450,505	0.00134	2,964,914	2,484,066	273,843	533,493	807,335	3,291,401
6	9	396,643,170	0.00151	2,960,931	2,479,020	275,327	599,514	874,841	3,353,860
7	10	395,768,329	0.00168	2,956,453	2,473,552	276,772	665,273	942,045	3,415,597
8	11	394,826,284	0.00185	2,951,480	2,467,664	278,177	730,736	1,008,913	3,476,577
9	12	393,817,371	0.00202	2,946,013	2,461,359	279,542	795,869	1,075,410	3,536,769
10	13	392,741,961	0.00219	2,940,056	2,454,637	280,865	860,637	1,141,502	3,596,140
11	14	391,600,459	0.00236	2,933,608	2,447,503	282,147	925,008	1,207,155	3,654,658
27	30	364,808,016	0.00514	2,766,461	2,280,050	296,406	1,874,688	2,171,094	4,451,144
28	31	362,636,921	0.00514	2,752,233	2,266,481	296,879	1,863,519	2,160,398	4,426,879
29	32	360,476,523	0.00514	2,738,078	2,252,978	297,351	1,852,406	2,149,758	4,402,736
30	33	358,326,766	0.00514	2,723,996	2,239,542	297,825	1,841,347	2,139,173	4,378,715
100	103	231,249,776	0.00514	1,898,682	1,445,311	332,928	1,187,608	1,520,537	2,965,848
101	104	229,729,239	0.00514	1,888,917	1,435,808	333,459	1,179,785	1,513,244	2,949,052
102	105	228,215,995	0.00514	1,879,202	1,426,350	333,990	1,172,000	1,505,990	2,932,340
103	106	226,710,004	0.00514	1,869,538	1,416,938	334,522	1,164,252	1,498,774	2,915,712
104	107	225,211,230	0.00514	1,859,923	1,407,570	335,055	1,156,541	1,491,596	2,899,166
105	108	223,719,634	0.00514	1,850,357	1,398,248	335,589	1,148,867	1,484,456	2,882,703

(Exhibit continued on next page …)

EXHIBIT 61-3 (continued)

Months from Now (1)	Months Seasoned* (2)	Outstanding Balance (3)	SMM (4)	Mortgage Payment (5)	Net Interest (6)	Scheduled Principal (7)	Prepayment (8)	Total Principal (9)	Cash Flow (10)
200	203	109,791,339	0.00514	1,133,751	686,196	390,372	562,651	953,023	1,639,219
201	204	108,838,316	0.00514	1,127,920	680,239	390,994	557,746	948,740	1,628,980
202	205	107,889,576	0.00514	1,122,119	674,310	391,617	552,863	944,480	1,618,790
203	206	106,945,096	0.00514	1,116,348	668,407	392,241	548,003	940,243	1,608,650
300	303	32,383,611	0.00514	676,991	202,398	457,727	164,195	621,923	824,320
301	304	31,761,689	0.00514	673,510	198,511	458,457	160,993	619,449	817,960
302	305	31,142,239	0.00514	670,046	194,639	459,187	157,803	616,990	811,629
303	306	30,525,249	0.00514	666,600	190,783	459,918	154,626	614,545	805,328
352	355	3,034,311	0.00514	517,770	18,964	497,226	13,048	510,274	529,238
353	356	2,524,037	0.00514	515,107	15,775	498,018	10,420	508,437	524,213
354	357	2,015,600	0.00514	512,458	12,597	498,811	7,801	506,612	519,209
355	358	1,508,988	0.00514	509,823	9,431	499,606	5,191	504,797	514,228
356	359	1,004,191	0.00514	507,201	6,276	500,401	2,591	502,992	509,269
357	360	501,199	0.00514	504,592	3,132	501,199	0	501,199	504,331

* Since the WAM is 357 months, the underlying mortgage pool is seasoned an average of three months, and therefore based on 100 PSA, the CPR is 0.8% in month 1 and the pool seasons at 6% in month 27.

passthrough rate), (2) the scheduled principal repayment (i.e., scheduled amortization), and (3) prepayments based on 100 PSA.

Let's walk through Exhibit 61-3 column by column.

Column 1: This is the number of months from now when the cash flow will be received.

Column 2: This is the number of months of seasoning. Since the WAM for this mortgage pool is 357 months, this means that the loans are seasoned an average of 3 months (360 months–357 months) now.

Column 3: This column gives the outstanding mortgage balance at the beginning of the month. It is equal to the outstanding balance at the beginning of the previous month reduced by the total principal payment in the previous month.

Column 4: This column shows the SMM based on the number of months the loans are seasoned—the number of months shown in Column (2). For example, for the first month shown in the exhibit, the loans are seasoned three months going into that month. Therefore, the CPR used is the CPR that corresponds to four months. From the PSA benchmark, the CPR is 0.8% (4 times 0.2%). The corresponding SMM is 0.00067. The mortgage pool becomes fully seasoned in Column (1) corresponding to month 27 because by that time the loans are seasoned 30 months. When the loans are fully seasoned the CPR at 100 PSA is 6% and the corresponding SMM is 0.00514.

Column 5: The total monthly mortgage payment is shown in this column. Notice that the total monthly mortgage payment declines over time as prepayments reduce the mortgage balance outstanding. There is a formula to determine what the monthly mortgage balance will be for each month given prepayments.[5]

Column 6: The *net* monthly interest (i.e., amount available to pay bondholders after the servicing fee) is found in this column. This value is determined by multiplying the outstanding mortgage balance at the beginning of the month by the passthrough rate of 7.5% and then dividing by 12.

Column 7: This column gives the scheduled principal repayment (i.e., scheduled amortization). This is the difference between the total monthly mortgage payment [the amount shown in Column (5)] and the gross coupon interest for the month. The gross coupon interest is found by multiplying 8.125% by the outstanding mortgage balance at the beginning of the month and then dividing by 12.

Column 8: The prepayment for the month is reported in this column. The prepayment is found by using equation (1). For example, in month 100, the beginning mortgage balance is \$231,249,776, the scheduled principal payment is \$332,928, and the SMM at 100 PSA is 0.00514301 (only 0.00514 is shown in the exhibit to save space), so the prepayment is:

$$0.00514301 \times (\$231,249,776 - \$332,928) = \$1,187,608$$

Column 9: The total principal payment, which is the sum of columns (7) and (8), is shown in this column.

Column 10: The projected monthly cash flow for this passthrough is shown in this last column. The monthly cash flow is the sum of the interest paid [Column (6)] and the total principal payments for the month [Column (9)].

Let's look at what happens to the cash flows for this passthrough if a different PSA assumption is made. Suppose that instead of 100 PSA, 165 PSA is

---

[5] The formula is presented in Chapter 19 of Frank J. Fabozzi, *Fixed Income Mathematics* (Chicago: Irwin Professional Publishing, 1997).

assumed. Prepayments are assumed to be faster. Exhibit 61-4 shows the cash flow for this passthrough based on 165 PSA. Notice that the cash flows are greater in the early years compared to Exhibit 61-3 because prepayments are higher. The cash flows in later years are less for 165 PSA compared to 100 PSA because of the higher prepayments in the earlier years.

E. Average Life

It is standard practice in the bond market to refer to the maturity of a bond. If a bond matures in five years, it is referred to as a "5-year bond." However, the typical bond repays principal only once: at the maturity date. Bonds with this characteristic are referred to as "bullet bonds." We know that the maturity of a bond affects its interest rate risk. More specifically, for a given coupon rate, the greater the maturity the greater the interest rate risk.

For a mortgage-backed security, we know that the principal repayments (scheduled payments and prepayments) are made over the life of the security. While a mortgage-backed has a "legal maturity," which is the date when the last scheduled principal payment is due, the legal maturity does not tell us much about the characteristic of the security as its pertains to interest rate risk. For example, it is incorrect to think of a 30-year corporate bond and a mortgage-backed security with a 30-year legal maturity with the same coupon rate as being equivalent in terms of interest rate risk. Of course, duration can be computed for both the corporate bond and the mortgage-backed security. (We will see how this is done for a mortgage-backed security in Reading 63.) Instead of duration, another measure widely used by market participants is the **weighted average life** or simply **average life**. This is the convention-based average time to receipt of principal payments (scheduled principal payments and projected prepayments).

Mathematically, the average life is expressed as follows:

$$\text{Average life} = \sum_{t=1}^{T} \frac{t \times \text{Projected principal received at time } t}{12 \times \text{Total principal}}$$

where T is the number of months.

The average life of a passthrough depends on the prepayment assumption. To see this, the average life is shown below for different prepayment speeds for the pass-through we used to illustrate the cash flow for 100 PSA and 165 PSA in Exhibits 61-3 and 61-4:

PSA speed	50	100	165	200	300	400	500	600	700
Average life (years)	15.11	11.66	8.76	7.68	5.63	4.44	3.68	3.16	2.78

F. Factors Affecting Prepayment Behavior

The factors that affect prepayment behavior are:

1. prevailing mortgage rate

2. housing turnover

3. characteristics of the underlying residential mortgage loans

The current mortgage rate affects prepayments. The spread between the prevailing mortgage rate in the market and the rate paid by the homeowner

EXHIBIT 61-4 Monthly Cash Flow for a $400 Million Passthrough with a 7.5% Passthrough Rate, a WAC of 8.125%, and a WAM of 357 Months Assuming 165 PSA

Months (1)	Months Seasoned* (2)	Outstanding Balance (3)	SMM (4)	Mortgage Payment (5)	Net Interest (6)	Scheduled Principal (7)	Prepayment (8)	Total Principal (9)	Cash Flow (10)
1	4	$400,000,000	0.00111	$2,975,868	$2,500,000	$267,535	$442,389	$709,923	$3,209,923
2	5	399,290,077	0.00139	2,972,575	2,495,563	269,048	552,847	821,896	3,317,459
3	6	398,468,181	0.00167	2,968,456	2,490,426	270,495	663,065	933,560	3,423,986
4	7	397,534,621	0.00195	2,963,513	2,484,591	271,873	772,949	1,044,822	3,529,413
5	8	396,489,799	0.00223	2,957,747	2,478,061	273,181	882,405	1,155,586	3,633,647
6	9	395,334,213	0.00251	2,951,160	2,470,839	274,418	991,341	1,265,759	3,736,598
7	10	394,068,454	0.00279	2,943,755	2,462,928	275,583	1,099,664	1,375,246	3,838,174
8	11	392,693,208	0.00308	2,935,534	2,454,333	276,674	1,207,280	1,483,954	3,938,287
9	12	391,209,254	0.00336	2,926,503	2,445,058	277,690	1,314,099	1,591,789	4,036,847
10	13	389,617,464	0.00365	2,916,666	2,435,109	278,631	1,420,029	1,698,659	4,133,769
11	14	387,918,805	0.00393	2,906,028	2,424,493	279,494	1,524,979	1,804,473	4,228,965
27	30	347,334,116	0.00865	2,633,950	2,170,838	282,209	3,001,955	3,284,164	5,455,002
28	31	344,049,952	0.00865	2,611,167	2,150,312	281,662	2,973,553	3,255,215	5,405,527
29	32	340,794,737	0.00865	2,588,581	2,129,967	281,116	2,945,400	3,226,516	5,356,483
30	33	337,568,221	0.00865	2,566,190	2,109,801	280,572	2,917,496	3,198,067	5,307,869
100	103	170,142,350	0.00865	1,396,958	1,063,390	244,953	1,469,591	1,714,544	2,777,933
101	104	168,427,806	0.00865	1,384,875	1,052,674	244,478	1,454,765	1,699,243	2,751,916
102	105	166,728,563	0.00865	1,372,896	1,042,054	244,004	1,440,071	1,684,075	2,726,128
103	106	165,044,489	0.00865	1,361,020	1,031,528	243,531	1,425,508	1,669,039	2,700,567
104	107	163,375,450	0.00865	1,349,248	1,021,097	243,060	1,411,075	1,654,134	2,675,231
105	108	161,721,315	0.00865	1,337,577	1,010,758	242,589	1,396,771	1,639,359	2,650,118

(Exhibit continued on next page ...)

EXHIBIT 61-4   (continued)

Months (1)	Months Seasoned* (2)	Outstanding Balance (3)	SMM (4)	Mortgage Payment (5)	Net Interest (6)	Scheduled Principal (7)	Prepayment (8)	Total Principal (9)	Cash Flow (10)
200	203	56,746,664	0.00865	585,990	354,667	201,767	489,106	690,874	1,045,540
201	204	56,055,790	0.00865	580,921	350,349	201,377	483,134	684,510	1,034,859
202	205	55,371,280	0.00865	575,896	346,070	200,986	477,216	678,202	1,024,273
203	206	54,693,077	0.00865	570,915	341,832	200,597	471,353	671,950	1,013,782
300	303	11,758,141	0.00865	245,808	73,488	166,196	100,269	266,465	339,953
301	304	11,491,677	0.00865	243,682	71,823	165,874	97,967	263,841	335,664
302	305	11,227,836	0.00865	241,574	70,174	165,552	95,687	261,240	331,414
303	306	10,966,596	0.00865	239,485	68,541	165,232	93,430	258,662	327,203
352	355	916,910	0.00865	156,460	5,731	150,252	6,631	156,883	162,614
353	356	760,027	0.00865	155,107	4,750	149,961	5,277	155,238	159,988
354	357	604,789	0.00865	153,765	3,780	149,670	3,937	153,607	157,387
355	358	451,182	0.00865	152,435	2,820	149,380	2,611	151,991	154,811
356	359	299,191	0.00865	151,117	1,870	149,091	1,298	150,389	152,259
357	360	148,802	0.00865	149,809	930	148,802	0	148,802	149,732

* Since the WAM is 357 months, the underlying mortgage pool is seasoned an average of three months, and therefore based on 165 PSA, the CPR is 0.8% × 1.65 in month 1 and the pool seasons at 6% × 1.65 in month 27.

affects the **incentive to refinance**. Moreover, the path of mortgage rates since the loan was originated affects prepayments through a phenomenon referred to as **refinancing burnout**. Both the spread and path of mortgage rates affect prepayments that are the product of refinancing.

By far, the single most important factor affecting prepayments because of refinancing is the current level of mortgage rates relative to the borrower's contract rate. The greater the difference between the two, the greater the incentive to refinance the mortgage loan. For refinancing to make economic sense, the interest savings must be greater than the costs associated with refinancing the mortgage. These costs include legal expenses, origination fees, title insurance, and the value of the time associated with obtaining another mortgage loan. Some of these costs will vary proportionately with the amount to be financed. Other costs such as the application fee and legal expenses are typically fixed.

Historically it had been observed that mortgage rates had to decline by between 250 and 350 basis points below the contract rate in order to make it worthwhile for borrowers to refinance. However, the creativity of mortgage originators in designing mortgage loans such that the refinancing costs are folded into the amount borrowed has changed the view that mortgage rates must drop dramatically below the contract rate to make refinancing economic. Moreover, mortgage originators now do an effective job of advertising to make homeowners cognizant of the economic benefits of refinancing.

The historical pattern of prepayments and economic theory suggests that it is not only the level of mortgage rates that affects prepayment behavior but also the path that mortgage rates take to get to the current level. To illustrate why, suppose the underlying contract rate for a pool of mortgage loans is 11% and that three years after origination, the prevailing mortgage rate declines to 8%. Let's consider two possible paths of the mortgage rate in getting to the 8% level. In the first path, the mortgage rate declines to 8% at the end of the first year, then rises to 13% at the end of the second year, and then falls to 8% at the end of the third year. In the second path, the mortgage rate rises to 12% at the end of the first year, continues its rise to 13% at the end of the second year, and then falls to 8% at the end of the third year.

If the mortgage rate follows the first path, those who can benefit from refinancing will more than likely take advantage of this opportunity when the mortgage rate drops to 8% in the first year. When the mortgage rate drops again to 8% at the end of the third year, the likelihood is that prepayments because of refinancing will not surge; those who want to benefit by taking advantage of the refinancing opportunity will have done so already when the mortgage rate declined for the first time. This is the prepayment behavior referred to as the refinancing burnout (or simply, burnout) phenomenon. In contrast, the expected prepayment behavior when the mortgage rate follows the second path is quite different. Prepayment rates are expected to be low in the first two years. When the mortgage rate declines to 8% in the third year, refinancing activity and therefore prepayments are expected to surge. Consequently, the burnout phenomenon is related to the path of mortgage rates.

There is another way in which the prevailing mortgage rate affects prepayments: through its effect on the affordability of housing and **housing turnover**. The level of mortgage rates affects housing turnover to the extent that a lower rate increases the affordability of homes. However, even without lower interest rates, there is a normal amount of housing turnover. This is attributed to economic growth. The link is as follows: a growing economy results in a rise in personal income and in opportunities for worker migration; this increases family mobility and as a result increases housing turnover. The opposite holds for a weak economy.

Two characteristics of the underlying residential mortgage loans that affect prepayments are the amount of seasoning and the geographical location of the underlying properties. **Seasoning** refers to the aging of the mortgage loans. Empirical evidence suggests that prepayment rates are low after the loan is originated and increase after the loan is somewhat seasoned. Then prepayment rates tend to level off, in which case the loans are referred to as fully seasoned. This is the underlying theory for the PSA prepayment benchmark discussed earlier in this chapter. In some regions of the country the prepayment behavior tends to be faster than the average national prepayment rate, while other regions exhibit slower prepayment rates. This is caused by differences in local economies that affect housing turnover.

G. Contraction Risk and Extension Risk

An investor who owns passthrough securities does not know what the cash flow will be because that depends on actual prepayments. As we noted earlier, this risk is called prepayment risk.

To understand the significance of prepayment risk, suppose an investor buys a 9% coupon passthrough security at a time when mortgage rates are 10%. Let's consider what will happen to prepayments if mortgage rates decline to, say, 6%. There will be two adverse consequences. First, a basic property of fixed income securities is that the price of an option-free bond will rise. But in the case of a passthrough security, the rise in price will not be as large as that of an option-free bond because a fall in interest rates will give the borrower an incentive to prepay the loan and refinance the debt at a lower rate. This results in the same adverse consequence faced by holders of callable bonds. As in the case of those instruments, the upside price potential of a passthrough security is compressed because of prepayments. (This is the negative convexity characteristic explained at Level I. The second adverse consequence is that the cash flow must be reinvested at a lower rate. Basically, the faster prepayments resulting from a decline in interest rates causes the passthrough to shorten in terms of the timing of its cash flows. Another way of saying this is that "shortening" results in a decline in the average life. Consequently, the two adverse consequences from a decline in interest rates for a passthrough security are referred to as **contraction risk**.

Now let's look at what happens if mortgage rates rise to 15%. The price of the passthrough, like the price of any bond, will decline. But again it will decline more because the higher rates will tend to slow down the rate of prepayment, in effect increasing the amount invested at the coupon rate, which is lower than the market rate. Prepayments will slow down, because homeowners will not refinance or partially prepay their mortgages when mortgage rates are higher than the contract rate of 10%. Of course this is just the time when investors want prepayments to speed up so that they can reinvest the prepayments at the higher market interest rate. Basically, the slower prepayments associated with a rise in interest rates that causes these adverse consequences are due to the passthrough lengthening in terms of the timing of its cash flows. Another way of saying this is that "lengthening" results in an increase in the average life. Consequently, the adverse consequence from a rise in interest rates for a passthrough security is referred to as **extension risk**.

Therefore, prepayment risk encompasses contraction risk and extension risk. Prepayment risk makes passthrough securities unattractive for certain financial institutions to hold from an asset/liability management perspective. Some institutional investors are concerned with extension risk and others with contraction risk when they purchase a passthrough security. This applies even for assets supporting specific types of insurance contracts. Is it possible to alter the cash flow of a passthrough so as to reduce the contraction risk or extension risk for institutional investors? This can be done, as we shall see, when we describe collateralized mortgage obligations.

4   COLLATERALIZED MORTGAGE OBLIGATIONS

As we noted, there is prepayment risk associated with investing in a mortgage passthrough security. Some institutional investors are concerned with extension risk and others with contraction risk. This problem can be mitigated by redirecting the cash flows of mortgage-related products (passthrough securities or a pool of loans) to different bond classes, called **tranches**,[6] so as to create securities that have different exposure to prepayment risk and therefore different risk/return patterns than the mortgage-related product from which they are created.

When the cash flows of mortgage-related products are redistributed to different bond classes, the resulting securities are called **collaterized mortgage obligations** (CMO). The mortgage-related products from which the cash flows are obtained are referred to as the collateral. Since the typical mortgage-related product used in a CMO is a pool of passthrough securities, sometimes market participants will use the terms "collateral" and "passthrough securities" interchangeably. The creation of a CMO cannot eliminate prepayment risk; it can only distribute the various forms of this risk among different classes of bondholders. The CMO's major **financial innovation** is that the securities created more closely satisfy the asset/liability needs of institutional investors, thereby broadening the appeal of mortgage-backed products.

There is a wide range of CMO structures.[7] We review the major ones below.

A. Sequential-Pay Tranches

The first CMO was structured so that each class of bond would be retired sequentially. Such structures are referred to as **sequential-pay** CMOs. The rule for the monthly distribution of the principal payments (scheduled principal plus prepayments) to the tranches would be as follows:

▶ Distribute all principal payments to Tranche 1 until the principal balance for Tranche 1 is zero. After Tranche 1 is paid off,

▶ distribute all principal payments to Tranche 2 until the principal balance for Tranche 2 is zero. After Tranche 2 is paid off,

▶ distribute all principal payments to Tranche 3 until the principal balance for Tranche 3 is zero. After Tranche 3 is paid off, ...

and so on.

---

[6] "Tranche" is from an old French word meaning "slice." In the case of a collateralized mortgage obligation it refers to a "slice of the cash flows."

[7] The issuer of a CMO wants to be sure that the trust created to pass through the interest and principal payments is not treated as a taxable entity. A provision of the Tax Reform Act of 1986, called the Real Estate Mortgage Investment Conduit (REMIC), specifies the requirements that an issuer must fulfill so that the legal entity created to issue a CMO is not taxable. Most CMOs today are created as REMICs. While it is common to hear market participants refer to a CMO as a REMIC, not all CMOs are REMICs.

To illustrate a sequential-pay CMO, we discuss FJF-01, a hypothetical deal made up to illustrate the basic features of the structure. The collateral for this hypothetical CMO is a hypothetical passthrough with a total par value of $400 million and the following characteristics: (1) the passthrough coupon rate is 7.5%, (2) the weighted average coupon (WAC) is 8.125%, and (3) the weighted average maturity (WAM) is 357 months. This is the same passthrough that we used in Section 3 to describe the cash flow of a passthrough based on some PSA assumption.

From this $400 million of collateral, four bond classes or tranches are created. Their characteristics are summarized in Exhibit 61-5. The total par value of the four tranches is equal to the par value of the collateral (i.e., the passthrough security).[8] In this simple structure, the coupon rate is the same for each tranche and also the same as the coupon rate on the collateral. There is no reason why this must be so, and, in fact, typically the coupon rate varies by tranche.

Now remember that a CMO is created by redistributing the cash flow—interest and principal—to the different tranches based on a set of payment rules. The payment rules at the bottom of Exhibit 61-5 describe how the cash flow from the passthrough (i.e., collateral) is to be distributed to the four tranches. There are separate rules for the distribution of the coupon interest and the payment of principal (the principal being the total of the scheduled principal payment and any prepayments).

While the payment rules for the disbursement of the principal payments are known, the precise amount of the principal in each month is not. This will depend on the cash flow, and therefore principal payments, of the collateral, which depends on the actual prepayment rate of the collateral. An assumed PSA speed allows the cash flow to be projected. Exhibit 61-6 shows the cash flow (interest, scheduled principal repayment, and prepayments) assuming 165 PSA. Assuming that the collateral does prepay at 165 PSA, the cash flow available to all four tranches of FJF-01 will be precisely the cash flow shown in Exhibit 61-6.

EXHIBIT 61-5	FJF-01—A Hypothetical 4-Tranche Sequential-Pay Structure	
Tranche	Par Amount ($)	Coupon Rate (%)
A	194,500,000	7.5
B	36,000,000	7.5
C	96,500,000	7.5
D	73,000,000	7.5
Total	400,000,000	

Payment rules:

1. *For payment of monthly coupon interest:* Disburse monthly coupon interest to each tranche on the basis of the amount of principal outstanding for each tranche at the beginning of the month.

2. *For disbursement of principal payments:* Disburse principal payments to tranche A until it is completely paid off. After tranche A is completely paid off, disburse principal payments to tranche B until it is completely paid off. After tranche B is completely paid off, disburse principal payments to tranche C until it is completely paid off. After tranche C is completely paid off, disburse principal payments to tranche D until it is completely paid off.

---

[8] Actually, a CMO is backed by a pool of passthrough securities.

| EXHIBIT 61-6 | Monthly Cash Flow for Selected Months for FJF-01 Assuming 165 PSA |

	Tranche A			Tranche B		
Month	Balance ($)	Principal ($)	Interest ($)	Balance ($)	Principal ($)	Interest ($)
1	194,500,000	709,923	1,215,625	36,000,000	0	225,000
2	193,790,077	821,896	1,211,188	36,000,000	0	225,000
3	192,968,181	933,560	1,206,051	36,000,000	0	225,000
4	192,034,621	1,044,822	1,200,216	36,000,000	0	225,000
5	190,989,799	1,155,586	1,193,686	36,000,000	0	225,000
6	189,834,213	1,265,759	1,186,464	36,000,000	0	225,000
7	188,568,454	1,375,246	1,178,553	36,000,000	0	225,000
8	187,193,208	1,483,954	1,169,958	36,000,000	0	225,000
9	185,709,254	1,591,789	1,160,683	36,000,000	0	225,000
10	184,117,464	1,698,659	1,150,734	36,000,000	0	225,000
11	182,418,805	1,804,473	1,140,118	36,000,000	0	225,000
12	180,614,332	1,909,139	1,128,840	36,000,000	0	225,000
75	12,893,479	2,143,974	80,584	36,000,000	0	225,000
76	10,749,504	2,124,935	67,184	36,000,000	0	225,000
77	8,624,569	2,106,062	53,904	36,000,000	0	225,000
78	6,518,507	2,087,353	40,741	36,000,000	0	225,000
79	4,431,154	2,068,807	27,695	36,000,000	0	225,000
80	2,362,347	2,050,422	14,765	36,000,000	0	225,000
81	311,926	311,926	1,950	36,000,000	1,720,271	225,000
82	0	0	0	34,279,729	2,014,130	214,248
83	0	0	0	32,265,599	1,996,221	201,660
84	0	0	0	30,269,378	1,978,468	189,184
85	0	0	0	28,290,911	1,960,869	176,818
95	0	0	0	9,449,331	1,793,089	59,058
96	0	0	0	7,656,242	1,777,104	47,852
97	0	0	0	5,879,138	1,761,258	36,745
98	0	0	0	4,117,879	1,745,550	25,737
99	0	0	0	2,372,329	1,729,979	14,827
100	0	0	0	642,350	642,350	4,015
101	0	0	0	0	0	0

(Exhibit continued on next page …)

EXHIBIT 61-6	(continued)

| Month | Tranche C | | | Tranche D | | |
	Balance ($)	Principal ($)	Interest ($)	Balance ($)	Principal ($)	Interest ($)
1	96,500,000	0	603,125	73,000,000	0	456,250
2	96,500,000	0	603,125	73,000,000	0	456,250
3	96,500,000	0	603,125	73,000,000	0	456,250
4	96,500,000	0	603,125	73,000,000	0	456,250
5	96,500,000	0	603,125	73,000,000	0	456,250
6	96,500,000	0	603,125	73,000,000	0	456,250
7	96,500,000	0	603,125	73,000,000	0	456,250
8	96,500,000	0	603,125	73,000,000	0	456,250
9	96,500,000	0	603,125	73,000,000	0	456,250
10	96,500,000	0	603,125	73,000,000	0	456,250
11	96,500,000	0	603,125	73,000,000	0	456,250
12	96,500,000	0	603,125	73,000,000	0	456,250
95	96,500,000	0	603,125	73,000,000	0	456,250
96	96,500,000	0	603,125	73,000,000	0	456,250
97	96,500,000	0	603,125	73,000,000	0	456,250
98	96,500,000	0	603,125	73,000,000	0	456,250
99	96,500,000	0	603,125	73,000,000	0	456,250
100	96,500,000	1,072,194	603,125	73,000,000	0	456,250
101	95,427,806	1,699,243	596,424	73,000,000	0	456,250
102	93,728,563	1,684,075	585,804	73,000,000	0	456,250
103	92,044,489	1,669,039	575,278	73,000,000	0	456,250
104	90,375,450	1,654,134	564,847	73,000,000	0	456,250
105	88,721,315	1,639,359	554,508	73,000,000	0	456,250
175	3,260,287	869,602	20,377	73,000,000	0	456,250
176	2,390,685	861,673	14,942	73,000,000	0	456,250
177	1,529,013	853,813	9,556	73,000,000	0	456,250
178	675,199	675,199	4,220	73,000,000	170,824	456,250
179	0	0	0	72,829,176	838,300	455,182
180	0	0	0	71,990,876	830,646	449,943
181	0	0	0	71,160,230	823,058	444,751
182	0	0	0	70,337,173	815,536	439,607
183	0	0	0	69,521,637	808,081	434,510
184	0	0	0	68,713,556	800,690	429,460
185	0	0	0	67,912,866	793,365	424,455
350	0	0	0	1,235,674	160,220	7,723
351	0	0	0	1,075,454	158,544	6,722
352	0	0	0	916,910	156,883	5,731
353	0	0	0	760,027	155,238	4,750
354	0	0	0	604,789	153,607	3,780
355	0	0	0	451,182	151,991	2,820
356	0	0	0	299,191	150,389	1,870
357	0	0	0	148,802	148,802	930

Note: The cash flow for a tranche in each month is the sum of the principal and interest.

To demonstrate how the payment rules for FJF-01 work, Exhibit 61-6 shows the cash flow for selected months assuming the collateral prepays at 165 PSA. For each tranche, the exhibit shows: (1) the balance at the end of the month, (2) the principal paid down (scheduled principal repayment plus prepayments), and (3) interest. In month 1, the cash flow for the collateral consists of a principal payment of $709,923 and an interest payment of $2.5 million (0.075 times $400 million divided by 12). The interest payment is distributed to the four tranches based on the amount of the par value outstanding. So, for example, tranche A receives $1,215,625 (0.075 times $194,500,000 divided by 12) of the $2.5 million. The principal, however, is all distributed to tranche A. Therefore, the cash flow for tranche A in month 1 is $1,925,548. The principal balance at the end of month 1 for tranche A is $193,790,076 (the original principal balance of $194,500,000 less the principal payment of $709,923). No principal payment is distributed to the three other tranches because there is still a principal balance outstanding for tranche A. This will be true for months 2 through 80. The cash flow for tranche A for each month is found by adding the amounts shown in the "Principal" and "Interest" columns. So, for tranche A, the cash flow in month 8 is $1,483,954 plus $1,169,958 or $2,653,912. The cash flow from months 82 on is zero based on 165 PSA.

After month 81, the principal balance will be zero for tranche A. For the collateral, the cash flow in month 81 is $3,318,521, consisting of a principal payment of $2,032,197 and interest of $1,286,325. At the beginning of month 81 (end of month 80), the principal balance for tranche A is $311,926. Therefore, $311,926 of the $2,032,196 of the principal payment from the collateral will be disbursed to tranche A. After this payment is made, no additional principal payments are made to this tranche as the principal balance is zero. The remaining principal payment from the collateral, $1,720,271, is distributed to tranche B. Based on an assumed prepayment speed of 165 PSA, tranche B then begins receiving principal payments in month 81. The cash flow for tranche B for each month is found by adding the amounts shown in the "Principal" and "Interest" columns. For months 1 though 80, the cash flow is just the interest. There is no cash flow after month 100 for Tranche B.

Exhibit 61-6 shows that tranche B is fully paid off by month 100, when tranche C begins to receive principal payments. Tranche C is not fully paid off until month 178, at which time tranche D begins receiving the remaining principal payments. The maturity (i.e., the time until the principal is fully paid off) for these four tranches assuming 165 PSA would be 81 months for tranche A, 100 months for tranche B, 178 months for tranche C, and 357 months for tranche D. The cash flow for each month for tranches C and D is found by adding the principal and the interest for the month.

The **principal pay down window** or **principal window** for a tranche is the time period between the beginning and the ending of the principal payments to that tranche. So, for example, for tranche A, the principal pay down window would be month 1 to month 81 assuming 165 PSA. For tranche B it is from month 81 to month 100.[9] In confirmation of trades involving CMOs, the principal pay down window is specified in terms of the initial month that principal is expected to be received to the final month that principal is expected to be received.

Let's look at what has been accomplished by creating the CMO. Earlier we saw that the average life of the passthrough is 8.76 years assuming a prepayment speed of 165 PSA. Exhibit 61-7 reports the average life of the collateral and the

---

[9] The window is also specified in terms of the length of the time from the beginning of the principal pay down window to the end of the principal pay down window. For tranche A, the window would be stated as 81 months, for tranche B 20 months.

EXHIBIT 61-7	Average Life for the Collateral and the Four Tranches of FJF-01				
Prepayment Speed (PSA)	**Average life (in years) for**				
	Collateral	**Tranche A**	**Tranche B**	**Tranche C**	**Tranche D**
50	15.11	7.48	15.98	21.02	27.24
100	11.66	4.90	10.86	15.78	24.58
165	8.76	3.48	7.49	11.19	20.27
200	7.68	3.05	6.42	9.60	18.11
300	5.63	2.32	4.64	6.81	13.36
400	4.44	1.94	3.70	5.31	10.34
500	3.68	1.69	3.12	4.38	8.35
600	3.16	1.51	2.74	3.75	6.96
700	2.78	1.38	2.47	3.30	5.95

four tranches assuming different prepayment speeds. Notice that the four tranches have average lives that are both shorter and longer than the collateral, thereby attracting investors who have a preference for an average life different from that of the collateral.

There is still a major problem: there is considerable variability of the average life for the tranches. We'll see how this can be handled later on. However, there is some protection provided for each tranche against prepayment risk. This is because prioritizing the distribution of principal (i.e., establishing the payment rules for principal) effectively protects the shorter-term tranche A in this structure against extension risk. This protection must come from somewhere, so it comes from the three other tranches. Similarly, tranches C and D provide protection against extension risk for tranches A and B. At the same time, tranches C and D benefit because they are provided protection against contraction risk, the protection coming from tranches A and B.

B. Accrual Tranches

In our previous example, the payment rules for interest provided for all tranches to be paid interest each month. In many sequential-pay CMO structures, at least one tranche does not receive current interest. Instead, the interest for that tranche would accrue and be added to the principal balance. Such a tranche is commonly referred to as an **accrual tranche** or a **Z bond**. The interest that would have been paid to the accrual tranche is used to pay off the principal balance of earlier tranches.

To see this, consider FJF-02, a hypothetical CMO structure with the same collateral as our previous example and with four tranches, each with a coupon rate of 7.5%. The last tranche, Z, is an accrual tranche. The structure for FJF-02 is shown in Exhibit 61-8.

Exhibit 61-9 shows cash flows for selected months for tranches A and B. Let's look at month 1 and compare it to month 1 in Exhibit 61-6. Both cash flows are based on 165 PSA. The principal payment from the collateral is $709,923. In FJF-01, this is the principal paydown for tranche A. In FJF-02, the interest for tranche

EXHIBIT 61-8	FJF-02—A Hypothetical 4-Tranche Sequential-Pay Structure with an Accrual Tranche	

Tranche	Par Amount ($)	Coupon Rate (%)
A	194,500,000	7.5
B	36,000,000	7.5
C	96,500,000	7.5
Z (Accrual)	73,000,000	7.5
Total	400,000,000	

Payment rules:

1. *For payment of monthly coupon interest:* Disburse monthly coupon interest to tranches A, B, and C on the basis of the amount of principal outstanding for each tranche at the beginning of the month. For tranche Z, accrue the interest based on the principal plus accrued interest in the previous month. The interest for tranche Z is to be paid to the earlier tranches as a principal paydown.

2. *For disbursement of principal payments:* Disburse principal payments to tranche A until it is completely paid off. After tranche A is completely paid off, disburse principal payments to tranche B until it is completely paid off. After tranche B is completely paid off, disburse principal payments to tranche C until it is completely paid off. After tranche C is completely paid off, disburse principal payments to tranche Z until the original principal balance plus accrued interest is completely paid off.

Z, $456,250, is not paid to that tranche but instead is used to pay down the principal of tranche A. So, the principal payment to tranche A in Exhibit 61-9 is $1,166,173, the collateral's principal payment of $709,923 plus the interest of $456,250 that was diverted from tranche Z.

The expected final maturity for tranches A, B, and C has shortened as a result of the inclusion of tranche Z. The final payout for tranche A is 64 months rather than 81 months; for tranche B it is 77 months rather than 100 months; and, for tranche C it is 113 months rather than 178 months.

The average lives for tranches A, B, and C are shorter in FJF-02 compared to our previous non-accrual, sequential-pay tranche example, FJF-01, because of the inclusion of the accrual tranche. For example, at 165 PSA, the average lives are as follows:

Structure	Tranche A	Tranche B	Tranche C
FJF-02	2.90	5.86	7.87
FJF-01	3.48	7.49	11.19

The reason for the shortening of the non-accrual tranches is that the interest that would be paid to the accrual tranche is being allocated to the other tranches. Tranche Z in FJF-02 will have a longer average life than tranche D in FJF-01 because in tranche Z the interest payments are being diverted to tranches A, B, and C.

Thus, shorter-term tranches and a longer-term tranche are created by including an accrual tranche in FJF-02 compared to FJF-01. The accrual tranche has appeal to investors who are concerned with reinvestment risk. Since there are no coupon payments to reinvest, reinvestment risk is eliminated until all the other tranches are paid off.

EXHIBIT 61-9	Monthly Cash Flow for Selected Months for Tranches A and B for FJF-02 Assuming 165 PSA

Month	Tranche A			Tranche B		
	Balance ($)	Principal ($)	Interest ($)	Balance ($)	Principal ($)	Interest ($)
1	194,500,000	1,166,173	1,215,625	36,000,000	0	225,000
2	193,333,827	1,280,997	1,208,336	36,000,000	0	225,000
3	192,052,829	1,395,531	1,200,330	36,000,000	0	225,000
4	190,657,298	1,509,680	1,191,608	36,000,000	0	225,000
5	189,147,619	1,623,350	1,182,173	36,000,000	0	225,000
6	187,524,269	1,736,446	1,172,027	36,000,000	0	225,000
7	185,787,823	1,848,875	1,161,174	36,000,000	0	225,000
8	183,938,947	1,960,543	1,149,618	36,000,000	0	225,000
9	181,978,404	2,071,357	1,137,365	36,000,000	0	225,000
10	179,907,047	2,181,225	1,124,419	36,000,000	0	225,000
11	177,725,822	2,290,054	1,110,786	36,000,000	0	225,000
12	175,435,768	2,397,755	1,096,474	36,000,000	0	225,000
60	15,023,406	3,109,398	93,896	36,000,000	0	225,000
61	11,914,007	3,091,812	74,463	36,000,000	0	225,000
62	8,822,195	3,074,441	55,139	36,000,000	0	225,000
63	5,747,754	3,057,282	35,923	36,000,000	0	225,000
64	2,690,472	2,690,472	16,815	36,000,000	349,863	225,000
65	0	0	0	35,650,137	3,023,598	222,813
66	0	0	0	32,626,540	3,007,069	203,916
67	0	0	0	29,619,470	2,990,748	185,122
68	0	0	0	26,628,722	2,974,633	166,430
69	0	0	0	23,654,089	2,958,722	147,838
70	0	0	0	20,695,367	2,943,014	129,346
71	0	0	0	17,752,353	2,927,508	110,952
72	0	0	0	14,824,845	2,912,203	92,655
73	0	0	0	11,912,642	2,897,096	74,454
74	0	0	0	9,015,546	2,882,187	56,347
75	0	0	0	6,133,358	2,867,475	38,333
76	0	0	0	3,265,883	2,852,958	20,412
77	0	0	0	412,925	412,925	2,581
78	0	0	0	0	0	0
79	0	0	0	0	0	0
80	0	0	0	0	0	0

C. Floating-Rate Tranches

The tranches described thus far have a fixed rate. There is a demand for tranches that have a floating rate. The problem is that the collateral pays a fixed rate and therefore it would be difficult to create a tranche with a floating rate. However, a floating-rate tranche can be created. This is done by creating from any fixed-rate tranche a floater and an inverse floater combination. We will illustrate the creation of a **floating-rate tranche** and an **inverse floating-rate tranche** using the hypothetical CMO structure—the 4-tranche sequential-pay structure with an accrual tranche (FJF-02).[10] We can select any of the tranches from which to create a floating-rate and inverse floating-rate tranche. In fact, we can create these two securities for more than one of the four tranches or for only a portion of one tranche.

In this case, we create a floater and an inverse floater from tranche C. A floater could have been created from any of the other tranches. The par value for this tranche is $96.5 million, and we create two tranches that have a combined par value of $96.5 million. We refer to this CMO structure with a floater and an inverse floater as FJF-03. It has five tranches, designated A, B, FL, IFL, and Z, where FL is the floating-rate tranche and IFL is the inverse floating-rate tranche. Exhibit 61-10 describes FJF-03. Any reference rate can be used to create a floater and the corresponding inverse floater. The reference rate for setting the coupon rate for FL and IFL in FJF-03 is 1-month LIBOR.

EXHIBIT 61-10	FJF-03—A Hypothetical 5-Tranche Sequential-Pay Structure with Floater, Inverse Floater, and Accrual Bond Tranches

Tranche	Par Amount ($)	Coupon Rate (%)
A	194,500,000	7.50
B	36,000,000	7.50
FL	72,375,000	1-month LIBOR + 0.50
IFL	24,125,000	$28.50 - 3 \times$ (1-month LIBOR)
Z (Accrual)	73,000,000	7.50
Total	400,000,000	

Payment rules:

1. *For payment of monthly coupon interest:* Disburse monthly coupon interest to tranches A, B, FL, and IFL on the basis of the amount of principal outstanding at the beginning of the month. For tranche Z, accrue the interest based on the principal plus accrued interest in the previous month. The interest for tranche Z is to be paid to the earlier tranches as a principal paydown. The maximum coupon rate for FL is 10%; the minimum coupon rate for IFL is 0%

2. *For disbursement of principal payments:* Disburse principal payments to tranche A until it is completely paid off. After tranche A is completely paid off, disburse principal payments to tranche B until it is completely paid off. After tranche B is completely paid off, disburse principal payments to tranches FL and IFL until they are completely paid off. The principal payments between tranches FL and IFL should be made in the following way: 75% to tranche FL and 25% to tranche IFL. After tranches FL and IFI are completely paid off, disburse principal payments to tranche Z until the original principal balance plus accrued interest are completely paid off.

---

[10] The same principle for creating a floating-rate tranche and inverse-floating rate tranche could have been accomplished using the 4-tranche sequential-pay structure without an accrual tranche (FJF-01).

The amount of the par value of the floating-rate tranche will be some portion of the $96.5 million. There are an infinite number of ways to slice up the $96.5 million between the floater and inverse floater, and final partitioning will be driven by the demands of investors. In the FJF-03 structure, we made the floater from $72,375,000 or 75% of the $96.5 million. The coupon formula for the floater is 1-month LIBOR plus 50 basis points. So, for example, if LIBOR is 3.75% at the reset date, the coupon rate on the floater is 3.75% + 0.5%, or 4.25%. There is a cap on the coupon rate for the floater (discussed later).

Unlike a floating-rate note in the corporate bond market whose principal is unchanged over the life of the instrument, the floater's principal balance declines over time as principal payments are made. The principal payments to the floater are determined by the principal payments from the tranche from which the floater is created. In our CMO structure, this is tranche C.

Since the floater's par value is $72,375,000 of the $96.5 million, the balance is par value for the inverse floater. Assuming that 1-month LIBOR is the reference rate, the coupon formula for the inverse floater takes the following form:

$$K - L \times (\text{1-month LIBOR})$$

where K and L are constants whose interpretation will be explained shortly.

In FJF-03, K is set at 28.50% and L at 3. Thus, if 1-month LIBOR is 3.75%, the coupon rate for the month is:

$$28.50\% - 3 \times (3.75\%) = 17.25\%$$

K is the cap or maximum coupon rate for the inverse floater. In FJF-03, the cap for the inverse floater is 28.50%. The determination of the inverse floater's cap rate is based on (1) the amount of interest that would have been paid to the tranche from which the floater and the inverse floater were created, tranche C in our hypothetical deal, and (2) the coupon rate for the floater if 1-month LIBOR is zero.

We will explain the determination of K by example. Let's see how the 28.5% for the inverse floater is determined. The total interest to be paid to tranche C if it was not split into the floater and the inverse floater is the principal of $96,500,000 times 7.5%, or $7,237,500. The maximum interest for the inverse floater occurs if 1-month LIBOR is zero. In that case, the coupon rate for the floater is

$$\text{1-month LIBOR} + 0.5\% = 0.5\%$$

Since the floater receives 0.5% on its principal of $72,375,000, the floater's interest is $361,875. The remainder of the interest of $7,237,500 from tranche C goes to the inverse floater. That is, the inverse floater's interest is $6,875,625 (= $7,237,500 − $361,875). Since the inverse floater's principal is $24,125,000, the cap rate for the inverse floater is

$$\frac{\$6,875,625}{\$24,125,000} = 28.5\%$$

In general, the formula for the cap rate on the inverse floater, K, is

$$K = \frac{\text{inverse floater interest when reference rate for floater is zero}}{\text{principal for inverse floater}}$$

The *L* or multiple in the coupon formula to determine the coupon rate for the inverse floater is called the *leverage*. The higher the leverage, the more the inverse floater's coupon rate changes for a given change in 1-month LIBOR. For example, a coupon leverage of 3 means that a 1-basis point change in 1-month LIBOR will change the coupon rate on the inverse floater by 3 basis points.

As in the case of the floater, the principal paydown of an inverse floater will be a proportionate amount of the principal paydown of tranche C.

Because 1-month LIBOR is always positive, the coupon rate paid to the floater cannot be negative. If there are no restrictions placed on the coupon rate for the inverse floater, however, it is possible for its coupon rate to be negative. To prevent this, a floor, or minimum, is placed on the coupon rate. In most structures, the floor is set at zero. Once a floor is set for the inverse floater, a cap or ceiling is imposed on the floater.

In FJF-03, a floor of zero is set for the inverse floater. The floor results in a cap or maximum coupon rate for the floater of 10%. This is determined as follows. If the floor for the inverse floater is zero, this means that the inverse floater receives no interest. All of the interest that would have been paid to tranche C, $7,237,500, would then be paid to the floater. Since the floater's principal is $72,375,000, the cap rate on the floater is $7,237,500/$72,375,000, or 10%.

In general, the cap rate for the floater *assuming a floor of zero for inverse floater* is determined as follows:

$$\text{cap rate for floater} = \frac{\text{collateral tranche interest}}{\text{principal for floater}}$$

The cap for the floater and the inverse floater, the floor for the inverse floater, the leverage, and the floater's spread are not determined independently. Any cap or floor imposed on the coupon rate for the floater and the inverse floater must be selected so that the weighted average coupon rate does not exceed the collateral tranche's coupon rate.

D. Structured Interest-Only Tranches

CMO structures can be created so that a tranche receives only interest. Interest only (IO) tranches in a CMO structure are commonly referred to as **structured IOs** to distinguish them from IO mortgage strips that we will describe later in this chapter. The basic principle in creating a structured IO is to set the coupon rate below the collateral's coupon rate so that excess interest can be generated. It is the excess interest that is used to create one or more structured IOs.

Let's look at how a structured IO is created using an illustration. Thus far, we used a simple CMO structure in which all the tranches have the same coupon rate (7.5%) and that coupon rate is the same as the collateral. A structured IO is created from a CMO structure where the coupon rate for at least one tranche is different from the collateral's coupon rate. This is seen in FJF-04 shown in Exhibit 61-11. In this structure, notice that the coupon interest rate for each tranche is less than the coupon interest rate for the collateral. That means that there is excess interest from the collateral that is not being paid to all the tranches. At one time, all of that excess interest not paid to the tranches was paid to a bond class called a "residual". Eventually (due to changes in the tax law that do not concern us here), structures of CMO began allocating the excess interest to the tranche that receives only interest. This is tranche IO in FJF-04.

Notice that for this structure the par amount for the IO tranche is shown as $52,566,667 and the coupon rate is 7.5%. Since this is an IO tranche there is no par amount. The amount shown is the amount upon which the interest payments

EXHIBIT 61-11	FJF-04: A Hypothetical Five–Tranche Sequential Pay with an Accrual Tranche, an Interest-Only Tranche, and a Residual Class	

Tranche	Par Amount	Coupon Rate (%)
A	$194,500,000	6.00
B	36,000,000	6.50
C	96,500,000	7.00
Z	73,000,000	7.25
IO	52,566,667 (Notional)	7.50
Total	$400,000,000	

Payment rules:

1. *For payment of monthly coupon interest:* Disburse monthly coupon interest to tranches A, B, and C on the basis of the amount of principal outstanding for each class at the beginning of the month. For tranche Z, accrue the interest based on the principal plus accrued interest in the previous month. The interest for tranche Z is to be paid to the earlier tranches as a principal pay down. Disburse periodic interest to the IO tranche based on the notional amount for all tranches at the beginning of the month.

2. *For disbursement of principal payments:* Disburse monthly principal payments to tranche A until it is completely paid off. After tranche A is completely paid off, disburse principal payments to tranche B until it is completely paid off. After tranche B is completely paid off, disburse principal payments to tranche C until it is completely paid off. After tranche C is completely paid off, disburse principal payments to tranche Z until the original principal balance plus accrued interest is completely paid off.

3. *No principal is to be paid to the IO tranche:* The notional amount of the IO tranche declines based on the principal payments to all other tranches.

will be determined, not the amount that will be paid to the holder of this tranche. Therefore, it is called a **notional amount**. The resulting IO is called a **notional IO**.

Let's look at how the notional amount is determined. Consider tranche A. The par value is $194.5 million and the coupon rate is 6%. Since the collateral's coupon rate is 7.5%, the excess interest is 150 basis points (1.5%). Therefore, an IO with a 1.5% coupon rate and a notional amount of $194.5 million can be created from tranche A. But this is equivalent to an IO with a notional amount of $38.9 million and a coupon rate of 7.5%. Mathematically, this notional amount is found as follows:

$$\text{notional amount for 7.5\% IO} = \frac{\text{original tranche's par value} \times \text{excess interest}}{0.075}$$

where

excess interest = collateral tranche's coupon rate − tranche coupon rate

For example, for tranche A:

excess interest = 0.075 − 0.060 = 0.015

tranche's par value = $194,500,000

$$\text{notional amount for 7.5\% IO} = \frac{\$194,500,000 \times 0.015}{0.075} = \$38,900,000$$

Similarly, from tranche B with a par value of $36 million, the excess interest is 100 basis points (1%) and therefore an IO with a coupon rate of 1% and a notional amount of $36 million can be created. But this is equivalent to creating an IO with a notional amount of $4.8 million and a coupon rate of 7.5%. This procedure is shown in Exhibit 61-12 for all four tranches.

E. Planned Amortization Class Tranches

The CMO structures discussed above attracted many institutional investors who had previously either avoided investing in mortgage-backed securities or allocated only a nominal portion of their portfolio to this sector of the bond market. While some traditional corporate bond buyers shifted their allocation to CMOs, a majority of institutional investors remained on the sidelines, concerned about investing in an instrument they continued to perceive as posing significant prepayment risk. This concern was based on the substantial average life variability, despite the innovations designed to mitigate prepayment risk.

In 1987, several structures came to market that shared the following characteristic: if the prepayment speed is within a specified band over the collateral's life, the cash flow pattern is known. The greater predictability of the cash flow for these classes of bonds, now referred to as **planned amortization class (PAC) bonds**, occurs because there is a principal repayment schedule that must be satisfied. PAC bondholders have priority over all other classes in the CMO structure in receiving principal payments from the collateral. The greater certainty of the cash flow for the PAC bonds comes at the expense of the non-PAC tranches, called the **support tranches** or **companion tranches**. It is these tranches that absorb the prepayment risk. Because PAC tranches have protection against both extension risk and contraction risk, they are said to provide **two-sided prepayment protection**.

To illustrate how to create a PAC bond, we will use as collateral the $400 million passthrough with a coupon rate of 7.5%, an 8.125% WAC, and a WAM of 357 months. The creation requires the specification of two PSA prepayment rates—a *lower PSA prepayment assumption* and an *upper PSA prepayment assumption*. In our illustration the lower PSA prepayment assumption will be 90 PSA and the upper PSA prepayment assumption will be 300 PSA. A natural question is: How does one select the lower and upper PSA prepayment assumptions? These are dictated by market conditions. For our purpose here, how they are determined is not important. The lower and upper PSA prepayment assumptions are referred to as the **initial PAC collar** or the **initial PAC band**. In our illustration the initial PAC collar is 90-300 PSA.

| EXHIBIT 61-12 | Creating a Notional IO Tranche | | |

Tranche	Par Amount	Excess Interest (%)	Notional Amount for a 7.5% Coupon Rate IO
A	$194,500,000	1.50	$38,900,000
B	36,000,000	1.00	4,800,000
C	96,500,000	0.50	6,433,333
Z	73,000,000	0.25	2,433,333

Notional amount for 7.5% IO = $52,566,667

The second column of Exhibit 61-13 shows the principal payment (scheduled principal repayment plus prepayments) for selected months assuming a prepayment speed of 90 PSA, and the next column shows the principal payments for selected months assuming that the passthrough prepays at 300 PSA.

The last column of Exhibit 61-13 gives the minimum principal payment if the collateral prepays at 90 PSA or 300 PSA for months 1 to 349. (After month 349, the outstanding principal balance will be paid off if the prepayment speed is between 90 PSA and 300 PSA.) For example, in the first month, the principal payment would be $508,169 if the collateral prepays at 90 PSA and $1,075,931 if the collateral prepays at 300 PSA. Thus, the minimum principal payment is $508,169, as reported in the last column of Exhibit 61-13. In month 103, the minimum principal payment is also the amount if the prepayment speed is 90 PSA, $1,446,761, compared to $1,458,618 for 300 PSA. In month 104, however, a prepayment speed of 300 PSA would produce a principal payment of $1,433,539, which is less than the principal payment of $1,440,825 assuming 90 PSA. So, $1,433,539 is reported in the last column of Exhibit 61-13. From month 104 on, the minimum principal payment is the one that would result assuming a prepayment speed of 300 PSA.

In fact, if the collateral prepays at any one speed between 90 PSA and 300 PSA over its life, the minimum principal payment would be the amount reported in the last column of Exhibit 61-13. For example, if we had included principal payment figures assuming a prepayment speed of 200 PSA, the minimum principal payment would not change: from month 1 through month 103, the minimum principal payment is that generated from 90 PSA, but from month 104 on, the minimum principal payment is that generated from 300 PSA.

This characteristic of the collateral allows for the creation of a PAC tranche, assuming that the collateral prepays over its life at a speed between 90 PSA to 300 PSA. A schedule of principal repayments that the PAC bondholders are entitled to receive before any other tranche in the CMO structure is specified. The monthly schedule of principal repayments is as specified in the last column of Exhibit 61-13, which shows the minimum principal payment. That is, this minimum principal payment in each month is the principal repayment schedule (i.e., planned amortization schedule) for investors in the PAC tranche. While there is no assurance that the collateral will prepay at a constant speed between these two speeds over its life, a PAC tranche can be structured to assume that it will.

Exhibit 61-14 shows a CMO structure, FJF-05, created from the $400 million, 7.5% coupon passthrough with a WAC of 8.125% and a WAM of 357 months. There are just two tranches in this structure: a 7.5% coupon PAC tranche created assuming 90 to 300 PSA with a par value of $243.8 million, and a support tranche with a par value of $156.2 million.

Exhibit 61-15 reports the average life for the PAC tranche and the support tranche in FJF-05 assuming various *actual* prepayment speeds. Notice that between 90 PSA and 300 PSA, the average life for the PAC bond is stable at 7.26 years. However, at slower or faster PSA speeds, the schedule is broken, and the average life changes, extending when the prepayment speed is less than 90 PSA and contracting when it is greater than 300 PSA. Even so, there is much greater variability for the average life of the support tranche.

1. Creating a Series of PAC Tranches

Most CMO PAC structures have more than one class of PAC tranches. A sequence of six PAC tranches (i.e., PAC tranches paid off in sequence as specified by a principal schedule) is shown in Exhibit 61-16 and is called FJF-06. The

EXHIBIT 61-13	Monthly Principal Payment for $400 Million, 7.5% Coupon Passthrough with an 8.125% WAC and a 357 WAM Assuming Prepayment Rates of 90 PSA and 300 PSA

Month	At 90 PSA ($)	At 300 PSA	Minimum Principal Payment Available to PAC Investors— the PAC Schedule ($)
1	508,169	1,075,931	508,169
2	569,843	1,279,412	569,843
3	631,377	1,482,194	631,377
4	692,741	1,683,966	692,741
5	753,909	1,884,414	753,909
6	814,850	2,083,227	814,850
7	875,536	2,280,092	875,536
8	935,940	2,474,700	935,940
9	996,032	2,666,744	996,032
10	1,055,784	2,855,920	1,055,784
11	1,115,170	3,041,927	1,115,170
12	1,174,160	3,224,472	1,174,160
13	1,232,727	3,403,265	1,232,727
14	1,290,844	3,578,023	1,290,844
15	1,348,484	3,748,472	1,348,484
16	1,405,620	3,914,344	1,405,620
17	1,462,225	4,075,381	1,462,225
18	1,518,274	4,231,334	1,518,274
101	1,458,719	1,510,072	1,458,719
102	1,452,725	1,484,126	1,452,725
103	1,446,761	1,458,618	1,446,761
104	1,440,825	1,433,539	1,433,539
105	1,434,919	1,408,883	1,408,883
211	949,482	213,309	213,309
212	946,033	209,409	209,409
213	942,601	205,577	205,577
346	618,684	13,269	13,269
347	617,071	12,944	12,944
348	615,468	12,626	12,626
349	613,875	12,314	3,432
350	612,292	12,008	0
351	610,719	11,708	0
352	609,156	11,414	0
353	607,603	11,126	0
354	606,060	10,843	0
355	604,527	10,567	0
356	603,003	10,295	0
357	601,489	10,029	0

EXHIBIT 61-14	FJF-05 CMO Structure with One PAC Tranche and One Support Tranche	
Tranche	**Par Amount ($)**	**Coupon Rate (%)**
P (PAC)	243,800,000	7.5
S (Support)	156,200,000	7.5
Total	400,000,000	

Payment rules:

1. *For payment of monthly coupon interest:* Disburse monthly coupon interest to each tranche on the basis of the amount of principal outstanding for each tranche at the beginning of the month.

2. *For disbursement of principal payments:* Disburse principal payments to tranche P based on its schedule of principal repayments. Tranche P has priority with respect to current and future principal payments to satisfy the schedule. Any excess principal payments in a month over the amount necessary to satisfy the schedule for tranche P are paid to tranche S. When tranche S is completely paid off, all principal payments are to be made to tranche P regardless of the schedule.

total par value of the six PAC tranches is equal to $243.8 million, which is the amount of the single PAC tranche in FJF-05. The schedule of principal repayments for selected months for each PAC bond is shown in Exhibit 61-17.

Exhibit 61-18 shows the average life for the six PAC tranches and the support tranche in FJF-06 at various prepayment speeds. From a PAC bond in FJF-05 with an average life of 7.26, six tranches have been created with an average life as short as 2.58 years (P-A) and as long as 16.92 years (P-F) if prepayments stay within 90 PSA and 300 PSA.

EXHIBIT 61-15	Average Life for PAC Tranche and Support Tranche in FJF-05 Assuming Various Prepayment Speeds (Years)	
Prepayment Rate (PSA)	**PAC Bond (P)**	**Support Bond (S)**
0	15.97	27.26
50	9.44	24.00
90	7.26	20.06
100	7.26	18.56
150	7.26	12.57
165	7.26	11.16
200	7.26	8.38
250	7.26	5.37
300	7.26	3.13
350	6.56	2.51
400	5.92	2.17
450	5.38	1.94
500	4.93	1.77
700	3.70	1.37

EXHIBIT 61-16	FJF-06: CMO Structure with Six PAC Tranches and a Support Tranche	

Tranche	Par Amount	Coupon Rate (%)
P-A	$85,000,000	7.5
P-B	8,000,000	7.5
P-C	35,000,000	7.5
P-D	45,000,000	7.5
P-E	40,000,000	7.5
P-F	30,800,000	7.5
S	156,200,000	7.5
Total	$400,000,000	

Payment rules:

1. *For payment of monthly coupon interest:* Disburse monthly coupon interest to each tranche on the basis of the amount of principal outstanding of each tranche at the beginning of the month.

2. *For disbursement of principal payments:* Disburse monthly principal payments to tranches P-A to P-F based on their respective schedules of principal repayments. Tranche P-A has priority with respect to current and future principal payments to satisfy the schedule. Any excess principal payments in a month over the amount necessary to satisfy the schedule for tranche P-A are paid to tranche S. Once tranche P-A is completely paid off, tranche P-B has priority, then tranche P-C, etc. When tranche S is completely paid off, all principal payments are to be made to the remaining PAC tranches in order of priority regardless of the schedule.

As expected, the average lives are stable if the prepayment speed is between 90 PSA and 300 PSA. Notice that even outside this range the average life is stable for several of the PAC tranches. For example, the PAC P-A tranche is stable even if prepayment speeds are as high as 400 PSA. For the PAC P-B, the average life does not vary when prepayments are in the initial collar until prepayments are greater than 350 PSA. Why is it that the shorter the PAC, the more protection it has against faster prepayments?

To understand this phenomenon, remember there are $156.2 million in support tranches that are protecting the $85 million of PAC P-A. Thus, even if prepayments are faster than the initial upper collar, there may be sufficient support tranches to assure the satisfaction of the schedule. In fact, as can be seen from Exhibit 61-18, even if prepayments are 400 PSA over the life of the collateral, the average life is unchanged.

Now consider PAC P-B. The support tranches provide protection for both the $85 million of PAC P-A and $93 million of PAC P-B. As can be seen from Exhibit 61-18, prepayments could be 350 PSA and the average life is still unchanged. From Exhibit 61-18 it can be seen that the degree of protection against extension risk increases the shorter the PAC. Thus, while the initial collar may be 90 to 300 PSA, the **effective collar** is wider for the shorter PAC tranches.

2. PAC Window

The length of time over which expected principal repayments are made is referred to as the window. For a PAC tranche it is referred to as the **PAC window**. A PAC window can be wide or narrow. The narrower a PAC window, the more it resembles a corporate bond with a bullet payment. For example, if the PAC schedule calls for just one principal payment (the narrowest window) in month

EXHIBIT 61-17		**Mortgage Balance for Selected Months for FJF-06 Assuming 165 PSA**					

	Tranche						
Month	**A**	**B**	**C**	**D**	**E**	**F**	**Support**
1	85,000,000	8,000,000	35,000,000	45,000,000	40,000,000	30,800,000	156,200,000
2	84,491,830	8,000,000	35,000,000	45,000,000	40,000,000	30,800,000	155,998,246
3	83,921,987	8,000,000	35,000,000	45,000,000	40,000,000	30,800,000	155,746,193
4	83,290,609	8,000,000	35,000,000	45,000,000	40,000,000	30,800,000	155,444,011
5	82,597,868	8,000,000	35,000,000	45,000,000	40,000,000	30,800,000	155,091,931
6	81,843,958	8,000,000	35,000,000	45,000,000	40,000,000	30,800,000	154,690,254
7	81,029,108	8,000,000	35,000,000	45,000,000	40,000,000	30,800,000	154,239,345
8	80,153,572	8,000,000	35,000,000	45,000,000	40,000,000	30,800,000	153,739,635
9	79,217,631	8,000,000	35,000,000	45,000,000	40,000,000	30,800,000	153,191,621
10	78,221,599	8,000,000	35,000,000	45,000,000	40,000,000	30,800,000	152,595,864
11	77,165,814	8,000,000	35,000,000	45,000,000	40,000,000	30,800,000	151,952,989
12	76,050,644	8,000,000	35,000,000	45,000,000	40,000,000	30,800,000	151,263,687
13	74,876,484	8,000,000	35,000,000	45,000,000	40,000,000	30,800,000	150,528,708
52	5,170,458	8,000,000	35,000,000	45,000,000	40,000,000	30,800,000	109,392,664
53	3,379,318	8,000,000	35,000,000	45,000,000	40,000,000	30,800,000	108,552,721
54	1,595,779	8,000,000	35,000,000	45,000,000	40,000,000	30,800,000	107,728,453
55	0	7,819,804	35,000,000	45,000,000	40,000,000	30,800,000	106,919,692
56	0	6,051,358	35,000,000	45,000,000	40,000,000	30,800,000	106,126,275
57	0	4,290,403	35,000,000	45,000,000	40,000,000	30,800,000	105,348,040
58	0	2,536,904	35,000,000	45,000,000	40,000,000	30,800,000	104,584,824
59	0	790,826	35,000,000	45,000,000	40,000,000	30,800,000	103,836,469
60	0	0	34,052,132	45,000,000	40,000,000	30,800,000	103,102,817
61	0	0	32,320,787	45,000,000	40,000,000	30,800,000	102,383,711
62	0	0	30,596,756	45,000,000	40,000,000	30,800,000	101,678,995
78	0	0	3,978,669	45,000,000	40,000,000	30,800,000	92,239,836
79	0	0	2,373,713	45,000,000	40,000,000	30,800,000	91,757,440
80	0	0	775,460	45,000,000	40,000,000	30,800,000	91,286,887
81	0	0	0	44,183,878	40,000,000	30,800,000	90,828,046
82	0	0	0	42,598,936	40,000,000	30,800,000	90,380,792
83	0	0	0	41,020,601	40,000,000	30,800,000	89,944,997
108	0	0	0	3,758,505	40,000,000	30,800,000	82,288,542
109	0	0	0	2,421,125	40,000,000	30,800,000	82,030,119
110	0	0	0	1,106,780	40,000,000	30,800,000	81,762,929
111	0	0	0	0	39,815,082	30,800,000	81,487,234
112	0	0	0	0	38,545,648	30,800,000	81,203,294
113	0	0	0	0	37,298,104	30,800,000	80,911,362

(Exhibit continued on next page ...)

EXHIBIT 61-17   (continued)

				Tranche			
Month	A	B	C	D	E	F	Support
153	0	0	0	0	1,715,140	30,800,000	65,030,732
154	0	0	0	0	1,107,570	30,800,000	64,575,431
155	0	0	0	0	510,672	30,800,000	64,119,075
156	0	0	0	0	0	30,724,266	63,661,761
157	0	0	0	0	0	30,148,172	63,203,587
158	0	0	0	0	0	29,582,215	62,744,644
347	0	0	0	0	0	29,003	1,697,536
348	0	0	0	0	0	16,058	1,545,142
349	0	0	0	0	0	3,432	1,394,152
350	0	0	0	0	0	0	1,235,674
351	0	0	0	0	0	0	1,075,454
352	0	0	0	0	0	0	916,910
353	0	0	0	0	0	0	760,026
354	0	0	0	0	0	0	604,789
355	0	0	0	0	0	0	451,182
356	0	0	0	0	0	0	299,191
357	0	0	0	0	0	0	148,801

120 and only interest payments up to month 120, this PAC tranche would resemble a 10-year (120-month) corporate bond.

PAC buyers appear to prefer tight windows, although institutional investors facing a liability schedule are generally better off with a window that more closely matches their liabilities. Investor demand dictates the PAC windows that dealers will create. Investor demand in turn is governed by the nature of investor liabilities.

3. Effective Collars and Actual Prepayments

The creation of a mortgage-backed security cannot make prepayment risk disappear. This is true for both a passthrough and a CMO. Thus, the reduction in prepayment risk (both extension risk and contraction risk) that a PAC offers investors must come from somewhere.

Where does the prepayment protection come from? It comes from the support tranches. It is the support tranches that defer principal payments to the PAC tranches if the collateral prepayments are slow; support tranches do not receive any principal until the PAC tranches receive the scheduled principal repayment. This reduces the risk that the PAC tranches will extend. Similarly, it is the support tranches that absorb any principal payments in excess of the scheduled principal payments that are made. This reduces the contraction risk of the PAC tranches. Thus, the key to the prepayment protection offered by a PAC tranche is the amount of support tranches outstanding. If the support tranches are paid off quickly because of faster-than-expected prepayments, then

| EXHIBIT 61-18 | Average Life for the Six PAC Tranches in FJF-06 Assuming Various Prepayment Speeds |

Prepayment Rate (PSA)	PAC Bonds					
	P-A	P-B	P-C	P-D	P-E	P-F
0	8.46	14.61	16.49	19.41	21.91	23.76
50	3.58	6.82	8.36	11.30	14.50	18.20
90	2.58	4.72	5.78	7.89	10.83	16.92
100	2.58	4.72	5.78	7.89	10.83	16.92
150	2.58	4.72	5.78	7.89	10.83	16.92
165	2.58	4.72	5.78	7.89	10.83	16.92
200	2.58	4.72	5.78	7.89	10.83	16.92
250	2.58	4.72	5.78	7.89	10.83	16.92
300	2.58	4.72	5.78	7.89	10.83	16.92
350	2.58	4.72	5.44	6.95	9.24	14.91
400	2.57	4.37	4.91	6.17	8.33	13.21
450	2.50	3.97	4.44	5.56	7.45	11.81
500	2.40	3.65	4.07	5.06	6.74	10.65
700	2.06	2.82	3.10	3.75	4.88	7.51

there is no longer any protection for the PAC tranches. *In fact, in FJF-06, if the support tranche is paid off, the structure effectively becomes a sequential-pay CMO.*

The support tranches can be thought of as bodyguards for the PAC bond-holders. When the bullets fly—i.e., prepayments occur—it is the bodyguards that get killed off first. The bodyguards are there to absorb the bullets. Once all the bodyguards are killed off (i.e., the support tranches paid off with faster-than-expected prepayments), the PAC tranches must fend for themselves: they are exposed to all the bullets. A PAC tranche in which all the support tranches have been paid off is called a **busted PAC** or **broken PAC**.

With the bodyguard metaphor for the support tranches in mind, let's consider two questions asked by investors in PAC tranches:

1. Will the schedule of principal repayments be satisfied if prepayments are faster than the initial upper collar?
2. Will the schedule of principal repayments be satisfied as long as prepayments stay within the initial collar?

a. Actual Prepayments Greater than the Initial Upper Collar

Let's address the first question. The initial upper collar for FJF-06 is 300 PSA. Suppose that actual prepayments are 500 PSA for seven consecutive months. Will this disrupt the schedule of principal repayments? The answer is: It depends!

There are two pieces of information we will need to answer this question. First, when does the 500 PSA occur? Second, what has been the actual prepayment experience up to the time that prepayments are 500 PSA? For example, suppose six years from now is when the prepayments reach 500 PSA, and also suppose that for the past six years the actual prepayment speed has been 90 PSA every month. What this means is that there are more bodyguards (i.e., support tranches) around than were expected when the PAC was structured at the initial collar. In establishing the schedule of principal repayments, it is assumed that the bodyguards would be killed off at 300 PSA. (Recall that 300 PSA is the upper collar prepayment assumption used in creating FJF-06.) But the actual prepayment experience results in them being killed off at only 90 PSA. Thus, six years from now when the 500 PSA is assumed to occur, there are more bodyguards than expected. In turn, a 500 PSA for seven consecutive months may have no effect on the ability of the schedule of principal repayments to be met.

In contrast, suppose that the actual prepayment experience for the first six years is 300 PSA (the upper collar of the initial PAC collar). In this case, there are no extra bodyguards around. As a result, any prepayment speeds faster than 300 PSA, such as 500 PSA in our example, jeopardize satisfaction of the principal repayment schedule and increase contraction risk. This does not mean that the schedule will be "busted"—the term used in the CMO market when the support tranches are fully paid off. What it does mean is that the prepayment protection is reduced.

It should be clear from these observations that the initial collars are not particularly useful in assessing the prepayment protection for a seasoned PAC tranche. This is most important to understand, as it is common for CMO buyers to compare prepayment protection of PACs in different CMO structures and conclude that the greater protection is offered by the one with the wider initial collar. This approach is inadequate because it is actual prepayment experience that determines the degree of prepayment protection, as well as the expected future prepayment behavior of the collateral.

The way to determine this protection is to calculate the **effective collar** for a seasoned PAC bond. An effective collar for a seasoned PAC is the lower and the upper PSA that can occur in the future and still allow maintenance of the schedule of principal repayments. For example, consider two seasoned PAC tranches in two CMO structures where the two PAC tranches have the same average life and the prepayment characteristics of the remaining collateral (i.e., the remaining mortgages in the mortgage pools) are similar. The information about these PAC tranches is as follows:

	PAC tranche X	PAC tranche Y
Initial PAC collar	180 PSA–350 PSA	170 PSA–410 PSA
Effective PAC collar	160 PSA–450 PSA	240 PSA–300 PSA

Notice that at issuance PAC tranche Y offered greater prepayment protection than PAC tranche X as indicated by the *wider* initial PAC collar. However, that protection is irrelevant for an investor who is considering the purchase of one of these two tranches today. Despite PAC tranche Y's greater prepayment protection at issuance than PAC tranche X, tranche Y has a much narrower effective PAC collar than PAC tranche X and therefore less prepayment protection.

The effective collar changes every month. An extended period over which actual prepayments are below the upper range of the initial PAC collar will result in an increase in the upper range of the effective collar. This is because there will be more bodyguards around than anticipated. An extended period of prepayments slower than the lower range of the initial PAC collar will raise the lower range of the effective collar. This is because it will take faster prepayments to make up the shortfall of the scheduled principal payments not made plus the scheduled future principal payments.

b. Actual Prepayments within the Initial Collar

The PAC schedule may not be satisfied even if the actual prepayments never fall outside of the *initial* collar. This may seem surprising since our previous analysis indicated that the average life would not change if prepayments are at either extreme of the initial collar. However, recall that all of our previous analysis has been based on a single PSA speed for the life of the structure.

The table below shows for FJF-05 what happens to the effective collar if prepayments are 300 PSA for the first 24 months but another prepayment speed for the balance of the life of the structure.

PSA from Year 2 on	Average Life
95	6.43
105	6.11
115	6.01
120	6.00
125	6.00
300	6.00
305	5.62

Notice that the average life is stable at six years if the prepayments for the subsequent months are between 115 PSA and 300 PSA. That is, the effective PAC collar is no longer the initial collar. Instead, the lower collar has shifted upward. This means that the protection from year 2 on is for 115 to 300 PSA, a narrower band than initially (90 to 300 PSA), even though the earlier prepayments did not exceed the initial upper collar.

F. Support Tranches

The support tranches are the bonds that provide prepayment protection for the PAC tranches. Consequently, support tranches expose investors to the greatest level of prepayment risk. Because of this, investors must be particularly careful in assessing the cash flow characteristics of support tranches to reduce the likelihood of adverse portfolio consequences due to prepayments.

The support tranche typically is divided into different tranches. All the tranches we have discussed earlier are available, including sequential-pay support tranches, floater and inverse floater support tranches, and accrual support tranches.

The support tranche can even be partitioned to create support tranches with a schedule of principal payments. That is, support tranches that are PAC tranches can be created. In a structure with a PAC tranche and a support tranche with a PAC schedule of principal payments, the former is called a **PAC I tranche** or **Level I PAC tranche** and the latter a **PAC II tranche** or **Level II PAC tranche** or **scheduled tranche** (denoted SCH in a prospectus). While PAC II tranches have greater prepayment protection than the support tranches without a schedule of principal repayments, the prepayment protection is less than that provided PAC I tranches.

The support tranche without a principal repayment schedule can be used to create any type of tranche. In fact, a portion of the non-PAC II support tranche can be given a schedule of principal repayments. This tranche would be called a **PAC III tranche** or a **Level III PAC tranche**. While it provides protection against prepayments for the PAC I and PAC II tranches and is therefore subject to considerable prepayment risk, such a tranche has greater protection than the support tranche without a schedule of principal repayments.

G. An Actual CMO Structure

Thus far we have presented some hypothetical CMO structures in order to demonstrate the characteristics of the different types of tranches. Now let's look at an actual CMO structure, one that we will look at further in Reading 63 when we discuss how to analyze a CMO deal.

The CMO structure we will discuss is the Freddie Mac (FHLMC) Series 1706 issued in early 1994. The collateral for this structure is Freddie Mac 7% coupon passthroughs. A summary of the deal is provided in Exhibit 61-19.

There are 17 tranches in this structure: 10 PAC tranches, three scheduled tranches, a floating-rate support tranche, and an inverse floating-rate support tranche.[11] There are also two "TAC" support tranches. We will explain a TAC tranche below. Let's look at all tranches.

First, we know what a PAC tranche is. There are 10 of them: tranches A, B, C, D, E, G, H, J, K, and IA. The initial collar used to create the PAC tranches was 95 PSA to 300 PSA. The PAC tranches except for tranche IA are simply PACs that pay off in sequence. Tranche IA is structured such that the underlying collateral's interest not allocated to the other PAC tranches is paid to the IO tranche. This is a notional IO tranche and we described earlier in this section how it is created. In this deal the tranches from which the interest is stripped are the PAC tranches. So, tranche IA is referred to as a **PAC IO**. (As of the time of this writing, tranches A and B had already paid off all of their principal.)

The prepayment protection for the PAC bonds is provided by the support tranches. The support tranches in this deal are tranches LA, LB, M, O, OA, PF, and PS. Notice that the support tranches have been carved up in different ways. First, there are scheduled (SCH) tranches. These are what we have called the PAC II tranches earlier in this section. The scheduled tranches are LA, LB, and M. The initial PAC collar used to create the scheduled tranches was 190 PSA to 250 PSA.

There are two support tranches that are designed such that they are created with a schedule that provides protection against contraction risk but not against extension. We did not discuss these tranches in this reading. They are called **target amortization class** (TAC) **tranches**. The support tranches O and OA are TAC tranches. The schedule of principal payments is created by using just a single PSA. In this structure the single PSA is 225 PSA.

Finally, the support tranche without a schedule (that must provide support for the scheduled bonds and the PACs) was carved into two tranches—a floater (tranche PF) and an inverse floater (tranche PS). In this structure the creation of the floater and inverse floater was from a support tranche.

Now that we know what all these tranches are, the next step is to analyze them in terms of their relative value and their price volatility characteristics when rates change. We will do this in Reading 63.

---

[11] Actually there were two other tranches, R and RS, called "residuals." These tranches were not described in the reading. They receive any excess cash flows remaining after the payment of all the tranches. The residual is actually the equity part of the deal.

EXHIBIT 61-19	Summary of Federal Home Loan Mortgage Corporation—Multiclass Mortgage Participation Certificates (Guaranteed), Series 1706

Total Issue: $300,000,000   Original Settlement Date: 3/30/94

Issue Date: 2/18/94

Tranche	Original Balance ($)	Coupon (%)	Average Life (yrs)
A (PAC Bond)	24,600,000	4.50	1.3
B (PAC Bond)	11,100,000	5.00	2.5
C (PAC Bond)	25,500,000	5.25	3.5
D (PAC Bond)	9,150,000	5.65	4.5
E (PAC Bond)	31,650,000	6.00	5.8
G (PAC Bond)	30,750,000	6.25	7.9
H (PAC Bond)	27,450,000	6.50	10.9
J (PAC Bond)	5,220,000	6.50	14.4
K (PAC Bond)	7,612,000	7.00	18.8
LA (SCH Bond)	26,673,000	7.00	3.5
LB (SCH Bond)	36,087,000	7.00	3.5
M (SCH Bond)	18,738,000	7.00	11.2
O (TAC Bond)	13,348,000	7.00	2.5
OA (TAC Bond)	3,600,000	7.00	7.2
IA (IO, PAC Bond)	30,246,000	7.00	7.1
PF (FLTR, Support Bond)	21,016,000	6.75*	17.5
PS (INV FLTR, Support Bond)	7,506,000	7.70*	17.5

* Coupon at issuance.

Structural Features

Cash Flow Allocation: Commencing on the first principal payment date of the Class A Bonds, principal equal to the amount specified in the Prospectus will be applied to the Class A, B, C, D, E, G, H, J, K, LA, LB, M, O, OA, PF, and PS Bonds. After all other Classes have been retired, any remaining principal will be used to retire the Class O, OA, LA, LB, M, A, B, C, D, E, G, H, J, and K Bonds. The Notional Class IA Bond will have its notional principal amount retired along with the PAC Bonds.

Other: The PAC Range is 95% to 300% PSA for the A - K Bonds, 190% to 250% PSA for the LA, LB, and M Bonds, and 225% PSA for the O and OA Bonds.

STRIPPED MORTGAGE-BACKED SECURITIES

In a CMO, there are multiple bond classes (tranches) and separate rules for the distribution of the interest and the principal to the bond classes. There are mortgage-backed securities where there are only two bond classes and the rule for the distribution for interest and principal is simple: one bond class receives all of the principal and one bond class receives all of the interest. This mortgage-backed security is called a **stripped mortgage-backed security**. The bond class that receives all of the principal is called the **principal-only class** or **PO class**. The bond class that receives all of the interest is called the **interest-only class** or **IO class**. These securities are also called **mortgage strips**. The POs are called **principal-only mortgage strips** and the IOs are called **interest-only mortgage strips**.

We have already seen interest-only type mortgage-backed securities: the structured IO. This is a product that is created within a CMO structure. A structured IO is created from the excess interest (i.e., the difference between the interest paid on the collateral and the interest paid to the bond classes). There is no corresponding PO class within the CMO structure. In contrast, in a stripped mortgage-backed security, the IO class is created by simply specifying that all interest payments be made to that class.

A. Principal-Only Strips

A principal-only mortgage strip is purchased at a substantial discount from par value. The return an investor realizes depends on the speed at which prepayments are made. The faster the prepayments, the higher the investor's return. For example, suppose that a pool of 30-year mortgages has a par value of $400 million and the market value of the pool of mortgages is also $400 million. Suppose further that the market value of just the principal payments is $175 million. The dollar return from this investment is the difference between the par value of $400 million that will be repaid to the investor in the principal mortgage strip and the $175 million paid. That is, the dollar return is $225 million.

Since there is no interest that will be paid to the investor in a principal-only mortgage strip, the investor's return is determined solely by the speed at which he or she receives the $225 million. In the extreme case, if all homeowners in the underlying mortgage pool decide to prepay their mortgage loans immediately, PO investors will realize the $225 million immediately. At the other extreme, if all homeowners decide to remain in their homes for 30 years and make no prepayments, the $225 million will be spread out over 30 years, which would result in a lower return for PO investors.

Let's look at how the price of the PO would be expected to change as mortgage rates in the market change. When mortgage rates decline below the contract rate, prepayments are expected to speed up, accelerating payments to the PO investor. Thus, the cash flow of a PO improves (in the sense that principal repayments are received earlier). The cash flow will be discounted at a lower interest rate because the mortgage rate in the market has declined. The result is that the PO price will increase when mortgage rates decline. When mortgage rates rise above the contract rate, prepayments are expected to slow down. The cash flow deteriorates (in the sense that it takes longer to recover principal repayments). Couple this with a higher discount rate, and the price of a PO will fall when mortgage rates rise.

Exhibit 61-20 shows the general relationship between the price of a principal-only mortgage strip when interest rates change and compares it to the relationship for the underlying passthrough from which it is created.

B. Interest-Only Strips

An interest-only mortgage strip has no par value. In contrast to the PO investor, the IO investor wants prepayments to be slow. The reason is that the IO investor receives interest only on the amount of the principal outstanding. When prepayments are made, less dollar interest will be received as the outstanding principal declines. In fact, *if prepayments are too fast, the IO investor may not recover the amount paid for the IO even if the security is held to maturity.*

Let's look at the expected price response of an IO to changes in mortgage rates. If mortgage rates decline below the contract rate, prepayments are expected to accelerate. This would result in a deterioration of the expected cash flow for an IO. While the cash flow will be discounted at a lower rate, the net effect

EXHIBIT 61-20	Relationship between Price and Mortgage Rates for a Passthrough, PO, and IO

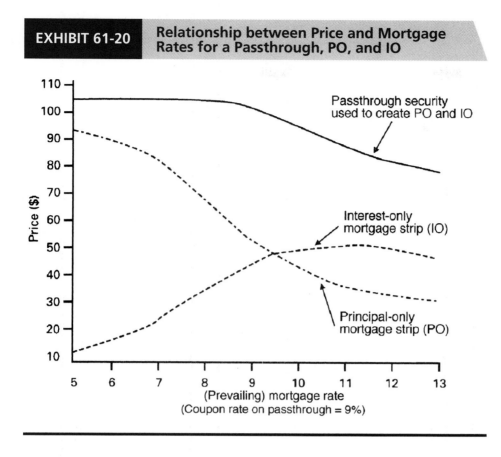

typically is a decline in the price of an IO. If mortgage rates rise above the contract rate, the expected cash flow improves, but the cash flow is discounted at a higher interest rate. The net effect may be either a rise or fall for the IO.

Thus, we see an interesting characteristic of an IO: its price tends to move in the same direction as the change in mortgage rates (1) when mortgage rates fall below the contract rate and (2) for some range of mortgage rates above the contract rate. Both POs and IOs exhibit substantial price volatility when mortgage rates change. The greater price volatility of the IO and PO compared to the passthrough from which they were created is due to the fact that the combined price volatility of the IO and PO must be equal to the price volatility of the passthrough.

Exhibit 61-20 shows the general relationship between the price of an interest-only mortgage strip when interest rates change and compares it to the relationship for the corresponding principal-only mortgage strip and underlying passthrough from which it is created.

An average life for a PO can be calculated based on some prepayment assumption. However, an IO receives no principal payments, so technically an average life cannot be computed. Instead, for an IO a **cash flow average life** is computed, using the projected interest payments in the average life formula instead of principal.

C. Trading and Settlement Procedures

The trading and settlement procedures for stripped mortgage-backed securities are similar to those set by the Public Securities Association for agency passthroughs described in Section III.C. IOs and POs are extreme premium and discount securities and consequently are very sensitive to prepayments, which are driven by the specific characteristics (weighted average coupon, weighted average maturity, geographic concentration, average loan size) of the underlying loans. Therefore, almost all secondary trades in IOs and POs are on a specified pool basis rather than on a TBA basis.

All IOs and POs are given a trust number. For instance, Fannie Mae Trust 1 is a IO/PO trust backed by specific pools of Fannie Mae 9% mortgages. Fannie Mae Trust 2 is backed by Fannie Mae 10% mortgages. Fannie Mae Trust 23 is another IO/PO trust backed by Fannie Mae 10% mortgages. Therefore, a portfolio manager must specify which trust he or she is buying.

The total proceeds of a PO trade are calculated the same way as with a passthrough trade except that there is no accrued interest. The market trades IOs based on notional principal. The proceeds include the price on the notional amount and the accrued interest.

6   NONAGENCY RESIDENTIAL MORTGAGE-BACKED SECURITIES

In the previous sections we looked at agency mortgage-backed securities in which the underlying mortgages are 1-to 4-single family residential mortgages. The mortgage-backed securities market includes other types of securities. These securities are called **nonagency mortgage-backed securities** (referred to as **nonagency securities** hereafter).

The underlying mortgage loans for nonagency securities can be for any type of real estate property. There are securities backed by 1- to 4-single family residential mortgages with a first lien (i.e., the lender has a first priority or first claim) on the mortgaged property. There are nonagency securities backed by other types of single family residential loans. These include home equity loan-backed securities and manufactured housing-loan backed securities. Our focus in this section is on nonagency securities in which the underlying loans are first-lien mortgages for 1- to 4-single-family residential properties.

As with an agency mortgage-backed security, the servicer is responsible for the collection of interest and principal. The servicer also handles delinquencies and foreclosures. Typically, there will be a master servicer and subservicers. The servicer plays a key role. In fact, in assessing the credit risk of a nonagency security, rating companies look carefully at the quality of the servicers.

A. Underlying Mortgage Loans

The underlying loans for agency securities are those that conform to the underwriting standards of the agency issuing or guaranteeing the issue. That is, only conforming loans are included in pools that are collateral for an agency mortgage-backed security. The three main underwriting standards deal with

1. the maximum loan-to-value ratio
2. the maximum payment-to-income ratio
3. the maximum loan amount

The **loan-to-value ratio** (LTV) is the ratio of the amount of the loan to the market value or appraised value of the property. The *lower* the LTV, the *greater* the protection afforded the lender. For example, an LTV of 0.90 means that if the lender has to repossess the property and sell it, the lender must realize at least 90% of the market value in order to recover the amount lent. An LTV of 0.80 means that the lender only has to sell the property for 80% of its market value in order to recover the amount lent.[12] Empirical studies of residential mortgage loans have found that the LTV is a key determinant of whether a borrower will default: the higher the LTV, the greater the likelihood of default.

As mentioned earlier in this reading, a nonconforming mortgage loan is one that does not conform to the underwriting standards established by any of the agencies. Typically, the loans for a nonagency security are nonconforming mortgage loans that fail to qualify for inclusion because the amount of the loan exceeds the limit established by the agencies. Such loans are referred to as jumbo loans. Jumbo loans do not necessarily have greater credit risk than conforming mortgages.

Loans that fail to qualify because of the first two underwriting standards expose the lender to greater credit risk than conforming loans. There are specialized lenders who provide mortgage loans to individuals who fail to qualify for a conforming loan because of their credit history. These specialized lenders classify borrowers by credit quality. Borrowers are classified as A borrowers, B borrowers, C borrowers, and D borrowers. A borrowers are those that are viewed as having the best credit record. Such borrowers are referred to as **prime borrowers**. Borrowers rated below A are viewed as **subprime borrowers**. However, there is no industry-wide classification system for prime and subprime borrowers.

B. Differences between Agency and Nonagency Securities

Nonagency securities can be either passthroughs or CMOs. In the agency market, CMOs are created from pools of passthrough securities. In the nonagency market, CMOs are created from unsecuritized mortgage loans. Since a mortgage loan not securitized as a passthrough is called a whole loan, nonagency CMOs are commonly referred to as **whole-loan CMOs**.

The major difference between agency and nonagency securities has to do with guarantees. With a nonagency security there is no explicit or implicit government guarantee of payment of interest and principal as there is with an agency security. The absence of any such guarantee means that the investor in a nonagency security is exposed to credit risk. The nationally recognized statistical rating organizations rate nonagency securities.

Because of the credit risk, all nonagency securities are **credit enhanced**. By credit enhancement it means that additional support against defaults must be obtained. The amount of credit enhancement needed is determined relative to a specific rating desired for a security rating agency. There are two general types of credit enhancement mechanisms: external and internal. We describe each of these types of credit enhancement in the next reading where we cover asset-backed securities.

---

[12] This ignores the costs of repossession and selling the property.

7   COMMERCIAL MORTGAGE-BACKED SECURITIES

Commercial mortgage-backed securities (CMBSs) are backed by a pool of commercial mortgage loans on income-producing property—multifamily properties (i.e., apartment buildings), office buildings, industrial properties (including warehouses), shopping centers, hotels, and health care facilities (i.e., senior housing care facilities). The basic building block of the CMBS transaction is a commercial loan that was originated either to finance a commercial purchase or to refinance a prior mortgage obligation.

There are two types of CMBS deal structures that have been of primary interest to bond investors: (1) multiproperty single borrower and (2) multiproperty conduit. Conduits are commercial-lending entities that are established for the sole purpose of generating collateral to securitize.

CMBS have been issued outside the United States. The dominant issues have been U.K. based (more than 80% in 2000) with the primary property types being retail and office properties. Starting in 2001, there was dramatic increase in the number of CMBS deals issued by German banks. An increasing number of deals include multi-country properties. The first pan-European securitization was Pan European Industrial Properties in 2001.[13]

A. Credit Risk

Unlike residential mortgage loans where the lender relies on the ability of the borrower to repay and has recourse to the borrower if the payment terms are not satisfied, commercial mortgage loans are **nonrecourse loans**. This means that the lender can only look to the income-producing property backing the loan for interest and principal repayment. If there is a default, the lender looks to the proceeds from the sale of the property for repayment and has no recourse to the borrower for any unpaid balance. The lender must view each property as a stand-alone business and evaluate each property using measures that have been found useful in assessing credit risk.

While fundamental principles of assessing credit risk apply to all property types, traditional approaches to assessing the credit risk of the collateral differs between CMBS and nonagency mortgage-backed securities and real estate-backed securities that fall into the asset-backed securities sector (those backed by home equity loans and manufactured housing loans). For mortgage-backed securities and asset backed securities in which the collateral is residential property, typically the loans are lumped into buckets based on certain loan characteristics and then assumptions regarding default rates are made regarding each bucket. In contrast, for commercial mortgage loans, the unique economic characteristics of each income-producing property in a pool backing a CMBS require that credit analysis be performed on a loan-by-loan basis not only at the time of issuance, but monitored on an ongoing basis.

Regardless of the type of commercial property, the two measures that have been found to be key indicators of the potential credit performance is the debt-to-service coverage ratio and the loan-to-value ratio.

The **debt-to-service coverage ratio** (DSC) is the ratio of the property's net operating income (NOI) divided by the debt service. The NOI is defined as

---

[13] Christopher Flanagan and Edward Reardon, *European Structures Products: 2001 Review and 2002 Outlook,* Global Structured Finance Research, J.P. Morgan Securities Inc. (January 11, 2002), pp. 12–13.

the rental income reduced by cash operating expenses (adjusted for a replacement reserve). A ratio greater than 1 means that the cash flow from the property is sufficient to cover debt servicing. The higher the ratio, the more likely that the borrower will be able to meet debt servicing from the property's cash flow.

For all properties backing a CMBS deal, a weighted average DSC ratio is computed. An analysis of the credit quality of an issue will also look at the dispersion of the DSC ratios for the underlying loans. For example, one might look at the percentage of a deal with a DSC ratio below a certain value.

As explained in Section 6.A, in computing the LTV, the figure used for "value" in the ratio is either market value or appraised value. In valuing commercial property, it is typically the appraised value. There can be considerable variation in the estimates of the property's appraised value. Thus, analysts tend to be skeptical about estimates of appraised value and the resulting LTVs reported for properties.

B. Basic CMBS Structure

As with any structured finance transaction, a rating agency will determine the necessary level of credit enhancement to achieve a desired rating level. For example, if certain DSC and LTV ratios are needed, and these ratios cannot be met at the loan level, then "subordination" is used to achieve these levels. By subordination it is meant that there will be bond classes in the structure whose claims on the cash flow of the collateral are subordinated to that of other bond classes in the structure.

The rating agencies will require that the CMBS transaction be retired sequentially, with the highest-rated bonds paying off first. Therefore, any return of principal caused by amortization, prepayment, or default will be used to repay the highest-rated tranche.

Interest on principal outstanding will be paid to all tranches. In the event of a delinquency resulting in insufficient cash to make all scheduled payments, the transaction's servicer will advance both principal and interest. Advancing will continue from the servicer for as long as these amounts are deemed recoverable.

Losses arising from loan defaults will be charged against the principal balance of the lowest-rated CMBS tranche outstanding. The total loss charged will include the amount previously advanced as well as the actual loss incurred in the sale of the loan's underlying property.

1. Call Protection

A critical investment feature that distinguishes residential MBS and commercial MBS is the call protection afforded an investor. An investor in a residential MBS is exposed to considerable prepayment risk because the borrower has the right to prepay a loan, in whole or in part, before the scheduled principal repayment date. Typically, the borrower does not pay any penalty for prepayment. When we discussed CMOs, we saw how certain types of tranches (e.g., sequential-pay and PAC tranches) can be purchased by an investor to reduce prepayment risk.

With CMBS, there is considerable call protection afforded investors. In fact, it is this protection that results in CMBS trading in the market more like corporate bonds than residential MBS. This call protection comes in two forms: (1) call protection at the loan level and (2) call protection at the structure level. We discuss both below.

a. Protection at the Loan Level

At the commercial loan level, call protection can take the following forms:

1. prepayment lockout

2. defeasance

3. prepayment penalty points

4. yield maintenance charges

A **prepayment lockout** is a contractual agreement that prohibits any prepayments during a specified period of time, called the lockout period. The lockout period at issuance can be from 2 to 5 years. After the lockout period, call protection comes in the form of either prepayment penalty points or yield maintenance charges. Prepayment lockout and defeasance are the strongest forms of prepayment protection.

With **defeasance**, rather than loan prepayment, the borrower provides sufficient funds for the servicer to invest in a portfolio of Treasury securities that replicates the cash flows that would exist in the absence of prepayments. Unlike the other call protection provisions discussed next, there is no distribution made to the bondholders when the defeasance takes place. So, since there are no penalties, there is no issue as to how any penalties paid by the borrower are to be distributed amongst the bondholders in a CMBS structure. Moreover, the substitution of the cash flow of a Treasury portfolio for that of the borrower improves the credit quality of the CMBS deal.

Prepayment penalty points are predetermined penalties that must be paid by the borrower if the borrower wishes to refinance. (A point is equal to 1% of the outstanding loan balance.) For example, 5-4-3-2-1 is a common prepayment penalty point structure. That is, if the borrower wishes to prepay during the first year, the borrower must pay a 5% penalty for a total of $105 rather than $100 (which is the norm in the residential market). Likewise, during the second year, a 4% penalty would apply, and so on.

When there are prepayment penalty points, there are rules for distributing the penalty among the tranches. Prepayment penalty points are not common in new CMBS structures. Instead, the next form of call protection discussed, yield maintenance charges, is more commonly used.

Yield maintenance charge, in its simplest terms, is designed to make the lender indifferent as to the timing of prepayments. The yield maintenance charge, also called the **make-whole charge**, makes it uneconomical to refinance solely to get a lower mortgage rate. While there are several methods used in practice for calculating the yield maintenance charge, the key principle is to make the lender whole. However, when a commercial loan is included as part of a CMBS deal, there must be an allocation of the yield maintenance charge amongst the tranches. Several methods are used in practice for distributing the yield maintenance charge and, depending on the method specified in a deal, not all tranches may be made whole.

b. Structural Protection

The other type of call protection available in CMBS transactions is structural. Because the CMBS bond structures are sequential-pay (by rating), the AA-rated tranche cannot pay down until the AAA is completely retired, and the AA-rated bonds must be paid off before the A-rated bonds, and so on. However, principal losses due to defaults are impacted from the bottom of the structure upward.

2. Balloon Maturity Provisions

Many commercial loans backing CMBS transactions are balloon loans that require substantial principal payment at the end of the term of the loan. If the borrower fails to make the **balloon payment**, the borrower is in default. The lender may extend the loan, and in so doing may modify the original loan terms. During the **workout period** for the loan, a higher interest rate will be charged, called the default interest rate.

The risk that a borrower will not be able to make the balloon payment because either the borrower cannot arrange for refinancing at the balloon payment date or cannot sell the property to generate sufficient funds to pay off the balloon balance is called **balloon risk**. Since the term of the loan will be extended by the lender during the workout period, balloon risk is a type of "extension risk". This is the same risk that we referred to earlier in describing residential mortgage-backed securities.

Although many investors like the "bullet bond-like" pay down of the balloon maturities, it does present difficulties from a structural standpoint. That is, if the deal is structured to completely pay down on a specified date, an event of default will occur if any delays occur. However, how such delays impact CMBS investors is dependent on the bond type (premium, par, or discount) and whether the servicer will advance to a particular tranche after the balloon default.

Another concern for CMBS investors in multitranche transactions is the fact that all loans must be refinanced to pay off the most senior bondholders. Therefore, the balloon risk of the most senior tranche (i.e., AAA) may be equivalent to that of the most junior tranche (i.e., B).

SUMMARY

► The basic mortgage-backed security is the mortgage passthrough security created from a pool of mortgage loans.

► Agency passthrough securities are those issued/guaranteed by Ginnie Mae, Fannie Mae, and Freddie Mac.

► The cash flow of a passthrough includes net interest, scheduled principal repayments (i.e., scheduled amortization), and prepayments.

► Any amount paid in excess of the required monthly mortgage payment is a prepayment; the cash flow of a mortgage-backed security is unknown because of prepayments.

► A projection of prepayments is necessary to project the cash flow of a passthrough security.

► The single monthly mortality (SMM) rate is the ratio of the amount of prepayments divided by the amount available to prepay (i.e., outstanding mortgage balance at the beginning of the month minus the scheduled principal payment for the month).

► The PSA prepayment benchmark is a series of conditional prepayment rates and is simply a market convention that describes in general the pattern of prepayments.

► A measure commonly used to estimate the life of a passthrough is its average life.

► The prepayment risk associated with investing in mortgage passthrough securities can be decomposed into contraction risk and extension risk.

► Prepayment risk makes passthrough securities unattractive for certain financial institutions to hold from an asset/liability perspective.

► The three factors that affect prepayments are (1) the prevailing mortgage rate, (2) normal housing turnover, and (3) characteristics of the underlying mortgage pool.

► Collateralized mortgage obligations are bond classes created by redirecting the interest and principal from a pool of passthroughs or whole loans.

► The creation of a CMO cannot eliminate prepayment risk; it can only transfer the various forms of this risk among different classes of bonds called tranches.

► From a fixed-rate CMO tranche, a floating-rate tranche and an inverse floating-rate tranche can be created.

► A notional interest-only tranche (also called a structured IO) can be created from the excess interest available from other tranches in the structure; excess interest is the difference between the collateral's coupon rate and a tranche's coupon rate.

► The amortization schedule for a planned amortization class is structured based on a lower PSA prepayment assumption and an upper PSA prepayment assumption—called the initial PAC collar.

► A planned amortization class (PAC) tranche has reduced average life variability, the better prepayment protection provided by the support tranches.

► If the collateral from which a PAC bond is created pays at a constant PSA rate that is anywhere within the initial PAC collar, the amortization schedule will be satisfied.

► Over time, the prepayment collar that will be able to support the PAC tranches (i.e., provide the prepayment protection) changes as the amount of the support tranches change.

▶ The effective collar is the lower and upper PSA prepayment rates that can occur in the future and still be able to satisfy the amortization schedule for the PAC tranche.

▶ The key to the prepayment protection for the PAC tranches is the support tranches.

▶ The support tranches are exposed to the greatest prepayment risk of all the tranches in a CMO structure and greater prepayment risk than the collateral (i.e., passthrough securities) from which a deal is created.

▶ Support tranches with a PAC schedule can be created from the support tranches; these tranches are still support tranches but they have better prepayment protection than other support tranches in the structure that do not have a schedule.

▶ A stripped mortgage-backed security is a derivative mortgage-backed security that is created by redistributing the interest and principal payments to two different classes.

▶ A principal-only mortgage strip (PO) benefits from declining interest rates and fast prepayments.

▶ An interest-only mortgage strip (IO) benefits from rising interest rates and a slowing of prepayments; if rates fall instead, the investor in an interest-only security may not realize the amount invested even if the security is held to maturity.

▶ Nonagency securities are not backed by any federal government agency guarantee.

▶ The underlying loans for nonagency securities are nonconforming mortgage loans—loans that do not qualify for inclusion in mortgage pools that underlie agency mortgage-backed securities.

▶ Credit enhancement is needed to support nonagency mortgage-backed securities.

▶ Credit enhancement levels are determined relative to a specific rating desired for a security and there are two general types of credit enhancement structures—external and internal.

▶ Commercial mortgage-backed securities are backed by a pool of commercial mortgage loans-loans on income-producing property

▶ Unlike residential mortgage loans where the lender relies on the ability of the borrower to repay and has recourse to the borrower if the payment terms are not satisfied, commercial mortgage loans are nonrecourse loans, and as a result the lender can only look to the income-producing property backing the loan for interest and principal repayment.

▶ Two measures that have been found to be key indicators of the potential credit performance of a commercial mortgage loan are the debt-to-service coverage ratio (i.e., the property's net operating income divided by the debt service) and the loan-to-value ratio.

▶ The degree of call protection available to a CMBS investor is a function of (1) call protection available at the loan level and (2) call protection afforded from the actual CMBS structure.

▶ At the commercial loan level, call protection can be in the form of a prepayment lockout, defeasance, prepayment penalty points, or yield maintenance charges.

▶ Many commercial loans backing CMBS transactions are balloon loans that require substantial principal payment at the end of the balloon term and therefore the investor faces balloon risk—the risk that the loan will extend beyond the scheduled maturity date.

PROBLEMS FOR READING 61

1. A. Complete the following schedule for a 30-year fully amortizing mortgage loan with a mortgage rate of 7.25% where the amount borrowed is $150,000. The monthly mortgage payment is $1,023.26.

Month	Beginning Mortgage	Mortgage Payment	Interest	Sch. Prin. Repayment	End-of-month balance
1	150,000.00	1,023.26			
2		1,023.26			
3		1,023.26			
4		1,023.26			
5		1,023.26			
6		1,023.26			
7		1,023.26			
8		1,023.26			
9		1,023.26			
10		1,023.26			
11		1,023.26			
12		1,023.26			
13		1,023.26			
14		1,023.26			

B. Complete the following schedule for the mortgage loan in part A given the following information:

Month	Beginning Mortgage	Mortgage Payment	Interest	Sch. Prin. Repayment	End-of-Month Balance
357	4,031.97	1,023.26			
358		1,023.26			
359		1,023.26			
360		1,023.26			

2. A. Suppose that the servicing fee for a mortgage loan is 0.5%. Complete the following schedule for the mortgage loan in the previous question. The column labeled "Servicing Fee" is the dollar amount of the servicing fee for the month. The column labeled "Net Interest" is the monthly interest after the servicing fee for the month.

Month	Beginning Mortgage	Mortgage Payment	Servicing Fee	Net Interest	Sch. Prin. Repayment	End-of-Month Balance
1						
2						
3						
4						
5						
6						

B. Determine for the first six months the cash flow for an investor who purchases this mortgage loan after the servicing fee is paid.

3. Explain why you agree or disagree with the following statement: "Since mortgage passthrough securities issued by Ginnie Mae are guaranteed by the full faith and credit of the U.S. government, there is no uncertainty about the cash flow for the security."

4. Consider the following mortgage pool.

Loan	Outstanding mortgage balance	Mortgage rate	Months remaining
1	$215,000	6.75%	200
2	$185,000	7.75%	185
3	$125,000	7.25%	192
4	$100,000	7.00%	210
5	$200,000	6.50%	180
Total	$825,000		

A. What is the weighted average coupon rate for this mortgage pool?

B. What is the weighted average maturity for this mortgage pool?

5. Mr. Jamison is looking at the historical prepayment for a passthrough security. He finds the following:

mortgage balance in month 42	=	$260,000,000
scheduled principal payment in month 42	=	$1,000,000
prepayment in month 42	=	$2,450,000

A. What is the SMM for month 42?

B. How should Mr. Jamison interpret the SMM computed?

C. What is the CPR for month 42?

D. How should Mr. Jamison interpret the CPR computed?

6. Using the Public Securities Association Prepayment benchmark, complete the following table:

Month	PSA	CPR	SMM
5	100		
15	80		
20	175		
27	50		
88	200		
136	75		
220	225		

7. Explain why 30 months after the origination of a mortgage pool, discussing prepayments in terms of one CPR and a PSA are identical.

8. Suppose that in month 140 the mortgage balance for a mortgage pool underlying a passthrough security is $537 million and that the scheduled principal repayment for month 140 is $440,000. Assuming 175 PSA, what is the amount of the prepayment for month 140?

9. Comment on the following statement: "The PSA model is a prepayment model."

10. Robert Reed is an assistant portfolio manager who has been recently given the responsibility of assisting Joan Soprano, the portfolio manager for the mortgage-backed securities portfolio. Ms. Soprano gave Mr. Reed a copy of the a Prudential Securities publication for November 1999 entitled *Mortgage and Asset-Backed Prepayment and Issuance*. An excerpt from the publication is given below:

GNMA 30 Year		Projected PSA				
		Dec	Jan	Feb	One Year	Long Term
6.0	1998	73	68	60	60	65
6.5	1998	113	102	92	91	90
7.0	1998	154	137	124	126	116
7.5	1993	181	166	150	155	138
8.0	1996	220	211	181	185	159
8.5	1994	283	272	223	205	173
9.0	1986	269	263	232	209	195

The mortgage rate at the time of the report was 8.13%.

Mr. Reed asks the following questions about the information in the above excerpt. Respond to each question.

A. What does "GNMA 30 YEAR" mean?

B. What does "8.5 1994" mean?

C. What do the numbers under "PROJECTED" mean?

D. Do the prepayment rates for "7.5 1993" apply to all GNMA issues in the market?

E. Why are the projected prepayments for "one year" and "long term" such that they increase with the coupon rate?

11. Suppose that you are analyzing prepayments of a passthrough security that was issued more than 15 years ago. The weighted average coupon (WAC) for the underlying mortgage pool was 13%. Suppose that the mortgage rate over the year of the analysis declined from 8% to 7% but prepayments for this mortgage pool you are analyzing did not increase. Explain why there is no increase in prepayments despite the lower mortgage rate relative to 13% being paid by borrowers and the decline in the mortgage rates over the year.

12. What type of prepayment risk is an investor interested in a short-term security concerned with when purchasing a mortgage-backed security?

13. Suppose that a portfolio manager is considering a collateralized mortgage obligation structure KMF-01. This structure has three tranches. The deal is a simple sequential pay and was issued several years ago. The tranches are A, B, and C with a coupon rate paid to each tranche each month and principal payments are made first to tranche A, then to tranche B, and finally to tranche C. Here is the status of the deal as of the time of the analysis:

Tranche	Coupon Rate	Par Amount Outstanding
A	6%	$3 million
B	7%	$8 million
C	8%	$30 million

Based on some prepayment rate, the projected principal payments (prepayments plus scheduled principal repayment) for the next four years for the collateral underlying this deal are as follows:

Month	Sch. Principal Repayment + Prepayments	Month	Sch. Principal Repayment + Prepayments
1	520,000	25	287,000
2	510,000	26	285,000
3	490,000	27	283,000
4	450,000	28	280,000
5	448,000	29	278,000
6	442,000	30	275,000
7	410,000	31	271,000
8	405,000	32	270,000
9	400,000	33	265,000
10	396,000	34	260,000
11	395,000	35	255,000
12	390,000	36	252,000
13	388,000	37	250,000
14	385,000	38	245,000
15	380,000	39	240,000
16	377,000	40	210,000
17	375,000	41	200,000
18	370,000	42	195,000
19	369,000	43	190,000
20	366,000	44	185,000
21	300,000	45	175,000
22	298,000	46	170,000
23	292,000	47	166,000
24	290,000	48	164,000

A. Compute the principal, interest, and cash flow for tranche A for the 48 months.

B. Compute the principal, interest, and cash flow for tranche B for the 48 months.

C. Compute the principal, interest, and cash flow for tranche C for the 48 months.

D. Compute the average life for tranche A.

14. Suppose that in the previous CMO structure, KMF-01, that tranche C is an accrual tranche that accrues coupon interest monthly. We will refer to this new CMO structure as KMF-02.

A. What is the principal repayment, interest, and cash flow for tranche A in KMF-02?

B. What is the principal balance for tranche C for the first five months?

C. What is the average life for tranche A in KMF-02 and contrast this with the average life for tranche A in KMF-01?

15. Explain why it is necessary to have a cap for the floater when a fixed-rate tranche is split into a floater and an inverse floater.

16. Suppose that a tranche from which a floater and an inverse floater are created has an average life of six years. What will be the average life of the floater and the inverse floater?

17. How does a CMO alter the cash flow from mortgages so as to redistribute the prepayment risk across various tranches in a deal?

18. "By creating a CMO, an issuer eliminates the prepayment risk associated with the underlying mortgages loans." Explain why you agree or disagree with this statement?

19. Ellen Morgan received a phone call from the trustee of a pension fund. Ms. Morgan is the portfolio manager for the pension fund's bond portfolio. The trustee expressed concerns about the inclusion of CMOs in the portfolio. The trustee's concern arose after reading several articles in the popular press where the CMO market was characterized as the sector of the mortgage-backed securities market with the greatest prepayment risk and the passthrough sector as the safest sector in terms of prepayment risk. What should Ms. Morgan say to this trustee regarding such statements made in the popular press?

20. What is the role of a support tranche in a CMO structure?

21. Suppose that the manager of a savings & loan association portfolio has decided to invest in mortgage-backed securities and is considering the following two securities: (i) a Fannie Mae passthrough security with a WAM of 310 months or (ii) a PAC tranche of a Fannie Mae CMO issue with an average life of 2 years. Which mortgage-backed security would probably be better from an asset/liability perspective?

22. Suppose that a PAC bond is created using prepayment speeds of 90 PSA and 240 PSA and the average life is 5 years. Will the average life for this PAC tranche be shorter than, longer than, or equal to 5 years if the collateral pays at 140 PSA over its life? Explain your answer.

23. Suppose that $1 billion of passthroughs are used to create a CMO structure, KMF-05. This structure includes a PAC tranche with a par value of $650 million and a support tranche with a par value of $350 million.

A. Which of the following will have the least average life variability: (i) the collateral, (ii) the PAC tranche, or (iii) the support tranche? Why?

B. Which of the following will have the greatest average life variability: (i) the collateral, (ii) the PAC tranche, or (iii) the support tranche? Why?

24. Suppose that the $1 billion of collateral in the CMO structure KMF-05 in the previous question was divided into a PAC tranche with a par value of $800 million and a support tranche with a par value of $200 million (instead of $650 million and $350 million). The new structure is KMF-06. Will the PAC tranche in KMF-06 have more or less protection than the PAC tranche in KMF-05?

25. Suppose that $500 million of passthroughs are used to create a CMO structure with a PAC tranche with a par value of $350 million (PAC I), a support tranche with a schedule (PAC II) with a par value of $100

million, and a support tranche without a schedule with a par value of $200 million.

  A. Will the PAC I or PAC II have less average life variability? Why?

  B. Will the support tranche without a schedule or the PAC II have the greater average life variability? Why?

26. In a CMO structure with several PAC tranches that pay off sequentially, explain what the structure effectively becomes once all the support tranches are paid off.

27. Suppose that for the first four years of a CMO, prepayments are well below the initial upper PAC collar and within the initial lower PAC collar. What will happen to the effective upper collar?

28. Consider the following CMO structure backed by 8% collateral:

Tranche	Par Amount	Coupon Rate
A	$400,000,000	6.25%
B	$200,000,000	6.75%
C	$225,000,000	7.50%
D	$175,000,000	7.75%

Suppose that the structurer of this CMO wants to create a notional IO tranche with a coupon rate of 8%. Calculate the notional amount for this notional IO tranche.

29. An issuer is considering the following two CMO structures:

Structure I:

Tranche	Par Amount	Coupon Rate
A	$150 million	6.50%
B	$100 million	6.75%
C	$200 million	7.25%
D	$150 million	7.75%
E	$100 million	8.00%
F	$500 million	8.50%

Tranches A-E are a sequence of PAC Is and F is the support tranche. Structure II:

Tranche	Par Amount	Coupon Rate
A	$150 million	6.50%
B	$100 million	6.75%
C	$200 million	7.25%
D	$150 million	7.75%
E	$100 million	8.00%
F	$200 million	8.25%
G	$300 million	?????

Tranches A-E are a sequence of PAC Is, F is a PAC II, and G is a support tranche without a schedule.

A. In Structure II tranche G is created from tranche F in Structure I. What is the coupon rate for tranche G assuming that the combined coupon rate for tranches F and G in Structure II should be 8.5%?

B. What is the effect on the value and average life of tranches A-E by including the PAC II in Structure II?

C. What is the difference in the average life variability of tranche G in Structure II and tranche F in Structure I?

30. What is a broken or busted PAC?

31. Assume that in FJF-01 in the chapter (see Exhibit 61-5 in the chapter), tranche C had been split to create a floater with a principal of $80,416,667 and an inverse floater with a principal of $16,083,333.

A. What would be the cap rate for the inverse floater if the coupon rate for the floater is 1-month LIBOR plus 1%?

B. Assuming that (1) the coupon formula for the floater is 1-month LIBOR plus 1% and (2) a floor is imposed on the inverse floater of zero, what would be the cap rate on the floater?

32. A. In assessing the prepayment protection offered by a seasoned PAC tranche, explain why the initial collars may provide limited insight?

B. What measure provides better information about the prepayment protection offered by a seasoned PAC tranche?

33. A. For a mortgage loan, is a higher or lower loan-to-value ratio an indication of greater credit risk? Explain why.

B. What is the empirical relationship between defaults and loan-to-value ratio observed by studies of residential mortgage loans?

34. A. What is a principal-only mortgage strip and an interest-only mortgage strip?

B. How does an interest-only mortgage strip differ with respect to the certainty about the cash flow from a Treasury strip created from the coupon interest?

C. How is the price of an interest-only mortgage strip expected to change when interest rates change?

35. A. An investor purchased $10 million par value of a 7% Ginnie Mae passthrough security agreeing to pay 102. The pool factor is 0.72. How much does the investor pay to the seller?

   B. Why would an investor who wants to purchase a principal-only mortgage strip not want to do so on a TBA basis?

36. Why can't all residential mortgage loans be securitized by either Ginnie Mae, Fannie Mae, or Freddie Mac?

37. Why is credit enhancement needed for a nonagency mortgage-backed security?

38. With respect to a default by the borrower, how does a residential mortgage loan differ from a commercial mortgage loan?

39. Why is the debt-to-service coverage ratio used to assess the credit risk of a commercial mortgage loan?

40. A. What types of provisions are usually included in a commercial loan to protect the lender against prepayment risk?

   B. In a commercial mortgage-backed securities deal, explain why the investor in a security may be afforded prepayment protection at the deal level.

41. What is balloon risk and how is it related to extension risk?

ASSET-BACKED SECTOR OF THE BOND MARKET

by Frank J. Fabozzi

READING

62

LEARNING OUTCOMES

The candidate should be able to:

a. illustrate the basic structural features of and parties to a securitization transaction;

b. explain prepayment tranching and credit tranching;

c. distinguish between the payment structure and collateral structure of a securitization backed by amortizing assets and non-amortizing assets;

d. distinguish among the various types of external and internal credit enhancements;

e. describe the cash flow and prepayment characteristics for securities backed by home equity loans, manufactured housing loans, automobile loans, student loans, SBA loans and credit card receivables;

f. describe a collateralized debt obligation (CDO) and the different types (cash and synthetic);

g. distinguish among the primary motivations for creating a collateralized debt obligation (arbitrage and balance sheet transactions).

INTRODUCTION   1

As an alternative to the issuance of a bond, a corporation can issue a security backed by loans or receivables. Debt instruments that have as their collateral loans or receivables are referred to as asset-backed securities. The transaction in which asset-backed securities are created is referred to as a **securitization**.

While the major issuers of asset-backed securities are corporations, municipal governments use this form of financing rather than issuing municipal bonds and several European central governments use this form of financing. In the United States, the first type of asset-backed security (ABS) was the residential mortgage loan. We discussed the resulting securities, referred to as mortgage-backed securities, in the previous reading. Securities backed by other types of assets (consumer and business loans and receivables) have been issued throughout the world. The largest sectors of the asset-backed securities market in the United States are securities backed by credit card receivables, auto loans, home equity loans, manufactured housing loans, student loans, Small Business Administration loans, corporate loans, and bonds (corporate, emerging market, and structured financial products). Since home equity loans and manufactured housing loans are backed by real estate property, the securities backed by them are referred to as **real estate-backed asset-backed securities**. Other asset-backed securities include securities backed by home improvement loans, health care receivables, agricultural equipment loans, equipment leases, music royalty receivables, movie royalty receivables, and municipal parking ticket receivables. Collectively, these products are called **credit-sensitive structured products**.

In this reading, we will discuss the securitization process, the basic features of a securitization transaction, and the major asset types that have been securitized. In the last section of this reading, we look at collateralized debt obligations. While this product has traditionally been classified as part of the ABS market, we will see how the structure of this product differs from that of a typical securitization.

There are two topics not covered in this reading. The first is the valuation of an ABS. This topic is covered in Reading 63. Second, the factors considered by rating agencies in rating an ABS transaction are not covered here.

2   THE SECURITIZATION PROCESS AND FEATURES OF ABS

The issuance of an asset-backed security is more complicated than the issuance of a corporate bond. In this section, we will describe the securitization process and the parties to a securitization. We will do so using a hypothetical securitization.

A. The Basic Securitization Transaction

Quality Home Theaters Inc. (QHT) manufacturers high-end equipment for home theaters. The cost of one of QHT's home theaters ranges from $20,000 to $200,000. Some of its sales are for cash, but the bulk of its sales are by installment sales contracts. Effectively, an installment sales contract is a loan to the buyer of the home theater who agrees to repay QHT over a specified period of time. For simplicity we will assume that the loans are typically for four years. The collateral for the loan is the home theater purchased by the borrower. The loan specifies an interest rate that the buyer pays.

The credit department of QHT makes the decision as to whether or not to extend credit to a customer. That is, the credit department will request a credit loan application form be completed by a customer and based on criteria established by QHT will decide on whether to extend a loan. The criteria for extending credit are referred to as **underwriting standards**. Because QHT is extending the loan, it is referred to as the **originator** of the loan. Moreover, QHT may have a department that is responsible for servicing the loan. **Servicing** involves collecting payments from borrowers, notifying borrowers who may be delinquent, and, when necessary, recovering and disposing of the collateral (i.e., home theater equipment in our illustration) if the borrower does not make loan repayments by a specified time. While the servicer of the loans need not be the originator of the loans, in our illustration we are assuming that QHT will be the servicer.

Now let's see how these loans can be used in a securitization. We will assume that QHT has $100 million of installment sales contracts. This amount is shown on QHT's balance sheet as an asset. We will further assume that QHT wants to raise $100 million. Rather than issuing corporate bonds for $100 million, QHT's treasurer decides to raise the funds via a securitization. To do so, QHT will set up a legal entity referred to as a **special purpose vehicle** (SPV). At Level I in our discussion of asset-backed securities we described the critical role of this legal entity; its role will become clearer in our illustration. In our illustration, the SPV that is set up is called *Homeview Asset Trust* (HAT). QHT will then sell to HAT $100 million of the loans. QHT will receive from HAT $100 million in cash, the amount it wanted to raise. But where does HAT get $100 million? It obtains those funds by selling securities that are backed by the $100 million of loans. These securities are the asset-backed securities we referred to earlier and we will discuss these further in Section 2.C.

In the prospectus, HAT (the SPV) would be referred to as either the "issuer" or the "trust." QHT, the seller of the collateral to HAT, would be referred to as the "seller." The prospectus might then state: "The securities represent obligations of the issuer only and do not represent obligations of or interests in Quality Home Theaters Inc. or any of its affiliates."

The transaction is diagrammed in panel a of Exhibit 62-1. In panel b, the parties to the transaction are summarized.

EXHIBIT 62-1   Securitization Illustration for QHT

Panel a: Securitization Process

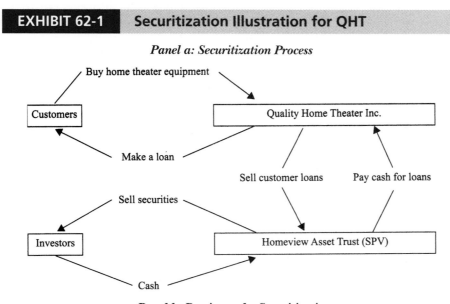

Panel b: Parties to the Securitization

Party	Description	Party in Illustration
Seller	Originates the loans and sells loans to the SPV	Quality Home Theaters Inc.
Issuer/Trust	The SPV that buys the loans from the seller and issues the asset-backed securities	Homeview Asset Trust
Servicer	Services the loans	Quality Home Theaters Inc.

The payments that are received from the collateral are distributed to pay servicing fees, other administrative fees, and principal and interest to the security holders. The legal documents in a securitization (prospectus or private placement memorandum) will set forth in considerable detail the priority and amount of payments to be made to the servicer, administrators, and the security holders of each bond class. The priority and amount of payments is commonly referred to as the "waterfall" because the flow of payments in a structure is depicted as a waterfall.

B. Parties to a Securitization

Thus far we have discussed three parties to a securitization: the seller of the collateral (also sometimes referred to as the originator), the special purpose vehicle (referred to in a prospectus or private placement memorandum as the issuer or the trust), and the servicer. There are other parties involved in a securitization: attorneys, independent accountants, trustees, underwriters, rating agencies, and guarantors. All of these parties plus the servicer are referred to as "third parties" to the transaction.

There is a good deal of legal documentation involved in a securitization transaction. The attorneys are responsible for preparing the legal documents. The first is the *purchase agreement* between the seller of the assets (QHT in our illustration) and the SPV (HAT in our illustration).[1] The purchase agreement sets forth the representations and warranties that the seller is making about the assets. The second is one that sets forth how the cash flows are divided among the bond classes (i.e., the structure's waterfall). Finally, the attorneys create the *servicing agreement* between the entity engaged to service the assets (in our illustration QHT retained the servicing of the loans) and the SPV.

An independent accounting firm will verify the accuracy of all numerical information placed in either the prospectus or private placement memorandum.[2] The result of this task results in a *comfort letter* for a securitization.

The **trustee** or **trustee agent** is the entity that safeguards the assets after they have been placed in the trust, receives the payments due to the bond holders, and provides periodic information to the bond holders. The information is provided in the form of *remittance reports* that may be issued monthly, quarterly or whenever agreed to by the terms of the prospectus or the private placement memorandum.

The underwriters and rating agencies perform the same function in a securitization as they do in a standard corporate bond offering. The rating agencies make an assessment of the collateral and the proposed structure to determine the amount of credit enhancement required to achieve a target credit rating for each bond class.

---

[1] There are concerns that both the creditors to the seller of the collateral (QHT's creditors in our illustration) and the investors in the securities issued by the SPV have about the assets. Specifically, QHT's creditors will be concerned that the assets are being sold to the SPV at less than fair market value, thereby weakening their credit position. The buyers of the asset-backed securities will be concerned that the assets were purchased at less than fair market value, thereby weakening their credit position. Because of this concern, the attorney will issue an opinion that the assets were sold at a fair market value.

[2] The way this is accomplished is that a copy of the transaction's payment structure, underlying collateral, average life, and yield are supplied to the accountants for verification. In turn, the accountants reverse engineer the deal according to the deal's payment rules (i.e., the waterfall). Following the rules and using the same collateral that will actually generate the cash flows for the transaction, the accountants reproduce the yield and average life tables that are put into the prospectus or private placement memorandum.

Finally, a securitization may have an entity that guarantees part of the obligations issued by the SPV. These entities are called guarantors and we will discuss their role in a securitization later.

C. Bonds Issued

Now let's take a closer look at the securities issued, what we refer to as the asset-backed securities.

A simple transaction can involve the sale of just one bond class with a par value of $100 million in our illustration. We will call this Bond Class A. Suppose HAT issues 100,000 certificates for Bond Class A with a par value of $1,000 per certificate. Then, each certificate holder would be entitled to 1/100,000 of the payment from the collateral after payment of fees and expenses. Each payment made by the borrowers (i.e., the buyers of the home theater equipment) consists of principal repayment and interest.

A structure can be more complicated. For example, there can be rules for distribution of principal and interest other than on a pro rata basis to different bond classes. As an example, suppose HAT issues Bond Classes A1, A2, A3, and A4 whose total par value is $100 million as follows:

Bond Class	Par Value (million)
A1	$ 40
A2	30
A3	20
A4	10
Total	$100

As with a **collateralized mortgage obligation (CMO)** structure described in the previous reading, there are different rules for the distribution of principal and interest to these four bond classes or tranches. A simple structure would be a sequential-pay one. As explained in the previous reading, in a basic sequential-pay structure, each bond class receives periodic interest. However, the principal is repaid as follows: all principal received from the collateral is paid first to Bond Class A1 until it is fully paid off its $40 million par value. After Bond Class A1 is paid off, all principal received from the collateral is paid to Bond Class A2 until it is fully paid off. All principal payments from the collateral are then paid to Bond Class A3 until it is fully paid off and then all principal payments are made to Bond Class A4.

The reason for the creation of the structure just described, as explained in the previous reading, is to redistribute the prepayment risk among different bond classes. Prepayment risk is the uncertainty about the cash flow due to prepayments. This risk can be decomposed into contraction risk (i.e., the undesired shortening in the average life of a security) or extension risk (i.e., the undesired lengthening in the average life of a security). The creation of these bond classes is referred to as **prepayment tranching** or **time tranching**.

Now let's look at a more common structure in a transaction. As will be explained later, there are structures where there is more than one bond class and the bond classes differ as to how they will share any losses resulting from defaults of the borrowers. In such a structure, the bond classes are classified as **senior bond classes** and **subordinate bond classes**. This structure is called a **senior-subordinate structure**. Losses are realized by the subordinate bond classes before there are any losses realized by the senior bond classes. For example, suppose that HAT issued $90 million par value of Bond Class A, the senior bond class, and $10 million par value of Bond Class B, the subordinate bond class. So the structure is as follows:

Bond Class	Par Value (million)
A (senior)	$90
B (subordinate)	10
Total	$100

In this structure, as long as there are no defaults by the borrower greater than $10 million, then Bond Class A will be repaid fully its $90 million.

The purpose of this structure is to redistribute the credit risk associated with the collateral. This is referred to as **credit tranching**. As explained later, the senior-subordinate structure is a form of credit enhancement for a transaction.

There is no reason why only one subordinate bond class is created. Suppose that HAT issued the following structure

Bond Class	Par Value (million)
A (senior)	$90
B (subordinate)	7
C (subordinate)	3
Total	$100

In this structure, Bond Class A is the senior bond class while both Bond Classes B and C are subordinate bond classes from the perspective of Bond Class A. The rules for the distribution of losses would be as follows. All losses on the collateral are absorbed by Bond Class C before any losses are realized by Bond Classes A or B. Consequently, if the losses on the collateral do not exceed $3 million, no losses will be realized by Bond Classes A and B. If the losses exceed $3 million, Bond Class B absorbs the loss up to $7 million (its par value). As an example, if the total loss on the collateral is $8 million, Bond Class C loses its entire par value ($3 million) and Bond Class B realizes a loss of $5 million of its $7 million par value. Bond Class A does not realize any loss in this scenario. It should be clear that Bond Class A only realizes a loss if the loss from the collateral exceeds $10 million. The bond class that must absorb the losses first is referred to as the **first loss piece**. In our hypothetical structure, Bond Class C is the first loss piece.

Now we will add just one more twist to the structure. Often in larger transactions, the senior bond class will be carved into different bond classes in order to

PRACTICE QUESTION 1

Suppose that the structure for an asset-backed security structure is as follows:

senior bond class	$380 million
subordinated bond class 1	$40 million
subordinated bond class 2	$20 million

The value of the collateral for the structure is $440 million and subordinated bond class 2 is the first loss piece.

a. What is the amount of the loss for each bond class if losses due to defaults over the life of the structure total $15 million?

b. What is the amount of the loss for each bond class if losses due to defaults over the life of the structure total $50 million?

c. What is the amount of the loss for each bond class if losses due to defaults over the life of the structure total $90 million?

redistribute the prepayment risk. For example, HAT might issue the following structure:

Bond Class	Par Value (million)
A1 (senior)	$35
A2 (senior)	28
A3 (senior)	15
A4 (senior)	12
B (subordinate)	7
C (subordinate)	3
Total	$100

In this structure there is both prepayment tranching for the senior bond class (creation of Bond Classes A1, A2, A3, and A4) and credit tranching (creation of the senior bond classes and the two subordinate bond classes, Bond Classes B and C).

As explained in the previous reading, a bond class in a securitization is also referred to as a "tranche." Consequently, throughout this reading the terms "bond class" and "tranche" are used interchangeably.

D. General Classification of Collateral and Transaction Structure

Later in this reading, we will describe some of the major assets that have been securitized. In general, the collateral can be classified as either amortizing or non-amortizing assets. **Amortizing assets** are loans in which the borrower's periodic payment consists of scheduled principal and interest payments over the life of the loan. The schedule for the repayment of the principal is called an **amortization schedule**. The standard residential mortgage loan falls into this category. Auto loans and certain types of home equity loans (specifically, closed-end home equity loans discussed later in this reading) are amortizing assets. Any excess payment over the scheduled principal payment is called a **prepayment**. Prepayments can be made to pay off the entire balance or a partial prepayment, called a **curtailment**.

In contrast to amortizing assets, non-amortizing assets require only minimum periodic payments with no scheduled principal repayment. If that payment is less than the interest on the outstanding loan balance, the shortfall is added to the outstanding loan balance. If the periodic payment is greater than the interest on the outstanding loan balance, then the difference is applied to the reduction of the outstanding loan balance. Since there is no schedule of principal payments (i.e., no amortization schedule) for a non-amortizing asset, the concept of a prepayment does not apply. A credit card receivable is an example of a non-amortizing asset.

The type of collateral—amortizing or non-amortizing—has an impact on the structure of the transaction. Typically, when amortizing assets are securitized, there is no change in the composition of the collateral over the life of the securities except for loans that have been removed due to defaults and full principal repayment due to prepayments or full amortization. For example, if at the time of issuance the collateral for an ABS consists of 3,000 four-year amortizing loans, then the same 3,000 loans will be in the collateral six months from now assuming no defaults and no prepayments. If, however, during the first six months, 200 of the loans prepay and 100 have defaulted, then the collateral at the end of six months will consist of 2,700 loans (3,000 − 200 − 100). Of course, the remaining principal of the 2,700 loans will decline because of scheduled principal repayments and any partial prepayments. All of the principal repayments from the collateral will be distributed to the security holders.

In contrast, for an ABS transaction backed by non-amortizing assets, the composition of the collateral changes. The funds available to pay the security holders are principal repayments and interest. The interest is distributed to the security holders. However, the principal repayments can be either (1) paid out to security holders or (2) reinvested by purchasing additional loans. What will happen to the principal repayments depends on the time since the transaction was originated. For a certain amount of time after issuance, all principal repayments are reinvested in additional loans. The period of time for which principal repayments are reinvested rather than paid out to the security holders is called the **lockout period** or **revolving period**. At the end of the lockout period, principal repayments are distributed to the security holders. The period when the principal repayments are not reinvested is called the **principal amortization period**. Notice that unlike the typical transaction that is backed by amortizing assets, the collateral backed by non-amortizing assets changes over time. A structure in which the principal repayments are reinvested in new loans is called a **revolving structure**.

While the receivables in a revolving structure may not be prepaid, all the bonds issued by the trust may be retired early if certain events occur. That is, during the lockout period, the trustee is required to use principal repayments to retire the securities rather than reinvest principal in new collateral if certain events occur. The most common trigger is the poor performance of the collateral. This provision that specifies the redirection of the principal repayments during the lockout period to retire the securities is referred to as the **early amortization provision** or **rapid amortization provision**.

Not all transactions that are revolving structures are backed by non-amortizing assets. There are some transactions in which the collateral consists of amortizing assets but during a lockout period, the principal repayments are reinvested in additional loans. For example, there are transactions in the European market in which the collateral consists of residential mortgage loans but during the lockout period principal repayments are used to acquire additional residential mortgage loans.

E. Collateral Cash Flow

For an amortizing asset, projection of the cash flows requires projecting prepayments. One factor that may affect prepayments is the prevailing level of interest rates relative to the interest rate on the loan. In projecting prepayments it is critical to determine the extent to which borrowers take advantage of a decline in interest rates below the loan rate in order to refinance the loan.

As with nonagency mortgage-backed securities, described in the previous reading, modeling defaults for the collateral is critical in estimating the cash flows of an asset-backed security. Proceeds that are recovered in the event of a default of a loan prior to the scheduled principal repayment date of an amortizing asset represent a prepayment and are referred to as an **involuntary prepayment**. Projecting prepayments for amortizing assets requires an assumption about the default rate and the recovery rate. For a non-amortizing asset, while the concept of a prepayment does not exist, a projection of defaults is still necessary to project how much will be recovered and when.

The analysis of prepayments can be performed on a pool level or a loan level. In **pool-level analysis** it is assumed that all loans comprising the collateral are identical. For an amortizing asset, the amortization schedule is based on the **gross weighted average coupon** (GWAC) and **weighted average maturity** (WAM) for that single loan. We explained in the previous reading what the WAC and WAM of a pool of mortgage loans is and illustrated how it is computed. In this reading, we refer to the WAC as gross WAC. Pool-level analysis is appropriate where the underlying loans are homogeneous. **Loan-level analysis** involves amortizing each loan (or group of homogeneous loans).

The **expected final maturity** of an asset-backed security is the maturity date based on expected prepayments at the time of pricing of a deal. The **legal final maturity** can be two or more years after the expected final maturity. The **average life**, or **weighted average life**, was explained in the previous reading.

Also explained in the previous reading is a tranche's **principal window** which refers to the time period over which the principal is expected to be paid to the bondholders. A principal window can be wide or narrow. When there is only one principal payment that is scheduled to be made to a bondholder, the bond is referred to as having a **bullet maturity**. Due to prepayments, an asset-backed security that is expected to have a bullet maturity may have an actual maturity that differs from that specified in the prospectus. Hence, asset-backed securities bonds that have an expected payment of only one principal are said to have a **soft bullet**.

F. Credit Enhancements

All asset-backed securities are credit enhanced. That means that support is provided for one or more of the bondholders in the structure. Credit enhancement levels are determined relative to a specific rating desired by the issuer for a security by each rating agency. Specifically, an investor in a triple A rated security expects to have "minimal" (virtually no) chance of losing any principal due to defaults. For example, a rating agency may require credit enhancement equal to four times expected losses to obtain a triple A rating or three times expected losses to obtain a double A rating. The amount of credit enhancement necessary depends on rating agency requirements.

There are two general types of credit enhancement structures: external and internal. We describe each type below.

1. External Credit Enhancements

In an ABS, there are two principal parties: the issuer and the security holder. The issuer in our hypothetical securitization is HAT. If another entity is introduced into the structure to guarantee any payments to the security holders, that entity is referred to as a "third party."

The most common third party in a securitization is a monoline insurance company (also referred to as a monoline insurer). A monoline insurance company is an insurance company whose business is restricted to providing guarantees for financial products such as municipal securities and asset-backed securities.[3] When a securitization has external credit enhancement that is provided by a monoline insurer, the securities are said to be "wrapped." The insurance works as follows. The monoline insurer agrees to make timely payment of interest and principal up to a specified amount should the issuer fail to make the payment. Unlike municipal bond insurance which guarantees the entire principal amount, the guarantee in a securitization is only for a percentage of the par value at origination. For example, a $100 million securitization may have only $5 million guaranteed by the monoline insurer.

Two less common forms of external credit enhancement are a **letter of credit** from a bank and a guarantee by the seller of the assets (i.e., the entity that sold the assets to the SPV—QHT in our hypothetical illustration).[4] The reason why these two forms of credit enhancement are less commonly used is because of the "weak link approach" employed by rating agencies when they rate securitizations. According to this approach, when rating a proposed structure, the credit quality of a security is only as good as the weakest link in its credit enhancement regardless of the quality of underlying assets. Consequently, if an issuer seeks a triple A rating for one of the bond classes in the structure, it would be unlikely to be awarded such a rating if the external credit enhancer has a rating that is less than triple A. Since few corporations and banks that issue letters of credit have a sufficiently high rating themselves to achieve the rating that may be sought in a securitization, these two forms of external credit enhancement are not as common as insurance.

There is credit risk in a securitization when there is a third-party guarantee because the downgrading of the third party *could* result in the downgrading of the securities in a structure.

2. Internal Credit Enhancements

Internal credit enhancements come in more complicated forms than external credit enhancements. The most common forms of internal credit enhancement are reserve funds, overcollateralization, and senior/subordinate structures.

---

[3] The major monoline insurance companies in the United States are Capital Markets Assurance Corporation (CapMAC), Financial Security Assurance Inc. (FSA), Financial Guaranty Insurance Corporation (FGIC), and Municipal Bond Investors Assurance Corporation (MBIA).

[4] As noted earlier, the seller is not a party to the transaction once the assets are sold to the SPV who then issues the securities. Hence, if the seller provides a guarantee, it is viewed as a third-party guarantee.

PRACTICE QUESTION 2

Suppose that the collateral for an asset-backed securities structure has a gross weighted average coupon of 9.5%. The servicing fee is 75 basis points. The tranches issued have a weighted average coupon rate of 7.5%. What is the excess spread?

a. Reserve Funds

Reserve funds come in two forms:

▶ cash reserve funds
▶ excess spread accounts

Cash reserve funds are straight deposits of cash generated from issuance proceeds. In this case, part of the underwriting profits from the deal are deposited into a fund which typically invests in money market instruments. Cash reserve funds are typically used in conjunction with external credit enhancements.

Excess spread accounts involve the allocation of excess spread or cash into a separate reserve account after paying out the net coupon, servicing fee, and all other expenses on a monthly basis. The excess spread is a design feature of the structure. For example, suppose that:

1. gross weighted average coupon (gross WAC) is 8.00%—this is the interest rate paid by the borrowers
2. servicing and other fees are 0.25%
3. net weighted average coupon (net WAC) is 7.25%—this is the rate that is paid to all the tranches in the structure

So, for this hypothetical deal, 8.00% is available to make payments to the tranches, to cover servicing fees, and to cover other fees. Of that amount, 0.25% is paid for servicing and other fees and 7.25% is paid to the tranches. This means that only 7.50% must be paid out, leaving 0.50% (8.00%—7.50%). This 0.50% or 50 basis points is called the **excess spread**. This amount is placed in a reserve account—the excess servicing account—and it will gradually increase and can be used to pay for possible future losses.

b. Overcollateralization

Overcollateralization in a structure refers to a situation in which the value of the collateral exceeds the amount of the par value of the outstanding securities issued by the SPV. For example, if $100 million par value of securities are issued and at issuance the collateral has a market value of $105, there is $5 million in overcollateralization. Over time, the amount of overcollateralization changes due to (1) defaults, (2) amortization, and (3) prepayments. For example, suppose that two years after issuance, the par value of the securities outstanding is $90 million and the value of the collateral at the time is $93 million. As a result, the overcollateralization is $3 million ($93 million − $90 million).

Overcollateralization represents a form of internal credit enhancement because it can be used to absorb losses. For example, if the liability of the structure (i.e., par value of all the bond classes) is $100 million and the collateral's value is $105 million, then the first $5 million of losses will not result in a loss to any of the bond classes in the structure.

c. Senior-Subordinate Structure

Earlier in this section we explained a senior-subordinate structure in describing the bonds that can be issued in a securitization. We explained that there are senior bond classes and subordinate bond classes. The subordinate bond classes are also referred to as junior bond classes or non-senior bond classes.

As explained earlier, the creation of a senior-subordinate structure is done to provide credit tranching. More specifically, the senior-subordinate structure is a form of internal credit enhancement because the subordinate bond classes provide credit support for the senior bond classes. To understand why, the hypothetical HAT structure with one subordinate bond class that was described earlier is reproduced below:

Bond Class	Par Value (million)
A (senior)	$ 90
B (subordinate)	10
Total	$100

The senior bond class, A, is credit enhanced because the first $10 million in losses is absorbed by the subordinate bond class, B. Consequently, if defaults do not exceed $10 million, then the senior bond will receive the entire par value of $90 million.

Note that one subordinate bond class can provide credit enhancement for another subordinate bond class. To see this, consider the hypothetical HAT structure with two subordinate bond classes presented earlier:

Bond Class	Par Value (million)
A (senior)	$ 90
B (subordinate)	7
C (subordinate)	3
Total	$100

Bond Class C, the first loss piece, provides credit enhancement for not only the senior bond class, but also the subordinate bond class B.

The basic concern in the senior-subordinate structure is that while the subordinate bond classes provide a certain level of credit protection for the senior bond class at the closing of the deal, the level of protection changes over time due to prepayments. Faster prepayments can remove the desired credit protection. Thus, the objective after the deal closes is to distribute any prepayments such that the credit protection for the senior bond class does not deteriorate over time.

In real-estate related asset-backed securities, as well as nonagency mortgage-backed securities, the solution to the credit protection problem is a well developed mechanism called the **shifting interest mechanism**. Here is how it works. The percentage of the mortgage balance of the subordinate bond class to that of the mortgage balance for the entire deal is called the **level of subordination** or the **subordinate interest**. The higher the percentage, the greater the level of protection for the senior bond classes. The subordinate interest changes after the deal is closed due to prepayments. That is, the subordinate interest shifts (hence the term "shifting interest"). The purpose of a shifting interest mechanism is to allocate prepayments so that the subordinate interest is maintained at an acceptable level to protect the senior bond class. In effect, by paying down the senior bond class more quickly, the amount of subordination is maintained at the desired level.

The prospectus will provide the shifting interest percentage schedule for calculating the **senior prepayment percentage** (the percentage of prepayments paid to the senior bond class). For mortgage loans, a commonly used shifting interest percentage schedule is as follows:

Year after issuance	Senior prepayment percentage
1–5	100%
6	70
7	60
8	40
9	20
after year 9	0

So, for example, if prepayments in month 20 are $1 million, the amount paid to the senior bond class is $1 million and no prepayments are made to the subordinated bond classes. If prepayments in month 90 (in the seventh year after issuance) are $1 million, the senior bond class is paid $600,000 (60% × $1 million).

The shifting interest percentage schedule given in the prospectus is the "base" schedule. The set of shifting interest percentages can change over time depending on the performance of the collateral. If the performance is such that the credit protection for the senior bond class has deteriorated because credit losses have reduced the subordinate bond classes, the base shifting interest percentages are overridden and a higher allocation of prepayments is made to the senior bond class.

Performance analysis of the collateral is undertaken by the trustee for determining whether or not to override the base schedule. The performance analysis is in terms of tests and if the collateral fails any of the tests, this will trigger an override of the base schedule.

It is important to understand that the presence of a shifting interest mechanism results in a trade-off between credit risk and contraction risk for the senior bond class. The shifting interest mechanism reduces the credit risk to the senior bond class. However, because the senior bond class receives a larger share of any prepayments, contraction risk increases.

G. Call Provisions

Corporate, federal agency, and municipal bonds may contain a call provision. This provision gives the issuer the right to retire the bond issue prior to the stated maturity date. The issuer motivation for having the provision is to benefit from a decline in interest rates after the bond is issued. Asset-backed securities typically have **call provisions**. The motivation is twofold. As with other bonds, the issuer (the SPV) will want to take advantage of a decline in interest rates. In addition, to reduce administrative fees, the trustee may want to call in the issue because the par value of a bond class is small and it is more cost-effective to payoff the one or more bond classes.

Typically, for a corporate, federal agency, and municipal bond the trigger event for a call provision is that a specified amount of time has passed.[5] In the case of asset-backed securities, it is not simply the passage of time whereby the trustee is permitted to exercise any call option. There are trigger events for exercising the call option based on the amount of the issue outstanding.

There are two call provisions where the trigger that grants the trustee to call in the issue is based on a date being reached: (1) call on or after specified date and (2) auction call. A **call on or after specified date** operates just like a standard call provision for corporate, federal agency, and municipal securities: once a specified date is reached, the trustee has the option to call all the outstanding bonds. In an **auction call**, at a certain date a call will be exercised if an auction results in the outstanding collateral being sold at a price greater than its par value. The premium over par value received from the auctioned collateral is retained by the trustee and is eventually distributed to the seller of the assets.

Provisions that allow the trustee to call an issue or a tranche based on the par value outstanding are referred to as **optional clean-up call provisions**. Two examples are (1) percent of collateral call and (2) percent of bond call. In a **percent of collateral call**, the outstanding bonds can be called at par value if the outstanding *collateral's* balance falls below a predetermined percent of the original collateral's balance. This is the most common type of clean-up call provision for amortizing assets and the predetermined level is typically 10%. For example, suppose that the value for the collateral is $100 million. If there is a percent of collateral call provision with a trigger of 10%, then the trustee can call the entire issue if the value of the call is $10 million or less. In a **percent of bond call**, the outstanding bonds can be called at par value if the outstanding *bond's* par value relative to the original par value of bonds issued falls below a specified amount.

There is a call option that combines two triggers based on the amount outstanding and date. In a **latter of percent or date call**, the outstanding bonds can be called if either (1) the collateral's outstanding balance reaches a predetermined level before the specified call date or (2) the call date has been reached even if the collateral outstanding is above the predetermined level.

In addition to the above call provisions which permit the trustee to call the bonds, there may be an **insurer call**. Such a call permits the insurer to call the bonds if the collateral's cumulative loss history reaches a predetermined level.

---

[5] As explained at Level I, the calling of a portion of the issue is permitted to satisfy any sinking fund requirement.

HOME EQUITY LOANS   3

A **home equity loan** (HEL) is a loan backed by residential property. At one time, the loan was typically a second lien on property that was already pledged to secure a first lien. In some cases, the lien was a third lien. In recent years, the character of a home equity loan has changed. Today, a home equity loan is often a first lien on property where the borrower has either an *impaired credit history* and/or the payment-to-income ratio is too high for the loan to qualify as a conforming loan for securitization by Ginnie Mae, Fannie Mae, or Freddie Mac. Typically, the borrower used a home equity loan to consolidate consumer debt using the current home as collateral rather than to obtain funds to purchase a new home.

Home equity loans can be either closed end or open end. A **closed-end HEL** is structured the same way as a fully amortizing residential mortgage loan. That is, it has a fixed maturity and the payments are structured to fully amortize the loan by the maturity date. With an **open-end HEL**, the homeowner is given a credit line and can write checks or use a credit card for up to the amount of the credit line. The amount of the credit line depends on the amount of the equity the borrower has in the property. Because home equity loan securitizations are predominately closed-end HELs, our focus in this section is securities backed by them.

There are both fixed-rate and variable-rate closed-end HELs. Typically, variable-rate loans have a reference rate of 6-month LIBOR and have periodic caps and lifetime caps. (A periodic cap limits the change in the mortgage rate from the previous time the mortgage rate was reset; a lifetime cap sets a maximum that the mortgage rate can ever be for the loan.) The cash flow of a pool of closed-end HELs is comprised of interest, regularly scheduled principal repayments, and prepayments, just as with mortgage-backed securities. Thus, it is necessary to have a prepayment model and a default model to forecast cash flows. The prepayment speed is measured in terms of a conditional prepayment rate (CPR).

A. Prepayments

As explained in the previous reading, in the agency MBS market the PSA prepayment benchmark is used as the base case prepayment assumption in the prospectus. This benchmark assumes that the conditional prepayment rate (CPR) begins at 0.2% in the first month and increases linearly for 30 months to 6% CPR. From month 36 to the last month that the security is expected to be outstanding, the CPR is assumed to be constant at 6%. At the time that the prepayment speed is assumed to be constant, the security is said to be **seasoned**. For the PSA benchmark, a security is assumed to be seasoned in month 36. When the prepayment speed is depicted graphically, the linear increase in the CPR from month 1 to the month when the security is assumed to be seasoned is called the **prepayment ramp**. For the PSA benchmark, the prepayment ramp begins at month 1 and extends to month 30. Speeds that are assumed to be faster or slower than the PSA prepayment benchmark are quoted as a multiple of the base case prepayment speed.

There are differences in the prepayment behavior for home equity loans and agency MBS. Wall Street firms involved in the underwriting and market making of securities backed by HELs have developed prepayment models for these deals. Several firms have found that the key difference between the prepayment behavior of HELs and agency residential mortgages is the important role played by the credit characteristics of the borrower.[6]

Borrower characteristics and the amount of seasoning (i.e., how long the loans have been outstanding) must be kept in mind when trying to assess prepayments for a particular deal. In the prospectus of a HEL, a base case prepayment assumption is made. Rather than use the PSA prepayment benchmark as the base case prepayment speed, issuer's now use a base case prepayment benchmark that is specific to that issuer. The benchmark prepayment speed in the prospectus is called the **prospectus prepayment curve** or PPC. As with the PSA benchmark, faster or slower prepayments speeds are a quoted as a multiple of the PPC. Having an issuer-specific prepayment benchmark is preferred to a generic benchmark such as the PSA benchmark. The drawback for this improved description of the prepayment characteristics of a pool of mortgage loans is that it makes comparing the prepayment characteristics and investment characteristics of the collateral between issuers and issues (newly issued and seasoned issues) difficult.

PRACTICE QUESTION 3

The base case prepayment for the Champion Home Equity Loan Trust 1996-1 is provided for the fixed-rate loans (referred to as Group One in the prospectus) and floating-rate loans (referred to as Group Two in the prospectus). The following is taken from the prospectus for the Group One loans:

The model used with respect to the fixed rate certificates (the "prepayment ramp") assumes that the home equity loans in loan Group One prepay at a rate of 4% CPR in the first month after origination, and an additional 1.5% each month thereafter until the 14th month. Beginning in the 15th month and each month thereafter, the prepayment ramp assumes a prepayment rate of 25% CPR.

What is the CPR assuming 150% PPC for the fixed-rate collateral for the following months:

Month	CPR	Month	CPR	Month	CPR
1		11		30	
2		12		125	
3		13		150	
4		14		200	
5		15		250	
6		16		275	
7		17		300	
8		18		325	
9		19		350	
10		20		360	

[6] Dale Westhoff and Mark Feldman, "Prepayment Modeling and Valuation of Home Equity Loan Securities," Chapter 18 in Frank J. Fabozzi, Chuck Ramsey, and Michael Marz (eds.), *The Handbook of Nonagency Mortgage-Backed Securities: Second Edition* (New Hope, PA: Frank J. Fabozzi Associates, 2000).

Since HEL deals are backed by both fixed-rate and variable-rate loans, a separate PPC is provided for each type of loan. For example, in the prospectus for the Contimortgage Home Equity Loan Trust 1998-2, the base case prepayment assumption for the fixed-rate collateral begins at 4% CPR in month 1 and increases 1.45455% CPR per month until month 12, at which time it is 20% CPR. Thus, the collateral is assumed to be seasoned in 12 months. The prepayment ramp begins in month 1 and ends in month 12. If an investor analyzed the deal based on 200% PPC, this means doubling the CPRs cited and using 12 months for when the collateral seasons. For the variable-rate collateral in the ContiMortgage deal, 100% PPC assumes the collateral is seasoned after 18 months with the CPR in month 1 being 4% and increasing 1.82353% CPR each month. From month 18 on, the CPR is 35%. Thus, the prepayment ramp starts at month 1 and ends at month 18. Notice that for this issuer, the variable-rate collateral is assumed to season slower than the fixed-rate collateral (18 versus 12 months), but has a faster CPR when the pool is seasoned (35% versus 20%).

B. Payment Structure

As with nonagency mortgage-backed securities discussed in the previous reading, there are passthrough and paythrough home equity loan-backed structures.

Typically, home equity loan-backed securities are securitized by both closed-end fixed-rate and adjustable-rate (or variable-rate) HELs. The securities backed by the latter are called **HEL floaters**. The reference rate of the underlying loans typically is 6-month LIBOR. The cash flow of these loans is affected by periodic and lifetime caps on the loan rate.

Institutional investors that seek securities that better match their floating-rate funding costs are attracted to securities that offer a floating-rate coupon. To increase the attractiveness of home equity loan-backed securities to such investors, the securities typically have been created in which the reference rate is 1-month LIBOR. Because of (1) the mismatch between the reference rate on the underlying loans (6-month LIBOR) and that of the HEL floater and (2) the periodic and life caps of the underlying loans, there is a cap on the coupon rate for the HEL floater. Unlike a typical floater, which has a cap that is fixed throughout the security's life, the effective periodic and lifetime cap of a HEL floater is variable. The effective cap, referred to as the **available funds cap**, will depend on the amount of funds generated by the net coupon on the principal, less any fees.

Let's look at one issue, Advanta Mortgage Loan Trust 1995-2 issued in June 1995. At the offering, this issue had approximately $122 million closed-end HELs. There were 1,192 HELs consisting of 727 fixed-rate loans and 465 variable-rate loans. There were five classes (A-1, A-2, A-3, A-4, and A-5) and a residual. The five classes are summarized below:

Class	Paramount ($)	Passthrough Coupon Rate (%)
A-1	9,229,000	7.30
A-2	30,330,000	6.60
A-3	16,455,000	6.85
A-4	9,081,000	floating rate
A-5	56,917,000	floating rate

The collateral is divided into group I and group II. The 727 fixed-rate loans are included in group I and support Classes A-1, A-2, A-3, and A-4 certificates. The 465 variable-rate loans are in group II and support Class A-5.

Tranches have been structured in home equity loan deals so as to give some senior tranches greater prepayment protection than other senior tranches. The two types of structures that do this are the non-accelerating senior tranche and the planned amortization class tranche.

1. Non-Accelerating Senior Tranches

A **non-accelerating senior tranche** (NAS tranche) receives principal payments according to a schedule. The schedule is not a dollar amount. Rather, it is a principal schedule that shows for a given month the share of pro rata principal that must be distributed to the NAS tranche. A typical principal schedule for a NAS tranche is as follows:[7]

Months	Share of Pro Rata Principal
1 through 36	0%
37 through 60	45%
61 through 72	80%
73 through 84	100%
After month 84	300%

The average life for the NAS tranche is stable for a large range of prepayments because for the first three years all prepayments are made to the other senior tranches. This reduces the risk of the NAS tranche contracting (i.e., shortening) due to fast prepayments. After month 84, 300% of its pro rata share is paid to the NAS tranche thereby reducing its extension risk.

The average life stability over a wide range of prepayments is illustrated in Exhibit 62-2. The deal analyzed is the ContiMortgage Home Equity Loan Trust 1997-2.[8] Class A-9 is the NAS tranche. The analysis was performed on Bloomberg shortly after the deal was issued using the issue's PPC. As can be seen, the average life is fairly stable between 75% to 200% PPC. In fact, the difference in the average life between 75% PPC and 200% PPC is slightly greater than 1 year.

In contrast, Exhibit 62-2 also shows the average life over the same prepayment scenarios for a non-NAS sequential-pay tranche in the same deal—Class A-7. Notice the substantial average life variability. While the average life difference between 75% and 200% PPC for the NAS tranche is just over 1 year, it is more than 9 years for the non-NAS tranche. Of course, the non-NAS in the same deal will be less stable than a regular sequential tranche because the non-NAS gets a greater share of principal than it would otherwise.

---

[7] Charles Schorin, Steven Weinreich, and Oliver Hsiang, "Home Equity Loan Transaction Structures," Chapter 6 in Frank J. Fabozzi, Chuck Ramsey, and Michael Marz, *Handbook of Nonagency Mortgage-Backed Securities: Second Edition* (New Hope, PA: Frank J. Fabozzi Associates, 2000).

[8] This illustration is from Schorin, Weinreich, and Hsiang, "Home Equity Loan Transaction Structures."

EXHIBIT 62-2	Average Life for NAS Tranche (Class A-9) and Non-NAS Tranche (Class A-7) for ContiMortgage Home Equity Loan Trust 1997-2 for a Range of Prepayments												

	% PPC												Avg. life difference 75% to 200% PPC
	0	50	75	100	120	150	200	250	300	350	400	500	
Plateau CPR	0	10	15	20	24	30	40	50	60	70	80	100	
Avg. Life													
NAS Bond	11.71	7.81	7.06	6.58	6.30	6.06	5.97	3.98	2.17	1.73	1.38	0.67	1.09
Non-NAS Bond	21.93	14.54	11.94	8.82	6.73	4.71	2.59	1.96	1.55	1.25	1.03	0.58	9.35

Calculation: Bloomberg Financial Markets.

Reported in Charles Schorin, Steven Weinreich, and Oliver Hsiang, "Home Equity Loan Transaction Structures," Chapter 6 in Frank J. Fabozzi, Chuck Ramsey, and Michael Marz, *Handbook of Nonagency Mortgage-Backed Securities: Second Edition* (New Hope, PA: Frank J. Fabozzi Associates, 2000).

2. Planned Amortization Class Tranche

In our discussion of collateralized mortgage obligations issued by the agencies in the previous chapter we explained how a planned amortization class tranche can be created. These tranches are also created in HEL structures. Unlike agency CMO PAC tranches that are backed by fixed-rate loans, the collateral for HEL deals is both fixed rate and adjustable rate.

An example of a HEL PAC tranche in a HEL-backed deal is tranche A-6 in ContiMortgage 1998-2. We described the PPC for this deal in Section III.A.1 above. There is a separate PAC collar for both the fixed-rate and adjustable-rate collateral. For the fixed-rate collateral the PAC collar is 125%–175% PPC; for the adjustable-rate collateral the PAC collar is 95%–130% PPC. The average life for tranche A-6 (a tranche backed by the fixed-rate collateral) is 5.1 years. As explained, the effective collar for shorter tranches can be greater than the upper collar specified in the prospectus. The effective upper collar for tranche A-6 is actually 180% PPC (assuming that the adjustable-rate collateral pays at 100% PPC).[9]

For shorter PACs, the effective upper collar is greater. For example, for tranche A-3 in the same deal, the initial PAC collar is 125% to 175% PPC with an average life of 2.02 years. However, the effective upper collar is 190% PPC (assuming the adjustable-rate collateral pays at 100% PPC).

The effective collar for PAC tranches changes over time based on actual prepayments and therefore based on when the support tranches depart from the initial PAC collar. For example, if for the next 36 months after the issuance of the ContiMortgage 1998-2 actual prepayments are a constant 150% PPC, then the effective collar would be 135% PPC to 210% PPC.[10] That is, the lower and

---

[9] For a more detailed analysis of this tranche, see Schorin, Weinreich, and Hsiang, "Home Equity Loan Transaction Structures."

[10] Schorin, Weinreich, and Hsiang, "Home Equity Loan Transaction Structures."

upper collar will increase. If the actual PPC is 200% PPC for the 10 months after issuance, the support bonds will be fully paid off and there will be no PAC collateral. In this situation the PAC is said to be a **broken PAC**.

4   MANUFACTURED HOUSING-BACKED SECURITIES

Manufactured housing-backed securities are backed by loans for manufactured homes. In contrast to site-built homes, manufactured homes are built at a factory and then transported to a site. The loan may be either a mortgage loan (for both the land and the home) or a consumer retail installment loan.

Manufactured housing-backed securities are issued by Ginnie Mae and private entities. The former securities are guaranteed by the full faith and credit of the U.S. government. The manufactured home loans that are collateral for the securities issued and guaranteed by Ginnie Mae are loans guaranteed by the Federal Housing Administration (FHA) or Veterans Administration (VA).

Loans not backed by the FHA or VA are called **conventional loans**. Manufactured housing-backed securities that are backed by such loans are called **conventional manufactured housing-backed securities**. These securities are issued by private entities.

The typical loan for a manufactured home is 15 to 20 years. The loan repayment is structured to fully amortize the amount borrowed. Therefore, as with residential mortgage loans and HELs, the cash flow consists of net interest, regularly scheduled principal, and prepayments. However, prepayments are more stable for manufactured housing-backed securities because they are not sensitive to refinancing.

There are several reasons for this. First, the loan balances are typically small so that there is no significant dollar savings from refinancing. Second, the rate of depreciation of mobile homes may be such that in the earlier years depreciation is greater than the amount of the loan paid off. This makes it difficult to refinance the loan. Finally, typically borrowers are of lower credit quality and therefore find it difficult to obtain funds to refinance.

As with residential mortgage loans and HELs, prepayments on manufactured housing-backed securities are measured in terms of CPR and each issue contains a PPC.

The payment structure is the same as with nonagency mortgage-backed securities and home equity loan-backed securities.

5   RESIDENTIAL MBS OUTSIDE THE UNITED STATES

Throughout the world where the market for securitized assets has developed, the largest sector is the residential mortgage-backed sector. It is not possible to provide a discussion of the residential mortgage-backed securities market in every country. Instead, to provide a flavor for this market sector and the similarities with the U.S. nonagency mortgage-backed securities market, we will discuss just the market in the United Kingdom and Australia.

A. U.K. Residential Mortgage-Backed Securities

In Europe, the country in which there has been the largest amount of issuance of asset-backed securities is the United Kingdom.[11] The largest component of that market is the residential mortgage-backed security market which includes "prime" residential mortgage-backed securities and "nonconforming" residential mortgage-backed securities. In the U.S. mortgage market, a nonconforming mortgage loan is one that does not meet the underwriting standards of Ginnie Mae, Fannie Mae, or Freddie Mac. However, this does not mean that the loan has greater credit risk. In contrast, in the U.K. mortgage market, nonconforming mortgage loans are made to borrowers that are viewed as having greater credit risk—those that do not have a credit history and those with a history of failing to meet their obligations.

The standard mortgage loan is a variable rate, fully amortizing loan. Typically, the term of the loan is 25 years. As in the U.S. mortgage market, borrowers seeking a loan with a high loan-to-value ratio are required to obtain mortgage insurance, called a "mortgage indemnity guarantee" (MIG).

The deals are more akin to the nonagency market since there is no guarantee by a federally related agency or a government sponsored enterprise as in the United States. Thus, there is credit enhancement as explained below.

Because the underlying mortgage loans are floating rate, the securities issued are floating rate (typically, LIBOR is the reference rate). The cash flow depends on the timing of the principal payments. The deals are typically set up as a sequential-pay structure. For example, consider the Granite Mortgage 00-2 transaction, a typical structure in the United Kingdom.[12] The mortgage pool consists of prime mortgages. There are four bond classes. The two class A tranches, Class A-1 and Class A-2, are rated AAA. One is a dollar denominated tranche and the other a pound sterling tranche. Class B is rated single A and tranche C is rated triple BBB. The sequence of principal payments is as follows: Class A-1 and Class A-2 are paid off on a pro rata basis, then Class B is paid off, and then Class C is paid off.

The issuer has the option to call the outstanding notes under the following circumstances:

▶ A withholding tax is imposed on the interest payments to noteholders

▶ a clean up call (if the mortgage pool falls to 10% or less of the original pool amount)

▶ on a specified date (called the "step up date") or dates in the future

For example, for the Granite Mortgage 00-02 transaction, the step up date is September 2007. The issuer is likely to call the issue because the coupon rate on the notes increases at that time. In this deal, as with most, the margin over LIBOR doubles.

---

[11] Information about the U.K. residential mortgage-backed securities market draws from the following sources: Phil Adams, "UK Residential Mortgage—Backed Securities," and "UK Non-Conforming Residential Mortgage-Backed Securities," in *Building Blocks,* Asset-Backed Securities Research, Barclays Capital, January 2001; Christopher Flanagan and Edward Reardon, *European Structured Products: 2001 Review and 2002 Outlook,* Global Structured Finance Research, J.P. Morgan Securities Inc., January 11, 2002; and "UK Mortgages—MBS Products for U.S. Investors," *Mortgage Strategist,* UBS Warburg, February 27, 2001, pp. 15–21.

[12] For a more detailed discussion of this structure, see Adams, "UK Residential Mortgage-Backed Securities," pp. 31–37.

Credit enhancement can consist of excess spread, reserve fund, and subordination. For the Granite Mortgage 00-2, there was subordination: Class B and C tranches for the two Class A tranche and Class C tranche for the Class B tranche. The reserve was fully funded at the time of issuance and the excess spread was used to build up the reserve fund. In addition, there is a "principal shortfall provision." This provision requires that if the realized losses for a period are such that the excess reserve for that period is not sufficient to cover the losses, as excess spread becomes available in future periods they are used to cover these losses. Also there are performance triggers that under certain conditions will provide further credit protection to the senior bonds by modifying the payment of principal. When the underlying mortgage pool consists of nonconforming mortgage loans, additional protections are provided for investors.

Since prepayments will reduce the average life of the senior notes in a transaction, typical deals have provision that permit the purchase of substitute mortgages if the prepayment rate exceeds a certain rate. For example, in the Granite Mortgage 00-02 deal, this rate is 20% per annum.

B. Australian Mortgage-Backed Securities

In Australia, lending is dominated by mortgage banks, the larger ones being ANZ, Commonwealth Bank of Australia, National Australia Bank, Westpac, and St. George Bank.[13] Non-mortgage bank competitors who have entered the market have used securitization as a financing vehicle. The majority of the properties are concentrated in New South Wales, particularly the city of Sydney. Rating agencies have found that the risk of default is considerably less than in the U.S. and the U.K.

Loan maturities are typically between 20 and 30 years. As in the United States, there is a wide range of mortgage designs with respect to interest rates. There are fixed-rate, variable-rate (both capped and uncapped), and rates tied to a benchmark.

There is mortgage insurance for loans to protect lenders, called "lenders mortgage insurance" (LMI). Loans typically have LMI covering 20% to 100% of the loan. The companies that provide this insurance are private corporations.[14] When mortgages loans that do not have LMI are securitized, typically the issuer will purchase insurance for those loans.

LMI is important for securitized transactions since it is the first layer of credit enhancement in a deal structure. The rating agencies recognize this in rating the tranches in a structure. The amount that a rating agency will count toward credit enhancement for LMI depends on the rating agency's assessment of the mortgage insurance company.

When securitized, the tranches have a floating rate. There is an initial revolving period—which means that no principal payments are made to the tranche holders but instead reinvested in new collateral. As with the U.K. Granite Mortgage 00-02 deal, the issuer has the right to call the issue if there is

---

[13] Information about the Australian residential mortgage-backed securities market draws from the following sources: Phil Adams, "Australian Residential Mortgage-Backed Securities," in *Building Blocks;* Karen Weaver, Eugene Xu, Nicholas Bakalar, and Trudy Weibel, "Mortgage-Backed Securities in Australia," Chapter 41 in *The Handbook of Mortgage-Backed Securities: Fifth Edition* (New York, NY: McGraw Hill, 2001); and, "Australian Value Down Under," *Mortgage Strategist,* UBS Warburg, February 6, 2001, pp. 14–22.

[14] The five major ones are Royal and Sun Alliance Lenders Mortgage Insurance Limited, CGU Lenders Mortgage Insurance Corporation Ltd., PMI mortgage insurance limited, GE Mortgage Insurance Property Ltd., and GE Mortgage Insurance Corporation.

an imposition of a withholding tax on note holders' interest payments, after a certain date, or if the balance falls below a certain level (typically, 10%).

Australian mortgage-backed securities have tranches that are U.S. dollar denominated and some that are denominated in Euros.[15] These global deals typically have two or three AAA senior tranches and one AA or AA—junior tranche.

For credit enhancement, there is excess spread (which in most deals is typically small), subordination, and, as noted earlier, LMI. To illustrate this, consider the Interstar Millennium Series 2000-3E Trust—a typical Australian MBS transaction. There are two tranches: a senior tranche (Class A) that was rated AAA and a subordinated tranche (Class B) that was AA–. The protection afforded the senior tranche is the subordinated tranche, LMI (all the properties were covered up to 100% and were insured by all five major mortgage insurance companies), and the excess spread.

AUTO LOAN-BACKED SECURITIES   6

Auto loan-backed securities represents one of the oldest and most familiar sectors of the asset-backed securities market. Auto loan-backed securities are issued by:

1. the financial subsidiaries of auto manufacturers
2. commercial banks
3. independent finance companies and small financial institutions specializing in auto loans

Historically, auto loan-backed securities have represented between 18% to 25% of the asset-backed securities market. The auto loan market is tiered based on the credit quality of the borrowers. "Prime auto loans" are of fundamentally high credit quality and originated by the financial subsidiaries of major auto manufacturers. The loans are of high credit quality for the following reasons. First, they are a secured form of lending. Second, they begin to repay principal immediately through amortization. Third, they are short-term in nature. Finally, for the most part, major issuers of auto loans have tended to follow reasonably prudent underwriting standards.

Unlike the sub-prime mortgage industry, there is less consistency on what actually constitutes various categories of prime and sub-prime auto loans. Moody's assumes the *prime* market is composed of issuers typically having cumulative losses of less than 3%; *near-prime* issuers have cumulative losses of 3–7%; and sub-prime issuers have losses exceeding 7%.

The auto sector was a small part of the European asset-backed securities market in 2002, about 5% of total securitization. There are two reasons for this. First, there is lower per capita car ownership in Europe. Second, there is considerable variance of tax and regulations dealing with borrower privacy rules in Europe thereby making securitization difficult.[16] Auto deals have been done in Italy, the U.K., Germany, Portugal, and Belgium.

---

[15] The foreign exchange risk for these deals is typically hedged using various types of swaps (fixed/floating, floating/floating, and currency swaps).

[16] Flanagan and Reardon, *European Structures Products: 2001 Review and 2002 Outlook*, p. 9.

A. Cash Flow and Prepayments

The cash flow for auto loan-backed securities consists of regularly scheduled monthly loan payments (interest and scheduled principal repayments) and any prepayments. For securities backed by auto loans, prepayments result from (1) sales and trade-ins requiring full payoff of the loan, (2) repossession and subsequent resale of the automobile, (3) loss or destruction of the vehicle, (4) payoff of the loan with cash to save on the interest cost, and (5) refinancing of the loan at a lower interest cost.

Prepayments due to repossession and subsequent resale are sensitive to the economic cycle. In recessionary economic periods, prepayments due to this factor increase. While refinancings may be a major reason for prepayments of mortgage loans, they are of minor importance for automobile loans. Moreover, the interest rates for the automobile loans underlying some deals are substantially below market rates since they are offered by manufacturers as part of a sales promotion.

B. Measuring Prepayments

For most asset-backed securities where there are prepayments, prepayments are measured in term of the conditional prepayment rate, CPR. As explained in the previous reading, monthly prepayments are quoted in terms of the single monthly mortality (SMM) rate. The *convention* for calculating and reporting prepayment rates for auto-loan backed securities is different. Prepayments for auto loan-backed securities are measured in terms of the **absolute prepayment speed**, denoted by ABS.[17] The ABS is the monthly prepayment expressed as a percentage of the original collateral amount. As explained in the previous reading, the SMM (monthly CPR) expresses prepayments based on the prior month's balance.

There is a mathematical relationship between the SMM and the ABS measures. Letting M denote the number of months after loan origination, the SMM rate can be calculated from the ABS rate using the following formula:

$$SMM = \frac{ABS}{1 - [ABS \times (M - 1)]}$$

where the ABS and SMM rates are expressed in decimal form.

For example, if the ABS rate is 1.5% (i.e., 0.015) at month 14 after origination, then the SMM rate is 1.86%, as shown below:

$$SMM = \frac{0.015}{1 - [0.015 \times (14 - 1)]} = 0.0186 = 1.86\%$$

---

[17] The only reason for the use of ABS rather than SMM/CPR in this sector is historical. Auto loan-backed securities (which were popularly referred to at one time as CARS (Certificates of Automobile Receivables)) were the first non-mortgage assets to be developed in the market. (The first non-mortgage asset-backed security was actually backed by computer lease receivables.) The major dealer in this market at the time, First Boston (now Credit Suisse First Boston) elected to use ABS for measuring prepayments. You may wonder how one obtains "ABS" from "absolute prepayment rate". Again, it is historical. When the market first started, the ABS measure probably meant "asset-backed security" but over time to avoid confusion evolved to absolute prepayment rate.

The ABS rate can be calculated from the SMM rate using the following formula:

$$ABS = \frac{SMM}{1 + [SMM \times (M - 1)]}$$

For example, if the SMM rate at month 9 after origination is 1.3%, then the ABS rate is:

$$ABS = \frac{0.013}{1 + [0.013 \times (9 - 1)]} = 0.0118 = 1.18\%$$

Historically, when measured in terms of SMM rate, auto loans have experienced SMMs that increase as the loans season.

STUDENT LOAN-BACKED SECURITIES

7

Student loans are made to cover college cost (undergraduate, graduate, and professional programs such as medical and law school) and tuition for a wide range of vocational and trade schools. Securities backed by student loans, popularly referred to as SLABS (student loan asset-backed securities), have similar structural features as the other asset-backed securities we discussed above.

The student loans that have been most commonly securitized are those that are made under the Federal Family Education Loan Program (FFELP). Under this program, the government makes loans to students via private lenders. The decision by private lenders to extend a loan to a student is not based on the applicant's ability to repay the loan. If a default of a loan occurs and the loan has been properly serviced, then the government will guarantee up to 98% of the principal plus accrued interest.[18]

Loans that are not part of a government guarantee program are called **alternative loans**. These loans are basically consumer loans and the lender's decision to extend an alternative loan will be based on the ability of the applicant to repay the loan. Alternative loans have been securitized.

A. Issuers

Congress created Fannie Mae and Freddie Mac to provide liquidity in the mortgage market by allowing these government sponsored enterprises to buy

---

[18] Actually, depending on the origination date, the guarantee can be up to 100%.

mortgage loans in the secondary market. Congress created the Student Loan Marketing Association (nicknamed "Sallie Mae") as a government sponsored enterprise to purchase student loans in the secondary market and to securitize pools of student loans. Since its first issuance in 1995, Sallie Mae is now the major issuer of SLABS and its issues are viewed as the benchmark issues.[19] Other entities that issue SLABS are either traditional corporate entities (e.g., the Money Store and PNC Bank) or non-profit organizations (Michigan Higher Education Loan Authority and the California Educational Facilities Authority). The SLABS of the latter typically are issued as tax-exempt securities and therefore trade in the municipal market. In recent years, several not-for-profit entities have changed their charter and applied for "for profit" treatment.

B. Cash Flow

Let's first look at the cash flow for the student loans themselves. There are different types of student loans under the FFELP including subsidized and unsubsidized Stafford loans, Parental Loans for Undergraduate Students (PLUS), and Supplemental Loans to Students (SLS). These loans involve three periods with respect to the borrower's payments—deferment period, grace period, and loan repayment period. Typically, student loans work as follows. While a student is in school, no payments are made by the student on the loan. This is the **deferment period**. Upon leaving school, the student is extended a **grace period** of usually six months when no payments on the loan must be made. After this period, payments are made on the loan by the borrower.

Student loans are floating-rate loans, exclusively indexed to the 3-month Treasury bill rate. As a result, some issuers of SLABs issue securities whose coupon rate is indexed to the 3-month Treasury bill rate. However, a large percentage of SLABS issued are indexed to LIBOR floaters.[20]

Prepayments typically occur due to defaults or loan consolidation. Even if there is no loss of principal faced by the investor when defaults occur, the investor is still exposed to contraction risk. This is the risk that the investor must reinvest the proceeds at a lower spread and in the case of a bond purchased at a premium, the premium will be lost. Studies have shown student loan prepayments are insensitive to the level of interest rates. Consolidations of a loan occur when the student who has loans over several years combines them into a single loan. The proceeds from the consolidation are distributed to the original lender and, in turn, distributed to the bondholders.

8   SBA LOAN-BACKED SECURITIES

The Small Business Administration (SBA) is an agency of the U.S. government empowered to guarantee loans made by approved SBA lenders to qualified borrowers. The loans are backed by the full faith and credit of the government. Most SBA loans are variable-rate loans where the reference rate is the prime rate.

---

[19] In 1997 Sallie Mae began the process of unwinding its status as a GSE; until this multi-year process is completed, all debt issued by Sallie Mae under its GSE status will be "grandfathered" as GSE debt until maturity.

[20] This creates a mismatch between the collateral and the securities. Issuers have dealt with this by hedging with the risk by using derivative instruments such as interest rate swaps (floating-to-floating rate swaps) or interest rate caps.

The rate on the loan is reset monthly on the first of the month or quarterly on the first of January, April, July, and October. SBA regulations specify the maximum coupon allowable in the secondary market. Newly originated loans have maturities between 5 and 25 years.

The Small Business Secondary Market Improvement Act passed in 1984 permitted the pooling of SBA loans. When pooled, the underlying loans must have similar terms and features. The maturities typically used for pooling loans are 7, 10, 15, 20, and 25 years. Loans without caps are not pooled with loans that have caps.

Most variable-rate SBA loans make monthly payments consisting of interest and principal repayment. The amount of the monthly payment for an individual loan is determined as follows. Given the coupon formula of the prime rate plus the loan's quoted margin, the interest rate is determined for each loan. Given the interest rate, a level payment amortization schedule is determined. It is this level payment that is paid for the next month until the coupon rate is reset.

The monthly cash flow that the investor in an SBA-backed security receives consists of

▶ the coupon interest based on the coupon rate set for the period

▶ the scheduled principal repayment (i.e., scheduled amortization)

▶ prepayments

Prepayments for SBA-backed securities are measured in terms of CPR. Voluntary prepayments can be made by the borrower without any penalty. There are several factors contributing to the prepayment speed of a pool of SBA loans. A factor affecting prepayments is the maturity date of the loan. It has been found that the fastest speeds on SBA loans and pools occur for shorter maturities.[21] The purpose of the loan also affects prepayments. There are loans for working capital purposes and loans to finance real estate construction or acquisition. It has been observed that SBA pools with maturities of 10 years or less made for working capital purposes tend to prepay at the fastest speed. In contrast, loans backed by real estate that are long maturities tend to prepay at a slow speed.

CREDIT CARD RECEIVABLE-BACKED SECURITIES　　9

When a purchase is made on a credit card, the issuer of the credit card (the lender) extends credit to the cardholder (the borrower). Credit cards are issued by banks (e.g., Visa and MasterCard), retailers (e.g., Sears and Target Corporation), and travel and entertainment companies (e.g., American Express). At the time of purchase, the cardholder is agreeing to repay the amount borrowed (i.e., the cost of the item purchased) plus any applicable finance charges. The amount that the cardholder has agreed to pay the issuer of the credit card is a receivable from the perspective of the issuer of the credit card. Credit card receivables are used as collateral for the issuance of an asset-backed security.

---

[21] Donna Faulk, "SBA Loan-Backed Securities," in *Asset-Backed Securities.*

A. Cash Flow

For a pool of credit card receivables, the cash flow consists of finance charges collected, fees, and principal. Finance charges collected represent the periodic interest the credit card borrower is charged based on the unpaid balance after the grace period. Fees include late payments fees and any annual membership fees.

Interest to security holders is paid periodically (e.g., monthly, quarterly, or semiannually). The interest rate may be fixed or floating—roughly half of the securities are floaters. The floating rate is uncapped.

A credit card receivable-backed security is a nonamortizing security. For a specified period of time, the lockout period or revolving period, the principal payments made by credit card borrowers comprising the pool are retained by the trustee and reinvested in additional receivables to maintain the size of the pool. The lockout period can vary from 18 months to 10 years. So, during the lockout period, the cash flow that is paid out to security holders is based on finance charges collected and fees. After the lockout period, the principal is no longer reinvested but paid to investors, the principal-amortization period and the various types of structures are described next.

B. Payment Structure

There are three different amortization structures that have been used in credit card receivable-backed security deals: (1) passthrough structure, (2) controlled-amortization structure, and (3) bullet-payment structure. The latter two are the more common. One source reports that 80% of the deals are bullet structures and the balance are controlled amortization structures.[22]

In a **passthrough structure**, the principal cash flows from the credit card accounts are paid to the security holders on a pro rata basis. In a **controlled-amortization structure**, a scheduled principal amount is established, similar to the principal window for a PAC bond. The scheduled principal amount is sufficiently low so that the obligation can be satisfied even under certain stress scenarios, where cash flow is decreased due to defaults or slower repayment by borrowers. The security holder is paid the lesser of the scheduled principal amount and the pro rata amount. In a **bullet-payment structure**, the security holder receives the entire amount in one distribution. Since there is no assurance that the entire amount can be paid in one lump sum, the procedure is for the trustee to place principal monthly into an account that generates sufficient interest to make periodic interest payments and accumulate the principal to be repaid. These deposits are made in the months shortly before the scheduled bullet payment. This type of structure is also often called a **soft bullet** because the maturity is technically not guaranteed, but is almost always satisfied. The time period over which the principal is accumulated is called the **accumulation period**.

C. Performance of the Portfolio of Receivables

There are several concepts that must be understood in order to assess the performance of the portfolio of receivables and the ability of the issuer to meet its interest obligation and repay principal as scheduled.

We begin with the concept of the **gross portfolio yield**. This yield includes finance charges collected and fees. **Charge-offs** represent the accounts charged off as uncollectible. **Net portfolio yield** is equal to gross portfolio yield minus

---

[22] Thompson, "MBNA Tests the Waters."

charge-offs. The net portfolio yield is important because it is from this yield that the bondholders will be paid. So, for example, if the average yield (WAC) that must be paid to the various tranches in the structure is 5% and the net portfolio yield for the month is only 4.5%, there is the risk that the bondholder obligations will not be satisfied.

Delinquencies are the percentages of receivables that are past due for a specified number of months, usually 30, 60, and 90 days. They are considered an indicator of potential future charge-offs.

The **monthly payment rate** (MPR) expresses the monthly payment (which includes finance charges, fees, and any principal repayment) of a credit card receivable portfolio as a percentage of credit card debt outstanding in the previous month. For example, suppose a $500 million credit card receivable portfolio in January realized $50 million of payments in February. The MPR would then be 10% ($50 million divided by $500 million).

There are two reasons why the MPR is important. First, if the MPR reaches an extremely low level, there is a chance that there will be extension risk with respect to the principal payments on the bonds. Second, if the MPR is very low, then there is a chance that there will not be sufficient cash flows to pay off principal. This is one of the events that could trigger early amortization of the principal (described below).

At issuance, portfolio yield, charge-offs, delinquency, and MPR information are provided in the prospectus. Information about portfolio performance is then available from Bloomberg, the rating agencies, and dealers.

D. Early Amortization Triggers

There are provisions in credit card receivable-backed securities that require early amortization of the principal if certain events occur. Such provisions, which as mentioned earlier in this reading are referred to as early amortization or rapid amortization provisions, are included to safeguard the credit quality of the issue. The only way that the principal cash flows can be altered is by the triggering of the early amortization provision.

Typically, early amortization allows for the rapid return of principal in the event that the 3-month average excess spread earned on the receivables falls to zero or less. When early amortization occurs, the credit card tranches are retired sequentially (i.e., first the AAA bond then the AA rated bond, etc.). This is accomplished by paying the principal payments made by the credit card borrowers to the investors instead of using them to purchase more receivables. The length of time until the return of principal is largely a function of the monthly payment rate. For example, suppose that a AAA tranche is 82% of the overall deal. If the monthly payment rate is 11% then the AAA tranche would return principal over a 7.5-month period (82%/11%). An 18% monthly payment rate would return principal over a 4.5-month period (82%/18%).

COLLATERALIZED DEBT OBLIGATIONS **10**

A **collateralized debt obligation** (CDO) is a security backed by a diversified pool of one or more of the following types of debt obligations:

▶ U.S. domestic high-yield corporate bonds

▶ structured financial products (i.e., mortgage-backed and asset-backed securities)

- ▶ emerging market bonds
- ▶ bank loans
- ▶ special situation loans and distressed debt

When the underlying pool of debt obligations are bond-type instruments (high-yield corporate, structured financial products, and emerging market bonds), a CDO is referred to as a **collateralized bond obligation** (CBO). When the underlying pool of debt obligations are bank loans, a CDO is referred to as a **collateralized loan obligation** (CLO).

A. Structure of a CDO

In a CDO structure, there is an asset manager responsible for managing the portfolio of debt obligations. There are restrictions imposed (i.e., restrictive covenants) as to what the asset manager may do and certain tests that must be satisfied for the tranches in the CDO to maintain the credit rating assigned at the time of issuance and determine how and when tranches are repaid principal.

The funds to purchase the underlying assets (i.e., the bonds and loans) are obtained from the issuance of debt obligations (i.e., tranches) and include one or more senior tranches, one or more mezzanine tranches, and a subordinate/equity tranche. There will be a rating sought for all but the subordinate/equity tranche. For the senior tranches, at least an A rating is typically sought. For the mezzanine tranches, a rating of BBB but no less than B is sought. As explained below, since the subordinate/equity tranche receives the residual cash flow, no rating is sought for this tranche.

The ability of the asset manager to make the interest payments to the tranches and payoff the tranches as they mature depends on the performance of the underlying assets. The proceeds to meet the obligations to the CDO tranches (interest and principal repayment) can come from (1) coupon interest payments of the underlying assets, (2) maturing assets in the underlying pool, and (3) sale of assets in the underlying pool.

In a typical structure, one or more of the tranches is a floating-rate security. With the exception of deals backed by bank loans which pay a floating rate, the asset manager invests in fixed-rate bonds. Now that presents a problem—paying tranche investors a floating rate and investing in assets with a fixed rate. To deal with this problem, the asset manager uses derivative instruments to be able to convert fixed-rate payments from the assets into floating-rate payments. In particular, interest rate swaps are used. This derivative instrument allows a market participant to swap fixed-rate payments for floating-rate payments or vice versa. Because of the mismatch between the nature of the cash flows of the debt obligations in which the asset manager invests and the floating-rate liability of any of the tranches, the asset manager must use an interest rate swap. A rating agency will require the use of swaps to eliminate this mismatch.

B. Family of CDOs

The family of CDOs is shown in Exhibit 62-3. While each CDO shown in the exhibit will be discussed in more detail below, we will provide an overview here.

The first breakdown in the CDO family is between cash CDOs and synthetic CDOs. A **cash CDO** is backed by a pool of cash market debt instruments. We described the range of debt obligations earlier. These were the original types of

EXHIBIT 62-3	CDO Family Tree

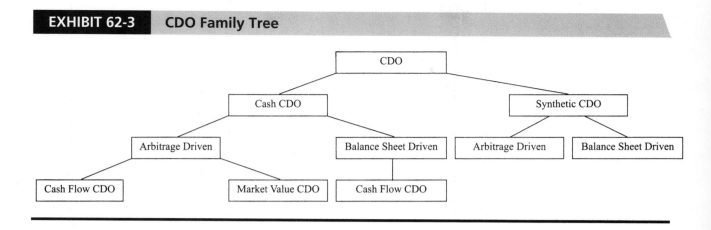

CDOs issued. A **synthetic CDO** is a CDO where the investor has the economic exposure to a pool of debt instrument but this exposure is realized via a credit derivative instrument rather than the purchase of the cash market instruments. We will discuss the basic elements of a synthetic CDO later.

Both a cash CDO and a synthetic CDO are further divided based on the motivation of the sponsor. The motivation leads to balance sheet and arbitrage CDOs. As explained below, in a **balance sheet CDO**, the motivation of the sponsor is to remove assets from its balance sheet. In an **arbitrage CDO**, the motivation of the sponsor is to capture a spread between the return that it is possible to realize on the collateral backing the CDO and the cost of borrowing funds to purchase the collateral (i.e., the interest rate paid on the obligations issued).

Cash CDOs that are arbitrage transactions are further divided in cash flow and market value CDOs depending on the primary source of the proceeds from the underlying asset used to satisfy the obligation to the tranches. In a **cash flow CDO**, the primary source is the interest and maturing principal from the underlying assets. In a **market value CDO**, the proceeds to meet the obligations depends heavily on the total return generated from the portfolio. While cash CDOs that are balance sheet motivated transactions can also be cash flow or market value CDOs, only cash flow CDOs have been issued.

C. Cash CDOs

In this section, we take a closer look at cash CDOs. Before we look at cash flow and market value CDOs, we will look at the type of cash CDO based on the sponsor motivation: arbitrage and balance sheet transactions. As can be seen in Exhibit 62-3 cash CDOs are categorized based on the motivation of the sponsor of the transaction. In an arbitrage transaction, the motivation of the sponsor is to earn the spread between the yield offered on the debt obligations in the underlying pool and the payments made to the various tranches in the structure. In a balance sheet transaction, the motivation of the sponsor is to remove debt instruments (primarily loans) from its balance sheet. Sponsors of balance sheet transactions are typically financial institutions such as banks seeking to reduce their capital requirements by removing loans due to their higher risk-based capital requirements. Our focus in this section is on arbitrage transactions because such transactions are the largest part of the cash CDO sector.

1. Cash CDO Arbitrage Transactions

The key as to whether or not it is economic to create an arbitrage CDO is whether or not a structure can be created that offers a competitive return for the subordinate/equity tranche.

To understand how the subordinate/equity tranche generates cash flows, consider the following basic $100 million CDO structure with the coupon rate to be offered at the time of issuance as shown below:

Tranche	Par Value	Coupon Rate
Senior	$80,000,000	LIBOR + 70 basis points
Mezzanine	10,000,000	10-year Treasury rate plus 200 basis points
Subordinate/Equity	10,000,000	—

Suppose that the collateral consists of bonds that all mature in 10 years and the coupon rate for every bond is the 10-year Treasury rate plus 400 basis points. The asset manager enters into an interest rate swap agreement with another party with a notional amount of $80 million in which it agrees to do the following:

▶ pay a fixed rate each year equal to the 10-year Treasury rate plus 100 basis points

▶ receive LIBOR

The interest rate agreement is simply an agreement to periodically exchange interest payments. The payments are benchmarked off of a notional amount. This amount is not exchanged between the two parties. Rather it is used simply to determine the dollar interest payment of each party. This is all we need to know about an interest rate swap in order to understand the economics of an arbitrage transaction. Keep in mind, the goal is to show how the subordinate/equity tranche can be expected to generate a return.

Let's assume that the 10-year Treasury rate at the time the CDO is issued is 7%. Now we can walk through the cash flows for each year. Look first at the collateral. The collateral will pay interest each year (assuming no defaults) equal to the 10-year Treasury rate of 7% plus 400 basis points. So the interest will be:

Interest from collateral: $11\% \times \$100,000,000 = \$11,000,000$

Now let's determine the interest that must be paid to the senior and mezzanine tranches. For the senior tranche, the interest payment will be:

Interest to senior tranche: $\$80,000,000 \times (\text{LIBOR} + 70 \text{ bp})$

The coupon rate for the mezzanine tranche is 7% plus 200 basis points. So, the coupon rate is 9% and the interest is:

Interest to mezzanine tranche: $9\% \times \$10,000,000 = \$900,000$

Finally, let's look at the interest rate swap. In this agreement, the asset manager is agreeing to pay some party (we'll call this party the "swap counterparty") each year 7% (the 10-year Treasury rate) plus 100 basis points, or 8%. But 8% of what? As explained above, in an interest rate swap payments are based on a notional amount. In our illustration, the notional amount is $80 million. The reason the asset manager selected the $80 million was because this is the amount of principal for the senior tranche which receives a floating rate. So, the asset manager pays to the swap counterparty:

Interest to swap counterparty: $8\% \times \$80,000,000 = \$6,400,000$

The interest payment received from the swap counterparty is LIBOR based on a notional amount of $80 million. That is,

Interest from swap counterparty: $\$80,000,000 \times$ LIBOR

Now we can put this all together. Let's look at the interest coming into the CDO:

Interest from collateral	$11,000,000
Interest from swap counterparty	$80,000,000 × LIBOR
Total interest received	$11,000,000 + $80,000,000 × LIBOR

The interest to be paid out to the senior and mezzanine tranches and to the swap counterparty include:

Interest to senior tranche	$80,000,000 × (LIBOR + 70 bp)
Interest to mezzanine tranche	$900,000
Interest to swap counterparty	$6,400,000
Total interest paid	$7,300,000 + $80,000,000 × (LIBOR + 70 bp)

Netting the interest payments coming in and going out we have:

Total interest received	$11,000,000 + $80,000,000 × LIBOR
Total interest paid	$ 7,300,000 + $80,000,000 × (LIBOR + 70 bp)
Net interest	$ 3,700,000 − $80,000,000 × (70 bp)

Since 70 bp times $80 million is $560,000, the net interest remaining is $3,140,000 (= $3,700,000 − $560,000). From this amount any fees (including the asset management fee) must be paid. The balance is then the amount available to pay the subordinate/equity tranche. Suppose that these fees are $634,000. Then the cash flow available to the subordinate/equity tranche for the year is $2.5 million. Since the tranche has a par value of $10 million and is assumed to be sold at par, this means that the annual return is 25%.

Obviously, some simplifying assumptions have been made. For example, it is assumed that there are no defaults. It is assumed that all of the issues purchased by the asset manager are noncallable and therefore the coupon rate would not decline because issues are called. Moreover, as explained below, after some period the asset manager must begin repaying principal to the senior and mezzanine tranches. Consequently, the interest rate swap must be structured to take this into account since the entire amount of the senior tranche is not outstanding for the life of the collateral. Despite the simplifying assumptions, the illustration does demonstrate the basic economics of an arbitrage transaction, the need for the use of an interest rate swap, and how the subordinate/equity tranche will realize a return.

2. Cash Flow CDO Structure

In a cash flow CDO, the objective of the asset manager is to generate cash flow (primarily from interest earned and proceeds from bonds that have matured, have been called, or have amortized) to repay investors in the senior and mezzanine tranches. Because the cash flows from the structure are designed to accomplish the objective for each tranche, restrictions are imposed on the asset managers. The conditions for disposing of issues held are specified and are usually driven by credit risk considerations. Also, in assembling the portfolio, the asset manager must meet certain requirements set forth by the rating agency or agencies that rate the deal.

There are three relevant periods. The first is the *ramp-up period*. This is the period that follows the closing date of the transaction where the manager begins investing the proceeds from the sale of the debt obligations issued. This period is usually less than one year. The *reinvestment period* or *revolving period* is where principal proceeds are reinvested and is usually for five or more years. In the final period, the portfolio assets are sold and the debt holders are paid off as described below.

a. Distribution of Income

Income is derived from interest income from the underlying assets and capital appreciation. The income is then used as follows. Payments are first made to the trustee and administrators and then to the asset manager.[23] Once these fees are paid, then the senior tranches are paid their interest. At this point, before any other payments are made, there are certain tests that must be passed.

These tests are called coverage tests and will be discussed later. If the coverage tests are passed then interest is paid to the mezzanine tranches. Once the mezzanine tranches are paid, interest is paid to the subordinate/equity tranche.

In contrast, if the coverage tests are not passed then there are payments that are made so as to protect the senior tranches. The remaining income after paying the fees and senior tranche interest is used to redeem the senior tranches (i.e., pay off principal) until the coverage tests are brought into compliance. If the senior tranches are paid off fully because the coverage tests are not brought into compliance, then any remaining income is used to redeem the mezzanine tranches. Any remaining income is then used to redeem the subordinate/equity tranche.

b. Distribution of Principal Cash Flow

The principal cash flow is distributed as follows after the payment of the fees to the trustees, administrators, and asset manager. If there is a shortfall in interest paid to the senior tranches, principal proceeds are used to make up the shortfall. Assuming that the coverage tests are satisfied, during the reinvestment period the principal is reinvested. After the reinvestment period or if the coverage tests are failed, the principal cash flow is used to pay down the senior tranches until the coverage tests are satisfied. If all the senior tranches are paid down, then the mezzanine tranches are paid off and then the subordinate/equity tranche is paid off.

c. Restrictions on Management

The asset manager in both a cash flow CDO and a market value CDO (discussed next) actively manage the portfolio. The difference is in the degree of active

---

[23] There are other management fees that are usually made based on performance. But these payments are made after payments to the mezzanine tranches.

management. In a cash flow CDO, the asset manager initially structures and then rebalances the portfolio so that interest from the pool of assets plus repaid principal is sufficient to meet the obligations of the tranches. In contrast, the asset manager in a market value CDO seeks to generate trading profits to satisfy a portion of the obligations to the tranches.

The asset manager for both types of CDOs must monitor the collateral to ensure that certain tests imposed by the rating agencies are being met. For cash flow CDOs there are two types of tests: quality tests and coverage tests.

In rating a transaction, the rating agencies are concerned with the diversity of the assets. There are tests that relate to the diversity of the assets. These tests are called **quality tests**. An asset manager may not undertake a trade that will result in the violation of any of the quality tests. Quality tests include (1) a minimum asset diversity score,[24] (2) a minimum weighted average rating, and (3) maturity restrictions.

There are tests to ensure that the performance of the collateral is sufficient to make payments to the various tranches. These tests are called **coverage tests**. There are two types of quality tests: par value tests and interest coverage ratio. Recall that if the coverage tests are violated, then income from the collateral is diverted to pay down the senior tranches.

3. Market Value CDO

As with a cash flow CDO, in a market value CDO there are debt tranches and a subordinate/equity tranche. However, because in a market value CDO the asset manager must sell assets in the underlying pool in order to generate proceeds for interest and repayment of maturing tranches, there is a careful monitoring of the assets and their price volatility. This is done by the frequent marking to market of the assets.

Because a market value CDO relies on the activities of the asset manager to generate capital appreciation and enhanced return to meet the obligations of the tranches in the structure, greater flexibility is granted to the asset manager with respect to some activities compared to a cash flow CDO. For example, while in a cash flow CDO the capital structure is fixed, in a market value CDO the asset manager is permitted to utilize additional leverage after the closing of the transaction.

D. Synthetic CDOs

A synthetic CDO is so named because the CDO does not actually own the underlying assets on which it has risk exposure. That is, in a synthetic CDO the CDO debt holders absorb the economic risks, but not the legal ownership, of a pool of assets.

1. Key Elements of a Synthetic CDO

In a synthetic CDO there is credit risk exposure to a portfolio of assets, called the **reference asset**. The reference asset serves as the basis for a contingent payment as will be explained later. The reference asset can be a bond market index such as a high-yield bond index or a mortgage index. Or, the reference asset can be a portfolio of corporate loans that is owned by a bank.

The credit risk associated with the reference asset is divided into two sections: (1) senior section and (2) junior section. In a typical synthetic CDO

---

[24] Rating agencies have developed measures that quantify the diversity of a portfolio. These measures are referred to as "diversity scores."

structure, the senior section is about 90% and the junior section is about 10%. (We'll see what we mean by 90% and 10% shortly.) The losses that are realized from the reference are first realized by the junior section up to a notional amount and then after that full loss is realized, the senior section begins realizing losses.

For example, let's suppose that the reference asset is a high-yield corporate bond index. An amount of credit risk exposure in terms of market value must be determined. Suppose that it is $500 million. The $500 million is referred to as the notional amount. Suppose further that the credit risk associated with the $500 million credit exposure is divided into a $450 million senior section and $50 million junior section. The $450 million is the notional amount for the senior section and the $50 million is the notional amount for the junior section. The first $50 million of loss to the reference asset due to a credit event (explained later) is absorbed by the junior section. Only after the junior section absorbs the first $50 million in loss will the senior section realize any loss.

You may wonder why we refer to senior and junior "sections" rather than senior and junior "note holders." The reason is that in a synthetic CDO structure, no debt obligations are issued to fund the senior section. However, for the junior section, debt obligations are issued. In our illustration, $50 million of junior notes are issued. They are issued in the same way as in a cash CDO structure. That is, there is typically several tranches of junior notes issued by the special purpose vehicle (SPV). There will be the most senior tranche of the junior notes and there will be the subordinate/equity tranche.

The proceeds received from the issuance of the junior notes are then invested by the asset manager. However, the investments are restricted to high quality debt instruments. This includes government securities, federal agency debentures, and corporate, mortgage-backed, and asset-backed securities rated triple A.

Now we introduce the key to a synthetic CDO—a credit derivative instrument. An interest rate derivative is used by an investor to protect against interest rate risk. (We actually illustrated the use of one type of interest rate derivative, an interest rate swap, earlier when we demonstrated the economics of an arbitrage CDO transaction.) A credit derivative, as the name indicates, is used to protect against credit risk. The type of **credit derivative** used in a synthetic CDO is a **credit default swap**. Here we discuss the essential elements of a credit default swap, just enough to understand its role in a synthetic CDO.

A credit default swap is conceptually similar to an insurance policy. There is a "protection buyer" who purchases protection against credit risk on the reference asset. In a synthetic CDO, the insurance buyer is the asset manager. The protection buyer (the asset manager in a synthetic CDO) pays a periodic fee (like an insurance premium) and receives, in return, payment from the protection seller in the event of a "credit event" affecting any asset included in the reference asset. Who is the seller of the protection seller? It is the SPV on behalf of the junior note holders.

As with an interest rate swap, a credit default swap has a notional amount. The notional amount will be equal to the senior section, $450 million in our example.

Let's clarify this by continuing with our earlier illustration and look at the return to the junior note holder in the structure. The junior note holders are getting payments that come from two sources:

(1) the income from the high quality securities purchased with the funds from the issuance of the **junior debt** obligations and

(2) the insurance premium (premium from the credit default swap) paid by the asset manager to the SPV

Effectively, the junior note holders are receiving the return on a portfolio of high-quality assets subsidized by the insurance premium (i.e., the payment from the credit default swap). However, this ignores the obligation of the junior note holders with respect to the credit default swap. If there is a credit event (discussed below) that requires the junior note holders to make a payment to the protection buyer, then this reduces the return to the junior note holders. As noted earlier, the effect on a particular tranche of the junior section depends on its priority. That is, the subordinate/equity tranche is affected first before the most senior tranche and the other tranches superior to the subordinate/equity tranche is affected.

So what becomes critical for the junior note holders' return is when it must make a payment. In credit derivatives, a payoff by the protection seller occurs when there is a **credit event**. Credit events are defined in the credit derivative documentation. On a debt instrument a credit event generally includes: bankruptcy, failure to pay when due, cross default/cross acceleration, repudiation, and restructuring. This credit event applies to any of the assets within the reference asset. For example, if a high-yield corporate bond index is the reference asset and Company X is in the index, a credit event with respect to Company X results in a payment to the protection buyer. If a designated portfolio of bank loans to corporations is the reference asset and Corporation Y's loan is included, then a credit event with respect to Corporation Y results in a payment to the protection buyer.

How much must be paid by the protection seller (the junior tranches in our illustration) to the protection buyer (the asset manager)? Should a credit event occur, there is an intent that the protection buyer be made whole: The protection buyer should be paid the difference between par and the "fair value" of the securities. How this is determined is set forth in the credit derivative agreement.

What is the motivation for the creation of synthetic CDOs? There exist two types: synthetic balance sheet CDOs and synthetic arbitrage CDOs. In the case of a synthetic balance sheet CDO, by embedding a credit default swap within a CDO structure, a bank can shed the credit risk of a portfolio of bank loans without having to notify any borrowers that they are selling the loans to another party, a requirement in some countries. No consent is needed from borrowers to transfer the credit risk of the loans, as is effectively done in a credit default swap. This is the reason synthetic balance sheet CDOs were initially set up to accommodate European bank balance sheet deals.

For a synthetic arbitrage CDO, there are several economic advantages of using a synthetic CDO structure rather than a cash CDO structure. First, it is not necessary to obtain funding for the senior section, thus making it easier to do a CDO transaction.[25] Second, the ramp-up period is shorter than for a cash CDO structure since only the high-quality assets need be assembled, not all of the assets contained in the reference asset. Finally, there are opportunities in the market to be able to effectively acquire the assets included in the reference asset via a credit default swap at a cheaper cost than buying the assets directly.[26] It because of these three advantages that issuance of synthetic CDO structures has increased dramatically since 2001 and is expected to continue to increase relative to cash CDO structures.

---

[25] It is for this reason that a nonsynthetic CDO structure is referred to as a "cash" CDO structure because cash is required to be raised to purchase all the collateral assets.

[26] For a more detailed discussion of these advantages and how it impacts the economics of a CDO, see Laurie S. Goodman and Frank J. Fabozzi, *Collateralized Debt Obligations: Structures and Analysis* (New York, NY: John Wiley & Sons, 2002).

SUMMARY

▶ An entity that wants to raise funds via a securitization will sell assets to a special purpose vehicle and is referred to as the "seller" in the transaction.

▶ The buyer of assets in a securitization is a special purpose vehicle and this entity, referred to as the issuer or trust, raises funds to buy the assets via the sale of securities (the asset-backed securities).

▶ There will be an entity in a securitization that will be responsible for servicing the loans or receivables.

▶ Third party entities in the securitization are attorneys, independent accountants, trustee, rating agencies, servicer, and possibly a guarantor.

▶ The waterfall of a transaction describes how the distribution of the cash flow will be distributed to the bond classes after fees are paid.

▶ In a securitization structure, the bond classes issued can consist of a senior bond that is tranched so as to redistribute prepayment risk and one or more **subordinate bonds**; the creation of the subordinate bonds provides credit tranching for the structure.

▶ The collateral for an asset-backed security can be either amortizing assets (e.g., auto loans and closed-end home equity loans) or nonamortizing assets (e.g., credit card receivables).

▶ For amortizing assets, projection of the cash flow requires projecting prepayments.

▶ For non-amortizing assets, prepayments by an individual borrower do not apply since there is no schedule of principal repayments.

▶ When the collateral is amortizing assets, typically the principal repayments are distributed to the security holders.

▶ When the collateral consists of non-amortizing assets, typically there is a lockout period, a period where principal repayments are reinvested in new assets; after the lockout period, principal repayments are distributed to the security holders.

▶ A structure where there is a lockout for principal repayments is called a revolving structure.

▶ One factor that may affect prepayments is the prevailing level of interest rates relative to the interest rate on the loan.

▶ Since a default is a prepayment (an involuntary prepayment), prepayment modeling for an asset-backed security backed by amortizing assets requires a model for projecting the amount that will be recovered and when it will be recovered.

▶ Cash flow analysis can be performed on a pool level or a loan level.

▶ The expected final maturity of an asset-backed security is the maturity date based on expected prepayments at the time of pricing of a deal; the legal final maturity can be two or more years after the expected final maturity.

▶ Average life is commonly used as a measure for the length of time an asset-backed security will be outstanding.

▶ With an asset-backed security, due to prepayments a bond that is expected to have a bullet maturity may have an actual maturity that differs from that specified in the prospectus and is therefore referred to as a soft bullet.

▶ Asset-backed securities are credit enhanced; that is, there must be support from somewhere to absorb a certain amount of defaults.

► Credit enhancement levels are determined relative to a specific rating desired for a security.

► There are two general types of credit enhancement structures: external and internal.

► External credit enhancements come in the form of third-party guarantees that provide for first loss protection against losses up to a specified level.

► External credit enhancement includes insurance by a monoline insurer, a guarantee by the seller of the assets, and a letter of credit.

► The most common forms of internal credit enhancements are reserve funds and senior/subordinate structures.

► The senior/subordinated structure is the most widely used internal credit support structure with a typical structure having a senior tranche and one or more non-senior tranches.

► For mortgage-related asset-backed securities and nonagency mortgage-backed securities there is a concern that prepayments will erode the protection afforded by the non-senior (i.e., subordinated) tranches after the deal closes.

► A shifting interest structure is used to protect against a deterioration in the senior tranche's credit protection due to prepayments by redistributing the prepayments disproportionately from the non-senior tranches to the senior tranche according to a specified schedule.

► With an asset-backed security, one of the following call provisions may be granted to the trustee: (1) percent of collateral call, (2) percent of bonds, (3) percent of tranche, (4) call on or after specified date, (5) latter of percent or date, or (6) auction call.

► The collateral for a home equity loan is typically a first lien on residential property and the loan fails to satisfy the underwriting standards for inclusion in a loan pool of Ginnie Mae, Fannie Mae, or Freddie Mac because of the borrower's impaired credit history or too high a payment-to-income ratio.

► Typically, a home equity loan is used by a borrower to consolidate consumer debt using the current home as collateral rather than to obtain funds to purchase a new home.

► Home equity loans can be either closed end (i.e., structured the same way as a fully amortizing residential mortgage loan) or open end (i.e., homeowner given a credit line).

► The monthly cash flow for a home equity loan-backed security backed by closed-end HELs consists of (1) net interest, (2) regularly scheduled principal payments, and (3) prepayments.

► Several studies by Wall Street firms have found that the key difference between the prepayment behavior of HELs and traditional residential mortgages is the important role played by the credit characteristics of the borrower.

► Studies strongly suggests that borrower credit quality is the most important determinant of prepayments, with the sensitivity of refinancing to interest rates being greater the higher the borrower's credit quality.

► The prospectus of an HEL offering contains a base case prepayment assumption regarding the initial speed and the amount of time until the collateral is expected to season.

► A prospectus prepayment curve is a multiple of the base case prepayments assumed in the prospectus (i.e., base case is equal to 100% PPC).

► Typically, home equity loan-backed securities are securitized by both closed-end fixed-rate and adjustable-rate (or variable-rate) HELs.

► Unlike a typical floater which has a cap that is fixed throughout the security's life, the available funds cap of a HEL floater is variable and depends on the amount of funds generated by the net coupon on the principal, less any fees.

► To provide stability to the average life of a senior tranche, closed-end home equity loan transactions will include either a non-accelerating senior (NAS) tranche or a planned amortization class (PAC) tranche.

► A NAS tranche receives principal payments according to a schedule based not on a dollar amount for a given month, but instead on a schedule that specifies for each month the share of pro rata principal that must be distributed to the NAS tranche.

► For a PAC tranche a schedule of the dollar amount for each month is specified.

► The structure of residential mortgage-backed securities outside the United States is similar to that of the nonagency mortgage market; there are internal and external credit enhancements.

► Auto loan-backed securities are issued by the financial subsidiaries of auto manufacturers, commercial banks, and independent finance companies and small financial institutions specializing in auto loans.

► The cash flow for auto loan-backed securities consists of regularly scheduled monthly loan payments (interest and scheduled principal repayments), and any prepayments.

► Prepayments on auto loans are not sensitive to interest rates.

► Prepayments on auto loan-backed securities are measured in terms of the absolute prepayment speed (denoted ABS) which measures monthly prepayments relative to the original collateral amount.

► Manufactured housing-backed securities are backed by loans on manufactured homes (i.e., homes built at a factory and then transported to a site).

► Manufactured housing-backed securities are issued by Ginnie Mae and private entities, the former being guaranteed by the full faith and credit of the U.S. government.

► A manufactured housing loan's cash flow consists of net interest, regularly scheduled principal, and prepayments.

► Prepayments are more stable for manufactured housing-backed securities because they are not sensitive to interest rate changes.

► SLABS are asset-backed securities backed by student loans.

► The student loans most commonly securitized are those that are made under the Federal Family Education Loan Program (FFELP) whereby the government makes loans to students via private lenders and the government guaranteeing up to 98% of the principal plus accrued interest.

► Alternative loans are student loans that are not part of a government guarantee program and are basically consumer loans.

► In contrast to government guaranteed loans, the lender's decision to extend an alternative loan is based on the ability of the applicant to repay the loan.

► Student loans involve three periods with respect to the borrower's payments—deferment period, grace period, and loan repayment period.

▶ Prepayments typically occur due to defaults or a loan consolidation (i.e., a loan to consolidate loans over several years into a single loan).

▶ Issuers of SLABs include the Student Loan Marketing Association (Sallie Mae), traditional corporate entities, and non-profit organizations.

▶ Student loan-backed securities offer a floating rate; for some issues the reference rate is the 3-month Treasury bill rate but for most issues the reference rate is LIBOR.

▶ Small Business Administration (SBA) loans are backed by the full faith and credit of the U.S. government.

▶ Most SBA loans are variable-rate loans where the reference rate is the prime rate with monthly payments consisting of interest and principal repayment.

▶ Voluntary prepayments can be made by the SBA borrower without any penalty.

▶ Factors contributing to the prepayment speed of a pool of SBA loans are (1) the maturity date of the loan (it has been found that the fastest speeds on SBA loans and pools occur for shorter maturities), (2) the purpose of the loan, and (3) whether or not there is a cap on the loan.

▶ Credit card receivable-backed securities are backed by credit card receivables for credit cards issued by banks, retailers, and travel and entertainment companies.

▶ Credit card deals are structured as a master trust.

▶ For a pool of credit card receivables, the cash flow consists of finance charges collected, fees, and principal.

▶ The principal repayment of a credit card receivable-backed security is not amortized; instead, during the lockout period, the principal payments made by credit card borrowers are retained by the trustee and reinvested in additional receivables and after the lockout period (the principal-amortization period), the principal received by the trustee is no longer reinvested but paid to investors.

▶ There are provisions in credit card receivable-backed securities that require early amortization of the principal if certain events occur.

▶ Since for credit card receivable-backed securities the concept of prepayments does not apply, participants look at the monthly payment rate (MPR) which expresses the monthly payment (which includes interest, finance charges, and any principal) of a credit card receivable portfolio as a percentage of debt outstanding in the previous month.

▶ The MPR for credit card receivable-backed securities is important because (1) if it reaches an extremely low level, there is a chance that there will be extension risk with respect to the principal payments and (2) if the MPR is very low, there is a chance that there will not be sufficient cash flows to pay off principal (which can trigger early amortization of the principal).

▶ To assess the performance of the portfolio of credit card receivables and the ability of the issuer to meet its interest obligation and repay principal as scheduled, an investor must analyze the gross portfolio yield (which includes finance charges collected and fees), charge-offs (which represents the accounts charged off as uncollectible), the net portfolio yield, gross portfolio yield minus charge-offs, and delinquencies (the percentage of receivable that are past due as specified number of months).

▶ There are three amortization structures that have been used in credit card receivable-backed security structures: (1) passthrough structure, (2) controlled-amortization structure, and (3) bullet-payment structure.

▶ A collateralized debt obligation is an asset-backed security backed by a diversified pool of debt obligations (high-yield corporate bonds, structured financial products, emerging market bonds, bank loans, and special situation loans and distressed debt).

▶ A collateralized bond obligation is a CDO in which the underlying pool of debt obligations consists of bond-type instruments (high-yield corporate and emerging market bonds).

▶ A collateralized loan obligation is a CDO in which the underlying pool of debt obligations consists of bank loans.

▶ In a CDO there is an asset manager responsible for managing the portfolio of assets.

▶ The tranches in a CDO include senior tranches, mezzanine tranches, and subordinate/equity tranche.

▶ The senior and mezzanine tranches are rated and the subordinate/equity tranche is unrated.

▶ The proceeds to meet the obligations to the CDO tranches (interest and principal repayment) can come from (1) coupon interest payments of the underlying assets, (2) maturing assets in the underlying pools, and (3) sale of assets in the underlying pool.

▶ CDOs are categorized based on the motivation of the sponsor of the transaction—arbitrage and balance sheet transactions.

▶ The motivation in an arbitrage transaction is for the sponsor to earn the spread between the yield offered on the debt obligations in the underlying pool and the payments made to the various tranches in the structure.

▶ In a balance sheet transaction the motivation of the sponsor is to remove debt instruments (primarily loans) from its balance sheet.

▶ The key as to whether or not it is economic to create an arbitrage transaction is whether or not a structure can offer a competitive return to the subordinated/equity tranche.

▶ Arbitrage transactions are classified as either cash flow CDOs or market value CDOs depending on where the primary source of the proceeds from the underlying asset is to come from to satisfy the obligation to the tranches.

▶ In a cash flow CDO the primary source is the interest and maturing principal from the underlying assets; in a market value CDO the proceeds to meet the obligations depends heavily on the total return generated from the portfolio.

▶ The three relevant periods in a CDO are the ramp up period, the reinvestment period or revolving period, and the final period where the portfolio assets are sold and the debt holders are paid off.

▶ In a CDO transaction, senior tranches are protected against a credit deterioration by coverage tests; a failure of coverage tests results in the paying off of the senior tranches until the coverage tests are satisfied.

▶ The tests imposed in a cash flow structure are quality tests (e.g., minimum asset diversity score, a minimum weighted average rating, and maturity restrictions) and coverage tests.

▶ Coverage tests are tests to ensure that the performance of the collateral is sufficient to make payments to the various tranches and include par value tests and interest coverage ratio.

▶ In market value structures the focus is on monitoring of the assets and their price volatility by the frequent **marking to market** of the assets.

▶ In a synthetic CDO a credit derivative instrument is used is to allow the CDO issuer to transfer the economic risk, but not the legal ownership of a reference asset.

▶ In a synthetic CDO, the credit derivative used is a credit **default swap** and this instrument allows the "protection buyer" (the asset manager in a synthetic CDO) to protect against default risk on a reference asset; the protection sellers are the tranches in the junior section of the CDO.

▶ In a synthetic CDO, the return to the junior note holders is based on the return from a portfolio of high-quality debt instruments plus the premium received in the credit default swap, reduced by the payment that must be made as a result of a credit event.

▶ There are synthetic balance sheet CDO transactions and synthetic arbitrage CDO transactions.

PROBLEMS FOR READING 62

1. Caterpillar Financial Asset Trust 1997-A is a special purpose vehicle. The collateral (i.e., assets) for the trust is a pool of fixed-rate retail installment sales contracts that are secured by new and used machinery manufactured primarily by Caterpillar Inc. The retail installment sales contracts were originated by the Caterpillar Financial Funding Corporation, a wholly-owned subsidiary of Caterpillar Financial Services Corporation. Caterpillar Financial Services Corporation is a wholly-owned subsidiary of Caterpillar Inc. The prospectus for the trust states that:

> "THE NOTES REPRESENT OBLIGATIONS OF THE ISSUER ONLY AND DO NOT REPRESENT OBLIGATIONS OF OR INTERESTS IN CATERPILLAR FINANCIAL FUNDING CORPORATION, CATERPILLAR FINANCIAL SERVICES CORPORATION, CATERPILLAR INC. OR ANY OF THEIR RESPECTIVE AFFILIATES."

The servicer of the retail installment sales contracts is Caterpillar Financial Services Corporation, a wholly-owned finance subsidiary of Caterpillar Inc. and is referred to as the servicer in the prospectus. For servicing the collateral, Caterpillar Financial Services Corporation receives a servicing fee of 100 basis points of the outstanding loan balance.

The securities were issued on May 19, 1997 and had a par value of $337,970,000. In the prospectus the securities are referred to as "asset-backed notes". There were four rated bond classes are:

Bond Class	Par Value
Class A-1	$ 88,000,000
Class A-2	$128,000,000
Class A-3	$108,100,000
Class B	$ 13,870,000

  A. In the prospectus, the term "Seller" is used. Who in this transaction would be the "Seller" and why?

  B. In the prospectus, the term "Issuer" is used. Who in this transaction would be the "Issuer" and why?

  C. Despite not having the waterfall for this structure, which bond classes do you think are the senior bonds?

  D. Despite not having the waterfall for this structure, which bond classes do you think are the subordinate bonds?

  E. Despite not having the waterfall for this structure, explain why there appears to be credit and prepayment tranching in this structure?

2. In the securitization process, what is the role played by the (a) attorneys and (b) independent accountants?

3. How are principal repayments from the collateral used by the trustee in a securitization transaction?

4. Suppose that the collateral for an asset-backed securities structure has a gross weighted average coupon of 8.6%. The servicing fee is 50 basis points. The tranches issued have a weighted average coupon rate of 7.1%. What is the excess servicing spread?

5. Suppose that the structure for an asset-backed security transaction is as follows:

senior tranche	$220 million
subordinate tranche 1	$ 50 million
subordinate tranche 2	$ 30 million

and that the value of the collateral for the structure is $320 million. Subordinate tranche 2 is the first loss tranche.

A. How much is the overcollateralization in this structure?

B. What is the amount of the loss for each tranche if losses due to defaults over the life of the structure total $15 million?

C. What is the amount of the loss for each tranche if losses due to defaults over the life of the structure total $35 million?

D. What is the amount of the loss for each tranche if losses due to defaults over the life of the structure total $85 million?

E. What is the amount of the loss for each tranche if losses due to defaults over the life of the structure total $110 million?

6. **A.** Explain why individual loans that are of a non-amortizing type are not subject to prepayment risk.

B. Explain why securities backed by collateral consisting of non-amortizing assets may expose an investor to prepayment risk.

7. An asset-backed security has been credit enhanced with a letter of credit from a bank with a single A credit rating. If this is the only form of credit enhancement, explain why this issue is unlikely to receive a triple A credit rating.

8. Why is it critical for monoline insurance companies that provide insurance for asset-backed security transactions to maintain a triple A credit rating?

9. What is the difference between a cash reserve fund and an excess servicing spread account?

10. Why is the assumption about how defaults may occur over the life of an asset-backed security transaction important in assessing the effectiveness of excess servicing spread as a form of internal credit enhancement?

11. **A.** Explain why a senior-subordinate structure is a form of internal credit enhancement.

B. Explain the need for a shifting interest mechanism in a senior-subordinate structure when the underlying assets are subject to prepayments.

12. **A.** What is meant by the "senior prepayment percentage" in a shifting interest mechanism of a senior-subordinate structure?

B. Why does a shifting interest mechanism affect the cash flow of the senior tranche and increase the senior tranche's exposure to contraction risk?

13. What is a "latter of percent or call date" call provision?

14. **A.** What is the cash flow of a closed-end home equity loan?

B. Indicate whether you agree or disagree with the following statement: "Typically, closed-end home equity loans are loans to borrowers of the highest credit quality."

15. The Izzobaf Home Equity Loan Trust 2000-1 is backed by fixed-rate closed-end home equity loans. The base case prepayment for this deal is specified in the prospectus as follows:

> The model used with respect to the loans (the "prepayment ramp") assumes that the home equity loans prepay at a rate of 5% CPR in the first month after origination, and an additional 1.8% each month thereafter until the 12th month. Beginning in the 12th month and each month thereafter, the prepayment ramp assumes a prepayment rate of 24.8% CPR.

What is the CPR assuming 200% PPC for the following months?

Month	CPR	Month	CPR	Month	CPR
1		11		30	
2		12		125	
3		13		150	
4		14		200	
5		15		250	
6		16		275	
7		17		300	
8		18		325	
9		19		350	
10		20		360	

16. James Tellmen is an assistant portfolio manager for a mortgage-backed securities portfolio. Mr. Tellmen's responsibility is to analyze agency mortgage-backed securities. Recently, the portfolio manager has been given authorization to purchase closed-end home equity loan-backed securities. Mr. Tellmen is analyzing his first structure in this sector of the asset-backed securities market. Upon reading the prospectus he finds that the base case prepayment is specified and believes that this prepayment assumption is the benchmark used in all closed-end home equity loan-backed securities. Explain why you agree or disagree with Mr. Tellmen.

17. Why is there is an available funds cap in an asset-backed security in which the collateral is adjustable-rate home equity loans?

18. Suppose that the base case shifting interest percentage schedule for a closed-end home equity loan-backed security is as follows:

Years after issuance	Senior prepayment percentage
1–4	100%
5	90%
6	80%
7	50%
8	20%
after year 8	0%

A. If there are prepayments in month 36 of $100,000, how much of the prepayments is paid to the senior tranche? How much is paid to the subordinate tranches?

B. If there are prepayments in the 8th year after issuance of $100,000, how much of the prepayments is paid to the senior tranche? How much is paid to the subordinate tranches?

C. If there are prepayments in the 10th year after issuance of $100,000, how much of the prepayments is paid to the senior tranche? How much is paid to the subordinate tranches?

19. Larry Forest is an analyst reviewing for the first time a closed-end home equity loan-backed structure in order to determine whether or not to purchase the deal's senior tranche. He understands how the shifting interest percentage schedule is structured so as to provide the senior tranches with protection after the deal is closed. However, he is concerned that the schedule in the prospectus will not be adequate if the collateral's performance deteriorates (i.e., there is considerably greater losses for the collateral than expected). Explain to Mr. Forest what provision is included in the prospectus for protecting the senior tranches if the performance of the collateral deteriorates.

20. How is a non-accelerating senior tranche provided protection to reduce contraction risk and extension risk?

21. **A.** What are the components of the cash flow for a manufactured housing-backed security?

B. What are the reasons why prepayments due to refinancing are not significant for manufactured housing loans?

22. Why are residential mortgage-backed securities outside the United States structured more like transactions in the nonagency U.S. market than the agency market.

23. **A.** What are the components of the cash flow for an auto loan-backed security?

B. How important are prepayments due to refinancing for auto loans?

24. What is the difference between a single monthly mortality rate and an absolute prepayment speed?

25. **A.** If the ABS for a security is 1.5% at month 21, what is the corresponding SMM?

B. If the SMM for a security is 1.9% at month 11, what is the corresponding ABS?

26. A trustee for a pension fund is working with a consultant to develop investment guidelines for the fund's bond portfolio. The trustee states that the fund should be able to invest in securities backed by student loans because the loans are fully guaranteed by the U.S. government. How should the consultant respond?

27. For a student loan-backed security, what is the difference between the deferment period and the grace period?

28. **A.** What are the components of the cash flow for a Small Business Administration-backed security?

B. What reference rate is used for setting the coupon interest and how often is the coupon rate reset?

29. **A.** What is the cash flow for a credit card receivable-backed security during the lockout or revolving period?

    B. How is the principal received from credit card borrowers handled during the lockout or revolving period?

    C. Explain why you agree or disagree with the following statement: "After the lockout period, the principal is paid to bondholders in one lump sum amount at the maturity date of the security."

30. A manager of a corporate bond portfolio is considering the purchase of a credit card receivable-backed security. The manager believes that an advantage of such securities is that there is no contraction risk and no extension risk. Explain why you agree or disagree with this view.

31. A. What is meant by the monthly payment rate for a credit card deal?

    B. What is the significance of the monthly payment rate?

    C. How is the net portfolio yield determined for a credit card deal?

32. What is a typical cash CDO structure?

33. Explain why you agree or disagree with the following statement: "The asset manager for a CDO is free to actively manage the portfolio without any constraints."

34. Explain why you agree or disagree with the following statement: "By using an interest rate swap, the asset manager for a CDO increases the risk associated with meeting the obligations that must be paid to the senior tranche."

35. What is the key factor in determining whether or not an arbitrage CDO can be issued?

36. Consider the following CDO transaction:

    1. The CDO is a $200 million structure. That is, the assets purchased will be $200 million.

    2. The collateral consists of bonds that all mature in 8 years and the coupon rate for every bond is the 8-year Treasury rate plus 600 basis points.

    3. The senior tranche comprises 75% of the structure ($150 million) and pays interest based on the following coupon formula: LIBOR plus 90 basis points.

    4. There is only one junior tranche ($30 million) with a coupon rate that is fixed. The coupon rate is the 8-year Treasury rate plus 300 basis points.

    5. The asset manager enters into an agreement with counterparty in which it agrees to pay the counterparty a fixed rate each year equal to the 8-year Treasury rate plus 120 basis points and receive LIBOR. The notional amount of the agreement is $150 million.

    A. How much is the equity tranche in this CDO?

    B. Assume that the 8-year Treasury rate at the time the CDO is issued is 6%. Assuming no defaults, what is the cash flow for each year and how is it distributed?

    C. Ignoring the asset management fee, what is the amount available each year for the equity tranche?

37. What are the elements of the return for the junior note holders in a synthetic CDO structure?

38. Why have banks issued synthetic balance sheet CDOs?

VALUING MORTGAGE-BACKED AND ASSET-BACKED SECURITIES

by Frank J. Fabozzi

LEARNING OUTCOMES

The candidate should be able to:

a. illustrate the computation, use, and limitations of the cash flow yield, nominal spread, and zero-volatility spread for a mortgage-backed security and an asset-backed security;

b. describe the Monte Carlo simulation model for valuing a mortgage-backed security;

c. describe path dependency in passthrough securities and the implications for valuation models;

d. illustrate how the option-adjusted spread is computed using the Monte Carlo simulation model and how this spread measure is interpreted;

e. evaluate whether mortgage-backed securities are rich or cheap, using option-adjusted spread analysis;

f. illustrate how effective duration is computed using the Monte Carlo simulation model;

g. discuss why the effective durations reported by various dealers and vendors may differ;

h. analyze the interest rate risk of a security given the security's effective duration and effective convexity;

i. explain other measures of duration used by practitioners in the mortgage-backed market (e.g., cash flow duration, coupon curve duration, and empirical duration), and describe the limitations of these duration measures;

j. determine whether the nominal spread, zero-volatility spread, or the option-adjusted spread should be used to evaluate a specific fixed income security.

Fixed Income Analysis for the Chartered Financial Analyst® Program, Second Edition, edited by Frank J. Fabozzi, Copyright © 2005 by CFA Institute. Reprinted with permission.

1

INTRODUCTION

In the two previous readings, we looked at mortgage-backed and asset-backed securities. Our focus was on understanding the risks associated with investing in these securities, how they are created (i.e., how they are structured), and why the products are created. Specifically, in the case of agency mortgage-backed securities we saw how prepayment risk can be redistributed among different tranches to create securities with a prepayment risk profile that is different from the underlying pool of mortgages. For asset-backed securities and nonagency mortgage-backed security, we saw how to create tranches with different degrees of credit risk.

What we did not discuss in describing these securities is how to value them and how to quantify their exposure to interest rate risk. That is, we know, for example, that a support tranche in a CMO structure has greater prepayment risk than a planned amortization class (PAC) tranche. However, how do we determine whether or not the price at which a support tranche is offered in the market adequately compensates for the greater prepayment risk? In this reading, we will describe and then apply a methodology for valuing mortgage-backed securities and some types of asset-backed securities—**Monte Carlo simulation**. A byproduct of a valuation model is the option-adjusted spread. We will see how the option-adjusted spread for a mortgage-backed or an asset-backed security is computed and applied. From a valuation model the effective duration and effective convexity of any security can be computed. We will explain how to compute effective duration and effective convexity using the Monte Carlo simulation model. However, in the case of mortgage-backed securities, there have been several alternative measures of duration used by practitioners. These measures will be identified along with their advantages and disadvantages.

Admittedly, the majority of this reading is devoted to the valuation of mortgage-backed securities and by extension to all real estate-related asset-backed securities. They are the most difficult asset-backed products to value and to quantify in terms of interest rate exposure. At the end of this reading, we provide a framework for determining which analytical measures discussed in this reading are appropriate for valuing any asset-backed security. In fact, the principles apply to all fixed income products.

2

CASH FLOW YIELD ANALYSIS

Let's begin with the traditional analysis of mortgage-backed and asset-backed securities—**cash flow yield analysis**. As explained at Level I, the yield on any financial instrument is the interest rate that makes the present value of the expected cash flow equal to its market price plus accrued interest. When applied to mortgage-backed and asset-backed securities, this yield is called a **cash flow yield**. The problem in calculating the cash flow yield of a mortgage-backed and asset-backed securities is that the cash flow is unknown because of prepayments. Consequently, to determine a cash flow yield, some assumption about the prepayment rate must be made. And, in the case of all but agency mortgage-backed securities, an assumption about default rates and recovery rates must be made.

The cash flow for mortgage-backed and asset-backed securities is typically monthly. The convention is to compare the yield on mortgage-backed and asset-backed securities to that of a Treasury coupon security by calculating the security's *bond-equivalent yield*. As explained at Level I, the bond-equivalent yield for a Treasury coupon security is found by doubling the semiannual yield to maturity. However, it is incorrect to do this for a mortgage-backed or an asset-backed security because the investor has the opportunity to generate greater reinvestment income by reinvesting the more frequent (i.e., monthly) cash flows. The **market convention** is to calculate a yield so as to make it comparable to the yield to maturity on a bond-equivalent basis. The formula for annualizing the monthly cash flow yield for a monthly-pay product is therefore:

$$\text{bond-equivalent yield} = 2[(1 + i_M)^6 - 1]$$

where i_M is the monthly interest rate that will equate the present value of the projected monthly cash flow equal to the market price (plus accrued interest) of the security.

To illustrate the calculation of the bond-equivalent yield, suppose that the monthly yield is 0.6%. That is, i_M is 0.006. Then

$$\text{bond-equivalent yield} = 2[(1.006)^6 - 1] = 0.0731 = 7.31\%$$

A. Limitations of Cash Flow Yield Measure

All yield measures suffer from problems that limit their use in assessing a security's potential return. The yield to maturity has two major shortcomings as a measure of a bond's potential return. To realize the stated yield to maturity, the investor must:

1. reinvest the coupon payments at a rate equal to the yield to maturity, and

2. hold the bond to the maturity date

As explained at Level I, the reinvestment of the coupon payments is critical and for long-term bonds can be as much as 80% of the bond's return. Reinvestment risk is the risk of having to reinvest the interest payments at less than the computed yield. Interest rate risk is the risk associated with having to sell the security before its maturity date at a price less than the purchase price.

These shortcomings are equally applicable to the cash flow yield measure:

1. the projected cash flows are assumed to be reinvested at the cash flow yield, and

2. the mortgage-backed or asset-backed security is assumed to be held until the final payout based on some prepayment assumption.

The importance of reinvestment risk, the risk that the cash flow will have to be reinvested at a rate less than the cash flow yield, is particularly important for many mortgage-backed and asset-backed securities because payments are monthly and both interest and principal must be reinvested. Moreover, an additional assumption is that the projected cash flow is actually realized. If the prepayment, default, and recovery experience is different from that assumed, the cash flow yield will not be realized.

B. Nominal Spread

Given the computed cash flow yield and the average life for a mortgage-backed or asset-backed security based on some prepayment, default, and recovery assumption, the next step is to compare the yield to the yield for a comparable Treasury security. "Comparable" is typically defined as a Treasury security with the same maturity as the security's average life. The difference between the cash flow yield and the yield on a comparable Treasury security is called the **nominal spread**.

Unfortunately, it is the nominal spread that some managers will use as a measure of relative value. However, this spread masks the fact that a portion of the nominal spread is compensation for accepting prepayment risk. For example, CMO support tranches have been offered at large nominal spreads. However, the nominal spread embodies the substantial prepayment risk associated with support tranches. The manager who buys solely on the basis of nominal spread fails to determine whether or not that nominal spread offered adequate compensation given the substantial prepayment risk faced by the holder of a support tranche.

Instead of nominal spread, managers need a measure that indicates the potential compensation after adjusting for prepayment risk. This measure is called the **option-adjusted spread**. We discussed this measure in Reading 60 where we covered the valuation of corporate and agency bonds with embedded options. Before discussing this measure for structured products, we describe another spread measure commonly quoted for structured products called the **zero-volatility spread**.

3   ZERO-VOLATILITY SPREAD

As explained at Level I, the proper procedure to compare any security to a U.S. Treasury security is to compare it to a portfolio of Treasury securities that have the same cash flow. The value of the security is then equal to the present value of all of the cash flows. The security's value, assuming the cash flows are default-free, will equal the present value of the replicating portfolio of Treasury securities. In turn, these cash flows are valued at the Treasury spot rates.

The **zero-volatility spread** is a measure of spread that the investor would realize over the entire Treasury spot rate curve if the mortgage-backed or asset-backed security is held to maturity. It is not a spread off one point on the Treasury yield curve, as is the nominal spread. The zero-volatility spread (also called the **Z-spread** and the **static spread**) is the spread that will make the present value of the cash flows from the mortgage-backed or asset-backed security when discounted at the Treasury spot rate plus the spread equal to the price of the security. A trial-and-error procedure (or search algorithm) is required to determine the zero-volatility spread. We illustrated this at Level I.[1]

Also as explained at Level I, in general, the shorter the maturity or average life of a structured product, the less the zero-volatility spread will differ from the nominal spread. The magnitude of the difference between the nominal spread and the zero-volatility spread also depends on the shape of the yield curve. The steeper the yield curve, the greater the difference.

One of the objectives of this reading is to explain when it is appropriate to use the Z-spread instead of the OAS. What will be seen is that if a structured

---

[1] Most common spreadsheet programs offer this type of algorithm.

product has an option and the borrower tends to take advantage of that option when interest rates decline, then the OAS should be used. If the borrower has an option but tends not to take advantage of it when interest rates decline, then the Z-spread should be used.

MONTE CARLO SIMULATION MODEL AND OAS　　　4

In Reading 60, we discussed one model that is used to value callable agency debentures and corporate bonds, the binomial model. This valuation model accommodates securities in which the decision to exercise a call option is not dependent on how interest rates evolved over time. That is, the decision of an issuer to call a bond will depend on the level of the rate at which the issue can be refunded relative to the issue's coupon rate, and not the path interest rates took to get to that rate. In contrast, there are fixed-income securities and derivative instruments for which the periodic cash flows are "interest rate path-dependent." This means that the cash flow received in one period is determined not only by the current interest rate level, but also by the path that interest rates took to get to the current level.

For example, in the case of passthrough securities, prepayments are interest rate path-dependent because this month's prepayment rate depends on whether there have been prior opportunities to refinance since the underlying mortgages were originated. This phenomenon is referred to as "prepayment burnout." Pools of passthroughs are used as collateral for the creation of CMOs. Consequently, there are typically two sources of path dependency in a CMO tranche's cash flows. First, the collateral prepayments are path-dependent as discussed above. Second, the cash flows to be received in the current month by a CMO tranche depend on the outstanding balances of the other tranches in the deal. Thus, we need the history of prepayments to calculate these balances.

Conceptually, the valuation of agency passthrough using the Monte Carlo model is simple. In practice, however, it is very complex. The simulation involves generating a set of cash flows based on simulated future mortgage refinancing rates, which in turn imply simulated prepayment rates.

Valuation modeling for agency CMOs is similar to valuation modeling for passthroughs, although the difficulties are amplified because the issuer has distributed both the prepayment risk and the interest rate risk into different tranches. The sensitivity of the passthroughs comprising the collateral to these two risks is not transmitted equally to every tranche. Some of the tranches wind up more sensitive to prepayment risk and interest rate risk than the collateral, while some of them are much less sensitive.

The objective is to figure out how the value of the collateral gets transmitted to the tranches in a deal. More specifically, the objective is to find out where the value goes and where the risk goes so that one can identify the tranches with low risk and high value: the tranches a manager wants to consider for purchase. The good news is that this combination usually exists in every deal. The bad news is that in every deal there are usually tranches with low value and high risk that managers want to avoid purchasing.

A. Simulating Interest Rate Paths and Cash Flows

To generate these random interest rate paths, the typical model used by Wall Street firms and commercial vendors takes as input today's term structure of interest rates and a volatility assumption. (We discussed these topics in Reading 60.)

The term structure of interest rates is the theoretical spot rate (or zero coupon) curve implied by today's Treasury securities. The simulations should be calibrated so that the average simulated price of a zero-coupon Treasury bond equals today's actual price.

On-the-run Treasury issues are often used in the calibration process. Some dealers and vendors of analytical systems use the LIBOR curve instead of the Treasury curve—or give the user a choice to use either the Treasury curve or the LIBOR curve. The reason is that some investors are interested in spreads that they can earn relative to their funding costs and LIBOR for many investors is a better proxy for that cost than Treasury rates. (We will discuss the different types of investors at Level III.)

As explained in Reading 60, every dealer and vendor of analytical systems employs an interest rate model. This is a model that assumes how interest rates will change over time. The interest rate models employed by most dealers and vendors of analytical systems are similar. However, one input to all interest rate models is the interest rate volatility assumption. It is that assumption that varies by dealer and vendor. As will be illustrated later in this reading, it is a critical input.

The volatility assumption determines the dispersion of future interest rates in the simulation. Today, many dealers and vendors do not use one volatility number for the yield of all maturities of the yield curve. Instead, they use either a short/long yield volatility or a term structure of yield volatility. A short/long yield volatility means that volatility is specified for maturities up to a certain number of years (short yield volatility) and a different yield volatility for longer maturities (long yield volatility). The short yield volatility is assumed to be greater than the long yield volatility. A term structure of yield volatilities means that a yield volatility is assumed for each maturity.

Based on the interest rate model and the assumed volatility, a series of interest rate paths will be generated. We will see shortly how a security is valued on each interest rate path. However, there is nothing that we have explained thus far that assures us that the values produced by the model will be arbitrage free. Recall from Reading 60 that the binomial interest rate tree by design is constructed to be arbitrage free. That is, if any of the on-the-run issues that were used to construct the binomial interest rate tree are valued using the tree, the model would produce a value for that on-the-run issue equal to its market value. There is nothing we described so far about the Monte Carlo simulation to assure this.

More specifically, in the case of Monte Carlo simulation for valuing mortgage-backed and asset-backed securities, the on-the-run Treasury issues are typically used. What assurance is there that if an on-the-run Treasury issue is valued using the Monte Carlo simulation model it will be arbitrage free? That is, what assurance is there that the value produced by the model will equal the market price? Nothing. That's right, nothing. What the model builder must do is "adjust" the interest rate paths so that the model produces the correct values for the on-the-run Treasury issues. A discussion of this adjustment process is not important to us. In fact, there are very few published sources that describe how this is done. The key point here is that no such adjustment is necessary in a binomial model for valuing corporate and agency bonds with embedded options because the tree is built to be arbitrage free. In the case of the Monte Carlo simulation model, the builder must make an arbitrary adjustment to the interest rate paths to get the model to be arbitrage free.

The simulation works by generating many scenarios of future interest rate paths. As just explained, the "raw" interest rate paths that are simulated must be "adjusted" so as to make the model generate arbitrage-free values for whatever benchmark interest rates are used—typically, the on-the-run Treasury issues. *So, in the remainder of this reading, when we refer to interest rate paths it is understood that it is the "adjusted" interest rate paths where "adjusted" means that each interest rate path is adjusted so that the model will produce arbitrage-free values.*

In each month of the scenario (i.e., path), a monthly interest rate and a mortgage refinancing rate are generated. The monthly interest rates are used to discount the projected cash flows in the scenario. The mortgage refinancing rate is needed to determine the cash flows because it represents the opportunity cost the borrower (i.e., mortgagor) is facing at that time.

If the refinancing rates are high relative to the borrower's original coupon rate (i.e., the rate on the borrower's loan), the borrower will have less incentive to refinance, or even a disincentive (i.e., the homeowner will avoid moving in order to avoid refinancing). If the refinancing rate is low relative to the borrower's original coupon rate, the borrower has an incentive to refinance.

Prepayments are projected by feeding the refinancing rate and loan characteristics into a prepayment model. Given the **projected** prepayments, the cash flows along an interest rate path can be determined.

To make this more concrete, consider a newly issued mortgage passthrough security with a maturity of 360 months. Exhibit 63-1 shows N "adjusted" simulated interest rate path scenarios—adjusted to be arbitrage free. Each scenario consists of a path of 360 simulated 1-month future interest rates. (The number of paths generated is based on a well known principle in simulation which will not be discussed here.) So, our first assumption that we make to get Exhibit 63-1 is the volatility of interest rates.

Exhibit 63-2 shows the paths of simulated mortgage refinancing rates corresponding to the scenarios shown in Exhibit 63-1. In going from Exhibit 63-1 to Exhibit 63-2, an assumption must be made about the relationship between the Treasury rates and refinancing rates. The assumption is that there is a constant

EXHIBIT 63-1	"Adjusted" Simulated Paths of Arbitrage-Free 1-Month Future Interest Rates*						
	Interest Rate Path Number						
Month	**1**	**2**	**3**	...	***n***	...	***N***
1	$f_1(1)$	$f_1(2)$	$f_1(3)$	...	$f_1(n)$	...	$f_1(N)$
2	$f_2(1)$	$f_2(2)$	$f_2(3)$	...	$f_2(n)$	...	$f_2(N)$
3	$f_3(1)$	$f_3(2)$	$f_3(3)$	...	$f_3(n)$	...	$f_3(N)$
...	...	...	...	...	...	...	...
t	$f_t(1)$	$f_t(2)$	$f_t(3)$	...	$f_t(n)$	...	$f_t(N)$
...	...	...	...	...	...	...	...
358	$f_{358}(1)$	$f_{358}(2)$	$f_{358}(3)$	...	$f_{358}(n)$	...	$f_{358}(N)$
359	$f_{359}(1)$	$f_{359}(2)$	$f_{359}(3)$	...	$f_{359}(n)$	...	$f_{359}(N)$
360	$f_{360}(1)$	$f_{360}(2)$	$f_{360}(3)$	...	$f_{360}(n)$	...	$f_{360}(N)$

Notation:

$f_t(n)$ = 1-month future interest rate for month t on path n

N = total number of interest rate paths

* As explained in the text, the "raw" interest rate paths that are simulated must be "adjusted" so as to make the model generate arbitrage-free values for whatever benchmark interest rates are used—typically, the on-the-run Treasury issues. The interest rates shown in the exhibit are the "adjusted" arbitrage-free interest rates.

EXHIBIT 63-2	Simulated Paths of Mortgage Refinancing Rates						
	Interest Rate Path Number						
Month	**1**	**2**	**3**	**...**	**n**	**...**	**N**
1	$r_1(1)$	$r_1(2)$	$r_1(3)$	...	$r_1(n)$	...	$r_1(N)$
2	$r_2(1)$	$r_2(2)$	$r_2(3)$	...	$r_2(n)$	...	$r_2(N)$
3	$r_3(1)$	$r_3(2)$	$r_3(3)$	...	$r_3(n)$	...	$r_3(N)$
...	...	...	...	...	...	...	...
t	$r_t(1)$	$r_t(2)$	$r_t(3)$	...	$r_t(n)$	...	$r_t(N)$
...	...	...	...	...	...	...	...
358	$r_{358}(1)$	$r_{358}(2)$	$r_{358}(3)$	...	$r_{358}(n)$	...	$r_{358}(N)$
359	$r_{359}(1)$	$r_{359}(2)$	$r_{359}(3)$	...	$r_{359}(n)$	...	$r_{359}(N)$
360	$r_{360}(1)$	$r_{360}(2)$	$r_{360}(3)$	...	$r_{360}(n)$	...	$r_{360}(N)$

Notation:

$r_t(n)$ = mortgage refinancing rate for month t on path n

N = total number of interest rate paths

spread relationship between the rate that the borrower will use to determine whether or not to refinance (i.e., the refinancing rate) and the 1-month interest rates shown in Exhibit 63-1. For example, for 30-year mortgage loans, model builders use the 10-year Treasury rate as a proxy for the refinancing rate.

Given the mortgage refinancing rates, the cash flows on each interest rate path can be generated. For agency mortgage-backed securities, this requires a

EXHIBIT 63-3	Simulated Cash Flows on Each of the Interest Rate Paths						
	Interest Rate Path Number						
Month	**1**	**2**	**3**	**...**	**n**	**...**	**N**
1	$C_1(1)$	$C_1(2)$	$C_1(3)$	...	$C_1(n)$	...	$C_1(N)$
2	$C_2(1)$	$C_2(2)$	$C_2(3)$	...	$C_2(n)$	...	$C_2(N)$
3	$C_3(1)$	$C_3(2)$	$C_3(3)$	...	$C_3(n)$	...	$C_3(N)$
...	...	...	...	...	...	...	...
t	$C_t(1)$	$C_t(2)$	$C_t(3)$	...	$C_t(n)$	...	$C_t(N)$
...	...	...	...	...	...	...	...
358	$C_{358}(1)$	$C_{358}(2)$	$C_{358}(3)$	...	$C_{358}(n)$	...	$C_{358}(N)$
359	$C_{359}(1)$	$C_{359}(2)$	$C_{359}(3)$	...	$C_{359}(n)$	...	$C_{359}(N)$
360	$C_{360}(1)$	$C_{360}(2)$	$C_{360}(3)$	...	$C_{360}(n)$	...	$C_{360}(N)$

Notation:

$C_t(n)$ = cash flow for month t on path n

N = total number of interest rate paths

prepayment model. For asset-backed securities and nonagency mortgage-backed securities, this requires both a prepayment model and a model of defaults and recoveries. So, our next assumption is that the output of these models (prepayments, defaults, and recoveries) are correct. The resulting cash flows are depicted in Exhibit 63-3.

B. Calculating the Present Value for an Interest Rate Path

Given the cash flows on an interest rate path, the path's present value can be calculated. The discount rate for determining the present value is the simulated spot rate for each month on the interest rate path plus an appropriate spread. The spot rate on a path can be determined from the simulated future monthly rates. The relationship that holds between the simulated spot rate for month T on path n and the simulated future 1-month rates is:

$$z_T(n) = \{[1 + f_1(n)][1 + f_2(n)] \cdots [1 + f_T(n)]\}^{1/T} - 1$$

where

$z_T(n)$ = simulated spot rate for month T on path n

$f_T(n)$ = simulated future 1-month rate for month t on path n

At Level I we explained the relationship between spot rates and forward rates.

Consequently, the interest rate path for the simulated future 1-month rates can be converted to the interest rate path for the simulated monthly spot rates as shown in Exhibit 63-4. Therefore, the present value of the cash flows for month T

EXHIBIT 63-4	"Adjusted" Simulated Paths of Monthly Arbitrage-Free Spot Rates						
	Interest Rate Path Number						
Month	**1**	**2**	**3**	**. . .**	**n**	**. . .**	**N**
1	$z_1(1)$	$z_1(2)$	$z_1(3)$	. . .	$z_1(n)$	. . .	$z_1(N)$
2	$z_2(1)$	$z_2(2)$	$z_2(3)$	. . .	$z_2(n)$	. . .	$z_2(N)$
3	$z_3(1)$	$z_3(2)$	$z_3(3)$	. . .	$z_3(n)$	. . .	$z_3(N)$
. . .	. . .	. . .	. . .	. . .	. . .	. . .	. . .
t	$z_t(1)$	$z_t(2)$	$z_t(3)$	. . .	$z_t(n)$	. . .	$z_t(N)$
. . .	. . .	. . .	. . .	. . .	. . .	. . .	. . .
358	$z_{358}(1)$	$z_{358}(2)$	$z_{358}(3)$	. . .	$z_{358}(n)$	. . .	$z_{358}(N)$
359	$z_{359}(1)$	$z_{359}(2)$	$z_{359}(3)$	. . .	$z_{359}(n)$	. . .	$z_{359}(N)$
360	$z_{360}(1)$	$z_{360}(2)$	$z_{360}(3)$	. . .	$z_{360}(n)$	. . .	$z_{360}(N)$

Notation:

$z_t(n)$ = spot rate for month t on path n

N = total number of interest rate paths

on interest rate path n discounted at the simulated spot rate for month T plus some spread is:

$$PV[C_T(n)] = \frac{C_T(n)}{[1 + z_T(n) + K]^T}$$

where

$PV[C_T(n)]$ = present value of cash flows for month T on path n
$C_T(n)$ = cash flow for month T on path n
$z_T(n)$ = spot rate for month T on path n
K = spread

The spread, K, reflects the risks that the investor feels are associated with realizing the cash flows.

The present value for path n is the sum of the present value of the cash flows for each month on path n. That is,

$$PV[\text{Path}(n)] = PV[C_1(n)] + PV[C_2(n)] + ... + PV[C_{360}(n)]$$

where $PV[\text{Path}(n)]$ is the present value of interest rate path n.

C. Determining the Theoretical Value

The present value of a given interest rate path can be thought of as the theoretical value of a passthrough if that path was actually realized. The theoretical value of the passthrough can be determined by calculating the average of the theoretical values of all the interest rate paths. That is, the theoretical value is equal to

$$\text{theoretical value} = \frac{PV[\text{Path}(1)] + PV[\text{Path}(2)] + ... + PV[\text{Path}(N)]}{N}$$

where N is the number of interest rate paths. The theoretical value derived from the above equation is based on some spread, K. It follows the usual practice of discounting cash flows at spot rates plus a spread—in this case the spread is K.

This procedure for valuing a passthrough is also followed for a CMO tranche. The cash flow for each month on each interest rate path is found according to the principal repayment and interest distribution rules of the deal.

D. Selecting the Number of Interest Rate Paths

Let's now address the question of the number of scenario paths, N, needed to value a security. The number of interest rate paths determines how "good" the estimate is, not relative to the truth but relative to the model used. The more paths, the more the average value produced tends to converge. It is simply a statistical sampling problem.

Most models employ some form of variance reduction to cut down on the number of sample paths necessary to get a good statistical sample.[2] Several vendor firms have developed computational procedures that reduce the number

---

[2] The variance reduction technique is described in books on management science and Monte Carlo simulation.

of paths required but still provide the accuracy of a full Monte Carlo analysis. The procedure is to use statistical techniques to reduce the number of interest rate paths to sets of similar paths. These paths are called **representative paths**. For example, suppose that 2,000 sample paths are generated. Using a certain statistical technique, these 2,000 sample paths can be collapsed to, say, 16 representative paths. The security is then valued on each of these 16 representative paths. The theoretical value of the security is then the *weighted* average of the 16 representative paths. The weight for a path is the percentage of that representative path relative to the total sample paths. Vendors often give the investor or portfolio manager the choice of whether to use the "full Monte Carlo simulation" or to specify a number of representative paths.

E. Option-Adjusted Spread

In Reading 60, we explained the option-adjusted spread (OAS). Specifically, we explained (1) how to compute the OAS for corporate and agency bonds with embedded options and (2) how to interpret the OAS and apply it in relative analysis. Below we cover the same issues for the OAS computed for mortgage-backed securities.

1. Computing the OAS

In the Monte Carlo model, the OAS is the spread that when added to all the spot rates on all interest rate paths will make the average present value of the paths equal to the observed market price (plus accrued interest). Mathematically, OAS is the value for K (the spread) that will satisfy the following condition:

$$\frac{\text{PV}[\text{Path}(1)] + \text{PV}[\text{Path}(2)] + \ldots + \text{PV}[\text{Path}(N)]}{N} = \text{market price}$$

where N is the number of interest rate paths. The left-hand side of the above equation looks identical to that of the equation for the theoretical value. The difference is that the objective is to determine what spread, K, will make the model produce a theoretical value equal to the market price.

The procedure for determining the OAS is straightforward and involves the same search algorithm explained for the zero-volatility spread. The next question, then, is how to interpret the OAS. Basically, the OAS is used to reconcile value with market price. On the *right*-hand side of the previous equation is the market's statement: the price of a structured product. The average present value over all the paths on the *left*-hand side of the equation is the model's output, which we refer to as the theoretical value.

2. Interpreting the OAS and Relative Value Application

What an investor or a portfolio manager seeks to do is to buy a mortgage-backed security where value is greater than price. By using a valuation model such as the Monte Carlo model, a portfolio manager could estimate the value of a security, which at this point would be sufficient in determining whether to buy a security. That is, the portfolio manager can say that this security is 1 point cheap or 2 points cheap, and so on. The model does not stop here. Instead, it converts the divergence between price and value into some type of spread measure since most market participants find it more convenient to think about spreads than price differences.

The OAS was developed as a measure of the spread that can be used to convert dollar differences between value and price. As we explained in Reading 60, in the binomial model a spread is measured relative to the benchmark interest rates used to generate the interest rate tree and which is therefore used to make the tree arbitrage free. The same is true in the case of the Monte Carlo simulation model. The spread is measured relative to the benchmark interest rates that were used to generate the interest rate paths and to adjust the interest rate paths to make them arbitrage free. Typically, for a mortgage-backed security the benchmark interest rates are the on-the-run Treasury rates. The OAS is then measuring the average spread over the Treasury spot rate curve, not the Treasury yield as explained in Reading 60. It is an average spread since the OAS is found by averaging over the interest rate paths for the possible Treasury spot rate curves. Of course, if the LIBOR curve is used, the OAS is the spread over that curve.

This spread measure is superior to the nominal spread which gives no recognition to the prepayment risk. As explained in Reading 60, the OAS is "option adjusted" because the cash flows on the interest rate paths are adjusted for the option of the borrowers to prepay. While we may understand the mechanics of how to compute the OAS and why it is appropriate to use the OAS rather than the nominal spread or Z-spread, the question is what does the spread represent? In Reading 60, a discussion of what compensation the OAS reflects for corporate and agency bonds with embedded options was presented. The compensation is for a combination of credit risk and liquidity risk. The compensation depends on the benchmark interest rates used in the analysis. For example, consider the use of Treasury interest rates and more specifically the Treasury spot rate curve since this is the benchmark typically used in the calculation of an OAS for a mortgage-backed security. If there is an OAS computed using the Treasury benchmark, then what is that OAS compensating?

Consider first Ginnie Mae mortgage passthrough securities. As explained at Level I, Ginnie Mae is an arm of the U.S. government. The securities it issues are backed by the full faith and credit of the U.S. government. Effectively, a Ginnie Mae mortgage-backed security is a Treasury security with prepayment risk. The OAS removes the prepayment risk (i.e., the option risk). Additionally, if the bechmark is Treasury rates, the OAS should not be compensation for credit risk. That leaves liquidity risk. While Ginnie Mae mortgage passthrough securities may not be as liquid as on-the-run Treasury issues, they are fairly liquid as measured by the bid-ask spread. Nevertheless, part of the OAS should reflect compensation for liquidity risk. There is one more risk that was not the focus of Reading 60, modeling risk. In our explanation of the Monte Carlo model, there were several critical assumptions and parameters required. If those assumptions prove incorrect or if the parameters are misestimated, the prepayment model will not calculate the true level of risk. Thus, probably a good part of the compensation for a Ginnie Mae mortgage passthrough security reflects payment for this model uncertainty.

If we consider CMOs issued by Ginnie Mae rather than the mortgage passthrough securities, the OAS would reflect the complexity associated with a particular tranche. For example, a planned amortization class (PAC) tranche would be less exposed to modeling risk than a support tranche in the same CMO structure. Hence, compensation for modeling risk would be greater for a support tranche than a PAC tranche in the same structure. Moreover, PAC tranches have greater liquidity than support tranches, so compensation is less for the former relative to the latter.

As we move from Ginnie Mae issued mortgage products to those issued by Freddie Mac and Fannie Mae, we introduce credit risk. As explained at Level I, Freddie Mac and Fannie Mae are government sponsored enterprises (GSEs). As such, there is no requirement that a GSE be bailed out by the U.S. government.

The GSEs are viewed as triple A rated. Consequently, in addition to modeling risk and liquidity risk, a portion of the OAS reflects credit risk relative to Treasury securities.

Moving on to nonagency mortgage-backed securities and real estate backed asset-backed securities, the OAS is compensating for: (1) credit risk (which varies depending on the credit rating for the tranche under consideration), (2) liquidity risk (which is greater than for Ginnie Mae, Fannie Mae, and Freddie Mac mortgage products), and (3) modeling risk.

F. Option Cost

The implied cost of the option embedded for a mortgage-backed or asset-backed security can be obtained by calculating the difference between the option-adjusted spread at the assumed volatility of interest rates and the zero-volatility spread. That is,

option cost = zero-volatility spread − option-adjusted spread

The option cost measures the prepayment (or option) risk embedded in the security. Note that the cost of the option is a byproduct of the option-adjusted spread analysis, not valued explicitly with some option pricing model.

G. Illustrations

We will use two deals to show how CMOs can be analyzed using the Monte Carlo model/OAS procedure discussed above—a simple structure and a PAC/support structure.[3]

1. Simple Structure

The simple structure analyzed is Freddie Mac (FHLMC) 1915. It is a simple sequential-pay CMO bond structure. The structure includes eight tranches, A, B, C, D, E, F, G, and S. The focus of our analysis is on tranches A, B, and C. All three tranches were priced at a premium.

The top panel of Exhibit 63-5 shows the OAS, the option cost, and effective duration[4] for the collateral and the three tranches in the CMO structure. However, tranche A had the smallest effective duration and tranche C had the largest effective duration. The OAS for the collateral is 51 basis points. Since the option cost is 67 basis points, the zero-volatility spread is 118 basis points (51 basis points plus 67 basis points).

At the time this analysis was performed, March 10, 1998, the Treasury yield curve was not steep. At Level I, we explained that when the yield curve is relatively flat the zero-volatility spread will not differ significantly from the nominal spread. Thus, for the three tranches shown in Exhibit 63-5, the zero-volatility spread is 83 basis points for A, 115 basis points for B, and 116 basis points for C.

---

[3] These illustrations are from Frank J. Fabozzi, Scott F. Richard, and David S. Horowitz, "Valuation of CMOs," Chapter 6 in Frank J. Fabozzi (ed.), *Advances in the Valuation and Management of Mortgage-Backed Securities* (New Hope, PA: Frank J. Fabozzi Associates, 1998).

[4] We will explain how to compute the effective duration using the Monte Carlo methodology in Section V.A.

| EXHIBIT 63-5 | OAS Analysis of FHLMC 1915 Classes A, B, and C (As of 3/10/98) |

All three tranches were trading at a premium as of the date of the analysis.

Base Case (Assumes 13% Interest Rate Volatility)

	OAS (in basis points)	Option Cost (in basis points)	Z-Spread (in basis points)	Effective Duration (in years)
Collateral	51	67	118	1.2
Tranche				
A	32	51	83	0.9
B	33	82	115	2.9
C	46	70	116	6.7

Prepayments at 80% and 120% of Prepayment Model (Assumes 13% Interest Rate Volatility)

	New OAS (in basis points)		Change in Price per $100 par (holding OAS constant)	
	80%	120%	80%	120%
Collateral	63	40	$0.45	−$0.32
Tranche				
A	40	23	0.17	−0.13
B	43	22	0.54	−0.43
C	58	36	0.97	−0.63

Interest Rate of Volatility of 9% and 17%

	New OAS (in basis points)		Change in Price per $100 par (holding OAS constant)	
	9%	17%	9%	17%
Collateral	79	21	$1.03	−$0.94
Tranche				
A	52	10	0.37	−0.37
B	66	−3	1.63	−1.50
C	77	15	2.44	−2.08

Notice that the tranches did not share the OAS equally. The same is true for the option cost. Both the Z-spread and the option cost increase as the effective duration increases. Whether or not any of these tranches were attractive investments requires a comparison to other tranches in the market with the same effective duration. While not presented here, all three tranches offered an OAS similar to other sequential-pay tranches with the same effective duration available in the market. On a relative basis (i.e., relative to the other tranches analyzed in the deal), the only tranche where there appears to be a bit of a bargain is tranche C. A portfolio manager contemplating the purchase of this last cash flow tranche can see that C offers a higher OAS than B and appears to bear less of the risk (i.e., has lower option cost), as measured by the option cost. The problem portfolio managers may face is that they might not be able to go out as long on the yield curve as tranche C because of effective duration, maturity, and average life constraints relative to their liabilities, for example.

Now let's look at modeling risk. Examination of the sensitivity of the tranches to changes in prepayments and interest rate volatility will help us to understand the interaction of the tranches in the structure and who is bearing the risk. How the deal behaves under various scenarios should reinforce and be consistent with the valuation (i.e., a tranche may look "cheap" for a reason).

We begin with prepayments. Specifically, we keep the same interest rate paths as those used to get the OAS in the base case (the top panel of Exhibit 63-5), but reduce the prepayment rate on each interest rate path to 80% of the projected rate. As can be seen in the second panel of Exhibit 63-5, slowing down prepayments increases the OAS and price for the collateral. The exhibit reports two results of the sensitivity analysis. First, it indicates the change in the OAS. Second, it indicates the change in the price, holding the OAS constant at the base case.

To see how a portfolio manager can use the information in the second panel, consider tranche A. At 80% of the prepayment speed, the OAS for this tranche increases from 32 basis points to 40 basis points. If the OAS is held constant, the panel indicates that the buyer of tranche A would gain $0.17 per $100 par value.

Notice that for all of the tranches reported in Exhibit 63-5 there is a gain from a slowdown in prepayments. This is because all of the sequential tranches in this deal are priced over par. (An investor in a tranche priced at a premium benefits from a slowdown in prepayments because the investor receives the higher coupon for a longer period and postpones the capital loss from a prepayment.) Also notice that while the changes in OAS are about the same for the different tranches, the changes in price are quite different. This arises because the shorter tranches have less duration. Therefore, their prices do not move as much from a change in OAS as a longer average life tranche. A portfolio manager who is willing to go to the long end of the yield curve, such as tranche C, would realize the most benefit from the slowdown in prepayments.

Also shown in the second panel of the exhibit is the second part of our experiment to test the sensitivity of prepayments: the prepayment rate is assumed to be 120% of the base case. The collateral loses money in this scenario because it is trading above par. This is reflected in the OAS of the collateral which declines from 51 basis points to 40 basis points. Now look at the three tranches. They all lost money because the tranches were all at a premium and the speeding of prepayments adversely affects the tranche.

Before looking at the last panel that shows the effect of a change in interest rate volatility on the OAS, let's review the relationship between expected interest rate volatility and the value of a mortgage-backed security. Recall that the investor in a mortgage-backed security has sold an option to homeowners (borrowers). Thus, the investor is short an option. The value of an option depends on expected interest rate volatility. When expected interest rate volatility decreases, the value of the option embedded in a mortgage-backed security decreases and therefore the value of a mortgage-backed security increases. The opposite is true when expected interest rate volatility increases—the value of the embedded option increases and the value of a mortgage-backed security decreases.

Now let's look at the sensitivity to the interest rate volatility assumption, 13% in the base case. Two experiments are performed: reducing the volatility assumption to 9% and increasing it to 17%. These results are reported in the third panel of Exhibit 63-5.

Reducing the volatility to 9% increases the dollar price of the collateral by $1.03 and increases the OAS from 51 in the base case to 79 basis points. However, this $1.03 increase in the price of the collateral is not equally distributed among the three tranches. Most of the increase in value is realized by the longer tranches. The OAS gain for each of the tranches follows more or less the effective durations of those tranches. This makes sense, because the longer the duration, the greater the risk, and when volatility declines, the reward is greater for the accepted risk. At the higher level of assumed interest rate volatility of 17%, the collateral is severely affected. The longer the duration, the greater the loss. These results for a decrease and an increase in interest rate volatility are consistent with what we explained earlier.

Using the Monte Carlo simulation/OAS analysis, a fair conclusion that can be made about this simple structure is: what you see is what you get. The only surprise in this structure is the lower option cost in tranche C. In general, however, a portfolio manager willing to extend duration gets paid for that risk in this structure.

2. PAC/Support Tranche Structure

Now let's look at how to apply the methodology to a more complicated CMO structure, FHLMC Series 1706. The collateral (i.e., pool of passthroughs) for this structure is Freddie Mac 7s (7% coupon rate). A partial summary of the deal is provided in Exhibit 63-6. That is, only the tranches we will be discussing in this section are shown in the exhibit.[5]

While this deal looks complicated, it is relatively simple compared to many deals that have been issued. Nonetheless, it brings out all the key points about application of OAS analysis, specifically, the fact that most deals include cheap bonds, expensive bonds, and fairly priced bonds. The OAS analysis helps identify how a tranche should be classified. A more proper analysis would compare the OAS for each tranche to a similar duration tranche available in the market.

All of the tranches in Exhibit 63-6 were discussed in Reading 61. At issuance, there were 10 PAC tranches, three scheduled tranches, a floating-rate support tranche, and an inverse floating-rate support. Recall that the "scheduled tranches" are support tranches with a schedule, referred to in Reading 61 as "PAC II tranches."

The first two PAC tranches in the deal, tranche A and tranche B, were paid off at the time of the analysis. The other PAC tranches were still available at the time of the analysis. The prepayment protection for the PAC tranches is provided by the support tranches. The support tranches in this deal that are shown in Exhibit 63-6 are tranches LA, LB, and M. There were other support tranches not shown in Exhibit 63-6. LA is the shortest average life support tranche (a scheduled (SCH) bond).

The collateral for this deal was trading at a premium. That is, the homeowners (borrowers) were paying a higher mortgage rate than available in the market at the time of the analysis. This meant that the value of the collateral would increase if prepayments slow down but would decrease if prepayments increase. What is important to note, however, is that a tranche could be trading at a discount, par, or

---

[5] This deal was described in Reading 61.

EXHIBIT 63-6	Summary of Federal Home Loan Mortgage Corporation—Multiclass Mortgage Participation Certificates (Guaranteed), Series 1706

Total Issue: $300,000,000   **Issue Date:** 2/18/94

Tranche	Original Balance ($)	Coupon (%)	Stated Maturity	Original Issue Pricing (225% PSA Assumed)	
				Average Life (yrs)	Expected Maturity
PAC Tranches					
C (PAC Bond)	25,500,000	5.25	4/15/14	3.5	6/15/98
D (PAC Bond)	9,150,000	5.65	8/15/15	4.5	1/15/99
E (PAC Bond)	31,650,000	6.00	1/15/19	5.8	1/15/01
G (PAC Bond)	30,750,000	6.25	8/15/21	7.9	5/15/03
H (PAC Bond)	27,450,000	6.50	6/15/23	10.9	10/15/07
J (PAC Bond)	5,220,000	6.50	10/15/23	14.4	9/15/09
K (PAC Bond)	7,612,000	7.00	3/15/24	18.8	5/15/19
Support Tranches					
LA (SCH Bond)	26,673,000	7.00	11/15/21	3.5	3/15/02
LB (SCH Bond)	36,087,000	7.00	6/15/23	3.5	9/15/02
M (SCH Bond)	18,738,000	7.00	3/15/24	11.2	10/15/08

premium even though the collateral is priced at a premium. For example, PAC C had a low coupon rate at the time of the analysis and therefore was trading at a discount. Thus, while the collateral (which was selling at a premium) loses value from an increase in prepayments, a discount tranche such as tranche C would increase in value if prepayments increase. (Recall that in the simple structure analyzed earlier, the collateral and all the tranches were trading at a premium.)

The top panel of Exhibit 63-7 shows the base case OAS, the option cost, and the effective duration for the collateral and tranches in Exhibit 63-7. The collateral OAS is 60 basis points, and the option cost is 44 basis points. The Z-spread of the collateral to the Treasury spot curve is 104 basis points.

The 60 basis points of OAS did not get equally distributed among the tranches—as was the case with the simple structure analyzed earlier. Tranche LB, the scheduled support, did not realize a good OAS allocation, only 29 basis points, and had an extremely high option cost. Given the prepayment uncertainty associated with this tranche, its OAS would be expected to be higher. The reason for the low OAS is that this tranche was priced so that its cash flow yield is high. Using the Z-spread as a proxy for the nominal spread (i.e., spread over the Treasury yield curve), the 103 basis point spread for tranche LB is high given that this appears to be a short average life tranche. Consequently, "yield buyers" (i.e., investors with a preference for high **nominal yield**, who may not be attentive to compensation for prepayment risk) probably bid aggressively for this tranche and thereby drove down its OAS, trading off "yield" for OAS. From a total return perspective, however, tranche LB should be avoided. It is a rich, or expensive, tranche. The other support tranche analyzed, tranche M, had an OAS of 72 basis points and at the time of this analysis was similar to that offered on comparable duration tranches available in the market.

EXHIBIT 63-7	OAS Analysis of FHLMC 1706 (As of 3/10/98)

Base Case (Assumes 13% Interest Rate Volatility)

	OAS (in basis points)	Option Cost (in basis points)	Z-Spread (in basis points)	Effective Duration (in years)
Collateral	60	44	104	2.6
PAC Tranches				
C (PAC)	15	0	15	0.2
D (PAC)	16	4	20	0.6
E (PAC)	26	4	30	1.7
G (PAC)	42	8	50	3.3
H (PAC)	50	12	62	4.9
J (PAC)	56	14	70	6.8
K (PAC)	57	11	68	8.6
Support Tranches				
LA (SCH)	39	12	51	1.4
LB (SCH)	29	74	103	1.2
M (SCH)	72	53	125	4.9

Prepayments at 80% and 120% of Prepayment Model (Assumes 13% Interest Rate Volatility)

	Base Case OAS	New OAS (in basis points)		Change in Price per $100 par (holding OAS constant)	
		80%	120%	80%	120%
Collateral	60	63	57	$0.17	−$0.11
PAC Tranches					
C (PAC)	15	15	15	0.00	0.00
D (PAC)	16	16	16	0.00	0.00
E (PAC)	26	27	26	0.01	−0.01
G (PAC)	42	44	40	0.08	−0.08
H (PAC)	50	55	44	0.29	−0.27
J (PAC)	56	63	50	0.50	−0.47
K (PAC)	57	65	49	0.77	−0.76
Support Tranches					
LA (SCH)	39	31	39	−0.12	0.00
LB (SCH)	29	39	18	0.38	−0.19
M (SCH)	72	71	76	−0.07	0.18

(Exhibit continued on next page …)

EXHIBIT 63-7	OAS Analysis of FHLMC 1706 (As of 3/10/98) (continued)

Interest Rate Volatility of 9% and 17%

	Base Case OAS	New OAS (in basis points)		Change in Price per $100 par (holding OAS constant)	
		9%	17%	9%	17%
Collateral	**60**	**81**	**35**	**$0.96**	**−$0.94**
PAC Tranches					
C (PAC)	15	15	15	0.00	0.00
D (PAC)	16	16	16	0.00	0.00
E (PAC)	26	27	24	0.02	−0.04
G (PAC)	42	48	34	0.21	−0.27
H (PAC)	50	58	35	0.48	−0.72
J (PAC)	56	66	41	0.70	−1.05
K (PAC)	57	66	44	0.82	−1.19
Support Tranches					
LA (SCH)	39	47	24	0.09	−0.18
LB (SCH)	29	58	−4	0.80	−0.82
M (SCH)	72	100	41	1.80	−1.72

The analysis reported in the top panel of Exhibit 63-7 help us identify where the cheap tranches are in the deal. The long average life and effective duration tranches in the deal are the PAC tranches G, H, J, and K. These tranches have high OAS relative to the other tranches and low option cost. They appear to be the cheap tranches in the deal. These PAC tranches had well protected cash flows and exhibited positive convexity (i.e., these tranches lose less in an adverse scenario than they gain in a positive scenario).

The next two panels in Exhibit 63-7 show the sensitivity of the OAS and the price (holding OAS constant at the base case) to changes in the prepayment speed (80% and 120% of the base case) and to changes in volatility (9% and 17%). This analysis shows that the change in the prepayment speed does not affect the collateral significantly, while the change in the OAS (holding the price constant) and price (holding OAS constant) for each tranche can be significant.

Tranches C and D at the time of the analysis were priced at a discount with short average lives. The OAS and price of these two tranches were not affected by a slowing down or a speeding up of the prepayment model. Tranche H was a premium tranche with a medium-term average life at the time of the analysis. Because tranche H was trading at a premium, it benefits from a slowing in prepayments, as the bondholder will receive the coupon for a longer time. Faster prepayments represent an adverse scenario. The PAC tranches are quite well-protected. The longer average life PACs will actually benefit from a reduced prepayment rate because they will be earning the higher coupon interest longer. So, on an OAS basis, the earlier conclusion that the long PACs were allocated a good part of the deal's value holds up under our first stress test (i.e., changing prepayments).

The sensitivity of the collateral and the tranches to changes in volatility are shown in the third panel of Exhibit 63-7. A lower volatility increases the value of the collateral, while a higher volatility reduces its value (This is consistent with our option cost equation in Section IV.E.) The long average life PACs continue to be fairly well-protected, whether the volatility is lower or higher. In the two volatility scenarios they continue to get a good OAS on a relative value basis, although not as much as in the base case if volatility is higher (but the OAS still looks like a reasonable value in this scenario). This reinforces the earlier conclusion concerning the investment merit of the long PACs in this deal. Note, however, that PAC tranches H, J, and K are more sensitive to the volatility assumption than tranches C, D, E, and G and therefore the investor is accepting greater **volatility risk** (i.e., the risk that volatility will change) with tranches H, J, and K relative to tranches C, D, E, and G.

5   MEASURING INTEREST RATE RISK

As explained at Level I and again in Reading 60, duration and convexity can be used to estimate the interest rate exposure to parallel shifts in the yield curve (i.e., a measure of level risk). In this section we will discuss duration measures for mortgage-backed securities. There are several duration measures that are used in practice. Two researchers who have done extensive work in measuring duration, Lakhbir Hayre and Hubert Chang, conclude that "No single duration measure will consistently work well for mortgage securities."[6] To that conclusion should be added that there are some measures that do not work at all.

A. Duration Measures

Duration is a measure of the price sensitivity to changes in interest rates. At Level I we have seen how to compute the duration of a security by shocking rates up and down and determining how the price of the security changes. Duration is then computed as follows:

$$\text{duration} = \frac{V_- - V_+}{2V_0(\Delta y)}$$

where

Δy = change in rate used to calculate new values (i.e., the interest rate shock)
V_+ = estimated value if yield is increased by Δy
V_- = estimated value if yield is decreased by Δy
V_0 = initial price (per \$100 of par value)

For bonds with embedded options such as mortgage-backed securities, the appropriate measure is effective duration and to capture the negative convexity of a bond with an embedded option, effective convexity should be computed. We will see how to calculate the effective duration for a mortgage-backed security using the Monte Carlo simulation model. Then we will see how the assumptions of the model impact the duration estimate. Dealers and vendors use other measures of duration that will be described later.

---

[6] Lakhbir Hayre and Hubert Chang, "Effective and Empirical Duration of Mortgage Securities", *The Journal of Fixed Income* (March 1997), pp. 17–33.

1. Effective Duration

To calculate effective duration, the value of the security must be estimated when rates are shocked up and down a given number of basis points. In terms of the Monte Carlo model, the yield curve used (either the Treasury yield curve or LIBOR curve) is shocked up and down and the new curve is used to generate the values to be used in the effective duration and effective convexity formulas. This is analogous to the process we used to compute effective duration and effective convexity using the binomial model in Reading 60.

In generating the prices when rates are shocked up and down, there is an assumption that the relationships assumed in generating the initial price do not change when rates are shocked up and down. Specifically, the yield volatility is assumed to be unchanged to derive the new interest rate paths for a given shock (i.e., the new Exhibit 63-1), the spread between the mortgage rate and the 10-year Treasury rate is assumed to be unchanged in constructing the new Exhibit 63-2 from the newly constructed Exhibit 63-1, and the OAS is assumed to be constant. The constancy of the OAS comes into play because when discounting the new cash flows (i.e., the cash flows in the new Exhibit 63-3), the current OAS that was computed is assumed to be the same and is added to the new rates in the new Exhibit 63-1.

We'll use an illustration by Lakhbir Hayre and Hubert Chang to explain the calculation of effective duration for a mortgage-backed security, a FNMA 7.5% TBA passthrough on May 1, 1996.[7] On that day, the base mortgage rate was 7.64%. The price of the issue at the time was 98.781 (i.e., 98-25). The OAS was 65 basis points. Based on a shock of 25 basis points, the estimated prices holding the OAS constant at 65 basis points were as follows:

V_- = 99.949 for a decrease in the yield curve of 25 basis points
V_+ = 97.542 for an increase in the yield curve of 25 basis points

The effective duration based on a Δy of 0.0025 is then

$$\frac{99.949 - 97.542}{2 \times 98.781 \times 0.0025} = 4.87$$

There are differences in the effective durations for a given mortgage-backed security reported by dealers and vendors of analytical systems. Several practitioners have explained and illustrated why there are differences in effective duration estimates reported by dealers and vendors. The differences result from, among others:[8]

1. differences in the amount of the rate shock used

2. differences in prepayment models

3. differences in option-adjusted spread

4. differences in the relationship between short-term interest rates and refinancing rates

At Level I, we discussed the first reason. As explained, the rate shock is the amount interest rates are increased and decreased to obtain the two values that

---

[7] Hayre and Chang, "Effective and Empirical Duration of Mortgage Securities."

[8] Sam Choi, "Effective Durations for Mortgage-Backed Securities: Recipes for Improvement", *The Journal of Fixed Income* (March 1996), pp. 24–30; and, Hayre and Chang, "Effective and Empirical Duration of Mortgage Securities."

are inserted into the effective duration formula. If the change is too large, there is the problem with picking up the effect of convexity.

Prepayment models differ across dealers and vendors. Some dealer models consistently forecast slower prepayments relative to other dealer models and others the reverse.

The effective duration is dependent on the OAS computed. Recall that the calculation of the OAS is a byproduct of the Monte Carlo model. Therefore, the computed value for the OAS depends on all of the assumptions in the Monte Carlo model. Specifically, it depends on the yield volatility assumed and the prepayment model employed. Dealers and vendors make different assumptions regarding yield volatility and use proprietary prepayment models. These can result in differences in OAS. Since the OAS is added to the new simulated short-term rates to compute the new values for V_- and V_+, a different OAS will result in different effective durations.

Finally, recall that in explaining the Monte Carlo simulation model that we stated that in moving from Exhibit 63-1 (the simulated short-term rates) to Exhibit 63-2 (the refinancing rates), an assumption must be made about the relationship between short-term rates and the 10-year Treasury rate (i.e., the rate used as a proxy for refinancing). Differences in models about how large the spread between these rates will be affects the value of a mortgage-backed security and therefore the values used in the duration equation when rates are shocked.

2. Other Duration Measures

There have been other measures proposed for estimating the duration of a mortgage-backed security. These measures include **cash flow duration, coupon curve duration**, and **empirical duration**. The first two duration measures are forms of effective duration in that they do recognize that the values that should be used in the duration formula should take into account how the cash flows may change due to changes in prepayments when interest rates change. In contrast, **empirical duration** is a duration that is computed statistically using observed market prices. Below we describe how each of these duration measures is calculated, as well as the advantages and limitations of each.

a. Cash Flow Duration

Recall from the general duration formula that there are two values that must be substituted into the numerator of the formula—the value if rates are decreased (V_-) and the value if rates are increased (V_+). With effective duration, these two values consider how changes in interest rates change the cash flow due to prepayments. This is done through the Monte Carlo simulation by allowing for the cash flows to change on the interest rate paths.

For **cash flow duration**, there is recognition that the cash flow can change but the analysis to obtain the cash flow is done following a static methodology. Specifically, the cash flow duration is calculated as follows:

Step 1: Calculate the cash flow based on some prepayment assumption.

Step 2: From the cash flow in Step 1 and the market price (V_0), compute the cash flow yield.

Step 3: Increase the cash flow yield by Δy and from a prepayment model determine the new prepayment rate at that higher cash flow yield. Typically, the prepayment rate will be lower than in Step 1 because of the higher yield level.

Step 4: Using the lower prepayment rate in Step 3 determine the cash flow and then value the cash flow using the higher cash flow yield as the discount rate. This gives the value (V_+).

Step 5: Decrease the cash flow yield by Δy and from a prepayment model determine the new prepayment rate at that lower cash flow yield. Typically, the prepayment rate will be higher than in Step 1 because of the lower yield level.

Step 6: Using the higher prepayment rate in Step 5 determine the cash flow and then value the cash flow using the lower cash flow yield as the discount rate. This gives the value (V_-).

From the change in basis points (Δy), the values for V_+ and V_- found in Steps 4 and 6, and the initial value V_0, the duration can be computed.

We can use the hypothetical CMO structure to illustrate how to calculate cash flow duration. Specifically, in FJF-2, there were four tranches, A, B, C, and Z. Let's focus on tranche C. Suppose that the price for this tranche is 100.2813. Then the cash flow duration is computed as follows:

Step 1: Suppose that the assumed prepayment rate for this tranche is 165 PSA.

Step 2: Based on the assumed prepayment rate of 165 PSA and the price of 100.2813, it can be demonstrated that the cash flow yield is 7%.

Step 3: Suppose that the cash flow yield is increased (i.e., shocked) by 25 basis points (from 7% to 7.25%) and suppose that some prepayment model projects a prepayment rate of 150 PSA. (Note that this is a slower prepayment rate than at 7%.)

Step 4: Based on 150 PSA, a new cash flow can be generated. The cash flow is then discounted at 7.25% (the new cash flow yield). It can be demonstrated that the value of this tranche based on these assumptions would be 98.3438. This is the value V_+.

Step 5: Suppose that the cash flow yield is decreased (i.e., shocked) by 25 basis points (from 7% to 6.75%) and suppose that some prepayment model projects a prepayment rate of 200 PSA. (Note that this is a faster prepayment rate than at 7%.)

Step 6: Based on 200 PSA, the new cash flow can be generated. The cash flow is then discounted at 6.75% (the new cash flow yield). It can be demonstrated that the value of this tranche based on these assumptions would be 101.9063. This is the value V_-.

Now we have the following information:

$$V_0 = 100.2813$$
$$V_+ = 98.3438$$
$$V_- = 101.9063$$
$$\Delta y = 0.0025$$

Then using the general form of duration, we obtain:

$$\text{duration} = \frac{101.9063 - 98.3438}{2(100.2813)(0.0025)} = 7.11$$

What type of duration measure is the cash flow duration—effective duration or modified duration? Technically, it is a form of effective duration because notice that in Steps 3 and 5 when the rate is changed, the cash flow is allowed to change. However, as has been stressed throughout, the valuation model that is used to get the new values to substitute into the duration formula is critical. The valuation model in the case of the cash flow duration is based on the naive assumption that there is a single prepayment rate over the life of the mortgage-backed security for any given interest rate shock. This is in contrast to the values produced by the Monte Carlo simulation model that does more sophisticated analyses of how the cash flow can change when interest rates change.

Why bother discussing the cash flow duration if it is an inferior form of effective duration? The reason is that it is a commonly cited duration measure and practitioners should be aware of how it is computed. Likewise, we did discuss in detail yield calculations at Level I despite their limitations.

An interesting question is how does this form of duration compare to modified duration. Recall from Level I and Reading 60 that modified duration does not assume that cash flows will change when rates are shocked. That is, in the steps discussed above to obtain cash flow duration, in Steps 3 and 5 it is assumed that the prepayment rate is the same as in Step 1.

To illustrate this, we'll once again use tranche C in FJF-2. In Step 3, the prepayment rate assumed is still 165 PSA despite the fact that rates are assumed to increase. That is, the cash flow is not assumed to change. Based on a cash flow yield of 7.25% and a prepayment rate of 165 PSA, the value of this tranche would decline to 98.4063. When the cash flow yield is assumed to decline to 6.75%, the prepayment rate is still assumed to be 165 PSA and the value of this tranche would be 102.1875. Then to calculate the modified duration we know:

$$V_0 = 100.2813$$
$$V_+ = 98.4063$$
$$V_- = 102.1875$$
$$\Delta y = 0.0025$$

The modified duration is then:

$$\text{duration} = \frac{102.1875 - 98.4063}{2(100.2813)(0.0025)} = 7.54$$

Thus, the modified duration is greater than the cash flow duration for this tranche.

It is important to reiterate that the modified duration is inferior to the cash flow duration because the former gives absolutely no recognition to how repayments may change when interest rates change. While cash flow duration is commonly cited in practice, it is a form of effective duration that does give some recognition that prepayments and therefore cash flow may change when interest rates change, but it is based on a naive assumption about how prepayments may change. The effective duration as computed using Monte Carlo simulation is superior to cash flow duration.

b. Coupon Curve Duration

The **coupon curve duration** uses market prices to estimate the duration of a mortgage-backed security. This approach, first suggested by Douglas Breeden,[9]

---

[9] Douglas Breeden, "Risk, Return, and Hedging of Fixed-Rate Mortgages," *The Journal of Fixed Income* (September 1991), pp. 85–107.

starts with the coupon curve of prices for similar mortgage-backed securities. The coupon curve represents generic passthrough securities of a particular issuer with different coupon rates. By rolling up and down the coupon curve of prices, the duration can be obtained. Because of the way it is estimated, this approach to duration estimation was referred to by Breeden as the "roll-up, roll-down approach." The prices obtained from rolling up and rolling down the coupon curve of prices are substituted into the duration formula.

To illustrate this approach, suppose that the coupon curve of prices for a passthrough security for some month is as follows:

Coupon	Price
6%	85.19
7%	92.06
8%	98.38
9%	103.34
10%	107.28
11%	111.19

Suppose that the coupon curve duration for the 8% coupon passthrough is sought. If the yield declines by 100 basis points, the assumption is that the price of the 8% coupon passthrough will increase to the price of the current 9% coupon passthrough. Thus, the price will increase from 98.38 to 103.34. Similarly, if the yield increases by 100 basis points, the assumption is that the price of the 8% coupon passthrough will decline to the price of the 7% coupon passthrough (92.06). Using the duration formula, the corresponding values are:

$$V_0 = 98.38$$
$$V_+ = 92.06$$
$$V_- = 103.34$$
$$\Delta y = 0.01$$

The estimated duration based on the coupon curve is then:

$$\text{duration} = \frac{103.34 - 92.06}{2(98.38)(0.01)} = 5.73$$

Breeden tested the coupon curve durations and found them to be relatively accurate in estimating the interest rate risk of generic passthrough securities.[10] Bennett Golub reports a similar finding.[11]

While the advantages of the coupon curve duration are the simplicity of its calculation and the fact that current prices embody market expectations, there are disadvantages. The approach is limited to generic mortgage-backed securities and difficult to use for mortgage derivatives such as CMOs.

---

[10] Breeden, "Risk, Return, and Hedging of Fixed-Rate Mortgages."

[11] See Bennett W. Golub, "Towards a New Approach to Measuring Mortgage Duration", Chapter 32 in Frank J. Fabozzi (ed.), *The Handbook of Mortgage-Backed Securities* (Chicago: Probus Publishing, 1995), p. 673.

c. Empirical Duration

When computing effective duration and cash flow duration, the values to be substituted into the duration formula are those based on some valuation model. For coupon curve duration, the observed market prices are used in the duration formula. In contrast, **empirical duration** is estimated statistically using historical market prices and market yields.[12] Regression analysis is used to estimate the relationship. Some firms such as PaineWebber use empirical duration, also called **implied duration**, as their primary measure of the duration of an MBS.

There are three advantages to the empirical duration approach.[13] First, the duration estimate does not rely on any theoretical formulas or analytical assumptions. Second, the estimation of the required parameters is easy to compute using regression analysis. Finally, the only inputs that are needed are a reliable price series and Treasury yield series.

There are disadvantages.[14] First, a reliable price series for the mortgage security may not be available. For example, there may be no price series available for a thinly traded mortgage **derivative security** or the prices may be matrix priced (i.e., priced by a pricing service based on issues with similar characteristics) or model priced rather than actual transaction prices. Second, an empirical relationship does not impose a structure for the options embedded in a mortgage-backed security and this can distort the empirical duration. This may occur after a sharp and sustained shock to interest rates have been realized. Finally, the volatility of the spread to Treasury yields can distort how the price of a mortgage-backed security reacts to yield changes.

6   VALUING ASSET-BACKED SECURITIES

From the description of the Monte Carlo model, it can be seen that the valuation process is complex. Rather than build their own valuation model, portfolio managers typically use a model of a third-party vendor of analytical systems or a model of a dealer firm to value mortgage-backed securities. But mortgage-backed securities are only one type of structured product. Asset-backed securities are also structured products. Is it necessary to use the Monte Carlo model for all asset-backed securities? Below we will explain the circumstances as to when the Monte Carlo model must be used and when it is sufficient to use the Z-spread.

---

[12] This approach was first suggested in 1986 in Scott M. Pinkus and Marie A. Chandoha, "The Relative Price Volatility of Mortgage Securities," *Journal of Portfolio Management* (Summer 1986), pp. 9–22 and then in 1990 by Paul DeRossa, Laurie Goodman, and Mike Zazzarino, "Duration Estimates on Mortgage-Backed Securities," *Journal of Portfolio Management* (Winter 1993), pp. 32-37, and more recently in Laurie S. Goodman and Jeffrey Ho, "Mortgage Hedge Ratios: Which One Works Best?" *The Journal of Fixed Income* (December 1997), pp. 23-33, and Laurie S. Goodman and and Jeffrey Ho, "An Integrated Approach to Hedging and Relative Value Analysis," Chapter 15 in Frank J. Fabozzi (ed.), *Advances in the Valuation and Management of Mortgage-Backed Securities* (New Hope, PA: Frank J. Fabozzi Associates, 1999).

[13] Golub, "Towards a New Approach to Measuring Mortgage Duration," p. 672.

[14] Golub, "Towards a New Approach to Measuring Mortgage Duration."

The model that should be used for valuing an asset-backed security (ABS) depends on the characteristic of the loans or receivables backing the deal. An ABS can have one of the following three characteristics:

Characteristic 1: The ABS does not have a prepayment option.

Characteristic 2: The ABS has a prepayment option but borrowers do not exhibit a tendency to prepay when refinancing rates fall below the loan rate.

Characteristic 3: The ABS has a prepayment option and borrowers do exhibit a tendency to prepay when refinancing rates fall below the loan rate.

An example of a Characteristic 1 type ABS is a security backed by credit card receivables. An example of a Characteristic 2 type ABS is a security backed by automobile loans. A security backed by closed-end home equity loans where the borrowers are high quality borrowers (i.e., prime borrowers) is an example of a Characteristic 3 type ABS. There are some real-estate backed ABS we discussed in Reading 62 where the verdict is still out as to the degree to which borrowers take advantage of refinancing opportunities. Specifically, these include securities backed by manufactured housing loans and securities backed by closed-end home equity loans to borrowers classified as low quality borrowers.

There are two possible approaches to valuing an ABS. They are the

1. zero-volatility spread (Z-spread) approach
2. option-adjusted spread (OAS) approach

For the Z-spread approach the interest rates used to discount the cash flows are the spot rates plus the zero-volatility spread. The value of an ABS is then the present value of the cash flows based on these discount rates. The Z-spread approach does not consider the prepayment option. Consequently, the Z-spread approach should be used to value Characteristic 1 type ABS. (In terms of the relationship between the Z-spread, OAS, and option cost discussed earlier in this reading, this means that the value of the option is zero and therefore the Z-spread is equal to the OAS.) Since the Z-spread is equal to the OAS, the Z-spread approach to valuation can be used.

The Z-spread approach can also be used to value Characteristic 2 type ABS because while the borrowers do have a prepayment option, the option is not typically exercised. Thus, as with Characteristic 1 type ABS, the Z-spread is equal to the OAS.

The OAS approach—which is considerably more computationally extensive than the Z-spread approach—is used to value securities where there is an embedded option and there is an expectation that the option is expected to be exercised if it makes economic sense for the borrower to do so. Consequently, the OAS approach is used to value Characteristic 3 type ABS. The choice is then whether to use the binomial model (or a comparable model) or the Monte Carlo simulation model. Since typically the cash flow for an ABS with a prepayment option is interest rate path dependent—as with a mortgage-backed security—the Monte Carlo simulation model is used.

VALUING ANY SECURITY   7

We conclude this reading with a summary of the approaches to valuing any fixed income security using the two approaches that we discussed in the previous section—the Z-spread approach and the OAS approach.

Below we match the valuation approach with the type of security.

1. For an *option-free bond* the correct approach is the Z-spread approach.

2. For a *bond with an embedded option where the cash flow is not interest rate path dependent* (such as a callable corporate or agency debenture bond or a putable bond) the correct approach is the OAS approach. Since the backward induction method can be used for such bonds, the binomial model or its equivalent should be used.

3. For a bond with an embedded option where the cash flow is interest rate path dependent (such as a mortgage-backed security or certain real estate-backed ABS) the correct approach is the OAS approach. However, because of the interest rate path dependency of the cash flow, the Monte Carlo simulation model should be used.

SUMMARY

▶ The cash flow yield is the interest rate that makes the present value of the projected cash flow for a mortgage-backed or asset-backed security equal to its market price plus accrued interest.

▶ The convention is to compare the yield on mortgage-backed and asset-backed securities to that of a Treasury coupon security by calculating the security's bond-equivalent yield. This measure is found by computing an effective semiannual rate and doubling it.

▶ The cash flow yield is based on three assumptions that thereby limit its use as a measure of relative value: (1) a prepayment assumption and default/recovery assumption, (2) an assumption that the cash flows will be reinvested at the computed cash flow yield, and (3) an assumption that the investor will hold the security until the last loan in the pool is paid off.

▶ The nominal spread is commonly computed as the difference between the cash flow yield and the yield on a Treasury security with the same maturity as the mortgage-backed or asset-backed security's average life.

▶ The nominal spread masks the fact that a portion of the spread is compensation for accepting prepayment risk.

▶ An investor or portfolio manager who buys solely on the basis of nominal spread fails to determine whether or not that nominal spread offers an adequate compensation for prepayment risk.

▶ An investor or portfolio manager needs a measure that indicates the potential compensation after adjusting for prepayment risk and this measure is the option-adjusted spread.

▶ The zero-volatility spread is a measure of the spread that the investor would realize over the entire Treasury spot rate curve if the mortgage-backed or asset-backed security is held to maturity.

▶ The zero-volatility spread is not a spread off one point on the Treasury yield curve, as is the nominal spread, but a spread that will make the present value of the cash flows from the mortgage-backed or asset-backed security when discounted at the Treasury spot rate plus the spread equal to the market price of the security plus accrued interest.

▶ The binomial model and other similar models that use the backward induction method can be used to value securities where the decision to exercise a call option is not dependent on how interest rates evolved over time—that is, the decision of an issuer to call a bond will depend on the level of the rate at which the issue can be refunded relative to the issue's coupon rate, and not the path interest rates took to get to that rate.

▶ Mortgage-backed securities and some types of asset-backed securities are products where the periodic cash flows are "interest rate path-dependent"—meaning that the cash flow received in one period is determined not only by the current interest rate level, but also by the path that interest rates took to get to the current level.

▶ The Monte Carlo simulation model for valuing mortgage-backed securities involves generating a set of cash flows based on simulated future mortgage refinancing rates, which in turn imply simulated prepayment rates.

► In the Monte Carlo simulation model there is nothing to assure that the simulated interest rates will generate arbitrage-free values of the benchmark securities used in the valuation process; consequently, the simulated interest rates must be adjusted so as to produce arbitrage-free values.

► The present value of a given interest rate path can be thought of as the theoretical value of a security if that path was actually realized.

► The theoretical value of a mortgage-backed security can be determined by calculating the average of the theoretical values of all the interest rate paths.

► In the Monte Carlo simulation model, the option-adjusted spread is the spread that when added to all the spot rates on all interest rate paths will make the average present value of the paths equal to the observed market price (plus accrued interest).

► The OAS is measured relative to the benchmark interest rates that were used to generate the interest rate paths and to adjust the interest rate paths to make them arbitrage free.

► Since typically for a mortgage-backed security the benchmark interest rates are the on-the-run Treasury rates, the OAS measures the average spread over the Treasury spot rate curve, not the Treasury yield curve.

► Depending on the mortgage product being valued, the OAS reflects credit risk, liquidity risk, and modeling risk.

► The OAS is superior to the nominal spread which gives no recognition to the prepayment risk.

► The implied cost of the option embedded in a mortgage-backed or an asset-backed security can be obtained by calculating the difference between the option-adjusted spread at the assumed interest rate volatility and the zero-volatility spread.

► The option cost measures the prepayment (or option) risk embedded in the security and is a byproduct of the option-adjusted spread analysis, not valued explicitly with some option pricing model.

► In valuation modeling of collateralized mortgage obligations, the objective is to figure out how the value and risks of the collateral get transmitted to the tranches in a deal.

► There are several duration measures for mortgage-backed securities that are used in practice—effective duration, cash flow duration, coupon curve duration, and empirical duration.

► For bonds with embedded options such as mortgage-backed securities, the appropriate measure is effective duration and to capture negative convexity, effective convexity should be computed.

► Effective duration is computed using Monte Carlo simulation by shocking the short-term interest rates for each interest rate path generated up and down and obtaining the new value for the security; the new values determined when rates are shocked up and down are used in the duration formula.

► There are differences in the effective duration reported for a given mortgage-backed security by dealers and vendors of analytical systems primarily due to differences in: (1) the amount of the rate shock used, (2) the prepayment model used, (3) the option-adjusted spread computed, and (4) the relationship between short-term interest rates and refinancing rates assumed.

► Cash flow duration and coupon curve duration measures are forms of effective duration in that they do recognize that the values that should be used in the duration formula should take into account how the cash flows may change due to changes in prepayments when interest rates change.

► Cash flow duration is based on an initial cash flow yield and initial prepayment rate and computes the new values when rates are shocked (i.e., when the cash flow yield is shocked) allowing the cash flow to change based on a new prepayment rate as determined by a prepayment model.

► Cash flow duration is superior to modified duration (which assumes that cash flows do not change when rates are shocked) but inferior to effective duration as computed using the Monte Carlo simulation model.

► The coupon curve duration begins with the coupon curve of prices for similar mortgage-backed securities and uses values in the duration formula found by rolling up and down the coupon curve of prices.

► Empirical duration is a duration measure that is computed statistically using regression analysis based on observed market prices and yields.

► Empirical duration imposes no structure on the embedded option.

► A limitation of empirical duration and coupon curve duration is that they are difficult to apply to CMOs because of a lack of valid market price data.

► The zero-volatility spread added to the spot rates can be used to value an asset-backed security if either (1) the security does not have a prepayment option or (2) the borrower has the right to prepay but it has been observed that the borrower does not tend to exercise that option if interest rates decline below the loan rate.

► The option-adjusted spread approach to valuation using the Monte Carlo simulation model is used for an asset-backed security if the borrower does have the right to prepay and it has been observed that the borrower does tend to refinance when interest rates decline below the loan rate.

► For any fixed income security, the valuation approaches that can be employed are the zero-volatility spread approach and the option-adjusted spread approach.

► For option-free bonds, the zero-volatility spread approach should be used.

► The choice of whether to use the binomial model (or a similar "nomial" model that uses the backward induction method) or the Monte Carlo simulation model for a security with an embedded option depends on the characteristics of the security.

► For corporate and agency debentures with an embedded option the binomial model or its equivalent should be used for valuation.

► For securities such as mortgage-backed and asset-backed securities (those where it is observed that borrowers do exercise the prepayment option) the Monte Carlo simulation model should be used since the cash flows are typically interest rate path dependent.

PROBLEMS FOR READING 63

1. Suppose that based on a prepayment assumption of 200 PSA the cash flow yield for a specific agency passthrough security is 7.5% and the stated maturity is 15 years. Suppose further that the average life of this security is 8 years. Assume the following yield curve for Treasuries:

Maturity	Yield
6-year	6.2%
8-year	6.3%
10-year	6.4%
15-year	6.6%

   A. What is the nominal spread for this agency passthrough security?

   B. What must occur over the life of this agency passthrough security for the cash flow yield of 7.5% to be realized?

2. Suppose that the monthly cash flow yield is 0.74%. What is the cash flow yield on a bond-equivalent basis?

3. Jane Howard is a corporate bond analyst. Recently she has been asked to extend her responsibilities to mortgage-backed securities. In researching the methodology for valuing mortgage-backed securities she read that these securities are valued using the Monte Carlo simulation model. She was unfamiliar with this approach to valuation because in valuing callable corporate bonds she used the binomial model. Explain to Ms. Howard why the Monte Carlo simulation method is used to value mortgage-backed securities rather than the binomial method.

4. The following questions have to do with the Monte Carlo simulation model.

   A. What assumption must be made in generating the path of short-term interest rates?

   B. Why must the paths of short-term interest rates be adjusted?

   C. In determining the path of refinancing rates, what assumption must be made?

5. Nat Hawthorne, a portfolio manager, discussed the valuation of a particular mortgage-backed security with his broker, Steven Ruthledge. Mr. Hawthorne is considering the purchase of the security and asked what valuation model the brokerage firm used. Mr. Ruthledge responded that the Monte Carlo simulation model was used. Mr. Hawthorne then asked about what prepayment assumption is used in the Monte Carlo simulation model. Mr. Ruthledge responded that for the particular security Mr. Hawthorne is considering, 175 PSA was assumed. Mr. Hawthorne was confused by the response because he did not believe that a particular PSA assumption was made in the Monte Carlo simulation model. Is Mr. Hawthorne correct? Explain your answer.

6. What interest rates are used to value a mortgage-backed security on each interest rate path when using the Monte Carlo simulation model?

7. Juan Rodriguez is the manager of a portfolio containing mortgage passthrough securities. He is reviewing output of his firm's analytical system for several passthrough securities that are in the portfolio. Below is a portion of the report for three passthrough securities:

| Passthrough | Price based on an assumed interest rate volatility of | | | |
	11%	13%	15%	16%
Security 1	100	98	95	93
Security 2	92	90	88	87
Security 3	102	104	106	107

Mr. Rodriguez believes that there is an error in the analytical system. Why does he suspect that there is an error?

8. Suppose that the pool of passthroughs used as collateral for a collateralized mortgage obligation is selling at a premium. Also suppose that one tranche in the deal, Tranche X, is selling at a discount and another tranche, Tranche Y, is selling at a premium.

A. Explain why a slowdown in prepayments will tend to increase the value of the collateral?

B. Explain why a slowdown in prepayments will not affect the value of Tranches X and Y in the same way.

9. Assume for simplicity that only ten interest rate paths are used in the Monte Carlo simulation model to a value Tranche W of a CMO deal. Suppose further that based on a spread of 70 basis points, the present value of the interest rate paths is as follows:

Interest rate path	1	2	3	4	5	6	7	8	9	10
PV for path	80	90	84	88	94	92	86	91	99	87

Based on the Monte Carlo simulation model and assuming a spread required by the market of 70 basis points, what is the theoretical value of Tranche W.

10. Jane Hubert is using an analytical system purchased by her firm to analyze mortgage-backed securities. The analytical system uses the Monte Carlo simulation model for valuation. She is given a choice when using the system to use either the "full Monte Carlo analysis" or "16 representative interest rate paths".

A. What is meant by "16 representative interest path paths"?

B. How is the theoretical value of a mortgage-backed security determined when representative paths are used?

C. What is the trade-off when using representative interest rate paths versus using the full Monte Carlo analysis?

11. A portfolio manager is using an analytical system to value Tranche K of a CMO deal. The Monte Carlo simulation model uses eight representative interest rate paths. The present value of each of the representative interest rate paths and the weight of each path are shown below:

Representative path	1	2	3	4	5	6	7	8
Weight of representative path	20%	18%	16%	12%	12%	12%	6%	4%
PV of representative path	70	82	79	68	74	86	91	93

What is the theoretical value of Tranche K?

12. Mr. Wacker is a bond analyst whose primary responsibility has been to manage the corporate bond portfolio. Recently, his firm's analyst responsible for the mortgage-backed securities portfolio left. Mr. Wacker was asked to monitor the mortgage-backed securities portfolio until an new analyst is hired. The portfolio contains only Ginnie Mae mortgage products. In reviewing the Ginnie Mae portfolio and the option-adjusted spread (OAS) for each security, he was troubled by the values he observed. He was told that the benchmark interest rates used in the calculation of the OAS are Treasury rates. Below are two questions raised by Mr. Wacker. Respond to each one.

A. "I don't understand why the Ginnie Mae securities in my portfolio have a positive OAS. These securities are backed by the full faith and credit of the U.S. government, so there is no credit risk. Why is there a positive OAS?"

B. "There are different types of Ginnie Mae mortgage products in the portfolio. There are passthroughs, sequential-pay CMO tranches, planned amortization class CMO tranches, and support CMO tranches. Why do they have different OASs?"

13. Suppose that 10 representative paths are used in the Monte Carlo simulation model and that each path has a weight of 10%. The present value for each representative path is based on discounting the cash flows on an interest rate path by the short-term interest rates on that path plus a spread. For the different spreads used, the present value of each representative path is shown below for Tranche L in a CMO deal:

Representative path	Present value if the spread used is			
	70 bps	75 bps	80 bps	85 bps
1	77	72	70	68
2	82	80	77	72
3	86	84	81	78
4	89	86	83	81
5	74	70	68	65
6	88	86	82	80
7	96	92	88	86
8	92	90	86	84
9	74	71	67	65
10	68	64	61	59

A. Suppose that the market price of Tranche L is 79.5. What is the option-adjusted spread?

B. Suppose instead of a market price for Tranche L of 79.5 the market price is 73.8. What is the option-adjusted spread?

14. Below are the results of a Monte Carlo simulation analysis using eight representative paths for two tranches of a CMO deal, Tranches M and N:

Representative path	1	2	3	4	5	6	7	8
PV of path for:								
Tranche M	60	55	90	105	110	50	48	70
Tranche N	86	85	89	91	84	92	87	86

One of the tranches is a PAC tranche and the other is a support tranche. Which tranche is probably the PAC tranche and which is probably the support tranche?

15. An analysis of an agency CMO structure using the Monte Carlo simulation model based on 12% volatility found the following:

	OAS (basis points)	Z-spread (basis points)	Effective duration
Collateral	90	130	8.0
Tranche			
PAC I A	50	60	1.5
PAC I B	70	80	3.0
PAC I C	30	120	5.0
PAC I D	30	150	9.0
PAC II A	80	150	4.0
PAC II B	20	280	6.0
Support S1	35	165	11.0
Support S2	50	190	14.0

A. What is the option cost for PAC I A, PAC II A, and Support S1?

B. Which of the PAC tranches appears to be expensive in the deal on a relative value basis?

C. PAC II tranches are support tranches with schedules. The four support tranches in the deal are therefore PAC II A, PAC II B, Support S1, and Support S2. Which of the support tranches appears to be expensive on a relative value basis?

D. Despite its low OAS of 20 basis points, why might a yield buyer be induced to purchase PAC II B?

16. How is the effective duration and effective convexity of a mortgage-backed security computed using the Monte Carlo simulation model? Be sure to explain what assumption is made regarding the option-adjusted spread when computing the effective duration and effective convexity.

17. Joel Winters is a junior portfolio manager of a corporate bond portfolio. A decision has been made to include mortgage-backed securities in the portfolio. Mr. Winters is considering the purchase of a CMO tranche called a support bond. Before he buys this tranche, he wants to know its effective duration. Because he does not have the use of an analytical system to compute effective duration, Mr. Winters contacts three dealers and inquires as to the effective duration for this tranche. He is given the following effective duration from the three dealer firms:

Dealer	1	2	3
Effective duration	8.1	4.6	11.6

Mr. Winters is puzzled by the significant variation in the effective durations, especially since all the dealers indicated that the Monte Carlo simulation model was used. In his experience with corporate bonds with embedded options he has never observed such a significant variation in the effective duration from dealer firm to dealer firm.

Explain to Mr. Winters why there is such a significant variation in the effective durations. Be sure to clearly identify the reasons for the variation in the effective durations.

18. Explain why you agree or disagree with the following statement: "If the collateral for a CMO deal has negative convexity, then all the tranches in the deal must have negative convexity. The only difference is the degree of negative convexity from one tranche to another."

19. A. What is the cash flow duration of a mortgage-backed security?

B. What are the limitations of cash flow duration as a measure of the price sensitivity of a mortgage-backed security to changes in interest rates?

20. Suppose that the coupon curve of prices for a passthrough security for some month is as follows:

Coupon	Price
7%	94.00
8%	97.06
9%	99.50
10%	102.60
11%	105.25
12%	106.19

What is the coupon curve duration for the 9% coupon passthrough?

21. Karen Brown is considering alternative measures for estimating the duration of some complex CMO tranches. One measure she is considering is empirical duration. Explain to Ms. Brown the difficulties of using empirical duration for complex CMO tranches.

22. Thomas Larken is a portfolio manager who is considering investing in the asset-backed securities market. In particular, Mr. Larken is considering investing in either credit card receivables, auto loan-backed securities, or prime home equity loan-backed securities. Examination of the nominal spreads in these three sectors of the market indicates that the largest nominal spread for AAA and AA issues is home equity loan-backed securities. Based on this analysis, Mr. Larken believes that the best sector in which to invest is in home equity loan-backed securities because it offers the greatest relative value as measured by the nominal spread. Explain whether or not you agree with Mr. Larken's assessment of the relative attractiveness of home equity loan-backed securities.

23. An investment banker has created an asset-backed security in which the collateral is the future royalties of a song writer. Which valuation approach do you think should be used to value this security, the zero-volatility spread or the option-adjusted spread?

24. Suppose that empirical evidence on prepayments for manufactured housing loans suggests that borrowers do not take advantage of refinancing when interest rates decline. Explain whether the zero-volatility spread approach or OAS approach is appropriate for valuing securities backed by manufacturing housing loans.

25. Evidence by Wall Street firms on home equity loans strongly suggests that high quality borrowers do take advantage of a decline in interest rates to refinance a loan. In contrast, low quality borrowers tend not to take advantage of a decline in interest rates to refinance.

    A. What is the appropriate valuation approach (option-adjusted spread approach or zero-volatility spread approach) to value home equity loan-backed securities where the underlying pool of loans are those of high quality borrowers? Explain why.

    B. What is the appropriate valuation approach (option-adjusted spread approach or zero-volatility spread approach) to value home equity loan-backed securities where the underlying pool of loans are those of low quality borrowers? Explain why.

APPENDIX A

Appendix A Solutions to End-of-Reading Problems

SOLUTIONS FOR READING 58

1. Credit risk is more general than the statement in the quote. Credit risk encompasses three types of risk: default risk, credit spread risk, and downgrade risk. The quote in the question refers to default risk only. (Credit spread risk is the risk that the credit spread will increase. Downgrade risk is the risk that the issue will be downgraded.) Thus, one should disagree with the statement in the question.

2. **A.** Information in addition to the credit rating that is provided by a rating agency includes rating watches (or credit watches), rating outlooks, and transition tables. The first two are useful in assessing default risk, while the last is useful for assessing downgrade risk.

    When an issue is put on rating watch (credit watch), this means that the rating agency is reviewing the issue with the potential for an upgrade or a downgrade. A rating outlook is a projection of whether an issue in the long term (from six months to two years) is likely to be upgraded (positive outlook), downgraded (negative outlook), or maintain its current rating (stable outlook).

    A rating transition table is published periodically by a rating agency. It shows the percentage of issues of each rating at the beginning of a period that was downgraded or upgraded by the end of the time period.

    B. A credit rating is a forward-looking assessment of credit risk. For long-term debt obligations, it is an assessment of (1) the probability of default and (2) the relative magnitude of the loss should a default occur. For short-term debt obligations, a credit rating is an assessment of only the probability of default.

3. The factors considered include strategic direction of management, financial philosophy, management's track record, succession planning, and control systems.

4. **A.** While there are various forms of back-up credit facilities, some forms are stronger than others. A back-up credit facility where the lender is contractually bound and contains no provisions that permit the lender to refuse to provide funds is the strongest form. There are non-contractual facilities such as lines of credit. For such facilities, the analyst should be concerned because the lender has the right to refuse to lend funds.

    B. A "material adverse change clause" in a back-up credit facility allows a bank to refuse funding if the bank feels that the borrower's financial condition or operating position has deteriorated significantly. Consequently, as explained in part a, this is a weaker form of back-up credit facility.

5. **A.** With high-yield issuers there tends to be more bank loans in the debt structure and the loans tend to be short term. Also, the loans tend to be floating rate rather than fixed. As a result, the analyst must look at the ability of the issuer to access short-term funding sources for liquidity to meet not only possible higher interest payments (when interest rates rise), but to pay off a maturing loan. High-yield issuers, however, have fewer alternatives for short-term funding sources than high-grade issuers.

B. At any given point in time, the cushion (as measured by coverage ratios) may be high. However, the concern is with future cash flows to satisfy obligations. If the coverage ratio is adequate and is predicted to change little in the future and the degree of confidence in the prediction is high, that situation would give greater comfort to a bondholder than one where the coverage ratio is extremely high but can fluctuate substantially in the future. Because of this variability it is difficult to assign a high degree of confidence to coverage ratios that are projected and there must be recognition that the coverage ratio may fall well below acceptable levels.

C. Financial flexibility means the ability to sustain operations should there be a down turn in business and to sustain current dividends without reliance on external funding.

D. Unfunded pension liabilities may not be listed as debt but they are effectively a form of borrowing by the firm. Hence, Moody's is considering them as part of the debt obligation. Guarantees represent potential liabilities if the corporate entity whose debt is guaranteed does not meet its obligations. If Moody's views the obligation as one that the company may have to satisfy, the obligation of the corporate entity whose debt is guaranteed is a form of borrowing and should be included in total debt.

E. Ratios represent a snapshot of a particular aspect of a firm's financial position at a given point in time. Ratings reflect an assessment of the future financial position and the assessment of future cash flows. This involves looking at a myriad of factors that impact future cash flows such as competition, potential earnings growth, and future capital requirements. This is a major limitation of ratio analysis as a sole indicator of an entity's financial strength—it is not forward looking in that it does not look at how factors in the future can alter cash flows.

6. By analyzing the statement of cash flows, creditors can examine such aspects of the business as (1) the source of financing for business operations, (2) the company's ability to meet its debt obligations, (3) the company's ability to finance expansion through operating cash flow, (4) the company's ability to pay dividends, and (5) the flexibility given to management in financing its operations.

7. A. Free operating cash flow, according to S&P, is obtained by reducing operating cash flow by capital expenditures.

Discretionary cash flow is found by reducing free operating cash flow by cash dividends.

Prefinancing financing cash flow is found by adjusting discretionary cash flow by (1) decreasing it by acquisitions and (2) increasing it by asset disposals, and then further adjusting by the net of other sources (uses) of cash.

B. Free operating cash flow according to S&P is the cash flow that can be used to pay dividends and make acquisitions. Reducing free operating cash flow by cash dividends gives discretionary cash flow that management can use to make acquisitions. Adjusting discretionary cash flow for managerial discretionary decisions for acquisition of other companies, the disposal of assets (e.g., lines of business or subsidiaries), and others sources or uses of cash gives prefinancing cash flow, which represents the extent to which company cash flow from all internal sources have been sufficient to cover all internal needs.

8. **A.** Since covenants deal with limitations and restrictions on the borrower's activities, certain covenants provide protection for a bondholder and this protection must be factored into the credit analysis.

   B. A negative covenant is one that requires the borrower not to take certain actions. An example of a negative covenant is a restriction on the company's ability to incur additional debt.

   C. A review of the covenants in a high-yield corporate issue may help the analyst understand management strategy regarding future funding and operational strategies to determine if they are consistent with what management is stating to investors. Loopholes in covenants may provide further clues as to management's future plans.

9. Agency risk is the risk that management will make decisions in its own self interest, thereby reducing firm value.

10. **A.** The motivation for developing a corporate governance rating is the belief that in the long run firms that focus on corporate governance and transparency will generate superior returns and economic performance and lower their cost of capital.

    B. Every firm that has developed a corporate governance rating uses its own criteria. Typically what is considered (using the S&P criteria) is ownership structure and external influences, shareholder rights and stakeholder relations, transparency, disclosure and audit process, and board structure and effectiveness.

11. **A.** The typical structure for a high-yield corporate issuer includes bank debt. This debt is senior to all other debt claims. As a result, bonds that are labeled "senior bonds" are subordinated to bank debt despite their title.

    B. The interest for a zero-coupon bond increases over time due to the accrual of the unpaid interest. As a result, assuming no other changes in the firm's debt structure, the percentage of a zero-coupon bond in the firm's debt structure increases over time. If these bonds are senior bonds (senior relative to the subordinated bonds, not to bank debt as discussed in part a), then the zero-coupon bond's percentage increases relative to the subordinated bonds. This may increase the credit risk of the subordinated bonds over time and adversely impact subordinated bondholders in the event of bankruptcy. Hence, in the quote Mr. Bernstein is stating that it is preferred to have zero-coupon bonds (or any deferred coupon bonds) as subordinated bonds rather than senior bonds.

12. In a holding company structure, the parent company issues debt as well as the operating subsidiaries. Consequently, the analyst in projecting the cash flows available to pay the creditors of the holding company must understand any restrictions on payments that can be made to the parent company (dividends or loans) by the operating subsidiaries.

13. In the risk-return spectrum, high-yield bonds are between high-grade corporate bonds and common stocks. High-yield corporate bonds have an equity component as evidenced by the higher correlation between stock returns and high-yield bond returns compared to high-grade bond returns and high-yield bond returns. Consequently, some portfolio managers such as Mr. Esser firmly believe that high-yield bond analysis should be viewed from an equity analyst's perspective. It is believed that the equity approach can provide more insight than traditional credit analysis. A manager using an equity approach, it is believed by Mr. Esser, will give that manager an

edge in identifying attractive issues for purchase or avoiding or disposing of unattractive issues relative to other managers who rely solely on traditional credit analysis.

14. Given the projected cash flow for the collateral under various scenarios, the next step is to determine how the cash flow would be distributed among the different tranches in the structure. So, by itself projection of the cash flow is insufficient because it will not indicate if any, or all, of the tranches (i.e., bonds) will realize a loss. The allocation of the cash flow in a given scenario will permit the determination of which tranches may realize losses and the extent of those losses.

15. A servicer may be required to make advances to cover interest payments to bondholders when there are delinquencies. Consequently, the servicer must have the financial capacity to fulfill this obligation. This requires an assessment of the financial condition of the servicer.

16. **A.** In a "true securitization" the role of the servicer is basically routine. There are basic daily administrative tasks performed and the cash flow does not depend to any significant extent on the servicer to perform. Where the role of the servicer is more than administrative in order to generate the cash flow, the transaction is referred to as a "hybrid transaction."

B. The analysis of a "hybrid transaction" uses both the standard methodology for evaluating an asset-backed security transaction and the analysis of a corporate entity—basically as a service business. The latter approach is referred to by S&P as a "quasi-corporate" approach. The final assessment of a rating agency is a subjective weighting of the credit quality using the two approaches. The more the transaction's cash flow is dependent on the performance of the servicer, the greater the weight given to the quasi-corporate approach.

17. The four basic categories are: (1) the issuer's debt structure; (2) the issuer's ability and political discipline to maintain sound budgetary policy; (3) the specific local taxes and intergovernmental revenues available to the issuer, as well as obtaining historical information on tax collection rates, and; (4) the issuer's overall socioeconomic environment.

18. **A.** The payment of the obligations of a revenue bond must come from the cash flow generated from the enterprise for which the bonds were issued. Thus, just as in the case of a corporate bond, the underlying principle in assessing an issuer's credit worthiness is whether or not sufficient cash flow will be generated to satisfy the obligations due bondholders.

B. A rate covenant specifies how charges will be set on the product or service sold by the enterprise. A rate covenant is included so the enterprise will set charges so as to satisfy both expenses and debt servicing, or to create a certain amount of reserves.

19. Because the issuer is a sovereign entity, if the issuer refuses to pay there is little legal remedy for the debt holder. Thus, it becomes necessary to understand the factors other than legal recourse that will increase the likelihood that the issuer will repay.

20. **A.** The reason for assigning two ratings is that the currency denomination of the payments may be either the local currency or a foreign currency. (Historically, the default frequency had differed by the currency denomination of the debt. It has been observed by rating agencies that defaults have been greater on foreign currency denominated debt.)

B. To generate sufficient local currency to satisfy its debt obligations denominated in its local currency, a government must be willing to raise taxes and control its domestic financial system. In contrast, a national government must purchase foreign currency to meet a debt obligation in that foreign currency. Consequently, a government has less control with respect to its exchange rate and faces exchange rate risk (i.e., depreciation of its currency) when it issues a foreign currency denominated bond.

The implication of this is that the factors a rating agency will emphasize in assessing the credit worthiness of a national government's local currency debt and foreign currency debt will differ to some extent. S&P, for example, focuses on domestic government policies that affect the likelihood of the government's ability to repay local currency denominated debt. For foreign currency debt, the same rating agency focuses on the interaction of domestic and foreign government policies. Specifically, the areas of analysis that S&P assesses is a country's balance of payments and the structure of its external balance sheet (i.e., the net public debt, total net external debt, and net external liabilities).

21. When analyzing domestic corporate bonds an analyst does factor in intangible and non-quantitative elements, the most important of which is the quality of management. Moreover, a factor that is considered in assessing the credit quality of a tax-backed municipal bond issue is the willingness of the issuing entity to generate funds to repay the obligation by raising taxes. So, the statement that intangible and non-quantitative elements are not considered in analyzing domestic corporate and domestic municipal bonds but only with sovereign bonds is incorrect.

22. All the financial ratios—actual and projected for 2001—clearly indicate that the credit worthiness of Krane Products is improving. Using as benchmarks the S&P median ratios, the coverage ratios were already by fiscal year 2000 approaching that of the median BBB rated issuer. The capitalization ratios, while improving, were still well below that of the median BBB rated issuer. Consequently, by fiscal year 2000 an analyst would have been well advised to monitor this issuer's credit for a possible upgrade and to examine how it was trading in the market. That is, was it trading like a BB or BBB credit?

If Ms. Andrews' projections are correct for fiscal year 2001, the ratios shown in the table are at least as good as the median BBB rated company. Consequently, based on her projections she would recommend the purchase of Krane Products Inc. bonds if that issuer's bonds continue to trade like a BB credit since, based on her analysis, the bonds are likely to be upgraded to BBB.

23. Credit scoring models tend to classify firms as likely to default, not only most of the firms that do eventually default, but also many firms that do not default. Some of the firms that appear to be troubled credits by credit scoring models hire new management and are then revitalized without defaulting. Thus, a credit analyst must recognize the possibility of a turnaround for a firm that the model has classified as likely to default. Furthermore, there are reasons why a firm may default that have nothing to do with the financial variables used in a credit scoring model.

24. Structural models and reduced form models are the two types of credit risk models for valuing corporate bonds.

The foundation of structural models, also know as "firm-value models," is the Black-Scholes-Merton option pricing model. The basic idea of these models is that a company defaults on its debt if the value of the assets of the company falls below a certain default point. The default process of a corporation is driven by the value of its assets. Since the value of any option depends on the volatility of the asset value in structural models, the probability of default is explicitly linked to the expected volatility of a corporation's asset value. Thus, in structural models, both the default process and recovery rates should a bankruptcy occur depend on the corporation's structural characteristics.

Reduced form models do not look "inside the firm," but instead model directly the probability of default or downgrade. That is, the default process and the recovery process are (1) modeled independently of the corporation's structural features and (2) are independent of each other.

SOLUTIONS FOR READING 59

Solutions are for Practice Questions found in Reading

1. A. The daily percentage change in yield for each trading day is shown below in the next to the last column:

t	y_t	$X_t = 100 [Ln (y_t/y_{t-1})]$	$(X_t - \bar{X})^2$
0	7.17400		
1	7.19400	0.27840	0.19820
2	7.21800	0.33306	0.24985
3	7.15100	−0.93257	0.58641
4	7.02500	−1.77770	2.59500
5	7.02400	−0.01424	0.02328
6	7.03000	0.08538	0.06360
7	7.02000	−0.14235	0.00060
8	6.96400	−0.80092	0.40211
9	6.90400	−0.86531	0.48792
10	6.89671	−0.10565	0.00374
11	6.85300	−0.63580	0.21996
12	6.87100	0.26231	0.18414
13	6.88300	0.17449	0.11648
14	6.87500	−0.11630	0.00255
15	6.87800	0.04363	0.04428
16	6.80400	−1.08172	0.83709
17	6.84300	0.57156	0.54517
18	6.79500	−0.70392	0.28850
19	6.79500	0.00000	0.02782
20	6.85400	0.86454	1.06365
21	6.81000	−0.64403	0.22775
22	6.77300	−0.54480	0.14289
23	6.86700	1.37832	2.38739
24	6.88700	0.29082	0.20942
25	6.88100	−0.08716	0.00634
	Total	−4.16994	10.91412

B. The daily standard deviation is computed as follows:

$$\text{sample mean} = \overline{X} = \frac{-4.16994\%}{25} = -0.166798\%$$

$$\text{variance} = \frac{10.91412\%}{25 - 1} = 0.4547550\%$$

$$\text{std dev} = \sqrt{0.4547550\%} = 0.67436\%$$

2. The daily standard deviation is 0.67436% and the annualized standard deviation based on an assumed number of trading days in a year is:

250 days	260 days	365 days
10.66%	10.87%	12.88%

1. Historically, four shapes have been observed for the yield curve. A positively sloping or normal yield curve is where the longer the maturity, the higher the yield. A flat yield curve is where the yield for all maturities is approximately the same. A negatively sloped or inverted yield curve is where yield decreases as maturity increases. A humped yield curve is where yield increases for a range of maturities and then decreases.

2. The slope of the yield curve is measured by the difference between long-term Treasury yields and short-term Treasury yields. While there is no industrywide accepted definition of the maturity used for the long-end and the maturity for the short-end of the yield curve, some market participants define the slope of the yield curve as the difference between the 30-year yield and the 3-month yield while other market participants define the slope of the yield curve as the difference between the 30-year yield and the 2-year yield. The more accepted measure is the latter. However, for some sectors of the bond market such as the mortgage sector, the slope of the yield curve is measured by the spread between the 10-year yield and 2-year yield.

3. Historically, the slope of the long end of the yield curve has been flatter than the slope of the short end of the yield curve.

4. **A.** Studies have shown that there have been three factors that affect Treasury returns: (1) changes in the level of yields, (2) changes in the slope of the yield curve, and (3) changes in the curvature of the yield curve.

   B. The most important factor is the change in the level of interest rates.

   C. The implication is that the manager of a Treasury portfolio should control for its exposure to changes in the level of interest rates. For this reason it is important to have a measure such as duration to quantify exposure to a parallel shift in the yield curve.

   D. The second most important factor is changes in the yield curve slope.

   E. The implication is that a measure such as duration must be supplemented with information about a portfolio's exposure to changes in the slope of the yield curve—a measure such as key rate duration.

5. **A.** One limitation is that there is a large gap between maturities for the on-the-run issues and a linear extrapolation is used to get the yield for maturities between the on-the-runs. A second limitation is that information is lost about the yield on other Treasury securities. Finally, one or more of the on-the-run issues may be on special in the repo market and thereby distort the true yield for these issues.

   B. Since there may be more than one Treasury issue for a given maturity and since there are callable securities and securities trading at a price different from par (leading to tax issues), a methodology for handling these problems must be used. The bootstrapping methodology does not deal with such problems.

6. **A** There are three problems with using the observed rates on Treasury strips (1) there is a liquidity premium for the observed yields in the strips market because strips are not as liquid as Treasury coupon securities; (2) the tax treatment of strips is different from that of Treasury coupon securities—the accrued interest on strips is taxed even

though no cash is received by the investor—resulting in the yield on strips reflecting this tax disadvantage; and, (3) there are maturity sectors where non-U.S. investors find it advantageous to trade off yield for tax advantages in their country that are associated with a strip.

B. A practitioner may restrict the use of Treasury strips to construct the theoretical spot rate curve to coupon strips because of the tax aspect mentioned in part a. Specifically, certain foreign tax authorities allow their citizens to treat the difference between the maturity value and the purchase price as a capital gain and tax this gain at a favorable tax rate. Some will grant this favorable treatment only when the strip is created from the principal rather than the coupon. Any such bias can be avoided by just using coupon strips.

7. The advantages are that (1) there are typically more points available to construct a swap curve than a government bond yield curve; (2) there are no distortions in yields caused by bonds being on special in the repo market; and (3) comparisons across countries are easier because there is almost no government regulation and no distortions caused by tax benefits.

8. If the country has a liquid swap market with a wide spectrum of maturities, a swap curve can be developed. By the bootstrapping methodology, the spot rate curve for that country can be derived.

9. **A.** The convention in the swap market is to quote the fixed rate (i.e., the swap rate) as a spread over an estimated government yield for a bond with the same maturity as the swap. That spread is called the swap spread.

   B. Since the credit risk in a swap is that the counterparty will fail to make the contractual payments and typically the counterparty is a high credit quality bank, the swap spread is a gauge of the credit risk associated with the banking sector.

10. **A.** The pure expectations theory postulates that no systematic factors other than expected future short-term rates affect forward rates. According to the pure expectations theory, forward rates exclusively represent expected future rates. Thus, the entire term structure at a given time reflects the market's current expectations of the family of future short-term rates.

   B. The pure expectations theory neglects the risks inherent in investing in bonds. If forward rates were perfect predictors of future interest rates, then the future prices of bonds would be known with certainty. The return over any investment period would be certain and independent of the maturity of the instrument acquired. However, with the uncertainty about future interest rates and, therefore, about future prices of bonds, these instruments become risky investments in the sense that the return over some investment horizon is unknown.

11. The broadest interpretation of the pure expectations theory asserts that there is no difference in the 4-year total return if an investor purchased a 7-year zero-coupon bond or a 15-year zero-coupon bond.

12. The local expectations form of the pure expectations theory asserts that the total return over a 6-month horizon for a 5-year zero-coupon bond would be the same as for a 2-year zero-coupon bond.

13. The first sentence of the statement is correct. Moreover, it is correct that studies have shown that forward rates are poor predictors of future interest rates. However, the last sentence of the statement is incorrect. Forward rates should not be ignored because they indicate break-even rates and rates that can be locked in. So, they play an important role in investment decisions.

14. The two interpretations of forward rates are that they are break-even rates and they are rates that can be locked in.

A. For the 1-year forward rate seven years from now of 6.4% the two interpretations are as follows:

(i) 6.4% is the rate that will make an investor indifferent between buying an 8-year zero-coupon bond or investing in a 7-year zero-coupon bond and when it matures reinvesting in a zero-coupon bond that matures in one year, and

(ii) 6.4% is the rate that can be locked in today by buying an 8-year zero-coupon bond rather than investing in a 7-year zero-coupon bond and when it matures reinvesting in a zero-coupon bond that matures in one year.

B. For the 2-year forward rate one year from now of 6.2% the two interpretations are as follows:

(i) 6.2% is the rate that will make an investor indifferent between buying a 3-year zero-coupon bond or investing in a 1-year zero-coupon bond and when it matures reinvesting in a zero-coupon bond that matures in two years, and

(ii) 6.2% is the rate that can be locked in today by buying a 3-year zero-coupon bond rather than investing in a 1-year zero-coupon bond and when it matures reinvesting in a zero-coupon bond that matures in two years.

C. For the 8-year forward rate three years from now of 7.1% the two interpretations are as follows:

(i) 7.1% is the rate that will make an investor indifferent between buying an 11-year zero-coupon bond or investing in a 3-year zero-coupon bond and when it matures reinvesting in a zero-coupon bond that matures in eight years, and

(ii) 7.1% is the rate that can be locked in today by buying an 11-year zero-coupon bond rather than investing in a 3-year zero-coupon bond and when it matures reinvesting in a zero-coupon bond that matures in eight years.

15. All expectations theories—the pure expectations theory, the liquidity preference theory, and the preferred habitat theory—share a hypothesis about the behavior of short-term forward rates and also assume that the forward rates in current long-term bonds are closely related to the market's expectations about future short-term rates. While the pure expectations theory postulates that no systematic factors other than expected future short-term rates affect forward rates, the liquidity preference theory and the preferred habitat theory postulate that there are other factors and therefore are referred to as biased expectations theories. The liquidity preference theory asserts that investors demand a liquidity premium for extending maturity so that the forward rates are biased by this premium. The preferred habitat theory asserts that investors must be induced by a yield premium in order to accept the risks associated with shifting funds out of their preferred sector and forward rates embody the premium for this inducement.

16. A. Proponents of the pure expectations theory would assert that an upward sloping yield curve is a market's forecast of a rise in interest rates. If that is correct, an expected rise in interest rates would mean that the manager should shorten or reduce the duration (i.e., interest rate risk) of the portfolio. However, the pure expectations has serious pitfalls and the forward rates are not good predictors of future interest rates.

B. The preferred habitat form of the biased expectations theory is consistent with the shape of the spot rate curve observed. The preferred habitat theory asserts that if there is an imbalance between the supply and demand for funds within a given maturity sector, market participants (i.e., borrowers and investors) will agree to shift their financing and investing activities out of their preferred maturity sector to take advantage of any such imbalance. However, participants will demand compensation for shifting out of their preferred maturity sector in the form of a yield premium. Consequently, any shape for the spot rate curve (and yield curve) can result, such as the one observed in the question. Therefore, the trustee's statement is incorrect.

(*Note:* The question only asked about *expectations* theories of the term structure of interest rates. Another theory, the market segmentation theory described in Level 1 asserts that when there are supply and demand imbalances within a maturity sector, market participants will not shift out of their preferred maturity sector. Consequently, different maturity sectors reflect supply and demand imbalances within each sector and the type of yield curve observed in the question is possible.)

17. A. Portfolio A is the bullet portfolio because its 10-year key rate duration dominates by far the key rate duration for the other maturities. Portfolio B is the laddered portfolio because the key rate durations after year 2 are roughly equal. Portfolio C is the barbell portfolio with the short end of the barbell at 5 years and the long end of the barbell at 20 years.

B. The bullet portfolio has the highest 10-year key rate duration and will therefore increase the most if the 10-year spot rate decreases while the key rates for the other maturities do not change much.

C. Adding up the key rate durations for each portfolio gives 6.2. This is the duration of all three portfolios if the spot rate for all key maturities changes by the same number of basis points—that is, a parallel shift in the spot rate for the key maturities.

18. The information for computing the daily standard deviation for yield volatility is shown below:

t	y_t	$X_t = 100 [\text{Ln} (y_t/y_{t-1})]$	$(X_t - \bar{X})^2$
0	5.854		
1	5.843	−0.18808	0.00060
2	5.774	−1.18793	1.04922
3	5.719	−0.95711	0.62964
4	5.726	0.12232	0.08176
5	5.761	0.60939	0.59753
6	5.797	0.62295	0.61868
7	5.720	−1.33717	1.37724
8	5.755	0.61002	0.59851
9	5.787	0.55450	0.51568
10	5.759	−0.48502	0.10330
	Total	−1.63613	5.57216825

$$\text{sample mean} = \overline{X} = \frac{-1.63613}{10} = -0.163613\%$$

$$\text{variance} = \frac{5.57216825}{10 - 1} = 0.6191298$$

$$\text{std dev} = \sqrt{0.6191298} = 0.786848\%$$

19. A. Using 250 days: $\sqrt{250}\,(0.786848\%) = 12.44\%$

B. Using 260 days: $\sqrt{260}\,(0.786848\%) = 12.69\%$

C. Using 365 days: $\sqrt{365}\,(0.786848\%) = 15.03\%$

20. This is not necessarily the case because with the same data there are still choices that the managers must make that may result in quite different estimates of historical volatility. These choices include the number of days to use and the annualization of the daily standard deviation.

21. Since the current level of the 2-year Treasury yield is 5%, then the annual standard deviation of 7% translates into a 35 basis point (5% times 7%) standard deviation. Assuming that yield volatility is approximately normally distributed, we can use the normal distribution to construct an interval or range for what the future yield will be. There is a 68.3% probability that the yield will be between one standard deviation below and above the expected value. The expected value is the prevailing yield. If the annual standard deviation is 35 basis points and the prevailing yield is 5%, then there is a 68.3% probability that the yield next year will be between 4.65% (5% minus 35 basis points) and 5.35% (5% plus 35 basis points). There is a 99.7% probability that the yield next year will be within three standard deviations. In our case, three standard deviations is 105 basis points. Therefore there is a 99.7% probability that the yield will be between 3.95% (5% minus 105 basis points) and 6.05% (5% plus 105 basis points).

22. A. Yield volatility can be estimated from the observed prices of interest rate options and caps. A yield volatility estimated in this way is called implied volatility and is based on some option pricing model. An input to any option pricing model in which the underlying is a Treasury security or Treasury futures contract is expected yield volatility. If the observed price of an option is assumed to be the fair price and the option pricing model is assumed to be the model that would generate that fair price, then the implied yield volatility is the yield volatility that when used as an input into the option pricing model would produce the observed option price.

B. The problems with using implied volatility are that (1) it is assumed the option pricing model is correct, and (2) since option pricing models typically assume that volatility is constant over the life of the option interpreting an implied volatility becomes difficult.

23. A. There are reasons to believe that market participants give greater weight to recent movements in yield when determining volatility. To incorporate this belief into the estimation of historical volatility, different weights can be assigned to the observed changes in daily yields. More specifically, observations further in the past should be given less weight.

B. Some market practitioners argue that in forecasting volatility the expected value or mean that should be used in the formula for the variance is zero.

SOLUTIONS FOR READING 60

Solutions are for Practice Questions found in Reading

1.

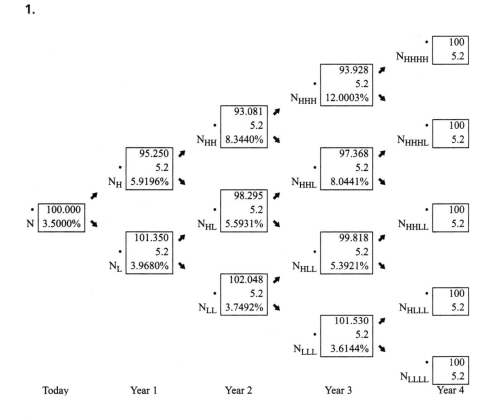

| Today | Year 1 | Year 2 | Year 3 | Year 4 |

2. The binomial interest rate tree is the one in Practice Question 1. Below is the tree with the values completed at each node. As can be seen, the root of the tree is 104.643, the arbitrage-free value found in the reading for this option-free bond.

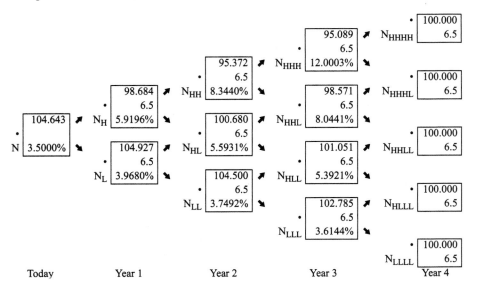

| Today | Year 1 | Year 2 | Year 3 | Year 4 |

Fixed Income Analysis for the Chartered Financial Analyst ® Program, Second Edition, edited by Frank J. Fabozzi, Copyright © 2005 by CFA Institute. Reprinted with permission.

3. A. The root of the binomial interest rate tree below shows that the arbitrage-free value of this bond is 102.108.

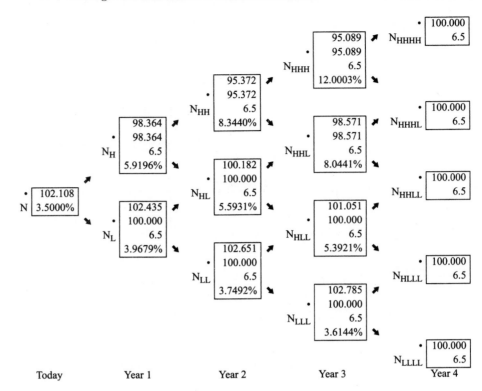

B. The arbitrage-free value at 20% is less than the arbitrage-free value at 10% (102.108 versus 102.899). This is because the value of the embedded call option is greater the higher the volatility.

4. The tree below shows that the OAS is −6 basis points for the 6.5% callable bond assuming 20% volatility. (Each 1-year rate is 6 basis points less than in Practice Question 1.)

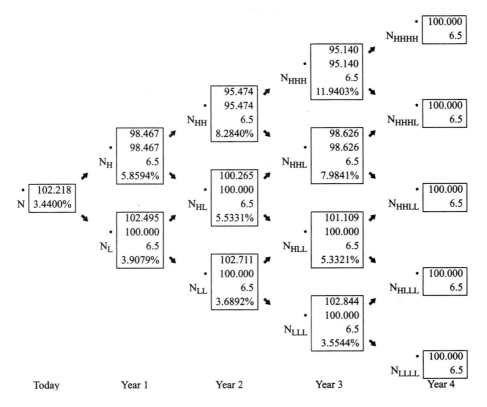

5. The tree below shows the arbitrage-free value for a putable bond with four years to maturity, a coupon rate of 6.5%, and putable in one year at 100 assuming a 20% volatility is 106.010.

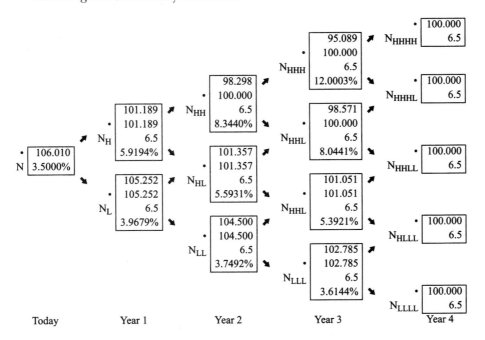

1. This statement is incorrect. While there are different models such as the binomial and trinomial models, the basic features of all these models are the same. They all involve assessing the cash flow at each node in the interest rate tree and determining whether or not to adjust the cash flow based on the embedded options. All these models require a rule for calling the issue and all require an assumption about the volatility of interest rates. The backward induction method is used for all these models.

2. The procedure for determining the value of a bond with an embedded option starts at the maturity date on the interest rate tree (i.e., the end of the tree) and values the bond moving backward to the root of the tree—which is today's value. Hence the procedure is called backward induction.

3. The reason is that in constructing the interest rate tree the on-the-run issues are used and interest rates on the tree must be such that if the on-the-run issue is valued using the tree, the model will produce the market value of the on-the-run issue. When a model produces the market value of the on-the-run issues it is said to be "calibrated to the market" or "arbitrage free."

4. **A.** In the interest rate tree, the forward rates for a given period are shown at each node. (In the illustrations in the reading, each period is one year.) Since there is more than one node for each period (after the root of the tree), there is not one forward rate for a given period but several forward rates.

   B. The binomial interest rate tree is constructed based on an assumption about interest rate volatility. If a different volatility assumption is made, a new interest rate tree is constructed and therefore there are different interest rates at the nodes for a given period and therefore a different set of forward rates.

5. **A.**

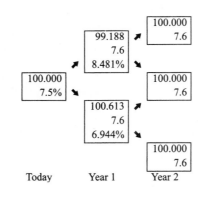

B.

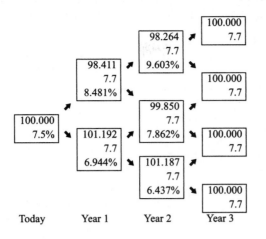

C. The value of an 8.5% coupon 3-year bond using the spot rates is as follows:

$$\frac{8.5}{(1.07500)} + \frac{8.5}{(1.07604)^2} + \frac{108.5}{(1.07710)^3} = \$102.076$$

D.

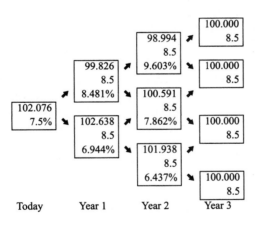

E. The value of this callable bond is 100.722.

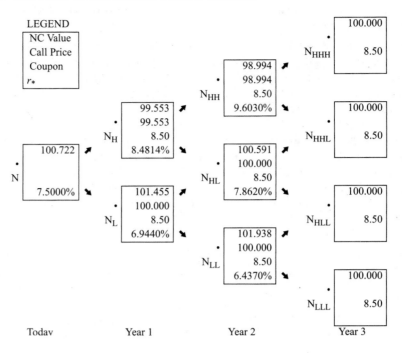

F. The value of the embedded call option is $1.354 which is equal to the value of the option-free bond ($102.076) minus the value of the callable bond ($100.722).

6. The statement is wrong. The option-adjusted spread is a byproduct (i.e., is obtained from) of a valuation model. Any assumptions that must be made in a valuation model to obtain the arbitrage-value of a bond also apply to the option-adjusted spread. For example, if a valuation model assumes that interest rate volatility is $x\%$, then the OAS is based on a volatility of $x\%$.

7. Despite the fact that both the dealer and the pricing service used the same model and same benchmark, there are other inputs to the model that could cause a 1 point difference. The major reason is probably that the two may have used a different volatility assumption. A second reason is that the call rule used by the two may be quite different.

8. One of the first questions should be what is the benchmark that the spread is relative to. The other key question is what is the assumed interest rate volatility.

9. This statement is not necessarily correct. An OAS can be computed based on any benchmark interest rates. For example, the on-the-run rates for the issuer or the on-the-run rates for issuers in the same bond sector and having the same credit rating can be used.

10. A. The value of a callable bond is equal to the value of an otherwise option-free bond minus the value of the embedded call option. The value of the embedded call option is higher the greater the assumed interest rate volatility. Therefore, a higher value for the embedded call option is subtracted from the value of the option-free bond, resulting in a lower value for the callable bond.

B. The value of a putable bond is equal to the value of an otherwise option-free bond plus the value of the embedded put option. The value of the embedded put option is higher the greater the assumed interest rate volatility. Therefore, a higher value for the embedded put option is added to the value of the option-free bond, resulting in a higher value of the putable bond.

11. While it is true that the value of a bond that is callable and putable is conceptually equal to the value of the option-free bond adjusted for the value of the put option and the value of the call option, this is not the procedure used in a model such as the binomial model that uses the backward induction method. The reason is that these embedded options exist simultaneously so that the exercise of one option would extinguish the value of the other option. What is done in the backward induction method is to value the callable/putable bond by simultaneously considering the two embedded options. The way this works is at each node it will be determined whether or not the call option will be exercised based on the call rule and then whether or not the put option will be exercised. If either option is exercised, the corresponding exercise value for the bond is used in subsequent calculations in the backward induction process.

12. There are two types of duration and convexity—modified and effective. Modified forms of duration and convexity assume that when interest rates change the cash flows do not change. In contrast, the effective forms assume that when interest rates change the cash flows may change. When the binomial model is used to determine the values when rates are increased and decreased, the new values reflect how the cash flows may change. That is, the cash flow at each node of the binomial interest tree when rates are shifted up and down are allowed to change depending on the rules for when an option will be exercised. Thus, the resulting duration and convexity are effective duration and convexity.

13. It is true that there is a standard formula for computing duration by shocking (i.e., changing) interest rates and substituting the values computed in the duration formula. However, for a bond with an embedded option, such as a callable bond, it is necessary to have a valuation model (such as the binomial model) to determine the value of the bond when interest rates are changed. Valuation models can give different values for the same bond depending on the assumptions used. For example, suppose that the vendor and the dealer use the same valuation model but employ (1) a different volatility assumption, (2) different benchmark interest rates, and (3) a different call rule. The values produced by the two models that are substituted into the (effective) duration formula can result in the difference of 5.4 versus 4.5.

14. It is assumed that the option-adjusted spread is constant when interest rates change.

15. The starting point is defining what the benchmark interest rates are that the spread is being measured relative to. It is based on the benchmark that one interprets what the option-adjusted spread is compensation for.

Manager 1 is wrong. The option-adjusted spread is adjusting any spread for the option risk. That is, it is netting out from the spread the option risk.

Manager 2 is partially correct. If the benchmark interest rates are the on-the-run Treasury issues, then the option-adjusted spread is indicating compensation for credit risk. But it also captures liquidity risk. Moreover, it is not necessarily true that the benchmark interest rates are the on-the-run Treasury rates.

Manager 3 is correct if the benchmark interest rates are the on-the-run Treasury issues. However, other benchmark interest rates have been used and in such cases Manager 3's interpretation would be incorrect.

Manager 4 is incorrect. Even if the benchmark interest rates are the rates for the issuer's on-the-run issues, the spread would not reflect compensation for credit risk.

16. It is incorrect to state that the 20 basis point OAS is a spread over the issuer's 10-year on-the-run issue. That is, it is not a spread over one point on the yield curve. Rather, from the issuer's on-the-run yield curve, the rates at each node on the interest rate tree are determined. These rates are the one-period forward rates. The OAS is the spread that when added to all these forward rates will produce a value for the callable bond equal to the market price of the bond. So, it is a spread over the forward rates in the interest rate tree which are in turn generated from the benchmark interest rates.

17. Without knowing the benchmark interest rate used to compute the OAS, no statement can be made. If the benchmark is the Treasury sector or a corporate sector with a higher credit quality than the issue being analyzed, then the statement is correct. However, if the benchmark is the issuer's yield curve, then an OAS of zero means that the issue is fairly priced.

18. A. The coupon rate on a floater is paid in arrears. This means that for a floater the rate determined in the current period is not paid until the end of the period (or beginning of the next period). This requires that an adjustment be made to the backward induction method.

B. The adjustment is made to the backward induction method by discounting the coupon payment to be made in the next period for a floater based on the beginning of the period reference rate.

C. A cap on a floater is handled by determining at each node if the cap is reached. At a node where the coupon rate exceeds the cap, the coupon rate is replaced by the capped rate.

19. A. A convertible bond grants the investor the option to call the common stock of the issuer. Thus, a convertible bond has an embedded call option on the common stock. However, most convertible bonds are callable. That is, there is a second embedded call option granting the issuer the right to retire the bond.

B. The complication that arises is that one of the options, the call on the common stock granted to the investor, depends on the future price of the common stock. However, the call on the bond granted to the issuer depends on future interest rates. Thus, valuing a callable convertible bond requires including in one valuation model both future stock price movements and future interest rate movements.

20. The conversion ratio is found by dividing the par value of $1,000 by the conversion price stated in the prospectus of $45 per share. The conversion ratio is then 22.22 ($1,000/$45).

21. A. conversion value = market price of common stock × conversion ratio
$$= \$25 \times 30 = \$750$$

B. market conversion price
$$= \frac{\text{market price of convertible bond}}{\text{conversion ratio}} = \frac{\$900}{30} = \$30$$

C. conversion premium per share
$$= \text{market conversion price} - \text{market price of common stock}$$
$$= \$30 - \$25 = \$5$$

D. conversion premium ratio

$$= \frac{\text{conversion premium per share}}{\text{market price of common stock}} = \frac{\$5}{\$25} = 20\%$$

E. premium over straight value $= \frac{\text{market price of convertible bond}}{\text{straight value}} - 1$

$$= \frac{\$900}{\$700} - 1 = 28.6\%$$

F. favorable income differential per share

$$= \frac{\text{coupon interest from bond} - \text{conversion ratio} \times \text{dividend per share}}{\text{conversion ratio}}$$

$$= \frac{\$85 - (30 \times \$1)}{30} = \$1.833$$

G. premium payback period $= \frac{\text{market conversion premium per share}}{\text{favorable income differential per share}}$

$$= \frac{\$5}{\$1.833} = 2.73 \text{ years}$$

22. A. If the price increases to $54, the conversion value will be

conversion value $= \$54 \times 30 = \$1,620$

Assuming that the convertible bond's price does not exceed the conversion value (that is why the question asked for an approximate return), then the return on the $900 investment in the convertible bond is:

$$\frac{\$1,620}{\$900} - 1 = 0.8 = 80\%$$

B. The return realized if $25 had been invested in the common stock is equal to:

$$\frac{\$54 - \$25}{\$25} = 1.16 = 116\%$$

C. The reason for the lower return by buying the convertible bond rather than the stock directly is that the investor has effectively paid $5 more for the stock.

23. A. If the price decreases to $10, the conversion value will be

conversion value $= \$10 \times 30 = \$300$

However, it is assumed in the question that the straight value is unchanged at $700. The convertible bond will trade at the greater of the straight value or the conversion value. In this case, it is $700. The return is then:

$$\frac{\$700}{\$900} - 1 = -0.22 = -22\%$$

B. The return realized if $25 had been invested in the common stock is equal to:

$$\frac{\$10 - \$25}{\$25} = -0.6 = -60\%$$

C. The return is greater for convertible bond because of the assumption made that the straight value did not change. If the straight value did decline, the loss would be greater than -22% but it would still be probably less than the loss on the direct purchase of the stock. The key here is that the floor (straight value) is what cushion's the decline—but it is moving floor.

24. A. If the stock price is low so that the straight value is considerably higher than the conversion value, the bond will trade much like a straight bond. The convertible in such instances is referred to as a "busted convertible."

B. Since the market value of a busted convertible is very close to that of a straight bond, the premium over straight value would be very small.

C. By restricting the convertible bonds in which Mr. Caywood would invest to higher investment grade ratings, he is reducing credit risk.

D. By seeking bonds not likely to be called, Mr. Caywood is reducing call risk that would result in a forced conversion to the common stock.

25. The measure assumes that the straight value does not decline.

26. A. A "factor" is the stochastic (or random) variable that is assumed to affect the value of a security. The two factors in valuing a convertible bond are the price movement of the underlying common stock (which affects the value of the embedded call option on the common stock) and the movement of interest rates (which affects the value of the embedded call option on the bond).

B. In practice, models used to value convertible bonds have been one-factor models with the factor included being the price movement of the underlying common stock.

SOLUTIONS FOR READING 61

1. A.

Month	Beginning Mortgage	Mortgage Payment	Interest	Sch. Prin Repayment	End of month balance
1	150,000.00	1,023.26	906.25	117.01	149,882.99
2	149,882.99	1,023.26	905.54	117.72	149,765.26
3	149,765.26	1,023.26	904.83	118.43	149,646.83
4	149,646.83	1,023.26	904.12	119.15	149,527.68
5	149,527.68	1,023.26	903.40	119.87	149,407.82
6	149,407.82	1,023.26	902.67	120.59	149,287.22
7	149,287.22	1,023.26	901.94	121.32	149,165.90
8	149,165.90	1,023.26	901.21	122.05	149,043.85
9	149,043.85	1,023.26	900.47	122.79	148,921.06
10	148,921.06	1,023.26	899.73	123.53	148,797.52
11	148,797.52	1,023.26	898.99	124.28	148,673.25
12	148,673.25	1,023.26	898.23	125.03	148,548.21
13	148,548.21	1,023.26	897.48	125.79	148,422.43
14	148,422.43	1,023.26	896.72	126.55	148,295.88

B.

Month	Beginning Mortgage	Mortgage Payment	Interest	Sch. Prin Repayment	End of month balance
357	4,031.97	1,023.26	24.36	998.90	3,033.07
358	3,033.07	1,023.26	18.32	1,004.94	2,028.13
359	2,028.13	1,023.26	12.25	1,011.01	1,017.12
360	1,017.12	1,023.26	6.15	1,017.12	0.00

2. A. The monthly servicing fee is found by dividing the servicing fee of 0.005 (50 basis points) by 12. The monthly servicing fee is therefore 0.0004167. Multiplying the monthly servicing fee by the beginning mortgage balance gives the servicing fee for the month.

Month	Beginning Mortgage	Mortgage Payment	Servicing Fee	Net Interest	Sch. Prin Repayment	End of month balance
1	150,000.00	1,023.26	62.50	843.75	117.01	149,882.99
2	149,882.99	1,023.26	62.45	843.09	117.72	149,765.26
3	149,765.26	1,023.26	62.40	842.43	118.43	149,646.83
4	149,646.83	1,023.26	62.35	841.76	119.15	149,527.68
5	149,527.68	1,023.26	62.30	841.09	119.87	149,407.82
6	149,407.82	1,023.26	62.25	840.42	120.59	149,287.22

B. The investor's cash flow is the sum of the net interest and the scheduled principal repayment.

Month	Net Interest	Sch. Prin Repayment	Investor cash flow
1	843.75	117.01	960.76
2	843.09	117.72	960.81
3	842.43	118.43	960.86
4	841.76	119.15	960.91
5	841.09	119.87	960.96
6	840.42	120.59	961.01

3. The statement is incorrect. While the guarantee by the U.S. government means that there will not be a loss of principal and that interest payments will be made in full, there is uncertainty about the timing of the principal repayments because the borrower may prepay at any time, in whole or in part.

4. A. and B. The weighted average coupon (WAC) and weighted average maturity (WAM) for the mortgage pool are computed below:

Loan	Outstanding mortgage balance	Weight in pool	Mortgage rate	Months remaining	WAC	WAM
1	$215,000	26.06%	6.75%	200	1.7591%	52.12
2	$185,000	22.42%	7.75%	185	1.7379%	41.48
3	$125,000	15.15%	7.25%	192	1.0985%	29.09
4	$100,000	12.12%	7.00%	210	0.8485%	25.45
5	$825,000	24.24%	6.50%	180	1.5758%	43.64
Total	$825,000	100.00%			7.02%	191.79

WAC = 7.02%   WAM = 192 (rounded)

5. A. The SMM is equal to

$$\frac{\$2,450,000}{\$260,000,000 - \$1,000,000} = 0.009459 = 0.9459\%$$

B. Mr. Jamison should interpret the SMM as follows: 0.9459% of the mortgage pool available to prepay in month 42 prepaid in the month.

C. Given the SMM, the CPR is computed using equation (2) in the reading:

$$CPR = 1 - (1 - SMM)^{12}$$

Therefore,

$$CPR = 1 - (1 - 0.009459)^{12} = 0.107790 = 10.78\%$$

D. Mr. Jamison should interpret the CPR as follows: ignoring scheduled principal payments, approximately 10.79% of the outstanding mortgage balance at the beginning of the year will be prepaid by the end of the year.

6. The CPR and SMM for each month are shown below:

Month	PSA	CPR	SMM
5	100	0.010	0.000837
15	80	0.024	0.002022
20	175	0.070	0.006029
27	50	0.027	0.002278
88	200	0.120	0.010596
136	75	0.045	0.003829
220	225	0.135	0.012012

7. According to the PSA prepayment benchmark, after month 30 the CPR is constant over the life of the security. Specifically, it is equal to

$$CPR = 6\% \times (PSA/100)$$

So, for example, if the assumed PSA is 225, the CPR for the life of the security is

$$CPR = 6\% \times (225/100) = 13.5\%$$

Thus, the statement is correct that one CPR can be used to describe the PSA 30 months after the origination of the mortgages.

8. The amount of the prepayment for the month is determined as follows:

$$(\text{Beginning mortgage balance} - \text{scheduled principal payment}) \times SMM$$

We know that

$$(\$537,000,000 - \$440,000) \times SMM$$

The CPR for month 140 assuming 175 PSA is

$$CPR = 6\% \times (175/100) = 10.5\%$$

The SMM is then

$$SMM = 1 - (1 - 0.105)^{0.08333} = 0.009201$$

Therefore, the prepayment in month 140 is

$$(\$537,000,000 - \$440,000) \times 0.009201 = \$4,936,889 \text{ (rounded)}$$

(Note: You will get a slightly different answer if you carried the SMM to more decimal places.)

9. The PSA model, or PSA prepayment benchmark, is not a prepayment model in that it does not predict prepayments for a mortgage-backed security. It is a generic benchmark that hypothesizes about what the pattern of prepayments will be over the life of a mortgage-backed security—that there is a prepayment ramp (that increases linearly) for 30 months, after which when the CPR is assumed to be constant for the life of the security.

10. A. GNMA refers to passthrough securities issued by the Government National Mortgage Association. "30-YEAR" indicates that the mortgage loans were originated with 30-year terms.

    B. This means GNMA 30-year passthrough securities with a coupon rate of 8.5% that were originated in 1994.

    C. These are the prepayment rates that are projected for various periods. The prepayment rates are expressed in term of the PSA prepayment benchmark. There is a prepayment rate projection for each of the subsequent three months, a prepayment rate projection for one year, and a long-term prepayment rate.

    D. First, the prepayments is only for 7.5% coupon GNMA issues originated in 1993. But there are many 7.5% coupon GNMA issues that were issued in 1993. The prepayments are for a generic issue. This means that when a specific Ginnie Mae 7.5% coupon originated in 1993 is delivered to the buyer, it can realize a prepayment rate quite different from the generic prepayment rate in the report, but on average, 1993 GNMA 7.5%'s are projected to have this prepayment rate.

    E. One factor that affects prepayments is the prevailing mortgage rate relative to the rate that borrowers are paying on the underlying mortgages. As noted in the question, the mortgage rate at the time was 8.13%. The higher the coupon rate, the higher the rate that the borrowers in the underlying mortgage pool are paying and the greater the incentive to prepay. So, as the coupon rate increases, prepayments are expected to be greater because of the incentive to prepay.

11. Since the mortgage passthrough being analyzed has been outstanding for more than 15 years, there have been probably several opportunities for borrowers in the underlying mortgage pool to refinance at a lower rate than they are paying. Consequently, the low mortgage rate of 8% relative to 13% may not result in an increase in prepayments and the same is true for a further decline over the year to 7%. This characteristic of prepayments is referred to as "prepayment burnout."

12. An investor in a short-term security is concerned with extension risk. This is the risk that the security's average life will increase.

13. A. For tranche A:

Month	Sch. Principal repayment/ prepayments	Beginning principal	Tranche A principal repayment	Interest at 6%	Cash flow
1	520,000	3,000,000	520,000	15,000	535,000
2	510,000	2,480,000	510,000	12,400	522,400
3	490,000	1,970,000	490,000	9,850	499,850
4	450,000	1,480,000	450,000	7,400	457,400
5	448,000	1,030,000	448,000	5,150	453,150
6	442,000	582,000	442,000	2,910	444,910
7	410,000	140,000	140,000	700	140,700
		Total	3,000,000		

From months 8 through 48, the principal repayment, interest, and cash flow are zero.

B. For tranche B:

Month	Sch. Principal repayment prepayments	Beginning principal	Tranche B principal repayment	Interest at 7%	Cash flow
1	520,000	8,000,000	0	46,667	46,667
2	510,000	8,000,000	0	46,667	46,667
3	490,000	8,000,000	0	46,667	46,667
4	450,000	8,000,000	0	46,667	46,667
5	448,000	8,000,000	0	46,667	46,667
6	442,000	8,000,000	0	46,667	46,667
7	410,000	8,000,000	270,000	46,667	316,667
8	405,000	7,730,000	405,000	45,092	450,092
9	400,000	7,325,000	400,000	42,729	442,729
10	396,000	6,925,000	396,000	40,396	436,396
11	395,000	6,529,000	395,000	38,086	433,086
12	390,000	6,134,000	390,000	35,782	425,782
13	388,000	5,744,000	388,000	33,507	421,507
14	385,000	5,356,000	385,000	31,243	416,243
15	380,000	4,971,000	380,000	28,998	408,998
16	377,000	4,591,000	377,000	26,781	403,781
17	375,000	4,214,000	375,000	24,582	399,582
18	370,000	3,839,000	370,000	22,394	392,394
19	369,000	3,469,000	369,000	20,236	389,236
20	366,000	3,100,000	366,000	18,083	384,083
21	300,000	2,734,000	300,000	15,948	315,948
22	298,000	2,434,000	298,000	14,198	312,198
23	292,000	2,136,000	292,000	12,460	304,460
24	290,000	1,844,000	290,000	10,757	300,757
25	287,000	1,554,000	287,000	9,065	296,065
26	285,000	1,267,000	285,000	7,391	292,391
27	283,000	982,000	283,000	5,728	288,728
28	280,000	699,000	280,000	4,078	284,078
29	278,000	419,000	278,000	2,444	280,444
30	275,000	141,000	141,000	823	141,823
		Total	8,000,000		

For months 31 through 48 the principal payment, interest, and cash flow are zero.

C. For tranche C:

Month	Sch. Principal repayment prepayments	Beginning principal	Tranche C principal repayment	Interest at 8%	Cash flow
1	520,000	30,000,000	0	200,000	200,000
2	510,000	30,000,000	0	200,000	200,000
3	490,000	30,000,000	0	200,000	200,000
4	450,000	30,000,000	0	200,000	200,000
5	448,000	30,000,000	0	200,000	200,000
6	442,000	30,000,000	0	200,000	200,000
7	410,000	30,000,000	0	200,000	200,000
8	405,000	30,000,000	0	200,000	200,000
9	400,000	30,000,000	0	200,000	200,000
10	396,000	30,000,000	0	200,000	200,000
11	395,000	30,000,000	0	200,000	200,000
12	390,000	30,000,000	0	200,000	200,000
13	388,000	30,000,000	0	200,000	200,000
14	385,000	30,000,000	0	200,000	200,000
15	380,000	30,000,000	0	200,000	200,000
16	377,000	30,000,000	0	200,000	200,000
17	375,000	30,000,000	0	200,000	200,000
18	370,000	30,000,000	0	200,000	200,000
19	369,000	30,000,000	0	200,000	200,000
20	366,000	30,000,000	0	200,000	200,000
21	300,000	30,000,000	0	200,000	200,000
22	298,000	30,000,000	0	200,000	200,000
23	292,000	30,000,000	0	200,000	200,000
24	290,000	30,000,000	0	200,000	200,000
25	287,000	30,000,000	0	200,000	200,000
26	285,000	30,000,000	0	200,000	200,000
27	283,000	30,000,000	0	200,000	200,000
28	280,000	30,000,000	0	200,000	200,000
29	278,000	30,000,000	0	200,000	200,000
30	275,000	30,000,000	134,000	200,000	334,000
31	271,000	29,866,000	271,000	199,107	470,107
32	270,000	29,595,000	270,000	197,300	467,300

(continued on next page …)

(continued)

Month	Sch. Principal repayment prepayments	Beginning principal	Tranche C principal repayment	Interest at 8%	Cash flow
33	265,000	29,325,000	265,000	195,500	460,500
34	260,000	29,060,000	260,000	193,733	453,733
35	255,000	28,800,000	255,000	192,000	447,000
36	252,000	28,545,000	252,000	190,300	442,300
37	250,000	28,293,000	250,000	188,620	438,620
38	245,000	28,043,000	245,000	186,953	431,953
39	240,000	27,798,000	240,000	185,320	425,320
40	210,000	27,558,000	210,000	183,720	393,720
41	200,000	27,348,000	200,000	182,320	382,320
42	195,000	27,148,000	195,000	180,987	375,987
43	190,000	26,953,000	190,000	179,687	369,687
44	185,000	26,763,000	185,000	178,420	363,420
45	175,000	26,578,000	175,000	177,187	352,187
46	170,000	26,403,000	170,000	176,020	346,020
47	166,000	26,233,000	166,000	174,887	340,887
48	164,000	26,067,000	164,000	173,780	337,780

D. The average life for tranche A is computed as follows:

Month	Tranche A principal repayment	Month × principal repayment
1	520,000	520,000
2	510,000	1,020,000
3	490,000	1,470,000
4	450,000	1,800,000
5	448,000	2,240,000
6	442,000	2,652,000
7	140,000	980,000
Total	3,000,000	10,682,000

$$\text{Average life} = \frac{\$10,682,000}{12\,(\$3,000,000)} = 0.30$$

14. A. The coupon interest that would be paid to tranche C is diverted as principal repayment to tranche A. In the table below, the total principal paid to tranche A is tranche A's principal repayment as in KMF-01 plus the interest diverted from tranche C.

Month	Beginning principal for tranche A	Principal repayment before C int*	Interest at 6%	Principal for Tranche C	Tranche C Diverted to Tranche A	Principal repayment for Tranche A	Cash flow
1	3,000,000	520,000	15,000	30,000,000	200,000	720,000	735,000
2	2,280,000	510,000	11,400	30,200,000	201,333	711,333	722,733
3	1,568,667	490,000	7,843	30,401,333	202,676	692,676	700,519
4	875,991	450,000	4,380	30,604,009	204,027	654,027	658,407
5	221,964	448,000	1,110	30,808,036	205,387	221,964	223,074
					Total	3,000,000	

* This is the amount before the accrued interest from Tranche C is allocated to Tranche A.

B. The principal balance for tranche C is increased each month by the amount of interest diverted from tranche C to tranche A. The principal balance for the first five months is shown in the fifth column of the schedule for part a.

C.

Month	Principal repayment for tranche A	Month × principal
1	720,000	720,000
2	711,333	1,422,667
3	692,676	2,078,027
4	654,027	2,616,107
5	221,964	1,109,822
	3,000,000	7,946,622

$$\text{Average life} = \frac{\$7,946,622}{12(\$3,000,000)} = 0.22$$

The average life is shorter for tranche A in KMF-02 relative to KMF-01 due to the presence of the accrual tranche.

15. There is typically a floor placed on an inverse floater to prevent the coupon rate from being negative. In order to fund this floor, the floater must be capped.

16. The principal payments that would have gone to the tranche used to create the floater and inverse floater are distributed proportionately to the floater and inverse floater based on their percentage of the par value. That is, if the floater's par value is 80% of the tranche from which it is created and the inverse floater 20%, then if $100 is received in principal payment $80 is distributed to the floater and $20 to the inverse floater. The effect is that the average life for the floater and the inverse floater will be the same as the tranche from which they are created, six years in this example.

17. A CMO redistributes prepayment risk by using rules for the distribution of principal payments and interest payments from the collateral. The collateral for a CMO has prepayment risk and its cash flow consists of interest payments and principal payments (both scheduled principal and prepayments). Prepayment risk consists of contraction risk and extension risk. In a CMO there are different bond classes (tranches) which are exposed to different degrees of prepayment risk. The exposure to different degrees of prepayment risk relative to the prepayment risk for the collateral underlying a CMO is due to rules as to how the principal and the interest are to be redistributed to the CMO tranches—hence, redistributing prepayment risk amongst the tranches in the structure. In the simplest type of CMO structure—a sequential-pay structure—the rules for the distribution of the cash flow are such that some tranches receive some protection against extension risk while other tranches in the CMO have some protection against contraction risk. In a CMO with PAC tranches, the rules for the distribution of the cash flow result in the PAC tranches having protection against both contraction risk and extension risk while the support tranches (non-PAC tranches) have greater prepayment risk than the underlying collateral for the CMO.

18. By creating any mortgage-backed security, prepayment risk cannot never be eliminated. Rather, the character of prepayment risk can be altered. Specifically, prepayment risk consists of contraction risk and extension risk. A CMO alters but does not eliminate the prepayment risk of the underlying mortgage loans. Therefore, the statement is incorrect.

19. Ms. Morgan should inform the trustee that the statement about the riskiness of the different sectors of the mortgage-backed securities market in terms of prepayment risk is incorrect. There are CMO tranches that expose an investor to less prepayment risk—in terms of extension or contraction risk—than the mortgage passthrough securities from which the CMO was created. There are CMO tranche types such as planned amortization classes that have considerably less prepayment risk than the mortgage passthrough securities from which the CMO was created. However, in order to create CMO tranches such as PACs, it is necessary to create tranches where there is considerable prepayment risk—prepayment risk that is greater than the underlying mortgage passthrough securities. These tranches are called support tranches.

20. A support tranche is included in a structure in which there are PAC tranches. The sole purpose of the support tranche is to provide prepayment protection for the PAC tranches. Consequently, support tranches are exposed to substantial prepayment risk.

21. The manager of an S&L portfolio is concerned with prepayment risk but more specifically extension risk. Moreover, to better match the average life of the investment to that of the S&L's funding cost, the manager will seek a shorter term investment. With the Fannie Mae PAC issue with an average life of 2 years the manager is buying a shorter term security and one with some protection against extension risk. In contrast, the Fannie Mae passthrough is probably a longer term average life security because of its WAM of 310 months and it will expose the S&L to substantial extension risk. Therefore, the Fannie Mae PAC tranche is probably a better investment from an asset/liability perspective.

22. Since the prepayments are assumed to be at a constant prepayment rate over the PAC tranche's life at 140 PSA which is within the PSA collar in which the PAC was created, the average life will be equal to five years.

23. A. The PAC tranche will have the least average life variability. This is because the PAC tranche is created to provide protection against extension risk and contraction risk—the support tranches providing the protection.

   B. The support tranche will have the greatest average life variability. This is because it is designed to absorb the prepayment risk to provide protection for the PAC tranche.

24. The PAC structure in KMF-06 will have less prepayment protection than in KMF-05 because the support tranche is smaller ($200 million in KMF-06 versus $350 for KMF-05).

25. A. The PAC II is a support tranche and as a result will have more average life variability than the PAC I tranche. Consequently, PAC I has the less average life variability.

   B. The support tranche without a schedule must provide prepayment protection for both the PAC I and the PAC II. Therefore, the support tranche without a schedule will have greater average life variability than the PAC II.

26. In a PAC tranche structure in which the PAC tranches are paid off in sequence, the support tranches absorb any excess prepayments above the scheduled amount. Once the support tranches are paid off, any prepayments must go to the PAC tranche that is currently receiving principal payments. Thus, the structure effectively becomes a typical (plain vanilla) sequential-pay structure.

27. If the prepayments are well below the initial upper PAC collar this means that there will be more support tranches available four years after the deal is structured than if prepayments were actually at the initial upper PAC collar. This means that there will be more support tranches to absorb prepayments. Hence, the effective upper collar will increase.

28. The notional amount of an 8% IO tranche is computed below:

Tranche	Par amount	Coupon rate	Excess interest	Excess dollar interest	Notional amount for an 8% coupon rate IO
A	$400,000,000	6.25%	1.75%	$7,000,000	$87,500,000
B	$200,000,000	6.75%	1.25%	$2,500,000	$31,250,000
C	$225,000,000	7.50%	0.50%	$1,125,000	$14,062,500
D	$175,000,000	7.75%	0.25%	$437,500	$5,468,750
				Notional amount for 8% IO	$138,281,250

29. A. The coupon rate for tranche G is found as follows:

$$\text{coupon interest for tranche F in Structure I} = \$500,000,000 \times 0.085$$
$$= \$42,500,000$$

$$\text{coupon interest for tranche F in Structure II} = \$200,000,000 \times 0.0825$$
$$= \$16,500,000$$

$$\text{coupon interest available to tranche G in Structure II} = \$42,500,000 -$$
$$\$16,500,000 = \$26,000,000$$

$$\text{coupon rate for tranche G} = \frac{\$26,000,000}{\$300,000,000} = 0.0867 = 8.67\%$$

B. There is no effect on the average life of the PAC tranches because the inclusion of the PAC II only impacts the support tranche in Structure I compared to Structure II.

C. There is greater average life variability for tranche G in Structure II than tranche F in Structure I because tranche G must provide prepayment protection in Structure II for not only the PACs but also tranche F.

30. A broken or busted PAC is a structure where all of the support tranches (the tranches that provide prepayment support for the PAC tranches in a structure) are completely paid off.

31. A. The formula for the cap rate on the inverse floater

$$\frac{\text{inverse floater interest when reference rate for floater is zero}}{\text{principal for inverse floater}}$$

The total interest to be paid to tranche C if it was not split into the floater and the inverse floater is the principal of $96,500,000 times 7.5%, or $7,237,500. The maximum interest for the inverse floater occurs if 1-month LIBOR is zero. In that case, the coupon rate for the floater is

1-month LIBOR + 1% = 1%

Since the floater receives 1% on its principal of $80,416,667, the floater's interest is $804,167. The remainder of the interest of $7,237,500 from tranche C goes to the inverse floater. That is, the inverse floater's interest is $6,433,333 (= $7,237,500 − $804,167). Since the inverse floater's principal is $16,083,333.33, the cap rate for the inverse floater is

$$\frac{\$6,433,333}{\$16,083,333} = 40.0\%$$

B. Assuming a floor of zero for inverse floater, the cap rate is determined as follows:

$$\text{cap rate for floater} = \frac{\text{collateral tranche interest}}{\text{principal for floater}}$$

The collateral tranche interest is $7,237,500. The floater principal is $80,416,667. Therefore,

$$\text{cap rate for floater} = \frac{\$7,237,500}{\$80,416,667} = 9\%$$

32. A. The PAC collar indicates the prepayment protection afforded the investor in a PAC tranche. Prepayment protection means the ability of the collateral to satisfy the PAC tranche's schedule of principal payments. The initial PAC collar only indicates the protection at issuance. As prepayments occur over time, the amount of the support tranches decline and, as a result, the PAC collars change. In fact, in the extreme case, if the support tranches pay off completely, there is no longer a PAC collar since there is no longer prepayment protection for the PAC tranche.

B. To assess the prepayment protection at any given time for the PAC tranche, the effective PAC collar is computed. This measure is computed by determining the PSA prepayment rate range that given the current amount of the support tranche would be able to meet the remaining PAC schedule.

33. A. For a mortgage loan, the higher the loan-to-value ratio, the greater the credit risk faced by a lender. The reason is that if the property is repossessed and sold, the greater the ratio, the greater the required sale price necessary to recover the loan amount.

B. Studies of residential mortgage loans have found that the loan-to-value ratio is a key determinant of whether a borrower will default and that the higher the ratio, the greater the likelihood of default.

34. A. Mortgage strips are created when the principal (both scheduled principal repayments plus prepayments) and the coupon interest are allocated to different bond classes. The tranche that is allocated the principal payments is called the principal-only mortgage strip and the tranche that is allocated the coupon interest is called the interest-only mortgage strip.

B. With an interest-only mortgage strip, there is no specific amount that will be received over time since the coupon interest payments depend on how prepayments occur over the security's life. In contrast, for a Treasury strip created from the coupon interest, the amount and the timing of the single cash flow is known with certainty.

C. Because prepayments increase when interest rates decrease and prepayments decrease when interest rates increase, the expected cash flow changes in the same direction as the change in interest rates. Thus, when interest rates increase, prepayments are expected to decrease and there will be an increase in the expected coupon interest payments since more of the underlying mortgages are expected to be outstanding. This will typically increase the value of an interest-only mortgage strip because the increase in the expected cash flow more than offsets the higher discount rates used to discount the cash flow. When interest rates decrease, the opposite occurs. So, an interest-only mortgage strip's value is expected to change in the same direction as the change in interest rates.

35. A. The purchase price per $100 par value is 1.02. Therefore

$$1.02 \times \$10,000,000 \times 0.72 = \$7,344,000$$

The investor pays $7,344,000 plus accrued interest.

B. Because the value and characteristics of a principal-only mortgage strip are highly sensitive to the underlying mortgage pool, an investor would not want the seller to have the option of which specific trust to deliver. If the trade is done on a TBA basis, the seller has the choice of the trust to deliver. To avoid this, a trade is done by the buyer specifying the trust that he or she is purchasing.

36. Ginnie Mae, Fannie Mae, and Freddie Mac have underwriting standards that must be met in order for a mortgage loan to qualify for inclusion in a mortgage pool underlying an agency mortgage-backed security. Mortgage loans that do qualify are called conforming loans. A loan may fail to be conforming because the loan balance exceeds the maximum permitted by the underwriting standard or the loan-to-value ratio is too high, or the payment-to-income ratio is too high. Loans that do not qualify are called nonconforming loans.

37. Since there is no implicit or explicit government guarantee for a non-agency mortgage-backed security, a mechanism is needed to reduce credit risk for bondholders when there are defaults. That is, there is a need to "enhance" the credit of the securities issued. These mechanisms are called credit enhancements of which there are two types, internal and external.

38. With a residential mortgage loans the lender relies on the ability of the borrower to repay and has recourse to the borrower if the payment terms are not satisfied. In contrast, commercial mortgage loans are nonrecourse loans which means that the lender can only look to the income-producing property backing the loan for interest and principal repayment. Should a default occur, the lender looks to the proceeds from the sale of the property for repayment and has no recourse to the borrower for any unpaid balance.

39. The figure used for "value" in the loan-to-value ratio is either market value or appraised value. In valuing commercial property, there can be considerable variance in the estimates of the property's market value. Thus, investors tend to be skeptical about estimates of market value and the resulting LTVs reported for properties in a pool of commercial loans. Therefore, the debt-to-service ratio is more objective, and a more reliable measure of risk.

40. A. Call protection at the loan level is provided in one or more of the following forms: (1) prepayment lockout, (2) defeasance, (3) prepayment penalty points, and (4) yield maintenance charges. A prepayment lockout is a contractual agreement that prohibits any prepayments during the lockout period (from 2 to 5 years). After the lockout period, call protection comes in the form of either prepayment penalty points or yield maintenance charges. With defeasance, rather than prepaying a loan, the borrower provides sufficient funds for the servicer to invest in a portfolio of Treasury securities that replicates the cash flows that would exist in the absence of prepayments. Prepayment penalty points are predetermined penalties that must be paid by the borrower if the borrower wishes to refinance. Yield maintenance charge provisions are designed to make the lender whole if prepayments are made.

B. A CMBS deal can be structured as a sequential-pay structure, thereby providing tranches some form of protection against prepayment risk at the structure level.

41. Typically commercial loans are balloon loans that require substantial principal payment at the end of the term of the loan. Balloon risk is the risk that a borrower will not be able to make the balloon payment because either the borrower cannot arrange for refinancing at the balloon payment date or cannot sell the property to generate sufficient funds to pay off the balloon balance. Since the term of the loan will be extended by the lender during the workout period, balloon risk is also referred to as extension risk.

SOLUTIONS FOR READING 62

Solutions are for Practice Questions found in Reading

1. Losses by bond class

	Total Loss	Senior Bond Class	Subordinate Bond Class 1	Subordinate Bond Class 2
a.	$15 million	zero	zero	$15 million
b.	$50 million	zero	$30 million	$20 million
c.	$90 million	$30 million	$40 million	$20 million

2. The excess servicing spread is determined as follows:

Gross weighted average coupon	=	9.50%
− Servicing fee	=	0.75%
Spread available to pay tranches	−	8.75%
− Net weighted average coupon	=	7.50%
Excess servicing spread	=	1.25% = 125 basis points

3. For month 1 the CPR is 4% as per the prospectus. Since we are interested in 150% PPC, the CPR in month 1 is 6% (1.5 × 4%). For month 2, 1.5% is added to 4%, so 100% PPC is 5.5%. Then 150% PPC is a CPR of 8.3% (= 1.5 × 5.5%). In month 15, the CPR is 25% for 100% PPC and for 150% PPC, the CPR is 37.5% (1.5 × 25%). For all months after month 15, the CPR is 37.5%.

Month	CPR	Month	CPR	Month	CPR
1	6.0%	11	28.5%	30	37.5%
2	8.3%	12	30.8%	125	37.5%
3	10.5%	13	33.0%	150	37.5%
4	12.8%	14	35.3%	200	37.5%
5	15.0%	15	37.5%	250	37.5%
6	17.3%	16	37.5%	275	37.5%
7	19.5%	17	37.5%	300	37.5%
8	21.8%	18	37.5%	325	37.5%
9	24.0%	19	37.5%	350	37.5%
10	26.3%	20	37.5%	360	37.5%

4. A. $\text{SMM} = \dfrac{0.02}{1 - \left[0.02 \times (11 - 1)\right]} = 0.025 = 2.5\%$

B. $\text{ABS} = \dfrac{0.017}{1 + \left[0.017 \times (21 - 1)\right]} = 0.0127 = 1.27\%$

SOLUTIONS FOR READING 62

1. **A.** Since Caterpillar Financial Funding Corporation sold the retail install-ment sales contracts to Caterpillar Financial Asset Trust 1997-A, Cater-pillar Financial Funding Corporation would be referred to in the prospectus as the "Seller."

   B. The special purpose vehicle in a securitization issues the securities and therefore is referred to as the "Issuer." In this transaction, Caterpillar Asset Financial Trust 1997-A is the "Issuer."

   C. Without having a full description of the waterfall for this structure, it appears that Bond Classes A-1, A-2, and A-3 are the senior classes.

   D. Without having a full description of the waterfall for this structure, it appears that Bond Class B is the subordinate class.

   E. Credit tranching in this structure was done by creating the senior and subordinate tranches. Prepayment tranching appears to have been done by offering three classes of the senior tranche.

2. **A.** In the securitization process, the attorneys prepare the legal documenta-tion which includes (i) the purchase agreement between the seller of the assets and the special purpose vehicle, (ii) how the cash flows are divided among the bond classes, and (iii) the servicing agreement between the entity engaged to service the assets and the special purpose vehicle.

   B. The independent accountant verifies the accuracy of all numerical infor-mation (e.g. yield and average life) placed in either the prospectus or private placement memorandum and then issues a comfort letter.

3. How the principal repayments from the collateral are used by the trustee in a securitization transaction depends on the waterfall which, in turn, is affected by the character of the collateral (amortizing versus non-amortizing). In a typical structure backed by amortizing assets, the principal repayments are distributed to the bond classes. In a typical structure backed by non-amortizing assets, the principal repayments for a specified period of time (the lockout period) are used to purchase new assets and after that period (assuming no early amortization provision is triggered), the princi-pal repayments are distributed to the bond classes. This structure is referred to as a revolving structure.

4. The excess servicing spread is determined as follows:

Gross weighted average coupon	=	8.60%
− Servicing fee	=	0.50%
Spread available to pay tranches	=	8.10%
− Net weighted average coupon	=	7.10%
Excess servicing spread	=	1.00% = 100 basis points

5. **A.** The amount of overcollateralization is the difference between the value of the collateral, $320 million, and the par value for all the tranches, $300 million. In this structure it is $20 million.

   B. If the losses total $15 million, then the loss is entirely absorbed by the overcollateralization. No tranche will realize a loss.

C. through e.

	Total Loss	Senior Tranche	Subordinate Tranche 1	Subordinate Tranche 2
c.	$35 million	zero	zero	$15 million
d.	$85 million	zero	$35 million	$30 million
e.	$110 million	$10 million	$50 million	$30 million

6. A. For a non-amortizing loan, there is no schedule for repayment of principal. Consequently, for individual loans of this type there can be no prepayments.

   B. While there may be no prepayments for individual loans that are non-amortizing, the securities that are backed by these loans may be prepayable. For example, credit card receivable-backed securities can be prepaid under certain conditions. Such conditions are referred to as "early amortization" or "rapid amortization" events or triggers.

7. The rating agencies take the weak-link approach to credit enhancement. Typically a structure cannot receive a rating higher than the rating on any third-party providing an external guarantee. Since the question specifies that the only form of credit enhancement is the letter of credit, then the rating will not exceed the single A rating of the bank providing the letter credit. Thus, a triple A rating is not likely.

8. Since credit agencies take the weak-link approach to credit enhancement, if an insurance company wants to offer bond insurance for an asset-backed security transaction where a triple A credit rating is sought, the insurance company must have a triple A credit rating.

9. Both a cash reserve fund and an excess servicing spread account are forms of internal credit enhancement. A cash reserve fund is provided by a deposit of cash at issuance. Excess servicing spread account is the cash available to absorb losses from the collateral after payment of interest to all the tranches and to the servicer.

10. The excess servicing spread account builds up over time in order to offset future losses. However, if losses occur early in the life of the collateral, there may not be enough time to accumulate the excess servicing spread to adequately cover future losses.

11. A. A senior-subordinate structure is a form of internal credit enhancement because it does not rely on the guarantee of a third party. Instead, the enhancement comes from within the structure by creating senior and subordinate tranches. The subordinate tranches provide credit protection for the senior tranche.

   B. Once a deal is closed, the percentage of the senior tranche and the percentage of the subordinate tranche change when the underlying assets are subject to prepayments. If the subordinate interest in a structure decreases after the deal is closed, the credit protection for the senior tranche decreases. The shifting interest mechanism seeks to prevent the senior tranche's credit protection provided by the subordinate tranche (or tranches) from declining by establishing a schedule that provides for a higher allocation of the prepayments to the senior tranche in the earlier years.

12. A. The senior prepayment percentage is the percentage of prepayments that are allocated to the senior tranche. The senior prepayment percentage is specified in the prospectus.

   B. Because the shifting interest mechanism results in a greater amount of the prepayments be paid to the senior tranche in the earlier years than in the absence of such a mechanism, the senior tranches are exposed to greater contraction risk.

13. The outstanding bonds in a structure can be called if either (1) the collateral outstanding reaches a predetermined level before the specified call date or (2) the call date has been reached even if the collateral outstanding is above the predetermined level.

14. A. The cash flow for a closed-end home equity loan is the same as for a standard mortgage loan: interest, regularly scheduled principal repayments (i.e., regular amortization), and prepayments.

   B. The statement is incorrect. Typically, a closed-end home equity loan borrower is a credit impaired borrower.

15. For month 1, the CPR for 100% PPC is 5%, so the CPR for 200% PPC is 10% (= 2 × 5%). For month 2, the CPR for 100% PPC is 5% plus 1.8% which is 6.8%. Therefore, the CPR for 200% PPC for month 2 is 13.6% (2 × 6.8%).

In month 12, the CPR for 100% PPC is

$$5\% + 1.8\% \times 11 = 24.8\%$$

Therefore, the CPR for 200% PPC is 49.6% (2 × 24.8%). For all months after month 12, the CPR for 200% CPR is 49.6%.

Month	CPR	Month	CPR	Month	CPR
1	10.0%	11	46.0%	30	49.6%
2	13.6%	12	49.6%	125	49.6%
3	17.2%	13	49.6%	150	49.6%
4	20.8%	14	49.6%	200	49.6%
5	24.4%	15	49.6%	250	49.6%
6	28.0%	16	49.6%	275	49.6%
7	31.6%	17	49.6%	300	49.6%
8	35.2%	18	49.6%	325	49.6%
9	38.8%	19	49.6%	350	49.6%
10	42.4%	20	49.6%	360	49.6%

16. The base case prepayment specified in the prospectus is called the prospectus prepayment curve (PPC). It is unique to each issuer and should be used instead of the generic PSA prepayment benchmark. However, it is not a generic prepayment benchmark for all closed-end home equity loan-securities as Mr. Tellmen assumes.

17. For adjustable-rate HELs, the reference rate is typically 6-month LIBOR. However, the floating-rate securities that these loans back typically are referenced to 1-month LIBOR in order to make them attractive to investors who fund themselves based on 1-month LIBOR. As a result, there will be a mismatch between the reference rate on the floating-rate HELs used as collateral and the securities backed by that collateral that will prevent the cap from being fixed over the life of the securities. In addition, there are periodic caps and a lifetime cap.

18. A. Since month 36 is in the first five years after issuance, the schedule specifies that all prepayments are allocated to the senior tranche and none to the subordinate tranches. Thus, the prepayments of $100,000 are allocated only to the senior tranche.

B. According to the schedule, if prepayments occur 8 years after issuance, 20% is allocated to the senior tranche and the balance is paid to the subordinate tranches. Since the prepayments are assumed to be $100,000, the senior tranche receives $20,000 and the subordinate tranches $80,000.

C. All prepayments that occur 10 years after issuance are paid to the subordinate tranches. Thus, the $100,000 of prepayments some time in year 10 are paid to the subordinate tranches.

19. The schedule in the prospectus is the base schedule. The schedule can change so as to allocate less to the subordinate tranches if the collateral's performance deteriorates after the deal is closed. Determination of whether or not the base schedule should be overridden is made by the trustee based on tests that are specified in the prospectus.

20. The protection is provided by establishing a schedule for the allocation of principal payments (both regularly scheduled principal payments and prepayments) between the NAS tranche and the non-NAS tranches such that contraction risk and extension risk are reduced. For example, a schedule would specify a lockout period for the principal payments to the NAS tranche. This means that the NAS tranche would not receive any payments until the lockout period ends and therefore contraction risk is mitigated. Extension risk is provided by allocating a large percentage to the NAS tranche in later years.

21. A. The cash flow is the same as for mortgage-backed securities backed by standard mortgage loans: (1) interest, (2) regularly scheduled principal repayments (amortization), and (3) prepayments.

B. The reasons why the securities backed by manufactured housing loans tend not to be sensitive to refinancing are:

1. the loan balances are typically small so that there is no significant dollar savings from refinancing.

2. the rate of depreciation of manufactured homes may be such that in the earlier years depreciation is greater than the amount of the loan paid off, making it difficult to refinance the loan.

3. typically borrowers are of lower credit quality and therefore find it difficult to obtain funds to refinance.

22. The deals are more akin to the nonagency market since there is no guarantee by a federally related agency or a government sponsored enterprise as in the United States. As such, the deals must be rated and therefore require credit enhancement.

23. A. The cash flow for auto-loan backed securities consists of: (1) interest, (2) regularly scheduled principal repayments (amortization), and (3) prepayments.

B. Prepayments due to refinancing on auto loans tend to be of minor importance.

24. A conditional prepayment rate measures prepayments relative to the amount outstanding in the previous year that could prepay. For a monthly CPR, called the single monthly mortality rate, SMM, prepayments are measured relative to the amount available in the previous month that was available to prepay.

   The absolute prepayment speed, denoted ABS, is the monthly prepayment expressed as a percentage of the *original* collateral amount.

25. **A.** $\text{SMM} = \dfrac{0.015}{1 - \left[0.015 \times (21 - 1)\right]} = 0.0214 = 2.14\%$

   B. $\text{ABS} = \dfrac{0.019}{1 + \left[0.019 \times (11 - 1)\right]} = 0.016 = 1.60\%$

26. The trustee is wrong. For certain student loans the government will guarantee up to 98% of the principal plus accrued interest (assuming the loans have been properly serviced). Moreover, there are securities backed by alternative student loans that carry no government guarantee.

27. While a student is in school, no payments are made by the student on the loan. This period is the deferment period. Upon leaving school, the student is extended a period of time (typically six months) when no payments on the loan must be made. This is called the grace period.

28. **A.** The cash flow for an SBA-backed security consists of (1) interest for the period, (2) the scheduled principal repayment, and (3) prepayments.

   B. The interest is based on a coupon formula where the prime rate is the reference rate. The rate on the loan is reset monthly on the first of the month or quarterly on the first of January, April, July, and October.

29. **A.** During the lockout period, only finance charges and fees collected are distributed to the bondholders.

   B. During the lockout period, principal paid by borrowers is reinvested in new receivables and not distributed to the bondholders.

   C. The statement is incorrect because principal repayment can be made by either (1) a bullet payment structure (as stated in the question), (2) a controlled amortization structure, or (3) a passthrough structure.

30. While there is no schedule of principal repayments for credit card borrowers, there is the potential risk of contraction for the securities. This is because there is a provision for early or rapid amortization if certain triggers are reached.

   There is also the potential for extension risk because principal repayment from the credit card borrowers and defaults and delinquencies may be such that the schedule specified for principal repayment of the security during the amortization period may not be adequate to completely pay off bondholders by the stated maturity.

   While these are nontrivial risks, neither of these occurs frequently.

31. **A.** The monthly payment rate (MPR) expresses the monthly payment of a credit card receivable portfolio as a percentage of debt outstanding in the previous month. The monthly payment includes finance charges, fees, and any principal repayment collected.

   B. There are two reasons why the MPR is important. First, if the MPR reaches an extremely low level, there is a chance that there will be extension risk with respect to the repayment of principal. The length of time until the return of principal is largely a function of the monthly payment rate. Second, if the MPR is very low, then there is a chance that there will not be sufficient cash flow to pay off principal. This is one of the events that could trigger early amortization of the principal.

C. The net portfolio yield for a credit card receivable portfolio is equal to the gross portfolio yield minus charge-offs. The gross portfolio yield includes finance charges collected and fees. From the gross portfolio yield charge offs are deducted. Charge-offs represent the accounts charged off as uncollectible.

32. The typical structure of a CDO is as follows. There is (1) a senior tranche (between 70% and 80% of the deal) with a floating rate, (2) different layers of subordinate or junior debt tranches with a fixed rate, and (3) an equity tranche.

33. The statement is incorrect. The asset manager responsible for purchasing the debt obligations for the portfolio will have restrictions that are imposed by the rating agencies that rate the securities in the deal (coverage and quality tests). There will be certain tests that must be satisfied for the tranches in the CBO to maintain its credit rating at the time of issuance.

34. The statement is not correct. In fact, it is because of interest rate swaps that the risk is reduced for the senior tranche. This is because the collateral is typically fixed-rate bonds and the senior tranche must be paid a floating rate. An interest rate swap is used to convert the fixed-rate payments from the collateral into floating-rate payments that can be made to the senior tranche.

35. The key determinant is whether or not the CDO can be issued such that the subordinate/equity tranche can be offered a competitive return.

36. A. Given that the senior tranche is $150 million and the junior tranche is $30 million, the equity tranche is $20 million ($200 million minus $180 million).

B. The collateral will pay interest each year (assuming no defaults) equal to the 8-year Treasury rate of 6% plus 600 basis points. So the interest will be:

Interest from collateral: 12% × $200,000,000 = $24,000,000

The interest that must be paid to the senior tranche is:

Interest to senior tranche: $150,000,000 × (LIBOR + 90 bp)

The coupon rate for the junior tranche is 6% plus 300 basis points. So, the coupon rate is 9% and the interest is:

Interest to junior tranche: 9% × $30,000,000 = $2,700,000

For the interest rate swap, the asset manager is agreeing to pay the swap counterparty each year 6% (the 8-year Treasury rate) plus 120 basis points, or 7.2%. Since the swap payments are based on a notional amount of $150 million, the asset manager pays to the swap counterparty:

Interest to swap counterparty: 7.2% × $150,000,000 = $10,800,000

The interest payment received from the swap counterparty is LIBOR based on a notional amount of $150 million. That is,

Interest from swap counterparty: $150,000,000 × LIBOR

The interest for the CBO is:

Interest from collateral $24,000,000
Interest from swap counterparty ....$150,000,000 × LIBOR
_____
Total interest received......................$24,000,000 + $150,000,000 × LIBOR

The interest to be paid out to the senior and junior tranches and to the swap counterparty include:

Interest to senior tranche..............$150,000,000 × (LIBOR + 90 bp)
Interest to junior tranche..................$2,700,000
Interest to swap counterparty..........$10,800,000
_____
Total interest paid...........................$13,500,000 + $150,000,000
                                                              × (LIBOR + 90 bp)

Netting the interest payments paid and received:

Total interest received ....$24,000,000 + $150,000,000 × LIBOR
− Total interest paid ......$13,500,000 + $150,000,000 × (LIBOR + 90 bp)
_____
Net interest.....................$10,500,000 − $150,000,000 × (90 bp)

> Since 90 bp times $150 million is $1,350,000, the net interest remaining is $9,150,000. This is the cash flow ignoring the asset management fee.

C. The amount available for the equity tranche is $9,150,000. This is the cash flow computed in part (b).

37. The return includes:

> the return on a portfolio of high-quality debt instruments
> plus
> the payment from the asset manager as part of the credit default swap
> minus
> the payment that must be made by a junior tranche due to a credit event

38. By issuing a synthetic CDO, a bank can remove the economic risk of bank loans without having to notify any borrowers that they are selling the loans to another party. Thus, no consent would be needed from borrowers to transfer loans, a requirement in some countries.

SOLUTIONS FOR READING 63

1. A. The convention is to determine the nominal spread relative to the spread on a Treasury security with the same maturity as the average life of the mortgage-backed security. Since the average life is 8 years, the benchmark Treasury issue is the 8-year issue. The nominal spread is then 7.5% minus the 6.3% of the 8-year Treasury issue. So, the nominal spread is 120 basis points.

B. For the 7.5% cash flow yield to be realized the following must occur:

  ► actual prepayments must be 200 PSA over the life of the security
  ► the monthly cash flow (interest plus principal repayment) must be reinvested at a rate of 7.5%
  ► the security must be held until the last mortgage pays off

2. The monthly cash flow yield, i_M, is 0.0074. Therefore,

$$\text{bond-equivalent yield} = 2[(1.0074)^6 - 1] = 0.0905 = 9.05\%$$

3. The binomial model used to value a corporate bond with an embedded option can handle securities in which the decision to exercise a call option is not dependent on how interest rates evolved over time. That is, the decision of a corporate issuer to call a bond will depend on the level of the rate at which the issue can be refunded relative to the issue's coupon rate. The decision to call does not depend on the path interest rates took to get to that rate. Ms. Howard must understand that this is not a characteristic of mortgage-backed securities. These securities are "interest rate path-dependent," meaning that the cash flow received in one period is determined not only by the interest rate level at that period, but also by the path that interest rates took to get to that rate.

For example, in the case of passthrough securities, prepayments are interest rate path-dependent because this month's prepayment rate depends on whether there have been prior opportunities to refinance since the underlying mortgages were originated. For CMOs there are typically two sources of path dependency in a CMO tranche's cash flows. First, the collateral prepayments are path-dependent as just described. Second, the cash flows to be received in the current month by a CMO tranche depend on the outstanding balances of the other tranches in the deal. Thus, we need the history of prepayments to calculate these balances.

4. A. To generate the path of short-term interest rates, an assumption about the volatility of short-term interest rates must be made.

B. If the short-term interest rates on each path are used without an adjustment, there is no assurance that the Monte Carlo simulation model will correctly value the on-the-run Treasury issues. An adjustment to the short-term interest rates is required in order to have the model properly price on-the-run Treasury issues so that the model will provide arbitrage-free values.

C. In moving from the short-term interest rates to the refinancing rates, it is necessary to make an assumption about the spread between these rates.

5. In the Monte Carlo simulation model, a prepayment *model* is used. The prepayment model provides a prepayment rate for each month on each interest rate path. Thus, no specific PSA prepayment assumption is made. Consequently, the statement by Mr. Ruthledge that a 175 PSA was made is inconsistent with the Monte Carlo simulation model. Therefore, Mr. Hawthorne should have been confused by Mr. Ruthledge's response.

6. On an interest rate path, the short-term interest rates are the forward rates. It is the forward rates plus an appropriate spread that is used to value a mortgage-backed security on an interest rate path.

7. The investor in a passthrough security has effectively sold a call option to borrowers (homeowners). The higher the assumed interest rate volatility the greater the value of this embedded call option and therefore the lower the price of a passthrough security. Securities 1 and 2 have the correct relationship between price and assumed interest rate volatility. Security 3 has the opposite relationship. Therefore, the error that Mr. Rodriguez discovered is with the relationship between assumed interest rate volatility and price for Security 3.

8. A. Since the collateral is trading at a premium, a slowdown in prepayments will allow the investor to receive the higher coupon for a longer period of time. This will increase the value of the collateral.

   B. Because Tranche Y is selling at a premium, its value will increase with a slowdown in prepayments. In contrast, because Tranche X is selling at a discount, a slowdown in prepayments will decrease its value. This is because for Tranche X, there will be less principal returned to be reinvested at the new, higher rates. Also, assuming that X was purchased when it was trading at a discount, there will be less of a capital gain realized (since principal is returned at par).

9. The theoretical value based on the ten interest rate paths is the average of the present value of the interest rate paths. The average value is 89.1.

10. A. Rather than sampling a large number of interest rate paths, some vendors of mortgage analytical systems have developed computational procedures that reduce the number of paths required. The procedure involves using statistical techniques to reduce the number of interest rate paths to sets of similar paths. These paths are called representative paths. The security is then valued on each of the representative interest rate paths—16 in the question.

   B. The theoretical value of a security when the representative interest rate paths are used is the weighted average of the 16 representative paths. The weight for a path is the percentage of that representative path relative to the total paths in a full Monte Carlo analysis.

   C. The trade-off between the full Monte Carlo analysis and the 16 representative paths is one of speed versus accuracy. The full Monte Carlo analysis provides the true value of the security—*true only based on all the assumptions of the model.* Using 16 representative sample is less accurate but requires less computational time.

11. The theoretical value is the weighted average of the present value of the representative interest rate paths. The weighted average of the present value of the representative interest rate paths is 77.94 as shown below:

Weight	PV	Weight × PV
0.20	70	14.00
0.18	82	14.76
0.16	79	12.64
0.12	68	8.16
0.12	74	8.88
0.12	86	10.32
0.06	91	5.46
0.04	93	3.72
Theoretical value		77.94

12. A. While there is no credit risk for a Ginnie Mae mortgage product, there is liquidity risk (relative to on-the-run Treasury issues) and modeling risk. The latter risk is due to the assumptions that must be made in valuing a mortgage-backed security. If those assumptions prove incorrect or if the parameters used as inputs are wrong, the valuation model will not calculate the true level of risk. A major portion of the compensation for a Ginnie Mae mortgage product reflects payment for this model uncertainty.

B. The OAS should differ by the type of Ginnie Mae mortgage product. The more complex the security to model and value, the greater the OAS should be to reflect the associated modeling risk. Moreover, the more complex the security, the less liquid the security tends to be. Consequently, the OAS will also differ because of liquidity risk.

13. Using the representative interest rate paths, the theoretical value of a mortgage-backed security is the weighted average of the present value of the paths. Since it is assumed in the question that each path has the same weight, the theoretical value is the simple average of the present values of the interest rate paths. For the four spreads, the average PV is given below:

Representative path	Present value if the spread used is			
	70 bps	75 bps	80 bps	85 bps
Average PV	82.6	79.5	76.3	73.8

A. The option-adjusted spread is the spread that will make the theoretical value equal to the market price. Since the question assumes that Tranche L has a market price of 79.5, then a spread of 75 basis points will produce a theoretical value equal to the market price of 79.5. Therefore, the OAS is 75 basis points.

B. If the price is 73.8 instead of 79.5, then the OAS is the spread that will make the theoretical value equal to 73.8. From the table above it can be seen that a spread of 85 basis points will produce a theoretical value equal to 73.8. Therefore, the OAS is 85 basis points.

14. Tranche M has a substantial variation in the present value for the paths. This is a characteristic of a support tranche since a support tranche is exposed to substantial prepayment risk. Tranche N has little variation in the present value for the paths and this is a characteristic of a PAC tranche. Therefore, Tranche M is probably the support tranche and Tranche N is probably the PAC tranche.

15. **A.** The option cost is the difference between the Z-spread and the OAS. Therefore,

> PAC I A: $60 - 50 = 10$ basis points
> PAC II A: $150 - 80 = 70$ basis points
> Support S1: $165 - 35 = 130$ basis points

B. Typically, the OAS increases with effective duration. The two longer PAC tranches, PAC I C and PAC I D, have lower OAS than the two shorter duration PACs. Therefore, the two longer duration PACs appear to be expensive.

C. On a relative value basis, all but PAC II A appear to be expensive. PAC II B has a lower OAS than PAC II A even though it has a higher effective duration. The other two support tranches without a schedule have a low OAS relative to their effective durations.

D. Investors who do not appreciate the significance of the option risk associated with a tranche can be induced to buy PAC II B because they look exclusively at the nominal spread. While the nominal spread is not provided as part of the information in the question, it can be estimated from the Z-spread. A Z-spread of 280 basis point is extremely appealing to investors for a security with no credit risk (since the deal is an agency CMO deal). Also, investors who do not realize that a PAC II is a support bond will believe that they have purchased a PAC tranche with a high "spread" to Treasuries.

16. The effective duration and effective convexity require the calculation of V_- and V_+. To calculate V_-, each path of short-term interest rates is decreased by a small number of basis points, say 25 basis points. Then, the cash flows are generated for each interest rate path. When the new cash flows are valued using the short-term interest rates plus a spread, the spread used is the original OAS. That is, it is assumed that the OAS does not change when interest rates are decreased. The same procedure is followed to compute V_+, but each path of short-term rates is increased by the same small number of basis points as was used to compute V_-. Again, it is assumed that the OAS does not change, so the new short-term interest rates plus the original OAS are used to discount the new cash flows on the interest rate paths.

17. First it is important to note that the CMO tranche is a support tranche and therefore has considerable prepayment risk. Despite Mr. Winters having been told that all the dealer firms used the Monte Carlo simulation model to compute the effective duration, there are assumptions in the model that can vary from dealer to dealer. This is the reason for the variation in the

effective duration. These different assumptions in computing the value of a mortgage-backed security include:

1. differences in the amount of the rate shock used

2. differences in prepayment models

3. differences in option-adjusted spread (recall that the OAS is held constant when rates are shocked)

4. differences in the relationship between short-term interest rates and refinancing rates

18. This statement is incorrect. From a collateral with negative convexity, tranches with both positive and negative convexity can be created. For example, a PAC bond that is well protected will have little prepayment risk and therefore positive convexity—effectively the convexity of an option-free bond. However, one or more of the other tranches in the deal would have to have more negative convexity than the collateral itself, since the tranching of the collateral can only reallocate prepayment risk; it cannot eliminate it entirely.

19. **A.** Cash flow duration is computed assuming that if interest rates are changed the prepayment rate will change when computing the new value.

B. The problem is that this duration measure is based on one initial prepayment speed and when rates are changed it is assumed the prepayment speed will change to another prepayment speed. It is a static approach because it considers only one prepayment speed if rates change. It does not consider the dynamics that interest rates can change in the future and therefore there is not just one potential cash flow or prepayment rate that must be considered in valuing a mortgage-backed security.

20. To compute the coupon curve duration the assumption is that if the yield declines by 100 basis points, the price of the 9% coupon passthrough will increase to the price of the current 10% coupon passthrough. Thus, the price will increase from 99.50 to 102.60. Similarly, if the yield increases by 100 basis points, the assumption is that the price of the 9% coupon passthrough will decline to the price of the 8% coupon passthrough (97.06). Using the duration formula, the corresponding values are:

$$
\begin{aligned}
V_0 &= 99.50 \\
V_+ &= 97.06 \\
V_- &= 102.60 \\
\Delta y &= 0.01
\end{aligned}
$$

The estimated duration based on the coupon curve is then:

$$
\frac{102.60 - 97.06}{2(99.50)(0.01)} = 2.78
$$

21. Empirical duration is computed using statistical analysis. It requires good price data for the tranche whose empirical duration is to be computed. A major problem with applying empirical duration to complex CMO tranches is that a reliable series of price data is often not available for a thinly traded mortgage product or the prices may be matrix priced or model priced rather than actual transaction prices. The second problem is that an

empirical relationship does not impose a structure for the options embedded in a mortgage-backed security and this can distort the empirical duration. Finally, the volatility of the spread to Treasury yields can distort how the price of a mortgage-backed security reacts to yield changes.

22. The nominal spread of an asset-backed security hides the associated option or prepayment risk. For auto loan-backed securities, refinancing is not an important factor and therefore prepayment risk is not significant. For credit card receivables, there is prepayment risk only at the security level—that is, a credit card borrower cannot prepay because there is no schedule of payments but a security can be prepaid if certain rapid or early amortization triggers are realized. However, prepayment risk is not significant. In contrast, for home equity loan-backed securities prepayment risk is significant and the nominal spread reflects that risk. Consequently, assessing relative value for these three types of asset-backed securities based on the nominal spread is incorrect because the spread is not adjusted for the prepayment risk. Home equity loan-backed securities offer a higher nominal spread because of the prepayment risk.

23. The appropriate valuation approach depends on whether or not the borrower has an option to prepay. Furthermore, even if the borrower has the right to prepay, it depends on whether or not the borrower will take advantage of this option to prepay when interest rates decline. Since the security involves future royalties, there is no prepayment option. Consequently, there is no option value and the appropriate valuation approach is the zero-volatility spread.

24. While there is an option to prepay, if the empirical evidence is correct that borrowers do not prepay when rates decline, then the option value is zero. Consequently, the zero-volatility spread approach is the appropriate approach since the OAS is equal to the zero-volatility spread.

25. **A.** Since high quality borrowers are observed to take advantage of refinancing opportunities, there is a value to the prepayment option. Consequently, the option-adjusted spread approach is appropriate when the underlying pool of home equity loans are those of high quality borrowers.

   B. Since low quality borrowers may prepay but have been observed not to take advantage of refinancing opportunities, there is very little value to the prepayment option. Since the option cost has a value of zero, the zero-volatility spread is equal to the option-adjusted spread. Consequently, the zero-volatility spread approach can be used to value securities backed by a pool of home equity loans of low quality borrowers.

   However, there is a caveat here regarding the behavior of low quality borrowers. The answer ignores the adverse selection impact of borrowers who upgrade their credit profile and refinance out, leaving a potentially longer average life, and worse credit, pool.

GLOSSARY

Abnormal rate of return The amount by which a security's actual return differs from its expected rate of return which is based on the market's rate of return and the security's relationship with the market.

Abnormal return Return on a stock beyond what would be predicted by market movements alone. Cumulative abnormal return (CAR) is the total abnormal return for the period surrounding an announcement or the release of information.

Absolute priority rule The hierarchy whereby claims are satisfied in corporate liquidation.

Accounting A detailed report to the trust beneficiaries by a trustee of his stewardship, also used to discharge the trustee.

Accounting earnings Earnings of a firm as reported on its income statement.

Accounting profit Total revenues minus total explicit costs.

Accounting Standards Board (ASB) The Accounting Standards Board issues Financial Reporting Standards (FRSs) for the United Kingdom. It took over the task of setting accounting standards from the Accounting Standards Committee in 1990.

Accounts payable A liability that results from the purchase of goods or services on open account, that is, without a signed note payable.

Accounts receivable Amounts owed to a company by customers as a result of delivering goods or services and extending credit in the ordinary course of business. Also referred to as *trade receivables*.

Accrual accounting The system of recording financial transactions as they come into existence as a legally enforceable claim, rather than when they settle.

Accrued expenses payable Incurred costs or expenses that have not been paid. Also referred to as *accruals*.

Accrued interest Interest earned but not yet due and payable. This is equal to the next coupon to be paid on a bond multiplied by the time elapsed since the last payment date and divided by the total coupon period. Exact conventions differ across bond markets.

Accumulate Wall Street expression for buying on a large scale over time, typically by an institution. "Accumulation" of a stock is said to occur if a number of institutions are gradually adding to their holdings.

Accumulated other comprehensive income Cumulative gains or losses reported in shareholders' equity that arise from changes in the fair value of available-for-sale securities, from the effects of changes in foreign-currency exchange rates on consolidated foreign-currency financial statements, from certain gains and losses on financial derivatives and from adjustments for under-funded pension plans.

Acquisition The purchase of an entire company or a controlling interest in a company.

Active management Attempts to achieve portfolio returns more than commensurate with risk, either by forecasting broad market trends or by identifying particular mispriced sectors of a market or securities in a market.

Active portfolio In the context of the Treynor-Black model, the portfolio formed by mixing analyzed stocks of perceived nonzero alpha values. This portfolio is ultimately mixed with the passive market index portfolio.

Actual change in cash and equivalents A term used on the cash flow analysis statement that consists of the change in cash and cash equivalents between reporting periods.

Additional information Information that is required or recommended under the GIPS standards and is not considered as "supplemental information" for the purposes of compliance.

Additions Assets transferred to a trust after the initial funding.

Adjustable-rate mortgage A mortgage whose interest rate varies according to some specified measure of the current market interest rate.

Adjusted operating cash flow Reported operating cash flow adjusted for the reclassification of selected nonoperating items and for nonrecurring items of operating cash flow. See also *sustainable operating cash flow*.

Adjusted EBITDA Conventional earnings before interest, taxes, depreciation, and amortization (EBITDA) with additional adjustments for other noncash or nonrecurring items of revenue, expense, gain, and loss.

Administrative fees All fees other than the trading expenses and the investment management fee. Administrative fees include custody fees, accounting fees, consulting fees, legal fees, performance measurement fees, or other related fees. These administrative fees are typically outside the control of the investment management firm and are not included in either the gross-of-fees return or the net-of-fees return. However, there are some markets and investment vehicles where administrative fees are controlled by the firm.

Adverse selection The likelihood that individuals who seek to borrow money may use the funds that they receive for unworthy, high-risk projects.

Agency conflict An ethical problem that can arise any time one person (i.e., agent) is hired to perform a service or act in the interest of another (i.e., principal).

Agency problem Conflicts of interest among stockholders, bondholders, and managers.

Agency trade A trade in which a broker acts as an agent only, not taking a position on the opposite side of the trade.

Aggregate demand (1) The relationship between the quantity of real GDP demanded and the price level. (2) The total of all planned expenditures for the entire economy.

Aggregate production function The relationship between the quantity of real GDP supplied and the quantities of labor and capital and the state of technology.

Aggressive Implies a concentrated portfolio holding smaller capitalization stocks than the general market, often with higher price/earnings and lower yields, together with low reserves. Often implies unusual volatility.

Aggressive cost capitalization Cost capitalization that stretches the flexibility of generally accepted accounting principles beyond its intended limits, resulting in reporting as assets items that should have been expensed.

AICPA The American Institute of Certified Public Accountants. The AICPA is the national association of CPAs in the United States.

AIMR (1) The Association for Investment Management and Research (AIMR®) awards the CFA® certification and sets professional standards that must be applied by its members worldwide. (2) A standard performance presentation system. For information call 804-980-3547 or go to *http://www.aimr.org.*

Allocative efficiency A situation in which we cannot produce more of any good without giving up some of another good that we value more highly.

Alpha The abnormal rate of return on a security in excess of what would be predicted by an equilibrium model like CAPM or APT.

Alphabet stock *See tracking stock.*

Alternative investments Hedge funds, venture capital pools, options and other derivatives, real estate, and other non-stock or -bond market securities.

American Depositary Receipt (ADR) A certificate of ownership issued by a U.S. bank to promote local trading in a foreign stock. The U.S. bank holds the foreign shares and issues ADRs against them.

American option An option contract that can be exercised at any time until its expiration date.

American terms With reference to U.S. dollar exchange rate quotations, the U.S. dollar price of a unit of another currency.

Amortizing swap An interest rate swap with a decreasing notional principal amount.

Anomalies (1) Security price relationships that appear to contradict a well-regarded hypothesis; in this case, the efficient market hypothesis. (2) Patterns of returns that seem to contradict the efficient market hypothesis.

Antitrust law A law that regulates and prohibits certain kinds of market behavior, such as monopoly and monopolistic practices.

Antitrust legislation Laws that restrict the formation of monopolies and regulate certain anticompetitive business practices.

Appraisal ratio The signal-to-noise ratio of an analyst's forecasts. The ratio of alpha to residual standard deviation.

Appreciation An increase in the exchange value of one nation's currency in terms of the currency of another nation.

Arbitrage The simultaneous purchase of an undervalued asset or portfolio and sale of an overvalued but equivalent asset or portfolio, in order to obtain a riskless profit on the price differential. Taking advantage of a market inefficiency in a risk-free manner.

Arbitrage pricing theory An asset pricing theory that is derived from a factor model, using diversification and arbitrage arguments. The theory describes the relationship between expected returns on securities, given that there are no opportunities to create wealth through risk-free arbitrage investments.

Arbitrage pricing theory (APT) A theory that posits that the expected return to a financial asset can be described by its relationship with several common risk factors. The multifactor APT can be contrasted with the single-factor CAPM.

Arithmetic mean (AM) A measure of mean annual rates of return equal to the sum of annual holding period rates of return divided by the number of years.

Ask price The price at which a market maker is willing to sell a security (also called *offer price*).

Asset allocation Dividing of investment funds among several asset classes to achieve diversification.

Asset allocation decision Choosing among broad asset classes such as stocks versus bonds.

Asset class Securities that have similar characteristics, attributes, and risk/return relationships.

Assets Amounts owned; all items to which a business or household holds legal claim.

Assets under management (AUM) The total market value of the assets managed by an investment firm.

Asset turnover (ATO) The annual sales generated by each dollar of assets (sales/assets).

Asymmetric information Possession of information by one party in a financial transaction but not by the other party.

At-the-money option An option for which the strike (or exercise) price is close to (at) the current market price of the underlying asset.

Auction market A market where all traders in a good meet at one place to buy or sell an asset. The NYSE is an example.

Autonomous expenditure The sum of those components of aggregate planned expenditure that are not influenced by real GDP. Autonomous expenditure equals investment, government purchases, exports, and the autonomous parts of consumption expenditure and imports.

Available-for-sale security A default classification for an investment in a debt or equity security that is not classified as either a held-to-maturity security or a trading security.

Average cost pricing rule A rule that sets price to cover cost including normal profit, which means setting the price equal to average total cost.

Average tax rate The total tax payment divided by total income. It is the proportion of total income paid in taxes.

BA *Banker's acceptance.*

Backwardation Condition in which *spot price* of commodity exceeds price of *future* (cf. *contango*).

Balanced budget A government budget in which tax revenues and expenditures are equal.

Balanced fund A mutual fund with, generally, a three-part investment objective: (1) to conserve the investor's principal, (2) to pay current income, and (3) to increase both principal and income. The fund aims to achieve this by owning a mixture of bonds, preferred stocks, and common stocks.

Balance of payments A system of accounts that measures transactions of goods, services, income, and financial assets between domestic households, businesses, and governments and residents of the rest of the world during a specific time period.

Balance of payments accounts A country's record of international trading, borrowing, and lending.

Balance sheet A financial statement that shows what assets the firm controls at a fixed point in time and how it has financed these assets.

Balloon payment Large final payment (e.g., when a loan is repaid in installments).

Bank overdraft Checks presented for payment that exceed a company's bank balance. A book overdraft becomes a bank overdraft when outstanding checks are presented for payment.

Barriers to entry Legal or natural constraints that protect a firm from potential competitors.

Barter The direct exchange of goods and services for other goods and services without the use of money.

Base year The year that is chosen as the point of reference for comparison of prices in other years.

Basis point A hundredth of a percent; thus 75 basis points equals three-quarters of 1 percentage point.

Basis swap An interest rate swap involving two floating rates.

Bear market Widespread decline in security prices (cf. *bull market*).

Behavioral finance (1) Involves the analysis of various psychological traits of individuals and how these traits affect how they act as investors, analysts, and portfolio managers. (2) Branch of finance that stresses aspects of investor irrationality.

Benchmark A standard measurement used to evaluate the performance of a portfolio. The benchmark may be some passive index or the aggregate performance on a universe of comparable portfolios (see *composite*).

Benchmark bond A bond representative of current market conditions and used for performance comparison.

Benchmark portfolio A comparison standard of risk and assets included in the policy statement and similar to the investor's risk preference and investment needs, which can be used to evaluate the investment performance of the portfolio manager.

Beta A standardized measure of systematic risk based upon an asset's covariance with the market portfolio.

Bid–asked spread The difference between a dealer's bid and asked price.

Bid–ask spread The difference between the quoted ask and the bid prices.

Bidder The acquiring firm.

Bid price The price at which a dealer is willing to purchase a security.

Big Board Colloquial term for the New York Stock Exchange.

Bilateral arbitrage With reference to currencies, an arbitrage involving two currencies only.

Binomial model An option valuation model predicated on the assumption that stock prices can move to only two values over any short time period.

Black-Scholes formula An equation to value a call option that uses the stock price, the exercise price, the risk-free interest rate, the time to maturity, and the standard deviation of the stock return.

Black-Scholes option pricing model A valuation equation that assumes the price of the underlying asset changes continuously through the option's expiration date by a statistical process known as *geometric Brownian motion*.

Black-Scholes or Black-Scholes-Merton formula A standard option pricing formula derived by F. Black and M. Scholes and also by R. Merton.

Block A large stock transaction (e.g., ten thousand shares or more).

Blue chip A large, stable, well-known, widely held, seasoned company with a strong financial position, usually paying a reasonable dividend.

Boilerplate Standard terms and conditions, e.g., in a debt contract.

Bond A security issued by a borrower that obligates the issuer to make specified payments to the holder over a specific period. A *coupon bond* obligates the issuer to make interest payments called coupon payments over the life of the bond, then to repay the *face value* at maturity.

Bond indenture The contract between the issuer and the bondholder.

Bond rating Rating of the likelihood of bond's default.

Book entry Registered ownership of stock without issue of stock certificate.

Book overdraft A negative cash balance for reporting purposes consisting of the excess of outstanding checks over a stated bank cash balance.

Books A shorthand reference to shareholder as opposed to income tax financial information.

Book-to-market effect The tendency for stocks of firms with high ratios of book-to-market value to generate abnormal returns.

Book value An accounting measure describing the net worth of common equity according to a firm's balance sheet.

Bottom-up Developing a portfolio by focusing on individual securities.

Bourse A French term often used to refer to a stock market.

Broker An agent who executes orders to buy or sell securities on behalf of a client in exchange for a commission.

Brokered market A market where an intermediary (a broker) offers search services to buyers and sellers.

Budget constraint All of the possible combinations of goods that can be purchased (at fixed prices) with a specific budget.

Budget deficit The amount by which government spending exceeds government revenues.

Bullet payment Single final payment, e.g., of a loan (in contrast to payment in installments).

Bull market Widespread rise in security prices (cf. *bear market*).

Bund Long-term German government *bond*.

Business cycle The periodic but irregular up-and-down movement in production.

Business risk The variability of operating income arising from the characteristics of the firm's industry. Two sources of business risk are sales variability and operating leverage.

Buy-and-hold strategy A passive portfolio management strategy in which securities (bonds or stocks) are bought and held to maturity.

Buyback Repurchase agreement.

Cable The exchange rate between U.S. dollars and sterling.

Callable bond A bond that the issuer may repurchase at a given price in some specified period.

Call auction See *fixing*.

Call option A contract that gives its holder the right to buy an asset, typically a financial instrument, at a specified price through a specified date.

Call protection An initial period during which a callable bond may not be called.

Call provision Provision that allows an issuer to buy back the *bond* issue at a stated price.

Call provisions Specifies when and how a firm can issue a call for bonds outstanding prior to their maturity.

Cap agreement A contract that on each settlement date pays the holder the greater of the difference between the reference rate and the cap rate or zero; it is equivalent to a series of call options at the reference rate.

Capital The tools, equipment, buildings, and other constructions that businesses now use to produce goods and services.

Capital account A component of the balance of payments that reflects unrequited (or unilateral) transfers corresponding to capital flows entailing no compensation (in the form of goods, services, or assets). Examples include investment capital given (without future repayment) in favor of poor countries, debt forgiveness, and expropriation losses.

Capital accumulation The growth of capital resources.

Capital allocation decision Allocation of invested funds between risk-free assets versus the risky portfolio.

Capital allocation line (CAL) A graph showing all feasible risk–return combinations of a risky and risk-free asset.

Capital appreciation A return objective in which the investor seeks to increase the portfolio value, primarily through capital gains, over time to meet a future need rather than dividend yield.

Capital asset pricing model (CAPM) An equilibrium theory that relates the expected return of an asset to its market risk (see *beta*).

Capital budget List of planned investment projects, usually prepared annually.

Capital budgeting A project analysis in which a project's receipts and outlays are valued over a project's life.

Capital consumption The decrease in the capital stock that results from wear and tear and obsolescence.

Capital controls Legal restrictions on the ability of a nation's residents to hold and trade assets denominated in foreign currencies.

Capital Employed (Real Estate) The denominator of the return expressions, defined as the "weighted-average equity" (weighted-average capital) during the measurement period. Capital employed should not include any income or capital return accrued *during* the measurement period. Beginning capital is adjusted by weighting the cash flows (contributions and distributions) that occurred during the period. Cash flows are typically weighted based on the actual days the flows are in or out of the portfolio. Other weighting methods are acceptable; however, once a methodology is chosen, it should be consistently applied.

Capital expenditures Expenditures made in the purchase of long-term productive assets, such as property, plant, and equipment, whose cost is amortized against income in future periods.

Capital gain The positive difference between the purchase price and the sale price of an asset. If a share of stock is bought for $5 and then sold for $15, the capital gain is $10.

Capital gains The amount by which the sale price of a security exceeds the purchase price.

Capital goods Producer durables; nonconsumable goods that firms use to make other goods.

Capitalization Long-term debt plus *preferred stock* plus *net worth*.

Capitalized interest Interest incurred during the construction period on monies invested in assets under construction that is added to the cost of the assets.

Capitalized operating cost Expenditure that is reported as an asset to be amortized against future revenue.

Capital lease A lease that transfers, in an economic sense, the risks and rewards of ownership to the lessee without transferring title. Lease payments made are comprised of interest and principal. Property held under a capital-lease agreement is accounted for as an asset. This cost is amortized over the relevant useful life.

Capital loss The negative difference between the purchase price and the sale price of an asset.

Capital market Financial market (particularly the market for long-term securities).

Capital market instruments Fixed-income or equity investments that trade in the secondary market.

Capital market line (CML) The line from the intercept point that represents the risk-free rate tangent to the original efficient frontier; it becomes the new efficient frontier since investments on this line dominate all the portfolios on the original Markowitz efficient frontier.

Capital markets Includes longer-term, relatively riskier securities.

Capital rationing Shortage of funds that forces a company to choose between worthwhile projects.

Capital stock The total quantity of plant, equipment, buildings, and inventories.

Capital structure Mix of different securities issued by a firm.

CAPM Capital asset pricing model.

Capture hypothesis A theory of regulatory behavior that predicts that the regulators will eventually be captured by the special interests of the industry being regulated.

Capture theory A theory of regulation that states that the regulations are supplied to satisfy the demand of producers to maximize producer surplus—to maximize economic profit.

Carve-out Public offering of shares in a subsidiary.

Cash Currency, coin, and funds on deposit that are available for immediate withdrawal without restriction. Money orders, certified checks, cashier's checks, personal checks, and bank drafts are also considered cash.

Cash after operations A Uniform Credit Analysis®–defined cash flow amount that consists of gross cash profit less cash operating expense.

Cash and carry Purchase of a security and simultaneous sale of a *future*, with the balance being financed with a loan or *repo*.

Cash cost of revenue A term used on the cash flow analysis statement that consists of cash payments to vendors and other suppliers, including employees, for the purchase of products and the procurement of services provided to customers.

Cash earnings Net income plus goodwill amortization.

Cash equivalents   Short-term and highly liquid investments readily convertible into known amounts of cash and close enough to maturity that there is insignificant risk of changes in value from interest rate movements.

Cash flow   An unspecified term that may refer to either total cash flow or operating cash flow. In most cases, use of the term refers to operating cash flow.

Cash flow after debt service   A term used on the cash flow analysis statement that consists of cash flow from operations less required principal payments on long-term debt capital leases.

Cash flow after dividends   A term used on the cash flow analysis statement that consists of cash flow after debt service less dividends paid.

Cash flow analysis   The search for the fundamental drivers that underlie a company's cash flow stream and affect its sustainability.

Cash flow analysis statement   A cash flow statement designed to facilitate analysis by creditors, equity investors, and analysts that provides multiple partitions of the overall change in cash and cash equivalents and highlights sustainable and nonrecurring sources and uses of cash. An example of the cash flow analysis statement is provided in Exhibit 9.4.

Cash flow available for debt service   A term used on the cash flow analysis statement that consists of core operating cash flow plus other cash income minus other cash expense and minus income taxes paid. Cash flow available for debt service is cash flow available for the payment of interest and required principal payments on debt and capital leases.

Cash flow drivers   The fundamental factors of growth and changes in profitability and efficiency that serve to increase and decrease core operating cash flow.

Cash flow from operations   A term used on the cash flow analysis statement that consists of cash flow available for debt service less total interest paid. The term also is used to refer to cash provided or used by operating activities and operating cash flow as those terms are defined by generally accepted accounting principles.

Cash flow impact   The measured effects of cash flow drivers of growth and changes in profitability and efficiency on core operating cash flow.

Cash flow tracking   Determining whether cash flows are associated with nonrecurring items of revenue, gain, expense, and loss. The timing of the cash flows is also investigated.

Cash from revenue   A term used on the cash flow analysis statement that consists of cash collections from customers for product sales and services provided.

Cash from sales   A Uniform Credit Analysis®–defined cash flow amount that consists of gross collections from customers for sales made and services provided.

Cash gross margin   A term used on the cash flow analysis statement that consists of cash from revenue minus cash cost of revenue.

Cash operating expense   A Uniform Credit Analysis®–defined cash flow amount that consists of cash paid for sales and marketing, general and administrative, and research and development expenditures. The term is defined the same way on the cash flow analysis statement.

Cash production costs   A Uniform Credit Analysis®–defined cash flow amount that consists of payments made for inventory purchased or manufactured and services provided.

Cash settlement   A procedure for settling futures contracts in which the cash difference between the futures price and the spot price is paid instead of physical delivery.

Cash surrender value of life insurance   That portion of a life insurance premium that will be returned to the policyholder in the event the policy is canceled.

Caution   One of the three components of the standard of prudence governing trustees; avoidance of undue risk and attentiveness to the protection of trust property.

CD   Certificate of deposit.

Central bank   A bank's bank and a public authority that regulates a nation's depository institutions and controls the quantity of money.

CEO   Chief executive officer.

Certificate of deposit   An unsecured evidence of indebtedness of a bank, which may be sold to others. Usually with a face value of $100,000 or more and bearing interest below the prime rate.

Ceteris paribus   Other things being equal—all other relevant things remaining the same.

CFTC   Commodity Futures Trading Commission.

CFO   Chief financial officer.

Chaebol   A Korean conglomerate.

Change in accumulated other comprehensive income   A term used on the cash flow analysis statement that refers to the change in accumulated other comprehensive income between reporting periods.

Change in cash and equivalents after external financing   A term used on the cash flow analysis statement that refers to the change in cash before external financing plus cash provided from external financing minus cash used in external financing adjusted for the change in accumulated other comprehensive income.

Change in cash before external financing A term used on the cash flow analysis statement that consists of cash flow after dividends minus cash paid for investments, capital expenditures, and intangibles.

Chapter 11 Bankruptcy procedure designed to reorganize and rehabilitate defaulting firm.

Chapter 7 Bankruptcy procedure whereby a debtor's assets are sold and the proceeds are used to repay creditors.

Characteristic line Regression line that indicates the systematic risk (beta) of a risky asset.

CHIPS Clearinghouse Interbank Payments System.

Classical growth theory A theory of economic growth based on the view that real GDP growth is temporary and that when real GDP per person increases above subsistence level, a population explosion brings real GDP back to subsistence level.

Clayton Act A federal antitrust law passed in 1914. Section 7, which is most relevant to mergers and acquisitions, prohibits the acquisition of stock and assets of a company when the effect is to lessen competition.

Clearinghouse An organization that settles and guarantees trades in some financial markets.

Closed-end fund An investment company with a fixed number of shares. New shares cannot be issued and the old shares cannot be redeemed. Shares are traded in the marketplace, and their value may differ from the underlying net asset value of the fund.

CMOs Collateralized mortgage obligations.

COD Cash on delivery.

Coefficient of variation (CV) A measure of relative variability that indicates risk per unit of return. It is equal to: standard deviation divided by the mean value. When used in investments, it is equal to: standard deviation of returns divided by the expected rate of return.

Collar (1) An upper and lower limit on the interest rate on a floating-rate note. (2) An options strategy that brackets the value of a portfolio between two bounds.

Collateral A specific asset pledged against possible default on a bond. Mortgage bonds are backed by claims on property. Collateral trust bonds are backed by claims on other securities. Equipment obligation bonds are backed by claims on equipment.

Collateralized mortgage obligation (CMO) A mortgage pass-through security that partitions cash flows from underlying mortgages into classes called tranches that receive principal payments according to stipulated rules.

Collateral trust bonds A mortgage bond wherein the assets backing the bond are financial assets like stocks and bonds.

Commercial bank A firm that is licensed by the Comptroller of the Currency in the U.S. Treasury or by a state agency to receive deposits and make loans.

Commercial paper Short-term unsecured debt issued by large corporations.

Commingled fund Typically, an investment pool run by a bank, in which participation is represented by accounting units rather than shares.

Commission recapture Credit for brokerage generated is then applied to such services as custody and appraisal.

Commitment fee Fee charged by bank on an unused *line of credit*.

Common stock Equities, or equity securities, issued as ownership shares in a publicly held corporation. Shareholders have voting rights and may receive dividends based on their proportionate ownership.

Company cost of capital The expected return on a portfolio of all the firm's securities.

Comparative advantage The ability to produce a good or service at a lower opportunity cost than other producers.

Compensating balance Non-interest-bearing demand deposits to compensate banks for bank loans or services.

Competitive environment The level of intensity of competition among firms in an industry, determined by an examination of five competitive forces.

Competitive market A market that has many buyers and many sellers, so no single buyer or seller can influence the price.

Competitive strategy The search by a firm for a favorable competitive position within an industry within the known competitive environment.

Complete portfolio The entire portfolio, including risky and risk-free assets.

Composite A universe of portfolios with similar investment objectives.

Composition Voluntary agreement to reduce payments on a firm's debt.

Compound interest Reinvestment of each interest payment on money invested to earn more interest (cf. *simple interest*).

Concentration ratio   The percentage of all sales contributed by the leading four or leading eight firms in an industry; sometimes called the *industry concentration ratio*.

Concentration ratios   Measures of the percentage of total industry revenues accounted for by a certain number of firms, usually the top four or eight.

Conglomerate   A combination of unrelated firms.

Conglomerate merger   *Merger* between two companies in unrelated businesses (cf. *horizontal merger, vertical merger*).

Constant growth model   A form of the dividend discount model that assumes dividends will grow at a constant rate.

Consumer Price Index (CPI)   An index that measures the average of the prices paid by urban consumers for a fixed "basket" of the consumer goods and services.

Consumption   The use of goods and services for personal satisfaction. Can also be viewed as spending on new goods and services out of a household's current income. Whatever is not consumed is saved. Consumption includes such things as buying food and going to a concert.

Consumption expenditure   The total payment for consumer goods and services.

Consumption function   The relationship between amount consumed and disposable income. A consumption function tells us how much people plan to consume at various levels of disposable income.

Consumption goods   Goods bought by households to use up, such as food and movies.

Contango   A situation in a futures market where the current contract price is greater than the current spot price for the underlying asset.

Contestable market   A market in which firms can enter and leave so easily that firms in the market face competition from potential entrants.

Continuous compounding   Interest compounded continuously rather than at fixed intervals.

Contraction   A business fluctuation during which the pace of national economic activity is slowing down.

Contract price   The transaction price specified in a forward or futures contract.

Controller   Officer responsible for budgeting, accounting, and auditing in a firm (cf. *treasurer*).

Convenience yield   An adjustment made to the theoretical forward or futures contract delivery price to account for the preference that consumers have for holding spot positions in the underlying asset.

Conversion factors   The adjustments made to Treasury bond futures contract terms to allow for the delivery of an instrument other than the standardized underlying asset.

Conversion parity price   The price at which common stock can be obtained by surrendering the convertible instrument at par value.

Conversion premium   The excess of the market value of the convertible security over its equity value if immediately converted into common stock. Typically expressed as a percentage of the equity value.

Conversion price   *Par value* of a *convertible bond* divided by the number of shares into which it may be exchanged.

Conversion ratio   The number of shares of common stock for which a convertible security may be exchanged.

Conversion value   The value of the convertible security if converted into common stock at the stock's current market price.

Convertible   A bond or preferred stock that offers the investor the right to convert his holding into common stock under set terms.

Convertible bond   A bond with an option allowing the bondholder to exchange the bond for a specified number of shares of common stock in the firm. A *conversion ratio* specifies the number of shares. The *market conversion price* is the current value of the shares for which the bond may be exchanged. The *conversion premium* is the excess of the bond's value over the conversion price.

Convexity   A measure of the degree to which a bond's price-yield curve departs from a straight line. This characteristic affects estimates of a bond's price volatility for a given change in yields.

Core operating cash flow   A term used on the cash flow analysis statement that consists of cash gross margin minus cash operating expense. Core operating cash flow is cash flow generated by core or central operations, before income taxes, other cash income and interest paid.

Corporate bonds   Long-term debt issued by private corporations typically paying semiannual coupons and returning the face value of the bond at maturity.

Corporate trustee   A bank or trust company having federal or state authority to serve as a trustee.

Corporation   A legal entity that may conduct business in its own name just as an individual does; the owners of a corporation, called shareholders, own shares of the firm's profits and enjoy the protection of limited liability.

Correlation   See *covariance*.

Correlation coefficient A statistic in which the covariance is scaled to a value between minus one (perfect negative correlation) and plus one (perfect positive correlation).

Cost of capital Opportunity cost of capital.

Cost of carry The cost associated with holding some asset, including financing, storage, and insurance costs. Any yield received on the asset is treated as a negative carrying cost.

Cost-of-service regulation Regulation based on allowing prices to reflect only the actual cost of production and no monopoly profits.

Counterparty Party on the other side of a *derivative* contract.

Country risk Uncertainty due to the possibility of major political or economic change in the country where an investment is located. Also called *political risk*.

Coupon The interest rate on a bond, expressed as a percentage of its face (not market) value. At one time bonds (and indeed stocks) contained coupons resembling postage stamps, which one "clipped" or cut periodically and presented for payment of interest (or dividends).

Coupon rate A bond's interest payments per dollar of par value.

Covariance A measure of the degree to which returns on two risky assets move in tandem. A positive covariance means that asset returns move together. A negative covariance means they vary inversely.

Covenant Clause in a loan agreement.

Covered call A trading strategy in which a call option is sold as a supplement to a long position in an underlying asset or portfolio of assets.

Covered interest arbitrage A trading strategy involving borrowing money in one country and lending it to another designed to exploit price deviations from the interest rate parity model.

Covered option *Option* position with an offsetting position in the underlying asset.

Creative cash flow reporting Any and all steps used to alter operating cash flow and, in the process, provide a more positive signal about a firm's sustainable cash-generating ability. Creative cash flow reporting may entail steps taken within the boundaries of generally accepted accounting principles, beyond those boundaries, or by the inclusion of nonrecurring amounts in operating cash flow.

Creative response Behavior on the part of a firm that allows it to comply with the letter of the law but violates the spirit, significantly lessening the law's effects.

Credit analysis An active bond portfolio management strategy designed to identify bonds that are expected to experience changes in rating. This strategy is critical when investing in high-yield bonds.

Credit derivative Contract for *hedging* against loan default or changes in credit risk (see *default swap*).

Credit enhancement Contract for *hedging* against loan default or changes in credit risk (see *default swap*).

Credit risk See Default risk.

Credit scoring A procedure for assigning scores to borrowers on the basis of the risk of default.

Cross-rate The exchange rate between two currencies, derived from their exchange rates with a third currency.

Crowding-out effect The tendency for a government budget deficit to decrease in investment.

Cum dividend With dividend.

Cumulative abnormal return See *abnormal return*.

Cumulative preferred stock Stock that takes priority over *common stock* in regard to dividend payments. Dividends may not be paid on the common stock until all past *dividends* on the *preferred stock* have been paid.

Currency The bills and coins that we use today.

Currency appreciation The rise in the value of one currency in terms of another currency.

Currency depreciation The fall in the value of one currency in terms of another currency.

Currency exposure The sensitivity of the asset return, measured in the investor's domestic currency, to a movement in the exchange rate.

Currency swap A contract to exchange streams of fixed cash flows denominated in two different currencies.

Current account A category of balance of payments transactions that measures the exchange of merchandise, the exchange of services, and unilateral transfers.

Current asset Asset that will normally be turned into cash within a year.

Current income A return objective in which the investor seeks to generate income rather than capital gains; generally a goal of an investor who wants to supplement earnings with income to meet living expenses.

Current liability Liability that will normally be repaid within a year.

Current ratio A ratio representing the ability of the firm to pay off its current liabilities by liquidating current assets (current assets/current liabilities).

Current yield A bond's annual coupon payment divided by its price. Differs from yield to maturity.

Custodians Agents who hold property in safekeeping for others, usually without inherent investment management responsibility.

Customer acquisition costs Initial direct costs incurred in adding to a company's customer base, including direct-response advertising, commissions, and related administrative costs. When capitalized, prospective customer-related revenues must be expected to exceed amounts capitalized. Depending on the industry, such costs may have other names, including subscriber acquisition costs and policy acquisition costs.

Cyclical company A firm whose earnings rise and fall with general economic activity.

Cyclical developments Changes in business activity that are caused by moves in the overall economy between expansion and recession.

Cyclical industries Industries with above-average sensitivity to the state of the economy.

Cyclicals Some industries are perennially subject to the vagaries of the business cycle: mining, steel, construction, automobiles, chemicals, machine tools, and the like. It is impossible to get away from the cyclical effect in business, just as there is always alternation between good and bad weather, so a cyclical company will have an irregular earnings pattern, and usually an irregular stock price pattern too.

Cyclical stock A stock with a high beta; its gains typically exceed those of a rising market and its losses typically exceed those of a falling market.

Cyclical surplus or deficit The actual surplus or deficit minus the structural surplus or deficit.

Data mining (data snooping) Excessive search to find interesting (but probably coincidental) behavior in a body of data.

DCF Discounted cash flow.

DDM Dividend discount model.

Dealer An agent that buys and sells securities as a principal (for its own account) rather than as a broker for clients. A dealer may function, at different times, as a broker or as a dealer. Sometimes called a *market maker*.

Debenture Unsecured *bond*.

Debentures Bonds that promise payments of interest and principal but pledge no specific assets. Holders have first claim on the issuer's income and unpledged assets. Also known as *unsecured bonds*.

Debt issue costs The cost of issuing debt, including appraisal and recording fees, and commitment fees paid separately to a lender.

Decision tree Method of representing alternative sequential decisions and the possible outcomes from these decisions.

Decline stage The fourth and final stage of a company's life cycle during which revenue declines and earnings turn to losses. Depending on the amount of noncash expenses reported, such as depreciation and amortization expense, operating cash flow may remain positive until very late in the decline stage.

Default premium A differential in promised yield that compensates the investor for the risk inherent in purchasing a corporate bond that entails some risk of default.

Default risk The risk that an issuer will be unable to make interest and principal payments on time.

Default swap *Credit derivative* in which one party makes fixed payments while the payments by the other party depend on the occurrence of a loan default.

Defeasance Practice whereby the borrower sets aside cash or *bonds* sufficient to service the borrower's debt. Both the borrower's debt and the offsetting cash or bonds are removed from the balance sheet.

Defensive competitive strategy Positioning the firm so that its capabilities provide the best means to deflect the effect of the competitive forces in the industry.

Defensive industries Industries with little sensitivity to the state of the economy.

Defensive stock A stock whose return is not expected to decline as much as that of the overall market during a bear market (a beta less than one).

Deferred revenue Revenue that is collected in advance of being earned and is reported as a liability. Also known as *unearned revenue*.

Deferred tax assets Future tax benefits that result from (1) the origination of a deductible temporary difference, that is, a tax deduction that can be used in a future period, or (2) a loss or tax-credit carryover. These future tax benefits are realized upon the reversal of deductible temporary differences. In addition, realization can occur by the offsetting of a loss carryforward against taxable income or a tax credit carryforward against taxes currently payable.

Deferred tax liabilities Future tax obligations that result from the origination of taxable temporary differences. Upon origination, these temporary difference cause pretax financial income to exceed taxable income. These future tax obligations are paid later when temporary differences reverse, now causing taxable income to exceed pretax book income.

Defined benefit pension plan A pension plan to which the company contributes a certain amount each year and promises to pay employees a specified income after they retire. The benefit size is based on factors such as workers' salary and time of employment.

Defined benefit plan A retirement plan that specifies the amount an employee collects after different periods of employment.

Defined benefit plans Pension plans in which retirement benefits are set according to a fixed formula.

Defined contribution pension plan A pension plan in which worker benefits are determined by the size of employees' contributions to the plan and the returns earned on the fund's investments.

Defined contribution plan A retirement plan with benefits based on the earnings of the contributions made, taking account of the length of employment.

Defined contribution plans Pension plans in which the employer is committed to making contributions according to a fixed formula.

Deflation The situation in which the average of all prices of goods and services in an economy is falling.

Degree of operating leverage Percentage change in profits for a 1% change in sales.

Delta The change in the price of the option with respect to a $1 change in the price of the underlying asset; this is the option's *hedge ratio,* or the number of units of the underlying asset that can be hedged by a single option contract.

Delta hedge A dynamic hedging strategy using options with continuous adjustment of the number of options used, as a function of the delta of the option.

Demand The relationship between the quantity of a good that consumers plan to buy and the price of the good when all other influences on buyers' plans remain the same. It is described by a demand schedule and illustrated by a demand curve.

Demand curve A curve that shows the relationship between the quantity demanded of a good and its price when all other influences on consumers' planned purchases remain the same.

Demand for labor The relationship between the quantity of labor demanded and the real wage rate when all other influences on a firm's hiring plans remain the same.

Demand-pull inflation An inflation that results from an initial increase in aggregate demand.

Dependent variable A variable whose value changes according to changes in the value of one or more independent variables.

Depreciation Reduction in the value of capital goods over a one-year period due to physical wear and tear and also to obsolescence; also called *capital consumption allowance.* Can also be viewed as a decrease in the exchange value of one nation's currency in terms of the currency of another nation.

Depreciation proxy for replacement capital expenditures A term used on the cash flow analysis statement that consists of depreciation and amortization of property, plant, and equipment used in operations and serves as an approximation of the cost of replacing that portion of property, plant, and equipment consumed by operations during a reporting period.

Depression An extremely severe recession.

Deregulation The elimination or phasing out of regulations on economic activity.

Derivatives Securities bearing a contractual relation to some underlying asset or rate. Options, futures, forward, and swap contracts, as well as many forms of bonds, are derivative securities.

Descendants The direct parental line, including children, grandchildren, great-grandchildren, and so on.

Devaluation Deliberate downward adjustment of a currency against its fixed parity.

Diff Differential swap.

Dilution Reduction in shareholders' equity per share or earnings per share that arises from some changes among shareholders' proportionate interests.

Diminishing marginal returns The tendency for the marginal product of an additional unit of a factor of production is less than the marginal product of the previous unit of the factor.

Directed brokerage A manager is asked to direct business to a specified broker, usually to pay for services.

Direct exchange rate The amount of local or domestic currency required to purchase one unit of foreign currency.

Direct Investments (Private Equity) An investment made directly in venture capital or private equity assets (i.e., not via a partnership or fund).

Direct quote For foreign exchange, the number of U.S. dollars needed to buy one unit of a foreign currency (cf. *indirect quote*).

Direct-response advertising Advertising designed to elicit sales to customers who can be shown to have responded specifically to the advertising in the past. Such costs can be capitalized when persuasive historical evidence permits formulation of a reliable estimate of the future revenue that can be obtained from incremental advertising expenditures.

Discontinued operations Net income and the gain or loss on disposal of a discontinued business segment or separately measured business unit.

Discount A bond selling at a price below par value due to capital market conditions.

Discounted cash flow (DCF) Future cash flows multiplied by *discount factors* to obtain *present value.*

Discount factor *Present value* of $1 received at a stated future date.

Discounting The conversion of a future amount of money to its present value.

Discount rate (1) Rate used to calculate the present value of future cash flows. (2) The interest rate at which the Fed stands ready to lend reserves to depository institutions.

Discretionary account An account of a customer who gives a broker the authority to make buy and sell decisions on the customer's behalf.

Disposable income Aggregate income minus taxes plus transfer payments.

Dissident A shareholder, or group of shareholders, who oppose current management and may try to use the proxy process to gain control of the company or to try to get the company to take certain actions, such as payment of certain dividends. Dissidents often try to have their representatives placed on the board of directors.

Diversifiable risk Risk attributable to firm-specific risk, or nonmarket risk. *Nondiversifiable* risk refers to systematic or market risk.

Diversification (1) Spreading a portfolio over many investments to avoid excessive exposure to any one source of risk. (2) In mergers and acquisitions, a term that refers to buying companies or assets outside the companies' current lines of business.

Divestiture The sale of a component of the company, such as a division.

Dividend Payment by a company to its stockholders.

Dividend discount model (DDM) A formula stating that the intrinsic value of a firm is the present value of all expected future dividends.

Dividend payout ratio Percentage of earnings paid out as dividends.

Dividend reinvestment plan (DRIP) Plan that allows shareholders to reinvest dividends automatically.

Dividends Portion of a corporation's profits paid to its owners (shareholders).

Dividends paid A term used on the cash flow analysis statement that refers to cash disbursements for dividends on common and preferred stock.

Dividend yield Annual dividend divided by share price.

Dow Jones Industrial Average (DJI or DJIA) A price-weighted average of thirty industrial companies.

Duration The average maturity of a bond. The longer the duration, the more sensitive will be the price to interest rate changes.

Dynamic hedging Constant updating of hedge positions as market conditions change.

Early stage With reference to venture capital financing, the stage associated with moving into operation and before commercial manufacturing and sales have occurred. Includes the start-up and first stages.

Earnings before interest, taxes, depreciation, and amortization (EBITDA) An earnings-based measure that often serves as a surrogate for cash flow. The measure actually represents working capital provided by operations before interest and taxes.

Earnings before interest and taxes (EBIT) Net income measured before interest expense and before income tax expense. EBIT has a long history of being used as a basis for measuring fixed-charge coverage.

Earnings management The practice of using flexibility in accounting rules to improve the apparent profitability of the firm.

Earnings momentum A strategy in which portfolios are constructed of stocks of firms with rising earnings.

Earnings multiplier model A technique for estimating the value of a stock issue as a multiple of its future earnings per share.

Earnings retention ratio Plowback ratio.

Earnings surprise A company announcement of earnings that differs from analysts' prevailing expectations.

Earnings yield The ratio of earnings to price, E/P.

EBIT Earnings before interest and taxes.

EBITDA Earnings before interest, taxes, depreciation, and amortization.

Economic depreciation The change in the market value of capital over a given period.

Economic efficiency A situation that occurs when the firm produces a given output at the least cost.

Economic exposure Risk that arises from changes in real exchange rates (cf. *transaction exposure, translation exposure*).

Economic growth (1) Increases in per capita real GDP measured by its rate of change per year. (2) The expansion of production possibilities that results from capital accumulation and technological change.

Economic growth rate The percentage change in the quantity of goods and services produced from one year to the next.

Economic income   Cash flow plus change in *present value.*

Economic model   A description of some aspect of the economic world that includes only those features of the world that are needed for the purpose at hand.

Economic profit   A firm's total revenue minus its opportunity cost.

Economic profits   Total revenues minus total opportunity costs of all inputs used, or the total of all implicit and explicit costs.

Economic rent   A payment for the use of any resource over and above its opportunity cost.

Economic rents   Profits in excess of the competitive level.

Economic risk   As used in currency risk management, the risk that arises when the foreign currency value of a foreign investment reacts systematically to an exchange rate movement.

Economics   The social science that studies the choices that individuals, businesses, governments, and entire societies make and how they cope with scarcity and the incentives that influence and reconcile those choices.

Economic theory   A generalization that summarizes what we think we understand about the economic choices that people make and the performance of industries and entire economies.

Economic value added (EVA)   (1) The spread between ROA and cost of capital multiplied by the capital invested in the firm. It measures the dollar value of the firm's return in excess of its opportunity cost. (2) Internal management performance measure that compares net operating profit to total cost of capital. Indicates how profitable company projects are as a sign of management performance.

Economic welfare   A comprehensive measure of the general state of economic well-being.

Economies of scale   The reduction of a company's average costs due to increasing output and spreading out fixed costs over higher output levels.

Economies of scope   The ability of a firm to utilize one set of inputs to provide a broader range of outputs or services.

Effective duration   Direct measure of the interest rate sensitivity of a bond (or any financial instrument) based upon price changes derived from a pricing model.

Efficient frontier   The set of all efficient portfolios for various levels of risk.

Efficient market   A market in which any relevant information is immediately impounded in asset prices.

Efficient Market Hypothesis   Crudely, the belief that since all information about stocks is available, their current market price represents their true value. If this were true, certain investors would not achieve consistently superior results, which they do, and since all information about a chess game is available to both opponents, there should not be consistently superior players. All information is never known, judgment is unevenly distributed, and decision making is imperfectly organized and moved by great tides of emotion.

Efficient portfolio   A portfolio that provides the best expected return for a given level of risk.

Effective duration   Percentage change in bond price per change in the level of market interest rates.

Effective tax rate   The income tax provision divided by income before the income tax provision.

Efficiency   The case in which a given level of inputs is used to produce the maximum output possible. Alternatively, the situation in which a given output is produced at minimum cost.

Efficient capital market   A market in which security prices rapidly reflect all information about securities.

Efficient diversification   The organizing principle of modern portfolio theory, which maintains that any risk-averse investor will search for the highest expected return for any level of portfolio risk.

Efficient frontier   The set of portfolios that has the maximum rate of return for every given level of risk, or the minimum risk for every potential rate of return.

Efficient market   Market in which security prices reflect information instantaneously.

Efficient portfolio   Portfolio that offers the lowest risk (*standard deviation*) for its *expected return* and the highest expected return for its level of risk.

EFT   Electronic funds transfer.

Electronic crossing networks   Order-driven trading systems in which market orders are anonymously matched at prespecified times at prices determined in the primary market for the system.

Emerging Issues Task Force (EITF)   The EITF assists the Financial Accounting Standards Board through the timely identification, discussion, and resolution of financial accounting issues based on existing authoritative literature.

Emerging markets   Often, countries so defined by the International Finance Corporation (IFC), based on their per capita income.

Empirical   Relying on real-world data in evaluating the usefulness of a model.

Empirical duration   Measures directly the interest rate sensitivity of an asset by examining the percentage price change for an asset in response to a change in yield during a specified period of time.

Employee Retirement Income Security Act (ERISA)   Governs most private pension and benefit plans.

Endogenous growth theory   A theory of economic growth that does not assume that the marginal productivity of capital declines as capital is added.

Endowment funds   Organizations chartered to invest money for specific purposes.

Endowments   The various resources in an economy, including both physical resources and such human resources as ingenuity and management skills.

Entrepreneurship   The human resource that organizes labor, land, and capital. Entrepreneurs come up with new ideas about what and how to produce, make business decisions, and bear the risk that arise from their decisions.

EPS   Earnings per share.

Equilibrium   The situation when quantity supplied equals quantity demanded at a particular price.

Equilibrium price   The price at which the quantity demanded equals the quantity supplied.

Equities   Another name for shares. The capitalization of a company consists of "equity"—or ownership—represented by common or preferred shares (stock), and debt, represented by bonds, notes, and the like. (In England, "corporation stock" means municipal bonds, incidentally.)

Equity   (1) *Common stock* and *preferred stock*. Often used to refer to common stock only. (2) *Net worth*.

Equity carve-out   The issuance of equity in a division or part of a parent company that then becomes a separate company.

Equity security   An ownership interest in an enterprise, including preferred and common stock.

Equity swap   A swap transaction in which one cash flow is tied to the return to an equity portfolio position, often an index such as the Standard and Poor's 500, while the other is based on a floating-rate index.

ESOP   Employee stock ownership plan.

Estimated rate of return   The rate of return an investor anticipates earning from a specific investment over a particular future holding period.

Euribor   Interbank offer rate for short-term deposits in euros. Euribor is determined by an association of European banks.

Euro   The common currency of many European countries.

Eurobond   A bond underwritten by a multinational syndicate of banks and placed mainly in countries other than the country of the issuer; sometimes called an *international bond*.

Eurocurrency market   Interbank market for short-term borrowing and lending in a currency outside of its home country. For example, borrowing and lending of U.S. dollars outside the United States. Thus, it is an offshore market escaping national regulations. This is the largest money market for several major currencies.

Eurodollar deposit   Dollar deposit with a bank outside the United States.

Eurodollar market   The U.S. dollar segment of the Eurocurrency market.

Eurodollars   Dollar-denominated deposits at foreign banks or foreign branches of American banks.

European option   A European option can be exercised only on the expiration date. Compare with an American option, which can be exercised before, up to, and on its expiration date.

European terms   With reference to U.S. dollar exchange rate quotations, the price of a U.S. dollar in terms of another currency.

European Union (EU)   A formal association of European countries founded by the Treaty of Rome in 1957. Formerly known as the EEC.

EVA   Economic value added.

Event study   Research methodology designed to measure the impact of an event of interest on stock returns.

Excess cash margin (ECM)   An interpretive ratio used to measure the relationship between adjusted operating cash flow and adjusted operating earnings. The ratio measures in percent terms the excess of cash margin (adjusted operating cash flow to revenue) over net margin (adjusted operating earnings to revenue). The ratio is calculated as ((Adjusted operating cash flow − Adjusted operating earnings)/Revenue) × 100). Increases in the ratio over time indicate that adjusted operating cash flow is growing faster or declining slower than adjusted operating earnings. Decreases in the ratio over time indicate that adjusted operating cash flow is growing slower or declining faster than adjusted operating earnings.

Excess return   Rate of return in excess of the risk-free rate.

Exchange of assets   Acquisition of another company by purchase of its assets in exchange for cash or shares.

Exchange rate   Price of a unit of one country's currency in terms of another country's currency.

Exchange rate risk   Uncertainty due to the denomination of an investment in a currency other than that of the investor's own country.

Exchange-traded funds (ETFs) A type of mutual fund traded like other shares on a stock market, having special characteristics particularly related to redemption, and generally designed to closely track the performance of a specified stock market index.

Exchanges National or regional auction markets providing a facility for members to trade securities. A seat is a membership on an exchange.

Executor The legal representative of a person who dies with a will.

Exercise price The transaction price specified in an option contract; also known as the *strike price*.

Exercise price (striking price) Price at which a call option or put option may be exercised.

Expansion A business cycle phase between a trough and a peak—phase in which real GDP increases.

Expectations theory Theory that forward interest rate (forward exchange rate) equals expected spot rate.

Expected rate of return The return that analysts' calculations suggest a security should provide, based on the market's rate of return during the period and the security's relationship to the market.

Expected return Average of possible returns weighted by their probabilities.

Expected return–beta relationship Implication of the CAPM that security risk premiums (expected excess returns) will be proportional to beta.

Expected utility The average utility arising from all possible outcomes.

Exports The goods and services that we sell to people in other countries.

Ex-Post After the fact.

Extended amortization period An amortization period that continues beyond a long-lived asset's economic useful life.

External financing A term used on the cash flow analysis statement that consists of net debt and equity capital raised from external sources.

Externality A consequence of an economic activity that spills over to affect third parties. Pollution is an externality. Can also be viewed as a situation in which a private cost (or benefit) diverges from a social cost (or benefit); a situation in which the costs (or benefits) of an action are not fully borne (or gained) by the two parties engaged in exchange or by an individual engaging in a scarce-resource-using activity.

Extra dividend *Dividend* that may or may not be repeated (cf. *regular dividend*).

Extraordinary item Gain or loss that is unusual and infrequent in occurrence.

Face value The amount paid on a bond at redemption and traditionally printed on the bond certificate. This face value excludes the final coupon payment. Sometimes referred to as *par value*.

Factor beta Sensitivity of security returns to changes in a systematic factor. Alternatively, factor loading; factor sensitivity.

Factoring Arrangement whereby a financial institution buys a company's *accounts receivable* and collects the debt.

Factor loading See *factor beta*.

Factor model A way of decomposing the factors that influence a security's rate of return into common and firm-specific influences.

Factor portfolio A well-diversified portfolio constructed to have a beta of 1.0 on one factor and a beta of zero on any other factor.

Factor sensitivity See *factor beta*.

Factors of production The productive resources that businesses use to produce goods and services.

Fair value (1) The amount at which an asset could be acquired or sold in a current transaction between willing parties in which the parties each acted knowledgeably, prudently, and without compulsion. (2) The theoretical value of a security based on current market conditions. The fair value is the value such that no arbitrage opportunities exist.

FASB Financial Accounting Standards Board.

Federal Deposit Insurance Corporation (FDIC) A government agency that insures the deposits held in banks and most other depository institutions; all U.S. banks are insured this way.

Federal funds Non-interest-bearing deposits by banks at the Federal Reserve. Excess reserves are lent by banks to each other.

Federal funds rate The interest rate that depository institutions pay to borrow reserves in the interbank federal funds market.

Fictitious revenue Revenue recognized on a nonexistent sale or service transaction.

Fiduciary A person who supervises or oversees the investment portfolio of a third party, such as in a trust account, and makes investment decisions in accordance with the owner's wishes.

Fiduciary relationship An arrangement under which a person (the fiduciary) has a duty to act for another's benefit (the beneficiary).

FIFO The first-in first-out accounting method of inventory valuation.

Film production costs Costs incurred in producing a motion picture, including costs to obtain a screenplay; compensation of cast members, directors, producers, extras and other staff; set construction and operations; wardrobe and accessories; sound synchronization; on-location costs; and postproduction costs such as music, special effects and editing.

Financial account   A component of the balance of payments covering investments by residents abroad and investments by nonresidents in the home country. Examples include direct investment made by companies, portfolio investments in equity and bonds, and other investments and liabilities.

Financial Accounting Standards Board (FASB)   The principal standard-setting body in the United States. Its primary standards are Statements of Financial Accounting Standards (SFASs).

Financial assets   Financial assets such as stocks and bonds are claims to the income generated by real assets or claims on income from the government.

Financial capital   Funds used to purchase physical capital goods such as buildings and equipment.

Financial engineering   Combining or dividing existing instruments to create new financial products.

Financial innovation   The development of new financial products—new ways of borrowing and lending.

Financial intermediaries   Institutions that transfer funds between ultimate lenders (savers) and ultimate borrowers.

Financial intermediation   The process by which financial institutions accept savings from businesses, households, and governments and lend the savings to other businesses, households, and governments.

Financial lease (capital lease, full-payout lease)   Long-term, noncancelable lease (cf. *operating lease*).

Financial risk   The variability of future income arising from the firm's fixed financing costs, for example, interest payments. The effect of fixed financial costs is to magnify the effect of changes in operating profit on net income or earnings per share.

Firm   (1) An economic unit that hires factors of production and organizes those factors to produce and sell goods and services. (2) For purposes of the GIPS standards, the term "firm" refers to the entity defined for compliance with the GIPS standards.

Firm-specific risk   See *diversifiable risk*.

Fiscal policy   The government's attempt to achieve macroeconomic objectives such as full employment, sustained economic growth, and price level stability by setting and changing taxes, making transfer payments, and purchasing goods and services.

Fixed costs   Costs that do not vary with output. Fixed costs include such things as rent on a building. These costs are fixed for a certain period of time; in the long run, they are variable.

Fixed-income security   A security such as a bond that pays a specified cash flow over a specific period.

Fixed investment   Purchases by businesses of newly produced producer durables, or capital goods, such as production machinery and office equipment.

Fixing   A method for determining the market price of a security by finding the price that balances buyers and sellers. A fixing takes place periodically each day at defined times. Sometimes called a *call auction*.

Flexible exchange rates   Exchange rates that are allowed to fluctuate in the open market in response to changes in supply and demand. Sometimes called *floating exchange rates*.

Flexible exchange rate system   A system in which exchange rates are determined by supply and demand.

Floating-rate bond   A bond whose interest rate is reset periodically according to a specified market rate.

Floating-rate note (FRN)   Short- to intermediate-term bonds with regularly scheduled coupon payments linked to a variable interest rate, most often LIBOR.

Floor   A contract on an interest rate, whereby the writer of the floor periodically pays the difference between a specified floor rate and the market interest rate if, and only if, this difference is positive. This is equivalent to a stream of put options on the interest rate.

Floor agreement   A contract that on each settlement date pays the holder the greater of the difference between the floor rate and the reference rate or zero; it is equivalent to a series of put options on the reference rate.

Floor-plan financing   A loan arrangement that is typically used to finance durable goods inventory such as automobiles, mobile homes, recreational vehicles, boats and motorcycles, where the underlying inventory is pledged as loan security. Any outstanding loan balance is linked directly to inventory levels, increasing as inventory levels increase and requiring repayment as inventory levels decline.

Flow   A quantity measured per unit of time; something that occurs over time, such as the income you make per week or per year or the number of individuals who are fired every month.

Foreign bond   A bond issued on the domestic capital market of another country.

Foreign currency risk premium   The expected movement in the (direct) exchange rate minus the interest rate differential (domestic risk-free rate minus foreign risk-free rate).

Foreign direct investment   The acquisition of more than 10 percent of the shares of ownership in a company in another nation.

Foreign exchange   The purchase (sale) of a currency against the sale (purchase) of another.

Foreign exchange expectation   A relation that states that the forward exchange rate, quoted at time 0 for delivery at time 1, is equal to the expected value of the spot exchange rate at time 1. When stated relative to the current spot exchange rate, the relation states that the forward discount (premium) is equal to the expected exchange rate movement.

Foreign exchange market   A market in which households, firms, and governments buy and sell national currencies.

Foreign exchange rate   (1) The price of one currency in terms of another. (2) The possibility that changes in the value of a nation's currency will result in variations in the market value of assets.

Forex   Foreign exchange.

Forward contract   An agreement between two counterparties that requires the exchange of a commodity or security at a fixed time in the future at a predetermined price.

Forward discount   A situation where, from the perspective of the domestic country, the spot exchange rate is smaller than the forward exchange rate with a foreign country.

Forward discount or premium   Refers to the percentage difference between the forward exchange rate and the spot exchange rate (premium if positive, discount if negative).

Forward exchange rate   Exchange rate fixed today for exchanging currency at some future date (cf. *spot exchange rate*).

Forward interest rate   (1) Interest rate fixed today on a loan to be made at some future date (cf. *spot interest rate*). (2) Rate of interest for a future period that would equate the total return of a long-term bond with that of a strategy of rolling over shorter-term bonds. The forward rate is inferred from the term structure.

Forward premium   A situation where, from the perspective of the domestic country, the spot exchange rate is larger than the forward exchange rate with a foreign country.

Forward rate   A short-term yield for a future holding period implied by the spot rates of two securities with different maturities.

Forward rate agreement (FRA)   A transaction in which two counter-parties agree to a single exchange of cash flows based on a fixed and floating rate, respectively.

Franchise factor   A firm's unique competitive advantage that makes it possible for a firm to earn excess returns (rates of return above a firm's cost of capital) on its capital projects. In turn, these excess returns and the franchise factor cause the firm's stock price to have a *P/E* ratio above its base *P/E* ratio that is equal to $1/k$.

Franchise value   In P/E ratio analysis, the present value of growth opportunities divided by next year's expected earnings.

Free cash flow   Cash not required for operations or for reinvestment.

Free cash flow hypothesis   Theory put forward by Michael Jensen, which asserts that the assumption of debt used to finance leveraged takeovers will absorb discretionary cash flows and help eliminate the agency problem between management and shareholders. It is assumed that with the higher debt service obligations, management would apply the company's cash flows to activities that are in management's interest and not necessarily in shareholders' interests.

Free cash flow to equity   This cash flow measure equals cash flow from operations minus capital expenditures and debt payments.

Full price (or dirty price)   The total price of a bond, including accrued interest.

Funded debt   Debt maturing after more than one year (cf. *unfunded debt*).

Funds   Traditionally defined as working capital, that is, the excess of current assets over current liabilities.

Funds from operations (FFO)   A term used by real estate investment trusts (REITs) and defined as net income or loss excluding gains or losses from debt restructuring and sales of property, plus depreciation and amortization of real estate assets.

Futures contract   A standardized contract to buy (sell) an asset at a specified date and a specified price (futures price). The contract is traded on an organized exchange, and the potential gain/loss is realized each day (marking to market).

Futures option   The right to enter a specified futures contract at a futures price equal to the stipulated exercise price.

Futures price   The price at which a futures trader commits to make or take delivery of the underlying asset.

GAAP   Generally accepted accounting principles.

GAAP operating cash flow   Cash flow from operating activities computed in accordance with generally accepted accounting principles. Also see *reported operating cash flow.*

Game theory   A tool that economists use to analyze strategic behavior—behavior that takes into account the expected behavior of others and the mutual recognition of independence.

Gamma   How a security's price changes affect an option's **delta** (*q.v.*). Low for small price changes and high for large ones.

GDP deflator   One measure of the price level, which is the average of current-year prices as a percentage of base-year prices.

Gearing   Financial leverage.

Generally accepted accounting principles (GAAP)   A common set of standards and procedures for the preparation of general-purpose financial statements that either have been established by an authoritative accounting rule-making body, such as the Financial Accounting Standards Board (FASB), or have over time become common accepted practice.

General Partner (Private Equity) (GP)   A class of partner in a partnership. The GP retains liability for the actions of the partnership. In the PRIVATE EQUITY world, the GP is the fund manager and the LIMITED PARTNERS (LPs) are the institutional and high-net-worth investors in the partnership. The GP earns a management fee and a percentage of profits.

General Utilities Doctrine   A component of the Tax Code that provided tax benefits for the sale of assets or liquidating distributions. It was repealed by the Tax Reform Act of 1986.

Generic   See *plain-vanilla.*

Geometric mean (GM)   The *n*th root of the product of the annual holding period returns for *n* years minus 1.

Global   Of a fund or portfolio, invested both in the United States and abroad.

Global Investment Performance Standards™ (GIPS®)   A global industry standard for the ethical presentation of investment performance results promulgated by the Association for Investment Management and Research.

Globalization   Tendency toward a worldwide investment environment, and the integration of national capital markets.

Golden parachute   Employment contract of upper management that provides a larger payout upon the occurrence of certain control transactions, such as a certain percentage share purchase by an outside entity or when there is a tender offer for a certain percentage of the company's shares.

Gold standard   An international monetary system in which the parity of a currency is fixed in terms of its gold content.

Goods   All things from which individuals derive satisfaction or happiness.

Goods and services   The objects that people value and produce to satisfy their wants.

Goodwill   An intangible asset representing the amount paid in the acquisition of either significant influence or control of an entity over the fair value of the acquired entity's identifiable net assets.

Governance   The oversight of a firm's management.

Government budget deficit   The deficit that arises when federal government spends more than it collects in taxes.

Government debt   The total amount of borrowing that the government has borrowed. It equals the sum of past budget deficits minus budget surpluses.

Great Depression   A decade (1929–1939) of high unemployment and stagnant production throughout the world economy.

Greenmail   Situation in which a large block of stock is held by an unfriendly company, forcing the target company to repurchase the stock at a substantial premium to prevent a takeover.

Gross capital expenditures   Capital expenditures before subtraction for the proceeds derived from the disposal of productive assets.

Gross cash profit   A Uniform Credit Analysis (UCA)®–defined cash flow amount that consists of cash collected from sales less cash paid to suppliers.

Gross domestic product (GDP)   Total value of a country's output produced by residents within the country's physical borders.

Gross investment   The total amount spent on purchases of new capital and on replacing depreciated capital.

Gross margin   Revenue minus cost of goods sold. Also referred to as *gross profit.*

Gross national product (GNP)   Total value of a country's output produced by residents both within the country's physical borders and abroad.

Growth accounting   A method of calculating how much real GDP growth results from growth of labor and capital and how much is attributable to technological change.

Growth cash flow profile The capacity of a firm to generate core operating cash flow as it grows reflecting a combination of its operating cushion and operating working capital requirements.

Growth company A company that consistently has the opportunities and ability to invest in projects that provide rates of return that exceed the firm's cost of capital. Because of these investment opportunities, it retains a high proportion of earnings, and its earnings grow faster than those of average firms.

Growth investing Emphasizes the future over apparent immediate undervaluation. Thus, usually implies buying companies with higher than average price-earnings ratios and lower dividend yields.

Growth-related capital expenditures, net of dispositions A term used on the cash flow analysis statement that consists of capital expenditures required to replace productive capacity consumed during a reporting period and to add infrastructure needed to maintain revenue growth. It is computed as capital expenditures net of cash received for dispositions of property, plant, and equipment less the depreciation proxy for replacement capital expenditures.

Growth stage The second period in a company's life cycle during which operating earnings turn positive and revenue increases faster than the rate of growth in the overall economy. Operating cash flow may be negative during the early part of the growth stage of a company's life cycle and turn positive as the firm becomes more established.

Growth stock A stock issue that generates a higher rate of return than other stocks in the market with similar risk characteristics.

Hedge fund An investment vehicle designed to manage a private, unregistered portfolio of assets according to any of several strategies. The investment strategy often employs arbitrage trading and significant financial leverage (e.g., short selling, borrowing, derivatives) while the compensation arrangement for the manager typically specifies considerable profit participation.

Hedge ratio (1) The percentage of the position in an asset that is hedged with derivatives. (2) The number of derivative contracts that must be transacted to offset the price volatility of an underlying commodity or security position.

Hedging (1) Buying one security and selling another in order to reduce risk. A perfect hedge produces a riskless portfolio. (2) The process of reducing the uncertainty of the future value of a portfolio by taking positions in various derivatives (e.g., forward and futures contracts).

Hedging demands Demands for securities to hedge particular sources of consumption risk, beyond the usual mean-variance diversification motivation.

Herfindahl index A measure of industry concentration equal to the sum of the squared market shares of the firms in the industry.

Highly leveraged transaction (HLT) Bank loan to a highly leveraged firm (formerly needed to be separately reported to the Federal Reserve Board).

High-yield bond A bond rated below investment grade. Also referred to as *speculative-grade bonds* or *junk bonds.*

Holding company A company that owns the stock of other corporations. A holding company may not engage in actual operations of its own but merely manages various operating units that it owns an interest in.

Holding-period return The rate of return over a given period.

Horizontal merger The joining of firms that are producing or selling a similar product.

Hot issue A newly issued stock that is in strong demand; often it will go to a premium over its original issue price.

Human capital The knowledge and skill that people obtain from education, on-the-job training, and experience.

Hurdle rate Minimum acceptable rate of return on a project.

Illiquidity premium Extra expected return as compensation for limited liquidity.

IMM International monetary market.

Implicit costs Expenses that managers do not have to pay out of pocket and hence do not normally explicitly calculate, such as the opportunity cost of factors of production that are owned; examples are owner-provided capital and owner-provided labor.

Implied volatility The volatility of an asset that is implicit in the current market price of an option (using a standard Black-Scholes-Merton formula).

Imports The goods and services that we buy from people in other countries.

Imputation tax system Arrangement by which investors who receive a *dividend* also receive a tax credit for corporate taxes that the firm has paid.

Incentive A reward that encourages or a penalty that discourages an action.

Incentives Rewards for engaging in a particular activity.

Incentive system A method of organizing production that uses a market-like mechanism inside the firm.

Income approach Measuring national income by adding up all components of national income, including wages, interest, rent, and profits.

Income beneficiary A person entitled to all or a share of the income of a trust.

Income effect The effect of a change in income on consumption, other things remaining the same.

Income elasticity of demand The responsiveness of demand to a change in income, other things remaining the same. It is calculated as the percentage change in the quantity demanded divided by the percentage change in income.

Income from continuing operations After-tax net income before discontinued operations, extraordinary items, and the cumulative effect of changes in accounting principle.

Income fund A mutual fund providing for liberal current income from investments.

Income statement A financial statement showing a firm's revenues and expenses during a specified period.

Income stock *Common stock* with high *dividend yield* and few profitable investment opportunities (cf. *growth stock*).

Income tax provision Income tax expense as computed on income before taxes and reported on the income statement.

Income taxes payable Income taxes currently due and payable to a taxing authority.

Indenture The legal agreement that lists the obligations of the issuer of a bond to the bondholder, including payment schedules, call provisions, and sinking funds.

Independent variable A variable whose value is determined independently of, or outside, the equation under study.

Index fund A portfolio designed to replicate the performance of an index.

Indexing A passive bond portfolio management strategy that seeks to match the composition, and therefore the performance, of a selected market index.

Index model A model of stock returns using a market index such as the SP 500 to represent common or systematic risk factors.

Index option A call or put option based on a stock market index.

Indirect exchange rate The amount of foreign currency required to purchase one unit of domestic currency.

Indirect-method format A format for the operating section of the cash flow statement that presents the derivation from net income of cash flow provided by operating activities. The format starts with net income and adjusts for nonoperating items, noncash income and expense, and changes in operating-related working capital accounts.

Indirect quote For foreign exchange, the number of units of a foreign currency needed to buy one U.S. dollar (cf. *direct quote*).

Industry life cycle Stages through which firms typically pass as they mature.

Inflation The rate at which the general level of prices for goods and services is rising.

Inflation-adjusted return A rate of return that is measured in terms of real goods and services; that is, after the effects of inflation have been factored out.

Inflation rate The percentage change in the price level from one year to the next.

Information An attribute of a good market that includes providing buyers and sellers with timely, accurate information on the volume and prices of past transactions and on all currently outstanding bids and offers.

Information ratio Statistic used to measure a portfolio's average return in excess of a comparison, benchmark portfolio divided by the standard deviation of this excess return.

Initial margin The amount that an investor must deposit to open a position in futures and some other derivatives; also used to refer to the initial equity required when a stock is purchased using borrowed money.

Initial public offering (IPO) A company's first public issue of *common stock*.

Innovation Transforming an invention into something that is useful to humans.

In play When the market believes that a company may be taken over. At this time, the stock becomes concentrated in the hands of arbitragers and the company becomes vulnerable to a takeover and the target of a bid.

Input list List of parameters such as expected returns, variances, and covariances necessary to determine the optimal risky portfolio.

Inside information Nonpublic knowledge about a corporation possessed by corporate officers, major owners, or other individuals with privileged access to information about a firm.

Insider trading Trading by officers, directors, major stockholders, or others who hold private inside information allowing them to benefit from buying or selling stock.

Institution A retirement fund, bank, investment company, investment advisor, insurance company, or other large pool of investment buying power.

Intangible asset Nonmaterial asset, such as technical expertise, a trademark, or a patent (cf. *tangible asset*).

Interest   The payment for current rather than future command over resources; the cost of obtaining credit. Also, the return paid to owners of capital.

Interest cover   Times interest earned.

Interest rate   The number of dollars earned per dollar invested per period.

Interest rate collar   The combination of a long position in a cap agreement and a short position in a floor agreement, or vice versa; it is equivalent to a series of range forward positions.

Interest rate effect   One of the reasons that the aggregate demand curve slopes downward: Higher price levels increase the interest rate, which in turn causes businesses and consumers to reduce desired spending due to the higher price of borrowing.

Interest rate parity   An arbitrage process that ensures that the forward discount or premium equals the interest rate differential between two currencies.

Interest rate risk   The uncertainty of returns on an investment due to possible changes in interest rates over time.

Interest rate swap   An agreement calling for the periodic exchange of cash flows, one based on an interest rate that remains fixed for the life of the contract and the other that is linked to a variable-rate index.

Intermediate   Of bonds, usually five to seven years' maturity.

Intermediate goods   Goods used up entirely in the production of final goods.

Internal rate of return (IRR)   Discount rate at which investment has zero net present value.

Internal-use software development costs   Costs incurred in developing new software applications for a company's own use and not for licensing to customers. Internal-use software development costs are capitalized once the preliminary project stage is completed.

Internal Valuation (Real Estate)   An INTERNAL VALUATION is an advisor's or underlying third-party manager's best estimate of MARKET VALUE based on the most current and accurate information available under the circumstances. An INTERNAL VALUATION could include industry practice techniques, such as discounted cash flow, sales comparison, replacement cost, or a review of all significant events (both general market and asset specific) that could have a material impact on the investment. Prudent assumptions and estimates MUST be used, and the process MUST be applied consistently from period to period, except where a change would result in better estimates of MARKET VALUE.

International Accounting Standard (IAS)   An accounting standard issued by the International Accounting Standards Committee. This committee has been replaced by the International Accounting Standards Board (IASB). IAS standards have been adopted by the IASB.

International Accounting Standards Board (IASB)   An international standard setting body. Its principal standard-setting products are International Financial Reporting Standards (IFRSs). The IASB assumed its duties from the International Accounting Standards Committee (IASC). Existing International Accounting Standards issued by the IASC were adopted by the IASB.

International CAPM   An equilibrium theory that relates the expected return of an asset to its world market and foreign exchange risks.

International Financial Reporting Standard (IFRS)   A financial reporting standard issued by the International Accounting Standards Board.

International Fisher relation   The assertion that the interest rate differential between two countries should equal the expected inflation rate differential over the term of the interest rates.

International monetary market (IMM)   The financial futures market within the Chicago Mercantile Exchange.

International Swaps and Derivatives Association (ISDA)   An association of swap dealers formed in 1985 to promote uniform practices in the writing, trading, and settlement procedures of swaps and other derivatives.

In the money   An option that has positive intrinsic value.

Intrinsic value   The portion of a call option's total value equal to the greater of either zero or the difference between the current value of the underlying asset and the exercise price; for a put option, intrinsic value is the greater of either zero or the exercise price less the underlying asset price. For a stock, it is the value derived from fundamental analysis of the stock's expected returns or cash flows.

Inventory investment   Changes in the stocks of finished goods and goods in process, as well as changes in the raw materials that businesses keep on hand. Whenever inventories are decreasing, inventory investment is negative; whenever they are increasing, inventory investment is positive.

Inventory turnover   The number of times during a year that inventory is sold and replaced. Calculated by dividing cost of goods sold by ending inventory.

Inverse relationship   A relationship between variables that move in opposite directions.

Invested Capital (Private Equity) The amount of paid-in capital that has been invested in portfolio companies.

Investing Buying an asset, such as a bond, corporate stock, rental property, or farm, with reasonably determinable underlying earnings.

Investment (1) Any use of today's resources to expand tomorrow's production or consumption. *Can also be viewed as* spending by businesses on things such as machines and buildings, which can be used to produce goods and services in the future. The investment part of total output is the portion that will be used in the process of producing goods in the future. (2) The current commitment of dollars for a period of time in order to derive future payments that will compensate the investor for the time the funds are committed, the expected rate of inflation, and the uncertainty of future payments.

Investment Advisor (Private Equity) Any individual or institution that supplies investment advice to clients on a per fee basis. The investment advisor inherently has no role in the management of the underlying portfolio companies of a partnership/fund.

Investment bankers Firms specializing in the sale of new securities to the public, typically by underwriting the issue.

Investment company A firm that issues (sells) shares, and uses the proceeds to invest in various financial instruments or other assets.

Investment Company Act of 1940 One of several pieces of federal legislation passed after the October 1929 stock market crash and the Great Depression. This law regulated the activities and reporting requirements of investment companies, which are firms whose principal business is the trading and management of securities.

Investment decision process Estimation of intrinsic value for comparison with market price to determine whether or not to invest.

Investment demand The relationship between investment and real interest rate, other things remaining the same.

Investment grade Bonds rated AAA to BBB.

Investment-grade bond Bond rated BBB and above or Baa and above. Lower-rated bonds are classified as speculative-grade or junk bonds.

Investment horizon The time period used for planning and forecasting purposes or the future time at which the investor requires the invested funds.

Investment management company A company separate from the investment company that manages the portfolio and performs administrative functions.

Investment Management Fee The fee payable to the investment management firm for the on-going management of a portfolio. Investment management fees are typically asset based (percentage of assets), performance based (based on performance relative to a benchmark), or a combination of the two but may take different forms as well.

Investment portfolio Set of securities chosen by an investor.

Investment strategy A decision by a portfolio manager regarding how he or she will manage the portfolio to meet the goals and objectives of the client. This will include either active or passive management and, if active, what style in terms of top-down or buttom-up or fundamental versus technical.

IPO Initial public offering.

IRR Internal rate of return.

IRS Internal Revenue Service.

Joint venture When companies jointly pursue a certain business activity.

Junior debt Subordinated debt.

Just-in-time System of inventory management that requires minimum inventories of materials and very frequent deliveries by suppliers.

Keiretsu A network of Japanese companies organized around a major bank.

Keynesian An economist who believes that left alone, the economy would rarely operate at full employment and that to achieve full employment, active help from fiscal policy and monetary policy is required.

Labor The work time and work effort that people devote to producing goods and services.

Labor force Individuals aged 16 years or older who either have jobs or are looking and available for jobs; the number of employed plus the number of unemployed.

Labor productivity Total real domestic output (real GDP) divided by the number of workers (output per worker).

Labor unions Worker organizations that seek to secure economic improvements for their members; they also seek to improve the safety, health, and other benefits (such as job security) of their members.

Land The natural resources that are available from nature. Land as a resource includes location, original fertility and mineral deposits, topography, climate, water, and vegetation.

Later stage With respect to venture capital financing, the stage after commercial manufacturing and sales have begun. Later-stage financing includes second-stage, third-stage, and mezzanine financing.

Law of demand The observation that there is a negative, or inverse, relationship between the price of any good or service and the quantity demanded, holding other factors constant.

Law of diminishing returns As a firm uses more of a variable input, with a given quantity of other inputs (fixed inputs), the marginal product of the variable input eventually diminishes.

Law of one price The rule stipulating that equivalent securities or bundles of securities must sell at equal prices to preclude arbitrage opportunities.

LBO Leveraged buyout.

Lease Long-term rental agreement.

Lease receivables Amounts due from customers on long-term sales-type lease agreements.

Lessee User of a leased asset (cf. *lessor*).

Lessor Owner of a leased asset (cf. *lessee*).

Letter of credit Letter from a bank stating that it has established a credit in the company's favor.

Letter stock Privately placed *common stock*, so-called because the *SEC* requires a letter from the purchaser that the stock is not intended for resale.

Leverage (1) The relation between the value of the asset position and the amount of equity invested. (2) Leverage (in England "gearing") is of two sorts: financial and sales. If a company is capitalized half in stock and half in bonds, for instance, a 10 percent change in profits will produce roughly a 20 percent change in earnings per share.

Leveraged buyout (LBO) When an investor or group borrows money, usually on the security of a company's own assets, to take control of it, usually expecting to sell assets to reduce this debt.

Leverage ratio Ratio of debt to total capitalization of a firm.

Liabilities Amounts owed; the legal claims against a business or household by nonowners.

Life cycle The progression of a firm through various stages of its organizational life, consisting of start-up, growth, maturity, and decline, during which earnings and operating cash flow have certain characteristic relationships.

LIFO The last-in first-out accounting method of valuing inventories.

LIFO liquidation A reduction in the physical quantity of an inventory that is accounted for using the LIFO method. A LIFO liquidation usually produces a nonrecurring increase in earnings because the older costs associated with the liquidated units are lower than current inventory costs.

Limit order An order to buy or sell a security at a specific price or better (lower for a buy order and higher for a sell order).

Limited liability A legal concept whereby the responsibility, or liability, of the owners of a corporation is limited to the value of the shares in the firm that they own.

Limited partnership *Partnership* in which some partners have *limited liability* and general partners have unlimited liability.

Linear relationship A relationship between two variables that is illustrated by a straight line.

Line of credit Agreement by a bank that a company may borrow at any time up to an established limit.

Liquid Term used to describe an asset that can be quickly converted to cash at a price close to fair market value.

Liquid asset Asset that is easily and cheaply turned into cash—notably cash itself and short-term securities.

Liquidating dividend *Dividend* that represents a return of capital.

Liquidation The sale of all of a company's assets whereby the firm ceases to exist.

Liquidation value Net amount that could be realized by selling the assets of a firm after paying the debt.

Liquidity (1) The degree to which an asset can be acquired or disposed of without much danger of any intervening loss in nominal value and with small transaction costs. Money is the most liquid asset. (2) The extent to which a stock trades widely in the market, and can thus be purchased or sold without excessively influencing the price. Also, a company's net asset position, particularly in cash or cash equivalents.

Liquidity preference theory Theory that the forward rate exceeds expected future interest rates.

Liquidity premium (1) Additional return for investing in a security that cannot easily be turned into cash; (2) difference between the forward interest rate and the expected spot interest rate.

Liquidity risk Uncertainty due to the ability to buy or sell an investment in the secondary market.

London Interbank offered rate (LIBOR) The rate at which international banks lend on the Eurocurrency market. This is the rate quoted to a top-quality borrower. The most common maturities are one month, three months, and six months. There is a LIBOR for the U.S. dollar and a few other major currencies. LIBOR is determined by the British Banking Association in London. See also *Euribor.*

Long position The buyer of a commodity or security or, for a forward contract, the counterparty who will be the eventual buyer of the underlying asset.

Long run (1) The time period during which all factors of production can be varied. (2) A period of time in which the quantities of all resources can be varied.

Long-run average cost curve The locus of points representing the minimum unit cost of producing any given rate of output, given current technology and resource prices.

Long-term receivables Amounts due from customers, typically on an installment basis, which extend beyond one year.

LP Linear programming.

LYON Liquid yield option note.

Macroeconomics The study of the behavior of the economy as a whole, including such economywide phenomena as changes in unemployment, the general price level, and national income.

MACRS Modified accelerated cost recovery system.

Maintenance margin The minimum margin that an investor must keep on deposit in a margin account at all times.

Management buyout An **LBO** (*q.v.*), led by insiders.

Management fee The compensation an investment company pays to the investment management company for its services. The average annual fee is about 0.5 percent of fund assets.

Mandatorily redeemable preferred stock Preferred stock that carries an unconditional obligation to be repurchased at a specified or determinable date, making the shares a hybrid security between debt and equity.

Margin (1) Cash or securities set aside by an investor as evidence that he or she can honor a commitment. (2) The percent of cost a buyer pays in cash for a security, borrowing the balance from the broker. This introduces leverage, which increases the risk of the transaction.

Margin account The collateral posted with the futures exchange clearinghouse by an outside counterparty to insure its eventual performance; the *initial* margin is the deposit required at contract origination while the *maintenance* margin is the minimum collateral necessary at all times.

Margin call A request by an investor's broker for additional capital for a security bought on margin if the investor's equity value declines below the required maintenance margin.

Margin deposit The amount of cash or securities that must be deposited as guarantee on a futures position. The margin is a returnable deposit.

Marginal benefit The benefit that a person receives from consuming one more unit of a good or service. It is measured as the maximum amount that a person is willing to pay for one more unit of the good or service.

Marginal cost The opportunity cost of producing one more unit of a good or service. It is the best alternative forgone. It is calculated as the increase in total cost divided by the increase in output.

Marginal cost pricing A system of pricing in which the price charged is equal to the opportunity cost to society of producing one more unit of the good or service in question. The opportunity cost is the marginal cost to society.

Marginal costs The change in total costs due to a one-unit change in production rate.

Marginal product The increase in total product that results from a one-unit increase in the variable input, with all other inputs remaining the same. It is calculated as the increase in total product divided by the increase in the variable input employed, when the quantities of all other inputs are constant.

Marginal revenue The change in total revenue that results from a one-unit increase in the quantity sold. It is calculated as the change in total revenue divided by the change in quantity sold.

Marginal tax rate The part of each additional dollar in income that is paid as tax.

Mark to market Reflecting current market value changes in an appraisal.

Marked to market The settlement process used to adjust the margin account of a futures contract for daily changes in the price of the underlying asset.

Market All of the arrangements that individuals have for exchanging with one another. Thus, for example, we can speak of the labor market, the automobile market, and the credit market.

Market analysis Great tides flow in the market, and an unemotional investor may be able to improve his odds by taking them into account. In the euphoric times when almost every new issue goes to a premium, and everybody you meet is bullish, the veteran cuts back. In the midst of gloom, when sound values are being jettisoned because they are "going lower," when many companies sell in the market for less than their cash in the bank, and when the subscription services are bearish, he reappears with his bushel basket and sweeps in the bargains.

Of course, euphoria can progress to a manic condition, and gloom degenerate into despair. Nevertheless, it is helpful to know the patient's current status, as measured by odd-lot short sales, mutual fund cash, brokers' credit balances, net advances, and the like. They can be studied in figures or shown in graphic form, like the graphs produced by a lie detector (heartbeat, breathing, sweating, etc.). This is quite different from the astrology of "double tops" and so forth that the **chartists** (*q.v.*) invoke.

Marketability discount   A discount applied to the value of some securities, such as securities in closely held companies, based on their comparatively lower liquidity.

Market capitalization (market cap)   The number of shares a company has outstanding times the price per share.

Market demand   The demand of all consumers in the marketplace for a particular good or service. The summation at each price of the quantity demanded by each individual.

Market failure   A state in which the market does not allocate resources efficiently.

Market impact   With reference to execution costs, the difference between the actual execution price and the market price that would have prevailed had the manager not sought to trade the security.

Market maker   An institution or individual quoting firm bid and ask prices for a security and standing ready to buy or sell the security at those quoted prices. Also called a *dealer.*

Market model   (1) Model suggesting a linear relationship between actual returns on a stock and on the market portfolio. (2) A method that is used in event studies. Regression analysis is used to compute the return that is attributable to market forces. It is used to compute "excess returns" that may be attributable to the occurrence of an event.

Market order   An order to buy or sell a security immediately at the best price available.

Market portfolio   The portfolio that includes all risky assets with relative weights equal to their proportional market values.

Market power   The ability to influence the market, and in particular the market price, by influencing the total quantity offered for sale.

Market price of risk   A measure of the extra return, or risk premium, that investors demand to bear risk. The reward-to-risk ratio of the market portfolio.

Market risk premium   The amount of return above the risk-free rate that investors expect from the market in general as compensation for systematic risk.

Market risk (systematic risk)   Risk that cannot be diversified away.

Market return   The standard (typically the SP 500) against which stock portfolio performance can be measured.

Market share test   The percentage of a market that a particular firm supplies, used as the primary measure of monopoly power.

Market timer   An investor who speculates on broad market moves rather than on specific securities.

Market timing   Trying to catch short-term market movements. Extremely difficult.

Market Value   The current listed price at which investors buy or sell securities at a given time.

Market value added (MVA)   External management performance measure to compare the market value of the company's debt and equity with the total capital invested in the firm.

Marking to market   Procedure whereby potential profits and losses on a futures position are realized daily. The daily futures price variation is debited (credited) in cash to the loser (winner) at the end of the day.

Master limited partnership (MLP)   A limited partnership whose shares are publicly traded. Its key advantage is that it eliminates the layer of corporate taxation because MLPs are taxed like partnerships, not corporations.

Maturity strategy   A portfolio management strategy employed to reduce the interest rate risk of a bond portfolio by matching the maturity of the portfolio with its investment horizon. For example, if the investment horizon is 10 years, the portfolio manager would construct a portfolio that will mature in 10 years.

MBO   Management buyout.

MDA   Multiple-discriminant analysis.

Means of payment   A method of settling a debt.

Mean-variance analysis   Evaluation of risky prospects based on the expected value and variance of possible outcomes.

Measurement error   Errors in measuring an explanatory variable in a regression that leads to biases in estimated parameters.

Merger   (1) Acquisition in which all assets and liabilities are absorbed by the buyer (cf. *exchange of assets, exchange of stock*); (2) more generally, any combination of two companies.

Mezzanine section   A middle section on the balance sheet positioned between liabilities and shareholders' equity, where claims that have elements of both, including minority interests, typically are reported.

Microcap   Refers to companies with a market capitalization in the $100 million to $300 million range.

Microeconomics The study of the choices that individuals and businesses make, the way those choices interact, and the influence governments exert on them.

Midcap Companies with a market capitalization in the $3 billion to $4 billion range.

Minimum-variance frontier Graph of the lowest possible portfolio variance that is attainable for a given portfolio expected return.

Minority interest in equity The interest in the equity of an entity that reflects the portion of shareholders' equity owned by noncontrolling or third-party investors, or investors outside the consolidated entity.

MLP See *master limited partnership.*

Modern portfolio theory (MPT) Principles underlying analysis and evaluation of rational portfolio choices based on risk–return trade-offs and efficient diversification.

Modified accelerated cost recovery system (MACRS) Schedule of *depreciation* deductions allowed for tax purposes.

Modified duration Measure of a bond's price sensitivity to interest rate movements. Equal to the duration of a bond divided by one plus its yield to maturity.

Monetarist An economist who believes that the economy is self-regulating and that it will normally operate at full employment, provided that monetary policy is not erratic and that the pace of money growth is kept steady.

Monetarists Macroeconomists who believe that inflation in the long run is always caused by excessive monetary growth and that changes in the money supply affect aggregate demand both directly and indirectly.

Monetary policy The Fed conducts the nation's monetary policy by changing in interest rates and adjusting the quantity of money.

Money Any medium that is universally accepted in an economy both by sellers of goods and services as payment for those goods and services and by creditors as payment for debts.

Money illusion Reacting to changes in money prices rather than relative prices. If a worker whose wages double when the price level also doubles thinks he or she is better off, that worker is suffering from money illusion.

Money market (1) The market for short-term debt securities with maturities of less than one year. (2) Includes short-term, highly liquid, and relatively low-risk debt instruments.

Money supply The amount of money in circulation.

Monopolist The single supplier of a good or service for which there is no close substitute. The monopolist therefore constitutes its entire industry.

Monopolization The possession of monopoly power in the relevant market and the willful acquisition or maintenance of that power, as distinguished from growth or development as a consequence of a superior product, business acumen, or historical accident.

Monopoly A market structure in which there is one firm, which produces a good or service that has no close substitute and in which the firm is protected from competition by a barrier preventing the entry of new firms.

Monte Carlo simulation Method for calculating the probability distribution of possible outcomes, e.g., from a project.

Mortgage-backed security Ownership claim in a pool of mortgages or an obligation that is secured by such a pool. Also called a *pass-through,* because payments are passed along from the mortgage originator to the purchaser of the mortgage-backed security.

Moving average The continually recalculating average of security prices for a period, often 200 days, to serve as an indication of the general trend of prices and also as a benchmark price.

Multifactor CAPM Generalization of the basic CAPM that accounts for extra-market hedging demands.

Multifactor model An empirical version of the APT where the investor chooses the exact number and identity of the common risk factors used to describe an asset's risk-return relationship. Risk factors are often designated as *macroeconomic* variables (e.g., inflation, changes in gross domestic product) or *microeconomic* variables (e.g., security-specific characteristics like firm size or book-to-market ratios).

Multifactor models Model of security returns positing that returns respond to several systematic factors.

Multiple Short for price-earnings multiple.

Multiplier The amount by which a change in autonomous expenditure is magnified or multiplied to determine the change in equilibrium expenditure and real GDP.

Municipal bonds Tax-exempt bonds issued by state and local governments, generally to finance capital improvement projects. General obligation bonds are backed by the general taxing power of the issuer. Revenue bonds are backed by the proceeds from the project or agency they are issued to finance.

Must A required provision for claiming compliance with the GIPS standards.

Mutual fund An investment company that pools money from shareholders and invests in a variety of securities, including stocks, bonds, and money market securities. A mutual fund ordinarily stands ready to buy back (redeem) its shares at their current net asset value, which depends on the market value of the fund's portfolio of securities at the time. Mutual funds generally continuously offer new shares to investors.

Mutual fund theorem A result associated with the CAPM, asserting that investors will choose to invest their entire risky portfolio in a market-index mutual fund.

Mutually exclusive projects Two projects that cannot both be undertaken.

NASDAQ National Association of Securities Dealers Automated Quotations. It is the trading system for the over-the-counter market.

Nash equilibrium The outcome of a game that occurs when player A takes the best possible action given the action of player B and player B takes the best possible action given the action of player A.

National income (NI) The total of all factor payments to resource owners. It can be obtained by subtracting indirect business taxes from NDP.

Natural monopoly A monopoly that arises from the peculiar production characteristics in an industry. It usually arises when there are large economies of scale relative to the industry's demand such that one firm can produce at a lower average cost than can be achieved by multiple firms.

Negative relationship A relationship between variables that move in opposite directions.

Neoclassical growth theory A theory of economic growth that proposes that real GDP grows because technological change induces a level of saving and investment that makes capital per hour of labor grow.

Net asset value (NAV) (1) The market value of the assets owned by a fund. (2) The value of each share expressed as assets minus liabilities on a per-share basis.

Net capital expenditures Gross capital expenditures minus proceeds from the disposal of productive assets.

Net cash after operations A Uniform Credit Analysis®–defined cash flow amount that consists of cash after operations plus other cash income minus other cash expense and minus income taxes paid.

Net debt Total debt minus cash on hand.

Net exports The value of exports minus the value of imports.

Net income plus depreciation Often referred to as traditional cash flow, its calculation removes an important noncash expense from net income.

Net investment Net increase in the capital stock—gross investment minus depreciation.

Net operating loss carryover Tax benefits that allow companies to use net operating losses in certain years to offset taxable income in other years.

Net present value (NPV) A measure of the excess cash flows expected from an investment proposal. It is equal to the present value of the cash inflows from an investment proposal, discounted at the required rate of return for the investment, minus the present value of the cash outflows required by the investment, also discounted at the investment's required rate of return. If the derived net present value is a positive value (i.e., there is an excess net present value), the investment should be acquired since it will provide a rate of return above its required returns.

Net public debt Gross public debt minus all government interagency borrowing.

Net working capital Current assets minus current liabilities.

Net worth (1) The difference between assets and liabilities. (2) Book value of a company's *common stock*, surplus, and *retained earnings*.

Network effect A situation in which a consumer's willingness to purchase a good or service is influenced by how many others also buy the item.

New entrant An individual who has never held a full-time job lasting two weeks or longer but is now seeking employment.

New growth theory A theory of economic growth based on the idea that real GDP per person grows because of the choices that people make in the pursuit of ever greater profit and that growth can persist indefinitely.

New issue Common stocks or bonds offered by companies for public sale.

Nominal GDP The value of the final goods and services produced in a given year valued at the prices that prevailed in that same year. It is a more precise name for GDP.

Nominal interest rate The interest rate in terms of nominal (not adjusted for purchasing power) dollars.

Nominal values The values of variables such as GDP and investment expressed in current dollars, also called money values; measurement in terms of the actual market prices at which goods and services are sold.

Nominal yield A bond's yield as measured by its coupon rate.

Noncontrolling interest Generally, minority interest. However, the term is used to reflect a minority shareholder interest when the definition of control is extended beyond a simple majority share ownership interest. Any interest in an entity besides that of a controlling shareholder.

Nondiversifiable risk See *systematic risk*.

Nonqualified stock option An option to purchase stock that requires payment of ordinary income taxes by the option holder on the date of exercise on income equal to the excess of the market price of the purchased stock over the exercise price of the option. The company issuing the option receives an expense deduction equal to the ordinary income of the option holder.

Nonrecurring cash flow Operating cash flow that appears infrequently or that may appear with some regularity but is very irregular in amount. In addition, even though included in operating cash flow, nonrecurring cash flow often is not closely tied to the core operating activities of the firm.

Nonsystematic risk Nonmarket or firm-specific risk factors that can be eliminated by diversification. Also called *unique risk* or *diversifiable risk*. Systematic risk refers to risk factors common to the entire economy.

Normal distribution Symmetric bell-shaped distribution that can be completely defined by its mean and *standard deviation*.

Normal rate of return The amount that must be paid to an investor to induce investment in a business; also known as the *opportunity cost of capital*.

Note Unsecured debt with a maturity of up to 10 years.

Notes Intermediate-term debt securities with maturities longer than 1 year but less than 10 years.

Notes payable Promissory notes that are evidence of a debt and state the terms of interest and principal payment.

Notional principal (1) Principal amount used to calculate swap payments. (2) The principal value of a swap transaction, which is not exchanged but is used as a scale factor to translate interest rate differentials into cash settlement payments.

NPV Net present value.

NYSE New York Stock Exchange.

Objectives The investor's goals expressed in terms of risk and return and included in the policy statement.

Off-balance-sheet financing Financing that is not shown as a liability in a company's balance sheet.

Offensive competitive strategy A strategy whereby a firm attempts to use its strengths to affect the competitive forces in the industry and, in so doing, improves the firm's relative position in the industry.

Offer price The price at which a market maker is willing to sell a security (also called *ask price*).

Official reserves The amount of reserves owned by the central bank of a government in the form of gold, Special Drawing Rights, and foreign cash or marketable securities.

One third rule The rule that, with no change in technology, a 1 percent increase in capital per hour of labor brings, on the average, a one third of 1 percent increase in real GDP per hour of labor.

Open account Arrangement whereby sales are made with no formal debt contract. The buyer signs a receipt, and the seller records the sale in the sales ledger.

Open-end fund An investment company that continuously offers to sell new shares, or redeem them, at prices based on the market value of the assets owned by the fund (net asset value).

Open interest The number of futures contracts outstanding.

Operating cash flow Cash flow from operating activities computed in accordance with generally accepted accounting principles.

Operating cushion Operating profit before depreciation and amortization expense.

Operating earnings An earnings measure that excludes selected items of nonrecurring gain, revenue, loss, and expense. This is not a GAAP measure, and its determination may vary widely among different companies.

Operating income See *operating profit*.

Operating lease A lease that does not transfer the risks and rewards of ownership to the lessee. Operating lease payments are expensed as incurred.

Operating leverage The use of fixed-production costs in the firm's operating cost structure. The effect of fixed costs is to magnify the effect of a change in sales on operating profits.

Operating loss carryforward For tax purposes only, losses are first carried back for 2 years, eliminating previous profits and producing a tax refund. If losses remain, then these may be carried forward for as long as 20 years. These losses will shield future profits from taxation. Corporations also may elect to forgo the loss carryback and only carry the loss forward for 20 years.

Operating payables   Amounts due vendors, including accounts payable and notes payable for purchases made.

Operating profit   Core pretax profit from central operations calculated as revenue minus cost of goods sold, selling, general and administrative expense, and research and development expense.

Operating receivables   Customer-related receivables including accounts receivable, notes receivable, and, for contractors, cost plus profit recognized in excess of amounts billed customers.

Operating working capital   Current assets, including operating receivables, inventory, and prepaid expenses, that are used in operations minus current liabilities, including operating payables and accrued expenses payable that are incurred in operations.

Opportunity cost   (1) The highest-valued, next-best alternative that must be sacrificed to obtain something or to satisfy a want. (2) With reference to execution costs, the loss (or gain) incurred as the result of failure or delay in the execution of a trade, or failure to complete a trade in full.

Opportunity cost of capital   The normal rate of return, or the available return on the next-best alternative investment. Economists consider this a cost of production, and it is included in our cost examples.

Optimal portfolio   The portfolio on the efficient frontier that has the highest utility for a given investor. It lies at the point of tangency between the efficient frontier and the curve with the investor's highest possible utility.

Optimal risky portfolio   An investor's best combination of risky assets to be mixed with safe assets to form the complete portfolio.

Option   See *call option, put option.*

Option-adjusted spread   A type of yield spread that considers changes in the term structure and alternative estimates of the volatility of interest rates. It is spread after adjusting for embedded options.

Option contract   An agreement that grants the owner the right, but not the obligation, to make a future transaction in an underlying commodity or security at a fixed price and within a predetermined time in the future.

Option delta   Hedge ratio.

Option premium   The purchase price of a call option or put option that reflects both an intrinsic value for the option represented by the difference between the option's exercise price and the market price of the asset covered by the option and the time value of money.

Options Clearing Corporation (OCC)   A company designed to guarantee, monitor margin accounts, and settle exchange-traded option transactions.

Order-driven market   A market without active market makers in which buy-and-sell orders directly confront each other; an auction market.

Origin   The intersection of the y axis and the x axis in a graph.

OTC   Over-the-counter.

Other cash income (expense)   A Uniform Credit Analysis®–defined cash flow amount that consists of cash receipts and disbursements that are not part of core operations. The term is defined the same way on the cash flow analysis statement. Other cash income examples include collections for interest, dividends, rents, royalties, and miscellaneous collections. Other cash expense examples include payments for corporate restructuring, severance, and litigation.

Out-of-the-money option   An option that has no intrinsic value.

Overdraft   A negative cash balance.

Overnight   A deal from today to the next business day.

Over-the-counter (OTC)   Informal market that does not involve a securities exchange. Specifically used to refer to the Nasdaq dealer market for *common stocks.*

Overweighted   A condition in which a portfolio, for whatever reason, includes more of a class of securities than the relative market value alone would justify.

Paid-In Capital (Private Equity)   The amount of committed capital a limited partner has actually transferred to a venture fund. Also known as the *cumulative drawdown amount.*

Partnership   A business owned by two or more joint owners, or partners, who share the responsibilities and the profits of the firm and are individually liable for all the debts of the partnership.

Par value   (1) The principal amount repaid at maturity of a bond. Also called *face value.* (2) The officially determined value of a currency.

Par yield curve   The yield curve drawn for government coupon bonds of different maturities that trade at, or around, par.

Passive investment strategy   See *passive management.*

Passive management   Buying a well-diversified portfolio to represent a broad-based market index without attempting to search out mispriced securities.

Passive portfolio   A market index portfolio.

Passive strategy   See *passive management.*

Pass-through security   Pools of loans (such as home mortgage loans) sold in one package. Owners of pass-throughs receive all principal and interest payments made by the borrowers.

Pass-through securities *Notes* or *bonds* backed by a package of assets (e.g., mortgage pass-throughs, *CARs*, *CARDs*).

Patent A government-sanctioned exclusive right granted to the inventor of a good, service, or productive process to produce, use, and sell the invention for a given number of years.

Payables Accounts payable.

Payables turnover The number of times during a year that operating payables are repaid and reincurred. Calculated by dividing cost of goods sold by ending operating payables.

Payback The time required for the added income from the convertible security relative to the stock to offset the conversion premium.

Payout ratio *Dividend* as a proportion of earnings per share.

Peak The point at which a business cycle turns from expansion into recession.

Peer group comparison A method of measuring portfolio performance by collecting the returns produced by a representative universe of investors over a specific period of time.

P/E ratio Share price divided by earnings per share.

Per capita Latin, meaning "by the head." Distributing to "issue per capita" means to distribute trust property to persons who take, in their own right, an equal portion of the property.

Perfect competition An industry structure characterized by certain conditions, including many buyers and sellers, homogeneous products, perfect information, easy entry and exit, and no barriers to entry. The existence of these conditions implies that each seller is a price taker.

Performance appraisal The assessment of an investment record for evidence of investment skill.

Performance attribution The attribution of investment performance to specific investment decisions (such as asset allocation and country weighting).

Performance presentation standards (PPS) A comprehensive set of reporting guidelines created by the Association for Investment Management and Research (AIMR) (now the CFA Institute), in an effort to fulfill the call for uniform, accurate, and consistent performance reporting.

Perpetuity An investment without any maturity date. It provides returns to its owner indefinitely.

Personal income (PI) The amount of income that households actually receive before they pay personal income taxes.

Personal trust An amount of money set aside by a grantor and often managed by a third party, the trustee. Often constructed so one party receives income from the trust's investments and another party receives the residual value of the trust after the income beneficiaries' death.

Physical capital All manufactured resources, including buildings, equipment, machines, and improvements to land that is used for production.

PIK Pay-in-kind bond.

Plain-vanilla Refers to a security, especially a bond or a swap, issued with standard features. Sometimes called *generic*.

Planning horizon The long run, during which all inputs are variable.

Point One percent (1%).

Poison pill A right issued by a corporation as a preventative antitakeover defense. It allows right holders to purchase shares in either their own company or the combined target and bidder companies at a discount, usually 50%. This discount may make the takeover prohibitively expensive.

Poison put A *covenant* allowing the *bond*holder to demand repayment in the event of a hostile *merger*.

Policy acquisition costs See *customer acquisition costs*.

Policy statement A statement in which the investor specifies investment goals, constraints, and risk preferences.

Political risk Possibility of the expropriation of assets, changes in tax policy, restrictions on the exchange of foreign currency for domestic currency, or other changes in the business climate of a country.

Pooling of interest Method of accounting for *mergers* (no longer available in the USA). The consolidated balance sheet of the merged firm is obtained by combining the balance sheets of the separate firms (cf. *purchase accounting*).

Portfolio A group of investments. Ideally, the investments should have different patterns of returns over time.

Portfolio investment The purchase of less than 10 percent of the shares of ownership in a company in another nation.

Portfolio management Process of combining securities in a portfolio tailored to the investor's preferences and needs, monitoring that portfolio, and evaluating its performance.

Positive market feedback A tendency for a good or service to come into favor with additional consumers because other consumers have chosen to buy the item.

Positive relationship A relationship between two variables that move in the same direction.

Poverty A situation in which a household's income is too low to be able to buy the quantities of food, shelter, and clothing that are deemed necessary.

Preferences A description of a person's likes and dislikes.

Preferred habitat theory Holds that investors prefer specific maturity ranges but can be induced to switch if risk premiums are sufficient.

Preferred stock A class of stock with priority rights, both as to dividends and in liquidation, over the common stock of the same company. Corporations pay a much lower income tax on dividends from their investments in other corporations (where it has already been taxed) than on direct business earnings. Preferred stock is usually priced at the level that makes it attractive to a corporation, taking account of this tax exemption, and as a result is rarely tax-efficient for individuals.

Premature revenue Revenue recognized for a confirmed sale or service transaction in a period prior to that called for by generally accepted accounting principles.

Premium (1) A bond selling at a price above par value due to capital market conditions. (2) The purchase price of an option.

Prepaid expenses Costs or expenses that have been paid in advance of being incurred. Also referred to as *prepaids*.

Present value The value of a future amount expressed in today's dollars; the most that someone would pay today to receive a certain sum at some point in the future.

Present value of growth opportunities (PVGO) *Net present value* of investments the firm is expected to make in the future.

Presumptive remaindermen Those persons who, if a trust were to terminate at any given time, are entitled to take the then trust corpus.

Price controls Government-mandated minimum or maximum prices that may be charged for goods and services.

Price discrimination Selling a given product at more than one price, with the price difference being unrelated to differences in cost.

Price-driven market A market in which dealers (market makers) adjust their quotes continuously to reflect supply and demand; also known as a *dealer market*.

Price–earnings multiple See *price–earnings ratio*.

Price–earnings ratio The ratio of a stock's price to its earnings per share. Also referred to as the *P/E multiple*.

Price effect The effect of a change in the price on the quantity of a good consumed, other things remaining the same.

Price level The average level of prices as measured by a price index.

Price momentum A portfolio strategy in which you acquire stocks that have enjoyed above-market stock price increases.

Price risk The component of interest rate risk due to the uncertainty of the market price of a bond caused by changes in market interest rates.

Price war A pricing campaign designed to capture additional market share by repeatedly cutting prices.

Primary market The market in which newly issued securities are sold by their issuers, who receive the proceeds.

Prime rate Benchmark lending rate set by U.S. banks.

Principal (1) The outstanding balance on a loan. (2) The corpus or capital of a trust, as distinguished from the income produced.

Principal-agent problem The problem of devising compensation rules that induce an agent to act in the best interest of a principal.

Principal trade A trade through a broker who guarantees full execution at specified discount/premium to the prevailing price.

Private equity *Equity* that is not publicly traded and that is used to finance business start-ups, *leveraged buy-outs*, etc.

Private information Information that is available to one person but is too costly for anyone else to obtain.

Private placement A new issue sold directly to a small group of investors, usually institutions.

Private trusts A term used to identify trusts created by individuals for individuals, either during life or under will.

Producer Price Index (PPI) A statistical measure of a weighted average of prices of goods and services that firms produce and sell.

Product differentiation The distinguishing of products by brand name, color, and other minor attributes. Product differentiation occurs in other than perfectly competitive markets in which products are, in theory, homogeneous, such as wheat or corn.

Production Any activity that results in the conversion of resources into products that can be used in consumption.

Productivity curve A relationship that shows how real GDP per hour of labor changes as the amount of capital per hour of labor changes with a given state of technology.

Productivity growth slowdown A slowdown in the growth rate of output per person.

Profit The income earned by entrepreneurship.

Profitability index Ratio of a project's *NPV* to the initial investment.

Profit margin See *return on sales.*

Pro forma Projected.

Pro-forma earnings A measure of earnings performance that selectively excludes nonrecurring as well as some noncash items.

Program trading Coordinated buy orders and sell orders of entire portfolios, usually with the aid of computers, often to achieve index arbitrage objectives.

Property rights Social arrangements that govern the ownership, use, and disposal of resources or factors of production, goods, and services that are enforceable in the courts.

Proprietorship A business owned by one individual who makes the business decisions, receives all the profits, and is legally responsible for the debts of the firm.

Prospectus Summary of the *registration* statement providing information on an issue of securities.

Protective put A trading strategy in which a put option is purchased as a supplement to a long position in an underlying asset or portfolio of assets; the most straightforward form of *portfolio insurance.*

Proxy An instrument empowering an agent to vote in the name of the shareholder.

Proxy contest When a dissident shareholder or group of shareholders try to take control of the board of directors or use the process to enact certain changes in the activities of the company.

Proxy vote Vote cast by one person on behalf of another.

Prudent investor rule An investment manager must act in accord with the actions of a hypothetical prudent investor.

Public good A good or service that is both nonrival and nonexcludable—it can be consumed simultaneously by everyone and from which no one can be excluded.

Purchase accounting Method of accounting for *mergers.* The assets of the acquired firm are shown at market value on the balance sheet of the acquirer (cf. *pooling of interest*).

Purchasing power The value of money for buying goods and services. If your money income stays the same but the price of one good that you are buying goes up, your effective purchasing power falls, and vice versa.

Purchasing power parity (PPP) A theory stating that the exchange rate between two currencies will exactly reflect the purchasing power of the two currencies.

Pure plays Companies that operate within clearly defined market boundaries.

Put option A contract that gives its holder the right to sell an asset, typically a financial instrument, at a specified price through a specified date.

Put options Options to sell a security (stock or bond) within a certain period at a specified price.

q Ratio of the market value of an asset to its replacement cost.

Qualified Institutional buyers (QIBs) Institutions that are allowed to trade unregistered stock among themselves.

Quality of earnings The realism and conservatism of the earnings number and the extent to which we might expect the reported level of earnings to be sustained.

Quantity demanded The amount of a good or service that consumers plan to buy during a given time period at a particular price.

Quick ratio A measure of liquidity similar to the current ratio except for exclusion of inventories (cash plus receivables divided by current liabilities).

Quota A quantitative restriction on the import of a particular good, which specifies the maximum amount that can be imported in a given time period.

Random walk Describes the notion that stock price changes are random and unpredictable.

Rate of return The future financial benefit to making a current investment.

Rational expectation The most accurate forecast possible, a forecast that uses all the available information, including knowledge of the relevant economic forces that influence the variable being forecasted.

Real assets Tangible assets and intangible assets used to carry on business (cf. financial assets).

Real Estate Real estate investments include:
- Wholly owned or partially owned properties,
- Commingled funds, property unit trusts, and insurance company separate accounts,
- Unlisted, private placement securities issued by private real estate investment trusts (REITs) and real estate operating companies (REOCs), and
- Equity-oriented debt, such as participating mortgage loans or any private interest in a property where some portion of return to the investor at the time of investment is related to the performance of the underlying real estate.

Real Estate Investment Trust (REIT) An entity that may invest in real estate or mortgages on real estate and whose earnings are exempt from federal taxation. REITs must meet certain strict requirements contained in the Internal Revenue Code including distribution of at least 90 percent of their earnings to shareholders to avoid taxation of profit at the corporate level.

Real exchange rate The exchange rate adjusted by the inflation differential between the two countries.

Real foreign currency risk The risk that real prices of consumption goods might not be identical in different countries. Also known as *real exchange rate risk*, or *purchasing power risk*.

Real Gross Domestic Product (real GDP) The value of final goods and services produced in a given year when valued at constant prices.

Real income A household's income expressed as a quantity of goods that the household can afford to buy.

Real interest rate The nominal interest rate adjusted for inflation; the nominal interest rate minus the inflation rate.

Real option The flexibility to modify, postpone, expand or abandon a project.

Real options Options embedded in a firm's real assets that give managers valuable decision-making flexibility, such as the right to either undertake or abandon an investment project.

Real rate of interest The nominal rate of interest minus the anticipated rate of inflation.

Realized capital gains Capital gains that result when an appreciated asset is sold; realized capital gains are taxable.

Real values Measurement of economic values after adjustments have been made for changes in the average of prices between years.

Real wage rate The quantity of goods and services that an hour's work can buy. It is equal to the money wage rate divided by the price level.

Rebalancing Realigning the proportions of assets in a portfolio as needed.

Receivables Accounts receivable.

Receivables days The number of days it would take to collect the ending balance in operating receivables at the year's average rate of revenue per day. Calculated by dividing 365 by receivables turnover.

Receivables turnover The number of times during a year that operating receivables are collected and replaced with new revenue transactions. Calculated by dividing revenue by ending operating receivables.

Receiver A bankruptcy practitioner appointed by secured creditors in the United Kingdom to oversee the repayment of debts.

Recession There are two common definitions of recession. They are: (1) A business cycle phase in which real GDP decreases for at least two successive quarters. (2) A significant decline in activity spread across the economy, lasting for more than a few months, visible in industrial production, employment, real income, and wholesale-retail trade.

Reclassification adjustment An adjustment to reported operating cash flow that moves a cash flow item from one classification to another, such as from operating cash flow to investing cash flow or from financing cash flow to operating cash flow. An example would be the reclassification of a tax benefit from stock options from operating cash flow to financing cash flow. The goal of these reclassifications is to produce a more sustainable measure of operating cash flow.

Record date Date set by directors when making dividend payment. *Dividends* are sent to stockholders who are registered on the record date.

Recycling The reuse of raw materials derived from manufactured products.

Registration Process of obtaining *SEC* approval for a public issue of securities.

Registration statement Required to be filed with the SEC to describe the issue of a new security.

Regression analysis In statistics, a technique for finding the line of best fit.

Regression equation An equation that describes the average relatinship between a dependent variable and a set of explanatory variables.

Regular dividend *Dividend* that the company expects to maintain in the future.

Regulation Rules administrated by a government agency to influence economic activity by determining prices, product standards and types, and conditions under which new firms may enter an industry.

Reinvestment Profits (or depreciation reserves) used to purchase new capital equipment.

Relative price The ratio of the price of one good or service to the price of another good or service. A relative price is an opportunity cost.

Relative return A portfolio's return compared with its benchmark.

Remainder The trust corpus existing at the termination of the life beneficiary's interest.

Rent The income that land earns.

Replacement capital expenditures Capital expenditures required to replace productive capacity consumed during a reporting period.

Replacement cost Cost to replace a firm's assets. "Reproduction" cost.

Repo Repurchase agreement.

Reported operating cash flow Cash flow from operating activities computed in accordance with generally accepted accounting principles. Also see *operating cash flow*.

Repurchase agreement (RP, repo, buy-back) Purchase of Treasury securities from a securities dealer with an agreement that the dealer will repurchase them at a specified price.

Required principal payments on long-term debt and capital lease obligations A term used on the cash flow analysis statement that consists of the current portion of long-term debt and capital lease obligations at the beginning of the year.

Required rate of return The return that compensates investors for their time, the expected rate of inflation, and the uncertainty of the return.

Reserves (1) Cash in a bank's vault plus the bank's deposits at Federal Reserve banks. (2) The fixed-income component of a portfolio, notably shorter-term highly liquid instruments.

Residual claim Refers to the fact that shareholders are at the bottom of the list of claimants to assets of a corporation in the event of failure or bankruptcy.

Residual income After-tax profit less the *opportunity cost of capital* employed by the business (see also *economic value added*).

Residual risk The **specific risk** contained in a security, as distinct from the general market risk.

Residuals Parts of stock returns not explained by the explanatory variable (the market-index return). They measure the impact of firm-specific events during a particular period.

Residual Value (Private Equity) The remaining equity that a limited partner has in the fund. (The value of the investments within the fund.) Also can be referred to as *ending market value* or *net asset value*.

Resources Things used to produce other things to satisfy people's wants.

Restatement of the Law Third, Trusts A book of rules and principles promulgated by the American Law Institute, concerning the conduct of a trustee in the management of a trust. It serves as a guide for lawyers, trustees, and investment advisors.

Restricted cash Cash set aside for a particular purpose either through a legal restriction related to a third party or through a more informal internal company restriction.

Restructuring charge Costs associated with restructuring activities, including the consolidation and/or relocation of operations or the disposition or abandonment of operations or productive assets. Such charges may be incurred in connection with a business combination, a change in an enterprise's strategic plan, or a managerial response to declines in demand, increasing costs, or other environmental factors.

Restructuring charges Also referred to as *big bath write-offs*. In a merger context it refers to a company's taking large write-offs following an acquisition, which lowers current income but may carry the implication that future income may be higher.

Restructuring reserve A liability reflecting restructuring costs to be paid or realized in future periods.

Retained earnings Earnings that a corporation saves, or retains, for investment in other productive activities; earnings that are not distributed to stockholders.

Return on assets (ROA) A profitability ratio; earnings before interest and taxes dividend by total assets.

Return on equity (ROE) (1) An accounting ratio of net profits divided by equity. (2) An excellent definition is profit margin × turnover × leverage, where profit margin is sales ÷ profits, turnover is sales ÷ assets, and leverage is assets ÷ equity. It is extremely high in industries with high RD that is expensed rather than capitalized and added to equity, such as pharmaceuticals.

Return on investment (ROI) Generally, book income as a proportion of net book value.

Return on sales (ROS), or profit margin The ratio of operating profits per dollar of sales (EBIT divided by sales).

Revenue bond A bond that is serviced by the income generated from specific revenue-producing projects of the municipality such as toll roads or athletic stadiums.

Reverse synergy $4 - 1 = 5$; where, following a sell-off, the remaining parts of a company are more valuable than the original parent business.

Revolving credit Legally assured *line of credit* with a bank.

Reward-to-variability ratio Ratio of a portfolio's risk premium to its standard deviation.

Risk A situation in which more than one outcome might occur and the probability of each possible outcome can be estimated.

Risk arbitrage Speculation on perceived mispriced securities, usually in connection with merger and acquisition targets.

Risk averse The assumption about investors that they will choose the least risky alternative, all else being equal.

Risk aversion Describes the fact that investors want to minimize risk for the same level of expected return. To take more risk, they require compensation by a risk premium.

Risk budgeting In a portfolio management context, the setting of risk limits for individual managers.

Risk-free asset An asset with a certain rate of return; often taken to be short-term T-bills.

Risk-free rate The interest rate that can be earned with certainty.

Risk-neutral See *risk-averse*.

Risk premium An expected return in excess of that on risk-free securities. The premium provides compensation for the risk of an investment.

Risk–return trade-off If an investor is willing to take on risk, there is the reward of higher expected returns.

Risky asset An asset with uncertain future returns.

Rival A good or service or a resource is rival if its use by one person decreases the quantity available for someone else.

ROI Return on investment.

RP Repurchase agreement.

Rule 144a *SEC* rule allowing *qualified institutional buyers* to buy and trade unregistered securities.

Russell 1000 Index The 1000 largest companies in the Russell 3000 index.

Russell 3000 Index The 3000 largest U.S. companies, capital-weighted, which represent about 98 percent of the investible equity market.

Russell 2000 Index The 2000 smallest companies in the Russell 3000 index.

Safe harbor Practices that satisfy such requirements as the Prudent Investor Rule.

Sale and leaseback A sale followed by the immediate leaseback of the asset sold by its previous owner.

Salvage value Scrap value of plant and equipment.

Sampling A technique for constructing a passive index portfolio in which the portfolio manager buys a representative sample of stocks that comprise the benchmark index.

Sarbanes-Oxley Act An act of Congress signed into law on July 30, 2002, that tightened the oversight of firms that audit public companies, added criminal penalties for earnings management activities, and took steps generally to improve company internal controls and corporate governance.

Saving The act of not consuming all of one's current income. Whatever is not consumed out of spendable income is, by definition, saved. Saving is an action measured over time (a flow), whereas savings are a stock, an accumulation resulting from the act of saving in the past.

Scatter diagram (1) A diagram that plots the value of one economic variable against the value of another. (2) Plot of returns of one security versus returns of another security. Each point represents one pair of returns for a given holding period.

Scenario analysis Analysis of the profitability of a project under alternative economic scenarios.

Seasonal factors Natural ebbs and flows in business activity occurring annually that are caused by changes in the seasons.

Seasoned issue Issue of a security for which there is an existing market (cf. *unseasoned issue*).

SEC Securities and Exchange Commission.

Secondary boycott A boycott of companies or products sold by companies that are dealing with a company being struck.

Secondary issue (1) Procedure for selling blocks of *seasoned issues* of stock; (2) more generally, sale of already issued stock.

Secondary market The market in which outstanding securities are bought and sold by owners other than the issuers. Purpose is to provide liquidity for investors.

Sector rotation An investment strategy which entails shifting the portfolio into industry sectors that are forecast to outperform others based on macroeconomic forecasts.

Sector rotation strategy An active strategy that involves purchasing stocks in specific industries or stocks with specific characteristics (low *P/E*, growth, value) that are anticipated to rise in value more than the overall market.

Securities Stocks and bonds.

Securities Exchange Act of 1934 The federal law that established the Securities and Exchange Commission. It also added further regulations for securities markets. The law has been amended several times since its initial passage. One of the amendments that is relevant to mergers is the Williams Act of 1968.

Securitization Substitution of tradable securities for privately negotiated instruments.

Securitized accounts receivable A financing arrangement where accounts receivable are pooled and an undivided interest in the receivables pool, which represents a claim on the entire pool of receivables, is sold, effectively creating a security that is backed by the receivables. It is accounted for as a sale of accounts receivable.

Security analysis Determining correct value of a security in the marketplace.

Security characteristic line A plot of the excess return on a security over the risk-free rate as a function of the excess return on the market.

Security market line (SML) The line that reflects the combination of risk and return of alternative investments. In CAPM, risk is measured by systematic risk (beta).

Self-interest The choices that you think are the best for you.

Sell-off A general term describing a sale of a part of a company. It also includes other more specific transactions, such as divestitures or spin-offs.

Senior debt Debt that, in the event of bankruptcy, must be repaid before *subordinated debt* receives any payment.

Sensitivity analysis Analysis of the effect on project profitability of possible changes in sales, costs, and so on.

Separation property The property that portfolio choice can be separated into two independent tasks: (1) determination of the optimal risky portfolio, which is a purely technical problem, and (2) the personal choice of the best mix of the risky portfolio and the risk-free asset.

Services Mental or physical labor or help purchased by consumers. Examples are the assistance of physicians, lawyers, dentists, repair personnel, housecleaners, educators, retailers, and wholesalers; things purchased or used by consumers that do not have physical characteristics.

Settlement price The official closing price of a futures contract set by the clearinghouse at the end of the day and used for marking to market.

Settlor The creator of an inter vivos trust; also same as *grantor, trustor,* or *creator.*

Share of stock A legal claim to a share of a corporation's future profits; if it is common stock, it incorporates certain voting rights regarding major policy decisions of the corporation; if it is preferred stock, its owners are accorded preferential treatment in the payment of dividends.

Share-the-gains, share-the-pains theory A theory of regulatory behavior in which the regulators must take account of the demands of three groups: legislators, who established and who oversee the regulatory agency; members of the regulated industry; and consumers of the regulated industry's products or services.

Sharpe measure A relative measure of a portfolio's benefit-to-risk ratio, calculated as its average return in excess of the risk-free rate divided by the standard deviation of portfolio returns.

Sharpe ratio The ratio of mean excess return (return minus the risk-free rate) to standard deviation of returns (or excess returns).

Shortage A situation in which quantity demanded is greater than quantity supplied at a price below the market clearing price.

Short hedge A hedge involving the sale of forward or futures contracts to cover the risk of a long position in the spot market.

Short interest rate A one-period interest rate.

Short position The seller of a commodity or security or, for a forward contract, the counterparty who will be the eventual seller of the underlying asset.

Short run The short run in microeconomics has two meanings. (1) For the firm, it is the period of time in which the quantity of at least one input is fixed and the quantities of the other inputs can be varied. The fixed input is usually capital—that is, the firm has a given plant size. (2) For the industry, the short run is the period of time in which each firm has a given plant size and the number of firms in the industry is fixed.

Short sale The sale of shares not owned by the investor but borrowed through a broker and later repurchased to replace the loan. Profit is earned if the initial sale is at a higher price than the repurchase price.

Should Encouraged (recommended) to follow the recommendation of the GIPS standards but not required.

Signal (1) Action that demonstrates an individual's unobservable characteristics (because it would be unduly costly for someone without those characteristics to take the action). (2) An action taken by an informed person (or firm) to send a message to uninformed people or an action taken outside a market that conveys information that can be used by that market.

Simulation Monte Carlo simulation.

Single-factor model A model of security returns that acknowledges only one common factor. See *factor model.*

Sinking fund Bond provision that requires the issuer to redeem some or all of the bond systematically over the term of the bond rather than in full at maturity.

Skill One of the three components of the standard of prudence governing trustees; familiarity with business matters.

Slope The change in the value of the variable measured on the y-axis divided by the change in the value of the variable measured on the x-axis.

Soft dollars The value of research services that brokerage houses supply to investment managers "free of charge" in exchange for the investment managers' business.

Software development costs Costs incurred in developing new software applications. Software development costs incurred in developing software for licensing to customers are capitalized once technological feasibility is reached.

Sovereign risk The risk that a government may default on its debt.

SPE Special purpose entity.

Specialist A trader who makes a market in the shares of one or more firms and who maintains a "fair and orderly market" by dealing personally in the stock.

Specialization The division of productive activities among persons and regions so that no one individual or one area is totally self-sufficient. An individual may specialize, for example, in law or medicine. A nation may specialize in the production of coffee, computers, or cameras.

Special purpose entity (SPE) An entity established by a corporate sponsor to carry out a limited business activity on behalf of the sponsor. The sponsor need not consolidate the SPE provided the sponsor is not a controlling owner and the entity's equity is sufficient to absorb any expected losses that may be generated. Also known as a *variable interest entity* (*VIE*).

Speculating Guessing, by buying an asset that has no underlying earnings, or about whose future price one knows little, such as art or gold.

Speculation Undertaking a risky investment with the objective of earning a greater profit than an investment in a risk-free alternative (a risk premium).

Speculative company A firm with a great degree of business and/or financial risk, with commensurate high earnings potential.

Speculative stock A stock that appears to be highly overpriced compared to its intrinsic valuation.

Spin-off A type of sell-off in which a parent company distributes shares on a pro rata basis to its shareholders. These new shares give shareholders ownership rights in a division or part of the parent company that is sold off.

Split When a stock reaches a high price, the management of the company will split it two for one, three for two, or whatever, to create a lower price per share and thus facilitate trading. The dividend may be raised at the same time.

In a "reverse split," a low-priced stock, often of a failing company, is consolidated to bring the price per share up to a reasonable level. On the Canadian exchanges such stocks are thereafter called "Consolidated Gold Bug" (or whatever).

Split-off A type of sell-off in which shareholders of a parent company exchange their shares in the parent company for shares in the sold off entity.

Split-up When the parent company spins off all of its component parts and ceases to exist.

Spot exchange rate Exchange rate on currency for immediate delivery (cf. *forward exchange rate*).

Spot price Price of asset for immediate delivery (in contrast to forward or futures price).

Spot rate The required yield for a cash flow to be received at some specific date in the future—for example, the spot rate for a flow to be received in one year, for a cash flow in two years, and so on.

Spread (1) A trading strategy where long and short positions in two call (or two put) option contracts having the same underlying asset but different exercise prices or expiration dates are combined to create a customized return distribution. (2) Difference between the ask and the bid quotations. Also refers to a mark-up paid by a given borrower over the market interest rate paid by a top-quality borrower. (3) Difference between the price at which an *underwriter* buys an issue from a firm and the price at which the underwriter sells it to the public.

Squeeze The possibility that enough long positions hold their contracts to maturity that supplies of the commodity are not adequate to cover all contracts. A *short squeeze* describes the reverse: short positions threaten to deliver an expensive-to-store commodity.

Stagflation The combination of recession and inflation.

Staggered board Also called a *classified board*. This is an antitakeover measure in which the election of directors is split in separate periods so that only a percentage of the total number of directors come up for election in a given year. It is designed to make taking control of the board of directors more difficult.

Stakeholder Any entity that is affected by the actions of a company, which may include shareholders, management, workers, communities, consumers, and so on.

Standard deviation of return A common measure of risk, often calculated using a time series of returns observed over the past. Equal to the square root of the variance.

Standard error In statistics, a measure of the possible error in an estimate.

Standstill agreement   An agreement that a potential hostile bidder enters into with the target corporation whereby the bidder agrees, in exchange for some consideration, not to purchase more than an agreed-upon number of shares.

Start-up stage   The opening period in a company's life cycle during which operating losses often are reported and operating cash flow is consumed.

Statement of cash flows   A financial statement showing a firm's cash receipts and cash payments during a specified period.

Stock   The quantity of something, measured at a given point in time—for example, an inventory of goods or a bank account. Stocks are defined independently of time, although they are assessed at a point in time.

Stock dividend   *Dividend* in the form of stock rather than cash.

Stock exchanges   Secondary markets where already-issued securities are bought and sold by members.

Stock option   A contract that gives its holder the right to buy (call option) or sell (put option) an interest in stock at a specified price through a specified date.

Stock selection   An active portfolio management technique that focuses on advantageous selection of particular stocks rather than on broad asset allocation choices.

Stock split   Issue by a corporation of a given number of shares in exchange for the current number of shares held by stockholders. Splits may go in either direction, either increasing or decreasing the number of shares outstanding. A *reverse split* decreases the number outstanding.

Stock warrant   A contract, similar to an option, that gives its holder the right to buy stock at a specified price through a specified date. Warrants may be granted with the issue of other securities such as bonds or preferred stock, or may be granted with the issue of common stock, giving its holder the right to purchase additional shares. When granted as a form of compensation, stock warrants are more likely to be referred to as stock options.

Straight-line depreciation   An equal dollar amount of *depreciation* in each period.

Strategic alliance   A more flexible alternative to a joint venture whereby certain companies agree to pursue certain common activities and interests.

Strategic asset allocation   The allocation to the major investment asset classes that is determined to be appropriate, given the investor's long-run investment objectives and constraints.

Strategies   All the possible actions of each player in a game.

Strategy   Any rule that is used to make a choice, such as "Always pick heads."

Strike price   Price at which an option can be exercised (same as *exercise price*).

Structural change   Economic trend occurring when the economy is undergoing a major change in organization or in how it functions.

Structured note   A bond with an embedded derivative designed to create a payoff distribution that satisfies the needs of a specific investor clientele.

Style analysis   An attempt to explain the variability in the observed returns to a security portfolio in terms of the movements in the returns to a series of benchmark portfolios designed to capture the essence of a particular security characteristic such as size, value, and growth.

Subordinate (junior) bonds   Debentures that, in case of default, entitle holders to claims on the issuer's assets only after the claims of holders of senior debentures and mortgage bonds are satisfied.

Subordinated debt (junior debt)   Debt over which *senior debt* takes priority. In the event of bankruptcy, subordinated debtholders receive payment only after senior debt is paid off in full.

Subscriber acquisition costs   See *customer acquisition costs.*

Subsidy   A payment that the government makes to a producer.

Subsistence real wage rate   The minimum real wage rate needed to maintain life.

Substitute   A good that can be used in place of another good.

Substitutes   Two goods are substitutes when either one can be used for consumption to satisfy a similar want—for example, coffee and tea. The more you buy of one, the less you buy of the other. For substitutes, the change in the price of one causes a shift in demand for the other in the same direction as the price change.

Substitution effect   The tendency of people to substitute cheaper commodities for more expensive commodities.

Sunk costs   Costs that have been incurred and cannot be reversed.

Supermajority   Provision in a company's charter requiring a majority of, say, 80 percent of shareholders to approve certain changes, such as a *merger.*

Supplemental Information   Any performance-related information included as part of a compliant performance presentation that supplements or enhances the required and/or recommended disclosure and presentation provisions of the GIPS standards.

Supply A schedule showing the relationship between price and quantity supplied for a specified period of time, other things being equal.

Supply curve The graphical representation of the supply schedule; a line (curve) showing the supply schedule, which generally slopes upward (has a positive slope), other things being equal.

Supply shock An event that influences production capacity and costs in the economy.

Supply-side economics The notion that creating incentives for individuals and firms to increase productivity will cause the aggregate supply curve to shift outward.

Surcharge A court-imposed penalty levied against a trustee for committing a breach of trust.

Surplus A situation in which quantity supplied is greater than quantity demanded at a price above the market clearing price.

Sustainable cash flow worksheet A worksheet that begins with reported operating cash flow and then adds and subtracts three different layers of nonrecurring operating cash flow items. Additions and subtractions also are made for reclassified operating cash flow items. Income tax adjustments are made where appropriate. Three different measures of sustainable cash flow are produced after the three different layers of adjustments have been recorded.

Sustainable financial performance See *sustainable operating cash flow.*

Sustainable growth rate A measure of how fast a firm can grow using internal equity and debt financing and a constant capital structure. Equal to retention rate × *ROE*.

Sustainable operating cash flow (SOCF) Cash flow that is derived from renewable sources, supported by profitable operations, and is available to meet a firm's discretionary needs. Generally, reported operating cash flow is a useful starting point for computing sustainable operating cash flow. However, adjustments are needed for reclassifications of operating items and for nonrecurring items. Also referred to as *sustainable cash flow.* See also *adjusted operating cash flow.*

Swap A contract whereby two parties agree to a periodic exchange of cash flows. In certain types of swaps, only the net difference between the amounts owed is exchanged on each payment date.

Swap spread A measure of the risk premium for an interest rate swap, calculated as the difference between the agreement's fixed rate and the yield on a Treasury bond with the same maturity.

Swaption An option to enter into a swap contract at a later date.

SWOT analysis An examination of a firm's Strengths, Weaknesses, Opportunities, and Threats. This analysis helps an analyst evaluate a firm's strategies to exploit its competitive advantages or defend against its weaknesses.

Synergy 2 + 2 = 5; a combination of businesses in which the combined entity is more valuable than the sum of the parts.

Systematic risk (1) The variability of returns that is due to macroeconomic factors that affect all risky assets. Because it affects all risky assets, it cannot be eliminated by diversification. (2) Market risk.

Tactical asset allocation Short-term adjustments to the long-term asset allocation to reflect views on the current relative attractiveness of asset classes.

Take-or-pay In *project finance,* arrangement where parent company agrees to pay for output of project even if it chooses not to take delivery.

Tangible asset Physical asset, such as plant, machinery, and offices (cf. *intangible assets*).

Tap Procedure by which a borrower can keep issuing additional amounts of an old bond at its current market value. This procedure is used for bond issues, notably by the British and French governments, as well as for some short-term debt instruments.

Targeted stock See *tracking stock.*

Tariff A tax that is imposed by the importing country when an imported good crosses its international boundary.

Tariffs Taxes on imported goods.

Tax A shorthand reference to the tax return income statement.

Tax adjustments Restatements of nonrecurring items of operating cash flow to place them on an after-tax basis. For example, an outsized tax-deductible pension contribution of $50 million would be reduced to an after-tax amount of $30 million if a combined federal and state marginal tax rate of 40 percent is assumed: $50 million × (1 − 40 percent) = $30 million.

Tax bracket A specified interval of income to which a specific and unique marginal tax rate is applied.

Tax credits A direct dollar-for-dollar reduction in taxes payable.

Tax loss carryforward Current tax-return losses that exceed tax-return earnings in the loss carryback period may be carried forward. The current net operating loss (NOL) carryforward period is 20 years.

T-bill Treasury bill.

Technological change The development of new goods and better ways of producing goods and services.

Technology (1) Any method of producing a good or service. (2) Society's pool of applied knowledge concerning how goods and services can be produced.

TED spread Difference between *LIBOR* and U.S. *Treasury bill* rate.

Temporary difference A difference between the book and tax basis of both assets and liabilities. Alternatively, a temporary difference is a difference between book and tax return earnings that will reverse at some future point in time. Temporary differences give rise to deferred tax assets and liabilities.

Tender offer An offer made directly to shareholders. One of the more common ways hostile takeovers are implemented.

Tenor Maturity of a loan.

Term bond A bond that has a single maturity date.

Term structure See *yield curve.*

Term structure of interest rates The relationship between term to maturity and yield to maturity for a sample of comparable bonds at a given time. Popularly known as the *yield curve.*

Term to maturity Specifies the date or the number of years before a bond matures or expires.

Terms of trade The quantity of goods and services that a country exports to pay for its imports of goods and services.

Testamentary trust A trust created by will.

The Fed The Federal Reserve System; the central bank of the United States.

Theory of contestable markets A hypothesis concerning pricing behavior that holds that even though there are only a few firms in an industry, they are forced to price their products more or less competitively because of the ease of entry by outsiders. The key aspect of a contestable market is relatively costless entry into and exit from the industry.

Third parties Parties who are not directly involved in a given activity or transaction.

Thrift institutions Financial institutions that receive most of their funds from the savings of the public; they include mutual savings banks, savings and loan associations, and credit unions.

Tick Minimum amount the price of a security may change.

Time deposit A deposit in a financial institution that requires notice of intent to withdraw or must be left for an agreed period. Withdrawal of funds prior to the end of the agreed period may result in a penalty.

Time-series graph A graph that measures time (for example, months or years) on the *x*-axis and the variable or variables in which we are interested on the *y*-axis.

Time premium The difference between an option's total market value and its intrinsic value.

Time value (of an option) The part of the value of an option that is due to its positive time to expiration. Not to be confused with present value or the time value of money.

Tobin's Q Ratio of market value of the firm to replacement cost.

Top-down With respect to investment approaches, the allocation of money first to categories such as asset classes, countries, or industry followed by the selection of individual securities within category.

Total cash flow The change in reported cash and cash equivalents during a reporting period.

Total cost The cost of all the productive resources that a firm uses.

Total costs The sum of total fixed costs and total variable costs.

Total fixed cost The cost of the firm's fixed inputs.

Total income The yearly amount earned by the nation's resources (factors of production). Total income therefore includes wages, rent, interest payments, and profits that are received, respectively, by workers, landowners, capital owners, and entrepreneurs.

Total interest paid A term used on the cash flow analysis statement that consists of cash payments for interest on debt and capital leases, including capitalized interest.

Total return A return objective in which the investor wants to increase the portfolio value to meet a future need by both capital gains and current income reinvestment.

Total revenue The value of a firm's sales. It is calculated as the price of the good multiplied by the quantity sold.

Total revenues The price per unit times the total quantity sold.

Total Value (Private Equity) Residual value of the portfolio plus distributed capital.

Tracking error The standard deviation of the difference in returns between an active investment portfolio and its benchmark portfolio; also called *tracking error volatility.*

Tracking portfolio A portfolio constructed to have returns with the highest possible correlation with a systematic risk factor.

Tracking stock   An issuance of equity that represents an interest in the earnings of a division of a company.

Trade balance   The balance of a country's exports and imports; part of the current account.

Trade credit   Accounts receivable.

Tradeoff   An exchange—giving up one thing to get something else.

Trading rule   A formula for deciding on current transactions based on historical data.

Trading turnover   The percentage of outstanding shares traded during a period of time.

Tranche   Refers to a portion of an issue that is designed for a specific category of investors. French for "slice."

Transaction cost   (1) The cost of executing a trade. Low costs characterize an operationally efficient market. (2) All of the costs associated with exchanging, including the informational costs of finding out price and quality, service record, and durability of a product, plus the cost of contracting and enforcing that contract. Can also be viewed as all costs associated with making, reaching, and enforcing agreements.

Transfer payments   Money payments made by governments to individuals for which in return no services or goods are concurrently rendered. Examples are welfare, Social Security, and unemployment insurance benefits.

Treasurer   Principal financial manager (cf. *controller*).

Treasury bill   Short-term, highly liquid government securities issued at a discount from the face value and returning the face amount at maturity.

Treasury bond   A U.S. government security with a maturity of more than 10 years that pays interest periodically.

Treasury note   A U.S. government security with maturities of 1 to 10 years that pays interest periodically.

Treasury stock   A corporation's issued stock that has subsequently been repurchased by the company and not retired.

Trend   The general tendency for a variable to move in one direction.

Triangular arbitrage   With respect to currencies, an arbitrage involving three currencies only.

Trough   The transition point between recession and recovery.

Trust agreement   The document that creates an inter vivos trust, between a grantor and a trustee, for the benefit of the beneficiaries.

Trust indenture   A trust agreement.

Trust instrument   A trust agreement.

Turnover   The ratio of the trading activity of a portfolio to the assets of the portfolio.

Unanticipated inflation   Inflation at a rate that comes as a surprise, either higher or lower than the rate anticipated.

Unbilled receivables   Cost plus profit recognized on contracts in excess of amounts billed customers.

Uncertainty   A situation in which more than one event might occur but it is not known which one.

Uncovered interest rate parity   The assertion that expected currency depreciation should offset the interest differential between two countries over the term of the interest rate.

Underlying   Refers to a security on which a derivative contract is written.

Underpricing   Issue of securities below their market value.

Underweighted   A condition in which a portfolio, for whatever reason, includes less of a class of securities than the relative market value alone would justify.

Underwriter   Firm that buys an issue of securities from a company and resells it to investors.

Unearned revenue   See *deferred revenue*.

Unemployment   The total number of adults (aged 16 years or older) who are willing and able to work and who are actively looking for work but have not found a job.

Unemployment rate   The percentage of the people in the labor force who are unemployed.

Unique risk   See *diversifiable risk*.

Unlimited liability   A legal concept whereby the personal assets of the owner of a firm can be seized to pay off the firm's debts.

Unrealized capital gains   Capital gains that reflect the price appreciation of currently held unsold assets.

Unsystematic risk   Risk that is unique to an asset, derived from its particular characteristics. It can be eliminated in a diversified portfolio.

Unwind   The negotiated termination of a forward or futures position before contract maturity.

U.S. interest rate differential   A gap equal to the U.S. interest rate minus the foreign interest rate.

Valuation analysis   An active bond portfolio management strategy designed to capitalize on expected price increases in temporarily undervalued issues.

Valuation process   Part of the investment decision process in which you estimate the value of a security.

Value   The maximum amount that a person is willing to pay for a good. The value of one more unit of the good or service is its marginal benefit.

Value additivity   Rule that the value of the whole must equal the sum of the values of the parts.

Value-at-risk (VAR)   A money measure of the minimum loss that is expected over a given period of time with a given probability.

Value chain   The set of transformations to move from raw material to product or service delivery.

Value stocks   Stocks that appear to be undervalued for reasons besides earnings growth potential. These stocks are usually identified based on high dividend yields, low *P/E* ratios, or low price-to-book ratios.

Value-weighted index   An index calculated as the total market value of the securities in the sample. Market value is equal to the number of shares or bonds outstanding times the market price of the security.

VAR   Value-at-risk.

Variable costs   Costs that vary with the rate of production. They include wages paid to workers and purchases of materials.

Variable principal redemption (VPR)   A class of debt securities whose principal redemption at maturity is not fixed but tied to changes in the value of another economic entity, such as a stock index or commodity price.

Variation margin   Profits or losses on open positions in futures and option contracts that are paid or collected daily.

Vendor financing   Amounts owed vendors for purchased goods or services, reported as accounts payable.

Venture capital   Capital to finance a new firm.

Vertical merger   A merger of companies that operate at different levels or stages of the production process in the same industry. For example, a company with large oil reserves buying a pipeline company for a gasoline retailer is an example of forward integration. A consumer electronics retail chain that buys a brand name manufacturer would be an example of backward integration.

Volatility   A measure of the uncertainty about the future price of an asset. Typically measured by the standard deviation of returns on the asset.

Volatility risk   The risk in the value of options portfolios due to unpredictable changes in the volatility of the underlying asset.

WACC   Weighted-average cost of capital.

Wages   The income that labor earns.

Warrant   An instrument that allows the holder to purchase a specified number of shares of the firm's common stock from the firm at a specified price for a given period of time.

Wealth   The stock of assets owned by a person, household, firm, or nation. For a household, wealth can consist of a house, cars, personal belongings, stocks, bonds, bank accounts, and cash.

Weighted-average cost of capital (WACC)   *Expected return* on a portfolio of all the firm's securities. Used as *hurdle rate* for capital investment.

Well-diversified portfolio   A portfolio spread out over many securities in such a way that the weight in any security is close to zero.

White knight   A friendly potential acquirer sought out by a target company threatened by a less welcome suitor.

Wholesale Price Index (WPI)   A price index defined on a basket of goods produced.

Wi   When issued.

Williams Act of 1968   An amendment of the Securities and Exchange Act of 1934 that regulates tender offers and other takeover-related actions, such as larger share purchases.

Window dressing   Toward the end of a reporting period, particularly at year end, mutual funds and banks will sometimes round up their holdings to even thousands, or sell positions that have gone down and thus constitute an eyesore.

Withholding tax   A tax levied by the country of source on income paid.

Working-age population   The total number of people aged 16 years and over who are not in jail, hospital, or some other form of institutional care.

Working capital   Current assets minus current liabilities.

Workout period   Realignment period of a temporary misaligned yield relationship.

World Bank   A supranational organization of several institutions designed to assist developing countries. The International Bank for Reconstruction and Development (IBRD) and the International Finance Corporation (IFC) are the more important members of the World Bank group.

Writer of an option   A term used for the person or institution selling an option and therefore granting the right to exercise it to the buyer of the option.

***x* axis**   The horizontal axis in a graph.

***y* axis**   The vertical axis in a graph.

Yield   The promised rate of return on an investment under certain assumptions.

Yield curve   A curve showing the relationship between yield (interest rate) and maturity for a set of similar securities. For example, the yield curve can be drawn for U.S. Treasuries or for LIBOR. Typically, different yield curves are drawn for zero-coupon bonds (zero-coupon yield curve) and for coupon bonds quoted at par (par yield curve).

Yield to maturity The total yield on a bond obtained by equating the bond's current market value to the discounted cash flows promised by the bond. Also called *actuarial yield*.

Yield spread The difference between the promised yields of alternative bond issues or market segments at a given time relative to yields on Treasury issues of equal maturity.

Zero-beta portfolio The minimum-variance portfolio uncorrelated with a chosen efficient portfolio.

Zero-coupon bond A bond that pays its par value at maturity but no periodic interest payments. Its yield is determined by the difference between its par value and its discounted purchase price. Also called *original issue discount (OID) bonds*.

Z-score Measure of the likelihood of bankruptcy.

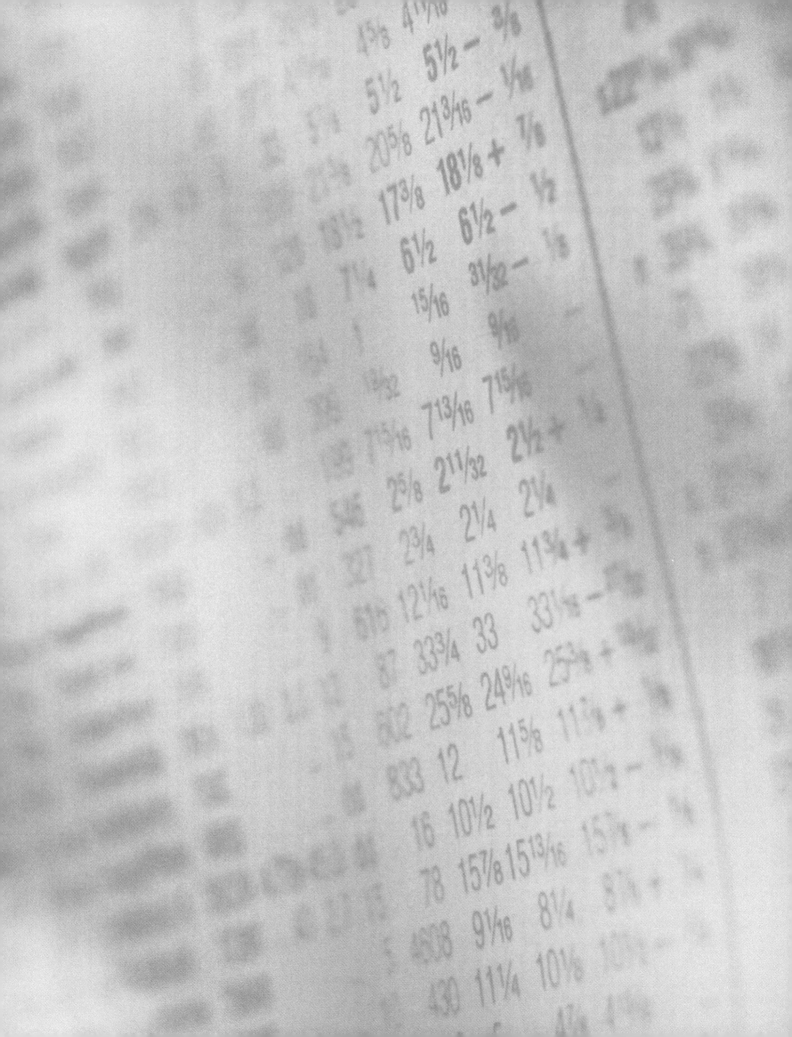

Page numbers followed by n refer to footnootes.

A

Aaker, David, V4: 227

AAR. *See* average accounting rate of return (AAR)

Aaron Rents, Inc., V2: 235–236

Aastrom Biosciences, Inc., V2: 375–376

abandonment options as real options, V3: 54, 56–57

Abate, James A., V4: 611

Abbey National (U.K.), V3: 269

Abbott Laboratories, V3: 189–190

ABG Gas Supply, LLC, V2: 195–197

abnormal earnings, V4: 572, 575

abnormal return, V4: 23; V6: 420

ABO. *See* accumulated benefit obligation (ABO)

ABS. *See* asset-backed sector (ABS) bonds

absolute prepayment speed (ABS), V5: 240

absolute priori rule, V5: 19

absolute return objective, V6: 447

absolute valuation model, V4: 27–29

Acacia Research Corp., V2: 252

accountability, V3: 133, 169

accounting conventions, V1: 571–572

accounting estimates, V4: 495n5

accounting income
    capital budgeting cash flows and, V3: 8–9
    project analysis/evaluation, V3: 61–64

accounting information, equity analysis and, V4: 18–14, 22

accounting methods, V4: 62. *See also* national accounting standards
    aggressive practices, V4: 595–596
    balance sheet adjustments for fair value, V4: 591–592
    cash flow and, V4: 536
    changes in, V4: 595
    clean surplus relationship, V4: 588–589
    earnings per share (EPS), V4: 498
    global differences in, V4: 135–147, 327
    goodwill, V4: 594
    intangible assets, V4: 592–495
    international considerations, V4: 551, 596–597

international harmonization of, V4: 137–139
    nonrecurring items, V4: 595
    residual income valuation model, V4: 588–596

Accounting Principles Board (APB)
    Opinion No. 16, V2: 102
    Opinion No. 18, V2: 22

accounting rate of return, V3: 26–27

accounting risk, V3: 169

Accounting Trends and Techniques (AICPA), V2: 87

accounts payable
    on cash flow analysis statement, V2: 410
    cash flow and, V2: 321–322, 329
    extending payment terms on, V2: 284–285

accounts receivable, classification of, V2: 290–295, 328

accreting swaps, V6: 256

accrual accounting, V2: 25, 441

accruals to revenue ratio, V2: 423

accumulated benefit obligation (ABO), V2: 67. *See also* pensions

accumulated postretirement benefit obligation (APBO), V2: 83

accumulation period, V5: 244

acid-test ratio, V5: 13–14

Acme Boot, V5: 31

acquisitions, V4: 11, 11n3. *See also* business combinations; mergers
    affecting earnings analysis, V2: 459–460
    cash flow and, V2: 213–214, 259–263
    defined, V2: 99
    standards for, V2: 100

Acree Products, V3: 249

active investment approach, V6: 439–440

active investment managers/styles, V4: 13, 17n10

active portfolio
    in construction of optimal risky portfolio, V6: 424–426
    in Treynor-Black portfolio construction, V6: 420

active portfolio management, V6: 411–432
    introduction, V6: 411–413
    alpha forecasts, V6: 427–429
    lure of, V6: 411–413
    market timing, V6: 414–418

multifactor models, V6: 426–427
    objectives of active portfolios, V6: 413–414
    security selection, V6: 418–426
    summary, V6: 430–431

active risk management, in trusts, V1: 187

active strategy, V4: 23, 67

Activision, Inc., V2: 247

activity ratios, V2: 3, 468–469

actual returns
    above required returns, V4: 310–311
    vs. expected returns, V6: 374

A.D.A.M., Inc., V2: 248

ADC. *See* All Digital Component Corporation (ADC)

add-on interest, V6: 15

additional compensation arrangements, V1: 15, 76–77

Adelphia, V3: 139–140

adjusted beta, V6: 380

adjusted book value per common shares, V2: 450–451

adjusted coefficient of variation, V1: 279–280, 280n26

adjusted operating cash flow. *See* sustainable operating cash flow (SOCF)

adjusted present value (APV), V3: 26–27; V4: 432n2

administrative prudence, V1: 181

Adolf Coors Co., V2: 428

ADR. *See* American Depository Receipts (ADRs)

ADS (American depository shares), V3: 246

Advanced Power Technology, Inc., V2: 259, 260–261, 262

Advanta Mortgage Loan Trust, V5: 233–234

advertising, capitalizing cost of, V2: 239

Aerotechnique S.A., V3: 108

Africa, economic growth trends in, V1: 399

after-tax cost of debt, V4: 259–260

age, demographics of, V1: 581–589

agency costs, V3: 209

agency costs of equity, V3: 209

agency note futures contracts, V6: 289

agency problem, V3: 136

agency relationships, V3: 136–141; V5: 22–26